THE LAST KAISER

THE LAST KAISER

A biography of

WILHELM II

German Emperor and King of Prussia

Tyler-Whittle, *Michael Sidney*

NYT

Times BOOKS

First published in Great Britain in 1977 by William Heinemann Ltd.

Library of Congress Cataloging in Publication Data

Tyler-Whittle, Michael Sidney, 1927–
    The last Kaiser.

    Includes bibliographical references and index.
    1. Wilhelm II, German Emperor, 1859–1941.
2. Germany—Kings and rulers—Biography. 3. Germany—
History—William II, 1888–1918. I. Title.
DD229.T94   1977   943.08'4'0924 [B]   77-79047
ISBN 0-8129-0716-7

TO

Gore Vidal

AUTHOR'S NOTE

The First World War began between the Alliance of the German and Austrian Empires and the Triple Entente of Russia, France and England. To each side were added allies by open or secret treaties and, at the end of the war, the Entente Powers for technical reasons were calling themselves 'The Allied and Associated Powers' and their enemies 'The Central Powers'. This seems to make for confusion and I have consistently referred to one power block as the Alliance and the other as the Entente. I fear, though, that I have been less consistent in describing my own countrymen, sometimes using the word British but more often English. This is not because I am unaware of the correct title of the sovereign and government and people of Great Britain, but to use the full and formal description in a book of this kind would be hideously ugly and inconvenient. I trust that those Scots, Welshmen and Ulstermen who value devolution will be charitably tolerant. In the main text, though not in the Reference Notes, I have rendered in English all names and titles where it has been possible. Chlodwig, for example, is rendered as Clovis, though Wolfgang remains Wolfgang because it has no English equivalent. Two exceptions to this practice are my use of the words Kaiser and Tsar, for William – unlike his father and grandfather – preferred the German to the French title and is generally known as the Kaiser, and, with the rise of pan-Slavism, the Emperors of Russia reverted to the Slav form of their title. There are some footnotes which might be of interest to the general reader, but the Reference Notes have been marked with small and unobtrusive numbers in the text and put where they properly belong, at the back of the book.

T.W.

CONTENTS

ILLUSTRATIONS

ACKNOWLEDGMENTS

I am grateful to Her Majesty The Queen for her gracious permission to the republication of material from the Royal Archives that is subject to copyright, and to H.I.H. Prince Louis Ferdinand, Head of the Royal House of Prussia, H.R.H. Princess Alice Countess of Athlone, and Lord Sysonby for similar kind permission to reproduce copyright material.

Not being a trained historian I have had to depend upon professionals for background and I am fortunate that modern German history has been so well investigated. I wish to thank the Librarians and their Assistants of the University Library, Cambridge, the Bodleian, and the British Library, and the Director and Librarian of the British Institute in Naples. I owe much to many historiographers and their work is mentioned in the Reference Notes, but my debt of gratitude is by far the largest to the late Senatore Luigi Albertini, Sir Alan Bullock, Professor Fritz Fischer, Professor Gerhard Masur, the late Professor Gerhard Ritter, Mr A. J. P. Taylor, Professor Hugh Trevor-Roper, the late Sir John Wheeler-Bennett, and, above all, to that fine scholar of the period, Dr John Röhl, who has been exceedingly generous with information and advice.

Fellow biographers of the Kaiser and commentators on his life and times have kept me busy for many months. I have read dozens of volumes as well as a plethora of articles, press reports, speeches, historical archives and memoirs written by a large variety of interested persons from ex-Imperial Chancellors to the Kaiser's American dentist. But only one biography has been my constant standby, the least subjective, best documented and, because the author is himself an historian, the most dependable and useful: Mr Michael Balfour's *The Kaiser and his Times*. I am extremely grateful for his help and his ready permission to use his material.

Then I must record my obligation and sincere thanks to those who in various ways have gone out of their way to give me help, amongst them Cecilia, Gräfin von Sternberg, the Rev'd Alan Coldwells, Lord Denham, Mr Duncan Ellison, Mr Jeffrey Finestone, Lord Mowbray and Stourton, Dr Arthur Plant, Mr Roger Smith and Mr Desmond Stewart. Finally, I acknowledge with great gratitude the kind interest of Mr Gore Vidal, to whom this book is affectionately dedicated, for his constant encouragement and a wide variety of information.

T.W.

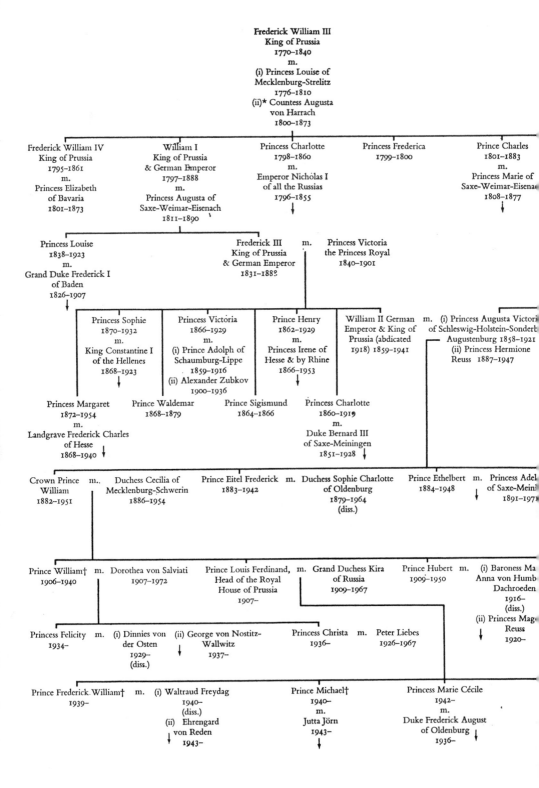

Frederick William III
King of Prussia
1770–1840
m.
(i) Princess Louise of
Mecklenburg-Strelitz
1776–1810
(ii)★ Countess Augusta
von Harrach
1800–1873

Frederick William IV
King of Prussia
1795–1861
m.
Princess Elizabeth
of Bavaria
1801–1873

William I
King of Prussia
& German Emperor
1797–1888
m.
Princess Augusta of
Saxe-Weimar-Eisenach
1811–1890

Princess Charlotte
1798–1860
m.
Emperor Nicholas I
of all the Russias
1796–1855

Princess Frederica
1799–1800

Prince Charles
1801–1883
m.
Princess Marie of
Saxe-Weimar-Eisenach
1808–1877

Princess Louise
1838–1923
m.
Grand Duke Frederick I
of Baden
1826–1907

Frederick III
King of Prussia
& German Emperor
1831–1888

m.

Princess Victoria
the Princess Royal
1840–1901

Princess Sophie
1870–1932
m.
King Constantine I
of the Hellenes
1868–1923

Princess Victoria
1866–1929
m.
(i) Prince Adolph of
Schaumburg-Lippe
1859–1916
(ii) Alexander Zubkov
1900–1936

Prince Henry
1862–1929
m.
Princess Irene of
Hesse & by Rhine
1866–1953

William II German
Emperor & King of
Prussia (abdicated
1918) 1859–1941

m.

(i) Princess Augusta Victoria
of Schleswig-Holstein-Sonderburg-
Augustenburg 1858–1921
(ii) Princess Hermione
Reuss 1887–1947

Princess Margaret
1872–1954
m.
Landgrave Frederick Charles
of Hesse
1868–1940

Prince Waldemar
1868–1879

Prince Sigismund
1864–1866

Princess Charlotte
1860–1919
m.
Duke Bernard III
of Saxe-Meiningen
1851–1928

Crown Prince
William
1882–1951

m..

Duchess Cecilia of
Mecklenburg-Schwerin
1886–1954

Prince Eitel Frederick
1883–1942

m.

Duchess Sophie Charlotte
of Oldenburg
1879–1964
(diss.)

Prince Ethelbert
1884–1948

m.

Princess Adelaide
of Saxe-Meiningen
1891–1971

Prince William†
1906–1940

m.

Dorothea von Salviati
1907–1972

Prince Louis Ferdinand,
Head of the Royal
House of Prussia
1907–

m.

Grand Duchess Kira
of Russia
1909–1967

Prince Hubert
1909–1950

m.

(i) Baroness Maria
Anna von Humboldt-
Dachroeden
1916–
(diss.)
(ii) Princess Magdalene
Reuss
1920–

Princess Felicity
1934–

m.

(i) Dinnies von
der Osten
1929–
(diss.)

(ii) George von Nostitz-
Wallwitz
1937–

Princess Christa
1936–

m.

Peter Liebes
1926–1967

Prince Frederick William†
1939–

m.

(i) Waltraud Freydag
1940–
(diss.)
(ii) Ehrengard
von Reden
1943–

Prince Michael†
1940–
m.
Jutta Jörn
1943–

Princess Marie Cécile
1942–
m.
Duke Frederick August
of Oldenburg
1936–

THE ANCESTRY & DESCENDANTS OF
WILLIAM II
a modified table compiled by Jeffrey Finestone
★ = contracted a morganatic marriage
† = renounced all rights of succession
↓ signifies that children were, or have
been, born of the marriage

Princess Alexandrine	Prince Ferdinand	Princess Louise	Prince Albert	Christian
1803–1892	1804–1806	1808–1870	1809–1872	Duke of Schleswig-Holstein-
m.		m.	m.	Sonderburg-Augustenburg
nd Duke Paul Frederick		Prince Frederick	(i) Princess Marianne	1798–1869
Mecklenburg-Schwerin		of the Netherlands	of the Netherlands (diss.)	m.
1800–1842		1797–1881	1810–1883	Countess Louise
↓		↓	(ii)★ Rosalie von Rauch	Danneskiold-Samsöe
			(Countess von Hohenhau)	1796–1867
			1820–1879	│
			↓	Duke Frederick
				1829–1880
				m.
				Princess Adelaide of
				Hohenlohe-Langenburg
				1835–1900

Princess Caroline Mathilde	Duke Ernest Gunther	Princess Louise Sophie	Princess Feodora
1860–1932	1863–1921	1866–1952	1874–1910
m.	m.	m.	
Duke Frederick Ferdinand of	Princess Dorothea of	Prince Frederick Leopold	
Schleswig-Holstein-	Saxe-Coburg and Gotha	of Prussia	
Sonderburg-Glücksburg	1881–1967	1865–1931	
1855–1934		↓	
↓			

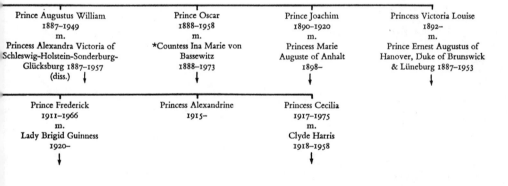

Prince Augustus William	Prince Oscar	Prince Joachim	Princess Victoria Louise
1887–1949	1888–1958	1890–1920	1892–
m.	m.	m.	m.
Princess Alexandra Victoria of	★Countess Ina Marie von	Princess Marie	Prince Ernest Augustus of
Schleswig-Holstein-Sonderburg-	Bassewitz	Auguste of Anhalt	Hanover, Duke of Brunswick
Glücksburg 1887–1957	1888–1973	1898–	& Lüneburg 1887–1953
(diss.) ↓	↓	↓	↓

Prince Frederick	Princess Alexandrine	Princess Cecilia
1911–1966	1915–	1917–1975
m.		m.
Lady Brigid Guinness		Clyde Harris
1920–		1918–1958
↓		

Princess Kira	Prince Louis Ferdinand	Prince Christian	Princess Xenia
1943–	1944–	Sigismund	1949–
m.	m.	1946–	m.
Thomas Liepsner	Countess Donata zu		Per-Edvard Lithander
1945–	Castell-Rüdenhausen		1945–
↓	1950– ↓		↓

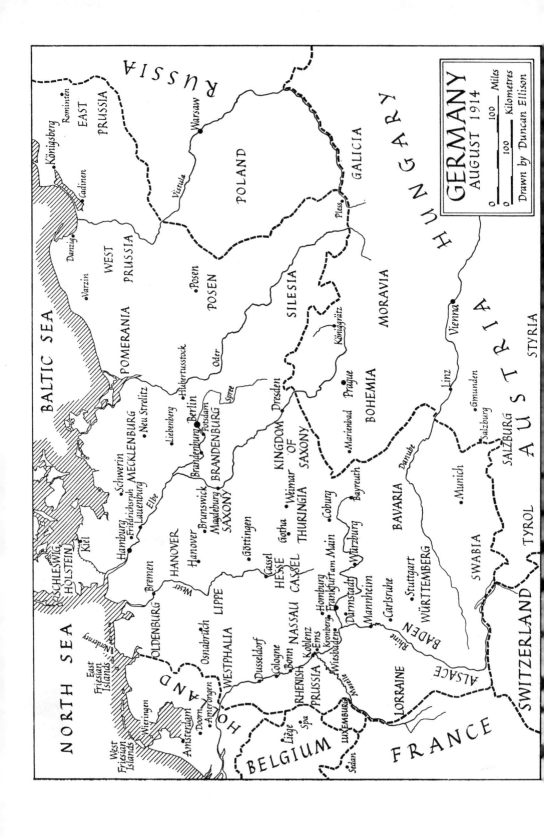

THE LAST KAISER

CHAPTER ONE

Hohenzollern and Saxe-Coburg-Gotha

'The poor lamb to the sacrifice'

QUEEN VICTORIA ON THE MARRIAGE OF
THE PRINCESS ROYAL

I

In April 1851 King Frederick William IV of Prussia wrote to Prince Albert to enquire if it was really safe for his brother and his family to attend the Great Exhibition in London.[1] Naturally he had no intention of being there himself. Nor would any crowned head who vividly recalled the revolutions of three years before when most of Europe had exploded with political agitation. In Berlin the barricades had gone up. As the King himself confessed: 'we all lay flat on our bellies;'[2] and his reactionary brother William, known to Berliners as the Grapeshot Prince, had been forced to shave off his whiskers, disguise himself, and fly the city, first to the Island of Peacocks near Potsdam, and thence to the safety of England.[3] The King of the French had done the same, arriving at Newhaven wigless and in goggles and calling himself 'Mr Smith'.[4] In the end only Louis-Philippe had lost his throne in what was to be called 'the revolution in dressing-gown and slippers',[5] but everywhere there had been rumbles, concessions ground from unwilling sovereigns, mob violence, barricade murders; and even that monolith of autocracy, the Hapsburg empire, had at last been forced to abandon Latin as its official language.[6] The agitators who had caused all this were still about and proliferating, and, according to the Emperor Nicholas of Russia, who had sent a friendly letter to the Prussian King, they were making for London like iron filings to a magnet. No-one would be safe there. The Emperor Nicholas himself had refused passports to all his people for fear of 'contamination'.[7]

Prince Albert was exceedingly vexed. In the face of much opposition he had worked hard to make his International Exhibition of Arts and Sciences not only a demonstration of modern progress but also a means of strengthening the brotherhood of mankind. The English aristocrats, who did not care for him, had opposed at every point, especially because the exhibition was to be contained in a vast conservatory sketched out originally by a duke's gardener on blotting-paper.[8] It might be a marvel of engineering and glazing, they said, but in the House of Commons it was seriously averred that this great 'palace of crystal' would succumb to hailstorms and kill exhibitors and visitors by the thousand. Others said that the London sparrows who perched outside might crush the whole structure with the weight of their droppings, and others that the thousands trapped inside would soil the exhibits before anyone could see them. This last problem was resolved by the old Duke of Wellington, who suggested releasing sparrowhawks within the building. The Prime Minister too had put in a word of criticism, saying he believed the saluting guns on Opening Day would shatter the glass to smithereens.

Having faced so many objections and obstacles it was especially galling to the Prince that the Queen's fellow sovereigns had refused her invitations one by one, and he wrote a tart reply to the King of Prussia that there was *no* fear in London of political contamination or physical assault, but as he could not absolutely guarantee anyone's safety he would withdraw the invitation.[9] This caused Frederick William IV to reflect. He was godfather to the Prince of Wales, and the Grapeshot Prince was godfather to Prince Alfred. Moreover he owed something to England for offering his brother asylum during the year of revolution. He changed his mind. The day before the official Opening on May Day in 1851, William, the Prince of Prussia, with his Princess, Augusta, and their two children, arrived at Victoria Station to be met by a pale but welcoming Prince Albert and driven through the streets in an open carriage. There was great cheering, a warm spontaneous greeting from the Londoners and the masses who had poured into the capital to see the Exhibition. Only the press was unwelcoming, *The Times* being the most hostile of all. But neither royalties minded. They were accustomed to abuse. Over thirteen years before the young Queen Victoria had been given advice by her uncle, the King of the Belgians, which she had never forgotten. 'If all the Editors,' King Leopold had written, 'of the papers in the countries where the liberty of the press exists were to be assembled, we should have a *crew* to which you would *not* confide a dog that you value, still less your honour and reputation.'[10]

It may be concluded that the visit was satisfactory in some degree to all parties.

The Prince of Prussia was a believer in absolutism, but Prince Albert tried to drench him with his theories for a liberal united Germany under the leadership of an enlightened Prussia. Nevertheless he remained polite, was impressed by the massiveness and comprehensiveness of the exhibition, and especially by the opening, when the weather was perfect, 35,000 people went through the turnstiles, no terrorists put in an appearance, several organs and massed choirs sang the 'Hallelujah Chorus' and the National Anthem, the cannon fired salutes (and failed to dislodge a single pane of glass), the English Princes itched in the great heat because they were kitted out in their 'Highland things', and an illustrious Chinaman was swept into the Diplomatic Corps and made a deep oriental obeisance which charmed the Queen – though it was all a great mistake and afterwards he confessed to being a Mr He Sing who usually showed people over his moored junk at a shilling a head.[11] The Prince of Prussia's main and abiding interest being the army, he could not be expected to show much enthusiasm for raw materials, machinery, manufactures and fine arts; nor even for the ingenious exhibits such as the Lord's Prayer inscribed on a sixpence, an 'alarm' bed that hurled the sleeper out at a pre-arranged hour, a physician's walking-stick with a convenient enema apparatus stuffed in its handle, and a pulpit connected by gutta-percha tubes to the pews of the deaf; though he might have approved of a machine for making fifty million medals a week, and he certainly admired the deft and apparently effortless way the English had for arranging such pageantry and spectacles.[12] But his chief interest was in his son Frederick, or Fritz as he was always called, who had been selected as a possible bridegroom for Queen Victoria's eldest daughter. The match had been dreamed up many years before by Prince Albert and Baron Stockmar, the German Merlin at the English Court.[13] Prince William was ultra-conservative but no ninny. He knew perfectly well that Albert planned to slip the liberal Princess Royal like a ferret into the warren of Prussian reaction. He knew equally well that Prussian reaction was very durable, and that there were real advantages in an alliance between the two royal houses. He did not worry in the least if the young people cared for one another. He had been forced to abandon the love of his life and marry a princess he could not abide, a princess moreover whose great pride was in being the granddaughter of Paul I of Russia, despite the fact that he was 'a brute with a death's head' and out of his mind. Prince William was not in the least a romantic, yet it pleased him to see that the plan for young Fritz seemed to be moving along very cosily.

In the Queen of England, the Princess of Prussia found a new and lasting friend. Both Victoria and Augusta were intelligent and emotional and both dearly wanted female confidantes. And the Queen was enraptured by the Princess's evident appreciation of all that Albert had attempted in organizing the Exhibition. Both mothers watched indulgently over Prince Fritz, aged twenty, escorting the Princess Royal, half his age, in the Crystal Palace. Rather it was the other way about and he was escorted because the Princess had several times visited the stands beforehand, and she knew exactly what was what. Pertly she guided him here and there, speaking almost faultless German, because the Prince's English was far from perfect; and, despite her youth, well aware of what was in store for her. For his part the young Prince was amazed by her precocity, by her freedom from too much restraint, a luxury denied to Prussian royalty, and most of all by the obvious affection which existed between her parents and which was so lacking between his. Supposedly their marriage too had been pre-arranged, yet while the Prince and Princess of Prussia disliked each other and bickered endlessly in public, Prince Albert and Queen Victoria were evidently much in love.

From his apartments at Windsor – he did not attend the opening, being melancholy and valetudinarian by disposition – Baron Stockmar foresaw that his plans were bearing fruit. Like Prince Albert he longed for a large and liberally constituted Germany. He also relished the power of arranging things. By a series of strange coincidences he had risen from being a lowly physician to the royal house of Saxe-Coburg to a position of unique importance in Europe. Fortuitously he had been at the deathbeds of both Princess Charlotte of Wales and Queen Victoria's father. With a barely observed skill he had eased King Leopold on to the throne of the Belgians and, more important, had guaranteed that new kingdom's neutrality by a promise from the Great Powers. Appositely he had been at hand at the very moment of Queen Victoria's accession, and afterwards had promoted the suit of Prince Albert of Saxe-Coburg. Many of his schemes had hatched. Now he lived in partial exile from his wife and family, devising educational regimes for princes, touching here and there a vital political string in many kingdoms, and, above all pleasure, royal matchmaking, spreading the Coburgs through the royal courts of Europe. Already they were in London, Portugal, and Belgium. Now he trusted and believed they were to have influence in Prussia.

Prince Albert, close to exhaustion, did not allow himself to rest. Not so indelicate as to mention any sort of formal arrangement even to the Prince of Prussia, he yet continued to drench that impervious gentleman with his political ideals for the future of Germany. Prince William listened politely. Very probably he would one day succeed his brother because Frederick William IV was childless. Then he would see. He did not care to commit himself outright. Prince Albert made a more elaborate attack on the impressionable Fritz. To his joy the young man seemed to respond. He asked if Prince Albert would perhaps occasionally oblige him with a letter or memorandum. It is questionable whether he was truly aware of what he was doing. Prince Albert was famous in the chancelleries of Europe for immense letters and memoranda. Enthusiastically he took Fritz's autograph book and wrote firmly the text of all that he hoped were their joint political aspirations:

> May Prussia be merged in Germany, and not Germany in Prussia
> Albert.[14]

2

Four years passed. They were eventful. Louis-Napoleon offered himself as candidate for the French Presidency, was elected, and soon after proclaimed himself Napoleon III, Emperor of the French.[15] There was war in the Crimea. France and England were at last allies. Strange bedfellows. Albert in one of his interminable letters to the Prince of Prussia said they were having to exchange visits with the Corsican's nephew. The Waterloo Chamber at Windsor was temporarily renamed the Music Room and precautions were being taken in St George's Chapel to see that George III did not turn in his grave.[16] The victor of Waterloo, old Wellington, died. So did the Emperor of Russia. Queen Victoria was left half a million pounds by an eccentric miser and bore her eighth child, the haemophiliac Prince Leopold. The Queen's Marine Residence at Osborne, built to the design of Prince Albert, was completed, and a place bought on Deeside where he began to design another royal property. In Prussia the bourgeoisie discovered their new monarchical constitution was more monarchical than parliamentarian. King Frederick William IV and the army continued to hold power. Smoking was again forbidden in the streets and could only be indulged in the *Konditorei* – a combination of reading room, sweet shop and coffee house.[17] Schopenhauer was the popular philosopher, Meyerbeer the fashionable composer, and that momentous word *Realpolitik* was coined.[18] Busy at his military duties, the young Prince Frederick of Prussia heard Court gossip that the Princess Royal of England had been publicly rebuked by her mother for flirting with officers at a review.[19] From his mother he heard regular reports of the Princess Royal's maturing because Queen Victoria – a dashing, hectic letter-writer – was frequently in correspondence with her new friend Augusta, the Princess of Prussia.

In 1855, after the English Royal Family had paid a visit to Paris, and the Queen had stood at Napoleon's tomb during a mighty thunderstorm while an equally mighty organ played the English National Anthem,[20] it was decided in Prussia that the time was right for Prince Frederick to propose himself for a fortnight or more. This he did and was told he would be welcome at the new family home of Balmoral for some stalking half way through

September. Count von Moltke accompanied him as A.D.C. and to give fatherly advice and encouragement.[21] They were received with great cordiality and ill-concealed excitement.

Prince Albert, though he abominated child marriages and was deeply attached to his fourteen-year-old eldest daughter, felt he could not allow his political dream to be shattered. Prince Frederick was now twenty-four. Safely married to the Princess Royal they would together save Germany from Prussian junkerdom, Russian despotism, and French licence. There was always a dreadful chance that the prize might be snapped from under their noses. He was gratified when the young Prince shot a stag on his first day out.

Queen Victoria, although she had been plotting the match by correspondence with the Princess of Prussia, and although she thought Prince Fritz's grown whiskers and moustache very fetching, had the strong maternal feelings proper to the occasion. She confided to her Journal that she found the visit heartbreaking as it would almost certainly decide the future of her eldest child.[22] She was in a conspicuous state of agitation.

The young Princess's feelings may be judged from the fact that four days after the Prince's arrival she pressed his hand hard when 'accidentally' they were left unchaperoned for a time; his from the fact that he slept badly, and barely slept at all the night before he asked if he might see the Queen and the Prince alone. He put his proposal with great delicacy, saying that he hoped he might belong to their family.

The Queen seized his hand. It was as good as saying yes, but she insisted that no marriage took place until her daughter was at least seventeen and that no formal proposal could be made until after she had been Confirmed the following spring, a token at that time of coming out into Society.[23]

Prince Frederick agreed, but he might have saved himself the trouble. Letters were sent off to Stockmar, relations and Ministers of the Crown, all marked secret, but containing such news that inevitably it would seep down to the press. Five days after his first offer, Prince Frederick was given permission to present the Princess with a bracelet. The Queen was in a high state of nerves. So too was her husband who began to claim he was suffering from acute rheumatism, pains which were probably symptomatic.[24] The Prussian Prince grew visibly more excited, as did the young Princess. Only Moltke remained calm. He remained so on the 29th when receiving the momentous news that a proposal had been formally made and formally accepted; that a sprig of white heather had changed hands; that the Princess and the Queen were in nervous hysterics, and Prince Albert absolutely incapacitated by rheumatism. He and his young master left on October 1st. Two days afterwards the Princess Royal sent a thick, forty-page letter in their wake. Moltke remarked dryly: "How the news must have accumulated!'[25]

3

The fish hooked, and Prince Albert's rheumatism somewhat abated, there followed what ought to have been a very pleasant interval between the formal betrothal of the happy pair and their marriage in 1858. In fact, it was a difficult time for all. In Berlin there was evidence that Frederick William IV was going out of his mind. A talented draughtsman, eloquent speaker, and unique amongst Hohenzollern monarchs in that he could not sit a horse, things were becoming too much for him and he was escaping into a world of his own.* His brother William, the Prince of Prussia, tended to be regarded as the *de facto* centre of affairs and eventually became Regent.

In England Queen Victoria's nervous system also suffered because her half-brother Charles died and she found the business of carrying her ninth and last child, who was born in April 1857, more trying than ever before. Added to this she began to resent the fact that her eldest daughter although so young was counted grown-up, and no longer could she occasionally enjoy *dîner à deux* with Albert, now created Prince Consort by Letters Patent. Always *dîner* had to be *à trois*. Failing to understand the special relationship which always exists between a man and his first daughter, she claimed she was being neglected, and found it no help to be told by her husband that she must pull herself together. Then there was the positively monumental task of preparing for her daughter's departure – such a trousseau it was, English to the last detail, and included twenty pairs of goloshes and a huge quantity of sponges. Moreover the closer grew the date the more she clung to her child.

'It's like taking a poor lamb to the sacrifice,' she moaned for all to hear.

Each Court found fault with the other, not a happy augury for the future. It was customary in the Hohenzollern family for their heirs to be married in Berlin and for brides to go there. Queen Victoria energetically put paid to this idea, writing to her Secretary of State for Foreign Affairs:

> *Whatever may be the usual practice of Prussian Princes, it is not every day that one marries the daughter of the Queen of England.*[27]

The Prussians for their part resented being treated by the English newspaper editors as though they were a petty German state and not an important

---

* From the latest studies it seems unlikely that he was suffering from the disease porphyria transmitted to the Houses of Stewart, Hanover and Brandenburg-Prussia by Mary, Queen of Scots, and which included amongst its most notable victims Frederick the Great of Prussia and George III of England.[26]

sovereign nation with an illustrious history. Grimly they held to their decision that the future Princess Frederick of Prussia was to have an entirely German Household. Queen Victoria exclaimed it was 'heartless', but had to give way. Nevertheless she insisted that her daughter's nominated physician be sent over to learn sound English methods.

When the marriage day arrived the Queen was in such a state of nerves that sitting still for the required length of time to take a daguerrotype was quite beyond her. A blurred mess was the result with the Prince Consort looking ill and drawn and the bride made rather less than pretty by anxiety. For all that there was a thick January fog, the day went well; though, emotionally, everyone was preparing for *the* day, that of departure.

The Times then sounded a muted clarion of gloom:

> *We only trust and pray that the policy of England and Prussia may never present any painful alternative to the Princess now about to leave our shores.*

The English Royal Family echoed it. Prince Frederick looked on with dismay as his bride's lips trembled and she cried and cried, her brothers and sisters howled, the Prince Consort sobbed and Queen Victoria shrieked. Such agitation. A Cockney brewer's drayman had called out on the way to Gravesend: 'Be good to 'er, or we'll 'ave 'er back'.[28]

The Royal Yacht made a good crossing and afterwards they went by train to Berlin, calling at important places on the track so that notables could pay their respects. One gift, a colossal apple pie presented to her by the burgomaster of Wittenberg, delighted the Princess, but later when a Prussian Field Marshal, Count von Wrangel, joined the suite to pay his compliments, he inadvertently sat on the pie and ruined it.[29]

In Berlin they were given a chilling reception in both senses of the word. The weather was icy and they had to ride in evening dress in an open carriage to be welcomed by the extremely odd old King and the Queen who did not care for England or Englishwomen. In their first home, the Old Palace in Berlin, there was a peculiar lack of comfort. The apartments had not been used nor, on account of the smells, bugs and bats, did it appear that they had been cared for since Frederick William III had died there eighteen years before, and the Princess had to pass through his gloomy death-chamber every time she went from her boudoir to her bedroom. One of her German ladies-in-waiting declared that no-one could have washed in the old days.

> *If you were lucky you found a basin, the size of an entrée dish of some precious porcelain, Dresden or Carl Theodore, and a bottle of water of priceless ruby glass.*[30]

The young Princess Frederick would have borne better with dirt and the discomfort if there had been any prospect of making improvements, but permission for the least change had to be obtained from the King who was mad, and she had to endure no wardrobe space or chests of drawers for all her massive trousseau, and surly and inefficient servants. Anyone less in love and less determined than she would have found everything unbearable, but she had been trained by her father to achieve her destiny in the shaping of Germany's history, and to carry that out she would have tolerated any discomfort.

Unhappily and quite unconsciously her adoring father had given her a very heavy burden. She was to enlighten her husband and, through him, Prussia and never forget that she was an Englishwoman brought up according to English ways and methods – and that they were undoubtedly the best. Already he had himself forgotten that, on leaving Coburg to marry Queen Victoria, he had vowed to his sorrowing, swooning grandmother: 'I shall never cease to be a true German, Coburger and Gothaner'.[31]

CHAPTER TWO

Cradle and Nursery

'You must not hide him away with a blush'

THE PRINCE CONSORT TO HIS ELDEST
DAUGHTER

I

Prince Frederick William Victor Albert was the first fruit of that meeting in the Crystal Palace. When he was born on January 27th, 1859, there was enormous excitement in Berlin. Prince William, the Regent, had made diligent preparations with a saluting battery to announce the birth of a royal prince or princess or even twins; and, as the cannon began to thunder, he threw his customary parsimony to one side, rushed out of his dingy palace, and took a cab to see his grandchild. Meanwhile Count von Wrangel, that same veteran Field Marshal who had sat on the giant apple pie, took it upon himself to announce the birth of a prince to the waiting crowds outside the palace. Impatient, not wishing to waste a second by opening the window, he smashed the glass, stuck his head through the aperture and roared: 'It's a prince, and a hefty recruit into the bargain.'[1]

These are undisputed facts. More disputed is the actual location of Prince William's birth. Most probably he was born in one of the two royal palaces on Unter den Linden – the other was occupied by the Regent – which had been handed over as Prince Frederick's Berlin residence the previous November and which, in time, became known as the Crown Prince's Palace. Less likely is that he was born at the Old Palace where his parents had first settled as a young married couple. Still less probable is the story that he was born in Potsdam, sixteen miles away to the south-west, at Babelsberg, a mock Windsor Castle structure built by the Regent which his son and daughter-in-law had been allowed to use five months after their marriage. Princess Frederick detested the place as her taste was not in accord with the Princess of Prussia and there was not a square inch of space for her own considerable collection of paintings, keepsakes, curios, and memento mori. Moreover her bedroom was directly over the palace kitchen, stifling in hot weather, and perpetually redolent of cooking greens. In any case Babelsberg was a summer residence and the birth took place in January. Yet only if he had been born at Babelsburg could the extravagant story surrounding William's birth have had any foundation.[2] This, in brief, was that the Princess's physician, Dr Wegner – who had been invited to England to see how things were done, and had actually attended the last confinement of Queen Victoria – was so resentful of the fact that a Scotch doctor had been sent over to keep an eye on things he insisted on the foreigner being lodged in Berlin, an hour's fast drive from Potsdam. Then, when the Princess's labour began, he was so casual about sending for the Scot that a note was posted rather than sent by special messenger, and it did not reach its destination for thirty-six hours. By this time the Princess was in a very bad way indeed, the birth being a breech-presentation complicated by *placenta previa*. When the hated foreigner arrived he was told by one of the German doctors it was no use, neither mother nor son could be saved. One version reads that he spoke in English; another that he used Latin which, though three-quarters dead, the learned Princess immediately understood, and used all her will power to assist the Scotch doctor in what he had to do.[3] As a result both she and her firstborn lived.

This and other stories persisted in print down to 1971, and will doubtless be resurrected again. They demonstrate the strong antipathy at that time between the Prussians and the English. Certainly many at the Prussian Court felt an animosity against the English wife of the Heir Apparent. The English newspapers, which were read widely in Berlin, did not help her situation but it appears she had done little to help herself. In the year since her arrival in the country Princess Frederick had indiscreetly compared the many differences between the two countries. She disliked eating dinner in full evening dress half-way through the afternoon. She abhorred the long, tedious and apparently meaningless ceremonies. She took an interest in politics which was promptly squashed. She would leave her carriage and walk about as she thought incognito, indifferent to or unaware of the fact that the breadth of her coachman's hat ribbon told everyone that a member of the royal family was in the neighbourhood, and this was squashed as well.[4] She loathed the Prussian addiction to uniforms, especially their boots, and loathed Prussian plumbing, Prussian etiquette, and her inability to entertain savants rather than her stuffy relations. The last was the worst of all. She missed the freedom of her old life, the intellectual pursuits she had been taught to admire and enjoy.

With a strange lack of shrewdness in two otherwise shrewd people, her parents did not encourage her to be less complaining and more discreet. Unwisely they persuaded Stockmar to let his son Baron Ernest go to Berlin as her Private Secretary. The Prince Consort wrote to say he quite understood her feelings and her homesickness and that he regretted Fritz had 'taken up the game of soldiering'.[5] Twice he visited her in the first twelve months of the marriage. Her brother, the Prince of Wales, spent three weeks in Berlin and reminded her of all things English. Queen Victoria, who confined herself to one visit which was not a great success – 'tears flowed fast'[6] – wrote endlessly about the topics she now at last could discuss with her daughter, as well as the importance of opening medicines, draught screens, the importance of calling herself 'Victoria, Princess Royal, Princess Frederick William of Prussia'. And she begged her:

Never, dear child, let go what you owe to your country.

In fact, she bombarded Berlin with such torrents of possessive parental advice that she threw the Princess into a state of nerves and, very delicately, through the Stockmars, the Foreign Secretary and the Prince Consort, had to be persuaded to lessen the flood for the sake of her daughter at this delicate time.[7] Some of the advice from England was sound, the rest served to stimulate the Princess's Englishness which was certain to ruffle a proud and sensitive people like the Prussians.*

However much she had suffered, and however indiscreet she had been during the past year, the birth of an heir restored her own personal joy and put her in general favour. No-one appeared to mind now that her nursemaid was a Mrs Hobbs, her midwife Mrs Innocent, and that Dr Martin continued to stay on for the time being.

It was Mrs Innocent the midwife who, on the day following the birth after the little Prince had been proudly presented to his grandparents and an illustrious gathering of courtiers, remarked to Dr Martin that there was something wrong with his arm. It appeared to be loose in its socket. It had a bluish tinge. Clearly in the difficult circumstances of delivery someone had bungled. And in the anxious business of getting the baby to use its lungs and cry the slight deformity had not been noticed. Now that it was noticed a scapegoat had to be found. There was no lack of them. And the most implausible theories were propounded: that the modest English practice of keeping the Princess covered throughout the delivery had caused the trouble; that this could have been put right if it had been seen and treated at once; and that instantly the Princess '*whose enthusiasms were all for beauty and aesthetic harmony, was hard, hostile, bitter, whenever she recalled the coming of the Prince into the world*'.[8] This last was written with hindsight, and after Prince William

---

* An extraordinary fact, which everyone appeared to have overlooked, was that the Princess could scarcely lay claim to be English at all. She was Guelph-Coburg. Her closest English ancestor, that is, as opposed to Welsh or Scotch or British, had died in 1503.

had fallen out with his mother, and contradicts the other report that both Prince and Princess Frederick were delighted with their son, were sorry for his misfortune, but were determined that it should make no difference. Mrs Hobbs should gently massage his arm each day. Specialists in manipulation should do all that could be done. And William should be treated as any other member of the family.*

The young Prince was christened soon after his birth according to the simple rite of the Evangelical Church of Prussia but with the complication of having no less than forty-two sponsors.[10] The four grandparents thought this excessive number lessened the honour of being a godparent, but Queen Victoria insisted that from their privileged position they would have the greatest influence on the child. To some extent she was correct.

No-one so forceful and sure of herself as William's maternal grandmother could fail to have a profound influence. In his book *My Early Life*, written as an old man in Holland, the Kaiser recorded his precocious first memory of being at Osborne in the summer of 1861. He was then two and a half years old, and from that time whether she was indulging him or rebuking him he never failed to love and respect Queen Victoria. They could have cross words; to her Prime Minister she once described her grandson's actions as 'too *vulgar* and too absurd, as well as untrue, almost *to be believed*';[11] and he, on one occasion, referred to her as 'an old hag';[12] but she had a closer understanding of him than almost anyone in his family. He was immensely proud of the indomitable little queen with her vast empire, great charm, and manner so grand that though she dressed frumpishly, and was once mistaken for a washerwoman, she could yet make great men quail.

The child's maternal grandfather was to have a less abiding influence, for he was to die within three years, but it was to be lasting. All the Prince Consort had learnt from Stockmar and from his studies of political economy was to affect William through his mother for many years. They had some proclivities in common, too. Both preferred the society of men to that of women; both in their heart claimed, as Frederick the Great had done, to despise the masses, yet both were concerned for their welfare.[13] Both were inventors and not very successful ones. It is pleasant to compare the Prince Consort's discovery for the conversion of sewage into agricultural manure which 'owing to a slight miscalculation, proved to be impracticable',[14] and his grandson's plans for a ship which would do everything but float.[15]

Inevitably, because they were closer at hand and part of his milieu, the

* One of the sourest of all stories concerning this event is that, under pressure from the Princess of Prussia and Queen Victoria, Princess Frederick gave up nursing her baby and that years later he was informed she had done so because she found his deformity so repugnant.[9]

child's paternal grandparents had the more forceful sway over his develop-
ment. They were an ill-assorted couple. Their portraits show them as benign;
he, tall, white-whiskered, handsome in a miliatry fashion; she, be-jewelled,
dark with fine features that could be alive with fun or calm with repose.

The Princess of Prussia was the more sparkling of the two, yet she had
less effect upon her grandson. She would indulge him and later his brothers
and sisters, but it was only to please herself. To them she was a fairy figure
because she had personally known Goethe at her father's court of Saxe-
Weimar, and they could not understand why she cared so little for food or
ordinary comforts.[16] In fact, because of the bitterness between her and her
husband, which neither troubled to conceal and which made them live
virtually separate lives, she became increasingly neurotic, developed unfortunate and very close relationships with her ladies-in-waiting, and took to
absenting herself from Berlin for long periods at a time.[17] She would go to
her castle at Koblenz where amongst the German princely families she became known, not entirely affectionately, as the 'Dragon of the Rhine'.[18]
One of the cleverest women of her time, she would relax her brain by reading
French novels, had enormous energy and, according to her daughter-in-
law, 'could stand more fatigue and excitement than anyone I know'.[19] A
custom at the Prussian Court was for her to have open 'Thursdays' during
Lent, when the entire royal family, the Diplomatic Corps, and specially
commanded guests were obliged to put in an appearance. The procedure and
menu never varied, and the *cercling* bored and exhausted everyone except
apparently the indomitable Princess of Prussia, who had been taught the
art as a child, circumnavigating a lawn in Weimar and speaking appropriately to each tree and shrub as she passed it.[20] At one point in William's
life she took him up, and was not then an especially good influence on him.
Otherwise she looked on him with a kindly eye and wrote reams about him
to her co-grandmother in England.

To the little William, 'Grandmama' was always Queen Victoria and
'Grandpapa', the Prince of Prussia, Regent, until the death of his mad
brother in 1861 when he became King William. He loved both passionately,
far more than his parents.

William I was that contradiction in terms, a kindly martinet. As a boy
of sixteen he had fought courageously against Napoleon at Leipzig, but
lacked the courage to try a lobster at the battle banquet afterwards because
he had never eaten one before.[21] This he soon remedied in secret and thereafter developed the eccentric habit of eating lobster salad at midnight, a
practice he carried on with few interruptions for the next seventy-five
years.[22] It was one of his few extravagances. Frugal by nature, his 'royal
train' was a single small coach halted at station restaurants for dinner, his

bedroom in Berlin was decorated with prints of Prussian and Russian uniforms, a large picture of his mother laid out for burial, a Crucifix, and an
army bed; and, not holding with the expense of bathrooms, he borrowed a
tub from a nearby hotel once a fortnight in which he was scrubbed with army
soap and scrubbing brushes by his valet, Eysel.[23] Essentially Prussian he
had accepted the impossibility of marrying into a non-sovereign princely
family, and had pined for his first love, Princess Eliza Radziwill, all his life.
This pining had not, however, prevented him from using the covered
archway from his palace on Unter den Linden to the Netherland Palace
presumably for assignations;[24] nor had it helped soothe the antagonism he
felt for the wife who had been forced on him. Unless they were actually
in the middle of a formal ceremonial, he never missed an opportunity of
making his feelings plain. They quarrelled, at the top of their voices, in front
of the whole court. Newcomers were startled and embarrassed. No-one else
worried very much. Autocratic in the extreme, if the King was crossed by
anyone he would grind his teeth and shout; but he always had time and a
smile for his eldest grandson William who remembered that the happiest
days of his early life were when he was allowed to dine with Grandpapa. On
these occasions the ogre became a charming old man, though his frugality
remained the same. After the meal he would mark the champagne bottle to
check on thieving servants and go off to change into his second-best trousers
before he left for the theatre.[25]

These, and loving though not uncritical parents, and a galaxy of nurses,
footmen, grooms and other factotums, were the lodestars of William's
existence in his infancy.

2

In the spring of 1859 William's parents moved into apartments in Frederick
the Great's superb New Palace at Potsdam. There was not much space as
yet, for the palace had been used for pensioned ladies-in-waiting and they
had to die off one by one before their apartments could be taken over; but
it was so much more beautiful a place than Babelsberg, and did not smell of
cooking greens.

It had been the Prince Consort's suggestion that they move there. His
artistic eye at once took in its possibilities, and once the Regent's permission
had been obtained, he sent plans for cleaning and re-furbishing, and making
plantations outside which were at once put into effect. Obligingly the
ladies-in-waiting began to die off and eventually the full beauty of the palace
was revealed.

At a later stage Disraeli was to call it 'A Paradise of Rococo' which was possibly an understatement. It had several galleries and magnificent stair-cases and a private theatre, the servants' quarters and kitchens being in an entirely separate building. The Tassen Zimmer was a great curiosity; a room where coffee was taken modelled in the shape of a cup with furniture constructed to add to the illusion. No less so, right at the centre of the palace was the Muschel-Saal, which had walls covered with every variety of shell arranged in intricate arabesques and patterns of roses, stars and spirals. The middle pillars of the room were stuccoed with amber from the Baltic, lapis lazuli, malachite, onyx, jasper, alabaster and porphyry, and different coloured, highly-polished pieces of quartz. The giant Marble Hall had stupendous stucco work by Pedrozzi, and each of the many reception rooms differed in furnishings and decorations. There was one with hunting decorations and superb furniture by the brothers Spindler; another, the Green Damask room, had a wide outlook on the park as far as the great fountain, and Watteaus and Poussins on the walls; and so on. The cupola was topped by a trio of scarcely draped nude ladies holding a crown, the three who had caused Frederick the Great the most trouble in his lifetime – Catherine the Great, the Empress Maria Theresa, and Madame de Pompadour.[26]

When they moved into the palace the Prince and Princess Frederick found the interior in a great muddle and mess. Furniture had wandered from apartment to apartment and it took some investigation and fine judgement to discover where each piece properly belonged. The Princess was in her element doing this. She was not her father's daughter for nothing. Slowly, and patiently because kindness dictated she should not rush the pensioned ladies-in-waiting, she restored the Palace to what it once had been, a pride of the Kingdom of Prussia. Her detractors were not grateful. They sniffed and called it 'The Palace of the Medicis'.[27] She did not greatly mind. The New Palace was to be her family home for almost thirty years.

During the summer months it was in these elegant surroundings – for even the nurseries were beautiful – that the young Prince William first became aware of things. Taken for airings in the pleasure grounds, or by the river Havel, or, for treats, to the other palaces at Potsdam, the exquisite Sans Souci adorned with fountains, statuary and artificial ruins, and the Marble Palace, he must inevitably have absorbed some of the beauty. His nurses dutifully reported that he enjoyed the drumming of the Lehrbataillon, a battalion of infantry composed of drafts from different regiments trained together at Potsdam to ensure unity of drill throughout the army; and certainly he delighted in the peal of bells from the Garrison Church which at each hour played the tune of the first line of the hymn 'Always be faithful and sincere'.[28]

In the winter months at the Crown Prince Palace he went out less, adored

Mrs Hobbs and his mother and father, and hated a Fräulein von Dobeneck, a preceptress who was brought in even at this early stage to form his character and increase his potentiality for learning. Presumably she was Stockmar-chosen and therefore reliable. To the baby William she was 'Dokka', and a source of menace.

He grew used to medical gentlemen prodding him about and examining his left arm and side. They left him to Mrs Hobbs' gentle massaging until he grew a little when they tried the latest methods of manipulation; forcing him to wear braces, clamps, a medical boot, subjecting him to galvanic shocks which it was hoped would work the small arm into growth and re-adjust his unbalanced left side. Their reports to his parents were not optimistic. Medical reports on royal children seldom were – in case of accidents. But it seemed clear that the child's left arm would not develop and it gave an appearance of atrophying. The general weakness of his left side, which, as soon as he could walk, gave him an unbalanced tottery look, could doubtless be corrected by regular exercise, manipulation, more iron braces, and the Prussian spirit.

Quite understanding what his perfectionist daughter might be going through, the Prince Consort wrote to advise her: 'You must not hide him away with a blush, as you used to hide your drawings in the portfolio.'[29] Her reply was non-committal. Nevertheless she was careful at Christmas to include with the Berlin present for Windsor of a boar's head and an album of photographs, a bust of little William's head.

It is impossible now to know whether or not her first instinct had been to hide her child away with a blush. Her subsequent attentiveness to William, her letters to her mother despairing at the pain and indignities the small child had to suffer, show that she was fully aware of his deformity – unlike some mothers who will not face the most obvious facts – but that in a common-sense sort of fashion she would not draw too much attention to it at home.

The Princess herself was unceasingly active during the formative years of her first child. Within the year she gave him a sister, Charlotte, and this time, and with her other children, she did not suffer the awful experiences of that first delivery.*

Then, politically she was absorbed in the sudden expansion of liberal ideas. The Bourbons were driven from Naples, the Federal States set about correcting the Confederacy, and the Emperor of Russia actually emancipated the serfs. As if to even the balances the mad King of Prussia died, her reactionary father and mother-in-law became King and Queen and she and her husband

* This caused an amusing contretemps in the Windsor nursery with the three-year-old Princess Beatrice who, when required to do something she felt disinclined to do, claimed that she had no time as she was busy writing to her niece.[30]

were Crown Prince and Princess. Soon after this her grandmother died in England and Queen Victoria nearly went out of her mind with remorse because, quite understandably, she had not got on at all well with the old lady. Rushing to console her mother, then rushing back to her family in Berlin, the Princess found the Court there agog with the news that the Queen of England was being restrained in a padded cell. Even Queen Augusta believed the story. The Princess sent off an urgent plea to her father to make Mama pull herself together and stop this ugly whispering in the Courts of Europe. In June she returned with her husband and son to Buckingham Palace and Osborne. Papa with the aid of Stockmar had done all that was necessary. The rumours had died. Mama was given to hysterical outbursts. No more. But Papa himself looked strained. He was goodness itself with her little William, dandling him in a napkin in the Osborne dining-room, but he looked distant, waxy, overfat, not at all himself. Five months later when the Crown Princess was carrying her third child, and under no circumstances was allowed to travel, came the thunder-clap from Windsor. Her adored father was dead. The Crown Prince at once left for England. His wife was distraught. At one, totally unexpected stroke she had lost a father, mentor, comforter, and dearest friend; but, when the first burst of grief had quietened, she saw, with horrible clarity, that her mother had lost more. Theirs she knew, had been a great love. They had quarrelled occasionally. As recently as three months before Queen Victoria had admitted that her husband was not perfect, indeed he could be very trying; but this had been but a tiff. Theirs was one of the happiest royal mar-riages in history and now suddenly one of the pair was dead, the other a widow of forty-two. Loving her husband as she did, the Crown Princess understood more than most what her mother had to go through, but she was quick to defend her brother, the Prince of Wales, when Mama blamed him for the tragedy. He had been having an affair with an actress, and to correct him his father had gone down to Cambridge where he was an undergraduate, and there had caught the fatal chill. The Crown Princess agreed that her brother should be married off as soon as possible – and she spent much of her energies that year in finding him a suitable bride – but she would not agree that he had killed off Papa.[31] Her husband agreed with her and went to some trouble to calm his nerve-racked mother-in-law. He promised to return to England in March and open the Second Exhibition in the place of the dead Prince Consort and to return a third time in June to give Princess Alice away in her marriage to Prince Louis of Hesse-Darmstadt. Under no circumstances was the Prince of Wales to be allowed to do these chores. He was packed off to Egypt and the Holy Land to be out of his mother's eyesight, returning via 'that Sodom and Gommorah, Paris'.[32]

It is alleged that King William behaved badly about the Prince Consort's death; that for some time he had been putting all letters from England at the back of the fire unopened;[33] that he had joined the general rejoicing because a certain Captain Macdonald, disputing his right to a seat in a railway carriage at Bonn Station, had laid about him with a cane and, in the legal process which landed him in gaol, the local public prosecutor had condemned the behaviour of the British travellers in Germany as 'rude, boorish and arrogant';[34] that he had ostentatiously crowned himself King at Königsberg 'by God's Grace', thereby re-declaring a doctrine of Divine Right thrown out by the English two hundred years before and which was quite odious to the Prince Consort; and, finally, after a week's short mourning, he went off for his usual two months' cure at Ems, made no pretence and grief, and condoled with his daughter-in-law not directly but through Queen Victoria.[35] Certainly he was becoming more and more rigidly reactionary and blamed the Crown Princess for fouling the Prussian nest with liberalism.

It is alleged that, in return, the Crown Princess was openly hostile to the King, calling him stupid in the presence of other people, and making sure that her insults got back to him.[36] Certainly she was trying to continue her father's work of liberalizing Germany and realized that the King's political myopia stood in her way.

How much influence she had on her husband is questionable. They were reported to be very much in love and the stronger character in any love match does not necessarily maintain sway. He might have been ready to sacrifice his forcefulness as a token of affection. Like Queen Victoria the Crown Princess was more of a wife than a mother and she was more intensely practical than her husband, who had romantic dreams of the great Empire of Charlemagne but who was easily discouraged, deeply depressed at times, and given to violent bursts of temper.[37] The evidence suggests he was mildly *unter dem Pantoffel*. His first son gives this impression. When he was about three years of age, having been surrounded largely by women, Prince William possibly expected his big, bearded uniformed father to put his foot down as often and as noisily as his big, whiskered and uniformed grandfather. But he was disappointed. One day the Crown Prince stopped eating at luncheon and, no doubt jokingly, his little son at once piped up: 'Go on eating, darling, your little wife wishes it'.[38] This innocent remark caused great outward amusement at the table. Interior feelings were subdued. Yet whoever was *unter dem Pantoffel* there are many joyous pictures of the Crown Prince and Princess together: she laying aside her needlework to re-fill his tobacco pipes; both of them on boating trips on the Havel, picknicking out in the countryside near Potsdam; driving with their children through the pleasure gardens of the Lustgarten and Wilhelmplatz to visit the market gardens in the little town, making directly for those where winter violets were cultivated.

In August 1862 Prince Henry was added to the nursery. Queen Victoria condoled with her daughter at being confined in such hot weather. 'Spring is the only time for campaigns. [as she oddly called them in a letter] All of you were spring flowers.'

Hot weather or no, the Crown Princess was soon up and about again. Within a month she was at Coburg for a family reunion. With her she took William. Some of the party stayed with Duke Ernest at his hilltop Castle Kalenberg, but most were with Queen Victoria at Reinhardtsbrunn, a large palace eight miles from Coburg which the Prince Consort's father had saved from ruin and made very comfortable. It was there that the family gathered and, inevitably, there was at first a great grieving over a lost husband and father. But then there was rejoicing because the Prince of Wales had just become engaged to Princess Alexandra of Denmark and, from the way he looked and spoke, it seemed as if he really loved her. No doubt secret feminine confidences were shared; that Princess Alice, so very happy with her Louis, would have her first child in the following April; and that Prince Alfred, now in the Royal Navy, had turned out as bad as his brother and had had what the Queen called 'a fall' – if not several. Great astonishment was expressed over the King of Prussia's determination to abdicate if his ox-headed Parliament would not let through the laws he wanted, and even more when the King himself arrived at Coburg and spoke gloomily of ending up on a scaffold in the Berlin Forum Fredericianum like Charles I in Whitehall.[39] The party brightened perceptibly when, as mysteriously as he had arrived, he went away again.

Queen Victoria was at some pains to remind William of his maternal grandfather. She took him for rides with her in the park and the forests, and bade him never forget Grandpapa Albert, and be loving and obedient to his parents; and when, after tea one day on the lawn, he rode into her presence on a donkey with Mrs Hobbs holding a parasol over his head, she was enchanted, gave him a kiss and a cake, and said he was a brave boy.[40]

William liked Reinhardtsbrunn. The woods came down to the wide water meadows. All the local people were friendly and had the time to talk – quite unlike the Berliners who were always on the run. It was a peaceful, beautiful country place. Nevertheless William must have sensed that a good deal was going on in the house. Arrangements were being made. Uncle Bertie of Wales was to go with Papa and Mama on a long sea cruise. Apparently Grandpapa of Prussia was no longer worried. He had a new Minister-President of his Parliament who was so much more obliging, a Junker called Otto von Bismarck.[41]

William was taught to apportion his time as his mother had been. So much had to be allowed for study, so much for play, so much, in his case, for medical manipulation, so much for ablutions, and so forth. Quite early in his life he showed that he preferred this methodical way of living. A less valued inheritance was the strong self-will of his mother, and the anger and moodiness of his ordinarily placid father. Unless Mrs Hobbs was at hand to restrain the one or placate the other, his rages could be tempestuous and his megrims pitiful. Unhappily at the marriage of his uncle, the Prince of Wales, to Princess Alexandra of Denmark, Mrs Hobbs was at home in the Crown Prince's Palace nurseries looking after Charlotte and Henry, or Charly and Harry as they were now called, and Prince William of Prussia got himself into scrape after scrape. He turned sullen when reproved for throwing an aunt's muff out of the carriage window in Windsor High Street, and caused long faces by addressing his grandmother and the Sovereign of England as 'Duck';[42] but his naughtiness exceeded all bounds when, wearing the kilt like his bachelor uncles, the Princes Arthur and Leopold, he grew bored with the long wedding ceremony and to relieve the tedium, prised the cairngorm from his dirk and hurled it across St George's Chapel. Corrected by Prince Leopold, his temper flew. He drew his dirk and brandished it. And when Prince Arthur objected, he promptly bit him in the leg.[43] When made to apologize afterwards he observed truly that at least he had gone willingly to the monotonous ceremony unlike the bride's youngest brother who, obsessed with a toy donkey, had put back his head and howled and made a fearful scene when driven into St George's Chapel.[44] He capped these events on the way home to the safety of Mrs Hobbs by declaring that the Princess of the Netherlands* who was sharing their carriage was 'an ugly old monkey'.[45]

At that age he must have been perceptive enough to realize that while his own heart raced at the thought of going home, the prospect was apparently making his parents more and more despondent. If anyone had told him that very moment they were considering living mostly in England and only part of the year in Germany he would not have believed it. In fact they were so depressed by the reactionary policies of Bismarck, the new Minister-President who was also Foreign Secretary of Prussia, that the Crown Princess had already suggested the move to Queen Victoria, who had said she would be delighted to find them a home.[46]

When they reached Berlin the Crown Prince intended to sound his father's views and if necessary ask for his permission to live chiefly abroad.

He did this even while Mrs Hobbs was hugging Prince William and simultaneously scolding him for his wickedness at Windsor, and the old King was at first angry and then cold. He said he would continue to support

* Princess Frederick of the Netherlands was a younger sister of the King of Prussia.

his Minister who knew the value of militarism, authoritarianism and patriotism. As for his disloyal son, who seemed to prefer liberalism and parliamentarianism, he was quite indifferent where he lived. So long as he left his sons behind the Crown Prince could take himself off to Tokyo or Togoland for all that the old King cared. This resolved the Crown Prince and Princess. They would have to stay where they were. As the Berliners put it, things were 'going to the cuckoo' but, rather than run away, they felt obliged to remain and face increasing hostility at Court. Solemnly they pledged themselves to speak out if and when anything unconstitutional took place.[47] They had less than a month to wait. Bismarck muzzled the press with immense bribes (taken from the revenues of the Cologne–Minden railway) and ordered censorship. The Crown Prince made a speech at Danzig: 'I knew nothing of this order beforehand. I was absent [from the Council] and not one of those who advised it.' Instantly there was a furore.[48] The King demanded that his son deny the statement. The Crown Prince refused. He was harangued, harassed, and threatened with imprisonment in a fortress. The Crown Princess immediately thought of her secretary's father Baron Stockmar. But the old man was dying. Before the appeal could reach him he was dead. He was mourned by half the royal families of Europe, but none mourned him more than the Crown Prince and Princess who so desperately required his sage advice. In the end, under great pressure, the Crown Prince gave way. He was forced to give a solemn undertaking that never again would he make a public announcement without prior permission from his father.

At the end of this exhausting episode the Crown Prince and Princess found themselves isolated. Baron Ernest Stockmar could stand the situation no longer. He begged to be excused on long leave. He would like, he said, to return to Gotha. He felt like a squeezed orange.[49] Robert Morier, at the British Embassy, was their one dependable friend left and it could only be a question of time before Bismarck managed to get him transferred.

It was against this hushed and sinister political background that William and his brothers and sisters grew up. They could barely fail to have been aware of it.

3

Prince William had his own especial worries which no-one could share and which greatly grieved his parents. Besides his congenital infirmity he had a tendency to catch colds, no matter how careful his nurses were, and they had a dreadful effect upon him. Not only did his colds last longer than anyone else's, but they aggravated all sorts of other weaknesses. As a man he had an almost pathological fear of infection, and no-one with a cold would dare to approach him at Court or, if possible, admit that he had one; and his oft-quoted remark that the cold he had was not a little one but a big one because everything about him was big sounds less clownish and big-headed if it is remembered that in fact his colds never *were* little ones.[50] When he was a small boy of three his mother wrote to Osborne:

William has inflamed eyes and is shut up in his room which makes him look like a cheese. His eyes discharge a good deal of matter and are much swollen; he had this before [five months previously] *but it was only one eye then and now it is both. Wegner says it proceeds from cold.*[51]

It was not only a question of colds. The ordinary course of childhood ailments, which Charly and Harry shrugged off so cheerfully, seemed so much worse when he caught them.

Precisely when his father was tilting a first hopeless lance at Bismarck's tyranny, William was confronted with a new machine which, it was hoped, would cure the weakness on the left side of his neck. His mother described it in a letter:

The machine consists of a belt round the waist to which is affixed an iron rod or bar which passes up the back to which a thing looking very like the bridle of a horse is attached. The head is strapped into this and then turned as required with a screw which moves the iron. When the head is firm in the leather strap it is made to turn towards the left so as to stretch the muscles of the right side of the neck ...

This was to be worn for an hour a day. If it did not bring good results, some of the sinews of his neck would have to be cut.[52]

Most of the heavy and enduring equipment used in the last century now excites admiration. Heavy drawers and doors closed with such a heavy, soapy chunk; tantalus cases and cigar humidors, the first cameras and wireless sets with coils and earphones; even the camping equipment of explorers were all beautifully, satisfyingly constructed. But in a modern age of light metal alloys and plastics, it is difficult to imagine the sheer solidity of orthopaedic apparatus a hundred years ago. The young Prince, understandably, did not care for them.

The Crown Princess wrote from the New Palace:

Poor Willie is so tormented with all these machines and things, that it makes him cross and difficult to manage. Poor child really he is sadly tried. He is so very funny sometimes. He had a sergeant who comes in the morning to make him do exercises, in order that he should be made to hold himself upright and use his left arm. When he does not wish to do his exercises he begins to say his prayers. ...[53]

It would be wrong, perhaps, to make too much of the child's considerable handicaps. As a boy and man the Prince largely overcame them. How much, and in what way, he might have compensated for them later lies beyond the capacity even if, properly, it lies within the terms of reference of a biographer, but it is worth recalling that some great men have been equally crippled. The 1st Earl of Halifax, an outstanding English statesman, had a similar withered arm, and the late President Franklin D. Roosevelt ruled firmly from a wheelchair, his legs encased in irons.

However formidable and tedious these treatments, it is almost certain they were a help. When the time came for Prince William to leave the tutelage of women at the age of seven, he was much stronger than anyone could have expected.

By this time he had seen his father ride out to fight against the Danes, and return in triumph a few weeks later, determined to rearrange his timetable so that he could see more of his children. It did not involve much adjustment because, apart from parades, reviews and manoeuvres, he had barely anything to do. Neither the King nor Bismarck would give him responsible work. But his decision gave great pleasure to William and Harry.

The Crown Prince took them for long walks, taught them to swim and to row on the Havel. Later he taught them to sail. He took them to museums and galleries and on visits to relations. Their favourite visit was to the dowager Queen Elizabeth who lived in the exquisite Sans Souci Palace in summer and at the Charlottenburg Palace in winter. They saw endless mementoes of Frederick the Great and Voltaire the philosopher, but neither Voltaire's workroom, nor the Marble Room, nor the gilded Music Room where Frederick had played his flute at Sans Souci, nor even the Polignac marbles at Charlottenburg interested them quite as much as a modern curiosity, a wooden model of Jerusalem which had removable domes. Allowed to raise them in turn they would gaze enchanted at the interior of the building. Though sometimes taciturn with his fellow officers and generally silent at family gatherings, the Crown Prince was a good talker with his sons. He taught them much. They heard a great deal about a good man, President Lincoln, who was assassinated, and another, Garibaldi, who was not; and rather less – possibly because their father could not trust his tongue – about that very controversial figure, Bismarck. To William especially his father passed on his own enthusiasm for the history of Greece and his fascination with archaeology; and the two would take down from the library shelf the heavy volume *German Treasures of the Holy Roman Empire* by Bock, and William watched and listened spellbound while his father turned the pages, explaining the illustrations, and dreamed his romantic dream out loud of restoring the glories of the Empire.[54]

Close as he was to his father, the little prince was naturally even closer to his mother. At a time when, in most of Europe, the inclination of parents and the possessiveness of nursemaids combined to keep children shut away save for small and regularly appointed periods of time when they were released to be appreciated, shown off, or scolded by their progenitors, the children of the Crown Prince and Princess were fortunate to be born in a country where this apartness existed less than anywhere else, and into an enlightened family. Parents and children always breakfasted together. At second breakfast or luncheon the children were present unless there were exceptionally important guests. The Crown Prince had made a resolve to see as much as possible of his children, and the Crown Princess apportioned part of every day to their general supervision.

In her first years as Crown Princess she was an extraordinarily active woman, subscribing to all the leading English and German newspapers and periodicals,* writing endless letters, gardening, taking lessons in mathematics and chemistry, and much interesting herself in hospitals, sanitation, schools, homes for fallen women, and, above all, in politics. She barely wasted a second of her day and, considering her preoccupation, it was surprising how much William saw of his mother in the early years. One of William's happier memories was watching her at work in her studio. It was a large, light, fascinating room with heaps of portfolios and albums and music, music stands, a piano, shelves, desks, easels and a mess of painting things. The Crown Princess had inherited from her mother a talent for water-colouring which a professional might have envied. William himself came to admire seascapes and painted some very adequate studies of his own. When later he had mastered his letters his mother liked him to read to her as she painted. As time passed, and his reading improved, he chose English books, the more amusing the better. At the funny parts her brush would be taken from the paper and she would laugh out loud, her round face growing redder and redder.[55] William read well. His English was good. Grammatically it was actually better than his mother's, though, in writing the language, he lacked her verve – or breathlessness of explanation. He would also read to her while she embroidered in her library; another fascinating apartment as it was a glazed gallery or arch with windows, like a Bridge of Sighs, which stretched from the Crown Prince's Palace to that of the Crown Princess. The open shelves were crammed with volumes in German, English, French and Italian. William was always very happy alone with his mother, though until the miraculous discovery of Bornstedt his time with her was rationed.

Bornstedt was found entirely by a happy accident because one afternoon

* In addition to the *Quarterly*, the *Fortnightly*, the *Saturday* and the *Edinburgh*, she also took the *Journal of Mining and Metallurgy*.[56]

the Crown Princess's coachman sleepily took a wrong turning and she found herself in an unknown, hidden and derelict village. The church was falling down, the cottages dirty and unkempt where the peasants slept higgledy-piggledy on straw with their boots on and ate only with their hands, and the one large farm was tumbledown and half smothered in weeds. The single existing asset of the place was an avenue of poplars leading to the farm; yet to the Crown Princess and to her husband who enthusiastically joined in her plans it had the superlative advantage of being a bolthole. Here, hidden away, though only a mile in a straight line from the Potsdam New Palace, they could take their children from time to time and live serene lives of privacy. They bought the property and transformed the cottages and church; built a school; largely reconstructed the farmhouse and outbuildings, and laid out pleasure gardens, vegetable plots, and fruit cages. The Crown Prince became a farmer owning cows, a squire so beneficent that the village children said in awe that he came from the Kingdom of God.[57] The Crown Princess made butter and cheese in her own dairy. The children rode a pair of Shetland ponies sent over by their English grandmother, helped make haycocks, hunted wild flowers and butterflies and played in the meadows and fell in the stream. In the evenings their father smoked his little tobacco pipe, and their mother sang *lieder* by Schubert and Schumann.[58] To all of them the discovery of Bornstedt made a lasting difference, although they could not be there for long periods and had perforce to follow the Court in its migrations back and forth between Potsdam and Berlin.

In January 1866 Prince William left Mrs Hobbs with some reluctance and the despotic 'Dokka' with none at all,* and moved into the schoolroom. He felt considerably more important than Charly or Harry or little Sigismund who had been added to the nursery two years before. Now he had his own military governor, a Captain von Schrötter of the artillery whom he immediately liked, and a tutor from Potsdam named Schüler who was excellent and to whom he was soon very much attached. Best of all a Sergeant Klee was selected to instruct him in drumming, and he drummed away, making a tremendous noise, to his heart's content. He was then a very happy small boy.[59]

* Sixty years later in *My Early Life*, he described her as 'a great gaunt dame of firm character and her method by no means excluded the use of the palm.'

CHAPTER THREE

Boyhood

'I have my doubts whether he is the right man'

BARON ERNEST VON STOCKMAR

I

On April 12th, 1866, Princess Victoria, named Moretta in the family, was born to the Crown Princess. The confinement was easy but the birth premature, a sign of the Crown Princess's uneasy state of mind. She was becoming morbidly afraid of Bismarck, who in May was made a count. His calumnies were ceaseless and she suspected that she and her husband were being spied on and their letters opened. Moreover his activities at that time were scarcely likely to win her approval. He was insistent that Prussia should be on a parity with the Empire of Francis Joseph in German affairs but rather than try to win this in the field of diplomacy he showed he had an almost mediaeval conception of war and used it as a political bludgeon to gain his point. That summer he mounted a campaign financed by a Jewish banking friend, Gerson Bleichröder and hurled Prussia and her allies onto the Austrians.[1] The Crown Princess considered this: *A mistake caused by the uncontrolled power of an unprincipled man,*[2] and she was distressed at the departure of her husband at the head of his troops. Her distress turned to anguish when her youngest son Sigismund suddenly contracted meningitis and within two days, because all the able doctors were at the front, he died.[3] Her nerves went astray and nothing seemed to bring her any relief. Exactly a fortnight after the child's death Bismarck's planned war ended in triumph at the battle of Königgrätz, but not even this, nor the news that her husband had been awarded the highest Prussian award for valour, Pour le Mérite, on the field of battle, could lighten her grief. She was also much concerned because her sister Alice of Hesse-Darmstadt had just borne a child and Hesse-Darmstadt had supported Austria. If the Tsar had not been married to a Hessian and brought some pressure to bear on King William the whole state would have been swallowed up. As it was, Alice's country was much diminished in treasure and territory. Schleswig and Holstein became totally Prussian. Hesse-Cassel, Nassau and Frankfurt were seized, and the unhappy King of Hanover lost his entire kingdom and a great part of his huge personal fortune, which Bismarck personally appropriated and used exclusively for corrupt practices such as bribing the press. As a reward for his leadership Count Bismarck was voted a grant of £40,000 by a grateful Prussian Parliament and he bought a large country estate with the money.[4] Now, in addition to being Minister-President and Foreign Minister of Prussia, he was also Chancellor of the new North German Federation. His personal power had been greatly extended.

2

It is a strange and, up to the present, unexplained phenomenon that with so many excellent men and women available for selection some royal families have a knack of failing badly when they choose tutors and governesses for their children. To give but three examples: Prince Albert, urged on by Stockmar, turned out a perfectly adequate clergyman tutor whom his sons liked and appointed in his place a martinet barrister whom they loathed, despite the fact that the gentleman's mother had died insane and his father bankrupt;[5] Queen Victoria appointed a French governess for her younger daughters and discovered she was teaching them a number of undesirable things, amongst them how to deceive their Mama;[6] and the Emperor Francis Joseph chose a bullying military man to supervise his heir's upbringing who, within a year, so worked on the boy's nerves that the Empress felt obliged to intervene.[7]

It seems inexplicable that the Crown Prince and Princess should have made the same blunder. Their eldest son could happily have been left with Herr Schüler, to whom he was devoted and who had all the necessary qualifications for such a position of trust, but Schüler was sent back to Potsdam High School and another was put in his place.

Dr George Hinzpeter had been brought to the Crown Prince's notice at the house of a friend.[8] Then he had become known to Robert Morier at the British Embassy who thought highly of his political ideals because his views on social reform and national economy happened to coincide with his own. The Crown Princess saw Hinzpeter herself and was impressed by his guarantee to mould the boy 'on the lines of the old Prussian simplicity'. Only Baron Ernest von Stockmar, seeing Hinzpeter on one of his now infrequent descents upon Berlin, rang a note of doubt. He wrote to Morier at the British Embassy:

I have seen your friend Hinzpeter and talked to him for three hours. He is a very superior man, but I have my doubts whether he is the right man. I am afraid he wants 'Gemuet' and is a hard Spartan idealist.

Another point which everyone overlooked was Hinzpeter's strict Calvinism. This is surprising. A well-informed group such as the Crown Princess's circle shǒuld have been aware that no dogma or ideology has had such an effect upon Western Christendom as John Calvin's doctrines of predestination, election and final perseverance – in fine, that the Almighty selects certain people for salvation; they alone can be saved and then only if they persevere, and the rest – no matter how hard they try – are irredeemably damned from the womb. Discounting, as it does, free-will, moral responsibility, and Divine love and mercy, it seems to make God into a selective monster. Its adherents are few but utterly determined.* It was also curious to put the future Head of the Lutheran Prussian Evangelical Church into the care of a Calvinistic zealot. They were living in the age of Renan's *Vie de Jésus*, Darwin's *Origin of Species*, and Higher Criticism, nevertheless religion was taken seriously in education and it seems inexplicable that Hinzpeter's religion should not have been an objection to his appointment. William himself claimed that Hinzpeter never made an attempt to proselytize him or his brother.[9] He gave them the Bible and Hymn Book and nothing else. But the disciplines and tenets of strict Calvinism are exceedingly combustible and could not have been kept permanently doused. Further it is questionable if it was wise or kind to put a sensitive boy, who had already suffered more frustration and bodily pain than most children, in the absolute control of so strict and humourless a man. Baron Ernest in saying Hinzpeter was 'a hard Spartan idealist' put his finger on the point, yet no-one paid much attention. Morier liked Hinzpeter's political views. The Crown Prince admired his lofty view of kingship. The Crown Princess, who described William at this time as 'a dear interesting charming boy', was quite aware of his failings.[10] He was by no means an easy child. Indeed at times he could be very captious and rebellious and arrogant. He needed humbling, and a firm hand. In that year of crises for the family he was placed into the exceedingly firm hands of Dr Hinzpeter.

William in *My Early Life* showed a suitable gratitude for all that Hinzpeter had done for him; yet in the same volume he describes the driving willpower which the tutor used to force him to become a good rider. Despite his physical handicap, a royal prince must be able to ride. William quoted

* Calvinism, in its first extreme form, has for centuries been losing ground. It has been much modified in the main Presbyterian and strict Baptist Churches. But its original severity is still found in isolated evangelical churches, and quite frequently in individual Calvinists like Hinzpeter.

at length Hinzpeter's own description of this lesson. An abstract is sufficient here:

> When the Prince was eight and a half years old, a lackey still had to lead his pony by the rein because his balance was so bad. . . . So long as this lasted, he could not learn to ride: it had to be overcome, no matter at what cost. Neither groom nor riding-master would do it. Therefore the tutor, using a moral authority over his pupil that by now had become absolute, set the weeping Prince on his horse, without stirrups and compelled him to go through the various paces. He fell off continually: every time, despite his prayers and tears, he was lifted up and set upon its back again. After weeks of torture the difficult task was accomplished: he had got his balance.[11]

The Prince added wryly that the result justified the method.

> But the lesson was a cruel one and my brother Henry often howled with pain when compelled to witness the martyrdom of my youth.[12]

Formal education under Hinzpeter was at first a surprise after being indulged in the nursery. It was not simply a question of learning Latin, history, geography, English and French, at which William did well because he had a quick memory, or of mathematics at which he did less well because he could see no sense in it, but of learning the special Spartan virtues of frugality – dry bread for breakfast, tenacity – twelve hours a day of study and physical exercise, and renunciation – handing round cakes to visitors but never taking one oneself. As he himself remarked: 'The strain on a boy of seven was pretty severe'.[13] Perhaps the biggest strain was that no word of praise ever fell from the tutor's lips. His green-speckled eyes never lit up with encouraging warmth. Neither William, nor Harry, who joined him in 1868, were ever encouraged, or ever given an approving word no matter how hard they had tried or how successful they had been.[14] But, though they were unaware of it at the time, William and Harry did enjoy a special privilege because of Hinzpeter. On Wednesday and Saturday afternoons he took them to foundries, workshops, factories, gardener's sheds, and farms, not only to let them see how the special work was done but also who was doing it. They saw things of which their contemporaries in the royal school-rooms of Europe were entirely ignorant. Very early they learnt about social inequalities and social injustices. It was a part of the tutor's lofty idea of sovereignty that a monarch must know all about his people. He must also know his kingdom. To further this purpose he took the boys on expeditions to the coast and into the country. Some were didactic; to Essen, for example, where the boys went down a mine and over the huge steel works of the

Krupp family, and to Gotha, where William saw his future Empress for the first time, and where they visited a mediaeval copperworks and a glass factory. And they also went to places to enjoy boating or walking. Their royal position was never forgotten but they were allowed to go to folk-plays and fairs and were not overprotected from the coarseness and brutality of the day. So far as Hinzpeter was concerned each experience was a lesson learnt. He noted without comment, but presumably with approval, when Prince William showed his disgust at the goose game at a fair on the Flemish coast. A well soaped goose was hung by the head from a pole and grabbed at by passers by. Generally it slid through their hands, but in the end the goose would have its head torn off by a triumphant peasant.[15] On the same holiday the King of the Belgians, of whom Hinzpeter did not approve, sent the boys a basket of delicious fruit from his hothouses. Renunciation was commanded. Neither boy was allowed to touch a single fruit.[16] Sometimes a chosen companion was permitted to go on these expeditions, but the choice was limited to scions of the princely houses of the North German Federation, and occasionally the boys joined their parents on a holiday, though the word holiday was something of an exaggeration. With only slight modification, the daily work routine, almost as immutable as the laws of the Medes and Persians, continued without interruption.

3

No-one in Prussia could consider himself anyone unless he was in the Officer Corps or the Reserve Officer Corps, and it was next to impossible to enter either without the right background. It was not difficult to achieve the ennobling 'von', as Bleichröder did for financing the Austrian War and being Bismarck's banker,[17] but that by no means entitled a man to a commission in the Reserve Officer Corps and permission to wear the uniform of a smart regiment. Even Bismarck had been content with a mere lieutenancy in the Reserve until the Austrian campaign, when he quickly promoted himself temporary major-general; and thereafter he gave up the frock coat of the Minister-President and for ever wore military uniform as Chancellor.[18] Inevitably army service was obligatory to all princes of the House of Hohen-zollern.

On January 27th, 1869, Prince William received his commission from his grandfather the King, and simultaneously was invested with the Order of the Black Eagle and permitted to wear the uniform of the first infantry regiment of the Guards.

It was not a purely formal occasion. To a certain extent the ten-year-old boy had earned his commission. His military governor had seen to that. For months beforehand like any other recruit he had been woken at dawn and made to parade for inspection by a sergeant major with a fat notebook stuck between the two top buttons of his tunic. Searching eyes looked for any traces of powder from his whitened belt, or for marks of 'Cupid paste' with which he had previously polished his buttons using a button-stick. Then like all the Grenadiers he drilled, and was trained in 'Up', 'Lie down' and 'Assault', and finally in guard-mounting.[19] This had been followed by breakfast – dry bread – and a twelve-hour day with Dr Hinzpeter. He felt he deserved his lieutenancy. Thereafter he had to parade on occasion with his regiment though he could barely keep up with the long-legged men and was forced to run. Then there were anniversary parades, church parades, and the autumn parade in Berlin followed by manoeuvres. Hinzpeter made sure these military exercises did not take him away too much from his schoolwork. Time lost had to be made up. For a lieutenant aged ten it could not have been an easy life.

In the early months of 1869 William and Harry, under the supervision of Dr. Hinzpeter, made up a party at Oeynhausen. The intention was that Harry should take a cure then as he was delicate and had been ailing for some time. The doctors hoped the change and the waters would put him right. There was not, however, to be much rest for anyone else. Three boys, sons of their parents' friends, accompanied them, and the five together made a model school for Hinzpeter to practise on. Then, for the first time, William's left ear began to trouble him. It was always on his left, weak side that things went wrong. He suffered considerable pain. At Potsdam his parents were alarmed to hear a report that the complaint was of a scrofulous nature.

Earlier than had been planned the party returned home for the ear to be examined by specialists. They hurt William a good deal, scraping and probing and sucking at his ear with a pump and washing it out. But the diagnosis must have been satisfactory for he was able to take part in a military parade and help entertain his relations from Hesse-Darmstadt, or Hesse as the truncated Grand-Duchy was now called. He liked his Uncle Louis and Aunt Alice. They were kind and civil, complimenting him on his commission and his part in the parade; but the cousins nearest to him in age were girls. Victoria, the eldest, was four years younger than he, and Elizabeth, whom everyone called Ella, was a tease. Irene had been born in the Austrian war. The only boy amongst them was a baby like William's youngest brother Waldemar. The Khedive of Egypt was then in Prussia on a state visit, and William discovered that his sister Charly and Cousin Victoria were kissing the Khedive's son to keep him happy.[20] He thought this most undignified. When all their guests had left the Crown Prince and Princess announced to

their children that they were all to go for a family holiday on the island of
Norderney in the North Sea. They hoped that the sea air would be good for
William and Harry and they themselves needed a rest. Berlin and Potsdam
had become uncomfortably oppressive.

The family holiday was a success. For once Hinzpeter's twelve-hour programme was set aside so that the boys could recover their health and enjoy
being with their family. Spirits were high, appetites, keen; and there were
boating and swimming parties, painting parties, botanical forays and many
expeditions: to Heligoland much further out in the North Sea, then still
a British possession; to the other Friesian Islands for picnics and fishing; and
on the last day, a very hot one, in a paddle-steamer which shook them
relentlessly, all the way to the new naval harbour at Wilhelmshaven where
the boys saw ironclads for the first time in their lives. They looked over the
largest ship, the *König Wilhelm* and had tea aboard before rattling over
unpaved roads to the railway station and thence by Bremen home again to
Potsdam.[21]

It had been a good holiday. Both the Crown Prince and Princess felt
more relaxed. Harry was much stronger and now resolved to make the
navy his career. William's ear trouble had cleared up enough for him to go
soldiering again. Then came news that they were all to go to the south of
France for the winter. At last the King had given his son a job to do. It was
not much – merely to represent him at the opening of the Suez Canal – but
it was something. The Crown Princess had discovered she was carrying her
seventh child and wanted the company of her sister Princess Alice. As Prince
Louis of Hesse was also to go to Egypt this was a convenient arrangement
and his wife and baby son joined the Crown Princess with her three children
in Cannes. With their ladies-in-waiting, private secretaries, the ubiquitous
Hinzpeter, governesses, stewards, English nannies and a large number of
servants, they settled into an hotel. Soon they were joined by other members
of the Prussian royal family. The French Riviera had not yet succumbed to
catering for the fast set of Europe and it had a climate which was a great
attraction for northerners. A cousin of the Crown Prince's proposed
himself, then one of his ailing aunts plus her husband and daughter, then
another ailing aunt. All these princes and princesses had their Households
and personal servants. When the Crown Prince and Prince Louis sailed
from Villefranche they left a substantial German colony behind them in
Cannes.[22]

Their departure coincided with one of the most serious crises of William's
boyhood. For no explicable reason he developed a dread of damnation and
hellfire. It terrified him by day and night. We do not know to whom he
confided his fears but Hinzpeter was certainly aware of his trouble and

attributed it to the awakening of conscience.[23] The boy could have expected only cold comfort from his tutor. Eventually the horrors passed. Possibly Cannes itself – being a new place to him and full of interest – helped him to throw off some of the burden; and once he was himself again he and Harry so much enjoyed themselves that they counted their holiday at Cannes as the best one they had ever had.[24]

Hinzpeter kept them at their lessons, but even he could not resist the southern sun. He took the princes on instructive walks: to the fish market to examine fish and crustaceans they had never seen before, to enclosed orange groves where they were able to pick the fresh fruit with their own hands, up into the hills behind Cannes to botanize and collect butterflies. He was content to allow a footman in bare feet or fisherman's waders to assist the boys in making a collection of marine life which they kept in improvised aquariums or sundried on eucalyptus branches. They were indeed so happy that when the Crown Prince and Prince Louis returned from Cairo with stories of mummies and the Sphinx, the Valley of the Kings, the difficulty of riding on camels, and the extraordinary luxury of oriental hospitality at the opening of the canal, it was decided that after Christmas at the hotel, a villa should be taken for Hinzpeter and his pupils and they should stay on for another three months.

When their parents had gone, the two Prussian princes continued to dutifully visit their great aunts, one of whom got better, and the other got worse and died, and they continued making their very smelly natural history museum. For Harry's sake they made a special trip to Toulon so that he could admire the French Mediterranean fleet. William was more pleased by the variety of troops who marched along the chief road at Cannes with such verve. He would watch them and irresistibly join the gang of French urchins who marched alongside, glorying in the music of the bugles, the 'Clarion en tête.'[25]

4

William could have had no notion that within a few months those same French troops would be battling with Germany. No-one could. Count von Bismarck once more used war as a political bludgeon. He now wanted to unify all the non-Austrian princely states into a German Empire and scoop in Bavaria, Württemberg, Hesse and Baden. The best, to him the only way of achieving this was to invite their help in a defensive war against imperial France, and, by seizing on a small event and magnifying it, pulling secret strings, teasing Gallic pride, and tinkering with a telegram before issuing it for publication, he managed to trick the French into declaring war on

Germany. The four princely states were invited to assist against this un-
wonted aggression although in fact the Prussian General Staff was already so
well prepared and confident that Count Helmuth von Moltke, the Chief of
General Staff, spent most of mobilization day lying on a sofa reading *Lady
Audley's Secret*.[26]

The military plan proceeded. The French troops were numerous and
brave but ill-disciplined and inefficiently deployed. Their Emperor alone
had seen that Bismarck was using France for his own unscrupulous purposes
and bravely went to the front himself, leaving his Empress as Regent in
Paris. He suffered so badly from stone in the bladder that riding or the jolt
of carriage wheels caused him intense pain, but he did his best to unravel the
muddle at the front.[27] It was hopeless. Troops with or without arms and
food, marched hither and thither, often retracing their steps, but getting
nowhere and doing little. Disillusioned generals did not hesitate to blame
Napoleon III. They called him 'our golden ball and chain'.[28] The troops were
still less complimentary. Should anyone cry: 'Vive l'Empereur' they would
roar in chorus: 'Un, deux, trois – Merde!'[29]

The Germans moved steadily forward. At each French town they handed
a list of their requirements to the authorities, for each German soldier
measured rations of bread, meat, coffee, cigars and either wine or beer. If
these rations were not forthcoming the town was razed to the ground.[30]
Prussian efficiency and training were irresistible. Within a month Napoleon
III had surrendered. His Empress, courageous to the last, was forced to fly
from a republican mob. Aided by her American dentist, but making no
attempt to hide her identity, she reached England and set up house in Kent.
Her son was sent to her there. Her husband was imprisoned at Wilhelmshöhe
near Cassel. But Bismarck had not finished with the French. He continued
to fight with the Republic, besieged Paris, and, against the Crown Prince's
protests, he lost patience with the Parisians who were reduced to eating
sewer rats and pet dogs and animals from the zoo. Moltke gave the order to
shell the capital. The Republic surrendered, and by terms of the surrender
lost to Germany the provinces of Alsace and Lorraine and had to pay a huge
indemnity.

Chancellor Bismarck had every reason to be pleased with himself but his
eccentric master showed not the least interest in the project for which he
had planned the whole war.* The obstinate old gentleman said he did not
want to lead a new German Empire. He had no desire, he declared, to trade

* William I's oddness was more marked than ever. Out with his staff to look over
Paris he suddenly disappeared behind a bush for what they supposed was the obvious
reason. In fact he returned with the extraordinary explanation that he had found a
piece of chocolate in his pocket but, as it was too small to be shared out, he had retired
to eat the piece alone.[31]

the splendid crown of Prussia for a crown of filth.[32] Moreover of the four princely states still not in the confederation only one sovereign was in favour of an empire, the Crown Prince's brother-in-law the Grand Duke of Baden. Bismarck almost gave up but the Crown Prince, who had romantic dreams of a Second Reich, pressed the matter. Patiently he explained to his father that he would not be losing Prussia but adding to it. Bismarck bargained with the Kings of Württemberg and Bavaria and the Grand Duke of Hesse. They were given special privileges which only Saxony already enjoyed. Then with an annual pension of £15,000 he bribed the extravagant and erratic King Louis II of Bavaria to offer the imperial crown to the King of Prussia.* That, with few exceptions,† the Reichstag of the North German Federation was also in agreement was not of the least interest to King William.[33] He was, however, grudgingly impressed by the fact that the four southern states were prepared to accept him as German Emperor. It only remained to concoct a constitution for the new empire. Bismarck, of course, had one in his pocket tailored to suit his own requirements.[35] To please the old King there was to be an upper house for Princes and state delegates, and the *Reichstag* was to continue as before. In effect the constitution was an impossible compromise between absolutism and democratic government. No ministerial responsibility was written into it. The *Reichstag* could not dismiss a Chancellor, or even impeach him. Only the Emperor could appoint and dismiss. The Crown Prince described it as 'ingeniously contrived chaos',[36] but he did not protest. He wanted a Second Reich.

Thus it was that on January 18th, 1871‡ the grumpy King of Prussia stood on a dais in the Galerie des Glaces, Versailles, listened first to a chorale chanted by a military choir, then to an exhortation from his Court Chaplain, then to the singing of 'Now thank we all our God', and afterwards read out a declaration that the German Empire had been re-established. To a frantic waving of swords and helmets and the rolling of drums, a military band burst into patriotic music, and the Crown Prince kissed his father's hand, followed by all the other Princes present. At the conclusion of the ceremony the new German Emperor wrote to his wife to say that he had passed the most unhappy day of his life.

The Dragon of the Rhine herself, well known for her leanings towards Roman Catholicism and French culture, had not had a happy war. She kept very much to herself, and no-one even troubled to tell her officially she was

* King William's title was to be German Emperor not Emperor of Germany to avoid any territorial connotation.

† Not all deputies were in agreement. The exceptions were vocal and expressed fear that the creation of an empire would result in recurring wars with France.[34]

‡ The exact anniversary of the crowning, at Königsberg in 1701, of the first Hohenzollern as King in Prussia.

now *die Kaiserin-Königin*. She discovered it quite by accident from one of her negro footmen.

Nor, save from reports of her husband's gallantry, did the Crown Princess take much satisfaction in the war. She owned to her mother that she was proud to bear her new title of Imperial and Royal Highness, but things had not gone well for her personally. She was distressed because certain members of her family supported France, and because no-one in Berlin appeared to appreciate her hospital organization and nursing work. Stubbornly she had gone off to Homburg to be nearer the front and had set up a hospital there. But no sooner was this established and running well than she was ordered back to Berlin. Her hospital found little favour with the German medical profession. She was told that English methods were not suitable.[37]

Prince William and his brother Harry had enjoyed the war as boys naturally would. Their father had sent home captured Colours and Eagles and the keys of surrendered cities. Their tutor put up a large wall map and, in the time-honoured way, flags on pins showed advances and troop movements as news came from the front.[38] They were at Homburg with their mother when the great news arrived of the victory at Sedan. It arrived after they had gone to bed but, wakened by cheers and a torchlight procession, William and Harry rushed out in their nightshirts to see what was happening. The news so excited them that they spontaneously capered about and sang and cheered with everyone else. The next morning they were punished by Hinzpeter who was scandalized at such unSpartan and such unprincely behaviour.[39] They found this hard to bear.

On Prince William's thirteenth birthday his father noted in his journal:

> *May he grow up a good upright, true and trusty man, one who delights in all that is good and beautiful, a thorough German. . . . God grant we may guard him suitably against whatever is base, petty, trivial, and by good guidance train him for the difficult office he is to fill!*[40]

His mother's prayers for him were no less ardent. She wrote in a letter to her mother at the time:

> *I am sure you would be pleased with William if you were to see him – he has Bertie's pleasant, amiable ways – and can be very winning. He is not possessed of brilliant abilities, nor of any strength of character or talents, but he is a dear boy. . . . I am happy to say that between him and me there is a bond of love and confidence, which I feel sure nothing can destroy. He has very strong health and would be a very pretty boy were it not for that wretched unhappy arm which shows more and more, spoils his face (for it is on one side), his carriage, walk and figure, makes him*

awkward in all his movements, and gives him a feeling of shyness, as he feels his complete dependence, not being able to do a single thing for himself. It is a great additional difficulty in his education, and is not without its effect on his character. To me it remains an inexpressible source of sorrow![41]

This sad little jeremiad was understandable in a confidential letter between child and parent but the Crown Princess was scarcely being accurate. By this time William had shown many talents. His greatest interest was, of course, military science and the profession of arms, but he was also enthusiastic about natural history. He was an avid reader, liking Schiller, Kleist, Ebers, Freytag, Fontane and all the German Nibelungen, as well as the myths and legends of Greece and Rome, Scott, and Jules Verne, 'Robinson Crusoe', and, above all, the works of Fenimore Cooper, the American who lived in sunny Sorrento writing stories about Red Indians in the far west.[42] He also enjoyed painting, for which he had some talent, and when he could escape from Hinzpeter he would set up his easel beside his mother's and they both worked at the same subject. Nor was his mother correct to say that he was completely dependent. He had specially made guns for shooting and a knife-cum-fork apparatus for eating, and he took part in many sports and games, rode well, and held himself beautifully, and either he genuinely paid small attention to his disability, or he had the sense and courage to pretend it was not important. Whatever strain it might have imposed upon him, the boy would not let his 'wretched, unhappy arm' be an embarrassment.

Queen Victoria, who, some time before, had confided in her journal that she hoped her grandson would not grow into 'a conceited Prussian'[43] was not a little alarmed by the sudden aggrandizement of the Hohenzollerns. She strongly deprecated the emperor-worship cult which grew more powerful each day, and especially the extravagant titles of the Kaiser – the All Highest and Supreme War Lord. She wrote to her daughter that living in Palaces and never seeing ordinary people could not be good for the children. Patiently the Crown Princess did not point out that she herself and her brothers had been separated from everyone in a rigid quarantine of English royalty and that at Bornstedt, if nowhere else, her own children did live in a simple farmhouse and saw a good deal of ordinary mortals.

The year 1871 was memorable in many ways. In America the Tammany Ring was exposed, a serious attempt was made to stamp out bigamy in Utah, and a third of Chicago went up in flames.[44] In England the purchase of army commissions was abolished,* the Queen was attacked vituperatively

---

* The news was received with disgust in Berlin where the Officer and Reserve Officer Corps were composed entirely of aristocrats, and the practice was defended by

in the public prints, and Disraeli in the House of Commons warned his colleagues that the balance of power in Europe had been entirely destroyed by the Franco-Prussian war and the effects of this great change would mostly be felt in England.[45] In Paris there was a bloody civil war between the new Republic and rebel Communards. In Rome the Pope declared himself infallible. In the new German Empire, the Chancellor was made a Prince and given a large country estate much bigger than the one he had already, and Count von Moltke was promoted to the rank of Field Marshal. As French reparations made it possible for war loans to be repaid immediately there began a period of spending and speculation never known before. It was the beginning of a showy, materialist, vulgar time known as the *Gründerjahre*, which sensitive, cultured people abhorred.[46]

For Prince William it was the year when the victorious troops returned to their fatherland, and there was a spectacular entry into Berlin from Potsdam through the Brandenburg Gate. He himself took part in the parade, riding on a small dappled horse between his father and his uncle, the Grand Duke of Baden. There were flags, buntings, flowers, garlands, drums and military bands, but the Emperor William was a little distrait. Of late he had undoubtedly been growing even more eccentric: refusing to move from his shoddy old palace in Unter den Linden; wandering about in public wearing a tattered mess-jacket with half the buttons undone; ordering people to economize over the smallest items, and re-using envelopes himself with strips of paper and a pot of gum.[47] On this glorious day of victory he threw his marshals into disarray by going to the head of his troops and leading certain of them past the saluting dais where he should have been himself and where a startled Empress took his place. Afterwards he suddenly came to himself and did take the salute from the remaining troops. At this point his third brother, Prince Albert, had a mild stroke and was carried off parade. Then he himself was gently led to the Castle Square where he was to unveil a statue of his mad elder brother at whose feet had been laid fifty-six captured French Eagles and Colours. The Crown Prince prompted him to cut the tapes and the draperies fell off to reveal Frederick William IV with amiable features mounted on a charger. There was a tremendous roar of cannon from the saluting batteries, cheering, hurrahing and singing, and the old Emperor waved his sword.[48]

And for William 1871 was also memorable because he and his brothers

---

many people in England on the principle that commission purchase attracted into the army only those who were very rich and who would not risk the despoiling of their estates or fortunes in a frivolous war of aggression. England, they said, had suffered enough at the hands of a largely bourgeois army in the Great Rebellion against Charles I.

and sisters with their father and mother, nurses and tutors and governesses and a multitude of servants paid a visit to England. The Crown Prince fell ill quite soon. Exhausted by the war he easily caught an infection which turned to pneumonia and when he was sufficiently recovered he had a longing to return home for a convalescence at Wiesbaden. But he would not let his wife or children accompany him. They were to stay and enjoy a long holiday with Queen Victoria. The children much enjoyed Buckingham Palace and Windsor. They were permitted to make butter and cream cheese in the royal dairy at Frogmore and there William won a large cake in a lottery for the royal children, which probably accounted for the fact that he had to have a tooth drawn. As he made no protest about this, his grandmother presented him with a sovereign which he carried in his pocket until the revolution of 1918.[49] Then, down at Osborne, he and Harry fired off the brass cannons of the model fort once used by his uncles, and his little brother Waldemar almost gave the Queen a stroke by producing his pet crocodile and laying it at her feet.[50] Having read 'Le Fond de la Mer', William was much excited to go down in a diving bell off Portsmouth, and he and Harry were shown over Nelson's *Victory* and the cadet training ship *St Vincent*.[51] In return for his kindness to her grandchildren the elderly admiral who superintended the dockyard was invited to luncheon at Osborne. Deafness caused him to make a memorable faux pas. There was talk of the sailing-frigate *Eurydice* which had gone down in the Solent and the Admiral described her salvaging. The Queen found it a melancholy subject and changed it by asking after the Admiral's sister. 'Well, Ma'am,' he boomed in reply, not quite having caught the question, 'I am thinking of having her turned over, taking a good look at her bottom and having it well scraped'. The result was an uncontrollable explosion of laughter. The children gaped at their grandmama hiding her head in her napkin and shaking convulsively while the tears ran down her face. The Duke of Connaught and the other young members of her family were equally convulsed. The footmen fled behind the serving screen in the corner of the dining-room. The Admiral was somewhat mystified but seized the opportunity to get on with his luncheon.[52]

The Hohenzollerns' departure from England was a lugubrious occasion. The Crown Princess felt rested in one sense but the idea of returning to the calumnies and intrigues of Germany was abhorrent to her. Moreover she still had such a fondness for England that leaving gave her acute homesickness. She burst into tears and threw herself, sobbing, into her mother's arms. The Queen was equally moved. Her dear daughter was returning to the clutches of 'that monster', and she felt dreadfully for her. Their tears were contagious. All the children, from William to the youngest, howled as they said their last goodbye.

5

Details of a German student's career or *curriculum vitae* had to be entered regularly into an official record. This was the *Lebenslauf* of the *Abiturient* which was handed in to the authorities before a boy took the final school examinations and Hohenzollern princes were not exempt.[53] And William also kept a diary, but it is unlikely that he did more than make bare factual records such as when his brother Harry was commissioned in the Imperial Navy, when he shot his first pheasant, when he took part in military revues, the birth of a fourth sister in 1872, and notes on day to day affairs. A diary could not be considered private with Hinzpeter in the offing. Later in life he admitted that at the time he was very introspective. Doubtless he was also obstreperous. Puberty in its initial stages affects children's moods. The merriest can become morose, the easiest-going truculent, and the talkers can turn taciturn. The majority also go through what is now technically known as 'the revolt against the father principle', and are belligerent to their elders. William was no exception. He failed to understand why his father and mother should be distressed when Germany's former enemy, Napoleon III, died in exile – and he said so. Nor could he understand why they were relieved that the boom of economic expansion suddenly collapsed. Patiently they explained that the postwar *Gründerjahre* had resulted in a general lowering of taste. Building speculators had ruined parts of Berlin with what Walter Rathenau★ called 'terrible abortions of polytechnic beer imagination' and contemptuously referred to the German capital as 'Chicago on the Spree'.[54] William promptly said he liked that sort of building. And when there was a political struggle between Bismarck and the Roman Catholic Centre Party, William, in adolescent rebellion because he knew it would wound his parents, declared for Bismarck and Protestantism. Yet he was not consistently difficult. He won golden opinions on official occasions such as a visit to Vienna where the Empress Elizabeth struck him as so beautiful that, shyly gauche, he stood rooted to the spot and had to be prompted to do his duty, kiss her hand, and move on.[56] He was also helpful when visitors came to Berlin or Potsdam. One such guest was so fascinating that he stood out in his memory: the Shah of Persia, whose horses' tails were dyed pink,[57] had courteously left three of his wives[58] on the German frontier, but he tended to spit out on the carpet any food he did not find to his taste. Moreover lambs and goats had to be driven live into his apartments in the Crown

★ Walter Rathenau (1867–1922) was an exceptionally gifted German Jew, banker and industrialist, who served in both the Wilhelmine and Weimar governments. More than a mere big-business politician, he was known through Europe for his tast and intellectual interests. In 1922 he was murdered by anti-Semitic thugs.[55]

Prince's Palace for ceremonial slaughter, at the very idea of which all the younger Princes and Princesses set up a screeching.[59] William could be considerate and not contradictory and he often was. Nevertheless his parents were much relieved to discover that, whatever his mood, Bornstedt always had a magical effect upon him. The simple farm life instantly made him good humoured and he happily did his share in exercising dogs and grooming horses.

In 1873 William passed his qualifying examination which permitted him to proceed to a gymnasium, the German equivalent of a grammar or high school, and it was decided that he should be allowed to spread his wings a little away from his parents in the royal town of Cassel.[60] So that they should not spread too far his brother Harry was to accompany him and the ubiquitous Hinzpeter, but before that he had to be Confirmed. For this he was carefully prepared in the tenets held by the Prussian Evangelical Church, to which his grandmother the Empress added certain other important aspects of religious devotion from her quasi-catholic point of view.[61] Then he had to prepare himself. An important part of Confirmation was the presentation of a personal Confession of Faith. So that he should have the peace and the leisure to do this, he and his brother and their tutor took the newly-opened sleeping-car service to Scheveningen in Holland in the summer of 1874.[62] William walked alone on the sands constructing his Confession of Faith. As the future head of an empire both catholic and protestant it had to be as non-sectarian as possible, based on the Apostles' Creed, and individual. No-one was permitted to assist him.[63] But life was not all intense meditation on the sands at Scheveningen. Theoretically the party was incognito, William being addressed as Count von Bergh, though everyone knew who they were. They inspected and admired the uniforms of Dutch soldiers, bathed and went sailing, went over the State Museum and picture galleries and called on the Queen of the Netherlands. Excitedly they told her they had had to help lift a de-railed tramcar on to its tracks, and that they had seen a most ludicrous stained-glass window in the church at Gouda which showed Judith with the head of Holofernes on a dish. The latter description rather shocked the Queen who saw nothing in a stained-glass window to cause such levity until William explained that instead of the wine and glasses with which Judith had made Holofernes drunk, and which should have been on a table beside the bed where lay his headless trunk, the prim artist, presumably a total abstainer, had substituted a Chinese tea service complete to the last detail.[64]

At the beginning of September the ceremony took place in the Friedens-kirche in Potsdam. His father and mother, the Emperor and Empress and the Prince and Princess of Wales were present. William was calm. He read out his personal Confession of Faith, satisfactorily replied to the forty prepared questions put to him, listened to three sermons, and was Confirmed. There are important differences between the Lutheran and Anglican doctrines of the Eucharist, yet in the lax views of the Prussian and English royal families they amounted to much the same thing and after the Confirmation his uncle, the Prince of Wales, happily received Communion with the Prussian family. William was presented with a Bible by his English grandmother who had written a formal letter to be read out to him after the ceremony. It adjured him to be good.[65] Afterwards the Prince of Wales kicked the hated Prussian dust from her heels and went directly to her beloved Denmark, and the Prince went to Baden to gamble.

Confirmation had its social as well as religious significance. Thenceforth not only could William receive the Sacrament, but he was no longer counted a child. He was now a schoolboy.

CHAPTER FOUR

Schooldays

'Today is a sort of break up'

THE PRINCESS ROYAL ON HER SONS LEAVING
FOR CASSEL

I

The Princes William and Henry arrived in Cassel in a distinctly unroyal fashion; Hinzpeter's Spartan ideals struggling with his notion of what was correct for two grandsons of the Emperor.

They marched along the Harz Mountains; went up the Brocken from which they could see nothing, likewise the Regenstein; then they were turned out of Wernigerode Castle by the proprietor who distrusted their ragged appearance; were given a single, tiny and uncomfortable room in an inn where all the food had been eaten by other guests; took a train for a space; and finally, marched on the last long section of old country road down into Cassel.

Hinzpeter delighted in their arrival, describing it in his diary on September 12th, 1874 as *in the true manner of a travelling student*. How much his charges enjoyed the frugality is not mentioned, though Hinzpeter hints that they did (or ought to have done):

> *We cheerfully sat in the enclosure for yeomen of a coachman's beerhouse, partaking of sour beer and hard bread. It was raining and I held my umbrella over the luncheon to prevent the beer from becoming still more watery, for we needed strengthening after a hard march ...*

This was not all. Their arrival coincided with that of the Emperor, who was paying a short visit to the royal palace at Wilhelmshöhe just outside the city. But Hinzpeter considered it would never do for his charges to lose the value of *the moral sermon they had exemplified in word and deed* and forget for a moment that they were mere travelling students. So they walked around in the rain trying to avoid recognition.

44

So as not to be with the Emperor in Cassel [Hinzpeter continued] *we wander about in the surrounding country, obtain, with difficulty, a cup of coffee in some pleasure grounds, wherein we blissfully soak a pocketed crust of bread . . . and finally move on to our Fürstenhaus in Königsstrasse where the porter, in gala array, is only with difficulty persuaded that we represent the expected company.*[1]

It was barely surprising. The Fürstenhaus was part of the Electoral Palace and the porter had been instructed to expect two Prussian Princes, not a drenched and shabby trio, fortified from their hard march over the mountains with blissful draughts of coffee, weak and sour beer, and dried crusts.

No doubt, in their way, the boys had enjoyed themselves. In his *Lebenslauf* William confessed that he had left home for the first time not without uneasiness and when he first saw Cassel through the rain his heart sank.[2] But at least the two brothers were together. Harry was to go to the Cassel Polytechnic School to prepare for his naval career and he and William would see each other at infrequent intervals. Moreover, school hours in Germany at that time were so long that they allowed a boy little time for home-sickness.*

King Henry V in his Agincourt speech rightly remarked: 'Old men forget', and it may be that, in recalling his schooldays at Cassel fifty-two years after the event, the ex-Kaiser's memory was at fault. But at Doorn where he wrote of his childhood he had his old *Lebenslauf*, together with countless diaries which the historian Sir John Wheeler-Bennett saw on his visit in 1939 and which he called 'a little cache of history'.[3] Therefore his recollections have an authenticity uncommon in the generality of old men.

He could not have found it easy settling in with 'ordinary' boys. It has been maintained that he never did and always kept himself aloof.[4] Yet he had a natural talent for getting on terms of intimacy with the most unlikely people. A well-known story told against him in later life to illustrate his indiscreet bursts of candour was that on one occasion aboard the imperial yacht he was overheard discussing highly confidential state affairs with an Italian pilot taken on board at Bari.[5] It also demonstrated his capacity for striking up quick relationships. Hinzpeter would have guided him in his choice of companions, but friendship cannot be forced. Royal experiments in this direction have, again and again, proved a failure. Whoever chose them and by what means, cannot be known, but William records becoming

* William's hours were especially long. He got up at 5 and by 6 was already doing his preparation. From 8 to 12 he was at school. From 12 to 2 he exercised. From 2 to 4 he was at school again. There followed a private lesson with Hinzpeter. Dinner was from 5 to 6, followed by two hours' work, then extra tuition in French and English, which often went on until 9.

especially friendly with four boys: one who ultimately became Secretary for War, another who became a headmaster in Hamburg; another a Public Prosecutor; and the fourth a Judge of the Court of Appeal. Cassel Grammar School was not especially 'packed' with chosen pupils to rub shoulders with the heir to the throne, though the headmaster, Vogt, was well thought of in the educational world. Therefore the ultimate careers of William's four closest friends shows the teaching must have been excellent. It also speaks well for William that, though his beau idéal of all human achievement was to serve with honour in the Prussian Officer Corps, where anti-Semitism was rife, his friend Sommer, who became Judge of the Court of Appeal, was a Jewish boy. He remarks quite casually that his form chose him to be in charge of the stove, and that he was kept especially busy in the lower sixth when they were taught by a Dr Auth, who was jovial, fat, loved wine and an overheated classroom, and bore an uncanny resemblance to the Crown Princess's difficult guest who had slaughtered kids in his apartments, the Shah of Persia.[6]

William's chief interests were history and the pleasures of reading, but philology and mathematics he neither enjoyed nor mastered. Modern languages he spoke easily. Greek and Latin were the source of much interesting ancient history and deepened his knowledge of archaeology. While he was at Cassel German archaeologists under the encouragement of his father the Crown Prince, were excavating Olympia and Dr Schliemann was continuing his digs at Troy and Mycenae. Schliemann fascinated William. He was the complete romantic, basing all his amateur probes not on any recognized system of archaeological procedure but on the thoroughly unscientific and highly eccentric method of referring solely to the texts of Homer and Pausanias. His life story, too, was like something written by Jules Verne or Fenimore Cooper.*

Despite the many hours of study there were occasional diversions at Cassel. Hinzpeter arranged monthly dinners to which local notables were bidden to meet their future sovereign and his brother. He had a didactic

---

* The son of a pastor who took to drink, Schliemann was apprenticed to a grocer at fourteen, ran away to sea, was shipwrecked, and, when still in his 'teens, was found to have an astounding flair for finance and foreign tongues. At the age of thirty-seven he had made a fortune and could speak and write fifteen languages. In his forties he began adventuring, going to Mecca speaking perfect Arabic and having himself circumcised as a precaution against discovery. Then he took seriously to archaeology. For company he married a sixteen-year-old Greek girl recommended by the Archbishop of Athens taught her all about Homer and Pausanias, and began to dig. After his success at Troy he dug at Mycenae in South Greece and found, as he thought he would, the treasure-filled tombs of the murdered Agamemnon and his companions. On the face of one well-preserved skull was a gold mask. That night the romantic Schliemann telegraphed the King of Greece: 'I HAVE GAZED UPON THE FACE OF AGAMEMNON.'[7]

purpose for every move he made and these 'conciliation dinners' as he called them were to jostle up the classes together and let people become acquainted. They were not as jolly as he had hoped. The guests could not relax. Nor could the two princes.

More enjoyable were rare visits to the opera and theatre, swimming in the river Fulda, fencing with the cadets at the Military Academy especially with the épée, and riding either with their military riding master or less often with Hinzpeter who, not losing a single opportunity to improve his pupils, mixed business with pleasure and lectured them on history and natural history and made them recite to him. To make certain they were not wasting time, Hinzpeter would snatch moments when they were doing nothing and lolling about as boys do, make them sit upright, and read to them from the 'professional novels' of Ebers about strange lands and distant places, or sometimes from Scott and Dickens.[8]

Though sealed away in Cassel he and Harry must have learnt what was going on in the world. Hinzpeter, even if he had wished to do so, could not have set up a complete system of censorship. They must have puzzled over the disgrace of Count von Arnim who was a great friend of their grandmother but who, disliked by Bismarck, had been brought back from the Embassy in Paris to face trifling charges and be dismissed from the diplomatic service. After he had published a defensive pamphlet Bismarck had had Arnim sentenced to five years' imprisonment.[9] To learn that the Chancellor and not the Emperor had real power in Germany, and that he had an implacable hostility to their parents and to their grandmother was a hard lesson. Before they might have sensed it. Now they knew it. How well they learnt and received the lesson cannot be imagined, nor precisely what effect it had upon them. They would have heard of the uproar in America, celebrating their hundredth anniversary of freedom, and electing a president rudely known as 'Queen Victoria in breeches'.[10] They would have heard of their English grandmother's assuming the title of Empress of India. . . .

Much else besides happened in their grammar school days, though only once did they have an opportunity to talk over things with their parents. This was on a family holiday in Holland, at Scheveningen the watering-place where there was the Holofernes-Judith stained-glass window complete with tea set, and where William had wandered over the sands feeling wicked and concocting his Confession of Faith. This was a less serious holiday altogether. Possibly Hinzpeter thought it frivolous because everyone seemed to enjoy himself and pleasure he believed was in some way connected with sin. Prince William charitably commented: *Poor Hinzpeter had to content himself with making sour faces in the background.*

Far from the tensions of Berlin, and genuinely delighted to see the improvement in his sons, the Crown Prince organized their holiday with enthusiasm. It is unlikely that he discussed his anxieties with them. Instead he made sure that they all enjoyed themselves. They learnt lawn tennis, walked on the beaches, paid visits to Dutch relations and friends, bathed and went boating, and visited a pancake fair in Utrecht. Normally restricted to a Spartan diet, the boys looked longingly at the pancakes being cooked at all the stalls. 'Go, go,' urged their father, 'stuff yourselves full.' Afterwards William called them 'golden days.'[11]

2

In January 1877 Prince William successfully passed the *Abiturienten-Examen* with sixteen other sixth-formers at Cassel and was given his leaving certificate. In his *Lebenslauf* he wrote that his future studies would be political science and jurisprudence because it was intended that he should follow his father and English grandfather and be a student at Bonn University.*

Two days later, on his eighteenth birthday, Prince William came of age. By tradition the occasion was marked by a private but nonetheless glittering ceremony in Berlin. Queen Victoria had offered her grandson the Grand Commandership of the Order of the Bath but he wanted the Garter, one of the most illustrious Orders of chivalry in Christendom. Tactfully the Crown Princess wrote to her mother to say that already the Emperors of Russia and Austria and the King of Italy had sent the highest Orders they could, and Prussia had honoured not only the Prince of Wales but also the Dukes of Edinburgh and Connaught with the Black Eagle.

Willie [she wrote] *would be satisfied with the Bath, but the nation would not.* Queen Victoria swiftly yielded.[13]

On the morning of the 27th the British Ambassador arrived at the Crown Prince's Palace with the mantle, star, ribbon and garter of the Order and there the Crown Prince, as a Knight of the Garter himself, deputized for the Queen and invested his son. Afterwards they drove to the Old Palace where in the Kittersaal the young Prince was solemnly invested with the red mantle and Chain of the Black Eagle, and given the accolade by his grandfather. All members of the royal family were present, all officers of the Order, and, amongst the large throng, a reluctant guest, Prince Bismarck. He undoubtedly had the upper hand over the Crown Prince and Princess, and treated the Empress with less civility than he would have shown to one of his clerks, but

---

* That celebrated tuft-hunter Jowett tried but failed to get him for Balliol through Morier at the British Embassy.[12] However, as Kaiser, William was gratified to be given an honorary D.C.L. by Oxford, as well as hon. LL.Ds by Pennsylvania and Berlin, an hon. M.D. by Prague, and an hon. D. Sc. by Klausenburg.

he had thought the old Emperor reliable and now he was turning difficult. Only a few days before he had complained in a letter:

The Kaiser is cold and as hard as a stone. He shows no gratitude to me at all. He only keeps me on because he thinks I may still be of use to him.

This, like many things about Bismarck, was somewhat exaggerated. Nevertheless he sensed the old gentleman no longer had quite the same confidence in him. In fact the Emperor had been complaining of his Chancellor's touchiness, saying that he had to be handled gently, 'like a raw egg'.[14] With so much overt hostility about it is conceivable that Bismarck looked with particular interest at the centre of that afternoon's ceremony, Prince William.

For the Prince it was an inspiring day. He always venerated the knightly code of chivalry and regarded his investiture with some of the greatest Orders in Europe with a quasi-religious awe. And there was the simpler but, in its way, no less delicious sense of freedom which he achieved that day. Before going to Bonn he had to put in a nominal six months' service with the army, to which he looked forward, and when he was at Potsdam he now had his own set of apartments in the New Palace. He was no longer on top of his family, no longer under the absolute authority of his parents.[15] Best of all, amongst the burrs he shrugged off that day was his tutor. It might or might not have been significant that Dr Hinzpeter was no longer required to tutor Harry or take over the nine-year-old Prince Waldemar. He was permitted to retire to his hometown of Bielefeld.[16]

CHAPTER FIVE

The Young Prince

'It is impossible to find two nicer boys than William and Henry'

THE PRINCE OF WALES TO
QUEEN VICTORIA IN 1878

'This son has never really been mine'

THE CROWN PRINCESS ABOUT
PRINCE WILLIAM IN 1881

I

The Emperor William was now eighty years of age. Despite his odd diet which was a conglomeration of fruit, sorbets, potted meats, strong tea, tepid champagne, and a lobster salad every night, he appeared to be indestructible. His son aged forty-six had absolutely no hand in affairs and therefore he and his wife had a good deal of time on their hands. They travelled, studied, farmed at Bornstedt, interested themselves in a variety of matters. Not very long after William came of age the Hermes of Praxiteles was found at the German Olympia excavations, an enormously important discovery to archaeology and art. The Crown Prince was congratulated on all sides for initiating such a work.* And being so capable and determined, the Crown Princess was able to do things in the sphere of education and hygiene, yet always on a limited scale. Both felt their chief talents were being thwarted by the Chancellor, and that they would atrophy before the Crown Prince ever succeeded his father and wielded power. Therefore they were exceedingly concerned, more perhaps than most parents, when they discovered an almost total divergence between their liberal views and the political views of their son. They realized that it was not merely an extension of his ado-

---

* In 1927 doubts were raised on technical grounds as to whether the figure was a genuine Praxiteles or a Hellenistic or Roman copy but neither these nor other theories have gained wide acceptance.[1]

lescent contrariness. Under the influence of his fellow officers and a group at Court who fawned on the callow Prince, William developed the same exalted ideas of kingship as his grandfather. As a corollary he regarded the few Social Democrats in the Reichstag as a threat to the security of the state,* despised his mother's liberalism and openly disapproved of her imbuing his father with the same unpatriotic views. There was no proof as to who was at the back of this obstreperousness, but they had deep suspicions. Furthermore the boy was constantly being subjected to toad-eating and, never having a word of praise from Hinzpeter in all the twelve years of their association, his resistance to it was very low indeed, and he was much influenced by the sudden deluge of praise and deference from all quarters. Right-wing newspapers in the Zeitungsviertel, Berlin's Fleet Street, eulogized him, and he did not trouble himself to read the others. At the work which falls to princes of opening, launching, inspecting and visiting, he was complimented, praised, and so courted that he almost sank under the weight of sycophancy. Just at the time his father was being gravely congratulated on the success of the dig at Olympia, William dutifully visited a mine in Saxony where a coal-black miner, representing the spirit of the mines, stepped forward into a blaze of bengal lights and gave him a fulsome welcome: 'Welcome among us, Hohenzollern Prince! Rejoice, ye hills; rejoice ye vaulted caverns! Noble Prince, the star of Germany! Protect our mines, at home and afar!'[3] It was cream to a cat, very indigestible, not in the least good for him.

Whenever possible the Crown Prince gently tried to bring him down to earth again. The impulsive, passionate Crown Princess was less successful. William had achieved a degree of independence which she was obliged to respect but it distressed her to see how ardently Harry and Charly also longed to escape from her authority. She put it down to William's influence. He had a certain authority over his weaker brother Harry who went off to join the Navy in the spring of 1877, Charly too, was easily led by her eldest brother, and shattered her mother's nerves by being at one moment a hoyden and at the next a vapid social butterfly, and always objecting strongly to being told what to do.

With the exception of Harry all the children joined their parents for a last family holiday in 1877. First they went to Ostend where sea-bathing and sight-seeing were organized on 'Prince-Consort' lines and no-one had the time or energy for bickering. Afterwards they went to the Court of Hesse where Prince Louis had just succeeded his uncle as Grand Duke.[4] There the

---

* By this time the political doctrines of Marx, Engels and Lassalle had been absorbed by the Social Democratic Labour Party, but in the 1877 elections the party only gained 12 seats out of a total of 397.[2]

young cousins played games of tennis and went riding and boating while their elders reorganized the twelve Hesse palaces and shooting boxes which had been allowed to fall into a deplorable state. By the end of the holiday the Crown Princess was convinced that the sooner Charly was married and settled the better for everyone.

Strangely it was William who, literally, thrust his sister into the arms of a husband. Later that summer he and a party of young people were on the Island of Peacocks where, many years before, the Grapeshot Prince, now German Emperor, had taken refuge from the Berlin mob. A switchback railway had been built there for the enjoyment of King Frederick William IV's brothers and sisters, and Willy, working the controls, suddenly accelerated the machine so that his sister Charly clung to Prince Bernard of Saxe-Meiningen for support. It was love at first contact and he was eminently eligible, being heir to a reigning house and son of a Princess of Prussia. Charly's cousin, later Marie, Queen of Roumania, frankly described her as capable of being more charming than anyone she had ever known, with cat-like movements, a most melodious voice – 'a purr that could charm a tiger' – and a passion for smoking and jewellery, and yet, for all that, –

> One of the most fickle and changeable women. . . . With a single word of disdain [she] could shrivel up your ardent enthusiasm, make your dearest possession appear worthless or rob your closest friend of her charm.[5]

This is a cutting thumbnail sketch, almost certainly exaggerated and prejudiced but, to some extent, it ties in with other candid portraits of the Crown Prince and Princess's eldest daughter, and gives a hint, if nothing more, of how difficult she might well have been at home. Much relieved to be rid of their seventeen-year-old peevish and contrary daughter and to such a suitable *parti*, they gave their consent to an early marriage.

The wedding took place in February 1878. Some of the extra non-essential trimmings had to be cut out because King Victor Emmanuel ('lawless in his passion for women' according to Queen Victoria)[6] had died only nine days before, but no-one really minded. The Prince of Wales came over for the event and charmed all the stiff Prussian royalties by making them feel important. It was a great help to the Crown Princess who had been growing closer to her brother since their strong differences of opinion in 1870. She herself marvelled at Charly's coolness. It appeared she could not get away from her home quickly enough, and there was none of the sobbing that had attended her own marriage. Charly and Bernard were briskly married, briskly went off for their honeymoon, and briskly returned to lead a smart set in Berlin of which their elders disapproved; and that was that.[7]

2

Besides his quite normal bellicose attitude to his parents – which was shared by his younger brother and sister – three particular wedges were driven between William and his parents.

The first was his attachment to his grandfather the Emperor, whose part he took in all family discussions, and whose yearly round he followed with dog-like attachment. The German Season began at the New Year and continued through Lent to Easter. The Courts at the New Year and Court Balls were gatherings of great splendour. These were held in the state apartments of the Old Palace. The aristocracy of the sword, the *Schwertadel*, and of the service, the *Briefadel*, had the *entrée* to these events as well as the Diplomatic Corps. Invitations to the one annual Court Ball held at the Emperor's own shabby palace were much less restricted, and socially mattered more than anything, although the entertainment was neither lavish nor diverting. There were also anniversaries, visits to the Opera, and royal concerts in the Old Palace. Finally there were the formal Thursdays in Lent, and informal *soirées de la Bonbonnière* to which only five or six of the Empress's friends would be invited. After the season the Empress would generally go to Koblenz while the Emperor passed on his annual round, to Ems for the cure, to Koblenz to quarrel with his Empress, to Mainau on Lake Constance and on to Gastein for another cure, steins of beer, skittles and amateur theatricals. In the summer he liked to be at the Babelsberg Palace at Potsdam, which the Crown Princess had handed back to him with relief, and he spent the early autumn on manoeuvres and the late autumn shooting in Silesia.

To the passage of the Season and the annual round of the Emperor young Prince William attached a reverential importance which thoroughly irritated his father and mother. It attached him more closely to his grandfather, who liked to be liked, and to his grandmother, who at this time was not over-scrupulous about correcting him if he made disparaging remarks about his liberal parents. She would remind him that she and they held many views in common – the chief being a detestation of the Chancellor – but she did not put him down for disloyalty as she ought to have done.

The second wedge which levered William from his parents was his genuine affection for the Army. The most powerful part of the German Army was that of Prussia, and unlike other professional armies it was officered largely by aristocrats. The bourgeoisie had begun to penetrate the British and Russian armies, and were thrusting their way right to the top of the French. The Prussian Guards regiments, on the other hand, were only open to members of sovereign families, *Durchlaucht*, or *maisons comtales*, *Erlaucht*, or to

Junkers of the Kingdom of Prussia. The Junkers were generally small country gentry with long genealogies and corresponded to no other class of society in Europe. They would, if necessary, join their men in the farm work, but were intensely proud of their noble birth and their right to carry a sword for the King of Prussia. They constituted an inward-looking caste, and into this caste Prince William fitted very comfortably. He liked the bachelor mess life, the camaraderie of fellow officers, the beer drinkings and wine evenings, most of all the absolute and sincere respect for the King-Emperor as Supreme War Lord. Very quickly he must have realized that though there were an immense number of frenzied toasts to, and 'hochs' for, his grandfather, his father was hardly ever honoured in the same way, nor was the Crown Prince really popular. William, who in any case had always dearly loved his grand-father, aligned himself with his brother officers. He himself showed promise as a soldier. He worked hard and learned about battle-order tactics, the 'English attack', the skirmishing line, normal attack, volley-firing and 'turks', or rehearsed stunts in manoeuvres. But, though very keen, he was not uncritical of the fact that the methods of training in 1877 were almost precisely the same as they had been in the Napoleonic wars. For example a Prussian officer was never permitted to lie down or take cover, therefore in skirmishing formation, as they led their crawling skirmishers, they showed the exact position of their men. Certain reforms were looked for, and he regarded them as very necessary. Most of all he disliked useless red tape.[8] Forward-looking, enthusiastic, proud of German arms, he should have been at one with his father who had proved himself on many a battlefield; yet his alignment with his fellow officers on the side of the Emperor made this impossible.

The third and hardest wedge driven between the Crown Prince and Princess and their eldest son was driven in by Bismarck.

So far in these pages Otto von Bismarck has appeared as a tremendous force, generally malign. No serious historian has ever denied his greatness, nor his quite remarkable influence over the destiny of Europe. The despair of liberals and social democrats, who regarded him with loathing, he was the dynamic hero of the right wing. They regarded him as almost heaven-sent, the right man for the right place at a critical period in the history of Prussia and ultimately Germany.

His origins were less celestial. He had that requisite, Junker blood. Born in sandy Brandenburg a fortnight after Napoleon had arrived in Paris for his last desperate Hundred Days, he was the son of a poor and obscure Junker and a middle-class mother. Mr A. J. P. Taylor in his study of Bismarck notes that he did not care for his clever mother, though he took after her; that he disapproved of her character and standards, and wanted to be like his father.[9]* He loved the country, and resented it when his mother moved the family to Berlin. After grammar school – the best in the capital – he went to the University of Göttingen where he expressed his burgeoning adolescence in flamboyant ways, dressing fantastically, duelling, swilling great quantities of beer and having grand affairs. There he made two life-long friends: strangely, a naturalist of noble blood from the Baltic seaboard, and an American who was to become a diplomat.[10] Then he entered the civil service, to give small satisfaction and continue chasing ladies in a rich milieu of English people. It is said he even imagined himself in love with a daughter of the Duke of Cleveland. He did his obligatory army service with reluctance, and as soon as his mother died he went back to the family farms, ran wild, and earned himself the local nickname of 'the mad Junker'. Moderating his wildness, he read a great deal, studied religion, and embraced a Cromwellian sort of faith. It is not difficult to imagine him esteeming the Lord Protector's view that religion should be 'a loose net in which the consciences of godly men might flourish',[11] and that simultaneously one had to wrestle with the Scriptures and other revelations of God's will. He once lyrically described the statesman's function as being patient 'until he hears the step of God sounding through events and then spring forward and seize the hem of His garment'.[12] His faith led him to marry a lady who thought along similar lines, though whereas Johanna von Puttkamer was the perfect wife for him, being virtuous, understanding, patient and calm, he could in no way claim to possess the same qualities, being consistently unfaithful, obstinate, impatient and excitable to the point of frenzy.

Chance thrust Bismarck into politics. Too eccentric to please his neighbours, he was not elected directly to the Diet, but only as a substitute deputy. Then, quite unexpectedly, the elected deputy fell ill and retired, and Bismarck went back to Berlin. Belligerent by nature, he attacked bureaucracy, which put him willy-nilly on the side of the King. He became so reactionary that he was squeezed to the top of the monarchist pyramid in the Diet. When the 1848 year of revolution came he had a suggestion pat. In the light of subsequent events it is very interesting: that the King should abdicate, his brother, who had fled to England, should renounce his rights, and the young Prince Frederick should be placed on the throne. When the threat of real constitutional government died away, Bismarck abandoned his idea and remained a rigid believer in oligarchy. This eventually brought him office as envoy to France, and at a critical time when William, by then King of

* This unusual characteristic – for it is more common for a boy to adore his mother and dislike his father on account of subconscious budding sexual jealousy – actually put him in juxtaposition with young Prince William. Both shared the unenviable inheritance of being highly-strung.

Prussia, was facing a deadlock in the Diet, threatening to abdicate, and demanded that Bismarck should come to his aid. But Bismarck was not to be found. He was not working in Paris but was down in Biarritz enjoying a passionate love affair with the wife of the Russian Ambassador at Brussels. For days he would not reply to letters or telegrams. When he did deign to go to his King's help, he did so only on certain conditions. They were agreed to. Whether or not Bismarck had seized the hem of God's garment, he had begun the enjoyment of supreme power which lasted twenty-seven years.[13]

Almost fifteen of those years had passed by the time Prince William came of age. He had grown up in the shadow of Bismarck and had seen his iron grip on everything and everyone grow firmer. To an impressionable romantic boy of eighteen Bismarck had that special attraction of being larger than life. He was a tall man with a huge frame and a thirst and appetite to match. He was an epicure but also a glutton and, as is the habit in second-class Greek restaurants, he was served with everything all at once. From the heaped table he would gorge sausages, poultry, game, butcher's meat, bread, potatoes, roots and green vegetables, macaroni, cheese and fish besides quantities of excellent red and white wines, beer and brandy, and then flood all this with an ocean of champagne. Indeed he had vowed to consume five thousand bottles of champagne in his lifetime. He also had colossal furniture, the chairs tenoned and mortised and then cemented with the surest glue for neither nails nor even wooden pegs could withstand his weight and his tantrums when, as frequently happened, he lost all control and started smashing things. Even his pencils were in proportion – each like a small walking-stick. Bismarck was larger than life in everything: in his grievances and vendettas, in his determined search to find someone to blame when anything went wrong, in his loves and his hates. Once, no doubt deservedly, he had been unable to sleep after a gargantuan supper and a great swilling of champagne and he claimed the next morning: 'I have spent the whole night *hating*!'

At his age it would not necessarily have occurred to Prince William that by showing any interest in the fascinating Chancellor he was being unfilial. If it had done, most probably he would not have been concerned. Bismarck stood for many of the things which he himself thought good and right, whatever was thought in the Crown Prince's Palace. Like all late adolescents, William was intensely sentimental. In this present age, described by a United States Vice-President as that of the common man, sentimentality is at the root of student movements; then it was expressed in fervent discipleship to great men. To Prince William there could hardly have been a greater man than the Chancellor. He need not be partisan, but to refuse his hospitality and his advice should either be offered would be churlish. It would also deprive him of the chance to observe Germany's Great Man, an opportunity few were offered.

By this time Prince Bismarck was one of the richest landowners in the Empire, although his two large estates had exceedingly ugly and ill-furnished houses; one at Varzin buried in overcrowded, decaying woodlands; the other, ten times larger, at Friedrichsruh with an even uglier house – a former hotel where the bedrooms were still numbered and there was no electricity. Both Prince and Princess Bismarck were indifferent to its comfort and banal surroundings. Their official house in Berlin was inconvenient and in permanent chaos. Stuffed with unhung portraits, unread books, unlaid carpets, half unwrapped gifts from admirers, innumerable hunting trophies and unbeautiful bric-à-brac as well as thrown-aside clothes, it looked more like a pawnshop or the site of a perpetual jumble sale than the official residence of the most powerful man in Germany. Not, though, that Bismarck was often in residence. More and more he ruled the Empire from Varzin, 'five hours by train from Berlin, and then forty miles on bad roads', or from the more accessible Friedrichsruh, only two hours by train from the centre of affairs. These distances slowed down business but in no way prevented it, and Bismarck felt better in the country where he liked the feudal life, walking about his estates, occasionally thrashing his peasants with a walking cane, and, when he was not going through state papers, reading and eating and drinking. With the exception of his master the Emperor, whom he saw daily when he was in Berlin, he wasted no time in giving interviews or dining out. He went to Court only when he had to, saw the Diplomatic Corps once a year, and occasionally met the sovereign Kings and Princes of the Empire. Even the Crown Prince rarely saw him. Months and months would pass between their meetings. His elusiveness and unavailability were quite deliberate. Prolific in ideas, he had to assemble them like mercury escaped from a broken barometer, and ponder hard before expressing a conclusion on paper. Chiefly for this reason he did not care to talk business, not even with his own chosen ministers. But there were other reasons, too. He had a short temper and an irascible tongue which might lead him into a regrettable indiscretion. Talking from a podium was anathema to him, and though in his time he made long and exceedingly impressive speeches in the Reichstag, the shrillness of his voice, his pause for thought or a sip of brandy and water, his digressions, and his general unease would sometimes cause the deputies to cough him down or laugh outright. Then he would put up a lorgnette to gaze imperiously at the house, and on rare occasions lose his temper, shake his fist at them and utter wild threats.

To Prince William this astonishing statesman, who had relentlessly harassed his parents and remained steadily loyal to his adored grandfather, was an enigma of infinite interest.

3

Bonn is an ancient and charming city of monuments, parks, avenues, and prospects of the Rhine. The Romanesque cathedral stands on the shrines of two Roman soldiers martyred there in 253 A.D. Beethoven was born in the Bonnegasse, his house being now a museum; and he is honoured annually with a music festival in a modern complex of music halls and auditoriums called the Beethovenhalle. Since the division of Germany it has been the capital of the Federal Republic which has involved the erection of administrative buildings and a large extension of the city to house the Diplomatic Corps and deputies to the Bundeshaus. It has always been famous for its university which, since 1818, has been housed in the Poppelsdorfer Palace of the Prince Archbishop Electors of Cologne, a thirteenth-century castle with added landscaped pleasure grounds and botanic gardens.

Almost certainly it was even more beautiful when, in October 1877, Prince William went there as a student. He had passed his officer's exam and carried out his essential military training, and led his men in the autumn manoeuvres.[14] Now he was to prepare himself intellectually for the responsibility that one day would be his. His father accompanied him there, enthusing on the joys of student life. His son was sceptical. A villa of considerable dimensions had been taken for him and for his household. In theory he was a free and private individual at the university. In practice he was the grandson of the Kaiser and heir presumptive to the throne. The last entry in his *Lebenslauf* at Cassel had been his intention to study politial science and jurisprudence. To these subjects he now added history, German literature, the history of art, philosophy, physics and chemistry – a formidable target which his mother might have tackled and achieved but which was far too ambitious for him.* Unlike other students he was instructed privately, at home by carefully chosen teachers. Only for experimental chemistry did he go up to the Poppelsdorfer Palace. This was to be expected. The same limitations had been imposed on his father at Bonn and on his uncle the Prince of Wales first at Oxford, then at Cambridge. He was also required to entertain notables from time to time, as he had done at Cassel, whether they interested him or not. As at other German universities there were corps or clubs of students, who drank together and duelled amongst themselves at the slightest excuse, hoping to gain an honourable scar. At Bonn there were three, the Hanseatic, the Pfälzer and the Borussia, the last being the smartest.

---

* Amongst the miscellaneous information he took with him from Bonn was how to make a salad (he was instructed by the sister-in-law of his tutor in state government) and the words of the song 'Bonn, Bonn, what an ideal place you are to "bummel" in!' (taught him by the authoress, Carmen Sylva, who was Queen of Roumania).

The Prince was permitted to join the Borussia, to which his father had belonged, but not as a fully-fledged member. This was to prevent him from duelling. A final peculiar limitation was imposed upon his university life: that he must be available at any time if he was called on by the Emperor, his family, or the army for certain duties. It seems from his book *My Early Life* that he also imposed certain limitations upon himself: that, as happens with some young men, he was taking life seriously. He clearly did not approve of what he called 'high jinks' amongst his comrades in the Borussia, nor of their drinking bouts, although Bonn and Königswinter across the Rhine were famous for wine, especially for the delicious Dragon's Blood. He held himself somewhat aloof, not attending the regular carnivals, though whether or not this was at the orders of the Emperor is not stated. His chief amusements seem to have been playing croquet with the daughters of his neighbour, and dancing with them in the evenings. Then there was the Rhine to enjoy. He always liked boating and with chosen companions would take the night steamer to Koblenz and row back to Bonn the next day. Amateur theatricals also amused him, and he rejoiced in the close association of the students with the King's Hussars who were stationed at Bonn. Several times he was summoned by his grandmother to Koblenz Castle and professed to have enjoyed himself, and he rode or took a train or steamer to visit other castles on the Rhine, but from a variety of sources it seems that his chief delight was to go over to Hesse and visit his relations there.[15]

In the summer they would be at their summer palace, Wolfsgarten, set in the forest north of Darmstadt and only ten miles from the Rhine. This was an enchanted place, smelling of roses and hay and stables, but two wolves kept in a cage by the gates added a macabre touch. Here William felt very much at home. His Aunt Alice and Uncle Louis and their children* made him welcome and often his other aunt Princess Christian of Schleswig-Holstein would be over from Windsor with her jovial husband and their four children. Aunt Louise and Uncle Leopold were sometimes there as well. He liked to take the young people off for gallops in the rides, or to row on the lake. Or they would play croquet or tennis and he was not above stopping the games to read extracts from the Bible for their edification. It was noticed that he had a special fondness for his cousin Elizabeth or Ella as she was called in the family; and, as is often done, he showed it by making a fuss of her elder sister Victoria, teaching her to smoke and so successfully that she became an inveterate smoker at the age of sixteen and remained one until she died in England seventy-one years later. He was the oldest, unless the

---

* There were six surviving Hesse children: Victoria, Elizabeth, Irene, Ernest Louis, Alix, and Mary. Four years before William went to Bonn, another child, Frederick William, who was an haemophiliac, had fallen from an upstairs window and died.

Battenberg cousins were there, and certainly in his own eyes as well as everyone else's the most important. His liking for Ella was genuine enough. He was silent when she spoke. No-one else could quieten him so easily. It was necessary to make him aware that she was already promised to the Grand Duke Serge of Russia. He took it rather badly but only betrayed this by later actions. At the time he showed little. His cousins found him likeable but strange: abrupt, volatile, enormously energetic, but given to brooding. They called him 'The Only' which he swallowed with some difficulty, and 'William the Sudden' because of his excitability. The nickname he liked best himself and which was used the most appeared to have no meaning. Someone used it one day and that was that. 'Gondola Billy' was William's name at Wolfsgarten and Darmstadt.[16]

4

By 1878 Prince von Bismarck had got himself right at the centre of European affairs. The treaty which had ended the Russo-Turkish war satisfied neither Austria nor Britain. Bismarck therefore invited all interested parties to a Congress in Berlin, and said that he himself would preside. With reluctance in some quarters the invitation was accepted, and elaborate preparations were made to greet the representatives of the Powers. Bismarck cared nothing for the Balkans – though he once predicted that the next war would be started by 'some damned foolish thing in the Balkans'[17] – but he was interested in proving to the world that Berlin now stood in the place once occupied by Vienna and Paris; and nothing was to be too good for the congress. Feeling that he could not rely on the Crown Princess to keep her nose out of such a political box of tricks, he told the Crown Prince to take her for a holiday in England. They proposed themselves to the Princess of Wales for a visit to Marlborough House, and had gone on to Lord Salisbury's at Hatfield when they heard that an attempt had been made on the Emperor. It was the second time he had been shot at in two months, but whereas the first had been an insignificant affair, and at the Emperor's request, largely hushed up, this was much more serious. He had been fired at twice with a shotgun, and the slugs and shot had spread mainly over his back and sides, though some had penetrated his wrist and neck and forehead.[18] Miraculously he had not bled to death, but he was still far from well. The Crown Prince and Princess left at once for Germany.

Bismarck heard the news at Friedrichsruh. Once assured that, although badly wounded, the Emperor would survive, he astonished his secretary by thumping the ground with his stick and crying joyfully: '*Now* we can dissolve the Reichstag!'[19] Immediately he saw the political possibilities. He had been trying to rid himself of the National Liberals, who had helped him in his campaign against the Papacy but who now stubbornly refused to support his plan to outlaw the Social Democratic Party. Astutely Bismarck realized that a half-dead Emperor peppered with over thirty pellets of shot was magnificent political material. Fortunately the would-be assassin, a rich doctor, had turned the gun on himself and died of wounds before he could be questioned. It would be easy to suggest through his friends in the press that the villain had been a Socialist, then cause an outcry and agitate against the Social Democrats and their friends the National Liberals, dissolve the Reichstag, and have his own people returned in a general election. Bismarck instantly left for Berlin. Only one difficulty stood in the way of the consummation of his plan. The Crown Prince would expect to be appointed Regent and might not agree to a dissolution. In a typical Bismarckian fashion he overcame this problem. The Emperor had lost a lot of blood and he was eighty-one years old. He signed a document which gave his son authority to act as his deputy, not as Regent with authority to initiate policy. The Crown Prince was simply to carry on with the paper work. Bismarck still held the reins of power.

Prince William, who had come straight from Bonn and had been horrified to find his grandfather swathed in bandages and as pale as death, was required to help his parents.[20] There was indeed a lot of paper work; patents, commissions and other documents to sign and sand. It was William's first sight of state papers. It was also his first experience of an international conference. The Crown Prince and Princess had to deputize for the Emperor, welcome the delegates to the Berlin Congress, and be at the centre of all the balls, receptions and banquets.[21] They did it impressively; the Crown Prince tall and stately and dignified, the perfect foil to his small, vivacious wife. She was delighted to greet their recent host, Lord Salisbury, who was England's Foreign Secretary, and her mother's great friend Lord Beaconsfield, the Prime Minister. She sent him flowers and strawberries and, as he wrote to Queen Victoria, 'showered kindnesses' upon him. Beaconsfield was at his best, witty, vivacious, complimentary, even at one point thunderous – it looked as if he was to be outwitted so he prepared to leave the Congress, ordering his special train to be prepared. The bluff worked. Some time before he had called Bismarck 'really just another old Bonaparte', but he respected him all the same. Bismarck himself remarked: 'The old Jew. He's the man.'[22] And Dizzy turned out to be; showing oriental cunning in his dealings with Carathéodory Pasha, the Turkish delegate; exquisite politeness to the Italian, Corti; a chilly sort of belligerence to the ancient Russian Prime Minister, Gortchakoff; firmness to the Austrian Andrássy, glorious in his scarlet Hungarian general's uniform frogged with gold;[23] and sharing with the French delegate, a M. Waddington, who was half English and had once rowed in the university boat-race, an epicure's estimate of the food they were given. They decided the prize went to the Turkish Embassy when they had such a delicious pilaff that M. Waddington had two helpings.[24]

Although on the periphery of these great events, Prince William, as his father's eldest son, was present at many of the luxurious entertainments. It was his first introduction to the workings of that old diplomacy described by Sir Winston Churchill in *The World Crisis* as 'polite, discreet, pacific and on the whole sincere' which was to disintegrate into something less estimable during the power scramble after 1918.[25] Most of the real work of the Congress was of course done outside the magnificent hall where the delegates met.[26] The Balkans were torn apart and put together again at banquets and behind closed doors in hotels and embassies, even during the special treats arranged for the delegates' delectation. Much went on aboard the steamer which took them down the river Havel as the Crown Prince and Princess's guests on a visit to Potsdam; though a storm blew up and the steamer all but capsized – which one delegate wryly said would have solved their problems at a stroke. It was then that Lord Beaconsfield described New Palace as a 'Paradise of Rococo'. Sans Souci he also adored, though certain arrangements were found to be inadequate. As Prince Hohenlohe, theoretically the German delegate, remarked, there was only one porcelain receptacle and, not able to wait after the long journey, 'Europe collected round that'.[27]

Few of the delegates returned home entirely satisfied, except Lord Beaconsfield, who had had a previous agreement with Turkey confirmed that England should have the island of Cyprus.

Having learnt something from his parents' careful interpretation of this international attempt to achieve an acceptable balance of power in the Balkans, Prince William's education as an Heir Presumptive was further enlarged by a request from his father to represent the Emperor at the Silver Jubilee of the wedding of Leopold II of the Belgians and his Queen. He did not much care for it. As was the custom, he was given certain information about his host and hostess which seemed to make the celebration of their Silver Jubilee a farce. Apparently they loathed one another and had not lived together for some time. The Queen was a Hapsburg and longed to return to Austria or Hungary but was obliged to eke out a miserable existence all alone at Spa. Her only son had died, for which King Leopold had never forgiven her, and her three daughters were all destined for unsavoury fates. As for the King of the Belgians, rumour could not speak too badly of his lasciviousness, indifference to other people's feelings, cruelty to his children, avarice, hypocrisy and greed.

It could hardly have been pleasant for the young Prince to take part in such a piece of humbug, especially as he was forced to observe King Leopold's malice at first hand. When he introduced his ministers to William he did so in French, complimenting them on their excellence and loyalty, then he denigrated each in German for the benefit of the Prince, who was much embarrassed by the cruel sneers of his host. At the state banquet which celebrated the Silver Wedding the unhappy Queen's cousin, the Archduke Charles Louis, proposed the congratulatory toast. Either the grisly travesty became too much for him or he simply forgot his prepared speech for he abruptly finished with a feeble '*Hoch!*' King Leopold turned to the young Prince and said in a loud voice: 'My dear William, it is truly a rare gift of the gods to be a good speaker', which embarrassed William quite as much as it did the Archduke, and threw the company into a silence which would have been total had not the deaf brother of the King gone on talking. His talk was not edifying as he was criticizing each of the guests in turn, laughing at most, deriding even the grandest. The lady next to him tried to silence him but he paid no attention. She looked appealingly at the King, who did nothing to stop his brother. At the conclusion of this appalling scene the King told William it was better to let his brother run on sometimes as only in that way could he hear things no-one dared tell him. Finally there was a High Mass and Te Deum of thanksgiving for this extremely unhappy marriage, a piece of cynicism close to blasphemy.

From Brussels William travelled direct to the New Palace where his parents were entertaining the Duke and Duchess of Schleswig-Holstein-Sonderburg-Augustenburg. Earlier that year he had proposed himself as a guest at their house in Gotha. There were two grown-up daughters in the family, one, Princess Augusta Victoria, generally called Dona, who was about sixteen months older than he, to whom he had shown polite attention; the other, Princess Caroline, a year younger. There is no doubt that he had in fact lost his heart to his cousin Ella of Hesse and he was not a young man who easily accepts a refusal. Furthermore, though the Augustenburgs were *souverain*, and the Duke had been a friend and fellow officer of the Crown Prince for many years, they were not of the innermost Court Circle and there might be some objection from the Emperor to such a *parti*.

It is difficult to see quite what William wanted to do. Possibly he did not know himself. He had shown no detectable signs of enjoying what his grandmother stigmatized as a 'fall'. Lights blaze on the most secret doings of the great, yet William may have had loyal friends in the Army or at University who could keep still tongues and not scribble in diaries. The high probability is that he was still a virgin. Bismarck averred he had strong sexual appetites, and the Chancellor must have had sources of information denied to modern biographers. Therefore, if the Prince were to avoid the hell-fire painted in such detail and for so long by Dr Hinzpeter, he would wish to marry young. The problem evidently got on top of him because no sooner had the visitors departed from New Palace than he himself left. He records the event in 'My Early Life'.

> *In the beginning of September I went for the benefit of my health to Ilfracombe, a seaside resort in Devonshire. A very charming young scholar who collaborated in the* Monumenta Germaniae *came with me; to my deep regret he died not long after.*

Whether or not this friend actually died in Ilfracombe is not stated, but hearing that her grandson was unwell and in Devonshire, Queen Victoria kindly invited him to Balmoral. He was suitably grateful. Balmoral he already knew well. He liked the Highlanders, 'Unlike the English [he wrote] they have a great sense of humour.'*[28]

Despite his limitation he had also trained and trained and made himself into a first-class shot, and he was delighted to be sent out stalking. He had bagged his first stag in Wildpark at Potsdam two years before, but stalking in Scotland was a very different affair. Told what to do by his grandfather's old loader, William found himself crawling through thick heather, avoiding peat hags with the wriggling motion of a Prussian skirmisher, getting wet, midge-bitten, and almost exhausting himself before he was in position to take a shot. To his joy he brought down a fine old stag, an eight-pointer. Then to his further joy his grandmother gave him formal leave to wear the Royal Stewart tartan, and John Brown, her body-servant, fitted the young Prince out with a green hunting kit and a dress kilt for the evenings, silver buckled shoes, stockings, day and dress sporrans, a plaid fastened by a cairngorm clasp, a skean-dhu, a longer dirk and a basket-hilted claymore in a bandolier. William was enraptured, and compared the kilt favourably with Tyrolean, Styrian and Upper Bavarian gaiters as the knees were always covered.[30]

On this occasion he got on extremely well with his grandmother, was appreciative of her kindness, went out for drives with her, and showed an interest in the plantation and gardens laid out by his grandfather. She would have made an excellent confidante about his personal affairs because, not only was she genuinely interested in his future and a good matchmaker, but she also had the advantage of being Ella's grandmother, and also related to

---

* It is interesting that this view was shared by William's grandfather, the Prince Consort, and by Leopold I of the Belgians. The latter noted: 'In America it is said to be still worse, and a joyous person a rarity'.[29] It is to be presumed that senses of humour vary a great deal.

Dona. However there is no mention of any such confidence being passed. Queen Victoria's *Letters* – much tinkered with by her daughter, Princess Beatrice – and William's own history, *My Early Life*, are silent on the matter. Probably it was a good opportunity lost.

Feeling a good deal better, William proceeded to London, and thence to Paris. He recorded that he saw the sights, looked in on a trial, went up in a balloon, raised his hat to the President and went to the theatre. He was charmed, he said, with the surroundings of Paris, 'but the feverish haste and restlessness of Paris repelled me. I never wanted to see the French capital again.[31]'

The word Paris, and especially at that giddy period, suggested the liberal sowing of wild oats, yet no-one has even hinted that William went on the ran-tan. He returned to Germany in time to see his brother Harry off on a two-year cruise round the world and to give his father the Crown Prince a birthday gift he had bought in Paris. Afterwards he went back to his life as a student, in better spirits, but with his own personal problems not yet resolved.

5

A month after his return to Bonn William heard that diphtheria had struck the family at Hesse. His cousin Victoria first contracted the disease, and he was strictly forbidden to ride over to Darmstadt. Four days afterwards her sister Alix went down with the disease. Queen Victoria's own physician was sent to Darmstadt. The Crown Princess ordered a Bavarian specialist to go there immediately. Then William's youngest cousin May caught it, then Irene, then the Grand Duke, then their only surviving son, Ernest. Ella was sent away from the pestilent palace to her paternal grandmother.[32]

On November 16th a heartbroken Grand Duchess telegraphed her mother that May had died.

THE PAIN IS TERRIBLE BUT GOD'S WILL BE DONE[33]

She and the doctors and nurses toiled together to bring the others through, and though Irène was for a long time on the danger list, and everyone was certain that Ernest would die, they all pulled through. Very soon the Grand Duke was up and able to drive out in a closed carriage. The other children gathered strength. Ella was still kept away but it was hoped she could return home soon. The next tragedy occurred about a month after the first. The Grand Duchess herself, worn out with anxiety, sorrow and constant nursing, contracted the disease, and died on December 14th, the anniversary of her own father's death. She was buried four days later, her coffin draped in a Union Jack.[34]

Though the Prince of Wales, Prince Leopold and Prince Christian travelled from England to be there, the German Emperor, who had made a remarkable recovery, would not permit the Crown Prince and Princess or Prince William to attend for fear of infection. They dared not disobey.

The royal families of Europe have scarcely ever permitted private grief to alter arrangements. Thus Queen Victoria would no more permit the arranged marriage of her son Arthur to be postponed because of the death of her daughter Alice than she had allowed Princess Alice's own marriage to be postponed on account of the death of the Prince Consort. If possible there had to be seemliness, but continuity was the important thing. Events must proceed. For a year Prince Arthur had been engaged to Princess Margaret Louise of Prussia, the daughter of estranged parents. They were married at Windsor three months after the tragedy of Darmstadt. A large party travelled to Windsor from Berlin, including the Crown Prince and Princess and William, but not Charly, as she was soon to be confined. With them was the bride's father, Prince Frederick Charles of Prussia, a sadist who had punished his children by bending back their fingernails and digging his own into their quicks, and who upset Queen Victoria by saying on arrival how very sorry he was to be in England again.[35] Despite the presence of this ill-tempered ogre the Queen made it a great occasion as Prince Arthur was her favourite son. Yet hardly had the bridal pair gone for their honeymoon than there was another family tragedy. The Crown Prince and Princess were urgently summoned home by telegram. Their eleven-year-old son Waldemar had caught diphtheria.[36] The Crown Princess had a special affection for Waldemar. Of all her children he seemed most like her father in character and intellect and she had placed great hopes in him.[37] As they rushed to Berlin the Crown Prince brought all the force at his command to control the mounting hysteria in his wife. It would have been apparent to the most insensitive son that he was better out of the way by himself, and to William, feeling useless, unwanted, and once more far down in the list of his mother's affections, the journey must have been intolerable. Trying to be helpful, he kept an all-night vigil in the Friedenskirche for his brother. In *My Early Life* he starkly recorded: *On March 27th my brother, Waldemar, died of diphtheria. The grief of my parents for the loss of this splendid son was unspeakable; our pain deep and cruel beyond words.*[38]

The Crown Prince and Princess found the loss of Waldemar almost unbearable. Possibly the cleverest, certainly the most affectionate of their sons, for her at any rate it re-opened the wounds of losing Sigismund during the Austrian War. She was a strong-willed, determined woman, but this shock came close to breaking her, and her enemies were unrelenting in their hate. The minister of a strict Protestant sect in Berlin who deeply disapproved of the Crown Princess's unorthodox approach to Christianity actually maintained that the death of Prince Waldemar was God's way of forcing humility on the Crown Princess's proud, unfeeling heart. She read this with her own eyes in a newspaper.[39] Her husband and many of her closest friends said she was never the same woman again.

6

Such a double disaster could quite easily have had a traumatic effect on a highly-strung young man like Prince William. His student days would soon be concluded. After that he wished to live right away from home and the funereal gloom which enveloped his mother. His apartments at New Palace were no longer distant enough. He must have his own establishment, and this, by custom, would only be granted to him on marriage.

No doubt he still wished to make a match with Ella of Hesse. Much of his time at Bonn had been spent in writing romantic verses expressing his love for her. But she had never deceived him. She had never given any indication of returning his feelings. Even without those impediments, Ella was still too young to meet his immediate need, and there was to hand Dona of Schleswig-Holstein, of ripe, marriageable age, to whom he was not indifferent, and who had clearly shown her affection for him. . . .

The Prince lived up to his nickname of 'William the Sudden' and made a rapid decision. Barely a month after the death of his young brother he went blackcock shooting at Görlitz in Lower Silesia. Not far away was the principal residence of the Duke of Schleswig-Holstein-Sonderburg-Augustenburg. Casually, as it were, Prince William called there; asked formal permission from the Duke to speak to his eldest daughter, and Princess Dona was pleased to say yes.[40]

It could not have been easy for him. Thereafter he attempted to put his first love out of his mind, though he never properly succeeded. Always he had Ella's photograph on his desk.[41] For many years he could not bring himself to meet her except on unavoidable, ceremonial occasions, and he would not speak to her; and then, thirty-nine years later, he did his utmost, making desperate efforts, to save her from the Bolsheviks. Ella had been replaced by Dona, but chiefly for reasons of expediency.

A number of obstacles still had to be overcome before any sort of official betrothal could be announced or even considered as fixed. Any movement he made would have been subjected to intense Court gossip, but it is by no means certain that even his parents were in Prince William's confidence at the time. They would have known of his affection for Ella. Their second son Harry had been simultaneously showing a marked liking for Ella's younger sister Irène.[42] They would have noted William's attention to the Augusten-burgs, but he was not in the habit of confiding in them. He was a very independent young man. They would now have to be consulted officially. More important, so would the German Emperor, and Prince Bismarck, who had insulted William's future father-in-law at the time of the Schleswig-Holstein war. Brutally he had first addressed him correctly as 'Your Royal Highness', within minutes altered it to 'Your Highness', and had terminated the conservation by addressing him merely as 'Your Excellency'.[43] New he generally referred to him as 'that idiot of Holstein'.[44]

The Crown Prince and Princess had gone to Homburg after Waldemar's funeral and wanted to go on to Italy. But their presence was required at the formal celebration of the Golden Wedding of the German Emperor and Empress on June 11th. Still desolated they attended the long and elaborate ceremonies, during which the Emperor looked nervous and his Empress looked magnificent in a dress of cloth of gold encrusted in diamonds and a gold spangled wig as orange as any worn by Queen Elizabeth I. Bored with the long ceremony, Prince Bismarck flirted with the young princesses, and Prince William, well aware how his grandparents hated and raved at each other, must have thought the jubilee as farcical as the one he had attended in Belgium, except that this marriage, so unpalatable to both parties, had lasted exactly twice as long.

He broached the matter of his own marriage to his own parents. If they were disappointed they hid it well. No doubt they would be glad to see their temperamental son set up house elsewhere. The principle of 'revolt against the father' was very much in evidence that summer. When his parents approved of the election of Prince Alexander of Battenberg as sovereign Prince of Bulgaria and the possibility of a match between him and William's sister Moretta, he automatically disapproved.[45] When he found his mother reading the first part of *Das Kapital* and finding it fascinating,[46] he was flamingly anti-Socialist and said he approved of the new order that regiments of the guards were forbidden to read liberal publications.[47] Then when she expressed horror at the foundation of an Anti-Semitic League (by a half-Jewish journalist),[48] he was automatically contradictory – despite the fact that he really agreed with her. No doubt his young brother's death, a growing cynicism, possibly a sense of loneliness, and undoubtedly the nervous tension caused by having to decide between Ella and Dona all con-tributed to his aggressiveness. Willingly the Crown Prince and Princess forwarded his marriage, appealing to the Emperor for his permission.

There they met with an unexpected check.

Fond as he was of his grandson, William I did not consider the match entirely suitable. The Augustenburgs were royal but hardly royal enough, not sufficiently *ebenbürtig*. His son pleaded. Queen Victoria pleaded. The old gentleman would not change his mind. And the more he was resisted the more William wanted his Dona. Everyone became convinced he was deeply in love with her.

The summer passed uneasily. William formally ceased being a student. His *Lebenslauf* was completed and filed away. He requested his grandfather for permission to travel, especially to Egypt. Again a check. William could go with his parents to Italy for a time, but then he was to report to his regiment.[49] With all the egotism of the thwarted young male he probably did not pay much attention to the political crises of that time. In foreign and home affairs Bismarck was obliged to go against his own convictions. While Emperor William continued his policy of leaning towards Russia, meeting his nephew the Emperor and thrashing out their differences in private, Bismarck – though he saw no point in a 'treaty' in peacetime – made an alliance with Austria-Hungary and, by threats of resignation, forced his master to sign it.[50] It cemented his European reputation because it seemed that, as he had concluded his conflict with the Catholics and the National Liberals, the Austrians were looking to him to quell radicalism. At home he established his position by introducing agrarian and industrial protective tariffs, thereby throwing the Junkers and the bourgeois capitalists into a marriage of convenience and boosting the country's economy.[51] The working people at all levels immediately felt the benefit. They were better off than at any time since the boom years of the *Gründerjahre*, roistering in their corner pubs and toasting the Chancellor. This was anathema to the Social Democrats, who did not want a contented proletariat and taught that their political objects could only be achieved through suffering and self-sacrifice. Workmen with money in their pockets were not impressed by notices which read '*Workers, abstain from alcohol!*'[52] It was also anathema to Bismarck. Never had his position been more secure but, to his disgust, he felt he was a second Metternich.[53] However, the security gave him more leisure to attend to the pleas of the Heir Presumptive that he be allowed to marry. Fortuitously Dona's father died in January 1880, and this suited Bismarck and broke down the old Emperor's obstinacy. Now there seemed little against the match and much for it. The monarchy needed undershoring. Bismarck had been considerably alarmed by the attempt on his master the previous year. He was also alarmed by the spread of radicalism. Gladstone in an electioneering tour had stated that the people were really sovereign and that the Queen's assumption of the title of Empress of India was 'theatrical bombast and folly'.[54] Worse was the manic edge of radicalism, anarchy. In December 1879 the

King and Queen of Spain had been shot at by a demented waiter,[55] and early in the following February an attempt had been made on the Emperor of Russia in his own dining room. By an almost unique chance the Emperor was late for dinner. He had been detained for ten minutes by the French Ambassador; then, taking the Empress's arm he had led the procession of courtiers and guests to dine. Beyond the open doors were waiting servants in a dining room ablaze with candlelight – and suddenly there was a flash and a roar. The darkness and long silence which followed was eventually broken by the Emperor's voice. 'My children, let us pray.' Lights were brought. A few feet in front of the Emperor and Empress was a chasm. There was no trace of the dining room nor of a single living servant.[56] All in all Bismarck considered that yet another heir in direct succession to the Royal and Imperial Crowns of Prussia and Germany could only do good, and so he urged William's marriage on the old Emperor.

Appropriately on St Valentine's day, only nine days after the outrage in the Russian Winter Palace, a quiet formal betrothal took place between Prince Frederick William Victor Albert of Prussia and Princess Augusta Victoria Frederica Louisa Feodora Jenny of Schleswig-Holstein-Sonderburg-Augustenburg. Prince William was then promoted to the rank of captain and given his first real command – that of a company in the First Regiment of Foot Guards – but he disappointed his parents by being no more amenable as an engaged man than he had been as a single one. Princess Dona's bovine devotion to her William exasperated them because it appeared to inflate his ego. They may have forgotten the transports of their own first love. After June 2nd, when the Emperor made a public proclamation of their betrothal, William became harder and more censorious than ever. The Empress Marie of Russia, a great-aunt of Ella, died lonely and unwanted in the Winter Palace. William said it was a disgrace that the Emperor had installed his mistress in the same palace and that his wife's last hours were disturbed by his bastards playing in the room above. He was hyper-critical, too, of the Emperor's move to marry his lady and legitimize the bastards. All this was understandable, but he and his mother were too much alike for her to have let him preach his narrow morality in her drawing-room.* It must have been a relief to her when he went on manoeuvres with his company, or travelled about to visit his family for the last time as a bachelor. One of these visits was a disaster. He went to Sandringham for his Uncle's birthday on November 9th, chiefly because he had a tendresse for his beautiful Aunt Alix. Indeed despite all the many differences which had occurred and which were to occur

---

* It is legitimate to wonder whether or not William was aware that, as a young man, this same Emperor had stolen the heart of Queen Victoria, and that under different circumstance he might have been his grandfather.[57]

between them he always kept on his desk a portrait of his Aunt Alix, together with one of his first love, Ella of Hesse. On this occasion he threw his weight about and actually left Sandringham at the shortest notice two days before his uncle's birthday. It was the sort of hastiness people were beginning to associate with him. His uncle and aunt chose to regard it as studied rudeness. The result was one he must have regretted. His aunt's old dislike for all things Prussian was thoroughly re-vitalized, she refused to accompany her husband to William's wedding, and did not trouble to conceal her pleasure when things went awry.[58]

The royal bride was welcomed to Berlin on February 26th, 1881. Her ceremonial entry to the city was not without incident. Drawn by eight black horses wearing heavy red, brass-studded harness, the bridal carriage was chiefly of glass with painted panels; freezing in the winter and as suffocating as a greenhouse in the summer. With outriders, a coachman, coachman's pages and three footmen behind, the heavy coach swayed from side to side like a ship on the sea. Obliged to wear State attire, that is, semi-evening dress with a long train, the bride could have been neither comfortable nor warm as her carriage moved slowly along the beflagged and wreathed gravelled centre of Unter den Linden. At the head of the procession, by ancient right, rode the master butchers of Berlin, none of them very comfortable in their top hats and frockcoats, and few of them entirely at ease though tired working horses had been chosen for them.[59] In the procession was William the bridegroom, not in that capacity but as recently promoted honorary major and Captain of the Bodyguard. The Berliners were suitably appreciative of the pomp, and enjoyed the sudden flight of white doves, released from the Brandenburg Gate, but with their sardonic humour they probably enjoyed far more the sight of their Burgomaster making a totally inaudible speech of welcome and the bride making a totally inaudible reply, the unhappy, heaving master butchers, and certainly a float, advertising Singer sewing machines, which had been obtruded by an enterprising agent right into the middle of the royal procession.[60] On reaching the palace where she was to be lodged, the Princess was greeted by the Crown Prince, who presented her to the lined-up Grenadiers with William at their head and announced she was 'mother of the company'.[61]

The next day, a Sunday, the marriage service took place.

By tradition anyone having any connection with the bride or bridegroom was permitted to be there: old servants, nurses, tutors, fellow students, friends and relations, all received invitations. The Prince of Wales was present, so were representatives of the crowned heads of Europe, and it was noticed that, though he never ever attended royal functions if it could be avoided, Prince Otto von Bismarck had found the time, strength and health to be present. Politically his presence there was the equivalent of an ancient Roman portent in the sky.

After a short and simple service the guests filed past the German Emperor and Empress and the bridal couple, bowing to each in turn. There followed a dinner, for most at small round tables, for the chief royalties at a much larger table. On such a formal occasion the Great Officers of State played their part waiting upon the Imperial couple, and members of the high nobility took dishes from the pages to serve the other royal guests.

Then the company moved to the great White Hall where the silver and white decorations were a perfect foil to the brilliance of coloured dresses and uniforms. In the centre of the floor was a polished inlay of a crowned Prussian Eagle – to be avoided by everyone for it was as slippery as glass.[62] There the wedding Torch Dance took place, a ceremony unique to the Court of Prussia, protracted but beautiful and impressive. Everyone took his place. The Emperor and Empress on thrones, William and Dona on gilded chairs raised slightly above the level of the floor, the remaining royal ladies seated with their parti-coloured trains spread out at their feet; rows of pages dressed in red behind the chairs; the royal princes standing in their uniforms. At a word from an official most of the lights were extinguished. At the word from another the band of the Garde du Corps began to play slow and stately marches. The doors were thrown open and the Marshal of the Court carrying his wand of office led into the room twenty-four pages each carrying a resin torch. In time to the music they walked sedately round the hall before bowing to Prince and Princess William. Bridegroom and bride then descended from the dais, and, hand in hand, proceeded round the hall in the same stately tread. Returning, Princess William took the Emperor by her right hand, her brother the new Duke by the left, while Prince William took the hands of his mother and his mother-in-law, and the six circled the hall. So it continued, the bride and bridegroom taking out all the royal guests in turn; an ancient pageant of display in the sweet smell of resin, the wisps of torch smoke, and with Orders and jewels and sword hilts glittering in the flickering light.

CHAPTER SIX

Marriage

'The Prince is really a pearl'

COUNT HERBERT BISMARCK TO COUNT
PHILIP ZU EULENBURG

I

Within a very short time of Prince and Princess William's wedding power abruptly changed hands in two countries: nihilists at last assassinated the Emperor of Russia, blowing him into bloody gobbets, and President Garfield of the United States was shot by a disappointed tuft-hunter and died eighty days afterwards. But power passed less quickly elsewhere. In Germany where the Emperor was eighty-four, and in England where the Queen was sixty-one, both seemed immortal. Not that anyone, least of all their heirs, wished either harm; in fact, the Prince of Wales was sincerely horrified when yet another attempt was made on his mother, her assailant being soundly drubbed by Etonians' umbrellas. Yet what may be termed the Absalom-David fate, the place of royal heirs with long-lived parents, has never been sung. So thwarted was the Prince of Wales at being kept from the centre of affairs, so teased by the Queen's occasional threats to abdicate which he learnt, with a sinking heart, were no more real than the threat of a melancholy extrovert to hurl himself from cliffs, that he had been heard to declare, with no little bitterness and some blasphemy, that everyone had an Everlasting Father but only he was blessed with an Everlasting Mother.[1]

The Crown Prince, feeling that his own powers were already declining, was in the same uneasy state. His wife, for all her talents, had been crushed by the death of their two sons, the Chancellor's implacable hostility, and the indifference of their three eldest children. Evidently she was giving up all hope of bringing liberalism to Germany. He himself was more of a national liberal and less of a democrat than she, and could acknowledge the Chancellor's great achievements in the creation of the Second Reich. But, in his

73

frustration at being denied even the smallest vestige of power, he busied himself with external matters; patronizing the excavations at Pergamon as he had done at Olympia; farming at Bornstedt, and travelling with his wife and three younger daughters chiefly to Italy where, at Portofino, they lived lives of extreme simplicity. Yet he could not believe this was his destiny. He was unused to discussing his feelings, which, to some, made him seem insignificant, even secretive. Increasingly he grew world-weary. Occasionally, when his pride was hurt, he could be provoked into vitality and show a burst of anger. Otherwise he was silent and morose.[2]

Possibly Prince Bismarck counted on the fact that when his master died and the Crown Prince became Emperor he would still remain as Chancellor simply because there would be no viable alternative. He was ruthless with potential rivals, would expose real weaknesses, ridicule imagined ones, even persecute people with mild infractions of the law, as he had done in the case of Count von Arnim. He had only one particular dread: that, although the Crown Princess had been drained of her force by personal calamities, when the time came she would still find sufficient reserves of power and spirit to challenge his position. Deliberately he set out to crush those reserves; first, by persuading the Emperor to send his grandson rather than the Crown Prince as his representative on missions abroad, a calculated insult which made the Crown Princess weep with exasperation;[3] and, second, by taking her eldest son and making much of him. As we have seen William was susceptible to flattery and being frequently invited to luncheon by Germany's great man and allowed to talk with him afterwards was heady stuff.[4] If Bismarck was bored he concealed it and let the young man prattle on. It would pay one day. And gradually he had the Prince trained in civil administration and the workings of the Foreign Ministry, but only superficially.[5] When the Crown Prince made a formal and angry protest that it was wrong to permit his immature son to have any knowledge of the secrets of the nation, Bismarck merely put it at the back of the fire. The Crown Prince was right, of course, and he had not the slightest intention of revealing his secret methods to the callow young man, but he would not even give the Crown Prince the satisfaction of a reply.[6]

Only five months after his marriage the Prince was sent to welcome his uncle, the Duke of Edinburgh, and the British Reserve Fleet at Kiel. It was not an unimportant commission, but should, normally, have been the duty of the Crown Prince to represent his father and, as Bismarck intended, it drove the Crown Princess into a frenzy. William naturally was overjoyed, especially as his brother Harry was at Kiel Castle, and he did a thorough job – observing, amongst other details, how the old two- and three-deckers had been 'shaved down' and plated over.[7] On board his uncle's yacht was

Sir Arthur Sullivan, whose operettas were much enjoyed in Berlin. William gravely received the musician's bow, returned it, and then delighted the company by singing 'He polished up the handle of the big front door' from *Pinafore*.[8] Nothing had been overlooked to make the visitors feel welcome, and German foresight and thoroughness was well proved by the Commandant at Kiel who had once served in the Royal Navy and knew that British sailors ashore immediately got drunk. He therefore had a shed prepared amply strawed and with a guard at the door, and as the sailors reeled or were carried in they were kept under guard until they would be returned to their ships. There were banquets, concerts, fleet manoeuvres and, at the final salute, with flags signalling: 'Farewell. Prosperous voyage,' the Prince saw for the first and last time in his life a warship under full sail. The British fleet had just completed a complicated manoeuvre like a dance movement called 'the Gridiron' when the last ship of the last squadron began to fall astern. Evidently her engines were in trouble, but at once she broke all sails and, under a great expanse of canvas, surged ahead and kept to her station. Whether or not he was aware of the chagrin at the Crown Prince's Palace, the old Emperor was delighted with his grandson's report.

2

The social life of the Prince and Princess William settled into an ordered pattern.

It is alleged that William found his wife had not only brought the smallest of dowries from Primkenau, but also that he had a mother-in-law who showed clear signs of going off her head. The Dowager had a remarkable system of washing which involved dividing her body into twenty-four washable sections or 'hemispheres', and required a complete set of bowl, ewer, soap dish and towel for each one.[9] This excessive demand naturally threw the domestic arrangements into turmoil. Furthermore she was simply not to be trusted with men. Even at two state occasions she 'made unspeakable assaults upon her male neighbours at table', and when thwarted by being placed between her daughter and lady-in-waiting, she frequently lost her temper, broke glasses and swore most obscenely.[10] William ordained that her visits were to be restricted to three a year, and the duration should be one, two or three weeks, or as long as the household could stand it.[11] He liked his sister-in-law Princess Féodora but was not especially taken with his wife's brother Duke Ernest Gunther, a good-hearted man but too much of a *bon-vivant* for William's taste. Unfortunately he was also the sort of man who could not take a hint when it was time to terminate his visit. He was a clinger.[12]

William did not care for the Berlin smart set ruled over by his sister Charly. She had already presented her husband with a daughter, but this in no sense diminished her power as a leader of fashion and giddy hostess. Beside her Dona looked a little plain. William did not care for the comparison. They saw each other at Court and family anniversaries, seldom at other times.

The Emperor had made over for his grandson's use the Marble Palace at Potsdam. It was a large house on the Heiligensee, not especially comfortable as the inside was a jumble of oddly shaped halls and passages and flights of stairs and lacked all design. It was as though the rooms had been shaken from a pepperpot into a beautiful exterior. To compensate, there was a superb view of the Island of Peacocks and the Havel lakes, and the park had many eighteenth-century artificial grottoes. Unused Potsdam palaces quickly fell into a dreadful state of disrepair, and the Marble Palace was not fit to be lived in.[13] Dona wished to make certain alterations to which the Emperor gave his consent. Therefore to begin with the couple lived in a part of the old Town Palace at Potsdam where Frederick William I of Prussia had invented modern drill, increased the fire-power of the infantry by inventing iron ramrods, suffered from the agonies of porphyria – smashing dinner-services, and his servants' teeth and noses – and thrashing, starving and degrading his son and heir who was to become Frederick the Great. In these historic if macabre surroundings the young couple settled down to get to know each other.[14]

Doubtless each had habits which the other found irritating or offensive. She would have been alarmed to discover that he always kept a self-cocking loaded pistol in the half-open drawer of his night table;[15] and his hypochondria, although it was mostly justified, must have been very tiresome. Equally tiresome was his indifference to comfort. Either he was deliberately copying his grandfather's examples of frugality or Hinzpeter's lessons had bitten very deeply indeed, for he refused a soft chair if there was a hard one, bathed in a portable zinc affair and, using no sort of toilet water or brilliantine, made do with a common unscented soap for his bath, washing and shaving, and water for plastering down his hair.[16] His particular pride was his moustache. He often fondled it, though it did not yet turn up at the ends. Dona from her much poorer, almost Cinderella background, was very partial to luxuries of all kinds and she had strong views about what was fitting. William's false cuffs, attached to his shirt by buttons and loops of elastic, must have offended her; so must his taste in socks which, though never seen in public by anyone were nevertheless seen by her, and she considered that drab snuff-coloured socks, half yellow, half brown, were hardly royal.[17] He on his part did not approve of her many beauty preparations or vanities as he called them, and it must have been increasingly difficult to keep out of sight her huge and expanding collection of toilet waters, colognes, balsams, milk and fruit and cucumber preparations, beers, wines, spirits, vinegars, cordials, essences, bran-water, Ambrée *crème*, fat-powders, 'electricity' drops, opium, iodine, arsenic to ensure a fresh appearance, magnesium for whitening her nose and calves, and scented powders of all kinds.[18]

There were, naturally, other matters besides these small personal irritants. Because of his quicksilver mind and passionate interest in things William found his wife a bore, and, with her adequate but by no means outstanding education she was subdued by his apparent cleverness. She was slow and his rapidity of action alarmed her. Marriage to 'William the Sudden' cannot have been restful. He was enormously energetic and unless she was on a horse, when she became a dashing and fearless rider,[19] Dona was of the heavily-built, placid run of womankind. His religion was sincere but too ebullient and tolerant for her taste. She was a rigid evangelical, so much so that her carefully chosen ladies-in-waiting were known as the 'Hallelujah Aunts'.[20] She did good works, had pastors amongst her friends, and hoped one day to be in a position to found religious schools and build churches.

All differences put aside, two things guaranteed that their life together should be a success. First, William needed a pivot, a rock to which he could return from ceaseless and restless wanderings, and Dona was just that rock. Second, by happy chance, Dona happened to fall in love with William. He was good-looking and vigorous, and charmed her by being extremely jealous even if a manservant looked at her when she was in décolleté.[21] She was never truly happy away from him, but it was a discipline she often had to bear. Even in the first year of his marriage he was always on the go, at military exercises, or enjoying mess-life or learning statecraft under the tutelage of people appointed by Bismarck, or representing his grandfather on special occasions. But they were sometimes together and Dona met his physical needs, which Bismarck had noted were considerable, and with such ardour that it appears he was largely faithful to her. As a result she produced a string of six healthy sons and one daughter as regularly as a fruiting tree. In very many ways theirs was an excellent marriage, though there was never any doubt who was *unter dem Pantoffel*. He even chose her hats.

Dona accompanied her husband to the wedding of Crown Prince Rudolph of Austria-Hungary. He was marrying Stephanie, second daughter of that unloved and unlovely King Leopold II of the Belgians. They appeared to be devoted, and Dona, richly charged with sentimentality and already carrying her first child, was enchanted by the occasion. She and William were lodged in a small rococo châlet in the Schönbrunn pleasure gardens.

William was placed *à la suite* in his grandfather's regiment by the Emperor of Austria. The ceremonies were dignified and the banqueting luxurious.[22] Neither appreciated returning to the oppressive atmosphere at home.

By now the disapproval of the Crown Prince and Princess was almost tangible. To begin with, her mother-in-law had tried to like and help Dona, though she represented the type of German the Crown Princess found most repellent – but Dona, out of shyness and fright, had failed to respond. She was a stubborn young woman, as stubborn as the Crown Princess herself, and said she would not allow herself to be patronized or have her life managed for her. Furthermore, shyness and fright sometimes made her make gauche remarks, and maddened by her inanity her mother-in-law was quick to point out her mistakes. All this had shattered any hope of a conciliation between William and his parents. An opportunity had arisen to unite father and son because Schliemann, the archaeologist, had offered to present his entire collection of smuggled Trojan treasure – 'the treasure of Priam' – in exchange for the Freedom of Berlin and the Pour le Mérite – and both were ardent supporters of agreeing to the old villain's blackmail.[23] But their common interest soon died, and William quite rightly was angry when it seemed to him that his mother was bullying his wife.

When Dona had her first child, another William, the saluting guns thundered over the German capital, and the Crown Princess started a campaign to get her daughter-in-law's figure back in trim. She bought her corsets and pretty clothes and said she owed it to William to make herself attractive. In a daze of the post-natal depression which affects some women, Dona said she saw no point in going to the trouble as William had made it abundantly clear that he wanted to ensure the succession. This unspirited attitude must have infuriated the Crown Princess. Even more irritating was Dona's strongly expressed views on the unsuitability of a marriage between William's sister Moretta and Prince Alexander, the reigning Prince of Bulgaria. Called 'the Beau' in Berlin Society and Sandro by the family, Prince Alexander according to the Crown Prince was a most suitable *parti*. Dona disagreed because Sandro was a Battenberg. Her own claims to grandness being so very small, she made the Crown Princess speechless by her talk of the stamp of morganatic blood. It seemed to her mother-in-law scarcely a month or two since she had been begging the Emperor's permission for William to marry Dona in the teeth of those who claimed that a Holstein was not sufficiently *ebenbürtig*.

The relationship actually worsened at what should have been a happy family party, the Silver Wedding of the Crown Prince and Princess. The Prince of Wales was there, immensely pleased at having been made Colonel of the 5th Pomeranian Hussars, though the tight-fitting uniform hardly became his ample frame. This, however, he hoped to put right with frequent games of lawn tennis. But the Princess of Wales had positively refused to come to Berlin, which offended her Prussian relations.[24] This was the first damper on the celebrations. A second was that the Crown Princess had hoped everyone would enjoy the old Windsor entertainment of *tableaux vivants*, but only she and her brother and her kindly husband entered into the spirit of this English importation. Rehearsals were few and all were spoilt by quarrels between her children. On the day itself the performance was ruined by Charly who tried to steal everyone's thunder and Dona who wore an almost indecently close-fitting costume for a woman carrying a child, and who missed a cue. It was not an ordinary cue but one on which the whole of a *tableau* turned.[25] The Crown Princess found it difficult to contain her anger. It was certainly felt by Dona who went weeping to her husband. William championed her. He was already angry because his beautiful aunt Alix had remained in England and Charly had spoilt what he now regarded as 'odious theatricals'. Dona's distress angered him further. He was in no mood to listen to his uncle who bore down on him and said it was his mother's wish that they should have a private talk together. It is not recorded whether or not the talk took place nor how it was received. The Prince of Wales had certainly been charged to speak to his nephew about his studied rudeness to his parents, in going everywhere with a large suite so that they could never get near to him for a private talk, and in championing everything the Chancellor said, even when it was to their detriment. If anything was said, it did not appear to make any alteration in Prince William's manner. His mother had given Dona a beautiful dress to wear at the Venetian Ball which was to follow the *tableaux*, and he was in full accord with her decision not to wear it on any account. The sudden death of the Crown Prince's favourite uncle, Prince Charles of Prussia, and the prompt cancellation of the ball, saved the Crown Princess from this bodkin thrust in her relationship with William and Dona; but by this time she had in any case almost given up hope of ever being truly reconciled to them. It was a hard blow for a proud woman. Her brother, who was devoted to her, tried to keep up her spirits: he affected great indignation that Prince Charles had died so inopportunely. He had come to Berlin to wear his domino and dance, he said, not sing funeral dirges. . . .[26]

Later that year, in an attempt to smooth things with his nephew and show cordiality, the Prince of Wales sent William a complete set of Highland things. Instantly William had himself photographed full length trying to express by his attitude the air of a great chieftain. At the foot he caused to be printed the cryptic message '*I bide my time*', and liberally distributed copies to his family and friends.[27]

The Chancellor's health had been deteriorating for years. The battering he gave his huge frame and his digestive system had its effect in making him irritable and malicious and full of petty spite, but he was a colossus in European affairs; apparently indestructible. In the summer of 1883 he suffered a dramatic falling off. He felt ill, not merely unwell, but really ill. There was no need now for his distracted family to urge him to see a physician. He was frightened into it, but he did not send for the family doctor. He chose a new one, a Jew.

Bismarck held ambivalent views about the Jews. Anti-Semitism was bred in him as a Prussian Junker, but, as in most things, he stood far out beyond the ordinary. He had the practical view that one did not need to be a visionary liberal to see that the Jews in Germany were uncommonly useful. Politely he once remarked that the Jews could not be expelled from Germany without grave injury to the national welfare.[28] Less politely, in speaking on mixed marriages, he remarked that good results should come from the mating of 'a Christian stallion with a Jewish mare'.[29] His banker and the nation's was a Jew. Now in his illness he sent for a Jewish doctor named Schweninger. Not only was Schweninger a Jew but he also had a past, having once been caught *in flagrante delicto* in some unstated immoral act in a churchyard.[30] Nevertheless he was highly talented and, though middle-aged, he was prepared to take risks and experiment, a quality Bismarck appreciated.

The physician proved himself at the first consultation, showing right from the beginning that he was not in the least alarmed by Bismarck's brusque manner. After a brief examination he closed his bag and began to question the Chancellor about how much he ate and drank. Bismarck rapidly lost patience and remarked that he was not accustomed to being questioned; at which Schweninger bowed as if about to leave, and said the Chancellor evidently required a vet not a physician. It was an amazingly bold Daniel act, but the lion did not claw him. To everyone's surprise the Jewish physician became almost a part of the household. He first prescribed an exclusive diet of herrings and Bismarck kept to it. Then he established a diet regimen which Bismarck would have accepted from no-one else. Schweninger also insisted on exercise. Not for a decade had the Chancellor been heaved on to a horse. Now he began to take regular rides. He still ate and drank more than most people, but he lost 56 pounds, his temper improved, he slept better, and he was less prone to nervous outbursts. Schweninger was handsomely rewarded. The medical faculty of the University of Berlin was invited to make the Prince von Bismarck's personal physician a professor. It objected. The University was one of the youngest in Europe but at that time it was one of the most reactionary, opening its doors only to students who were attested graduates from a gymnasium. The thought of admitting a Jew who had once committed unspecified acts of indecency in a churchyard as a professor must have struck them as outrageous.[31] Nevertheless the Chancellor's fiat went forth. Ernst Schweninger was given his professorial chair.[32]

No longer bloated and savage-tempered, the Chancellor required far less patience when listening to the young Prince rattling on after luncheon parties. He was easy to draw out about his family and his work and William was full of stories about his amusements. He frequently shot with the Emperor of Austria and was once given the privilege of using the imperial butt which he reached in the dark and mist of early morning and which turned out to be a rocky protuberance over a sickening drop of 400 feet. On another shoot one of the guests, Count Wurm, claimed two stags with a *coup double*, and was much mortified when the keeper's report showed the *coup* had fallen at 8 a.m. on a mountain and the *double* at 3 p.m. in a valley.[33] William was also interesting himself in Naval affairs and on secret manoeuvres with the famous Captain Tirpitz had witnessed the arrest of an elderly gentleman caught spying on the fleet movements off Zoppot who had turned out to be Tirpitz's father.[34] The Chancellor listened. He was always prepared to hear anything at all about Austria – even their method of cavalry charging with sabres outstretched which the Prince admired and wanted to introduce into Germany.[35] As for the Navy, General Caprivi was at the head of it and Tirpitz was an expert on torpedo attacks and both were increasing in prestige and were therefore within Bismarck's rival-detecting antennae. It is reasonable to suppose that from listening to the plethora of the Prince's talk, the Chancellor did not go unrewarded. Choice morsels of useful information, given guilelessly, must have often dropped into his maw.

Bismarck showed no corresponding increase of patience with the Prince's mother, not relaxing his hostility for a minute, not even when she mourned her haemophiliac younger brother Leopold, who died in Cannes that spring. He had already firmly made up his mind that her plan to marry Princess Moretta to Prince Alexander the sovereign of Bulgaria must be scotched as soon as possible. Conceivably the Chancellor's chief reason was simply that the Crown Prince and Princess desired it. But his anxiety concerning rivals was now an obsession, and he had an idea that if the Crown Prince came to power he would make Prince Alexander his Chancellor. Then there might have been something in the rumour that he wished to use Princess Moretta as a political pawn or even marry her to his own son Count Herbert, whom he planned to make State Secretary for Foreign Affairs and who was at the base of his dynastic dreams. Yet Bismarck also had a sound political motive for disliking the match which was thoroughly appreciated by his master the

German Emperor: Prince Alexander, though placed in power by Russian influence, and a cousin by marriage of the new Emperor Alexander III, was showing marked anti-Russian feelings. Gradually he was getting rid of the Russian members of his Household. In the spring of 1884 he made a tour of European Courts, and his manner in Berlin made his feelings abundantly plain.[36]

In the same spring the 'royal mob', as Queen Victoria called it, descended upon little Darmstadt for the wedding of the Grand Duke's eldest daughter to Sandro's brother, Prince Louis of Battenberg, now a British subject and a sub-lieutenant in the Royal Navy. Once again private grief had not been allowed to alter a public royal arrangement. Although her dear son Leopold had died so recently, Queen Victoria was there in person to preside over the ceremonies. The Berlin contingent was led by the Empress Augusta, and included the Crown Prince and Princess, and Prince and Princess William. William's feelings may be imagined when, just before the marriage, the Grand Duke announced the engagement of his second daughter Ella to the Grand Duke Serge.[37] Then in a curiously ill-judged fashion, the Grand Duke himself was secretly married to a Madame Alexandrine de Kalomine only a few hours after his daughter's wedding. It was three days before the news leaked out. When it did the Empress Augusta swept off the Berlin party leaving Queen Victoria to deal with her son-in-law. This was done with great speed and efficiency. It was understandable perhaps that the Grand Duke should have consoled himself discreetly with the Polish wife of the Russian *chargé d'affaires* in Darmstadt, although the poor diplomat had gone off and divorced her, but marriage was quite out of the question. German divorce and annulment laws were easily managed. Exactly seventy days after his second marriage the Grand Duke found himself a widower once more.[38]

This was not the only fruit of the Darmstadt wedding. Princess Beatrice, Queen Victoria's youngest child, had conceived a passion for Prince Henry of Battenberg. She was her Mama's Benjamin, intended to be the comfort of her old age, and now she had become indispensable because the Queen's devoted factotum, John Brown, had died barely twelve months before. When the Princess bravely mentioned her attachment Queen Victoria's worst nature showed itself. Incredulity was followed by wrath which broke over her daughter's head in relentless waves. Then, although for weeks they were living under the same roof, the Princess was put into Coventry. They communicated only by small notes.[39]

In Berlin life was no more harmonious between William and his parents. Bismarck tormented them by arranging for William to go to Russia and represent the Emperor at the coming of age of Crown Prince Nicholas.

The Crown Prince and Princess of Prussia
with their children William, Charlotte, Henry
and Sigismund; a photograph taken in 1866
Radio Times Hulton Picture Library

William, aged eight, with
a cousin on a walking
tour arranged and
supervised by Dr Hinzpeter
Radio Times Hulton Picture Library

Georg Hinzpeter, Tutor to Prince William
and Prince Henry

William photographed in England while
on a long visit to his grandmother
Queen Victoria at Osborne
Mansell Collection

Prince Otto von Bismarck
Landesbildstelle Berlin

The young Prince in cuirassier uniform at the age
of twenty   *Radio Times Hulton Picture Library*

Princess Elizabeth of Hesse, William's
cousin Ella and his first love who married
Grand Duke Serge of Russia
Radio Times Hulton Picture Library

William and his chosen bride, Dona –
Princess Augusta Victoria of Schleswig-
Holstein-Sonderburg-Augustenburg
Radio Times Hulton Picture Library

The Emperor William I, the Crown Prince, Prince William of Prussia and his first son

Kaiser William II opening the
Reichstag in 1888
Landesbildstelle Berlin

Tenniel's famous *Punch* cartoon
'Dropping the Pilot'
Radio Times Hulton Picture Library

Baron von Holstein, the enigmatic Senior
Counsellor at the Wilhelmstrasse who
ensured continuity after the dismissal of
Bismarck   *Popperfoto*

General von Caprivi, Bismarck's successor
as Chancellor
Radio Times Hulton Picture Library

Prince Clovis zu Hohenlohe-Schillingsfurst, a 'spry young seventy-five',
third Chancellor of the Second Reich
Radio Times Hulton Picture Library

An idealized painting of the Kaiser as his subjects liked to see him; though it is worth noting that, despite his withered arm, he was a courageous and exceptionally capable rider

There he found a general fear of anarchy which was strangely unbelievable and oppressive. Otherwise he enjoyed himself and he got on well with both the Emperor and his heir.[40] Invited to write direct to the Emperor of Russia, that is, not through Bismarck or diplomatic channels, William accepted with alacrity and let himself go in a diatribe against his father and mother, his uncle of Wales, and the Prince of Bulgaria.

Espionage has moved far beyond the stage of the spy with carrier pigeons in his hat box and onion-juice invisible ink, and the superstates have not scrupled to tinker with recorded facts if it has given them a propaganda advantage. It follows that modern historians on both sides, and in between, can never now be entirely certain of the authenticity of their documentary evidence. Many of the Russian Imperial archives published after the Revolution and the German Imperial archives found in the rush on Berlin at the end of the Second World War, are probably not genuine, and all must be suspect. That admitted, here are two extracts from letters alleged to have been written by Prince William to the Emperor after his return to Berlin:

> *I only beg of you on no account to trust my English uncle. Do not be alarmed at anything you may hear from my father. You know him. He loves being contrary and is under my mother's thumb and she, in turn, is guided by the Queen of England and makes him see everything through English eyes. . . .*

> *We shall see the Prince of Wales here in a few days; we are not at all pleased at this appearance – pardon, he is your brother-in-law – with his duplicity and love of intrigue he will doubtless either try to encourage the Bulgarian – may Allah banish him to hell – or discuss politics with the ladies behind the scenes. I shall do my best to keep an eye on them but it is impossible to be everywhere.*[41]*

These extracts do not make pleasant reading. Bismarck's pupil had become his strongest ally. At all events, William's mission was accounted a great success. M. Giers, the Russian Foreign Minister, wrote: *Whoever had the idea of sending the Prince to us is to be much congratulated.*[42]†

Privately William must have been particularly pleased that his formal visit in May made it reasonable for him not to go to Ella's wedding to the Grand Duke Serge in June. An incident at the wedding banquet demonstrated Bismarck's unscrupulous cunning. Through his son Herbert he hinted to the Emperor of Russia that the German court strongly disapproved

---

* Both these letters are in English in the original.

† Prince William helped towards achieving Bismarck's most remarkable personal triumph, a meeting of the three Emperors, Francis Joseph, Alexander III and William in Poland that September, which renewed the Dreikaiserbund Alliance.

of Princess Victoria of Hesse having married a Battenberg. As a result, Prince Louis when he went into the banquet with his wife was not permitted to sit anywhere near her or her family, but with the officers of the Queen's yacht *Osborne* which had been sent over to take the English and Danish royalties home again. The Grand Duke of Hesse, now forgiven for his peccadillo, protested. The Emperor calmly replied that, after what he had heard from Berlin, he could hardly have placed Prince Louis with the royal family. Bismarck was not the sort of man to trouble himself about trifles like morganatic marriages, but he saw it as a convenient weapon, and one most likely to appeal to the Prussian Court, in his campaign against the marriage of Princess Moretta to Prince Louis' brother.[43] The latter, despite Prince William's curse, had not been confined by Allah to hell, and Bismarck knew he would have to use all means, fair and foul, to prevent the match.

At this unpropitious moment Queen Victoria's better nature prevailed. She changed her mind about Prince Henry and stipulated that if he would go to England and live permanently in the royal establishment with Beatrice, she would give her consent. He at once agreed.

There was uproar in Berlin. Those who esteemed the Almanach de Gotha were appalled that the daughter of a sovereign should marry the fruit of a morganatic marriage. Being his father's son, Prince Henry had managed to gain a commission in the splendid Gardes du Corps and they considered this should have been the height of his ambition. The marriage of Prince Louis to Princess Victoria had caused great offence already. This would be worse still. And in the background stood the third Battenberg brother who aspired to marry a daughter of the Crown Prince. Volleys of protest were fired at Queen Victoria. Empress Augusta did not spare her old friend. Nor, surprisingly, did the Crown Prince. In his letter he used the word 'stock' which enraged his mother-in-law as it implied the marriage was between animals. Then William and Dona added their objection. At this Queen Victoria boiled with wrath. Not even the Empress Augusta was spared, being reminded that the father of her son-in-law and his brothers and sisters were: *the children of a Fräulein von Geyersberg, a very bad woman, and they had been acknowledged by the whole of Europe as Princes of Baden.* Bastardy, the Queen raged, was considerably worse than morganatic marriage; and she would like Europe to know that morganatic marriages did not obtain in Great Britain and were disregarded. Prince Henry was a royal prince and should marry her daughter. Her most biting rejoinder was reserved for her eldest grandchild and his wife. She wrote to the Crown Princess:

The extraordinary impertinence and insolence and, I must add, great unkindness of Willie and the foolish Dona force me to say I shall not write to either. As for Dona, poor little insignificant princess, raised entirely by your kindness to the position she is in – I have no words. . . . As for Willie, that very foolish, undutiful, and, I must add, unfeeling boy, I have no patience with and I wish he could get a good 'skelping' as the Scotch say.[44]

This does not make very pleasant reading either. It is likely that his mother made sure William saw it. His delight at having been given command of the 1st Battalion of the 1st Regiment of Footguards, called 'The First Battalion of Christendom', was much spoilt by being called *an unfeeling boy*. He simmered when he heard that he would not be welcome at Windsor. Then the Prince of Wales likewise barred Sandringham. It was on this occasion that, much excited, William referred to his grandmother as 'an old hag'. His love-hate relationship with England was dancing from foot to foot.

Events in Berlin moved rapidly. Princess Moretta was heart-broken. She told her mother she was so much in love that if anything happened to Sandro Battenberg she would throw herself in a canal.[45] To William's delight the Emperor wrote a sharp letter to the Prince of Bulgaria in which he spoke strongly against the marriage, and Sandro, counting on the Emperor's great age, and wisely prepared to wait until the Crown Prince inherited the throne, undertook to renounce the idea for the time being.[46] It was not good enough for the Crown Princess. With the utmost vigour she promoted the projected marriage. It was the cause of yet another clash between her and her eldest son. There was a violent storm between them, and on this occasion unfortunately it was in public. Not even Bismarck could save William from the result of his conduct. He was advised to leave Potsdam for a time and withdraw from the Court. Sullenly he did so.[47] But Bismarck was no more satisfied than the Crown Princess with Prince Sandro's obvious attempt to play for time. He set to work to blast the Prince's reputation. Rumours began to spring up in the Bulgarian capital: that Prince Alexander was a homosexual and that two of his young and good-looking *aides* had been hurriedly recalled from Sofia by the Emperor of Russia. It was also said that he had venereal disease.[48] There were lewd whispers in Berlin that the Crown Princess really wanted Prince Sandro for herself. Bismarck permitted himself to remark that she was a wild woman and he was filled with horror at the uncurbed sensuousness which glowed in her eyes.[49] All the time he was plotting to have Prince Alexander's sovereignty rescinded by Russia. But simultaneously he himself was becoming increasingly neurotic about producing a dynasty and only felt safe when he installed his son Count Herbert as Secretary of State for Foreign Affairs. After that his enemies could do as they wished. The Marquis of Salisbury, now Queen Victoria's Prime Minister and Foreign Secretary, might raise his Cecil eyebrows and talk of 'Hateful Herbert',[50] but with his son at the centre of the web in the Wilhelmstrasse, the Chancellor felt secure.[51]

4

It has been noted that Prince William easily formed acquaintances but as a boy and a young man he made few intimate friends. His closest relationships were with his brother Harry and his sister Charly but by the time of his marriage they had grown away from him and Dona did not provide that close intimacy which is one of the greatest riches of princes. From these facts three possible conclusions may be reached. Either he was a 'loner' in the psychological sense and did not wish to give his whole confidence to anyone; or he was prevented by some inhibition from making close friendships; or he had too lofty a view of his own ultimate destiny to make such a thing possible – an idea which might have been implanted by Hinzpeter, who had exalted views of the mystique of sovereignty. Whichever is the correct interpretation, he found it more easy to be confiding as he grew older. Besides his own suite which was considerable but with whom he kept solely on terms of camaraderie, there was a large number of courtiers, officials and fellow officers who wished to get on with the Heir Presumptive and who claimed to be his friends. The Emperor being so very old, William found himself at the heart of a caucus which in other countries would have been called the heir's party. Bismarck gave his grand blessing to the party, and Count Herbert watched it with avuncular care. He was possibly a little too avuncular, offering, so it is said, to procure a mistress for the Prince should he feel the need of one. It is doubtful if William availed himself of the offer, especially as Dona got to hear of it and declared Count Herbert was thenceforth her deadly enemy.[52]

From this large number of acquaintances William made three friends who were to have much influence upon his life and history.

The first was General Count von Waldersee, twenty-seven years older than the Prince, who was Quartermaster-General, that is, Deputy Chief of Staff. He had been responsible for training William in how the General Staff was run, and had impressed his pupil by his quite phenomenal geographical bump for the lie of the land. He also spoke English and French and was full of vitality and an agreeable mixture of fun and religious fervour. Furthermore he had a touch of eccentricity which young men like in their elders but not in their contemporaries. He had a pet raven which perched on his golden shoulder straps and could never be touched by anyone. Physically he was unprepossessing, having the rigid carriage of the Prussian officer, a toothbrush moustache and short cut hair (what the Berliners called a peg-top), and the shape of a pear. But he had a bland manner and great charm. Moreover, he was within the inner circle, being a friend of Charly and married to a widow of Dona's uncle.

Countess von Waldersee, William's second particular friend, was an American from New York who charmed German society with her wit and intelligence. It was also said that she charmed William into her bed but this scarcely seems probable in view of the fact that she was twenty-one years older than he, and she enjoyed a great friendship with her niece by marriage, Dona – they shared a taste for hot-gospelling.[53] William did like pretty women. Daisy, Princess of Pless, the daughter of Mrs Cornwallis-West, a mistress of the Prince of Wales, said he could not have enough of their sympathy and understanding, but he was no Lothario.[54] Dona and he were often at the Waldersees' salon at General Staff Headquarters, and they all went to Wednesday meetings of the Court Preacher, Adolph Stöcker who struck at the Social Democrats by peppering his sermons with Christian Socialism and Anti-Semitism. Possibly it flattered William to be taken up by so able a soldier as Waldersee and he was entirely deceived by his artfulness. Called 'the Badger' by his contemporaries because of his liking for nosing underground,[55] Waldersee was a mischief-maker par excellence, fierce in his dislike of the Crown Prince and an encourager of William's disloyalty. In fact the General once went so far as to say that if ever there was a question of a *coup d'état* against the Crown Princess, William could count on him.[56] He did little good to the Prince or to his reputation. Countess Waldersee was better for him as her fierce evangelicalism forbade oversmoking, pornography and cursing, all of which William liked and perforce had to give up for the time being.[57]

Later in life when he had read Waldersee's published memoirs, William wrote:

> I considered him to be entirely trustworthy and truly devoted to me. What he entered in his diary of evenings, in the way of religion and other comments, I could not, of course, have known at that time.[58]

It was a mild, generous comment compared with Waldersee's outburst:

> Would to God that I were able to record any good thing coming from, or concerning, the Kaiser.[59]

William and Dona's third particular friend was to remain true for many years. Count Philip zu Eulenburg had many blessings: a happy childhood in a home he loved and which one day he was to inherit, a grand marriage to a granddaughter of the famous Swedish Field Marshal Count Sandels, three sons and three daughters, an aptitude for diplomacy which was never so exacting that he did not have time for a wide range of pleasures, and a keen intellect. He had served a number of months in the Paris Embassy where he became particularly friendly with yet another German who, later, was to play a considerable part in William's life, Bernard von Bülow; but Paris had sad associations for him and his wife. They lost their second child there and, as a kindness, Herbert von Bismarck quickly transferred Eulenburg to a post of greater responsibility. It was at this period of his life as Prussian Secretary of Legation at Munich, the Bavarian capital, that he first became friendly with Prince William. This was in May, 1886, at the spring shoot of Count Dohna at Prökelwitz in East Prussia, when the Prince was in temporary banishment from Potsdam.* Having friends in common they had, of course, met before but what had been a polite acquaintanceship now developed into a warm friendship.

At this stage of his life William was apt to love or hate and with extreme intensity, and, the shooting party putting them in close proximity, he was at once attracted by what could be called Eulenburg's non-Prussian tastes and talents. Not that the Count lacked the Prussian virtues. He rode beautifully and shot well. Eulenburg had a proper regard for efficiency and self-discipline, and he esteemed courage and chivalry; but he showed little arrogance and self-conceit although his accomplishments were many, and he had a quietness, almost a gentleness, about him not much in evidence amongst William's fellow officers in the mess. He was witty and amusing though he did not care for practical jokes which were very much in the mode and which William especially liked. It was noticeable that in all the years of their close friendship William never once played a practical joke on Eulenburg.[60] Undoubtedly William respected him as a man of the world with charm and languor and savoir-faire. Eulenburg was seldom dismissive and not overcritical, at any rate, to begin with, and it fascinated the Prince that he not only appreciated paintings but sketched well himself and encouraged William in his liking for painting seascapes; not only did he enjoy music, he actually composed it, writing and singing light romantic Rosenlieder and vigorous Nordic sagas, the Skaldengesänge. William was captivated by his songs. The shooting party at Prökelwitz took on a new and surprising aspect when Count zu Eulenburg sang song after song.

In his first enthusiasm for Eulenburg it is not likely that William noticed his weaknesses; his ambitiousness, for example, and his sentimentality, and his disastrous capacity for making enemies. All he saw was the hedonist, the

---

* Count Richard Dohna was either a sycophant or a very thoughtful host. Knowing of the Prince's liking for beachcombing, he had 'thunderbolts' strategically placed so that William should have the pleasure of finding them.

scholar, the sportsman, the diplomat, the soldier, the perfect friend, the confidant he could trust. Years later in exile the ex-Kaiser recognized that he had overestimated Eulenburg.

> *But that cannot alter the fact that he was one of the most charming men I have ever known. . . . As an entertaining companion he was sublime, he could seize on any trivial incident of a journey, make a fascinating story out of it, and tell it in such an interesting way that one had to listen to it. . . . As a 'cicerone' he was indispensable to me . . . He was my friend and as such he will remain in my memory.*[61]

From the beginning there was no mistaking his devotion to Eulenburg.

The Count's description of the start of the friendship was more critical but still warm. In his memoirs he frankly pointed out there could be small material advantage in allying himself to the Prince, as he was unlikely to come to the throne for a considerable time, and he did not hesitate to point out that the Prince's absorption in soldiering was holding up his maturing. Like the public school and university system in England which then guaranteed that the sons of the rich matured years after other boys, what was called 'the Potsdam life' in Prussia did the same for the scions of the nobility. In Prince William's case, it was particularly noticeable. Eulenburg summed up:

> *My attitude towards Prince William was cordial yet circumspect when in 1885* his friendship for me became ecstatic. He was twelve years my junior, and when I made his acquaintance, his father was going about in exuberant health. My attitude was cordial because his enthusiasm for my music, and my musical performances, which almost feverishly delighted him, was congenial to my artistic soul, and very likely flattered my vanity as well . . . But I also felt cordial towards the Prince because he entered so frankly not only into my artistic interests, but into all the others, and, moreover, showed so warm and eager a sympathy with my ardent love for wife and children that it might have been his personal possession.*[62]

Their relationship has been described as 'heliotrope-scented',[63] and whether physically expressed or not, the friendship probably had some sort of erotic content. Possibly William had not quite passed through the homosexual stage which the vast majority of human beings encounter – to emerge as heterosexual, bisexual, homosexual, or, in rare cases, a-sexual. Certainly 'the Potsdam Life', with its emphasis on *camaraderie*, the brotherhood of arms, and the Spartan ideal of soldierly fellowship, created a homo-erotic climate. William did have an extrovert habit of slapping his friends on the bottom

---

* Eulenburg's error. It was actually in 1886.

and pinching the cheeks of youngsters★ and it is evident from his own naïf description of his visit to Russia that he noticed good-looking men:

> *The* [Russian] *family picture was brightened by the cheery presence of a large number of quite young Grand Dukes. . . . The Chevalier Guard and* Garde à Cheval *recruits were a nice-looking lot, though the fact that hardly any of them had any hips made their white capes look as though they had been poured over their slim bodies. . . .*[64]

Rumours persist in Germany to this day that William was bi-sexual, just as they persist in England that the Prince Consort was the same. Like his grandfather, William preferred the company of men to that of women.[65] One recent biographer of the Prince Consort states that 'the more pronounced curves of his hips emphasized an androgynous element in his physique'.[66] And Daisy, Princess of Pless, said there was 'a great deal of the woman' in the Kaiser.[67] To continue the comparison, the Prince Consort begat nine children but, save in one absurd case, never had his name linked with another woman. His grandson fathered seven, rarely had his name linked with women, but was with his wife, that is, under the same roof, only one hundred days out of the 365 in the year. The point seems to be that, despite Bismarck's appraisal of William's prowess in the alcove, neither he nor his grandfather were sexual athletes, and both were deep-dyed romantics. Moreover William lived at a period when male friendships were the norm; men could set up house together (no-one, for example, has yet questioned the sex life of Holmes and Watson, or Higgins and Pickering) and curates were sought for who were 'good with boys' or 'good with young men'.

On the other hand, not all was innocence. It is of interest to the sociologist that what was termed 'the English vice' by the Germans was 'the German vice' to the English. It is scarcely believable that ultimately William did not come to know that Eulenburg, in addition to his taste for music, art and literature, had a partiality for good-looking young men. It was not uncommon in military circles where the offenders were called *Soldatentante*; nor even in royal circles. Young King Louis II of Bavaria, the patron of Wagner and builder of fantastic castles, was a homosexual; as was old King Charles of Württemberg who was then making a fool of himself over a sceneshifter in the royal theatre. Nor were William's English relatives free from accusations. Besides the Prince Consort there were also speculations about his grandson, Prince Albert Victor of Wales. It is difficult to judge from this distance of time, especially as documents might have been removed

---

★ But this bonhomie was not entirely confined to men. On occasion he also slapped women on their bare shoulders and it is alleged he was not above popping a spoon into their décolletage.[68]

from public archives or the scandal worked up by sensational journalists, but undoubtedly in the 'eighties there were rumours that Prince Albert Victor was bi-sexual, that he lacked ordinary circumspection, and that, under an assumed female name, he belonged to a notorious homosexual club in London.[69] Nevertheless there is not a shred of real evidence that William himself was ever a practising homosexual, and it is unlikely that such a thing could have been kept secret. Doubtless his first burst of passion for Eulenburg was part of his late maturing. William's well-known apologist, Emil Ludwig, permits himself to frown on 'the vanity of an idolized tenor and the folly of his idolizing devotee', yet he goes on to praise Eulenburg in the purplest of passages as:

> The first to open the gates of the garden of Romance to the young man who had been forced into the part of a hard-bitten Prussian Prince, and now was taking leave of adolescence poor alike in love and the dreams of youth.[70]

That is one way of acknowledging William's debt to Eulenburg. Another, and far more important in the history of Germany, is that during the years that followed Eulenburg gave William what he badly needed, comfort, encouragement and guidance. He exercised crucial influence that could have been malign. Historians are generally agreed that on the whole it was not.

5

Prince William could be as stubborn as his grandmother Queen Victoria. Now a colonel and given the command of Hussar Guards, he felt so sure of himself that he dared to brave her anger. When Prince and Princess Henry of Battenberg arrived at the New Palace to finish their continental honeymoon as the guests of the Crown Princess, they found themselves cold-shouldered by Prince and Princess William. And William continued obdurate in his opposition to the Moretta–Sandro marriage.

By September 1885 Sandro had proved himself so unpopular with the Russians that his cousin the Emperor removed him from the Army list and impregnated Bulgaria with agents whose sole purpose was to stir up trouble. But the Prince was immensely popular with his own subjects and led them to victory when the Serbs invaded Bulgaria. He then shed his vassalage to Russia and turned towards Turkey.[71] What followed reads more like the plot of a Ruritanian romance than exact history. Russia's reply was swift. Millions of roubles were spent on bribery and corruption and in spreading fresh calumnies against Prince Alexander. Inflamed with drink and the promises of quick promotion from the Russians, part of the Bulgarian army mutinied. Literally at bayonet-point the Prince was forced to sign a deed of abdication, then he was kidnapped by Russian agents, maltreated, and taken to Bessarabia. On his release he bravely retracted the abdication as having been made under duress, and he somehow managed to return to Bulgaria. But it was soon apparent that life would be made impossible for him if he tried to reign as sovereign prince. In September 1886 he was shot at in the cathedral and convinced by skilful Russian propaganda that he had failed as a ruler and could never succeed; he was persuaded to abdicate, this time voluntarily.[72] Immediately candidates were canvassed for election in his place. They included three kings, two royal dukes, several German pumpernickel princelings, two generals – Sherman of America and Brialmont of Belgium, a Croatian count, and, for good measure, a Turk.[73] Either through whimsy or to please the Russians, the Bulgarian Assembly proceeded to elect as Prince Alexander's successor his exact opposite. Prince Ferdinand of Coburg, called 'Foxy' by friends and enemies alike, was weak where Sandro had been strong, and whereas Sandro was essentially masculine, Prince Ferdinand wore bracelets, powdered his face and slept in pink, lace-trimmed nightgowns. According to one of the Crown Princess's ladies-in-waiting he would not last a year on the throne. But he was not called Foxy for nothing. He reigned over Bulgaria to everyone's satisfaction for thirty-one years.[74]

To Queen Victoria, her daughter and granddaughter, Prince Sandro's abdication was a disaster. To the German Emperor, Bismarck and Prince William, it underlined their view that Russia never would have tolerated such a marriage, nor would she tolerate it now.

William was warned by Bismarck that he might have to go on a mission to Russia to make sure of the matter. He did not wish to go. Considerable pain in his left ear had obliged him to take a two-month cure at Reichenhall,[75] and he was concerned for his new friend Eulenburg, who had had a bad summer. A hostile Bavarian government had deposed their amoral and amazingly extravagant monarch Louis II by declaring him insane, at which in a frenzy he had drowned himself and, with poetic justice, his physician in the deep waters of the Starnberg Lake. Eulenburg's Ambassador was on leave at the time and, as Prussian *chargé d'affaires* he was much concerned with the events. He reported to Herbert Bismarck his own belief King Louis had not been insane, but that Otto, his brother and successor, certainly was. A Prince Regent had been appointed who was antipathetic to the Crown Princess. Much harassed by this unexpected diplomatic emergency he proposed himself to Prince and Princess William, who were delighted to receive him at Reichenhall. After a short rest he accompanied Prince William to the Bayreuth Festival, where he was able to introduce him to the Wagner family. Herbert Bismarck in a letter to Eulenburg said he hoped that the

Wagnerian trombones would not damage the princely left ear, admitting:
  Six hours of the Music of the Future would inflame even my drums.
In a more serious vein he continued:

> *I am always afraid that the Prince will do too much, so energetic he is in everything; and he must be prevented from that, for his health is of quite inestimable importance to the German nation.*

His anxiety did not move Count Herbert to change his mind about the necessity for the Prince to take the long journey east. It would be for the second time that year, as he had already been on a winter bear-shooting expedition in Russia. William had warned his grandfather that his father would not care to be passed-over for this most important mission, but neither he nor Bismarck paid any attention. It had been decided.[76] The German Emperor and Crown Prince would go to the German Imperial manoeuvres in Alsace, while Prince William would travel to Brest-Litovsk where the Emperor of Russia was attending grand siege exercises. On returning to Potsdam from a hammering of Wagner at Bayreuth, he found that, as he had feared, his father was highly indignant at having been passed over.

William did not enjoy his mission. The massive Emperor – he was six feet four inches tall, immensely strong and in proportion to his vast empire – was not as cordial as on the young Prince's previous visit. He did not express any gratitude for Germany's refusal to aid the Prince of Bulgaria in any way; and when William with some callowness told him that the Chancellor would not stand in his way if he wished to take Constantinople, the giant Emperor growled that he had no need of Bismarck's permission; if he wanted the place he would take it. The best William could get out of him was a reiteration that he would hold to the alliance of the three emperors, but Russia, he said, was prepared for anything. He sent polite and fraternal messages to William's grandfather.

The German Emperor and Chancellor received the Prince's report with great gloom. Despite all Bismarck's efforts tension was growing between the German-Austrian group and the Slavs, with whom the Russians more and more associated themselves. Indeed it was at about this time, but not before, that the Autocrat, or Emperor of All the Russias, began to use the title Tsar, and his son the Crown Prince of All the Russias, that of Tsarevitch. One pleasant surprise awaited the Prince. His father had overcome his resentment and received him in a friendly way. He wanted to know all that had taken place in Brest-Litovsk. Afterwards they embraced. It was a tender mark of affection between them that had become rare. In the calamitous eighteen months which followed, it was to be rarer still.[77]

CHAPTER SEVEN

Three Kaisers

'There is no object in trying to draw the veil
of oblivion over these things'

PRINCE WILLIAM ON THE ILLNESS OF HIS
FATHER

I

The year 1887 is best remembered as the Golden Jubilee of Queen Victoria. For her, and for many members of her family, it was the year of the Crown Prince's agony.

Inevitably, because of emotional involvement, or because their professional skill was at stake, or their political career put in jeopardy, the printed recollection of the principals in the unfolding of that drama are mostly subjective, have varied considerably and even contradicted each other. This makes the presentation of the facts, so far as they concerned Prince William, particularly difficult.

It appears that, early in the new year when there was much to do at Court and the Crown Prince was recovering from a debilitating illness, he sensed some irritation in his throat. By March 6th the tone of his voice had altered and he sent for a specialist. After a careful examination he was told there was a small lump on the left vocal chord, a growth or polypus which would need attending to. He gave permission for a second opinion to be brought in, but so far as he was concerned it was no time to be ill. Everyone was preparing for the ninetieth birthday of the German Emperor on the 22nd. He had to make a speech proposing his father's health and afterwards he intended to announce the betrothal of his second son Prince Henry to Princess Irène of Hesse. The love of their childhood had continued and now they were to marry.

The ninetieth birthday was a great affair. The Emperor still maintained his frugal, unwholesome and indigestible diet and, though his whiskers were silver and outstanding, he had lost all his hair save a few strands which were waxed to the dome of his head each morning. Communicating with him was not easy as he was very deaf and faulty dentistry made his speech such a mumble that people could never be sure if he was speaking German or French.[1] He still however managed to quarrel with the Empress, who was equally indomitable, though she was crippled with rheumatism, had lost a breast to cancer, and shook like a jelly with Parkinson's disease. At the birthday she was described by an onlooker as 'looking like one dug up from the dead, bent double, painted and covered in precious stones, something of a skeleton and something of a witch'.[2] Yet she still had her sharp mind and her tongue. She snapped back at the aged Emperor with all her old vigour.

It was generally noticed that the Crown Prince's voice was hoarse.

Very soon after the celebration a second specialist burnt the polypus with galvanic cautery, an agonizing treatment which we know today was also dangerous.[3] As soon as he could travel the Crown Princess took him to Ems less for the cure than for a complete rest.[4] Perhaps only she was concerned at this stage. Simultaneously Prince William and Philip Eulenburg were shooting stags and singing *Rosenlieder* at Prökelwitz. Prince Henry and Princess Irène were preparing for their marriage. Everyone was looking forward to going to London for Queen Victoria's Jubilee in the following month. In the spring sunshine at Ems the Crown Prince seemed to improve and both he and his wife were optimistic when they returned to Berlin to see the specialist. They had been over sanguine. The wound caused by the cautery had not healed and the growth, of whatever kind it was, appeared to be larger.[5] An eminent surgeon was called in. He first tried to lassoo the growth with an apparatus like a rabbit snare. Afterwards he attempted to remove it with a ring knife.[6] Finally the patient was subjected to daily cauterizing of the swelling with red hot wires.[7] There was little improvement and the three medical attendants ultimately announced to the Crown Princess that the growth was probably malign and they advised an immediate operation.[8]

The Crown Prince was kept in ignorance of the nature of his illness[9] but as he was heir to the throne the German Emperor and Chancellor had to be informed. Presumably William was also informed at this stage. Bismarck, with characteristic thoroughness, summoned three more doctors. They confirmed their colleagues' diagnosis. An operation was provisionally fixed for May 20th, and it was generally agreed that it should be kept from the Crown Prince until the last moment. Bismarck demurred at this idea.[10] He seized on the suggestion of the Crown Prince's body physician that yet another opinion be sought.[11] He must be a laryngologist of international fame and Bismarck made the point that on political grounds he did not wish for an Austrian or French specialist. Prince William reports that Dr Wagner, his father's body-physician, proposed that Dr Morell MacKenzie be sent for from London.[12] His five colleagues and the Chancellor all agreed.[13]

Afterwards there was a great to-do about sending for an English (*sic*) doctor because it reflected on the competence of the German medical profession. A rash of accusations against the Crown Princess appeared in print for favouring one of her own nation. One authoritative German newspaper, *Norddeutsche Allemeine Zeitung*, went so far as to blame Queen Victoria as well as her daughter – who had, in fact, mildly questioned the wisdom of the German doctors' sending for MacKenzie – and angrily the Queen demanded through her Ambassador that the statement be refuted. To her amazement and increased rage, Count Herbert Bismarck refused on the curious grounds that it would only make matters worse.*[14] Most probably the Crown Princess's godson Major Frederick Ponsonby† was right in his objective comment:

> *Divorced from national prejudice, medical rivalry and political bias ...*
> *the weight of evidence proves that he [MacKenzie] was sent for not by a*
> *Princess of English birth who was reputed to have a bias against German*
> *doctors, but in consequence of the intervention of Prince Bismarck and*
> *on the advice of one of the German doctors to which the others assented.*[15]

Let this stand.

When MacKenzie arrived he cut a tiny section from the growth and sent it to Professor Virchow, a pathologist of European reputation. Virchow reported that the piece of tissue was too small for more than a superficial examination. MacKenzie cut a larger one and sent it off. Later he sent a third and fourth. Two conflicting and irreconcilable facts were now presented; that Virchow sat on the fence and remained non-committal,[16] and that he stated no trace of cancer could be found.[17] In light of what modern research has disclosed the latter is more probable. The six German doctors were convinced the growth was malign and carcinomous. MacKenzie with his wide experience of throat diseases would not accept this in the first stages. There were quarrels. The leading surgeon amongst the Crown Prince's German medical attendants declared their patient would die if he was not operated on. MacKenzie said that on the contrary the operation would kill him. In the light of hindsight it is interesting to note that two years afterwards this same surgeon performed the same operation on a patient with exactly the

---

* This fact was not brought to light until January 18th, 1928 when Sir Rennell Rodd, later Lord Rennell of Rodd, who had been Secretary of Embassy in Berlin forty years before, wrote an account of the episode in a letter to *The Times*.

† Major, later Sir Frederick Ponsonby, and afterwards first Lord Sysonby (1867–1935) was Equerry and Assistant Private Secretary to Queen Victoria and Edward VII, and for twenty-five years Keeper of the Privy Purse for George V.

same symptoms as the Crown Prince, and the patient died on the theatre table.[18] The Crown Princess, backed by the German Emperor and Chancellor, decided to accept MacKenzie's advice against an operation. The Crown Prince, who was to go to England for Queen Victoria's Jubilee would take his two personal German physicians and be under the special care of Dr MacKenzie.[19] It now seems clear that MacKenzie suspected that his royal patient had syphilis of the larynx, a diagnosis later confirmed by the German doctor Schmidt, who proposed that the Crown Prince be given large doses of potassium iodide, the usual treatment for advanced syphilis.[20] But the Crown Prince was no *bon viveur* like his English brother-in-law. In fact his public reputation was quite untarnished. If he had sown any wild oats it had been in Egypt seventeen years before at the opening of the Suez Canal, and the harvest had now come. It was not the sort of thing a physician blurts out. Apart from the Hippocratic Oath, discretion would require MacKenzie to be reticent and not blast the reputation of so well-loved and well-behaved a prince. The secret was well kept for a long time. Rumours appeared in the French newspapers in the following year, but they were entirely disregarded. Such a thing could not be believed of the Crown Prince Frederick.

As ignorant as everyone, Prince William took a powerful stand against the ascendancy of MacKenzie. In *My Early Life* he makes no bones about his hard feelings:

> *When one considers that, if the English doctor had not intervened, my father would in all human probability have been saved, one will understand how it was that I took every opportunity of opposing the most violent resistance to this ostrich policy. That my mother could not free herself from the Englishman's authority, even when the facts had become fully clear to everyone else, had the worst possible effect upon my relation with her.*[21]

Usually William was gentler in his reminiscences. This time circumstances made him act impulsively. Thoroughly caught up again in his love-hate relationship with England; warned that the old Emperor was becoming more and more enfeebled; told that there was a law which inhibited any dumb man from inheriting the Crown of Prussia – a rumour which was instantly squashed by Bismarck;[22] and toadied to by 'Badger' Waldersee and his wife, who saw themselves closer than ever to the fount of all authority in Germany, Prince William lacked the calmness and the judgement to stand aside and be non-committal. Early he declared himself against MacKenzie, and said publicly that he ought to go to the Jubilee as the Emperor's representative in place of his father.

While the doctors continued to quarrel over the Crown Prince, Prince William attended the laying of the foundation stone of the Emperor William canal at Kiel, and, at Harry's especial request, his dearly-loved grandfather attached him *à la suite* to the First Battalion of Marines so that he had a new uniform to be proud of and wear at the coming Jubilee. Congratulations poured in, save from one old Prussian general who peered at him over his pince-nez and remarked with the lofty contempt of the Prussian Army for anything naval: 'Dear me, you take an interest in that sort of thing, do you?'[23]

Sufficiently buoyant to recover from such a set-down, it hardened William's decision to wear Marine uniform at the Jubilee; but on his return home to Potsdam and calling at New Palace for news of his father, he received another set-down. His mother told him that his father would be going to London as the Emperor's representative. She was very determined and so was he. There was an angry scene in which William declared it was wrong for MacKenzie to give everyone false hopes.[24] A compromise was reached which placated William's pride and saved the Crown Prince from too much exhaustion. Prince William formally represented his grandfather, he and Dona being met with great formality and escorted everywhere they went. The Crown Prince and Princess were much more warmly received, not only by the Court but by the people, because they were 'close family'. The Crown Prince rode beside the Queen's carriage in his splendid white uniform with silver breastplate and eagle-crested helmet; the Crown Princess rode in the Queen's carriage with the Princess of Wales facing her mother.[25] William and Dona and their eldest son had their place in the procession, which was far less grand, and William found himself being given as a dining partner the dusky sister of King Kala Kana of Hawaii,[26] and Dona disliked having to give precedence to the Hawaian Queen.[27] Nor did he approve of the arrangements, deploring the misunderstandings and friction. There were indeed some unfortunate contretemps which varied in importance from one of the Queen's sons-in-law, Lord Lorne, being thrown from his horse even before the procession began[28] to the inadequate ventilation of marquees which a peer tried to remedy by cutting out a window with his rapier and pinking a housemaid's bottom.[29] In two senses Lord Ronald Sutherland Gower was wrong when he wrote in his book *Old Diaries*:

> It was impossible for the most fault-finding to pick a hole in any of the arrangements of this great and superb show of Royalty and People.[30]

There were faults and Prince William found them. He was somewhat soothed by being able to wear his new Marine uniform at the great Spithead review,[31] and by his grandmother's kindness in putting one of the royal yachts at his disposal for the journey to Flushing, but he did not like leaving his father in England to the care of Morell MacKenzie and when he arrived back in Germany he made this plain.

So far as is known no-one had yet mentioned to the Crown Prince that he might have cancer. Indeed his wife, by rigid self-control and careful censorship of newspaper reports, was at great pains to hide the possibility from him. But, though predisposed to melancholia and *Weltschmerz*, he was not an idiot. Intuitively he must have guessed that, whatever the nature of his illness, it might be mortal, and he had seized the opportunity of the Jubilee to bring from Germany three boxes of personal papers and deposit them for safe-keeping in the Royal Archives at Windsor.[32] This was some relief to him. So was a restful holiday at Osborne, then, afterwards, in the clear, clean Highland air. He and the Crown Princess with their suite stayed in a hotel in Braemar, driving daily to Balmoral. Queen Victoria unwisely entered the lists on the side of Dr MacKenzie by knighting him at her daughter's request. The German press squealed with indignation at this affront. Berlin society expressed disgust at the rumour that the Crown Prince's Court Marshal had accused the Crown Princess's Private Secretary of being her lover.[33] By October Scotland was too cold for a sick man. The party moved to Toblach in the Austrian Tyrol, and there at Innichen the Crown Prince decided his mausoleum should be modelled on the village church. In a macabre fashion the order was made there and then.[34] The cold drove them on, first to Venice and second to Baveno. All this time a series of anguished letters passed between the Crown Princess and her mother. Sir Morell MacKenzie came and went leaving an assistant when he was not present in person. The outcry in Berlin grew clamant. Some of it was pathetic – that no matter what his condition the Crown Prince ought to be in Berlin for the twenty-fifth anniversary of Bismarck's taking control of the state. Most said an ailing Emperor in the country and a Crown Prince out of it was not at all satisfactory for the German Nation. All were xenophobic and aimed at the Crown Princess for keeping on MacKenzie.

All his children save Charly were at Baveno for the Crown Prince's fifty-sixth birthday. William thought his father looked well but he took the opportunity of speaking about MacKenzie to his mother. For this he incurred 'her severe displeasure'.[35]

Soon after, on November 3rd, the Crown Prince and Princess went to San Remo where they had taken the Villa Zirio. There, beside the sea, and in the bland Mediterranean climate, he would be less likely to catch cold, and it was hoped, might make some sort of recovery. But it was at the Villa Zirio only twenty-four hours after their arrival that MacKenzie's assistant noticed a new and alarming change. He telegraphed to London and on arriving Sir Morell confirmed that what had formerly been a syphilitic larynx had altered in character so that it appeared to be cancerous.[36]

In the medical battles which followed the illness, and which were conducted in the indecency of the public prints, MacKenzie was blamed for failing to see six months before what evidently had been cancer. His fixed reply was that six months before the growth had not been carcinomous.

A little time before the Crown Prince had begged MacKenzie to deny the rumours of syphilis which were being printed in the French press, and, out of kindness, the doctor had done so – though he confessed to a colleague the French were probably right.[37] And at his wife's entreaty the Crown Prince had given up reading the German newspapers which maintained such sustained and bitter attacks upon them. Now, in light of MacKenzie being summoned from London and the concern which could no longer be hidden by anyone, he begged to be told the truth. He asked outright if he had cancer. The Scot replied: 'I am sorry to say, Sir, it looks very much like it, but it is impossible to be certain.' Later when he was quite certain, and his opinion was confirmed by German and Austrian laryngologists, he offered the Crown Prince an alternative, either to have an operation which would remove his voice and shorten his life, even possibly kill him, or to have a tracheotomy tube inserted in the neck when the need arose, that is, a hollow tube of metal through which he could breathe if the swelling continued and threatened to choke him. After some reflection the Crown Prince chose the latter.[38]

The German Emperor and Empress, William, Charly and Harry, Queen Victoria and Chancellor von Bismarck were officially informed; and on November 12th the German Official Gazette announced in an unsigned notice that 'the disease is due to the existence of a malignant new growth' which was cancerous.[39] Now that the world knew the Crown Prince wrote calmly in his diary: *Well, I shall evidently have to put my house in order.*[40]

Of prime importance was to get his War Diary of 1870–71, containing frank criticisms of Bismarck, to the safety of England. Guessing that the Chancellor had his spies in San Remo, he asked for the help of Sir Morell's assistant Dr Hovell. Their plan was ingenious. The three volumes of the diary were left on the big table in the largest drawing-room of the Villa Zirio for all to see. Then one night Dr Hovell was called out 'professionally', swept up the diaries, and, guessing that the French and English ports and railways would be watched, went directly to Berlin; there he woke the British Ambassador at an early hour, and, by the time the diaries were safely on their way in a diplomatic bag to England, Dr Hovell was back in San Remo.[41]

There were other, less important practical matters to deal with, and these the Crown Prince undertook with an outward calm that aroused everyone's admiration. Only to his wife could he show his real feelings. One day he burst into tears and bewailed his fate: 'To think that I should have such a horrid, disgusting illness, that I shall be an object of disgust to everyone, and a burden to you all. I had so hoped to be of use to my country. Why is Heaven so cruel to me? What have I done to be thus stricken down and condemned? What will become of you? . . .'[42]

Two days later the Crown Princess wrote to her mother: *William has just arrived, not by our wish, and just at present is rather in the way.*

Probably Queen Victoria had a more sensitive appreciation of William's difficulties and weaknesses than her daughter, and while agreeing that he could be exceedingly vexing and vexatious, she sought to be a conciliator. It was far too late. By this time nothing could alter William's Potsdam view that had his father been operated on in May he might have made a good recovery; and nothing could alter the Crown Princess's view that her son was unfeeling. Her grief and her fears and nervous exhaustion all combined to make it difficult for her to get on now with any of her three elder children. What had always been an unsatisfactory relationship deteriorated into something worse. They in turn, and especially William, doubted her professed passion for her husband and put down a large part of her grief to the frustration of her political hopes after such a very long time of waiting for power. When he arrived at San Remo, backed by his grandfather's authority and accompanied by Dr Schmidt of Frankfurt* and two other doctors, none was made welcome. He himself wrote:

> *My arrival gave little pleasure to my mother. Standing at the foot of the stairs, I had to allow a flood of her reproaches to pass over me, and to hear her decided refusal to allow me to see my father. . . . Then I heard a rustling at the top of the stairs, looked up and saw my father smiling a welcome to me. I rushed up the stairs, and with infinite emotion we held each other embraced. . . .*[43]

To his displeasure he was given two rooms in the Hotel Victoria, a place already crowded with reporters and cameramen with their cumbersome flashlight apparatus, most of them 'MacKenzie's creatures', and he carried out the Emperor's instructions to find out precisely what was wrong with his father with orderly precision. *I then called upon them* [the doctors], *in order of seniority, to give their verdict.* Only once, according to William,

---

* The doctor who virtually confirmed MacKenzie's first diagnosis by prescribing the accepted cure for syphilis.

did his mother lose her masterly self-control and then: *holding tightly to my arm, it was only after a considerable time that she again became mistress of herself.*[44]

The Crown Princess's version of what happened is different. She wrote to her mother:

> *You ask how Willy was when he was here! He was as rude, as dis-agreeable and as impertinent to me as possible when he arrived. . . . He began with saying he would not go out walking with me 'because he was too busy – he had to speak to the doctors.' I said the doctors had to report to me and not to him, upon which he said he had the 'Emperor's orders' and half turning his back to me, so I said I would go and tell his father how he behaved and ask that he should be forbidden the house – and walked away. Upon which he sent Ct. Radolinsky flying after me to say he had not meant to be rude and begged me to say nothing . . . so it all went on quite smoothly and we had many a pleasant little walk and chat together . . . When he has not got his head stuffed with rubbish at Berlin he is quite nice and traitable.*[45]

Possibly from this amalgam of opposite views the truth can be arrived at.

The Crown Princess, despite her immense will power and determination to protect her husband, on occasions broke down. She must at times have been close to hysteria. As for William, he was, as she said, rather 'stuffed with rubbish at Berlin'.

In the capital everything combined to inflate the Prince's ego. Because the Emperor was ill and the Crown Prince far away in San Remo and somebody had to have the authority to sign state documents, it was given to Prince William. It was a sensible move as he was on the spot but it hurt his father profoundly. Count Eulenburg wrote encouraging and wise letters from Munich and sent him a present to consolidate their friendship, and Dona bore his fourth son that winter, but no-one turned away the fawners who wanted to lick William's boots. There was no-one to check or guide him. His grandparents were too feeble and old to restrain him. The Chancellor, too, was feeling his age and only just managing to contain a highly tense political situation between Germany and Russia. The Tsar had arrived in Berlin and had barely been polite.* In return Bismarck had forbidden the Reichsbank to discount Russian bills in case a Russian military invasion

---

* At the railway station the Tsar's carriage was taken beyond the Chancellor waiting on a red mat so the old man had to thunder down the platform bellowing *'Je suis le prince Bismarck'*; to which a Russian aide made the acid comment, *'Ça explique mais ça n'excuse pas.'*[46]

should actually be underwritten by German money.[47] He had very little time or energy for anything else. But when he saw Prince William being flattered and attending Pastor Stöcker's Christian Socialist meetings, Bismarck proceeded to apply a brake. Through one of his hired newspapermen he rebuked the Prince for meddling in such things. He also personally rebuked him when, in indelicate anticipation, William drafted a proclamation to the German princes in the event of his accession. He advised the young man to burn it.[48] Made testy by the Chancellor's attitude, William had a temporary and, for him, unusual fit of anti-Semitism – no doubt under the influence of Stöcker – and announced that when he came to the throne the Jewish influence over the press would be stopped. That, explained the Minister of the Interior, would be a violation of the constitution. Carried out of depth by his own stupidity, William did what many proud young men do and made no attempt to regain land but plunged in further. Very well, he said grandly, then the Constitution itself would have to be got rid of.[49]

It must have been a relief for him to turn temporarily to military affairs which he understood and enjoyed, and seldom blundered. The Tsar's belligerent attitude moved the Emperor and Chancellor to order a review of the military situation and a report from the Chief of General Staff on the needs for a war on two fronts. William attended when the report was read out by Field Marshal Count von Moltke, still stiff-backed and lucid despite his eighty-eight years. It was he who had accompanied the Crown Prince, then Prince Frederick William, to Balmoral for the courting of the Princess Royal thirty-two years before. His report was masterly. Amongst his recommendations were that troops should be drafted to East Prussia, bridges built at great cost over the Vistula and the Nogat, and a network of railways and proper roads made in East Prussia, a largely trackless area of forests and lakes. All were accepted by that group of far-sighted, elderly men. Only William was young enough to realize in the 1914–1918 war just how far-sighted they had been.

2

The year 1888 was called in Germany the Year of the Three Kaisers.[50] January and February were melancholy months. Everyone's eyes were centred on the Emperor's Palace on Unter den Linden where the old soldier was slowly dying, and on the Villa Zirio far away where his son was equally stricken. Many eyes were also on Prince William's Berlin palace. The casual observer would have thought his life continued on an even tenor. He went on with his work at the Foreign Ministry, signed state documents for his grandfather, and gave his eldest son, not quite six, into the hands of a most carefully chosen tutor. He was promoted major general and changed his command, and watched with fascination the old Chancellor minimize the threat of a war with the Russians by the exceedingly risky but in this case successful practice of defying and teasing them. He announced to the world the secret terms of the Austro-German treaty and then introduced a new Army Law. 'Germany,' he roared at the Reichstag, 'must depend on her own strength. The Pike in the European Carp pond prevent us from becoming Carp.' The Pike paid attention.[51]

But William must have believed himself immersed in uncertainties. He felt that he could depend on Eulenburg though even his friend was writing to deplore of the 'social abyss' which was opening up before them. And he could depend on Harry and, possibly, Charly. Dona he would not have thought of in the context of being useful. He was not sure of the Bismarcks; nor, now, of the Waldersees. The place-hunters amongst his fellow officers and in Society were already at his elbow.

In his nervous uncertainty he undoubtedly made mistakes. He went again to San Remo where it had been necessary to perform a tracheotomy and insert a breathing-tube in the Crown Prince's neck. The air which was sucked in and out made a noise which was 'very horrid'. He could only now communicate by writing notes. William came charged with a command from the Emperor that the Crown Prince should return home as soon as possible. Aghast at the change in his father, who was emaciated and yellow and had a rasping cough, William begged that he should return to Berlin, and be among his own people, not stay in a strange land the focal point of a flock of journalists who waited like hungry vultures round the walls of the Villa Zirio.[52] Politically, too, it was important for him to be seen. Some Germans believed he was already dead.* But the Crown Princess knew that the weather was exceptionally cold in Berlin and she would not hear of her husband being moved. William could do nothing about it. No doubt he saw his mother's point of view that the blander climate of San Remo was much better for a sick man. He found it so himself. He had come to Italy directly from the funeral of a cousin in Bavaria and the cold had caused a recurrence of his old ear trouble. Not thinking, he cursed the pain in his father's presence and his father, who had borne so much, scribbled a note telling him to suffer without complaint.[53] Under the circumstances it was just parental rebuke, but humiliating all the same to a son as proud as William. He spent a miserable few days with his parents, then left. In his own words: 'Deeply depressed and hopeless I travelled back to Berlin.'[55]

* Count Radolinsky had turned up at the Villa Zirio a short time before certain that he would find the Crown Prince dead.[54]

His mother's version of the visit was sent off to Queen Victoria:

It all went straight between Willy and us and was quite harmonious. He left yesterday morning! Not one word of sympathy or affection did he utter, and I was distressed to see how very haughty he had become, and what tremendous airs he gives himself! It is no doubt the effect of being told so often that he may be Emperor in less than a year. His visit did not do any harm, and he did not meddle this time.[56]

Never very sure of himself, William must have been even less so at this time of his life than at any other, and the fruits of uncertainty are absent-mindedness or an air of abstraction, a gaucheness which could be mistaken for indifference, a tied tongue, and an embarrassment which in a nervous individual easily balloons into arrogance.

It is not often taken into account that William's self-confidence, boundless though it may have appeared, must have been eroded by the constant complaints about his lack of maturity and the tendency for his family to regard him as an overgrown schoolboy. Most probably at the beginning of 1888 he was nervously contemplating his future rôle as monarch simply because it had been drummed into him that as yet he was totally unfitted for it, and also because he was aware that sovereignty would inevitably isolate him to some extent from his pathetically few friends. He also had to face the prospect of losing a grandfather whom he had always loved and a father whom he had admired and with whom on many past occasions he had enjoyed most happy relations. In any assessment of his character these facts have an importance.

The Emperor William died as he had lived, without any fuss. He lay in his camp bed wearing a white uniform jacket and a red scarf and his life slowly slid away. The only chief difference was that he managed to smile at his wife who had been wheeled to his bedside and who held his hand for hours. Her palsy made her appear to be shaking it. He did not mind. On the other side of the camp bed sat his only daughter, the Grand Duchess of Baden, who had just lost her second son. At the foot stood Prince William straight from San Remo. Occasionally the old man mistook him for his son the Crown Prince and bade him hold fast to Russia. The Court Chaplains and the Emperor's valet were there as well as the great Officers of State and his Military Household. The Chancellor came in and out of the sickroom. Often Bismarck was in tears. At daybreak on March 9th the Emperor spoke to his daughter. She rose and went to his work-room and took from his desk the miniature of Princess Elisa Radziwill which had stood there for almost seventy years. She pressed it into her father's hands.[57] He asked for champagne, and sipped a little, but he could no longer mark the bottle.[58] At twenty past eight in the morning he died. Outside a snowstorm was whitening Berlin.

Frederick III reigned as Emperor and King for ninety days. His first act was to take the star of the Order of the Black Eagle and pin it to his wife's dress. He then made the journey to Berlin, not wishing to stop en route to be greeted by the German Princes, chiefly because it would have taxed his strength too much, but also because he had very small regard for those whom he described as 'Kings by the Grace of Napoleon'.[59] His own desire to be known as Frederick IV, thereby implying a connection with the mediaeval Hohenstaufen emperors, was respectfully scotched by the Chancellor, who telegraphed that he ruled as Emperor because he was Frederick III of Prussia. In this the Chancellor was supported by an unlikely combination of the new Empress Victoria and her eldest son, now William, the Crown Prince.[60]

William had already received a pointed telegram from San Remo:

I EXPRESS MY FIRM CONFIDENCE THAT YOU IN LOYALTY AND OBEDIENCE WILL BE AN EXAMPLE TO ALL[61]

Arrangements were made so that the new Emperor and Empress should move directly into the apartments of their daughter Charly in the Charlottenburg Palace. They were well-warmed, and, the palace being a little out of the city and surrounded by parkland, there was far less likelihood of dust – a hazard to the tracheotomy tube, than at any of the other Berlin palaces.

The Chancellor, with his Prussian ministers, met the Emperor at Leipzig. Affectionate greetings were exchanged. Though with some reservations, Frederick III valued Bismarck's services to the second Empire, and he had always been aware of the Chancellor's devotion for his father. There was to be no change in the status quo for the time being. One observer, who may well have been prejudiced, noted the 'Empress simply looked on'.

If the same observer is to be trusted the Empress did precisely the same when her son welcomed them at the Charlottenburg Palace. William kissed his father's hand and helped him to alight but felt unable to trust himself to speak. He was too upset and disturbed. When he went to greet his mother,

she turned her head aside, and seemed to busy herself with the Emperor, without making any sign that she noticed her son. He bit his lips, but kept silent.*[62]

* This is a quotation from *The Berlin Court Under William II* by 'Count Axel von Schwering', London, 1915. In a Publisher's Note about the pseudonym it is stated 'the high personage, through whom this remarkable document came into our possession, declares that the intimacy which existed between the author and his Imperial master

This would have had a profound effect on even the most insensitive son at such a time, and William was never insensitive. It explains if it does not excuse some of his subsequent behaviour towards his mother. His mourning for his grandfather was entirely genuine and he was particularly distressed because on the melancholy occasion of the funeral, his father was too ill to be present and could only stand weeping as he watched the cortège make its way to the mausoleum. The Prince of Wales had cut short the celebration of his own Silver Wedding and came over to represent his mother and he was a source of comfort to the new Emperor and Empress. But there was to be little comfort for Prince William in the days which followed. He was regarded by many in his mother's household as a rival and competitor, and being the type of man he was, a rival and competitor he became. It is alleged that, unable to tolerate the tension any longer and finding himself for a moment alone with his mother, he begged her to explain what had come between them; and that the Empress, considering this insolent, unbraided him for having attempted to dethrone his father. He energetically denied this but his mother would not listen. She shrugged and said one lie more or less hardly mattered in such an ungrateful son, a taunt which made him forget the respect he still owed her. He threatened to remind her of her words when he was master, left the rooms without permission, and slammed the door.[63] This is probably overstrong, but it indicates the bitterness that was hardening on both sides.

There is probably some truth in William's claim that he was hardly ever allowed to see his father during his short reign.[64] He would simply have caused an upset, and that was the last thing Empress Victoria wanted for her husband. She was pursuing her hope that Sandro would, after all, marry her daughter Moretta although it was hopeless because Bismarck still considered it out of the question and the Emperor was in no state to challenge his Chancellor even if he had wanted to. It was also tactless as it aggravated William into telling Sandro that he would regard anyone who worked for the marriage as an enemy of Germany and they would be dealt with as such.[65] Then Sandro's father opposed the match on the grounds that his son had already formed an attachment with an actress which had made him happy for the first time in many years.[66] Finally it was opposed by Queen Victoria herself.[67] That wise old lady paid a private visit to Berlin, to see her beloved

---

was so long-standing and close as to render it both logical and legitimate to believe all the details given in the Diary'. The publishers, Messrs Cassell of London, would reveal the author's real name in the interest of historical scholarship and to assist in verifying the authenticity of 'Schwering's' work, but, by ironic fate, their records on this book together with many others, were destroyed by the Germans' blitzkrieg of London in the Second World War. Enquiries made to many libraries, both national and belonging to universities, have met with no success.

son-in-law for the last time. She also met Bismarck and somewhat alarmed him with the power of her personality* and she paid a courtesy visit to her old friend the bereaved Empress William whom she found 'rather a ghastly sight'.[68] She did all she could for her daughter but begged her not to press the Sandro-Moretta match. If they did marry they would have to leave Germany and as Sandro had no money they would be obliged to live on a shoestring. It simply would not do, and certainly ought not to be contemplated without William's consent. She then saw William himself and, true to the family habit of treating him as an infant, she made him promise to behave better. Though she felt it keenly, the Queen refused to be emotional when she said a last goodbye to her son-in-law. She kissed him and accepted from him a bunch of forget-me-nots, but it was a sad, sad parting when her train drew out of the station and she left her distraught daughter to face the tragic days ahead.[69]

As long as he could the Emperor struggled on with his duties. It was only a token. Sovereign remedies poured in from well-wishers and sympathizers all over the world, carbolic acid from France, whisky from Scotland and ground mother-of-pearl from England, live worms from the United States; but nothing that anyone could do could alter the fact that he was dying.[70] Several times he was able to get out into the garden. There he would sit in a tent and make an attempt to work at his papers, or write notes to his wrinkled and shaking old mother who was brought to see him from time to time. He even took a drive in the Grunewald, and then into Berlin, where he was given a rapturous welcome by his subjects. But the Imperial power was slipping from him day by day. Only a month after Queen Victoria's visit her daughter wrote:

> William . . . is in a 'ring', a côterie, whose main endeavour is as it were to paralyze Fritz in every way. William is not conscious of this.[73]

It is impossible to judge how much William was being led by the nose. Certainly he did foolish things. The tracheotomy tube in his father's throat had to be replaced and the German physician who did the job bungled it and caused the Emperor great pain. It was swiftly put right but Sir Morell MacKenzie threatened to go home if that particular German was allowed to touch the imperial throat again. This sent the bungler off in high dudgeon. He was at once made a lot of by the anti-liberals, and ineptly the Crown

---

* Bismarck is reported to have mopped his brow after the audience, exclaiming: 'What a woman, one could do business with her!', and he called her 'a jolly little body!'[71] He was less complimentary when telling the story to Busch, one of his two personal assistants and his press secretary, saying: 'Grandmama behaved quite sensibly –'[72]

Prince asked him to dine. It was either an incredible piece of tactlessness, or a piece of spite (remembering Princess Daisy of Pless's remark that he had a strong feminine streak), or stupidly he was allowing himself to be used. Whatever the reason, he came out of the incident discreditably.[74]

Other things were to his credit. He bore with metaphorical advice from Eulenburg which a more cocksure man would have found intolerable. His friend sent him a picture bought at a bazaar in aid of the victims of some recent floods. Under it was inscribed the legend: *The arrogant utterance of the frog is classic, and teaches us emphatically not to let our heads swell* . . .[75]

William also behaved creditably when Waldersee finally over-reached himself by saying that all loyal subjects, military and civil, were exceedingly irritated by 'the petticoat government being exercised indirectly through the sick Emperor' and advised the Crown Prince to take no notice of orders emanating from the Charlottenburg Palace. Whatever he thought privately about 'petticoat government' William was not standing for this. He reminded Waldersee that, like every other German officer, he had just sworn an oath to the Emperor and said he would continue to obey orders emanating from the Charlottenburg Palace, even if they included the arrest of the Quartermaster-General for trying to seduce an officer from his duty. He added: 'If Count Waldersee is to be placed in front of a sandheap and shot, I should execute the command to the letter – with pleasure.' Count von Waldersee had shot his bolt, or, as the Berliners put it colloquially, had fired off his gunpowder.[76]

The Emperor almost died in April, and again in May, but he made a supreme effort to do his duty as a father when his son Harry married Princess Irène of Hesse on May 24th. The Court went out of mourning for the occasion. The Emperor put on full uniform and went to meet the bride in person when she reached Berlin, and at the wedding ceremony during the exchanging of rings he stood erect, his hand on the arm of his mother's bathchair, and his tracheotomy tube hissing and gurgling but taking not an inch from his regal bearing.[77] It was an impressive display of Prussian courage and determination that won everyone's admiration. His one-time A.D.C. Field Marshal Moltke declared afterwards: 'I have seen many brave men, but none as brave as the Emperor has shown himself today.'[78] His son William, touched to the heart, described his father as 'like a hero of old'.[79] Ella was there, too, with the Grand Duke Serge, which would have increased his own misery though, no more than his father, did he betray his feelings. Less self-disciplined, the Prince of Wales broke down, and when afterwards Count Herbert Bismarck spoke lightly of the Emperor as an incubus and said that a dumb man was unfit to reign, the Prince did nothing to conceal his profound shock. Later he told his mother: 'If I had not taken into consideration that good relations between Germany and England were essential, I should have thrown him out.'[80]

How close father and son were at this momentous time can only be conjectured. The Emperor, struggling against his disease and still trying to keep in touch with affairs, seldom saw his heir. It has been suggested that he was not dying quickly enough for William and his cronies,[81] but there is no evidence that William sat like a carrion bird waiting for his crown. Although inevitably he was growing away from people on being shown more deference, and beginning to suffer the inescapable pains of royal loneliness, he went on with his ordinary work in as ordinary a fashion as possible. In two ways he went to some trouble to please his father. The first was to suggest that the Emperor review a selected battalion of troops.[82] That evening His Imperial and Prussian Royal Highness, Major-General the Crown Prince William, was drinking beer in the mess when a royal messenger arrived from Charlottenburg. There was an instant silence. He took the letter from the salver and broke the seal. It was not the summons which his fellow officers instinctively expected but an imperial command.

The Emperor wished to see the men of the Crown Prince's own Second Guards' Infantry Brigade and ordered them to defile before him on the following afternoon. This was done, three regiments in columns of companies, and to band music and the rolling of drums, marching past their Supreme War Lord who sat helmeted and in uniform in a carriage, his son the Crown Prince a little to the rear. The Emperor was delighted and wrote to William thanking him.[83]

It was customary for the Court to move from Berlin at the end of May. The Emperor clearly wished to go home, as he put it, and it was his son who made all the arrangements. The railway was forbidden by the doctors as the vibrations would endanger the tracheotomy tube. To ride there by carriage would raise harmful dust. William proposed that the journey should be made by water. A canal connected the Charlottenburg Palace to the complex of waters between Berlin and Potsdam, and a new Imperial steam yacht, built to replace Emperor William's paddle boat, had just completed her trials. Having a low deck she could be boarded by a level gangway and no climbing was necessary. On May 31st the Emperor paid a filial visit to the Mausoleum where his father was entombed, and together with his Empress and all their children made the voyage from the Charlottenburg to the New Palace. It was a distressing journey as people collected on the banks of the Havel and hurled flowers on to the decks to show their affection for their dying Emperor,[84] and they were passing familiar landmarks he would never see again: the Island of Peacocks where the Emperor William had hidden in the revolution of 1848 and where, by manipulating the controls of a switchback, William had literally hurled his sister Charly into the arms of her future husband; the places where the Emperor had taken his sons bathing and boating and fishing and skating. William found himself so moved by the sight of his father saying goodbye to the places where they had all been happy together, that he took refuge on the bridge. There he found the Master gripping the wheel, his jaw set and tears streaming down his beard.[85]

At the New Palace ground-floor apartments had been prepared so that if the weather was fine the Emperor could step straight into the park of Sans Souci.* He was delighted to be home again and expressed a wish that thenceforth New Palace should be called Friedrichskron.[86] It was there that he enacted one piece of business which exasperated the right-wing politicians and pleased the left. He dismissed Robert von Puttkamer, a reactionary Minister of the Interior who had been found guilty of accepting bribes.[87]† He also received his last royal guest, his old friend King Oscar of Sweden, who said afterwards that Germany would not see his like again.‡ On the day afterwards Bismarck came to the Friedrichskron. The dumb and dying man made a last gesture of conciliation. He took his wife's hand and laid it in the Chancellor's. Both understood and both did what was expected of them, but too much had passed between them for the gesture to be sincere.

There are two accounts of the final cause of the Emperor's death. William in *My Early Life* wrote that he was told by the physician his father could no longer take nourishment as the inside of his throat was completely destroyed.[88] Another, more likely cause is that a piece of food went down the wrong way, lodged itself in the Emperor's lung and he contracted pneumonia.[89] By June 14th the doctors made it clear he had only a few hours to live. On his direct order the Empress had already received payment of three-quarters of her portion and the dowries of her unmarried daughters from a reluctant Bismarck, so their future was financially secure.[90] She now determined to secure the Emperor's diaries for the past ten years. She sent for the Berlin correspondent of the *New York Herald* and in the presence of Sir Morell MacKenzie gave him a sealed packet to take quickly to the British Embassy.

* It so happened that although the Emperor was quite often able to go out of doors the weather that June was quite extraordinary. Snow fell in many parts of northern Europe, a phenomenon that was not to take place again until June 1975. Then, afterwards, as in 1975, there was a perfect summer.

† The Empress's many enemies blamed her for Puttkamer's dismissal. In fact Bismarck himself agreed to the Emperor's proposal in return for his agreement to a cartel majority decision to prolong the life of future Reichstags from three to five years.

‡ It was a view held by many. The Prince of Wales bade his son George never to forget his uncle. 'He was one of the finest and noblest characters ever known.'[91]

Thence it was to be sent by military attaché to her mother.* The Emperor's will was also taken from Friedrichskron.[92]

On the morning of June 15th the Emperor's children and Dona and Bernard and Irène were sent for. The servants came in one by one to take their farewell. Then the physicians, who could do no more, one by one bowed stiffly to their patient from the foot of his bed. The Court Chaplains were present and one did all that was necessary. The Empress held her husband's hand. He feebly wrote a last message: *Victoria, I and the children. . . .* and then stopped. Its purpose was plain enough. He was happy to have his family with him.

He weakened perceptibly before their eyes. For hours they patiently watched in that hot stuffy room until after a long bout of unconsciousness he suddenly coughed, took three breaths, gave a barely perceptible wince and died.

The Empress kissed his hands and laid them by his side. Then she took from the wall a withered wreath of bays she had given him on his return from the Franco-Prussian war and laid it on his breast. She rested his sword on his arm, and a locket containing her portrait and a lock of her hair on his heart. Then she left the room.[93]

Lord Salisbury, casting a statesman's eyes over Europe, had exclaimed on the death of the Emperor William: 'This is the crossing of the bar. I can see the sea covered with white horses.' It would have been a much more relevant remark ninety-nine days afterwards when Emperor Frederick III died, to be succeeded by his son.[94]

* An extract from Queen Victoria's Journal dated June 17th, 1888, shows that the packet safely reached Balmoral. '*Colonel Swain arrived from Berlin . . . He had brought some papers, which Fritz had desired should be placed in my care.*'

CHAPTER EIGHT

The Great Stealer of Our People's Hearts

*'The Kaiser is like a balloon, if you don't
keep fast hold of the string, you never know
where he'll be off to.'*

PRINCE VON BISMARCK ON WILLIAM II
IN 1888

I

It was a personal and political misfortune that Kaiser William II – he preferred the German title to the French* – was rocketed into power at the
early age of twenty-nine. Unlike most heirs to the Prussian throne, who had
had ample time to prepare themselves for kingship, William had only the
ghostly, tense, short reign of his father. And, unlike most Prussian kings, he
had overall responsibility for some fifty million Germans. His Physician in
Ordinary, Dr Leuthold, confided to the Austro-Hungarian Ambassador that
the Kaiser had high qualities of mind and heart but he had been 'too long
at Potsdam'; in other words, that he knew too little of the world and viewed
events from the rather blinkered viewpoint of a Prussian officer.[2] It has to
be remembered as well that Bismarck's instruction in home administration
and foreign affairs had been kept to the minimum so that William should not
be too well informed politically. He also had limitations of character: some
were to disappear as he grew older; others were to emerge; all were to have
more news value than his merits. He was undoubtedly vain; enjoyed being
photographed and painted and struck attitudes. It displeased him that when
they were sitting at table his wife's long back made him appear shorter
than he was and he always sat on a cushion to make up his height.[3] He was
also inclined to morbidity. Everywhere he went he carried with him from
palace to palace, and imperial yacht to shooting-box, and even on visits to
friends, a gruesome load of *memento mori*, pictures of his dead relatives and

---

* At one point he also 'germanized' all royal menus and *Canapé d'anchois* became
Kleine fische zur divan, or, in English, little fishes on divans.[1]

113

friends all clad in shrouds. These he set up on a chest of drawers or whatever was handy beneath an oleograph of Christ Crucified.[4] Then, though full of bonhomie with his A.D.C's and other friends, he was strangely frigid with his sons. With his only daughter it was different. She was indulged and given the best of everything. There was no sign that he was jealous of his sons, and very occasionally he could relax with them, but on the whole he kept them on a tight rein. It is claimed that from the time he came to the throne he generally communicated with them through the Chief of his Military Cabinet and family matters were subject to 'Cabinet Orders'.[5] This may have been a by-product of Bismarck's persistent exaltation of the monarchical principle for more than twenty years. Like his grandfather William I, he believed himself appointed by God and only accountable to him, but unlike that humble and frugal monarch William thought this should be shown by dress, attitude and action. He understood better than most sovereigns the importance to his subjects of outward pomp, that it was in itself an *instrumentum regni*; though he carried his theories into wonderland when he declared to a startled fellow monarch: 'We Hohenzollerns are the bailiffs of God.'[6] He decided that as far as was possible his Court should be magnificent and the protocol inflexible and for all his sense of social obligation he still had a distaste for the 'mob' shared by his other grandfather, the Prince Consort, and by a large number of theoretical 'socialists' the world over. But the Kaiser's most striking defect was his quite extraordinary restlessness. So far it had been caged by protocol. Now he felt free to indulge in agitated gyrations which probably had their origin in some physical malfunction in his make-up. Easily bored and made fidgety at home, he woke at dawn to drag the protesting Kaiserin to join him in a gallop,[7] or he would make a sudden decision to leave *en garçon* for a distant place. His regular round did not establish itself until he had been Kaiser for about eighteen months. Thereafter, though supposed to be fixed, it was liable to sudden and inexplicable alterations. In the first four months of his reign he earned the nickname of the Travelling Kaiser and in Court circles his initials W. I. R. were interpreted as *Immer Reisefertig*, 'always ready to start'. This and other mild eccentricities rather endeared him to his more phlegmatic subjects. One of them remarked: 'He wants to be the bride at every wedding and the corpse at every funeral.'[8]

This is one side of the picture. He had of course several accomplishments and merits which have not been remembered quite as well as his limitations. One of his most important virtues was his serious concern for other people. This was a legacy from Hinzpeter who now found himself advising his ex-pupil on social matters. The English governess to his daughter, who was not in the least inclined to toady the Kaiser, reported that he was 'in every respect more democratic than his Court'.[9] Nor, though cast in the mould of a Prussian officer, was he anti-Semitic, anti-parvenu and anti-American. The declaration to the Federal Princes which Bismarck had advised him to burn showed that he had then a more enlightened and liberal view of their functions in the German Empire than had his liberal father. This view he was to modify as he grew older. But in one respect he did not alter; though a Protestant himself, he knew that religious intolerance harmed his empire. His own clever mother admitted that, though easily led, he too was clever[10] and yet neither, it is interesting to note, was fully educated in the sense that neither ever really understood or was prepared to appreciate an opponent's point of view in the world of ideas. Nonetheless William's intellectual inheritance from his parents and the Prince Consort was a rich one. All through his life he interested himself in archaeology and history, military science, painting and the plastic arts, and read a catholic selection of the literature of three languages. He took special pleasure in science and technology, could memorize a mass of technical data about the most out-of-the-way subjects such as agricultural machines, boilers, cranes, pumps, trams, electro-dynamos, dentistry and shipbuilding;[11] and he was proud of the industrial boom which made Berlin the centre of German banking instead of Frankfurt and earned her the title of world city. Added to these mental accomplishments was his power as a raconteur – few could match him at telling a story – and his skill as a yachtsman, swimmer, shot, horseman and whip.* He was also courageous, both physically and morally, absolutely tire-less and – a most important point in any assessment of his character – he had an acute sense of humour.[12]

William's conspicuous liking for being photographed shows us his appear-ance at the time he ascended the throne. His moustache with the swept-up ends, pomaded daily by a barber, was his most outstanding feature.† He looked taller than he was because he held himself so well. He had plenty of curly mouse-coloured hair, grown not in a Prussian 'peg-top' but carefully brushed back from a left-side parting. His atrophied left arm was not notice-able, carefully concealed by expert tailoring and by the Kaiser's own dex-terity. He wore rather more rings, mostly diamonds and sapphires, than suited the taste of his English relatives but this was in accord with his flam-boyance. As a boy he had been good-looking, as an old man he was to be the same. If he was less than handsome in photographs taken during his reign this was often because he tended to 'put on' a face, thrusting out his

* He often drove a brake with a team of stallions from the New Palace in Potsdam to the Old Palace in Berlin at an average of 12 m.p.h.[13]

† His barber Herr Haby was also noted for the invention of a lotion for whiskers called *Achievement*.[14]

short dimpled chin and gazing sternly. Away from the lens we are told that his bright blue restless twinkling eyes could turn grey and hard when he was angry; but generally they were kindly and matched his manners which were almost invariably genial to visitors. Indeed he could be captivating, and was always candid.[15] There appeared to be no humbug about him at all.* The historian Gerhard Masur, in his recent study, *Imperial Berlin*, remarks: 'Even his severest critics concede William's fascinating personality, his eagerness to impress all who came in contact with him.'[16] Yet he could and often did give the opposite impression when he was angry and in a spiteful or bullying mood.[18] What mattered most, as those percipient enemies, the widowed Empress and Prince von Bismarck, remarked, was not so much what the Kaiser himself did or said or intended to do and say but who was at his elbow.[19] Goethe had taught at his great grandfather's Court that the touchstone of greatness was to have a sense of proportion and maintain it.[20] William only possessed it in fits and starts.

This was the talented but, at that time, muddled and troubled prince who became Kaiser on the death of his father Frederick III.

2

There is no record of the widowed Empress making any sort of recognition that her eldest son was now Kaiser as she left the room after the death of Frederick III. She had a regard for the proprieties, therefore it must be assumed an excess of grief prevented her from doing the correct thing. But it was most unfortunate. William most certainly would have noticed the omission and interpreted it as a sign his mother intended to continue regarding him as her troublesome son rather than as her sovereign. It was a point about which, as we shall see, he was ultra-sensitive.

Half an hour later, still dazed with grief, the Empress went out of doors to cut white roses to put on her husband's body. Incredulously she saw soldiers. One, with great respect, begged her to return to the interior of the palace. He led her inside again. No-one, she was told, was permitted to leave the palace without a signed authority. The purpose became only too plain. In the Emperor Frederick's apartments, in her own, in fact in every part where documents might have been concealed, soldiers began a thorough search. William himself searched his mother's rooms.[21] When she came to

* It is interesting to note that A. J. Balfour, Lord Salisbury's nephew who succeeded him as Prime Minister and was acknowledged as one of the finest intellects, best talkers, and most genial mannered of his generation, said 'he had never spent a more stimulating hour' than one he spent with the Kaiser, and added that he and King George V were the only princes with whom he had ever managed to talk as man to man.[17]

hear of it Queen Victoria was exceedingly indignant although she herself had the safe-keeping of the very documents her grandson wanted and which had been smuggled out of Germany. To subject his mother to such hurtful treatment showed that William was determined to be master, but the very fact that he found nothing, after a most thorough search, showed that he did have a reason for making one. The pathetic result was that both sides had a fresh sense of grievance.

That same day a telegram arrived from Balmoral:

> I AM BROKENHEARTED. HELP AND DO ALL THAT YOU CAN FOR YOUR
> POOR DEAR MOTHER AND TRY TO FOLLOW IN YOUR BEST NOBLEST
> AND KINDEST OF FATHERS FOOTSTEPS
>
> GRANDMAMA V. R. I.[22]

It was a polite prod in the right direction though Queen Victoria did not herself think it would do much good. Her caustic description of the new rulers of Germany, William, Dona and Bismarck, showed her true feelings:

> *Two so unfit & one so wicked!*[23]

The Empress Frederick, as she was thenceforth to be called, pleaded with Dona to use her influence and hold William in check, which showed a naïve appreciation of their relationship. She also appealed to the Chancellor to grant her an interview. This he refused, explaining that he was too busy serving his new master.[24]

The new master was enjoying his power. Breaking a promise to his mother he ordered that an autopsy be carried out on his father's corpse. She was frantic, but it made no difference. German history demanded a true verdict of the Emperor Frederick's disease. It was also ammunition against Mac-Kenzie, who would undoubtedly print his view of the case. It was only with the greatest difficulty that the Kaiser had been prevented from putting MacKenzie under house arrest. The following day, Empress Frederick took her three young daughters to the farm at Bornstedt.[25]

Kaiser William had three immediate duties, the first being the equivalent of a declaration of accession, the taking of the oath of allegiance from the armed forces. It was a solemn ceremony to which he responded warmly:

> *We belong to each other – I and the army – we were born for each other*
> *and will cleave indissolubly to each other, whether it be the will of God*
> *to send us calm or storm.**[26]

---

* The Kaiser meant what he said. He regarded his union with his soldiers and sailors quite as holy and totally indissoluble as a good Christian marriage.

His second duty was to receive from the Minister of Justice a sealed letter which contained a direction from his mad great-uncle, Frederick William IV, that all his successors should refuse any sort of constitutional government. It had been initialled by William's grandfather and father. William himself burnt the letter; sealed and initialled the envelope, adding the words 'read and destroyed', and had it returned to the royal archives.[27]

The third duty was to bury his father. This was done soon after the autopsy with unseemly haste. Ludwig reported:

> *While the chapel was being decorated, the coffin stood among the hammering workmen like a toolchest.*

The general public was not invited. Nor were foreign princes though the Prince of Wales was there – for the third time within three months – accompanied by his wife and their elder son Prince Albert Victor, and Princess Louise's husband, Lord Lorne. Sensibly the Prince wrote to his mother a non-censorious account of the funeral, remarking on the exquisite music, the late Emperor's charger constantly neighing behind the hearse, and his sincere grief at parting from the best and noblest of men;[28] but in fact he thought it a hole-in-corner funeral, without any widespread expressions of grief,[29] inefficiently managed, and, despite the fact that it happened to be Waterloo Day and he was Colonel of the Blücher Hussars, by now he hated wearing his tight-fitting red uniform with all its Prussian associations. Privately he would have agreed with Eulenburg, who described the ceremony as

> *A hurried, far from imposing affair ... the clergy were laughing and chattering. Field-Marshal Blumenthal with the Standard over his shoulder, reeling about talking – it was horrible.*[30]

The Empress Frederick remained at Bornstedt while the funeral took place, but later she returned to Friedrichskron to sort out and pack up her own belongings and her husbands.' William had announced that he would be requiring the Palace himself. Something else would be found for her. The Prince of Wales had brought with him an open invitation from the Queen to her eldest daughter to come to England whenever and for as long as she wished. Touched and still in an access of grief the widowed Empress confided in her brother what humiliations she had had to endure. For some unknown reason William had already ordered that Friedrichskron (meaning the crown or chief delight of him who is rich in peace) should be once more called the New Palace. Writing paper embossed with the new name had been destroyed. Moreover she had produced the Emperor Frederick's will which contained, as she well knew, a clause charging William 'as a filial duty' to marry his sister Moretta to Prince Alexander, and William had paid not the slightest attention to this solemn wish. Instead he had written to Sandro that Bismarck still vetoed the idea, and that, anyway, both his grandfather and father had been against the match.[31] The Prince of Wales knew better than she exactly how things stood with Sandro and begged his sister to put the matter out of her mind. As for the rest, he did his best to assure for her future.

He forced himself to be pleasant with the Kaiser and Kaiserin and asked where his sister was to live in future. To this he received no satisfactory reply. Then he swallowed his pride and attempted to be pleasant to the Bismarcks, father and son. During the course of idle conversation, he asked if it had indeed been the late Emperor's intention to redress past wrongs, that is make territorial concessions to France and return the Duke of Cumberland's private fortune. Aghast at the thought of either proposition the Bismarcks spread it about that the Prince of Wales was as anti-Prussian as the Empress Frederick.[32] There was instantly a blazing row. The new Kaiser declared that his uncle had insulted the Emperor Frederick's memory by recommending the cession of all Alsace and Lorraine. It was always to be a festering sore between them. In a frank appraisal of what really happened the Prince of Wales's own Equerry wrote to Queen Victoria's Private Secretary:

> *The P. of W. to my certain knowledge went to Berlin imbued with the greatest anxiety to keep in well with his nephew, with the Chancellor e tutti quanti. The first 24 hours all was smooth but the Empress Frederick succeeded in inflaming him with her own personal animosity that very likely the P. of W. said more to Herbert Bismarck and to the Chancellor than was prudent ... the Germans make no allowance for the P. of W's brotherly feeling for his sister's sake. He not only made the pot boil over here, but stayed on longer than desirable and it went on boiling over. .... Every mistake the Empress made – she probably made about two big ones every day – was credited to the English influence of her brother's late visit. .... All cordiality, real friendship in Berlin is gone forever. The real beginning and cause for this is the Empress Frederick.[33]*

From all accounts this is the objective view of an Englishman who knew the Germans very well indeed. The event certainly hardened the mutual dislike of the Kaiser and his uncle and did little to improve the Empress Frederick's prospects.

The Kaiser showed his true feelings by sending one of his father's antipathetic A.D.Cs as Special Envoy to announce his succession to his grandmother. Not surprisingly he was given an icy reception. The Kaiser complained. His grandmother replied:

The Queen intended that it should be cold. She last saw him as her son-in-law's A.D.C. He came to her and never uttered one word of sorrow for his death, and rejoiced in the accession of his new master.[34]

Having made it clear she was standing for no nonsense, she wrote a personal letter to ask where William's mother was to live. She did not approve, she said, of the Villa Liegnitz at Potsdam which had been proposed 'An Empress could not well live in a little villa'.[35] She then proceeded to comment on rumours that William was about to pay visits to fellow sovereigns, hoping that at least he would let several months pass by before doing so. It was an outspoken reminder that he owed at least a token period of mourning to the memory of his father.

William showed that while he respected his grandmother he was not going to be intimidated by the Queen of England. He also made it clear he was standing for no nonsense. He dashed off a courteous reply to say he had offered the use of palaces in Berlin, Homburg and Wiesbaden and that she had only asked for a *pied à terre* in Potsdam, and finished by announcing that he was off to Russia at the end of the month:

The fate which hangs over nations does not wait until the etiquette of Court mourning has been fulfilled.[36]

His grandmother telegraphed her Prime Minister:

TRUST WE SHALL BE VERY COOL THOUGH CIVIL, IN OUR COMMUNI-
CATIONS WITH MY GRANDSON AND PRINCE BISMARCK WHO ARE BENT
ON A RETURN TO THE OLDEST TIMES OF GOVERNMENT.[37]

Lord Salisbury quite agreed with her. He had no good opinion of the new Kaiser. 'He's false,' he would mumble into his beard. 'He's false.'

All State and Court appointments had lapsed with the death of Frederick III. They had to be remade. In this the young Kaiser showed an aptitude for organization, a willingness to accept advice, and an unusually good judgement of character. The Chancellor and his son Count Herbert were re-appointed to their offices and recommended a new Head of the Civil Cabinet. They also approved the appointment of General von Hahnke as Head of the Military Cabinet and the replacement of the Minister of War. The latter was resentful of any change and dogmatic. Worst of all, he condescended to his new master. He found himself dismissed.[38] Simultaneously William retired a number of elderly generals to allow younger men with fresh ideas to be promoted and, though he was disinclined to do so, he felt he had to accept the resignation of Field Marshal von Moltke who, in his ninetieth year, declared he could no longer serve as Chief of General

Staff. Moltke was persuaded to remain as President of the Defence Committee with undiminished authority, but he refused to remain at the head of the Army.[39] For the post of Chief of General Staff he recommended General von Waldersee.[40] Hardly surprisingly this was an unattractive proposal to William, who only too clearly remembered the disgraceful occasion when Waldersee had over-reached himself. He discussed the problem with his new Head of the Military Cabinet, 'a master of lucid statement' and intellectually brilliant.[41] Hahnke was candid. Field Marshal von Moltke had been right to recommend Waldersee because of his exceptional qualities as a soldier, and the Kaiser was right to hesitate because Waldersee was undoubtedly a political intriguer. The answer was to contain him, restrict his badger-like activities, yet at the same time make use of his military expertise.[42] Acting on this advice the Kaiser appointed Waldersee, who expressed himself delighted with the honour. He was far from realizing he had 'fired his gunpoweder' by his infamous remarks about 'petticoat government'. It seems that even William's blunt warning that he would have executed him against a sand heap and with pleasure had been accepted by the General as a kind of deadpan joke. He had not even troubled to mention the interview in his diary, a sure sign of how unimportant he considered the whole matter. But William had not forgotten. He did as General von Hahnke suggested, trusted Waldersee's judgement solely in military matters and maintained outwardly an amiability towards him that he did not feel, but he never permitted the General to exercise any political influence whatever. The Kaiser underlined this minimizing of the Army's influence at Court – and astounded a large number of people – by abandoning altogether the *maison militaire* which both his grandfather and father had favoured. He appointed the four Great Officers of the Imperial Household who ranked at Court before everyone, even the heads of the princely mediatized houses, the Great Chamberlain, the Head Marshal, the Great Cupbearer, and the Chief Butler, and the less important posts of Great and Second Masters of Ceremonies and Master of the Horse. Philip Eulenburg's cousin Count August zu Eulenburg was made Minister of the Imperial Household, and William kept on Captain von Lyncker, who had looked after his own small princely household, as Master of the Imperial Household.[43] He also chose the Empress's Household, her Master of the Household, her Mistress of the Robes, fifteen ladies-in-waiting,* and her maids of honour.[44] In fact considering how many posts had to be filled and that Court Society was classified according to fifty

---

* One who served the Empress for a long time, the Duchess of Ratibor, 'a nice great and fat' lady married to 'a little weeny' husband, had the unusual accomplishment for a lady-in-waiting of being an excellent trumpeter. She would take her instrument to private parties and perform.[47]

categories,[45] the rapidity and sureness with which the Kaiser made the appointments was amazing. It is permissible to look into the future and say that almost always he showed excellent judgement in choosing members of the Households and lesser servants of the Court.

Having completed his lists, he then further astonished his subjects by announcing that he did not wish for a coronation.[46] Considering his liking for grandeur and the money he suddenly had at his disposal* it was an uncharacteristic decision but, as he told Bismarck, a coronation was not required constitutionally and his grandfather had done all that was necessary for his successors by crowning himself 'by the grace of God' in the chapel at Königsberg Castle. He attached more importance to the opening of his first Reichstag in the White Hall of the Old Palace a fortnight after his father's death. There was great pomp and pageantry and he undertook to carry on his grandfather's policies. The point was not missed.[48]

This done and his appointments made the Kaiser gave rein to his restlessness and set out on his first grand gadabout. He was accompanied by selected A.D.Cs and political advisers and his valet Schulze who had been his father's valet and was to remain in his service until he died in Holland long after the First World War. William was not content to travel modestly as grandfather had done, nor stop at stations to eat simple meals in chilly or overheated waiting rooms. A brand new Imperial train was quickly put together; twelve carriages painted dark blue and ivory outside and white and gold inside. The Kaiser's own drawing-room carriage was upholstered with blue silk and had many chandeliers, and his sleeping and bathing and dining carriages were no less luxurious. The suite had to make do with sleeping carriages, and other carriages contained the chef's galley and extensive wardrobes. Luggage vans were also attached. To pull this considerable load at the speed the Kaiser liked required the services of two locomotives, their engineers and footplatemen in tall hats and frock coats.[50] Only the Kaiser relished speed. His suite, unable to get elusive consommé out of bowls with curved-in rims, and always in danger of being showered with cutlets and carved joints and vegetables, preferred to jog along.[51] It made sleeping more agreeable too. But the Kaiser preferred to roar through the countryside. In Germany, although most of the railways were the property of the State, he had to pay mileage like everyone else; over the frontiers he was generally given his travelling free.[52]

His first gadabout was to Russia because his grandfather had ordered him to foster Russo-German goodwill. With him he took a huge collection of

* He was by far the richest inhabitant of that very rich city Berlin, having a fortune of over 140 million marks. Number two in the list of the city's many millionaires had only 47 million.[49]

gifts which varied from minor Orders in different degrees to photographs of himself in gold frames and a selection of jewelry.[53]

It showed how slow the pace of government was that in the summer and autumn of 1888 everything seemed to move in the right direction despite the fact that the new Kaiser was generally out of the country, and the German Chancellor – who also happened to be Foreign Minister, Prussian Minister-President and Minister of Trade – disappeared from Berlin soon after the Reichstag had been opened and for the next six months, as Mr A. J. P. Taylor puts it, he was 'living the life of Reilly at Varzin or Friedrichsruh'.[54] The taxes were collected and the police kept order. Everything else was theoretically under the thumb of Herbert von Bismarck at the Wilhelmstrasse.

In fact, while the Chancellor was meditating and, though on a diet, yet eating enough for two men, and planting trees (not cutting them down as he maliciously informed that great timber-feller Gladstone), and observing the birds and animals on his domains, he still kept a distant eye on the continuing vendetta against the Empress Frederick. Possibly he hoped she would be driven permanently from Germany.

The publication of a detailed report on her late husband's disease by his German physicians had disgusted the Empress Frederick as an indecent invasion into family privacy.[55] Then Sir Morell MacKenzie dismayed her by publishing an attack on the German physicians entitled *Frederick the Noble*. It only worsened matters. MacKenzie seemed unaware of the difference between defending his professional integrity in decent privacy and in abusing his medical colleagues. He even went so far as to say one of them was an habitual drunkard. The German press made hysterical counterattacks – one saying that really he was a Jew called Moritz Marcovicz. Sir Morell's colleagues in England would not support him. The Royal College of Physicians officially condemned his book.[56] The Empress Frederick appealed to her son to use his authority and stop this medical battle over his father's corpse. But he did nothing. It seemed to her that he never paid any attention to her requests; that no-one save her three youngest daughters and her devoted staff supported her in any way. According to protocol the mother of the sovereign and not his wife or grandmother came next in precedence at the Prussian and Russian Courts, yet the Empress Frederick was being cold-shouldered and being given third place after her mother-in-law, now the Empress William, and Dona, now the Empress Victoria. Ironically it was now the crippled, shaking Dragon of the Rhine to whom people addressed themselves as a source of authority. 'This house does not exist,'[57] she wrote despairingly to her mother; and the fact that courtiers and officials were treating her as a negligible quantity, and showing her lack of courtesy and consideration, began to frighten her. When William by Royal

Decree commanded that the literary remains of his father be unsealed and inspected, she quickly begged her mother to return the three boxes of documents and diaries which had been lodged in the English royal archives. German ministers of the Crown went through them with great thoroughness, depositing some, including the Emperor Frederick's Diary of the Franco-Prussian War period, in the domestic archives in Berlin. Apparently one of the then Crown Prince's greatest friends, a jurist and diplomat of distinction, had seen the diaries in 1873 and had copied extracts. By an unhappy coincidence, and without consulting the Empress Frederick or anyone else, this gentleman, Professor Geffcken, gave a précis, no more than twenty pages, for printing in the *Deutsche Rundschau*.* It demonstrated beyond shadow of doubt that some of the credit claimed by Bismarck for founding the Second Reich really belonged to the Emperor Frederick. This caused the self-exiled Chancellor to roar from Friedrichsruh that the précis was a forgery. A shrill protest came from the Kaiser that taking the extract was 'a theft of state papers' and Geffcken had committed lèse-majesté. This prompted the Chancellor to change his mind. The Kaiser was right. He actually attempted to have the editor of the *Deutsche Rundschau* prosecuted. As a contemporary critic put it, Bismarck tended to regard the creation of the Second Empire as his own specially made cheese and anyone who wanted a slice was a thief.[59] In the end nothing much came of it save that the Empress Frederick was blamed and her unpopularity thereby increased. The Chancellor sank back into his bucolic meditations. The Kaiser continued on his gadabout.

Having enjoyed his trip to Russia he now decided to propose himself to his other ally the Austrian Emperor and visit Vienna for the first time as Kaiser of Germany. It is uncertain whether or not he knew beforehand that his uncle the Prince of Wales would be in Vienna at that time. At all events he continued to antagonize his uncle by letting Emperor Francis Joseph know that the Prince of Wales's presence there at the same time would be unacceptable. The embarrassed Francis Joseph had to urge his English guest to move on.[60] Not content with humiliating his uncle, William then confided in his old friend Crown Prince Rudolph that 'if his uncle wrote him a very kind letter, he might perhaps answer it', which caused the Crown Prince to write to a friend: 'The Kaiser is bound to bring about a vast turmoil in Europe.'[61]

In fact the former friendship between Rudolph and William was quickly cooling. Rudolph was very much a Hapsburg in that he thought the new Kaiser's posturing somewhat ridiculous – which William with his acute

---

* A sophisticated journal founded by a German Jew in 1874 and described as 'the voice of Berlin's intellectual and cultural élite', it had a political bias to the right wing of the Liberal party. It corresponded roughly to the *Quarterly Review* and *Revue des Deux Mondes*. The Nazis suppressed the journal in 1942.[58]

sensibility was quick to detect. And Rudolph was very much a certain type of Hapsburg in that he soon found his wife a bore and was often on the rantan. William frankly wrote of their deteriorating relationship in *My Early Life*. He disapproved of Rudolph's cynical lack of faith in the Christian religion and of his mordant wit poured out at the expense of people who were in no position to reply. Most of all he disapproved of the fact that: 'his soul revolted from the Prussian idea'.[62]

The Kaiser returned to Germany to ride his white charger, splendid in the black and silver uniform of the Death's Head Hussars at the autumn manoeuvres, direct operations, sing emotional hymns in a gigantic marquee on Sunday, and cut dead the military attaché to the British Ambassador. Colonel Swaine was surprised because up to then he had always been on the most cordial terms with the Kaiser, but the Kaiser had not forgotten that Swaine also happened to be a close friend of the Prince of Wales, and it had been brought to his notice that his uncle had recently declared: 'William the Great needs to learn that he is living at the end of the nineteenth century and not in the Middle Ages'.[63] William was not prepared to stand for this. Notes were sent to his Ambassador in London concerning the Prince of Wales's offensive habit of treating him as a schoolboy nephew instead of as German Emperor. The Queen, the Prince, and Lord Salisbury were outraged. It made no difference. William was adamant about the respect due to his nation. Here was a growth of those plants of mutual dislike already sown some time before. Their budding, flowering and fruiting were to have great political consequences.

William's succession automatically increased the influence of his closest friend Count Philip zu Eulenburg. The recent publication of the first part of Eulenburg's correspondence makes clear that, both by letter and in person, he encouraged wise policies and discouraged wild ones.[64] In the first months of the reign they met in Munich, where Eulenburg was still Prussia's *chargé d' affaires*, though he was soon destined to be Ambassador at Oldenburg, and they discussed privately Geffcken's publication of the diary extracts. The Count was given the Hohenzollern Order and the Kaiser proposed himself for a shoot at Liebenberg and begged that the Countess should bring all her children and come and stay at New Palace in Potsdam. It was all very amiable.

The Kaiser made one more journey that year, to Rome. His sister Charly and her husband rushed ahead to be there in time to greet him, sycophancy which sickened the Empress Frederick. On his return he made a speech to the Municipal Council of Berlin protesting against the idea that he gadded about for fun. He informed the city fathers that his travelling was hard work. He was his country's first ambassador and representative.[65]

In the passage of time the problems of the Empress Frederick's future had partly resolved themselves. The offer of the Villa Liegnitz had been withdrawn. Instead she was to have the use of the State Palace at Potsdam whenever she wished. This was not likely to be often as she would have to give notice and ask permission. She had Bornstedt as her Potsdam retreat, her palace in Berlin, and recently she had bought a fine palace near Kronberg called the Villa Reiss which she intended to rebuild. It was to be renamed Friedrichshof, and characteristically she planned that it should be as much like an English country house as possible.* Gardeners and architects had already been set to work. Her feelings, though, had not altered, especially with regard to her three elder children. 'Seeing my sons side with our enemies makes me guess what Caesar felt when Brutus stabbed him'.[66] She lamented to her mother that William's first reception held in the White Hall that autumn was far too grand and colourful. Trumpets greeted the arrival of the new Emperor and Empress. There was a splendid dinner afterwards. The only one pathetic sign that Frederick III was still remembered was the black bows at the pages' knees.

The Empress Frederick's future would be in a backwater but at least it was now assured, and she thought a suitable time had arrived for her to do what she had longed to do for months and visit her mother in England. Lord Salisbury demurred. He explained that politically it would be expedient to postpone the visit until a later date. But Salisbury, though a formidable statesman, was no match for an alliance of Queen Victoria and the Empress Frederick. He gave way.

On a November morning the Kaiser accompanied his mother and three younger sisters to the railway station in Berlin and saw them off on their long journey. It was a token of his respect for her as a son. She saw it as a token of penitence for past wrongs.[68]

Queen Victoria had sent her yacht *Victoria & Albert* to Flushing. She honoured her daughter further by actually driving down to the docks to meet her, a thing she had never done before. The widowed Empress with two long white bands flowing over her black mourning threw herself into her weeping mother's arms. Behind her stood her three daughters, without the white bands, dressed from top to toe in black. They all had red eyes from so much crying.†[69] Two days after her arrival it was the Empress

---

* Its design was based on Flete Manor in Devonshire with German and Italian touches. Ultimately it became the property of H.R.H. Prince Philip of Hesse and now, under the name of *Schlosshotel Kronberg*, is described by Fodor's as 'a unique establishment, perhaps the best Castle Hotel in (Federal) Germany'.[67]

† To the Empress Frederick's embarrassment all through their long visit her mother insisted on giving her precedence, but the Queen knew what was important in German eyes and considered it might do some good for her daughter when she returned home.

Frederick's forty-eighth birthday. As a present her mother gave her a nose-gay and a handsome contribution towards a mausoleum.[70]

3

In the following year the Kaiser established his hectic routine. From the time he emerged from his matrimonial bed, heavily curtained and with the quilts and blankets clipped down to exclude any possibility of draughts, to the time he crawled back into it, William was forever on the go. First he rushed to his dressing-room to take a hot bath in an ordinary painted zinc tub, then baled over himself several pails of water in which sea-salt had been dissolved; then on to the barber's chair to be shaved and have his moustache brushed up by the ubiquitous Herr Haby; then to dress in whatever uniform was appropriate for the first activity of the day. That did not preclude changing later. Indeed the Emperor took an extravagant pleasure in wearing appropriate clothes, so much so that the joke went round he wore naval uniform when attending a performance of *The Flying Dutchman* and the uniform of a General of Engineers for a dinner of the Berlin Motor Club. He called his uncle, the Prince of Wales, an 'old peacock'; but his own vanity was noticeable and his collection of uniforms vast. Besides a considerable number of foreign uniforms he preserved a set of each of the three hundred and more Prussian regiments, and the many more of Bavaria, Württemberg and Saxony, plus naval and marine uniforms. Each had its accoutrements of badges, sashes, caps, hats, helmets, shakos, busbies, czapkas, cuirasses, shoulder points, knots, epaulettes, cords, belts and cartridge cases and a whole armoury of swords, lances and sidearms. His total military and naval wardrobe was so large that it had to be housed in a hall containing huge wardrobes and a Kammerdiener was on duty from morning to night to select at the shortest possible notice whatever his master might require. Dressed, he would generally take a gallop, breakfast, receive condensed reports prepared by the Foreign Office of world news,*[71] grant audiences, go hunting or review troops, take meals in messes or with the Empress, and occasionally go to the theatre or opera. In the evenings he often read English newspapers or books which had taken his interest, and sometimes enjoyed a game of billiards.

The Empire's curious constitution which put military and naval affairs beyond the control of the Reichstag save for the matter of voting supplies, which became monotonously automatic, made the Kaiser the only bridge

---

* Princess Daisy of Pless in her *Private Diaries* (London, 1950) asserts that these were printed in gold and that massed together they were known as the *Golden Journal*, but this is scarcely credible.[72]

between the two. Perforce he had to leave much in the hands of the Chancellor, his Secretaries of State for Foreign Affairs and the Interior, and his political advisers; and he did rather less paperwork – about two hours a day – than most of his contemporary sovereigns. Queen Victoria was always at her despatch boxes. The Emperor Francis Joseph was at his standing desk most of the day. The Tsar was an indefatigable worker. William refused, as he put it, to be drowned in detail. Nevertheless he had a strong sense of duty so far as the less attractive chores of royalty were concerned. He was indefatigable at ceremonious openings and dedications and speech-making and receiving deputations as well as attending all reviews, manoeuvres, Court hunts and other functions.

Being a respecter of tradition, William did not alter the formal structure of the Berlin season, though he livened it up. After the great hunt for Easter Eggs in Bellevue Park his annual round followed a certain pattern: At Whitsun came the Schrippen-Fest when the Potsdam garrison was given a special dinner instituted for them long before by Frederick the Great. This was a meal of beef, prunes and rice cooked in giant copper cauldrons, eaten at trestle tables traditionally decorated by pine and fir twigs; and it was not simply for soldiers but for the Diplomatic Corps and special visitors as well as the whole of the royal family.[73] In May the Kaiser continued his habit of going to Count Dohna's at Prökelwitz for shooting and long talks with Eulenburg. He liked also to be at the Wiesbaden Festival in that month. June was a time for visiting large cities and ended with the Kiel Regatta – an important occasion not only socially for the yachting but also because, though his most senior Secretaries of State and Ministers saw the Kaiser at fairly regular intervals, Kiel Week was the one and only chance in the whole year for the less important Ministers to see their master.[74] In July the Kaiser took an annual cruise to the Norwegian fiords in the *Hohenzollern*, a warship he had had altered to suit his needs as a private yacht. The Kaiserin had her own yacht, the *Iduna*, complete with a cook from Brighton who always called his mistress 'Mum'.[75]

At the beginning of August they went together to the end of the English Season at Cowes; thence the Court moved to Wilhelmsöhe near the Kaiser's old grammar school at Cassel, and on to military manoeuvres. September would find the family at New Palace for a short period, then travelling to the Kaiser's farm on the Baltic coast at Cadinen. The Kaiser himself would move on to the Russian frontier where he had a hunting lodge at Rominten, again accompanied by Philip Eulenburg and chosen companions. He had to be back in Potsdam for the Kaiserin's birthday on October 22nd but afterwards he almost invariably went on to stay with Prince Fürstenberg at Donaueschingen in Baden. Christmas was spent at New Palace and the

Court moved to the Old Palace in Berlin on New Year's Day for the beginning of another season.

This programme, though it seems to the modern mind colossal, was the minimum amount of movement within the German Court. William himself added to it considerably. His vitality was prodigious.

Early in 1889 when the young Kaiser was beginning to settle into his annual round, two scandals shook European Society. The first was the death in tragic circumstances of the Crown Prince of Austria. Rumours flew; that he had been seriously wounded out shooting and could not live; that he and his mistress had been found in bed dead from cyanide poisoning; that he had died after a duel; that he had been killed by a forester for seducing his daughter; that he had been hit over the head with a bottle by his cousin the Archduke John; that he had shot himself in an orgy. The official *Wiener Zeitung* announced that he had died of apoplexy, a later edition altering the cause of death to a heart attack. The British Ambassador hardly exaggerated when he reported: 'It is all mystery, mystery, mystery'. The facts appear to have been that the Crown Prince shot his mistress and then himself. A suicide could not be buried by Catholic rites. The Emperor ordered an autopsy on his son's body. This reported he had died from a self-inflicted wound and that he had a malformation of the skull which could have caused temporary insanity. No other official announcement was made. It was remembered that the Crown Prince was half a Wittelsbach, noted for their madness, and he had been depressed and suffering from headaches in the past months. Canon law was satisfied and Rudolph was laid to rest in the Hapsburg vault with one hundred and twelve ancestors. No crowned heads were invited apart from the Crown Princess's parents, the King and Queen of the Belgians. The dead girl was never mentioned officially and was buried in an abbey graveyard. The sensation was tremendous. The Papal Nuncio told William's Ambassador that his official conscience was clear, nevertheless it was the first time in history that a Nuncio in full canonicals had attended the funeral of 'a murderer and a suicide'.[76]

Less than a month after came the second royal scandal. Alexander of Battenberg, once sovereign Prince Alexander of Bulgaria, married his actress, changed his name to Count Hartenau, and determined to settle in Austria. The Kaiser was grimly satisfied. He had no strong fraternal feelings for his three youngest sisters. He, Harry and Charly had always been apart. 'My mother,' he said sourly when he heard the news, 'will have enjoyed her luncheon!'[77] He could estimate exactly how the scandal was being received in England. Princess Moretta was in a pathetic state. Now she could never marry her handsome, dashing Sandro. The Empress Frederick, her most ardent wish frustrated, was both angry and, at the same time, stricken by the thought that she was a principal cause of Moretta's present suffering. Queen Victoria, her own conscience not quite at ease, tried to be encouraging. She agreed with Princess Beatrice's husband who felt bitterly that his brother had been positively driven to take this drastic step. She sympathized most sincerely with Moretta. Privately she urged her daughter not to be in too great a hurry to find a substitute for Sandro. The Empress Frederick was not having that. There was an understanding between her daughter Sophie and Prince Constantine, the Duke of Sparta, who was heir to the throne of Greece. Later that year they were to be married. Moretta as an elder sister would feel it keenly if no-one was found for her. The Queen repeated her warning not to hurry. In any case Moretta should spend most of the summer with her. The girl was inclined to plumpness and had been trying to keep her figure by dieting. This, declared her grandmother, was nonsense. She should eat good plain food and have whisky and milk at eleven each morning. . . .[78] When they had all recovered a little from the shock, the Queen suggested tentatively to her daughter that perhaps Sandro and his lady were deeply in love. It was the sort of thing that happened in the novels of Marie Corelli which she had been enjoying lately. The Empress Frederick was very much her father's daughter. 'Marie Corelli writes rubbish for the semi-educated,' she snapped in irritation.[79] Queen Victoria did not invariably win word battles in her own family. Nevertheless she continued privately to enjoy romantic novels, and she was delighted when that summer she threw open a window at Windsor on a starry night and, being mistaken for a servant, was passionately wooed by the sentry on guard at the foot of the wall.[80]

One of the most level-headed of all constitutional monarchs, the Queen had exploded privately to her Household and to her Prime Minister about her grandson's behaviour, but she never failed to realize that her kingdom must come before family loyalties. When Bismarck toyed with the idea of some sort of Anglo-German alliance Lord Salisbury knew that he would have no more than a token protest from his Queen. Privately she was more than interested in the possibility of such an agreement, which Count Herbert von Bismarck went to London to negotiate. Nothing came of it in the end, but she believed that the attempt had been worthwhile. Evidently her grandson shared this view. He had had an amazingly active June, shooting at Prökelwitz, going on to Kiel and thence to Berlin to receive the Shah of Persia,* on to Dresden and Stuttgart and back again to Kiel. On the last day

---

* This in itself must have been an exhausting business for the Shah was not an easy guest. He travelled on to London from Berlin, and there he tried to buy the Marchioness of Londonderry to take home with him and, at a crowded Drawing Room, enquired of the Prince of Wales: 'Are these your wives? Have them beheaded and get prettier ones.'[81]

of the month he stepped aboard the *Hohenzollern* for his first Norwegian cruise, but his energy was by no means exhausted. He sent word to England that, with his grandma's permission, he would like to attend the Cowes Regatta and he begged her to accept the Honorary Colonelcy of the 1st Regiment of his Dragoon Guards. Smothering her personal feelings she accepted the regiment and invited William to Osborne for the Cowes Regatta. Best of all, so far as he was concerned, she determined to confer on him the rank of a British Admiral. His reply conveyed through the British Ambassador in Berlin was ecstatic and a trifle incoherent:

> ... *Fancy wearing the same uniform as St. Vincent and Nelson; it is enough to make one quite giddy. I feel something like Macbeth must have felt when he was suddenly received by the witches with the cry 'All hail, who art Thane of Glamis and of Cawdor too'.*[82]

The Queen's will that family quarrels must take second place prevailed. When the German party arrived in the Solent, the Prince of Wales himself with his brothers-in-law and his two sons went out to board the *Hohenzollern*, to meet the Kaiser and his brother Harry, and accompany him to Osborne. William was in English Admiral's uniform and determined to be pleasant. No-one could be more charming and so, though he was two and a half hours late in arriving, normally inexcusable in a household where punctuality was highly regarded, he was forgiven. He was affectionate with his grandmother and all his relations. On his second day at Osborne the Queen reviewed the German fleet, the ships playing *God Save the Queen* as she passed in the *Alberta*, and before dinner William presented to her a deputation of four officers of her own regiment. She got on famously with General von Hahnke, the Head of his Military Cabinet, and the third and last day of the visit the German-English cordiality was sealed when the Queen gave her grandson Harry the Garter, and the Kaiser gave his cousin Prince George of Wales the Black Eagle. For his grandmother there was a bust of himself in a helmet by Begas.[83]

William was delighted with the success of his visit. It made no difference to the hostility between Friederichshof and New Palace, but then he never supposed it would. Already he had worked out the reason for the antipathy and faced it so frankly that he had admitted it to the British Ambassador:

> *My mother and I have the same characters. I have inherited hers. That good stubborn English [sic] blood which will not give way is in both our veins. The consequence is that, if we do not happen to agree, the situation becomes difficult.*[84]

The Empress Frederick, in a less detached and far more bitter way, underlined this in a letter to Queen Victoria:

As he does not feel for his mother he cannot be surprised if she who gave him so much love and care, now can only remember with pain that he is her son ... He has it in his power to change this. I can do nothing, nor will I ever give way and humour him.[85]

William did not allow his mother's obduracy to prevent him from interesting himself in family life as a whole. His brother Harry's wife gave birth to a son, Waldemar, in that year of 1889. His cousin, the Prince of Wales's heir, gave the family a series of shocks between May and the end of October, first trying unsuccessfully for the hand of his cousin, Alicky of Hesse, then for the hand of Princess Hélène of Orleans, finally, being hurried off to India because of his instability and dissipation in London. There was a huge concourse of the royal mob at Athens in October for the marriage of the Kaiser's sister Sophie to the Duke of Sparta, when the Empress Frederick – who had a low opinion of Greek sanitation – craftily insinuated an English midwife as her daughter's 'housekeeper' against any future event. William enjoyed Athens. It stimulated a fresh gadabout. In November and December he visited Constantinople, Venice, Corfu, Italy, Berlin, Liebenberg, Berlin, Hanover, and back to Berlin.

The Kaiser saw a great deal of his friend Eulenburg that year. If they were not actually together they frequently wrote and telegraphed.

Inevitably their close association gave rise to grumbles from the jealous and suspicious. A legend grew that Eulenburg ruined the young Kaiser by fawning on him. The contrary appears to be the case. Eulenburg strengthened his character with shrewd and candid advice. Few others at that period either could or would. For example, in September that year he wrote to the Kaiser deprecating his excitability and passion for travelling. He did not mince his words, saying that William must not live so restless a life:

My nerves were once what Your Majesty's are now; and though I, by gracious permission, can set myself right by living as a mere private person, Your Majesty will never be able to give yourself such plenary indulgence. Therefore prohibitive measures are the only right ones – I mean that the pace of your life must be reduced as far as possible.[86]

Another legend grew up – nurtured by the aggrieved Waldersees – that Eulenburg had attempted to make the Kaiser into a 'visionary'. Evidently it was spurious. Had he succeeded we should have known more of it. It is true that Eulenburg himself, despite his intellectual qualities, had succumbed to the mania of the 'eighties – the American exported quack religion or mode of thought called spiritualism; and, at the beginning of their acquaintance he had interested the impressionable William in the subject. But he had the sense to see how this could harm him when he came to the throne and he warned him against spiritualism.[87] A full analysis of their friendship is difficult at this distance in time, but it is likely that William's hero-worship made Eulenburg more loved than loving. Yet the Count still had an undoubted affection for the Kaiser and evidently for his sake, and for Germany's, he was prepared to risk his young master's displeasure by giving him counsel, even strict warnings.

Such forthrightness gave him a very special position. Bismarck noted it. His wife got on well with the Count – calling him 'our northern bard Phili' – and because he did not see him as a potential rival for the Chancellorship, he decided to make use of Eulenburg. First he was to exercise restraint upon the Kaiser's impetuousness; and, second, he was to act as 'extra-representative of the Foreign Office attached to the Imperial person'. When approached by Count Herbert, Eulenburg agreed. No doubt at first he felt he could legitimately bask in both the Bismarckian and Imperial suns, although William showed undoubted signs of resenting Bismarck's indifference to his views on foreign affairs.

The Chancellor did not trouble himself to be tactful with his young master. He was mildly contemptuous of one so callow and untried and referred him to Count Herbert Bismarck at the Foreign Ministry. This might have been bearable to the Kaiser if Count Herbert had been the subtle manager his father thought he was. But he was not. His attitude was forceful and assertive.[88] Inevitably William jibbed. Eulenburg, from his position of privilege, counselled patience. There is evidence he soon came to the conclusion that Bismarck's astute method of retaining office by creating crises and then, as if by magic, solving them was a form of dictatorship that undermined the authority of the true source of power, the Kaiser. By November, 1888 he had allied himself to a cabal of civil servants who found the Chancellor's methods unacceptable yet still could not imagine Germany without him. The containing of the two Bismarcks was their aim and they knew that the success of all their plans depended on patience and looking for strategic opportunities.[89] The Kaiser, in his impetuosity, could damage the very thing he had set his heart on unless he was restrained. Eulenburg was his only brake and William continued to stir more and more restlessly under Bismarck's contemptuous disregard of his views and was looking for supporters. The Empress Frederick believed that the Waldersees came back into the sphere of influence over her son, but this is scarcely credible. William was faithful to the Head of his Military Cabinet who had warned him to 'contain' Waldersee and it is inconceivable that he should have readmitted so dangerous an intriguer into his circle of advisers. But he certainly expected support from his A.D.Cs and Civil and Military Cabinets in his attempt to prove himself.

The Tsar came to Germany in October. Ostensibly it was a courteous return visit to the Kaiser; in fact it was to talk to the old Chancellor who forgot his age and ailments and went up to Berlin to meet him. In the private interview the Tsar was gracious, bidding the Chancellor be seated while he himself remained standing – which was unroyal but psychologically acute – while they talked of a Reinsurance Treaty between them so secret that even the Kaiser hardly knew the terms. The Tsar suddenly dumbfounded the old man when they discussed future relations. 'Are you sure,' he asked kindly, 'that you will remain Chancellor?' He had already sensed the Kaiser's great resentment.[90]

As the winter passed the cabal gradually altered its aim. Bismarck was no longer to be permitted to grasp the authority which properly belonged to the Kaiser. An election was due in February. There was every reason to suppose the Chancellor's campaign would run on familiar lines.

The leader of the cabal was an isolated, retiring man, Count Herbert's Senior Counsellor at the Wilhelmstrasse, Baron Frederick von Holstein. Fifteen months before he had given a luncheon to selected guests at the famous Berlin restaurant Borchardt's that was to have a lasting effect upon the history of Europe. The guests were Count Philip zu Eulenburg, his cousin, Count August, who was Minister of the Imperial Household, and two influential imperial A.D.Cs.[91] Holstein was an habitué of Borchardt's and a known epicure who loved *primeurs*. Moreover he was a man of considerable political power who had been put on the first rung of the ladder by Prince von Bismarck and to whom he owed everything.* In view of the company, that excellent luncheon at Borchardt's had a conspiratorial air. There were other luncheons, too.

The traditional picture of Holstein is more likely a caricature than a portrait. Amongst a variety of non-complimentary nicknames he was called 'the Reich's Jesuit', 'the Mole', and 'the Spider',[92] and modern historiographers have been at some pains to get at the truth and de-daemonize him.[93] Yet a certain amount of mud has stuck, probably because so much was thrown. Here, in brief, is his controversial history.

In his youth Holstein had been a philanderer. He gained a reputation in London where he was serving in the Embassy during the Schleswig-Holstein War and allegedly disliked the English thereafter for their attitude to Prussia's actions.[94] Moved to Washington he compromised the wife of the

* It is not without interest that both *bons vivants* gave their names to almost identical gastronomic delicacies: *Steak Bismarck* being a fried egg on a beef steak, and *Schnitzel à la Holstein* being a fried egg on breaded and egged veal.

Chairman of the Senate Foreign Relations Committee, fought a duel, and was recalled.[95] Bismarck then used him as a spy in order to get rid of his Ambassador to Paris, the popular Count Harry von Arnim, a man under the protection of the Emperor himself and dearly loved by the Empress. When Holstein returned to Berlin he found himself cut by Arnim's many friends in Society. Doors were barred to him. He was ostracized, socially dead.[96] He had to turn to Bismarck for help, for the work which would replace his former life of pleasure associating with a variety of different and interesting ladies. He who had enjoyed the pleasures of the alcove on an international scale became, so they said, a woman-hater. He became a recluse; took lodgings where he was looked after by an old woman; dined and wined alone, giving minute and detailed instructions to Borchardt's chef before-hand, and gradually imposed upon the Bismarckian system of running the Foreign Ministry his own secret system which was scarcely observable or detectable.[97] It was alleged that he did this, undermining his master's power because the Prince's sons Herbert and Bill gave him scant respect and pulled his leg once too often.[98]

The Bismarckian system worked well enough. Discipline was strict. The staff had to be on call day and night. Senior officials had to be accessible for recall at a few minutes' notice. Urgent affairs, marked 'Cito', were put in red portfolios and dealt with in twenty-four hours. Every document was registered in and out. Ambassadors' reports were minuted by Count Herbert 'Not to be put before the Kaiser' or 'Not for the Kaiser' or 'Revise for the Kaiser', which showed precisely how much power the Kaiser had.[99] Count Herbert and his father were entirely satisfied at the smooth-working and exactness of the machine they had created. But unknown to them Holstein was mentally noting that certain documents were 'Not to be put before the Bis-marcks', 'Not for the Bismarcks' or 'Revise for the Bismarcks'. It was he, Holstein, and his subordinates who had the ultimate power.

His power mania was tied to a persecution complex. He would not show himself. No-one without an invitation could get into his sealed-off room at Borchardt's. No-one could penetrate his dingy rooms on the Grossbeeren-strasse where he had a large safe called by those who had suffered at his hands 'The Poison Cupboard'. It contained the skeletons of many noble families and those of 'useful people'. Anyone with anything to hide, even youthful indiscretions, feared the Spider. He had indexed lists of drug addicts, alcoholics, adulterers, paederasts, *Soldatentanten*, gamblers, debtors, bankrupts, even blackmailers – anyone with a habit or a deviation he wished to hide.[100] And at his office Holstein kept people at bay by two attendants in evening dress who under no circumstance would let anyone past unless he had *le droit de la porte*. This right was given to up-and-coming young men, especially if they were interested in food and happened to be handsome; but these gilded youths, once sucked dry of useful gossip, were quickly put aside and *le droit* was withdrawn. So fearful was he of people prying at his papers that Holstein would not leave his office for a moment and perforce had to make use of a chamber pot which he kept in a cupboard.[101] In theory he was in close contact with Count Herbert, whom he saw daily, but in reality neither was in the other's confidence. Prince Bismarck's description of the Senior-Counsellor as 'the man with the hyena eyes', and 'extremely useful as second or third in command but dangerous at the top' had either been overlooked by his son, or Holstein with his pebble eye-glasses, funereal dress, and amazing prowess as a walker, had mesmerized him.

How much of this is fantasy and how much fact has recently been the subject of much study. Possibly, in the effort to de-daemonize him, the grotesque old blackmailer of the Wilhelmstrasse has been too liberally whitewashed. Almost certainly, whatever the cause, he became a recluse which would exaggerate any tendencies to persecution mania. Equally certainly he loved intrigue and his chief loyalty was to himself. Legends were undoubtedly centred on him and some must have been rooted in fact.[102] Whatever the truth of his personality and character Holstein eagerly awaited the elections of February, 1890.

The month before an influenza epidemic originating in Russia swept over Europe. Amongst its many distinguished victims it claimed the Duke of Aosta, formerly King Amadeo of Spain, and the Kaiser's grandmother. The latter died quietly and no doubt she was very pleased to go. Undoubtedly, could she have done so, she would have much enjoyed her lying-in-state. It was of imperial magnificence. Dressed in cloth of gold, trimmed with ermine, a golden myrtle wreath over her wig, her eyelashes and eyebrows painted and lacquered, her veil gold-spangled, she lay in her coffin surrounded with flowers, as though, remarked her daughter-in-law, she lay in bed: 'She looked wonderfully well and really almost like a young person.' The Empress Frederick had rushed from Rome, too late to reach the deathbed but in time for the lying-in-state and the funeral which followed. Possibly she regretted her haste because no-one paid her the slightest attention. The Court officials gave her small respect. There was no-one even to hand her up and down the steps of the Old Palace chapel. Then she discovered that command of the Red Cross and other nursing and charitable activities which her mother-in-law had clung on to but for which, against the day, she had been preparing herself and making special studies, was to pass directly to Dona. It was another bitter blow and she complained.[103] William was in the middle of a struggle with his Chancellor and could not spare any thought for her predicament. Nevertheless, he was being so successful in his campaign that Bismarck, seizing at every chance, gave the Empress Frederick a longed-for moment of triumph. He went to her, cap in hand, to ask her to help settle the misunderstanding between himself and the Kaiser. She replied that she had no influence at all with her son. He, Bismarck himself, had totally destroyed it.[104]

Bismarck was indeed in a bad way. His second son, nicknamed Count Bill, declared: 'My father can no longer wield the sledge-hammer.' It was apt. Nor could he control his temper. Count Herbert did all he could to save a deteriorating situation but like a wounded bear his father blundered about and roared, aggravated beyond bearing because in so many matters this young sprig of a Hohenzollern was challenging his views.

Bismarck himself had legislated for social improvement but had not gone very far. William pointedly concocted a programme which included the regulation of working hours, wages, and factory inspection. His Chancellor spoke disparagingly of 'dingy humanitarians' and refused to countersign the Kaiser's programme, the first time he had done so since the foundation of the Empire. He also tried his old trick of creating a crisis and then 'heroically' curing it to concentrate his own power. The anti-Socialist laws were due for renewal and the Chancellor's attitude goaded the workers to vote for the Social Democrats at the 1890 Reichstag elections. They polled more votes than any other single party. Because of the second ballot system they only had 35 seats whereas the Catholic Centre with fewer votes had 108 seats, but it was a moral victory. As he had planned, almost everyone looked to Bismarck to save them from radicalism. He heightened the terror by declaring nothing could be done with the newly-elected Reichstag. The Second Reich itself must be dissolved and another created where the teaching of Marx and Lassalle would be outlawed. With his consummate skill at working on people he temporarily infected the Kaiser with his own enthusiasm. He said in one day he could arrange a 'rising' through *agents provocateurs*: 'Then you can give the people a smart dose of grapeshot.'[105] He overplayed his hand. William shouted and threatened all his life but he was never a man of violence.[106] Moreover he had a romantic notion to be a *roi des gueux*. Bismarck was informed that a repressive policy would not answer. The Chancellor reacted swiftly. To keep power he was now prepared to come to some sort of compromise with the Catholic Centre party and sent for its leader Louis Windthorst. Windthorst was cautious and afterwards said he had been to a political deathbed. William declared Bismarck had no right to negotiate with party leaders without his consent and politely reminded him he was not a Minister-President responsible to Parliament but a Chancellor responsible to the Emperor. Bismarck promptly invoked a statute of Frederick William IV which declared that all ministerial communications to the King of Prussia must pass through the Minister-President.

William calmly said the statute was out of date and inoperable if the Minister-President of Prussia spent the best part of every year miles away from Berlin. He ordered a fresh decree to be drawn up. Bismarck sidestepped. He brought up foreign policy. He mentioned Russia and the existence of a treaty. For no known reason, except again possibly to goad the Kaiser, he read out an ambassadorial report which stated that Tsar Alexander III had described William as '*Un garçon mal élevé et de mauvaise foi*'. White with anger, the Kaiser turned on his heel and left the room. His summary order that a fresh decree be drawn up to supersede that of Frederick William IV was refused by the Chancellor, who offered his resignation. To his astonishment and fury it was accepted. Worse, his resignation letter which was lengthy and abusive was suppressed, and the Kaiser's published reply accepting the resignation indicated that it was for reasons of health and age. William was becoming quite Bismarckian. The cabal had won.

The Chancellor had forgotten his own amusing aside about the Kaiser resembling a balloon, and he had let go of the string. His last few days in the Chancellery were not pleasant. Already his successor was sitting in a room there taking over control, which showed he had been chosen for some time.* The Prince himself hurriedly tried to sort out a multitude of documents to aid in the memoirs he intended to write. They filled over three hundred packing cases. The Princess tried to arrange the transport of the innumerable presents sent to her husband in the past twenty-eight years, her very ordinary furniture, an immense number of boxes of cigars, and thirteen thousand bottles of champagne. Ostentatiously they went to make their peace with the Empress Frederick, and put roses in the mausoleum of Emperor William I – 'my old master'. After that they received Holy Communion at home but when the pastor attempted to preach on the text 'Love your enemies' he found himself being vigorously thrust out of the room by Princess Johanna. Bismarck gave a dinner to all his old ministers, who with one exception had decided to stay on. It was a dismal meal. He refused to accept their return invitation to dine, and said not a word to any of his officials or old colleagues. The Kaiser promoted him to the rank of Colonel-General in the Prussian Army and created the Duke of Lauenburg (which title he said he would only use when he was travelling incognito), and he refused a gift of money, which he compared with a Christmas tip to the postman. When he left Berlin large crowds lined the streets. At the station he was given a guard of honour and a formal send-off. The band played a slow march. 'Really a first-class funeral,' he said as the train began to move.[108]

* Holstein and the cabal were aware of who would succeed Bismarck as Chancellor even before the candidate was.[107]

Old Field Marshal von Moltke, when he heard of the Chancellor's dismissal, commented: 'Not at all a nice story!'[109]

Considering his temperament, the Kaiser had shown a surprising degree of calm during the long crisis. If his motives for getting rid of Bismarck were chiefly personal, at least they coincided with historic necessity. All over the empire many thoughtful people were ready, if not eager, for a change from Bismarckianism. Yet when it came and Bismarck was no longer in charge, it seemed so extraordinary as to be impossible. Eventually there were grumbles from the older reactionaries, barely restrained rejoicing from the socialists. Count Waldersee, slavering in his hunger for Bismarck's place, said that the old Chancellor had lost his capacity for sustained effort but obstinately refused to hand work over to other people for fear they would get too much credit as a result. Holstein pointed out to Count Herbert that if it had not been for Professor Schweninger his father would have died long ago. 'As it is he is still alive but is getting old like anyone else.'[110] The Kaiser justified himself to his grandmother, Queen Victoria, and to the Emperor Francis Joseph, but for the present to no-one else.[111] So far as his countrymen were concerned he maintained the decencies (or was hypocritical – it depended on one's point of view) and said he grieved the loss of Germany's greatest statesman, but, at seventy-five, Prince Bismarck had become totally unable to bear the weight of full responsibility. The Bismarcks did not take shade under this courteous umbrella. In memoranda drawn up by the vituperative Count Herbert, and in unsigned yet unmistakable Bismarckian letters and articles printed in the press, the Kaiser was accused of everything from slyness to downright ingratitude. Wisely William chose not to reply in kind, knowing that in any slanging match with two such consummate politicians as the Bismarcks he would lose. He preferred to continue going through the polite motions expected of him. His chief aim was to soothe public apprehension and assure his subjects that continuity would be maintained. Employing his favourite metaphor, he sent off a telegram *en clair* to Hinzpeter which was a roundabout way of getting royal messages printed in the newspapers:

THE DUTY OF WATCH-KEEPING OFFICER IN THE SHIP OF STATE HAS NOW DEVOLVED UPON ME. THE COURSE REMAINS AS IT WAS. FULL STEAM AHEAD.[112]

This inspired *Punch*'s most famous political cartoon 'Dropping the Pilot', which Princess Johanna had framed and hung over her bed. Cotta, the publisher, offered the amazing price of £5,000 a volume for six volumes of the ex-Chancellor's memoirs; and as it became plainer and plainer that he was not to be sent for again, the old man started dictating his reminiscences.

Germany accepted Prince Bismarck's retirement and continued to honour him. Though many of his methods had been and continued to be disreputable, he was never to lose his hold upon the nation nor his place amongst the few great statesmen of Europe. William himself recognized this, describing his first Chancellor to his mother, and less with envy than in affection, as 'the great stealer of our people's hearts'.[113]

CHAPTER NINE

Full Steam Ahead

'I will lead you to days of glory'

THE KAISER TO THE BRANDENBURG
LANDTAG

I

The Kaiser's choice of General Georg Leo von Caprivi as Chancellor was a surprise to many. To the Waldersees it was a blow from which neither recovered. The Empress Frederick, believing that William was about to turn into a sort of Tsar and rule by ukase, said she did not know whether to laugh or cry. In a letter to her mother she declared that the only ministry suitable for William would be composed of that weaver of fantasies Jules Verne, the reactionary anti-Semitic composer Wagner, and Lord Randolph Churchill and Lord Charles Beresford – both known for their instability.[1] Possibly the appointment surprised even Caprivi because formerly, as head of the Navy, he had resigned when William poked a finger into his work, and since then he had been Divisional Commander at Hanover and had believed that he was quite out of imperial favour.[2] Nevertheless William I had had a good opinion of him, and so had Prince Bismarck, a combination which the Kaiser appreciated. He also trusted to his intuition, his flair for choosing ministers. As long as six weeks before Bismarck's fall he had told Caprivi of his destiny.

The appointment was not particularly popular. Being a Prussian soldier, Caprivi was regarded with foreboding by the Social Democrats, and, having something of a reputation as a radical, he was suspect to his fellow Junkers. But Caprivi was no extremist. His few friends called him 'the Seal' because he had whiskers, a large forehead and a round head. He also had that animal's amiability and ponderosity. Gently but firmly he continued the old policies save that the Reinsurance Treaty was not renewed with Russia,* and though

* This was not by the wish of the Kaiser, who never forgot his grandfather's advice

he was, perhaps, a little unimaginative and would be no political ball of fire, he became a much harder worker. Until he found his own ideas thwarted, especially his eagerness to have a larger Navy, the Kaiser was well satisfied with his new Chancellor. Other appointments had to be made. Rather ingenuously the Kaiser had hoped Bismarck's son would continue to manage the Foreign Ministry but Count Herbert was always ready to immolate himself for his father.* His refusal was couched in hysterical terms:

> *I am so bound up with my father by every fibre of my existence that my one and only joy is to live and work for him. . . I can scarcely imagine life without him. It would be like conditions depicted in our old Northern sagas where, if the wolf Fenris ever managed to swallow the sun there would be cold darkness, confusion and despair everywhere.*[3]

But he left behind him Baron von Holstein, who really mattered, and the appointed Minister, Baron Adolf Marschall von Bieberstein, the Baden envoy to Berlin, was an adequate replacement.† Eulenburg's influence continued. Extraordinarily enough, though Holstein served as Senior Counsellor at the Wilhelmstrasse for the next sixteen years he only met the Kaiser once in all that time. He knew how much his power rested on being elusive.

Imperial Germany continued on its course of full steam ahead. The arts were flourishing, industry burgeoning, order prevailed everywhere. The new Chancellor, unlike his predecessor, gave full information to all sound newspapers whatever their political leanings. It was a step in the right direction for the dissemination of truth and the education of the masses, but the pressmen said they really preferred the old days when Bismarck had bribed them with the fortune stolen from the House of Hanover. Another step in the right direction was an Imperial decree which stated:

* Once when he fell deeply in love Count Herbert was not permitted to marry simply because the lady was related to one of his father's enemies.[6]

† Prince Bismarck in an unsigned contribution to a Hamburg newspaper described Marschall as 'the incompetent limpet'.[7]

---

to hold fast to Russia, but Caprivi had the conservative army man's mistrust of Russia, and the new Foreign Minister was quite out of his depth at finding on his desk a treaty so secret that the Kaiser himself knew little about it. William gave way to his unfortunate advisers at the Wilhelmstrasse who should have known better, but he did not like doing so, and, on meeting the Tsar personally later in the year he swallowed the gross insult Bismarck had dragged up and did his best to restore good relations. The response was cordial. In *My Memoirs* he reports that the Tsar declared: 'As to the rapport between us, my dear William, the downfall of the prince will have the best of results; distrust will disappear.'[4] And he urged a looser and revised form of treaty. But again Caprivi would have none of it. Within 17 months of the meeting of the Kaiser and the Tsar Russia and France had concluded a treaty to act together in the event of a threat to peace.[5]

I cannot approve of entrance into the Corps of Officers being made to depend on excessively large private means; this only prevents sons of less well-endowed families who, however, in sentiment and conception of life are closely associated with the Corps of Officers, from entering the Army.[8]

The Army was not yet ready to accept the bourgeoisie into the Officers Corps, but the time could not be far off. William was sagacious enough to see this. A very short time after he showed the same prudence. Quite illegally and rashly, and simply to make trouble, Prince Bismarck had given foreign reporters certain information about internal affairs of the German Empire. It caused a flurry all over the world until it was skilfully calmed down by the Kaiser. He announced to the press:

His Majesty makes a distinction between the Prince Bismarck of the past and him of the present and would like to see anything avoided that could contribute to dimming, for the German people, the picture of their greatest statesman.[9]

It barely commended the Kaiser at Varzin and Friedrichsruh where old Bismarck now carefully laid out coins with the imperial eagle uppermost so that he should not see 'that false face'.

Count Philip zu Eulenburg was not best pleased to be transferred to the Court of Württemberg just after Bismarck's fall. It was promotion of a kind, but Stuttgart was an industrial and commercial centre with only a few pretensions to beauty.* Its Court was exceedingly odd, at its head strange old King Charles who was still in love with his scene-shifter. The Queen was so vague that she had not even heard of Bismarck's fall, and could only remember that she was the daughter of the Russian Emperor Nicholas I.† The King's sister was a massive princess with a hearty appetite and a passion for wearing purple velvet, so that from a distance she resembled a large plum. She was also the mother of the heir to the throne, Prince William, who, in the incredible ramifications of the Württemberg family, was not only an uncle's grandson but also his own nephew.[10] Then there was the Duchess Eugène, who alarmed the Court because she suffered from an especially active form of St Vitus' Dance and had to be pursued down the palace corridors by a dragoon sergeant who caught her from time to time and saved her from hurting herself or smashing the furniture.[11] Of all the possible available appointments Eulenburg would have chosen Stuttgart last, but he had a special duty there because Empress Frederick had finally found a husband

---

* Two of its three mediaeval churches and the *Akademie* where Schiller was a student were destroyed by Allied bombing in the Second World War.

† A petty know-all who once attempted to tell Pushkin how to write verse.

for Princess Moretta; an undistinguished, shy, and not very clever young soldier, Prince Adolf of Schaumburg-Lippe who was a close relative of Prince William the future King of Württemberg. There was to be a wedding in November. Ironically Eulenburg grew fond of his work in Stuttgart and became friendly with Prince William, so much so that for years he often re-visited the city. However he had barely settled in and seen the Kaiser's sister safely married off, when he received a note from Holstein to say that by William's special request he was to be sent back to Munich as Prussian Ambassador. Although it was a return to his own stamping-grounds, he did not altogether relish leaving the eccentric Court at Stuttgart which had certain attractions.

Princess Moretta's wedding to Prince Adolf of Schaumburg-Lippe took place in the chapel of the Old Palace in Berlin on November 19th. The general and gloomy view seemed to be that she was sealing her fate by making such an undistinguished marriage to such a sloppily dressed non-entity, but she was determined to be married and no-one now stood in her way.

The family gathering became an occasion for an explosive quarrel. Princess Sophie had had her first child in July, safely delivered by the mid-wife-housekeeper so thoughtfully insinuated into her household; and she now arrived in Berlin with the announcement that she proposed to adopt the Greek Orthodox faith. It was received very coldly.[12]

Dona, who was carrying her sixth child, was not as comfortable as usual on those occasions. And she had had a vexing summer. First she had been worried to death because the Tsar had sent her husband a troika with three wild Asiatic stallions to pull it and a Russian to drive it. She had begged him not to use such a dangerous vehicle but he would have insisted had not the driver asked for a larger wage and had to be sacked. Fortunately a German coachman, trying to manage the three stallions abreast,* had lost control and wrecked the troika.[13] After that Dona had had to receive the King of the Belgians whom she detested and who, by an unfortunate accident, scalded himself in a hastily improvised hot bath and could not sit a saddle that day at a review held in his honour.[14] His anger was great. So had been Dona's mortification as a hostess. Then it had been brought to her attention that her eldest son William was taking a lively and exceedingly precocious interest in the ladies.[15] After that she had excited her husband's anger, a thing she dreaded most in the world, by appearing at their shooting-lodge Hubertus-stock for a rut-of-hart shoot in a white dress which frightened away the deer. He made her eat supper alone with her lady-in-waiting and she had not

---

* Exceedingly difficult for one unaccustomed to a troika as the shaft horse trots while the two off horses canter.

enjoyed it in the least, despite the fact that the chef had produced her favourite dish of baked potatoes and cold pork.[16] Now, when she had barely recovered from these unnerving events, her evangelical feelings were outraged by her sister-in-law's announcement.

No sooner had Moretta and Adolf been seen off for a honeymoon in Cairo than she made a scene. She sent for Sophie and asked if what she had heard was true. On being told yes, and, apart from every other consideration, it seemed sensible that a future Queen of Greece should share her people's religion, Dona sternly warned her that she would end up in hell.[17] Moreover William as head of the Evangelical Church of Prussia would not give his consent. Sophie gave a sharp, impolite retort and left the room banging the door. It has been maintained that the Kaiser took the trouble to follow his sister all the way down to Homburg where she planned to stay with their mother and that, booted and spurred, he stood in the Empress Frederick's drawing-room and declared that if his sister apostatized, he would bar her from Germany.[18] He repeated the threat in a telegram to the King of Greece. But neither he nor Dona could persuade Sophie to change her mind. In the middle of the quarrel Dona's son, Joachim, was born prematurely, was much smaller than his brothers and evidently the runt of the litter. William instantly blamed his sister for upsetting Dona; though the probability is that Dona's accumulated anxieties plus far too much riding and tight corseting had caused the premature birth. Sophie still paid no attention. The following spring she was received into the Greek Church and at her mother's earnest request sent a long explanatory letter to William. He remained obdurate. She replied in an *en clair* telegram to her mother:

RECEIVED ANSWER. KEEPS TO WHAT HE SAID IN BERLIN. FIXES IT TO THREE YEARS. MAD. NEVER MIND. SOPHIE.[19]

2

By a careful study of the ups and downs in the life of the Kaiser it is possible to see that from time to time he experienced a type of climacteric when calm and deliberate proceedings were followed by a short or long period of irritability and instability. In this respect he was not unlike Oliver Cromwell, another highly controversial historical figure. Occasionally both gave way to red rages and lashed out with their tongues. Very probably both were victims of their physical and nervous health. A lady-in-waiting at William's court reported that he was in constant need of stimulants, often swallowing as many as five egg-cognacs in a day;[20] yet from modern medicine, a much more exact science than in his day, we may judge he was really more in need of some form of sedation, especially after political or family crises.

The consensus of opinion is that ridding himself of the Bismarcks, though he had done it with notable aplomb, had actually frayed his nerves a good deal.

He chafed under attacks in the newspapers:

> *Everything that was done* [he wrote in his Memoirs] *was painted in dark colours, made ridiculous and criticized from top to bottom, by a press that placed itself quite willingly at the disposal of the prince* [Bismarck] *and often out-Bismarcked Bismarck in its behaviour.*[21]

His feelings were bitter when, for no known reason, the press attacked his and Caprivi's excellent idea of exchanging the important island of Heligoland, then in British hands, for Zanzibar and Witu in East Africa, which were far less important to Germany. He reflected that had the agreement with Lord Salisbury been reached by Bismarck no doubt the press would have regarded it as a great piece of statesmanship. As it was, execration flooded over the Kaiser and his new Chancellor. It somewhat dismayed the stolid Caprivi working away at his desk. Its effect upon the volatile Kaiser can hardly be overestimated.

William showed a certain dignity when a memorial to his father was unveiled at Windsor and no-one troubled to tell him about it officially. He sent an A.D.C. to lay a wreath there, that was all.[22] Therefore he was all the more vexed when his mother protested because Berlin had offered to erect a statue to his father and, as the State was raising one, he had refused. He pointed out that his father had already been commemorated by Berlin in the Emperor Frederick Hospital, and as the State had commissioned Reinhold Begas to sculpt an equestrian memorial to Emperor William I* the state should do the same for his father. The Empress Frederick still protested and wrote to her mother that evidently William did not want any visual evidence of his father's popularity to go down to posterity.[23]

William was exasperated by her constant complaints and when, early in 1891, the Foreign Office proposed that the pulse of French feeling about Germany be taken by someone close to the Kaiser he decided that this was something that his mother could do and do well. She had always enjoyed France, paying several visits there incognito since the Franco-Prussian War, and she was the most likely member of the German Imperial Family to sow the seed of rapprochement between the two countries. Delighted, she set off

---

* This disastrous memorial, a mounted figure, surrounded by a plethora of winged victories, angels, symbols of peace and war, horses and lions, was always known affectionately by the Berliners as 'William in the Lion's Den'.[24]

with her daughter Princess Margaret on a semi-official visit to the Republic. It was a disastrous failure. *La mystique d'Alsace* – the will of the French people to be revenged for Sedan and their humiliation – the French newspapers suddenly exploded into powerful blasts concerning '*Insultes aux Français*'. The German press retaliated in kind and, though she herself had done nothing to contribute to the failure, the Empress Frederick quickly moved on to London to avoid being personally insulted.[25] William was enraged. His mother was given no more responsibility. Such was his state of excitement that he was almost taken in by a lunatic story spread by some shrewd foreign entrepreneurs who would have profited handsomely from a war, and nearly replaced his Ambassador to the French Republic with a general. Instead, at a banquet of the Brandenburg Provincial Landtag, the Kaiser showered abuse where it properly belonged, on the press:

> *A spirit of insubordination is abroad in the land; it takes many glittering and alluring disguises, thus confusing the minds of my people and those who are devoted to me; it presses into its service oceans of printers' ink and paper.*[26]

Within a week he received a letter from the one man who dared to try to restrain him: 'In your Majesty's gift of eloquence there lies a danger – that Your Majesty may make too great use of it.'[27] Eulenburg was in the process of leading Stuttgart, to the disappointment of King Charles and his Court, and going to Munich to present his credentials to the Prince Regent of Bavaria. He was faced with a difficult task because a large number of Bavarians wished to separate their country from the Reich. He was also directed to keep an eye on the Papal Nuncio. Nevertheless he found the time to collect press comments on the outspoken Brandenburg speech for forwarding to the Kaiser through the Foreign Minister.

Even his friend's advice could not subdue William's present excitability. Only three weeks afterwards he declared in a speech:

> *The Soldiers and the Army, not Parliamentary majorities and decisions, have welded the German Empire together. I put my trust in the Army.*[28]

His nerves were further frayed when Bismarck was elected to the Reichstag at a by-election, and of all things as a National Liberal. The old ogre never, in fact, took his seat; but the Kaiser was not to know that. He was in a constant state of apprehension.

Eulenburg went up to Potsdam to see him in June and deplored the fact that William was being fed information by people who revelled in gossip and slander. Anything which might be important or useful was being withheld.[29] Evidently the Kaiser and his Chancellor were not getting on. William had plans for building a large fleet and hoped that Caprivi, as a previous Head of the Navy, would co-operate; but the Chancellor said good relations with England were more important and the laying down of battleships was not the way to endear Germany to a maritime nation.

Such was the Kaiser's agitation and the Kaiserin's melancholy that those who wished them well were exceedingly anxious when they went on a State Visit to England early in June, 1891. It was felt that anything might happen, especially as only the month before a scandal at a country house called Tranby Croft had reached the courts, the Prince of Wales had been publicly revealed as a player of an illegal game for high stakes in disreputable company, and William had not hesitated to send a message that this was not the sort of behaviour he expected from the Colonel of the Blücher Hussars.[30] But, no matter how they really felt about one another, all the chief persons concerned had been intensely trained in the importance of good manners and observing strict protocol on royal occasions; a princely asset much underlined when there were State Visits from the heads of republican states. The Prince of Wales, correctly dressed in his Prussian uniform, accompanied by two of his brothers, went to meet their nephew the Kaiser and take him to Queen Victoria. There were presentations of suites, a State Dinner, a City Banquet at the Guildhall, revues and all the usual arrangements for a State Visit, and not once was a crack of dissent observable in the varnish of royal behaviour. When the Visit was officially finished, William politely telegraphed his sincere thanks and went off to Norway in the *Hohenzollern*. Dona remained privately in England, taking all her six sons with a quantity of tutors, governesses and nursemaids to a sea holiday at Felixstowe in Suffolk.

William proposed to return for the Cowes Regatta. He had a new yacht, *Meteor*, which he wished to enter in its class. General Caprivi, more sensitive to the Prince of Wales's present feelings than the Kaiser, suggested a year's postponement, and must have found William's candid reply somewhat shattering: 'The Hohenzollerns have never been popular in England. I am going to Cowes for the races and that is all there is to it.' He went, stayed at Osborne with a considerable suite, vexed his Uncle Bertie, somewhat bewildered his grandmother who had already hinted 'these regular visits are not quite desirable', and thoroughly enjoyed himself.[31]

No doubt the sea air and the restriction of life aboard gave him the rest he needed and he returned to Berlin refreshed. But in no time at all Waldersee contrived to get on his nerves. The Chief of General Staff so far forgot himself, or deliberately risked insulting the Kaiser, by giving a detailed analysis of army manoeuvres from which the Supreme War Lord emerged looking rather a fool. William hated criticism at third hand, especially from the press, though he did not mind criticism, however hostile, if it was expressed respectfully and in private, but he was not going to be made to look ridiculous before his own generals. He promptly got rid of Waldersee both from his command and, as well as he could, from Court by making him G.-O.-C. of the Hamburg District for the next nine years.[32]

His sudden decision won wide approval. Not many people cared for the Waldersees. The Count's successor, General Alfred von Schlieffen, was a slim, elegant officer with an eyeglass; modest, highly intelligent, and devoted to the practice of his profession. A legend had it that after an all night staff ride in East Prussia a young adjutant drew his attention to the beauties of a river in the early morning light. His reply was typical: 'An unimportant obstacle'.[33] His plan for a war on two fronts was to have an important effect upon the outcome of the First World War. The Kaiser was well satisfied with Schlieffen and the new Chief of the General Staff was far too much of a loyal Prussian officer ever to make it clear whether or not he was satisfied with the Kaiser.

Once again the strain of being calm and deliberate in ridding himself of a highly-placed nuisance such as Waldersee produced a reaction. William's nerves went astray. Uncharacteristically, when the King of Württemberg died in October and Eulenburg's friend Prince William came to the throne, the Kaiser gave him the barest token of mourning. This was not because of old King Charles' wayward love-life, for, to the Kaiser, royalty was royalty whatever it did, but simply because he chafed against the restraints of mourning. He and Dona slipped off to the hunting-lodge of Hubertusstock where he relieved his nervous tension by shooting from dawn to dusk, and Dona took the opportunity to wear some of her oldest clothes and a Berlin hat until the Hubertusstock postman refused to hand over the royal letters, mistaking her for the cook.[34] Like Queen Victoria, who many years before had been mistaken for a washerwoman on board her royal yacht, the Kaiserin did not mind in the least. William did. In his present state of agitation such a thing mattered.

In less than a month he had committed a blunder of the first magnitude, going to Munich, where Eulenburg was doing his best to contain the separatist movement, and there writing in the Town Hall album for distinguished visitors: 'Suprema Lex Regis Voluntas'*. There was an outcry at what the Empress Frederick described as the sort of thing only a Tsar or a Pope or a Bourbon or Charles I might have written.[35]† In fact it expressed William's firm opinion as it had been his grandfather's, but it did not help towards the

---

* A classical tag meaning the will of the king is the highest law.
† At Charles I's execution he was banned from making any sort of public appeal but to the few on the scaffold he gave his last determined view: 'A subject and a sovereign are clean different things.

unification of his Empire, and it was excellent propaganda for the Bavarian separatists.

A credible explanation for this almost incredible imperial gesture is offered by Sir Rennell Rodd* in his *Social and Diplomatic Memories*: that there were actually two books in the Munich Town Hall, one for great dignitaries called the Golden Book, the other for lesser notables. By accident the Kaiser was asked to sign the latter, which he did, and when the mistake was discovered the Regent of Bavaria begged him to sign the Golden Book as well. William genially said it was unnecessary but, when the Regent insisted, he agreed, writing the Latin tag to emphasize that the Regent's will, because he acted for the King of Bavaria, must be his law. But evidently the sorely-tried Prussian Ambassador to Bavaria did not think this plausible. Count Eulenburg wrote to his master:

> *Why your Majesty inscribed that motto I have no business to ask. But I should be guilty of a cowardly misdemeanour if I did not write of the evil effect in South Germany, where Your Majesty has appointed me overseer ... All parties without exception have been offended. ... To say that Your Majesty, by such an inscription, has very greatly added to the difficulties, and destroyed many of the hard-won victories, of those who are earnest in Your Majesty's service alone, is to say something which goes very much against the grain with me.*[36]

William humbly accepted this, but offered no explanation. Nor did he attempt to explain away his speech delivered that same month to military recruits. A tempestuous passage was undoubtedly tampered with by a hostile press as anti-monarchical propaganda and there are three different versions in existence. Here is one.

> *You have sworn loyalty to me. You have only one enemy and that is my enemy. In the present social confusion it may come about that I order you to shoot down your own relations, brothers or parents but even then you must follow my orders without a murmur.*[37]

Though aware that, like Queen Victoria, he was 'above' politics, William still had great powers and insisted that Germany was not and never could be a democracy in the English sense. And he held firmly to the beliefs taught by Hinzpeter, and to the example of his grandfather. Furthermore he was living in agitated times. There was a general scramble for colonies. Already Germany had acquired German South-West Africa, German East Africa, the Cameroons, Togoland, part of New Guinea, the Marshall, Brown and Solomon Islands, the Bismarck Archipelago and Heligoland. Politically

* Later Lord Rennell of Rodd.

Germany was the centre of both extreme reaction and extreme radicalism. Social Democrats attacked the Kaiser in the Reichstag, but no attempt was ever made to gag him or limit his powers by constitutional means, and only twice was he threatened, first in November 1900 by a demented old woman who threw an axe at him but missed[38] and, second, in 1903 when a feeble-minded youth hurled a piece of iron at him and wounded him under the right eye.[39] William rather suited his time, and it is notable that the entire era is called the Wilhelminian in German history. For all his grandiose eloquence, few monarchs have so easily got on with their subjects. He had an enviable common touch. But there is no doubt he opened his mouth far too wide and far too often.

His annual speech as Margrave to the Brandenburg Landtag was always an anxiety to his ministers. His speech of 1891 had brought a sharp protest from Eulenburg. In 1892 he worked himself into a passion of excitement about his divine mission, claimed Almighty God as the military ally of Prussia, and declared:

I will lead you to days of glory.[40]

His listeners were enraptured. He had gone straight to their Prussian hearts. Nevertheless his despairing mother declared she felt like an old hen that had hatched a duckling which was swimming away, and his friend Eulenburg reminded him that he could not so to speak separate his existence as Margrave of Brandenburg and Kaiser of Germany. The Bavarians, for instance, took an exceedingly poor view of the emphasis on Prussia and the speech had made 'very bad blood'.[41] At once penitent William telegraphed an apology to his friend admitting he was very wretched, needed to abstain from work, his condition having been caused by strain and over-exertion. Unhappily he sent the message *en clair*.[42] Even worse, in an *en clair* telegram sent later that year to Eulenburg in Bavaria he said:

DONT LOSE YOUR HEAD OVER THE SQUEALING OF THE IDIOTIC BAVARIAN LOYALISTS WHO FALL INTO EVERY TRAP LAID FOR THEM BY THE BERLIN FREE-THINKERS.

Caustically Eulenburg replied that he had once been given a little cypher book 'for special occasions' and begged the Kaiser to send a second *en clair* telegram saying that he was not to take the first in any way seriously. He finished: 'Does Your Majesty *want* a fight? If so, I am ready; but I beg for instructions.'[43]

William did not want a fight. He calmed his indignant Ambassador. Neither bore any resentment. That month they were shooting together at Prökelwitz and were as friendly as ever. On the Norwegian cruise in July they drank 'to brotherhood' and thenceforth the Kaiser always used the affectionate '*Du*' to him. But serving so mercurial a master was not easy.

William shot at Liebenberg, where the sport was good, and there gave his friend permission to wear Court Shooting-Dress. Eulenburg did not care for the distinction, chiefly because he disliked the green uniform coat with a military choker collar, and the high brown boots with silver spurs which he considered ugly; but also because he preferred the unique distinction of being ordinarily dressed. He confided to the privacy of his journal. '*It is like spiritual cod-liver oil to me. And I will not be dressed like the Imperial Household. I am something other than that.*'[44] He had so much to do at Liebenberg that he really did not wish to go on to Rominten, but duty obliged him to do so. In a revealing passage in his journal he wrote:

> *If I did not feel so much compassion for the poor Emperor no power on earth should prevent me from going back to Liebenberg and never leaving it again.*[45]

The first bright flush of their friendship was evidently dying down – at least so far as Philip Eulenburg was concerned.

3

It is not known if the Kaiser got on with his scandalous cousin Prince Albert Victor of Wales, who died from influenza in 1892, but it is known that he liked George the younger son and Princess May of Teck who, having been engaged to the elder brother, after a decent interval, now engaged herself to the younger. The friendship of all three augured well for the future of good relationships between Germany and England. When Prince George was created Duke of York, he left the Royal Navy and went to Heidelberg to read German, and was carefully instructed by his father to take his German uniform and boots and all Orders. It was a courtesy the Kaiser appreciated, and he made sure his cousin was warmly welcomed. When they met they spoke English because William was bilingual and Prince George had been far too long a sea-going, stamp-collecting naval officer to accept with any readiness the discipline of learning foreign languages.* Certainly he was made to feel more at home than William was in England.

Caprivi had been quite correct in estimating that the Kaiser's zeal for a German Navy would arouse the suspicions of English statesmen and William was politely warned by his diplomatic advisers that he could hardly expect a warm welcome. Queen Victoria added her own strong hints that it would not be

---

* Vexed by the constant corrections of his tutor, he is said to have exploded one day: 'Der, die or das Sonne is really very hot today, choose which you like, Professor'.[47]

politic for her grandson to become a regular attender at the Cowes Regatta. All these warnings and hints bounced off his resilient back. He simply announced that he would be coming and when he did arrive in the Solent he offered to send his band ashore to give his grandmama a concert. This she refused. She was in mourning for her grandson and her son-in-law.* It was no reason for German bands.[46] William was not to be put down. While respecting the Queen's mourning he enjoyed the yachting and the social life at Cowes. Evidently he planned to make the Regatta part of his annual round. His determination wavered when he arrived for Cowes Week in the following year and found himself involved in a crisis which threatened war between France and England with the possibility of Germany being drawn in. It cannot too often be stated that for all his verbal bravura the Kaiser dreaded the thought of involvement in a war. At once he had a *crise de nerfs*, refused to commit himself to the English, and went sailing all day aboard his yacht the *Meteor*. Philip Eulenburg, to whom he had personally offered the choice of the Embassies in London or Paris or Vienna and who had wounded and disappointed him by choosing Vienna, was left to spend the day entertaining the Prince of Wales, who was evidently ravenous as he breakfasted from ten until four,[48] and who was also in an ill-humour as he made a disgruntled reference to his nephew's deformity. It was to be hoped, he said, that the Kaiser would not damage himself on the heaving deck.† Eulenburg gave as good as he got: emphasizing his master's excellent balance despite his handicap, and his dash and his courage as a cavalry officer. At a review the year before he had been given an overspirited charger and despite pleadings from his staff that he make a change, he had insisted on riding and quelling the horse. The remark told. Being massive and oval the Prince of Wales was at some disadvantage in a saddle and shy of taking a jump.[49] Eulenburg did not underestimate the Prince's political and social force and decided he was 'a capable, amiable, but very crafty man – *not* our friend'.[50] When he returned from his day's sailing the Kaiser was vastly relieved to find the tension between France and England had relaxed. There was no further danger of war. Automatically, like a released Jack-in-the-Box, he was his merry self again. A cloud hung over Queen Victoria because her friend the Rector's wife had just toppled from an upstairs window and broken her neck; nevertheless she did her best for William, honouring him as German Emperor with a great dinner in the Durbar Room designed by Rudyard Kipling's

* Louis, Grand Duke of Hesse died on March 13th, 1892.

† Eulenburg in his diary gives the impression that the Kaiser took charge aboard the Prince of Wales's yacht and was on deck above their heads as they spoke. It is unlikely for two reasons. William had panicked and wished to get right away from his uncle, and the Prince of Wales would never have permitted his nephew to take charge of his yacht.

father.* And the rest of the week passed well. William's newly-married cousins the Duke and Duchess of York arrived from their honeymoon to be given a rapturous welcome by the family, bluejackets and volunteers, and nine hundred schoolchildren carrying green branches. Then in one race the Prince of Wales beat an American: '*Which* [noted his mother] *caused immense satisfaction*' and the Kaiser won the Queen's Cup.[51]

With his strong belief that the peace of Europe could best be kept by sovereign rulers, William was always eager to meet a fellow monarch. He was certain to be present at any family event, and he welcomed his grandmother to Germany on the occasion of the marriage of her nephew, the new Grand Duke of Hesse, to his cousin Victoria, daughter of the Duke of Edinburgh. The event took place in Coburg where there was a great gathering of the royal mob. Queen Victoria had rather given up her favourite hobby of matchmaking since the defection of Prince Sandro had caused her granddaughter such distress. William was about to take it up. He knew well and he liked the Tsarevitch, Nicholas, who so resembled the Duke of York that they might have been identical twins. He was in his confidence to the extent that he knew of Nicholas' brief and passionate affair with Mathilde Kschessinska, a dancer in the Imperial Ballet who entertained him in a rented house owned by Rimsky-Korsakov.[52] He also knew that on a visit to her sister Ella, Grand Duchess Serge, in 1889 Alix of Hesse had caught the Tsarevitch's eye.[53] She had then been seventeen with red-gold hair and he twenty-one, a gentle blue-eyed prince quite unlike his great bear of a father. Nicholas had promptly fallen in love. His parents strongly opposed his wish to marry her. Though she was granddaughter to Queen Victoria, first cousin to the Kaiser and sister to the Grand Duchess Serge, she came from what Carlyle contemptuously called 'a Pumpernickel Court'.[54] Moreover she was tomboyish, adventurous, and played the banjo. Worst of all she was half English, had been largely brought up by her grandmother as an English girl,[55] and the Russian Court was strongly prejudiced against England. It was a daily prayer of the Tsar's brother, Grand Duke Vladimir, that he would live long enough 'to hear England's death rattle'.[56] The match would not have been popular. Then the health of the huge Tsar gave way. He had a disease of the kidneys besides other ailments. It seemed impossible that so vital and strong a man should be close to collapse. Believing it was urgent for the

---

* The Kaiser already delighted in Kipling's prose and verse and especially the 'Barrack Room Ballads'. From the date of its publication in 1909, the poem 'If' became his favourite. Together with a lampshade on which Dona had painted in blue '*He who prevails over himself conquers*', a framed copy of 'If' stood on his desk thereafter. It is noteworthy that few sovereigns had such a talent for filling 'the unforgiving minute with sixty seconds' worth of distance run' and few have had such a happy 'common touch'.

safety of Russia for the Tsarevitch to marry quickly, the Tsar gave his reluctant consent. But Nicholas' battle was not yet won. He still had to overcome Princess Alix's strong aversion from changing her religion to Orthodoxy, an absolute necessity in a future Tsaritsa of Russia. Her sister Ella, who had happily and of her own choice accepted Orthodoxy, tried to help her over this difficulty and William, though still unable to talk to Ella except in exchanging the briefest civilities, added his voice to hers in urging Alix to change her religion. This appears strange in view of his treatment of his sister Sophie. Equally strange was his attempt to justify himself by explaining that it was diplomatically desirable to have a German Tsaritsa because one of his chief complaints about his own mother was that she had remained English and never become absorbed in her husband's country. Nevertheless, inconsistent or no, William was very determined on the match. He took Nicholas by the arm, led him to his room, buckled on his sword, told him to be a man, snatched some flowers from the table to present to Alix and launched him in her direction. This Alix assault failed. Princess Alix would not give up her religion. William then had a long talk with her, and being one of the most eloquent of the family he succeeded where others had failed. He drove his cousin to the house where the Tsarevitch was staying and made a second launching. This time she consented.[57] The Kaiser's hard work had put the delighted Tsarevitch under a great obligation to him. Thenceforth they would not only be 'cousins' by royal protocol, but cousins by marriage; in their letters (always written in English) they would address each other as 'Dearest Nicky' and 'Dearest Willy';[58] and, on the surface at any rate, their friendship became deeper and more enduring. William felt it was a cause for self-congratulation.

At home Dona had delighted him by presenting him with her seventh child and only daughter.[59] Part of the Hinzpeter severity accounted for William's treatment of his sons; or possibly the brutal example of Frederick the Great's father. He kept them at a distance and very seldom relaxed in their presence, though one snapshot taken of him striding out with five of his six growing sons in file at a Schrippenfest is a picture of a happy family. As is sometimes the way, he over-indulged his only daughter.[60] Her presence gave him a reason to be at home more frequently.

There are tales that there was a certain dingy sumptuousness about the Imperial Court, a mixture of splendour and the tawdry, economy and extravagance which was not very comfortable for guests. The Prince of Wales on an official visit to Berlin was well enough treated, though his servants grumbled at the distinct lack of comfort.[61] The Imperial Household had much to put up with. The Kaiser liked dachshunds, but they were not particular about finding a lamp-post; any convenient lady-in-waiting's dress would do. And being little dogs they snapped and often bit the calves of servants, tore at clothing, and worried to pieces any fan or glove unwisely left within their reach. William serenely walked through his palaces with a pair of these undesirable dogs always at his heels, not noticing or oblivious to the discomfiture they caused. When asked why he did not quietly poison the dachshunds, Count August zu Eulenburg acknowledged that he had considered it but if the Kaiser then decided to follow Prince Bismarck's example and keep Great Danes instead, they would be in terror of their lives.[62] The servants, naturally, had even more to put up with than members of the Household and the Kaiserin never did anything to improve their lot. Either it was not drawn to her attention, or she was a Mrs Jellaby, ever busy with her many outside charities and neglecting her own at home. Stories, probably legends, had it that the servants' bed linen and huckaback towels were in short supply and changed only once a month. Two bathrooms were allocated for the use of all the inside and outdoor servants. Their tin washbowls contained barely three pints of water, and the ration of windowless lavatories perpetually lighted by kerosene lamps was one to every twenty-six persons.[63]

A baffling density of bureaucracy, allied to inefficiency and the perquisite system, were a source of intense aggravation to the members of the Household. Large breakages could only be replaced by making application through the Court Marshal's Office, which then had to forward an enquiry asking for an estimate. Smaller breakages were even more annoying. There was no store of duplicates. A maid had to carry the broken pieces for inspection first by the Under Master of the Household, second by the House Marshal, third by the Court Marshal, and fourth by the Treasurer. This often resulted in delays and people having to do without a hand washbasin or a soap dish or even a chamber pot – which an indignant and deprived Duchess of Orleans described as essential to one's true comfort.[64]

Many of these tales were no doubt exaggerated because both above and below stairs at Courts were natural forcing grounds for jealousies and spite; and, though no doubt there was inefficiency and some degree of seediness, it is worth recalling that the chief setting of the Court in Berlin was in the magnificence of the Old Palace built by Andreas Schlüter in the late seventeenth century,* and at Potsdam in the rococo elegance of the New Palace. It would have been difficult not to take pleasure in such surroundings. Other royal establishments also had distinct advantages. Wilhelmshöhe, looted from the Electoral Landgraves of Hesse after the Austro-Prussian War, was a small Versailles exquisitely furnished in the First Empire style by Napo-

* Since blown to bits by the Russians and levelled and paved to make the new Marx-Engels Platz.

leon's brother Jerome who reigned there for seven years as King of West-phalia. Another favourite was the royal farm at Cadinen near the Baltic;* an ordinary stuccoed country house at the end of a chestnut avenue, with orchards and vegetable plots and an untidy garden complete with ornamental pool where large green frogs called Unken made a pitiful moaning noise all day and all night.[65] Nearby were cottages for the labourers, farm sheds and barns, and geese and chickens and pigs wandered round the yards. Cadinen was so totally unlike the New Palace that anyone fortunate enough to go there loved it, although, if the Kaiser was there too with his large suite, there was a squash and most of his Household lived on the royal train shunted on to a siding. Even further east, at Rominten, the Imperial Hunting Lodge was in two sections connected by an overhead gallery built entirely of massive Norwegian pines. This was also a favourite place, though it had a distinct disadvantage in that the doubled log walls were easily penetrated by smells and sound. Occasionally it was necessary to whisper, and, as the Kaiser's daughter's governess put it, a servant merely had to light a cigar in the basement and the Kaiserin up in her sitting-room was at once aware of it.[66]

The chief object in the Kaiserin's life was to eliminate minor irritations so that her husband should not be needlessly vexed. His temper was bound to affect everyone in the Household. Occasionally there were serious disasters. One will serve as an example. Annually there was a Hubertus hunt in November, a social occasion held in honour of St Hubert, patron of the chase, and so that the ladies could show off their new habits. A boxed boar was released at a given point to be hunted rather like a boxed stag and brought to bay in the shortest possible time. On the day before the Hubertus hunt in 1892 the Kaiser's sister Princess Charly arrived at the royal stables with her lady-in-waiting, both red-faced and fresh from a very hearty break-fast. When the Princess offered to ride à la Florence Dixie if someone would lend her a pair of breeches, it became evident she was tipsy. She then pro-ceeded to demonstrate how the Kaiserin mounted, thudding down into the saddle like a sack of flour. There were polite titters from other princesses and the ladies. The next day all Princesses of the Blood and ladies-in-waiting were barred from the hunt by order of the Kaiserin.[67] In this sort of authori-tarian way she controlled the Court.

One outrage, though, was beyond her power to manage.

Not long after the Hubertus hunt scandal envelopes began to arrive at Court containing montages based on photographs from Paris which 'in respect of erotic imagination left nothing to be desired'.[68] The originals' heads were obscured by cut-out photographs of the heads of well-known courtiers. Even the Kaiser and Kaiserin were defamed. One stark naked

* Then in East Prussia, now in the U.S.S.R.

female in a compromising situation had the face of the Kaiserin, her almost stark naked compromiser the face of Court Pastor Stöcker plus clerical bands. In addition to these obscene photographs the Court was inundated with anonymous letters either hinting at this and that or being outspoken. The outraged Kaiser ordered an auditor, vested with full powers of enquiry, to look into the matter, but he met with no success. By the volume of material posted anonymously there were evidently two hands at work. The police were brought into the case. They too failed.[69] Courtiers became quite neurotic, daily expecting to be held up to ridicule or suddenly exposed. It was as though Baron von Holstein had suddenly unlocked his Poison Cupboard.

In this nervous, uncomfortable setting the last of the Kaiser's sisters, Princess Margaret, was married to Prince Frederick Charles, son of the Landgrave of Hesse. William was not sure that he approved of the marriage. Though a direct descendant of George II of England and of a sovereign family, the Landgraves of Hesse had been landless, save for a handful of beautiful castles, since the Austro-Prussian war. Prince Frederick Charles seemed a poor match. Yet it was evident the couple were in love, and Margaret was young and of no special importance in the family.[70] The only person who spoilt the marriage was Dona's brother Duke Ernest Gunther of Holstein who gave the visiting Tsarevitch too lavish a bachelor entertainment of Roman punch and dancing girls which obliged him to miss a formal dinner at the Russian Embassy. William was exceedingly angry.[71] He was angrier still that the senders of obscene collages and poison pen letters remained undetected. The pornographers were tireless. More than two hundred (and one report alleges four hundred) were sent in less than two years. Then the Kaiser's Master of Ceremony, Baron von Schrader, received a particularly disgusting collage with his own photograph employed, and decided it could only be the work of his deadliest enemy at Court, Herr Leberecht von Kotze. It made no difference that Kotze happened to be a particular friend of the Kaiser. Schrader planted the seed of suspicion and it grew. The investigators then found on Kotze's writing table a piece of blotting paper which had blotted writing very like that used by the anonymous pornographers. Schrader denounced Kotze and, on this slender evidence, the Kaiser ordered his arrest.[72] Madame von Kotze then caught the Kaiser in the New Palace billiard-room and threw herself on her knees before him, imploring for a change of heart. Allegedly Dona and her younger children were walking in the garden outside and heard the appeals and screams and the Kaiser repeatedly saying No. This caused the young princess to demand: 'What is Papa doing to Auntie Kotze?' and the Kaiserin to reply that thenceforth they had no Auntie Kotze.[73] To everyone's acute embarrassment while Kotze was in gaol awaiting trial by a military tribunal the flow of collages and letters continued unchecked. It was Eastertide. As if in compensation for false imprisonment William sent his former friend a decorated egg, some bottles of Steinberger, and gave him back his uniform and rank.[74] Kotze was unforgiving, demanded a military trial which declared him innocent and then began on a series of duels with people who had believed in his guilt, emerging from them maimed but having killed his enemy Schrader on the field.[75] Having proved Kotze's innocence, the pornographers either became tired or they were discovered and warned off. The latter seems probable. It was understood that one was a close relation of the Kaiserin and he had been aided by his mistress. Nothing was said but it is significant that like his mother with her mysterious system of washing her twenty-four 'hemispheres' and her taste for grabbing at male courtiers, Dona's brother Duke Ernest Gunther had his time rationed at Court in future, a week at a time and no more. Further the Kaiser would not allow him to open any establishment of his own in the capital or at Potsdam on threat of being turned adrift.[76] In a sisterly way Dona tried to find him a suitable wife, but the first he refused because she was too gross, the second because though a princess she had already had a child by an unscrupulous footman. The third, Princess Marie of Edinburgh-Coburg, refused him.[77] Ernest Gunther's supposed accomplice was given sharper treatment. She was a French marquise without any rights in the German Empire. Two members of the political police took her to the frontier and warned her not to set foot in Germany again.[78]

How much of the moral erosion at his Court was kept from William is not known. He made decisions, but possibly they were based on less information than was really available. The Kaiserin could be a formidable woman and her policy was always to protect her husband. Being an impulsive, imaginative man, his pride would have been hurt by such a long and burning scandal at the centre of his own Court. On the other hand he had the advantage of being able to put unpleasantness behind him and reach out for compensations. Queen Victoria offered one opportune blessing giving him the Colonelcy of the 1st Royals. He could hardly wait to make a private visit to Osborne in his new uniform, to thank his grandmother and report himself to the senior military officer in the Household. This turned out to be General Sir Henry Ponsonby, the Queen's Private Secretary, who had no uniform at Osborne, and whose frock coat according to the Prince of Wales was a perfect fright. The Prince rushed off to find him a better one but by the time he returned the Kaiser had already reported to Sir Henry with a dramatic salute, and Sir Henry in his shabby old coat had shaken the Kaiser's hand and welcomed him in the name of the British Army.[79] After that

William went out with his Uncle Arthur the Duke of Connaught to review troops at Aldershot, including a squadron of the Royals, and dine with his officers. Thence he returned home by a 'roly-poly passage on an angry North Sea' for manoeuvres of his own army.[80]

During his absence Dona had been preparing a surprise to please him, painting with her own hands his favourite wicker basket seats. Her choice of colour, bright lilac, was bold. On his return home the Kaiser expressed himself touched by her thought. They both sat in the lilac chairs and for a long second, barely more, both were in perfect accord. Then it became only too clear the paint was not yet dry. William called it a 'sorry joke' and roared for turpentine.[81]

4

General von Caprivi did his best to be a conscientious Chancellor but the fact that he offered his resignation ten times in four and a half years indicates how difficult it was to replace Bismarck and initiate what the Kaiser termed the 'New Course'. Historians show us several Caprivis. One sees him as an honest man of moderation with administrative capabilities of a high order who agreed with the Kaiser's 'liberalism' and tried to implement worthwhile social legislation.[82] Another regards him as a political Don Quixote tilting at the windmills of social injustice without making any attempt to change the economic foundation on which they were based.[83] Yet another describes his policies as rational but 'politically weak', and only William's consistent support could have made them a success.[84] Inconsistency being a fruit of the grasshopper mind, Caprivi lacked this support. The whole picture reveals that in foreign affairs he bravely though unsuccessfully aimed for an alliance with England and some sort of rapprochement with France; and he rather rashly undertook to support Austria against Russia should there be trouble in the Balkans.[85] This reversal of his own policy infuriated Bismarck, smouldering in retirement, though nothing Caprivi did angered him more than his order to fell the trees in the Chancellery garden and let in more light.[86] In home affairs Caprivi indulged and approved of the Kaiser's general concern for the welfare of all his subjects, but in doing so he inaugurated some very controversial policies. For instance, during his chancellorship courts of industrial arbitration were set up and laws were passed which regulated the working hours of women and children; the anti-Socialist laws were allowed to lapse; the Poles in East Russia and the French in Alsace-Lorraine were given greater liberties; and a new Army Law was passed which reduced the period of compulsory service from three years to two.[87]

These innovations alienated Caprivi from the industrial magnates, reactionaries, and conservative soldiers. This was by no means all. Believing that Germany's destiny was to be a great industrial nation fed by cheap imports from abroad, he made no less than thirty-eight foreign trade treaties which had the immediate effect of ameliorating the conditions of the poor in Germany who, now they had cheaper food and the prospects of work, were far less inclined to emigrate to the Americas. But there was also an immediate effect upon the Junkers' agrarian interests in Prussia. There a newly-formed Landowners' Union declared that, as a Prussian nobleman and German general Caprivi was a traitor to his class, and the right-wing newspaper *Kreuzzeitung* announced: 'The German farmer will now be inclined to regard the Emperor as his political enemy.'[88] Caprivi then fell out with anti-clerical National Liberals by permitting the Minister of Education to put forward a bill to give the clergy control over religious education in Prussian schools.[89] So fierce was the outcry that, as was his wont, the Kaiser disappeared with two aides to his shooting lodge at Hubertusstock until things had sorted themselves out.[90] He returned to the capital to accept abandonment of the bill, the Education Minister's resignation, and Caprivi's idea that he hand over the Minister-Presidency of the Prussian government to an impeccably reactionary Prussian Junker, Count Botho zu Eulenburg, who was Philip Eulenburg's cousin. As Caprivi still remained at the head of the Prussian delegation to the Bundesrat there were obvious difficulties, but at the time it seemed a sensible way of placating the National Liberal and the Junker interests.

William made Caprivi a Count but he was no more comfortable with him than he had been with Bismarck. 'Caprivi,' he said candidly if a trifle rudely, 'you get on my nerves terribly'; – and the custom grew that they communicated largely either through Kiderlen, a subordinate of Holstein's at the Foreign Ministry, or through Eulenburg.[91]

Kaiser and Chancellor were agreed that Bismarck's continuous press attacks should not go unpunished. When Count Herbert married an Austrian lady, Caprivi instructed the German Embassy to decline any participation in the ceremony, and the Kaiser begged the Emperor Francis Joseph not to notice the ex-Chancellor.[92] The Bismarcks' prompt response was to send invitations only to close members of the two families concerned. Eulenburg wisely advised Caprivi that conciliation was better than what could only be a war of attrition. The Kaiser ought to bribe the old man into silence by the offer of the use of one of the royal palaces in Berlin. Caprivi disagreed and saw no reason to recommend it to his master. Meanwhile William had been told privately by his cousin Prince Albert that a rapprochement of some sort was most important. Should Bismarck die as the Kaiser's declared enemy posterity would not easily forgive him. This impressed William, especially when Bismarck suddenly took to his bed in September, 1893, and it was given out that he was seriously ill. Without reference to Caprivi, the Kaiser telegraphed his sympathies and begged him to move as soon as possible from Varzin to the more salubrious Friedrichsruh or make use of any of the imperial castles in Central Germany. Bismarck telegraphed his thanks but said that he would more easily recover in 'long-accustomed domestic surroundings'. William then sent a bottle of old Steinberger-Kabinett which he knew Bismarck would enjoy. He did.[93] Caprivi began to see that political life would be more tolerable if Bismarck's sting was drawn and he agreed to Eulenburg's original suggestion. He proposed to the Kaiser that one of the Berlin palaces be put at the Prince's disposal. William demurred. He did not want the Iron Chancellor on his doorstep. But he allowed himself to be persuaded by a combination of August and Philip Eulenburg and Caprivi. He telegraphed an offer. Bismarck refused, but he was sufficiently impressed by the cordial offer to make his first visit to Berlin since his dismissal and call on the Kaiser to congratulate him on his thirty-fifth birthday. On the arms of his sons Count Herbert and Count Bill he tottered up the flight of steps at the Old Palace to be greeted by the Kaiser, embraced, kissed, and led inside for talks. But William changed the subject if it turned to politics. He did the same at the celebratory luncheon, and during the drive which the two took together afterwards through the streets of Berlin. There was to be no more consultations on great affairs between the two. Bismarck was politically quiescent for the moment.*[94]

That Easter William showed he had not lost his sense of humour. Professor Quidde published a pamphlet *Caligula, a study in Roman Megalomania*, a satire aimed directly at the Kaiser. He did very well out of it, selling thousands of copies. Amongst his readers was the Kaiser. An English friend, Lord Lonsdale, came to stay in Berlin and William gave him a bust of himself. No special plinth was available, and one was rapidly taken from the classical heads which lined the corridor. 'No doubt Caligula's!' chuckled the Kaiser as he handed the sculpture over.[96] However his reaction was less cordial when a newspaper reported in the summer a calculation that in the previous 365 days the Kaiser had spent no less than 199 on gadding about,[97] and he was definitely perturbed when a comic paper called *Kladderadatsch* (a Berlin colloquialism for any mess or muddle or mix-up) launched an attack upon government by crony; that is, against the Kaiser communicating indirectly with his Chancellor through Eulenburg, Kiderlen and Holstein. The last three were called 'Troubadour', 'Dumpling', and 'Oyster friend', and in the

* Two years later he caused a fluttering by divulging the secret text of the Reinsurance Treaty, and William seriously considered arresting him for treason. He was persuaded to think better of it.[95]

very best type of Berlin humour – unlike that of any other – they were dealt
with very severely indeed. The writers were Bismarckian diplomatists,
though this was not known at the time, and the enraged Holstein tried in
vain to identify them. The attacks were so vituperative that legal action was
considered, but this did not suit the Kaiser who did not wish for more
publicity and graver comment about his unusual way of going about things.
Nor did it suit Holstein's policy of perpetual secrecy. Yet something had to
be done. Kiderlen challenged the editor of *Kladderadatsch* and wounded him.
Holstein, a noted duellist, called out three men who he considered might be
involved. All denied it and refused to fight. The frustration made him smart
still more and he told Eulenburg to bring pressure on the Kaiser to force at
least one to fight. Eulenburg refused, and, although the Kaiser, hearing by
roundabout means of Holstein's deep distress, tried to console him by making
him a Privy Councillor with the style of address of 'Your Excellency', he
remained disgruntled.[98] Eulenburg who was feeling the strain of his triple
rôle as appointed German Ambassador to Austria, Holstein's ambassador to
the Imperial Person, and messenger-boy between Palace and Chancellery,
gave vent to his feelings in his diary: 'If only I had three heads and one heart,
instead of three hearts and a solitary head.'[99]

Kaiser William might have echoed this wishful thinking. He had backed
Caprivi in all his liberal innovations yet, by the time of Bismarck's re-
appearance at Court in January 1894, his liberalism was crumbling beneath
the influence of his conservative military advisers and the unpopularity of
most of Caprivi's measures.[100] His original enlightened views of the place of
the Federal Princes in the Empire had altered so much since 1888 that when
Prince Louis of Bavaria denied in 1894 that they were in any sense vassals of
the Emperor, he met with William's strong displeasure. So did the new
young King of Württemberg when he told the Kaiser that, as none of the
Princes had sworn to uphold the constitution, there was nothing to prevent
them from subverting it. This changeabout might have been caused by the
accession of Prince Alfred, Duke of Edinburgh, to the Duchy of Saxe-
Coburg on the death of the old roué Duke Ernest. William cared no more
for him than he cared for his uncle the Prince of Wales. He would have
enjoyed treating Uncle Alfred as a vassal Prince.

The New Course ceased when Caprivi came into conflict with the Minister-
President of Prussia, Count Botho zu Eulenburg. Because of an eruption of
anarchical terrorism through Europe, during which the President of France
was stabbed to death on his way from a banquet, Count Botho wished to
introduce a renewal of the anti-Socialist laws. Caprivi would not have this
under any circumstances. The Kaiser recalled Bismarck's advice: 'The German Empire is all very well, la la! But you must try to make only Prussia

powerful.'[101] Though he desired to be a modern monarch, stand above party politics, and look after his people, William could not resist the Prussian siren voices. He supported Count Botho zu Eulenburg. In a speech at that most Prussian of places, Königsberg, he sounded a Prussian warning: 'To arms for religion, morality, and order against the parties of the revolution.'[102]

Caprivi was alone. He had offended everyone: the Junkers, the Army, the Navy, the heavy industrialists, the National Liberals, the clergy, the nationalists, and the Prussian Parliament. Even Holstein's support of him became lukewarm because, in his opinion, the Chancellor was less of a politician than a philosopher.[103]

William was shooting at Liebenberg in October 1894 when the Caprivi-Count Botho crisis came to a head. He was persuaded both would have to go.[104] Caprivi went home to live for five more years. Unlike William's other Chancellors he wrote no *apologia* or attack, nor did he publish any sort of reminiscences. Some have said that this was because he had nothing of importance to write, but he represented social conciliation in government and he never lost the conviction that he had failed his master at an important time. It is reported that he died of a broken heart.[105]

CHAPTER TEN

The Stumm Era

'The trident belongs in the German fist'

KAISER WILLIAM II

I

Amongst the Sovereigns of Europe the Kaiser shared only with the Tsar the Austrian Emperor and the Pope the actual not merely theoretical right to choose his own First Minister. When Count von Caprivi's downfall became inevitable there was much speculation in the press as to who would be his successor. Philip zu Eulenburg was the favourite. Earlier there had been thought of making him Foreign Minister in place of Marschall, but Eulenburg was never truly a fit man and he lacked the necessary energy to be ambitious. To speak for Germany from his vast and beautiful Embassy, the Neue Burg in Vienna, was quite enough for him, and sometimes he felt too much. The idea of being Foreign Minister was insupportable. He wrote to Bernard von Bülow: 'A poor barndoor fowl like me, cockered up into an eagle.'[1] Even less would he consider the higher, more splendid office.

The Kaiser held the extreme view that no-one could actually refuse an office or resign from it without his approval. 'It is I who dismiss my Ministers, not they me.'[2] Therefore Eulenburg had to work on his friend, and persuade him not to make the appointment. He was successful. Thereafter they discussed together who should follow Caprivi. William's cousin, the Grand Duke of Baden, proposed an interim Chancellor while the right man was searched for, and suggested Prince Clovis zu Hohenlohe-Schillingsfürst. Interim appointments were not altogether satisfactory. There was a living example in Rome, Pope Leo XIII, who had so successfully composed the Roman Catholics' difficulties with Germany. This pontiff had been elected in 1878 at the age of sixty-eight, simply because the state of his health was precarious and the other aspirants to the Papal Throne required a little time to forward their own interests; but no sooner was he elected than his health improved and he outlived them all. He now lived exclusively on thin gruel and soup and great quantities of snuff,* and at eighty-four was as vigorous as ever.[3] Nevertheless it became apparent that Hohenlohe for all his years suited Holstein. The Kaiser permitted himself to be persuaded by his cousin and by Holstein who thought Hohenlohe an admirable choice and no-one pointed out the imperial inconsistency in allowing Chancellor Bismarck to 'retire' at seventy-five on account of age and appointing another Chancellor in his seventy-seventh year.

One branch of the Hohenlohe family was related to Queen Victoria and therefore to the Kaiser. The Hohenlohe-Schillingsfürsts were also related to the Kaiserin on her mother's side and so the Prince took office with the exceptional advantage of being known as 'Uncle Clovis' in the imperial family. He had had an excellent political career as Bavarian Minister-President, German Ambassador in Paris, and more recently Governor of Alsace-Lorraine. Well-read, intelligent, witty, not easily ruffled, and eminently sensible, he has been called Germany's 'Salisbury', though his lineage was longer and more illustrious. Anyone more unlike Otto von Bismarck it would be difficult to imagine: unemotional, spare in speech, cool in judgement, small in stature, yet totally lacking in that self-protective aggressiveness common to little people, he was a spry 'young seventy-five'.[6] It was rumoured that during his time in Paris he had become the victim of blackmailers. If so, he paid up and made no fuss.[7] One of his brothers was a Cardinal and Grand Almoner to the everlasting Leo XIII; another was Chamberlain to the Emperor Francis Joseph; another took his subsidiary title as Duke of Ratibor and was married to Dona's trumpet-playing lady-in-waiting.[8] Hohenlohe's wife, with whom he usually spoke French, had brought him huge estates in Russia and one of her favourite pastimes was bear-shooting. His sons had brought him sadness. His heir first married a Greek princess and, after her death, an actress, then suffered a breakdown and had to be confined in a private asylum. Another son had married an Italian nineteen years older than himself.[9]

His appointment struck everyone as adventurous. He was a Bavarian and a devout Roman Catholic, which meant that both Chancellor and Foreign Minister were Southern Germans, and, unlike his predecessors in office, he had the self-confidence of a patrician and was an excellent delegator and team-leader. Caprivi's idealist attempt to be agreeable to the masses had left a sour taste in everyone's mouth, even in that of the Social Democrats. Prince Hohenlohe was more of a realist, and time and experience had made

---

* So great was his need for snuff that even the greatest public ceremonials were frequently interrupted by the cardinals flocking about the Holy Father to hide the fact that he was taking a pinch.[4]

him something of a cynic, He cared no more for the protective tariffs which made Prussian farmers rich than he did for any other self-interest.

With an apparent serenity he could not have felt, the new Chancellor got on excellently with the ebullient Kaiser, presided over the ministerial team, and did his best to satisfy the self-interested demands of the greater power lobbies: the Junkers who wanted even higher tariffs, railway concessions, tax relief, and direct subsidies; the industrialists who, in order to market their goods, required concessions from abroad and the colonies; the Centre Party which, though it had a large number of seats in the Reichstag, had never been admitted as an official state party and wanted to prove its members were as loyal to the nation as they were to the Roman Catholic Church; and the intelligentsia who were emotionally excited by the birth and growth of Greater Germany, and wished for a lavish and practical display of nationalism in foreign policies. Of the four the industrialists were the most pressing. Their success was ballooning. By 1900 they were producing more iron and steel than the British and were eternally preoccupied with finding markets.[10] For this reason the period was once named by German historians 'the Stumm era', after an autocratic deputy in the Reichstag, calling himself a 'Free Conservative', Baron Karl von Stumm-Halberg, who was king of the Saar heavy industry and would allow no Social Democrat or Christian Socialist meetings within his realm.[11]

Reaction was in vogue again. Landowners and industrialists felt it was in their interest to encourage and finance patriotic movements which sprang up to meet the needs of certain groups. The Eastern Marches Association had an obvious self-interest, so had the Colonial League and the Navy League. The committee members of each interlocked with one another and were not disinterested; Stumm and Krupp, for example, contributed to, or, rather, invested in, the Navy League and reaped ample profits from the Kaiser's naval armament programme. The most active body of all, the Pan-German League, had been founded as a protest at exchanging Heligoland for Zanzibar and Witu, a bargain scornfully described as 'a trouser button for a whole suit of clothes'.[12] The League was underwritten by leaders of heavy industry, and had a strong appeal to small professional men, especially teachers, clerks and shopkeepers, in other words 'patriotic theorists who sought to compensate by their country's aggrandizement for the inadequacies of their own lives'.*[13] They were anti-Semitic, anti-Pole, anti-everything non-German; and they were the first to use the sinister word *Herrenvolk* as a warcry. Numerically small – never more than 22,000 – they had shrill protesting voices.[14] In the

* The *Poujadistes* were a similar group seeking power in France after the Second World War. The same type frequently figures in some 'White' governments in Africa today.

'nineties Pan-Germans in Austria were loud in their anti-Semitism both in the Representative Chamber and out of it. It is worth recalling that a founder member in Germany, Alfred Hugenberg, later a director of Krupps, head of a film combine and the most powerful press baron in the Weimar Republic, was largely responsible for bringing Hitler to power.[15]

Both the Kaiser and his Chancellor tolerated the birth of these patriotic movements but no more. They shared the view that the Navy League might be useful (to the Kaiser's relief, Hohenlohe approved of his naval programme); and the Colonial League would help to find an outlet for the products of German industry; but neither cared for the excesses of the Pan-German League which were bound to cause trouble, especially their racialism. In the German Empire Jews were far better off than they were in Russia or France,[16] and once Stöcker's bad influence over him had passed William was singularly free from anti-Semitism. He had little patience when Princess Sophie of Weimar shot herself because her parents would not allow her to marry a Jewish banker.[17] The point was that she would not have been allowed to marry any sort of banker. In Wilhelminian Germany anti-Semitic parties did not prosper, and the cult was confined to isolated intellectuals of great prestige like Professor Henry von Treitschke,[18] head-in-the-air theorists like the expatriate Englishman Houston Stewart Chamberlain and his father-in-law the composer Wagner, and to lower middle class eccentrics like William Marr and the members of the Pan-German League.* William did not disguise his scorn for the Pan-Germans, saying in public that they were incapable of constructive thought.[19] His own racialist prejudice was the commonly held fear of what he called 'The Yellow Peril', but even this did not prevent him approving when the son of one of the four great officials at the Prussian Court, with exceptional precedence in Germany, married a Japanese lady.[20] He also once said in a speech to troops and settlers: 'Never forget that though the people you meet in S.W. Africa have skins of a different colour, they for all that possess hearts susceptible to feelings of honour. Handle such people gently.'[21]

William's new conservatism was a grudging acceptance of the old *status quo* simply because Caprivi's experiment in democracy had failed. His policy at home now was no policy. It was impossible to satisfy all self-interests. The age was so vital that a straightforward home policy was beyond his capacity or that of the Chancellor and the bureaucratic machine. They lived from day to day, adjusting and trimming here and there, compromising, trying to con-

---

* Wagner probably had a common reason for being anti-Semitic – a share of Jewish blood. Nietzsche believed he was the illegitimate son of a Jewish actor, Ludwig Geyer.[22] By strange coincidence William Marr, who coined the expression anti-Semitism, was also the son of a Jewish actor.[23]

tain any difficult situations and ameliorate the lot of persecuted minorities, aiming at one target only: the gradual expansion of German power so that the Fatherland should become a force to be reckoned with and her colonies sources of plenty.* There were few critics of this scheme, as it appeared to be to everyone's advantage, but some liberal philosophers and political thinkers saw in it the seeds of disaster. Perhaps the shrewdest of them was an old gentleman living in Berlin, formerly a journalist, war correspondent and travel-writer who only began his twenty-year-long career as a leading novelist when he was sixty. Theodor Fontane's value to German social history is great. In word pictures he painted old Berlin and the Mark of Brandenburg before the German industrial explosion. He was also a prophet. He knew that the régime created by Bismarck and carried on by the Kaiser had a limited life. He predicted the fall of all Empires, German, Dutch and English. 'The whole policy of colonization is madness' he wrote in 1897.[24] But only those of the Social Democrats who had fed on the strong meat of Marx, Engels and Lassalle might have agreed with him. Few else would. The German worker was not a revolutionary. Any tendency in that direction had been reduced by the recognition of his political party, its legal representation in the Reichstag, a system of social security, high employment and the possibility of emigration.[25] On the whole the German workers would have agreed with their Kaiser's aim to make the empire greater. Like him they wanted a powerful navy to protect German interests and her colonies. They wanted a World Policy.

At the Brandenburg Assembly in September 1895, William developed his theme of expansion and he promised: 'We are destined to great things, and I am leading you to marvellous times.'[26]

2

William's foreign policy was partly his own and partly Marschall's, but was mostly concocted in the background by Eulenburg and Holstein. Russia was to be weaned from the French and made to cooperate with Germany. The Kaiser thought this should not be too difficult. Alexander III had died and his 'Dearest Nicky' was now Tsar. He urged him to join in the defence of Europe 'from the inroads of the Great Yellow race'. It was an idea which appealed to Russia because she had ambitions in the Far East and was concerned about the growing power of Japan; and William had the wit to see that a Russia busily employed looking at Japan and China was less likely to pay attention to what was going on in Europe and the Near East.[27] For the time being England was to be kept at arm's length. When Salisbury noted

* Such was the Kaiser's appetite for colonies that a legend sprang up in Africa that Queen Victoria once gave her grandson Mount Kilimanjaro as a birthday present.

that the Ottoman Empire appeared to be on the point of disintegration and proposed that the corpse be divided amongst the Powers by international agreement, Holstein would have nothing to do with it.[28] And when Britain protested because the Boers of the Transvaal made an agreement with Germany to lay a railway from Delagoa Bay to Pretoria, thus permitting Germans to reach the Transvaal without crossing British Territory, Holstein vigorously defended the agreement. Britain continued to press that the Transvaal had only limited independence. By the London Convention of 1884 the Boers had undertaken to make no agreements with other countries. The Germans declared that as they had not been signatories to the Convention they were free agents. The railway was built and the Kaiser sent a telegram of congratulations on the opening of the new railway.[29] Then Dr Jameson made his famous raid into the Transvaal on December 29th, 1895, and Marschall ordered that a cruiser should steam to Delagoa Bay and Marines be landed if it was necessary to protect German interests. But, after an initial success, Jameson and his freebooters were surrounded by the Boers and forced to surrender. The Kaiser telegraphed his congratulations to President Kruger. Allegedly he wanted to land troops and Marschall tried to soothe him by proposing a telegram. Others support William's claim that he was persuaded to telegraph against his (and Holstein's) better judgement. Whatever the correct interpretation the telegram raised a hornet's nest.

The English were then and later acutely sensitive about what they called their internal, domestic and private affairs in South Africa. Although the German colony of South-West Africa lay alongside Cape Colony they regarded the Kaiser's act as an unwarranted interference. Only three weeks before they had been denounced as aggressors for penetrating Venezuela from British Guiana in a bellicose message from President Cleveland in Congress.* He had asserted the right of the United States to restrain the aggressors,[31] but this far more insulting and, as it turned out, quite unjustified attack, did not provoke the English as much as the Kaiser's telegram. For some reason which defies analysis, they had a strong feeling that, as their Queen's grandson and the son of the Princess Royal, William should support their policies.† The Prince of Wales spoke of it as a 'most gratuitous act of unfriendliness' as though his nephew really had a duty to be friendly, and he urged the Queen to give William 'a good snubbing'.[32] She wrote a calm and courteous personal letter expressing her deep regret

---

* It was Presidential election year and clearly Cleveland was trying to win votes. For the six months while the parties prepared their campaigns there was a very real danger of war with England. Then an international court of arbitration found for England and the episode was closed. It seems a discreditable piece of electioneering.[34]

† This is rather remarkable in view of the constant anti-German barrage from The Times and other British newspapers, and the return fire from the German press.

that her grandson should have sent such a telegram and saying that it had made a very painful impression on England.

> *The action of Dr. Jameson was of course very wrong and totally un-*
> *warranted, but considering the very peculiar position in which the*
> *Transvaal stands towards Great Britain I think it would have been far*
> *better to have said nothing.*[33]

There is still some doubt as to whether or not Dr Jameson had been en-couraged in his illegal act by the British Colonial Secretary, Mr Joseph Chamberlain, but there is no doubt that the Kaiser had already told the Tsar: 'Come what may, I shall never allow the British to stamp out the Transvaal'.[35]

William was receiving fifty abusive and mostly anonymous letters a day and he heard that the officers of the 1st Royals in England had hacked his portrait to bits and thrown them in the fire. He swallowed his pride and replied to his grandmother, giving her three reasons for having sent the telegram: first, that peace had suddenly been violated and he was glad it had been restored; second, that his subjects in the Transvaal and the German investments there needed protecting and he was glad Jameson's attack had failed; and third, because rebels had failed in their purpose. He went on to put some blame on the English press and the Germans, and say that he hoped England and Germany could be friends again. He finished: 'What would the Duke of Wellington and old Blücher say if they saw this?'[36] Ironically it was the verve and character of Dr Jameson which inspired Rudyard Kipling to write William's favourite poem 'If'.[37]

Queen Victoria quickly forgot her vexations because, only a few days afterwards, she received the news that Prince Henry of Battenberg had died of enteric fever on the Ashanti campaign. She was desolated with grief both for her daughter Beatrice and for herself. But the English did not forget. The Queen's Ambassador in Berlin said later that all the misunderstandings between the two countries dated from the Kruger telegram affair. Nor did William forget it. Three days after the despatch of the telegram he held two important conferences about enlarging the German fleet.[38]

Within a year – and it was the year of Queen Victoria's Diamond Jubilee – the Kaiser was again wrangling with England. There was trouble between Greece and Turkey over possession of Crete, and, because of his affection for and interest in the Turks the Kaiser took the Sultan's part despite the fact that his sister was married to the Greek Crown Prince. Again the English, who were inclined to be pro-Greek, were indignant at his 'shameful behaviour'.[39]

William would dearly have liked to have attended Queen Victoria's magnificent Diamond Jubilee that summer, not as a monarch but as a grand-son, but in view of recent events it was out of the question. Pointedly he was not even invited. His mother and three of his sisters were there and were accepted by the Londoners as 'family'.[40] However, Lord Ronald Sutherland Gower, who had remarked on the excellence of the arrangements for the Golden Jubilee ten years before, wrote:

> *The only jarring note was when a German general rode by, for the crowd groaned; and one felt what a fortunate thing it was that the German Emperor had not put in an appearance.*[41]

There can be no doubt that William would have heard about this demonstration so hostile to his country and to him personally. Many have remarked on his growing belief that he was a much misunderstood man.* That year he certainly was fraught. Only stolid, dependable Dona seemed to care. His friend Eulenburg sent nothing but long jeremiads from Vienna. The Federal Princes, led by the King of Saxony, were stirring restlessly and kicking against his authority as Kaiser.[42] And when, during the Greek-Turkish crisis, there was a calamitous fire in Paris at a charity bazaar in which 200 people lost their lives including the sister of the Empress of Austria, and he sent a handsome donation from his private fortune to the distress fund, he received small thanks. The French newspapers offensively called it a part repayment of the 1870 indemnity. He found work was an anodyne. All his energies were bent to the creation of a great Imperial Navy.

Cruisers and smaller ships were all that strict necessity required for the defence of Germany's coastline and her overseas colonies, but the Kaiser and the Navy League and Friedrich Krupp wanted a battle fleet. Trying to convince the Officer Corps that the glory of German arms should float as well as march was a task which took all William's considerable powers of persuasion. Trying to squeeze the necessary finance out of the Reichstag was an even more tedious affair. He gave lantern lectures at the New Palace to important deputies and men of influence. Mahan's *Influence of Sea Power on History* was one of his bedside books and he knew long passages by heart. He quoted these endlessly whenever the opportunity occurred.[43] Earlier in 1897 he had lambasted the Social Democrats, who were totally opposed to his policies, saying they were revolutionaries and godless and should be 'rooted out to the very last stump'.[44] Then, in the same excited strain, he caused a furore on his usual podium, the annual Brandenburg speech, in which he declared that, had his grandfather lived in the Middle Ages, he would have been canonized, and that Bismarck and Moltke had merely been his henchmen.[45]

Chancellor Hohenlohe urged that moderation was more likely to win the

---

* Princess Daisy of Pless noted that on one occasion when explaining how misunderstood he was, a tear stole down his cheek and landed on his cigar.

support of the Reichstag and, when the Kaiser impulsively proposed a coup, he forced him to think again by threatening to resign. William gave way over this but, nonetheless he still simmered with resentment against those who stood in his way. He wrote to his brother Harry that the offending deputies were 'unpatriotic louts and scoundrels', a comment which the Prince read out loud to his assembled ship's company.[46]

There was a change of ministers that spring and summer. Marschall, lukewarm in his keenness for a navy, was relieved of the Foreign Ministry and sent off to distant Constantinople to be Ambassador to the Sublime Porte,* and Bernard von Bülow replaced him. The Secretary of the Interior was likewise replaced. Most important of all to the Emperor was the retirement of Admiral von Hollman as Secretary for the Navy and his replacement by the energetic, highly intelligent Admiral Alfred von Tirpitz.[48] He had the thrust, the political know-how, and the organizing ability to get what the Kaiser most wanted.† He was like a bull terrier in that he sank his teeth into the cause of creating the Navy and he would not let go, and, unlike most sailors he had a light touch which charmed his adversaries in the Reichstag. He was as good a politician as an Admiral.

In the year of his appointment the new Secretary for the Navy visited Prince Bismarck at Friedrichsruh. It was a shrewd move because the old Chancellor still had an immense following and, though he was supposed to be on good terms with Hohenlohe, was still critical of his ministry. Moreover no German statesman had visited Bismarck for some time. It was a conciliatory gesture and Tirpitz hoped to gain his approval of the Navy programme. To his dismay he found the giant had shrunk.[50] He was still resentfully missing his wife who had died three years before and his world had narrowed to a bathchair. He passed his time brooding, or reading and re-reading the Bible, Schiller, Shakespeare and the novels of Dumas, father and son; nothing else.[51] He took great quantities of morphia and held hot water bottles to his cheeks to ease the pain of neuralgia. The great eater had

---

* He was not regretted by Holstein who, over a dinner at Borchardt's of trout, spring chicken and Steinberger on June 8th, declared to Philip Eulenburg that he had (mistakenly) discovered Marschall was one of the Kladderadatsch conspirators and had he not been eased from office he would have called him out. Evidently by now Holstein's persecution mania was grave. He warned Eulenburg: 'Anyone coming to the [Foreign] Office will have to bring a steel broom with him. Marschall has been conducting a secret, pernicious campaign against all Prussians, aristocrats and political functionaries'.[47]

† It is strange that these two, who were so largely responsible for creating the fresh irritant in international affairs, the Imperial German Navy, were more familiar with England and the English way of life than anyone else in power. Heredity and regular contact with England gave the Kaiser his knowledge and Tirpitz's came from his passion for English philology and the fact that both his wife and daughter were at Cheltenham Ladies' College.[49]

been reduced to finely chopped meat and could barely speak. But he drank one and a half bottles of champagne during the Admiral's visit which seemed to do him good, and then he expressed his firm opinion that Germany should keep within her frontiers.[52] Coastal defences and torpedo-carrying craft were excellent but he saw no purpose in an aggressive Grand Fleet.

Not even a visit from the Kaiser in December 1897 could make Bismarck lend his name to naval propaganda.* Instead he gave William a short lecture, not on the desirability of a Navy but on the necessity of being able to count on the Officer Corps if he wished to rule without his ministers.[53] The hint was not well received.

More to the Kaiser's taste was the tacit consent of Tsar Nicholas that Germany should take possession of the Bay of Kiao-Chow as a German coaling station,† and that same month a squadron, under the command of his brother, was sailing out to plant the Imperial flag. It was understood in the family that the incoherent Prince Harry's speeches were frequently written by his voluble elder brother in order to ensure consistency of policy, but occasionally he forgot his lines, or he was carried away and spoke extempore which invariably landed him in trouble. Unfortunately on this occasion he was thrown by an unexpected announcement that the Kaiser was arriving in person to dine on board. Then his brother solemnly charged him to carry the mailed fist to the East because two German Roman Catholic missionaries had recently been murdered in China and the Centre Party was causing a great pother at the Foreign Ministry. All this, together with the frantic excitement that hummed through Kiel, made Prince Harry let himself go with a vengeance. Even more unfortunately, it was not a simple quarter deck speech as he supposed but it was reported by the press and read throughout the world. He addressed his speech as follows:

> *Exalted Emperor, Puissant King and Master, Illustrious brother. . . . I will carry forth the evangel of Your Majesty's person; I will preach it to those who want to hear it and also to those who do not want to hear it . . . Our sublime, mighty, beloved Kaiser, King and Lord for all times for ever and ever – hurrah, hurrah, hurrah!'*[56]

Despite the mockery which poured over the German Navy and the German imperial family as a result of this astounding eulogy; and despite the Social Democrats, Bismarckians and Progressives; despite even the well-intentioned

---

* It was William's second visit to his ex-Chancellor. On the first occasion two years before, he had taken with him the thirteen year old Crown Prince and the boy had been agitated because one of Bismarck's Great Danes snapped at him from under the table at a celebratory banquet.[54]

† In March, 1898, China leased the territory to Germany for the term of ninety-nine years.[55]

warnings of the Empress Frederick who personally went to see Bülow and warn him that there were serious dangers of alienating England, the Kaiser's careful and considerate handling of the Army and Tirpitz's strategy in the Reichstag ensured the passage of a Navy Bill on March 28th, 1898.

In a state of high delight William, Tirpitz and Bülow at once began looking for fresh coaling stations to serve what was to be a much-enlarged fleet. A splendid opportunity soon offered itself. In February the American battleship *Maine* had exploded while lying in the harbour of Havana and American public opinion blamed a Spanish submarine.* By April the two countries were at war. Though personally he liked Americans, William supported Spain because she was a monarchy. But the size of the United States Navy made the result a foregone conclusion. When the war spread to the Far East the Kaiser hoped for some pickings from the spoils. He had his eye on Manila where, conveniently, twenty-five Germans happened to be living. Nevertheless when Bülow proposed to send a gunboat to protect their lives and interests, William refused. Shrewdly he judged it would be too provocative an act.[58] It would be wiser to negotiate for Manila, but America, then an imperialistic nation and thwarted of Canada though twice she had invaded it, was not going to part with a square yard of conquered territory. When the Spanish fleet was blown out of the water off Carita, the United States seized all seven thousand and more of the Philippine Islands. The Kaiser promptly made a bargain with Spain, offering 17 million marks for Mariana and Caroline Islands. Temporarily embarrassed, Spain was glad to accept.[59]

In that same month of July, 1898, William telegraphed his grandmother a report that he had just inspected the flagship of the English Training Squadron off Molde:

I VENTURE TO EXPRESS MY GRATIFICATION AT THE EVENT OF BEING ABLE TO SPEND SOME HOURS WITH SO MANY CHARMING BROTHER OFFICERS[60]

The term 'brother officers' was not lost upon Queen Victoria. William obviously valued his rank as an English Admiral. It was a friendly gesture. Only three days afterwards the Empress Frederick wrote from her new and beautiful home at Kronberg to her mother at Windsor:

I do know for a fact that William is MOST ANXIOUS for a rapprochement with England, and hopes with all his heart that England will COME forward in some sort of way and meet him half-way.[61]

* Not everyone did. For a long time the two countries had been squabbling over Cuba. When war broke out Queen Victoria expressed the majority opinion in her Journal: '*It is monstrous of America*'.[57]

Lord Salisbury was quick to tell the Queen that he agreed with his Colonial Minister that a policy of isolation was no longer satisfactory, but he committed the Government no further, and soon left for Contrexéville to take a three-week cure for gouty eczema followed by a further three-week *Nachkur* in the Vosges.[62] Temporarily he left his nephew Balfour to take care of Foreign Affairs, but in fact he could not escape the business of being Prime Minister. In exchange for an alliance the Kaiser wanted colonial and trade concessions, but whereas Chamberlain might have agreed, he could not carry the Cabinet with him and certainly not the Prime Minister.[63] Salisbury wrote from Contrexéville to the Queen that the British public would never tolerate territorial cessions. Vexed, he opined:

> *The German Emperor takes offence very easily. Lord Salisbury cannot in the least understand what it is he refers to when he speaks of his overtures having been received with 'something between a joke and a snub'.*[64]

This was myopic. If England was abandoning her isolationism and needed continental allies she had to look to Germany or to the Franco-Russian bloc. At all levels, except from the press angle, an Anglo-German alliance seemed the most 'natural'. William had responded accordingly, stating no precise proposals at this stage, but nevertheless making a gesture of friendliness which had been received with a chilly reserve. His Ambassador in London emphasized that there was no fear of Germany falling between two stools, and Bülow his Foreign Secretary was insistent that the other Powers needed Germany more than she needed them. He controlled his disappointment and his private feelings sufficiently to be able to lead three cheers for the Queen of England when the news of the battle of Omdurman reached him at a review of troops at Hanover. Nevertheless, though Lord Salisbury affected not to understand why, William did feel snubbed.

3

Two gods amongst statesmen fell in 1898.

Gladstone died on Ascension Day, his last characteristic wish that his family should pray for him, all fellow-Christians, and all unhappy and miserable people. He was buried in the north transept of Westminster Abbey, the Prince of Wales and his son the Duke of York acting as two of his pall-bearers.[65]

In July Bismarck fell into his last decline. He went very willingly. For years he had not been able to walk. Despite vast doses of morphia he had lived much of his extreme old age in pain. He had outlived Moltke and the two great friends of his youth. To one he had confided that his dependence upon God had lessened with the decline of his erotic passions, and so he no longer even had a need for the Almighty. His Jewish physician Schweninger could serve him no longer. His sons were sent for. They and their sister sat beside him during the last hours. Sometimes he sang to himself. Sometimes his daughter read Schiller's verse out aloud. Once he whistled *La donna è mobile*. When the end came it was as characteristic as Gladstone's. Offered a teaspoonful of champagne, he sat up, seized the glass, cried 'Forward!' in a loud voice, and drank the whole glassful. On July 30th he died just before eleven o'clock at night.[66]

The Kaiser was on his annual Norwegian cruise when he heard the news. He dictated an admirable Order of the Day to honour the memory of the great statesman, telegraphed his sympathies to Bismarck's children, proposed that the funeral should take place in Berlin cathedral and the mourning family might have use of the royal stalls, and steamed at once for Kiel. In death as in life Bismarck was hostile to his wishes. He had left careful instructions that under no circumstances was he to be buried in Berlin Cathedral but in the mausoleum at Friedrichsruh.*[67] William went there for the funeral accompanied by a large number of generals and admirals. They were coldly received. The Kaiser and his company stood on one side of the sarcophagus, the family on the other. The service was short. In one respect it was remarkable. The most unusual of contemporary monarchs was saying goodbye to the most unusual of all Prussian Junkers. It was the last meeting of two vital men both with talents and blemishes and surprising limitations. Half an hour after they had walked from the little station to the house the royal party had gone. By Bismarck's own order his epitaph was brief:

HERE LIES PRINCE BISMARCK
A FAITHFUL SERVANT OF EMPEROR WILLIAM THE FIRST[68]

It was the beginning of a campaign that was to last for a very long time. Only the day after his death Bismarck's press officer, Busch, released to the press a copy of his original letter of resignation which had been suppressed by the Kaiser. That same year he also published a polemic in three volumes entitled *Bismarck: Secret Passages from his Life* which had obviously been ready and waiting for the ex-Chancellor's death. Cotta, the publisher who had given so much for Bismarck's memoirs, now decided to issue the first volume.† Like its successor it was a badly made-up book, a discursive reminis-

---

* It was ugly and, strangely, cut off from the house by a railway line; but this could hardly have mattered to a man who had lived for twenty-seven years in a large hotel which he never bothered to convert to the comfort of an ordinary home.

† This was entitled *Erinnerung und Gedanke*, later reversed to *Gedanken und Erinnerungen*. There were three volumes; the first two dictated at sporadic intervals to Lothar Bucher, Bismarck's closest assistant for thirty years – for whose devoted services.

cence full of unconnected vignettes and padded out from a vast store of state and private documents by Bismarck's amanuensis. It was also incomplete because he had predeceased his master by six years, and it was the agglomeration he left behind which Cotta had set up against the day. Its publication caused a high wave of comment to wash over Europe. Though studded here and there with the jewels of Bismarck's undoubted literary excellence it was a cruel disappointment to his disciples. From it he emerged as a vindictive, relentless mocker. Scholars of all schools of thought were critical of its historical inadequacy. The Kaiser was enraged because this first volume was a frenzied Bismarckian trumpet blast against the House of Hohenzollern. This had the salutary effect of making him closer to his mother than at any time for years because they sympathized with each other. He addressed her as 'Most beloved Mama'. Neither looked forward to volume two.

To relieve the tensions of that year William decided to visit the Holy Land in the autumn. It would break with his usual routine but he considered that might be beneficial. Messrs Thomas Cook, the English travel agents, were commanded to make all the necessary arrangements for an extensive tour in October.[72]

On September 10th came the shattering news that the Empress of Austria had been assassinated by an Italian anarchist in Geneva. She had been stepping aboard a paddlesteamer on the Lake when the assassin leapt out and stabbed her to the heart.★ Within an hour she died.[73] It was a dramatic end to a dramatic, unhappy life. Her first-born, a daughter, had died as a child. Her brother-in-law, the delightful Maximilian, had gone off to be Emperor of Mexico but in a rebellion he had been betrayed to his enemies, shot by firing squad and bits of his mutilated corpse sold off in lots by public auction as souvenirs.[75] Her son, Crown Prince Rudolph, had at Mayerling met a tragic and scandalous end. Emotionally she had been unable to cope either with her devoted husband or with Court life in Vienna, and she had spent most of the past thirty-five years travelling incognito as Countess Hohenembs and becoming increasingly eccentric. She had hunted in Ireland, converting her sitting-room there into a gymnasium;[76] built a neo-Greek palace called the Achil-

★ H.R.H. Princess Alice, Countess of Athlone, recalls her mother telling her a soothsayer had predicted that of the beautiful Wittelsbach sisters one would die by fire, another by steel and a third by water. The Duchess d'Alençon had been burnt to death the year before at the Paris charity bazaar, Empress Elizabeth was stabbed to death, and a third sister was drowned.[74]

according to Mr. A. J. P. Taylor, he only once received a word of praise;[69] the third, written by Count Herbert about his father's fall, called the 'suppressed' volume, which did not appear until 1921. William read this in exile and most carefully annotated his copy.[70]

leion on Corfu where her Greek secretary read Homer out loud while she took the air;[77] went racing and gaming and spent a large fortune on fantastic clothes and equally fantastic health cures – for a time she lived on a diet of blood and milk, and even experimented with a curative diet of sand.[78] She also asked for the most bizarre presents, anything from a tiger to a fully equipped lunatic asylum.[79] But she had always kept the stately beauty which William had found so startling that, at the age of fourteen on first seeing her, he had forgotten his manners, lost his tongue and stared. He no sooner heard the news of her assassination than he travelled at once to Vienna to be with the Emperor. The lengthy obsequies were scarcely finished when the Queen of Denmark died, mother of William's Aunt Alix of Wales – whose portrait with that of Ella had adorned his desk for years. Then his own mother, at last less critical and much more of a friend, had an accident whilst riding in the Taunus forest. Her horse shied at a thrashing machine, threw her, and dragged her by the stirrup for a considerable distance. Typically she did not complain and refused to be fussed, but her backbone had been seriously damaged.[80]

The Kaiser's physical courage was never questioned but he was much affected by this series of hammerblows.* Once he had been assured that his mother was in no danger of her life he was glad to get away in late October on his Cook's tour of the Near East. It was a larger gadabout than usual, its nominal object to dedicate a German church built in Jerusalem. Dona and Bülow and Philip Eulenburg accompanied him, together with a bevy of soldiers and clergymen; but as he was not *en garçon* with his usual suite, but accompanied by the Kaiserin, his Foreign Secretary and his Ambassador to Vienna, the Powers looked on his pilgrimage with some suspicion.

His first stop was Constantinople, where he was greeted as an old friend by the reigning Sultan. Abdul Hamid II, the son of a consumptive Circassian slave girl, also enjoyed the unfriendly sobriquets of the Red Sultan, on account of the amount of blood he had shed, Abdul the Damned, and the Ogre of Yildiz Kiosk – his fortified palace on a hill above the city. The third Sultan to have considerable dealings with the Powers, he was by far the most wily. His father had been a slothful, egg-shaped ruler remembered only because he introduced the four-poster bed to Turkey. His uncle who succeeded was turned out in a palace *coup* and either committed suicide or was knocked on the head. Abdul's elder brother who was next in the line of succession was a sot and happy to hand over the sultanate in return for a short

---

* Evidently it also affected the Minister of Crathay Church by Balmoral who, to the Queen's barely stifled mirth, was so carried away by anxiety for his beloved sovereign that he begged in a extempore prayer that she might continue 'to skip like a he-goat upon the mountains!'

retirement in an alcoholic stupor. Abdul himself, though Sultan of the vast Ottoman Empire and Caliph of Islam and so the Shadow of God on Earth to some 300 million Moslems, was not much to look at; shrunken, with a great beaked nose and his wispy beard dyed red as custom demanded. Moreover he had such a morbid dread of electricity, diseases and crowds, that his life was one long neurotic agony of imprisoning himself behind a barricade of guards, none of whom he trusted, and employing over twenty thousand secret agents to spy upon the guards and upon each other. Apart from work, and he was a very hard worker, his only diversions from looking beneath and behind furniture for assassins and shooting down suspects with a pearl-handled revolver, were of a western character. He enjoyed the company of a Belgian mistress as well as his inherited seraglio, rowed on an artificial lake at Yildiz Kiosk, played Offenbach, and read Sherlock Holmes.[81] Despite his neuroses the Ogre of Yildiz could be charming. He had gone out of his way to be pleasant to the Kaiser on his first visit in 1889 and, as a result, had won his support in the Turkish-Greek dispute. He was charming again now, and though Dona complained of the dirt and she and her ladies spent anxious moments chasing insects which crept out of the walls with their hat pins,[82] William enjoyed the magnificence of the oriental Court, and was delighted by the Sultan's attentive friendliness. England's virtual seizure of Egypt from his Empire had turned the Sultan towards Germany and he had German officers reorganizing and training the Ottoman army. He was also prepared to make more than mere token signs of his friendship. It emboldened William to ask direct for the gift of the Dormition in the Holy Land, that is, the place where the body of the Blessed Virgin was said to have rested before her Assumption. He explained why he wished for it and the Sultan readily assented.[83] He also offered the Kaiser a guard of two Syrian soldiers to protect his person in the Holy Land, a gesture which was much appreciated.[84] This was by no means all. Important political concessions were also granted. Two months after the Kaiser's visit, Germany was permitted to build a harbour and railway terminal on the east side of the Bosphorus, lay a cable between Constanza and Constantinople, and the German dream – and English nightmare – of a railway from Berlin to Baghdad seemed closer to reality.[85]

Journeying on to Palestine the imperial pilgrimage found the heat overpowering. But nothing could daunt William if he was bent on enjoying himself. Flanked by his Syrian bodyguards he led his Court into Jerusalem and they visited the Holy Places which, though drab and dirty, were still impressive. In the presence of many general superintendents of the German Protestant churches, he dedicated the Church of the Redeemer built by Germans in Jerusalem; and, because he believed it important for imperial unity to show no partiality, he then presented to the German Roman Catholics in Palestine the site of the Dormition which had been given him by the Sultan.[86] With a German priest he discussed building plans and who should have responsibility for this holy place.*

It was in Palestine that the Kaiser was approached by the celebrated Austrian Zionist Theodor Herzl. He had come with four colleagues from Vienna to ask William's aid in the establishment of a colony of Jews in their original homeland. The first meeting was casual, by the roadside, but led to a second when the Kaiser received the five Zionists in his tent.[87] William was not unattracted by the plan. 'Your movement,' he said, 'with which I am thoroughly familiar, is based on a sound healthy idea. There is room here for everyone. My personal observation is that the land is arable. Only provide water and trees.'†[88] It is difficult to know what really lay behind William's broad approval of Herzl's scheme, and improper for a biographer to impute motive. It has been suggested that he was genuinely anxious to find a home for German Jews. For twenty-seven years, that is, since the founding of the Second Empire, German Jews had enjoyed full economic emancipation, and many had distinguished themselves in politics, the professions and the arts. The highest concentration, though there was never any ghetto, was in Berlin, and it is an as yet unexplained phenomenon that anti-Semitism always emerges when the Jewish minority reaches a certain proportion of the native inhabitants of a country.[91] Nine years after his meeting with Herzl the Kaiser was complaining of the number of Jews in his Empire. 'If I did not restrain my people, they would be Jew-baiting,' he declared.[92] His restraint was not all that successful: the university theorists, the Prussian Officer Corps, and the Pan-German League saw to that.

It is interesting that afterwards, in a handwritten memorandum, he denied ever meeting Herzl at all.[93] A number of explanations for this curious behaviour have been proposed, the most widely accepted being that he simply wished to avoid the embarrassment of having to go back on his general approval of Zionism. The truth is he suffered from a restrictive mental condition, common to imaginative children and excitable grown-ups, technically called *Pseudologia fantastica*, and, in ordinary parlance, tall-story telling. It is white lying as opposed to black lying, not likely to bring

* Ultimately he decided the monks of Beuron should go out and take possession both of the Dormition and the monastery which he had built next to it. This they did in 1906.[89]

† The last was a tall order. Almost a hundred years, and many miles of technological advance later, and despite the most inventive and economical use of water, Isaiah's prophecy 'the desert shall blossom as the rose' has yet to come to pass. Even Nabbatean irrigation schemes, desalination, cloud-seeding, 'acquifer'-mining, and breeding hybrid plants which can use brackish water, have not wholly solved the problem.[90]

the victim any advantage save the satisfaction of enjoying the sensation caused by making such an obviously detectable false statement. It is play-acting, no more. Eleven years later, for no apparent reason, the Kaiser was to deny that a certain physician had ever looked after his mother, the Empress Frederick; a denial quite as foolish and as pointless as his refusal to acknow-ledge meeting Herzl.[94] Between these two reported events and before and after them, the Kaiser must have shown other unreported manifestations of *Pseudologia fantastica*, but while the habit makes him appear silly, even chil-dish, it must not be considered a severe mental complaint. It lies more within the province of the moral theologian than in that of the psychiatrist. In Palestine the heat and the exotic surroundings stimulated William into a high state of nervousness. In fact, although he had a definite Christian piety and was on a pilgrimage, he found the infidel atmosphere far more attractive than the Jewish or the Christian. He appeared in public dressed as a Bedouin sheik; went on to Damascus where he was greeted ecstatically by the Sultan's subjects crying: '*Lululu, Lululu, Lululu, Lululu,*' as was their custom, and where, thinking less of St Paul than of Saladin, William laid a wreath on the latter's tomb, spoke movingly of the affection Haroun al-Raschid had had for Charlemagne, and concluded with the peroration:

> Let me assure his Majesty the Sultan and the three hundred millions
> of Moslems who, in whatever corner of the globe they live, revere
> in him their Caliph, that the German Emperor will ever be their
> friend.[95]

The needle of the European balance of power was already flickering dangerously. General Lord Kitchener of Khartoum, having slain ten thousand Dervishes, had proceeded up the Nile to a point called Fashoda where he found a steamer which had been brought in sections right across the continent to be bolted together and launched on the river. It was manned by a com-pany of Senegalese troops and nine French officers. The republican tricolour flew where he had planned to plant the Union Jack. Kitchener had the com-mon sense to exchange civilities rather than bullets and he left the affair to the statesmen.[96] The French and English confronted each other with welling indignation. Had France had the means and not been rent asunder by a resurrection of the Dreyfus affair, and had she not changed her Foreign Minister from an Anglophobe to an Anglophile halfway through the baring of sabres, there might well have been a war. But M. Delcassé the new Foreign Minister liked the English, and did not want them in the German camp. To the Kaiser's disappointment the threat of war died down and the two colonial powers sat down to work out a mutually agreeable settlement of their affairs in Africa. This left Germany in a difficult position. Neither

England, with a hundred million Moslems in the Indian sub-continent, nor Russia with her hunger for a way out of the Black Sea, regarded the Kaiser's euphoric Damascus speech with any sort of favour; and France, despite *l'affaire Dreyfus*, had not forgotten *l'affaire d'Alsace*. William's only allies seemed to be the old Emperor of Austria, King Humbert of Italy and the Ogre of Yildiz, and neither of the latter amounted to very much.

The medical profession states that men can and often do suffer the emotional stresses experienced by females in the menopause. If this was the case with the Kaiser it would explain his increased nervousness and tension in his early middle age. January 29th, 1899 was his fortieth birthday. He wrote to Queen Victoria that the strain of his office was 'often too heavy to bear' and described himself as 'her queer and impetuous colleague'.[97] She noted in her journal: 'I wish he were more prudent and less impulsive at such an age!'[98] Victoria herself enjoyed flattery. Some of her courtiers were fulsome. Already her portrait had appeared in one of Kempe's new windows in the Lady Chapel of Winchester Cathedral.[99] But she was an eminently level-headed old lady and could cope with such attentions. Her grandson found it more difficult, and the flattery was plastered on. One supposedly liberal Berlin newspaper, founded in the eighteenth century and renowned in the capital, the *Vossische Zeitung*, hailed him on his fortieth birthday in the most extravagant terms as an

> Emperor, a Caesar, more than a Napoleon, and that is true not only for us but for the whole world! In Europe today all eyes are turned towards the banks of the Spree, towards our old and lovely royal palace, in which the Idol, the God of the Day, does us the honour to reside![100]

This sort of fantastic toadying frequently gave William an inflated ego and made it easy for him to detect insults, imaginary or otherwise, and difficult to be forgiving. At this time he was especially annoyed with Lord Salisbury and his grandmother. He had set his heart on going to England for the Queen's eightieth birthday and presenting his seven children to her one by one. But she refused to invite him or his family to Osborne. She said it would be too much for her although, from her report of what she actually managed to do on her birthday, it seems that she had abounding reserves of energy and could easily have indulged her grandson.[101] Her Ambassador in Berlin, Sir Frank Lascelles, noted the Kaiser's bitter disappointment in 'not being able to carry out his cherished scheme'.[102] Bülow was also reported as saying he 'took the refusal badly'. It certainly gave William muscle to the strong line he took when, on the death of his Uncle Alfred's heir, Queen Victoria busied herself with the business of the succession but approached the two local diets without reference to him as Emperor. Refusing his consent, he threatened his grandmother and Lord Salisbury with the veto of the Reichstag. The Duke of Connaught then renounced his own rights and those of his son, and the young Duke of Albany was finally adopted as heir presumptive and sent over to learn German ways and serve in the Germany army.[103]

Having made his feelings clear about this piece of interference he sent for the English Military Attaché and informed him that he found his country's policies incomprehensible.

> *He said* [reported the Attaché to his Ambassador] *that for years he had been the one true friend to Great Britain on the continent of Europe, and had done everything to help her policy and assist her, and that he had received nothing in return but ingratitude.*[104]

The Kaiser felt with some justice that the English were liberally helping themselves to colonies all over the world and, in that English phrase untranslatable into any foreign tongue, they were 'not being fair'. He particularly wanted Samoa in the Pacific. Salisbury said it would have to be divided between the three Protective powers, England, Germany and the United States, and as there were only two islands such a division was impossible. His Olympian attitude and bad geography, for there happened to be three islands not two, maddened William.[105] He snapped to the English Ambassador in Berlin: 'Tell your people to behave themselves properly!'[106] and three days after her eightieth birthday he dashed off an indignant letter to his grandmother. It was very revealing.

> *... I am most sorry to have to state that popular feeling in Germany is just now very bitter on England. .... Lord Salisbury's government must learn to respect and treat us as equals. .... I so ardently hoped to get over for your birthday.*[107]

And he point blank refused an invitation to Cowes which had been offered as a sop. She replied in kind.

> *I doubt whether any sovereign ever wrote in such terms to another, and that sovereign his own grandmother, about their Prime Minister.*[108]

William was quite unrepentant. On the contrary he remained obdurate and if anything his nervousness increased. When the Tsar, Commander in Chief of the largest, though by no means the most efficient army in the world, proposed a disarmament conference William said it was a ludicrous suggestion. Disarmament was out of the question in the Stumm era, but at the Tsar's instigation a Court of Arbitration to settle international disputes was set up at the Hague. William grudgingly had promised his support but now he regretted it.

So that he shan't make a fool of himself before Europe [he wrote of the Tsar] *I have to agree to nonsense! But for my part I'll go on trusting and appealing to God and my sharp sword! And . . . the whole concern!*[109]

This was a private comment. He was less reticent in his opinion of the Reichstag, which was clearly going to block a bill for the protection of non-strikers which he wanted passed. Publicly, that is through his usual medium of telegraphing his old tutor *en clair* for release to the press, he announced that he was going to give Hinzpeter's native town a statue of Frederick the Great and called it:

A SYMBOL THAT IN THAT ANCESTOR AS IN MYSELF THERE RESIDES
AN INFLEXIBLE WILL WHICH WILL PROCEED IN FACE OF ALL RESISTANCE
TO THE GOAL FELT TO BE RIGHT[110]

It was a strong hint that if the deputies blocked his bill he might dissolve the Reichstag and carry on without it. There was an uproar.

Philip Eulenburg, though he was a sick man, took his master to task. On the Norwegian cruise that summer he walked ashore with William and advised him to be calmer and not to go too far. The constitution, he said, was like a masterpiece under a glass dome; break the glass and there would be trouble. He capped this with a message from the grave. On his deathbed Cardinal Hohenlohe had begged him to warn the Kaiser if ever it should be necessary that a number of highly placed persons would depose him should he behave irresponsibly and return to the idea of absolute monarchy. Eulenburg drew the sting from this startling warning by saying that he realized the Kaiser's intentions were good, and his policy was modern-minded, even progressive, but he must not be so demonstrative.[111] William replied with spirit that he claimed the right of free speech like any other German, but the hint was taken.[112] Unfortunately it threw him into a still higher state of nervous agitation and Surgeon-General Leuthold, also aboard the *Hohenzollern*, declared it was folly to continue the cruise for too long.[113] Fortuitously the Kaiserin, who was on holiday at Berchtesgaden – not then in the least the sinister name it was to become later – slipped and fractured her calf bone, and William persuaded himself his duty was at her side.[114] In the clear mountain air he was calmer. He was also restored to a better frame of mind by detecting a change in Lord Salisbury's policy. Evidently the British government had decided that something really must be done to appease the wrathful Kaiser. The Queen was persuaded to repeat her invitation for him to stay at Osborne for Cowes. Once more he refused, this time on account of Dona's accident, but he said he would like to propose himself for November at Windsor.[115] His grandmother accepted. But Willam still had a shot in his locker to show how deeply he had been hurt by the English side of his

family. Although he would not go himself, he sent his yacht *Meteor* to
Cowes where it won the Queen's Cup. After the race he sent a telegram to
his uncle the Prince of Wales in his capacity as Commodore of the Yacht
Squadron:

YOUR HANDICAPS ARE APPALLING.[116]

The English government decided that something extra was necessary.
Samoa was handed over to Germany. William called it 'the pearl in my
crown' and made Bülow a count for his part in the negotiations. Further,
with great reluctance the Prince of Wales undertook to invite his nephew to
Sandringham after the Windsor visit. These small concessions were well
worth the while. When the Boer War broke out in October that year,
though everyone in Europe seemed to support the Boers, William was on
the side of England.

4

In that summer of 1899 when he reminded the Kaiser of the fragility and
importance of the constitution Eulenburg was himself in a highly nervous
state. For many years, as the confidant of the Kaiser he had invited the
malice of ambitious men and his private life had not been discreet.[117] Bülow
owed much to him for his advancement and, Iago-like, found gratitude an
unpleasant pill to swallow. Then Holstein must have been soured by envy
of Eulenburg's power. Moreover he was critical of William's personal rule[118]
and decided he could best attack the Kaiser through his friend. The intrigue
was such that that Eulenburg was slow in realizing Bülow's hostility. In
March, 1896 he confided to him his belief that the Wilhelmstrasse's aim was
'to throttle the Kaiser'.[119] When Bülow became Foreign Secretary he found
in the secret archives a memorandum which alleged Eulenburg had been
blackmailed by the proprietor of a Viennese bathing establishment at about the
same time as Emperor Francis Joseph's youngest brother, a rakish homosexual known as 'the Archduke of the Bath' by the Viennese, had been
banished from the Empire.[120] Bülow mentioned this to Eulenburg who
promptly suffered what he himself later described as a nervous breakdown.[121] He went to Carlsbad and Gastein for the cures, but for months he
was prostrate with gout and nervous exhaustion.[122] Then, trying to keep up
appearances in Vienna, it had been observed that he was quieter, kept to his
duties, and did not enjoy social activities. Frequently he fainted.[123] Holstein
sent him badgering letters and then, suddenly, after twelve years' uninter-
rupted correspondence, he shut up like an oyster.[124] Eulenburg was terrified.
It is now clear that he was or had been a practising homosexual and that

Holstein as well as Bülow had evidence of the fact.[125] Exposure would not only ruin him socially but also, by implication, greatly harm the Kaiser. The most effective solution was to retire as quickly as possible into private life but, being unaware of the real reason for his friend's nervous state, William would not hear of it.

Somehow Eulenburg kept going. He was in a scared and despondent state when on the Norwegian cruise he conveyed the Cardinal's solemn warning from the grave, but he would have served his master better by being frank about his own disastrous affairs. As Holstein was aiming at the throne through him he certainly owed William a full explanation, but he was a proud man as well as a frightened one, and he remained silent. As it was his lack of candour landed him in an appalling position. Making one last attempt to sweeten his enemy he paid a personal visit to the Wilhelmstrasse that September. Holstein was not at home to him. Eulenburg's fright increased. He wrote in his journal: 'That was the end of the end.'[126] Then, in the next month when the Boer War broke out, the Kaiser announced his intention of making his old friend a prince. He did so after a shoot at Liebenberg and was rather put out to meet with an alarmed refusal. But Eulenburg was cornered and unable to explain why he did not wish for the honour. He had to give way. No sooner had he said goodbye to the Kaiser and the imperial train departed than he went to the station buffet and ordered a glass of cognac, something he had never done before.[127] On New Year's Day 1900 he and Count Dohna became Prussian Princes.* On January 27th he was nominated an hereditary member of the Prussian Upper House. By July such was the deterioration of his nervous system that on board the *Hohenzollern* he once more tried to resign, but William would not let him. With the lack of sympathy and understanding often characteristic of men who are seldom seriously ill themselves, he said he could not possibly do without his friend in Vienna.[128] Supposing that Holstein was sharpening his claws before making a final pounce, the new Prince miserably accepted his fate.

The Kaiser was delighted when he withdrew his request. It was another little victory. Recently he had been enjoying an unusual series of personal triumphs. He had broken the resistance of the universities to accept long overdue reforms by an imperial decree,[130] and the Reichstag had passed a second and most satisfying Naval Law so that the shipyards and factories of Stumm, Krupp and Woermann were humming.[131] And, for once, his relations with England were extremely amiable. The Duke and Duchess of York had

---

* Eulenburg wrote in his diary on that date: 'The visits of congratulation went on and on – and *nobody* could see into my heart. . . . I knew perfectly well that this 'elevation' could not fail to stir all the venomous elements into one deadly poison. . . . I could not help feeling a sort of terror.'[129]

kindly asked him to stand sponsor to their third son Harry,[132] and though
the German press was violently pro-Boer, the Kaiser was not. He had telegraphed his delighted congratulations on the relief of Kimberley,[133] his profound sympathies to the Prince of Wales who was shot at by a halfwit in
Brussels,[134]★ and, still determined to present his family in some form or
other, he had sent for his grandmama's eighty-first birthday a large clock
surrounded by photographs of himself, Dona, their six sons and one daughter.[135] Yet family concerns were still worrying William. His mother had never
recovered from her fall and the doctors had finally diagnosed cancer of the
spine. She was faced with a daunting ordeal and, as often happens on these
occasions, sympathy made her son forget their bitter quarrels of the past and
remember the better times. Frequently he went to visit her.[136] Together they
followed each British defeat and victory in South Africa with the keenest
interest; his presence reminding her of how much she felt she must forgive
but never could forget. Simultaneously he was having trouble with his eldest
son William, the Crown Prince, who had passed out as a member of the
Officer Corps and was now serving with his regiment surrounded by idle
toadies. Ironically another David and Absalom problem was building up.
When the Crown Prince came of age he found he had no more freedom than
before. His father kept a watchful eye on everything he did; therefore, to
annoy his father, the Crown Prince led a very fast life indeed. Dona, to whom
William might have looked for some comfort in these family troubles, was
appalled when he let it be known that he was planning to send her three
youngest boys to the military academy at Plön. Her maternal instincts were
strong. She longed to keep her children with her. Three had already gone,
now three more were to leave her at a very young age. She wept, sulked, and
was not at all herself.[137]

Besides these family worries the Kaiser had suffered a number of petty
vexations which, balled together, chafed seriously at his nerves. He had
ambitious plans to beautify Berlin with an Avenue of Victory and had
ordered it to be decorated by thirty-two colossal statues in white marble of
those who had ruled the Brandenburg Mark, and already the Berliners were
criticizing his gift even before the statues had been placed in position.†[138]

★ The Kaiser was particular outraged by the fact that the boy was allowed to escape
punishment by the Belgians. With characteristic vigour he wrote to the Prince of
Wales: 'Either the laws are ridiculous, or the jury are a set of d—d, bl—y scoundrels; which is
the case I am unable to decide. With best love to Aunty and Cousins.'

† They were right to be apprehensive. When, six months later, the Avenue was
officially opened, the thirty-two very ordinary but terribly obvious sculptures were
derided. One of the honoured Margraves of Brandenburg had been Otto the Idle who
never set foot in the territory and simply wanted to sell it. Another long-forgotten
Margrave had been given the face of Prince Philip Eulenburg. The Berliners promptly
called it 'Doll's Avenue'.[142]

Then his friend Archduke Francis Ferdinand who was heir to the Austro-Hungarian throne, had thrown the Emperor and everyone else into a state of great indignation by contracting a mésalliance with a mere countess. The Emperor Francis Joseph had made him swear on the Gospels in the presence of his Privy Council, the Prince-Bishop of Vienna and the Prince-Primate of Hungary that his marriage was morganatic.[139] William wondered how, as Kaiser, he ought to treat this most delicate and vexing question. Worst of all for his nervous system, the German *chargé d'affaires* had been assassinated in riots in Peking on July 5th during the Boxer Rebellion. The Chinese Emperor offered his apologies and said he would organize processions of burnt offerings to atone, but William was totally unsatisfied. He telegraphed from Brunsbuettel Koog to Queen Victoria, who had also lost a number of subjects in the same riot:

THIS MEANS SERIOUS BUSINESS. WILLIAM I.R.[140]

Count von Waldersee was given another chance. He was appointed commander of a punitive expedition and because it was composed of several nationalities he was jokingly called World Marshal.[141] As preparations for the expedition were made and the great white *Hohenzollern* cruised in Norwegian waters order after order was sent off from the signal room. Surgeon-General Leuthold watched the Kaiser's mounting excitement with a good deal of apprehension, and Prince Eulenburg tried to put his own serious troubles aside and calm his friend. By 1900 four bulky volumes of Imperial speeches had already been printed, many of them harmful to the Kaiser and to his country. Eulenburg could see that another speech was burgeoning. William refused to be calmed. He worked out what he should say to the departing expeditionary force. If he stuck to this outline all would be well, but everyone in the world knew that he was so easily carried away by his own oratory. The *Hohenzollern* made for Bremerhaven and there the astute Eulenburg arranged for officials to invite aboard all the newspapermen who had come down for the send-off. He told them the Kaiser was very much upset by the insult put upon the German nation and then dictated the text of the speech the Kaiser intended to deliver later in the day. What he called 'that horrid little gang of reporters'[143] were delighted to have the speech in shorthand – copy so early obtained was rare – and they rushed for the Berlin train. It was a clever ruse and ought to have worked, but one reporter had been missed by the officials and not invited aboard. It was from his pen that the world heard one of the Kaiser's more dramatic outbursts.*[144] Bülow, present in his capacity as Foreign Secretary, noticed a

* Eulenburg claims the credit for this attempt to baffle the press for the Kaiser's sake. Bülow in his *Memoirs* does the same for himself.[145]

box on a pole beside the quay and wondered if it could be a hoist for drying
coir ropes or hoses or perhaps some sort of naval apparatus unknown to him.
He was startled to see the Kaiser climb up into the box and use it as a pulpit.[146] The speech went well but then, as Eulenburg had feared, William was
carried away by excitement. After a reasonable beginning he exploded:

> *Live up to Prussia's traditional steadfastness! Show yourselves Christians,*
> *happily enduring in the face of the heathens. May Honour and Fame attend*
> *your colours and arms! . . . No pardon will be given, and prisoners will not*
> *be made. Anyone who falls to your hand falls to your sword. Just as the*
> *Huns and their King Etzel created for themselves a thousand years ago a*
> *name which men still respect, you should give the name of Germany such*
> *cause to be remembered in China for a thousand years that no Chinaman,*
> *whether his eyes be slit or not, will dare to look a German in the face. . . .*[147]

It was an unhappy speech. Few took exception to the Kaiser's insistence on
no quarter. It was the rule in the East and had been carried out by the British
without comment in the Indian Mutiny. But the speech gave the world the
false impression that William was no mere sabre-rattler but actually ready
to draw his sword, and the equally false belief that Germans were in some
way related to Huns.[148] It was also rather a farcical speech because, by the
time the World Marshal arrived on the scene, Peking had already fallen to
a force of Indians, Japanese, Russians, Americans and English. Waldersee
promptly entered the diplomatic area, imposing terms on the Chinese which
for months they found unacceptable while he enjoyed a liaison with the wife
of a former Chinese envoy to Berlin. Her slit eyes certainly dared to look one
German in the face.[149]

Explosions of imperial emotion were generally followed by a period of
some restraint, but there was no repose for William after the Bremerhaven
speech. Three days later the King of Italy was shot at and killed by an
Italian-American anarchist. This upset the Kaiser a great deal. Then, on the
very same day, he heard that his Uncle Alfred, the reigning Duke of Saxe-
Coburg, had died of cancer. He made all the necessary arrangements for
Prince Charles, the young Duke of Albany, to succeed to the duchy and
sincerely condoled with Queen Victoria. Then he was appalled to learn that
she herself was failing. Not only had he a sincere affection for his grandmother, but he anticipated the rule of his uncle Edward with dismay.
Another distressing event took place in late autumn. Prince Hohenlohe
finally took exception to the many inferences – by direct comment and
cartoons in the press – that he was a supernumerary. He protested, sent in his

* This is part of the version printed by the semi-official newspaper *Nordwestdeutscher*
Zeitung which differs slightly from the official *Reichsanzeiger*.

resignation, and William felt obliged to accept it.[150] At eighty-two Uncle Clovis thankfully retired from the business of trying to conciliate the executive and the legislature. In his place, as had been planned long before, Bülow took control. Eulenburg wrote to congratulate his supposed friend:

> *Your motto must be 'Pacify Germany, and never wound the Emperor'.*
> *God help you keep your balance on the tight-rope appointed for your*
> *feet.*[151]

The Kaiser, equally histrionically, said: 'Bülow be my Bismarck!'

Bülow like a number of leading German politicians had an animal sobriquet. Holstein was the Spider. Caprivi had been the Seal. Bülow appropriately was called the Eel.

The Prussian Kingdom was to celebrate its duocentenary at the beginning of 1901. Simultaneously the German Empire came closer to an alliance with England than at any other time. Baron von Eckardstein,* *chargé d'affaires* of the German Embassy, saw Mr Joseph Chamberlain at a Chatsworth party and an alliance was proposed. The details would have to be worked out later but the essential point was that England could no longer afford isolationism: she had to choose between the Triple Alliance of Germany, Austria-Hungary and Italy and the Dual Entente of France and Russia. Eckardstein and Count von Hatzfeldt-Wildenburg, who had been German Ambassador for the past sixteen years, begged Bülow not to close this open door. Holstein and the Wilhelmstrasse broadly favoured an advantageous and carefully negotiated alliance but were mistrustful of the English and determined to make as few concessions as possible. And, though well-intentioned, Eckardstein was something of a botcher and Hatzfelt-Wildenburg was ill. Most important of all, Bülow was secretly convinced that England would involve Germany in a disastrous war with Russia.[152]

Diplomacy requires time. During this time, while Eckardstein was reporting to Berlin and Berlin was cabling back instructions, Queen Victoria lay dying. The Kaiser at once left his anniversary celebrations and with the Duke of Connaught, who was England's representative in Berlin for the event, he hurried to be with her at the end. Eckardstein was waiting at the harbour. On the train to London he told his master of the English proposals. The Kaiser gave instructions that a telegram be sent to Bülow which began:

---

* His book of reminiscences *Ten Years at the Court of St. James* explains much of the personal antipathy between the Kaiser and his uncle. He was jovial and a hearty eater and much liked in England, and at one Saturday to Monday in the country he caused a flurry of concern because an illicit assignation had been arranged, the lady leaving her bedside plate of sandwiches outside her door as a signal, and the Baron, happening to pass, saw the sandwiches and gobbled them up.[153]

SO 'THEY COME' IT SEEMS JUST AS WE EXPECTED THIS IS WHAT WE HAVE
WAITED FOR –

The Chancellor smiled benignly on the idea and sabotaged it throughout the
negotiations.[154]

William was received at Victoria by the Prince of Wales in Prussian
uniform and together they travelled to Osborne on the Isle of Wight.
There his 'unparalleled Grandmama' died in his arms. With the late Queen's
Resident Medical Attendant, he measured her for her coffin. With the
Duke of Connaught he lifted her frail and tiny body into the inner shell.[155]
He surprised everyone by his tenderness, his obvious sorrow, but he
annoyed the Germans, above all Dona, who disliked being left at home,
and Bülow, who was appalled at the thought of his master's limitless opportunities for committing Germany to a policy he detested. Certainly the
Kaiser added many energetic pleas to those of Eckardstein that Bülow seize
the opportunity of an alliance,* but he thought it out of place to discuss
affairs with the English Ministers until his grandmother was buried. Much
of his time he spent with his English relations and criticizing the Crown
Prince who had hurried over after him. Whatever his private feelings, the
new King Edward VII showed gratitude for his nephew's attentions. He was
also glad to note that he seemed to be on much better terms with his mother,
showing genuine distress at the pain she was enduring and which she bore so
courageously, describing her as 'wrapped in an aura of poetry'.[156] He made
the Kaiser a British Field Marshal, Prince Harry a Vice-Admiral of the Royal
Navy, and gave the Order of the Garter to the Crown Prince.[157] William
behaved impeccably at the funeral and impressed the English crowds a great
deal.† He in turn showed only too clearly how much he felt the loss of his
grandmother. Scarcely anyone could believe that the Victorian era was over.
All over the world people who had never known her wondered how affairs
could be managed without the Queen of England. The future seemed
uncertain, full of menace. To William, who had loved and admired her just
as he had his grandfather William I, her death meant far more. It was as
though a prop had been cut from beneath him. Flying in the face of public
opinion at home in Germany he honoured the general whom his grandmother had loved to honour. He conferred the Order of the Black Eagle on

* Strangely, Edward as Prince of Wales had been at the same Chatsworth Saturday
to Monday as Chamberlain and Eckardstein; but so far was he kept from affairs, even
at this stage, that he knew nothing of the possibility of an Anglo-German alliance until
after his mother's death.

† Not all sovereigns were as well behaved. Characteristically the spade-bearded
King of the Belgians caused grave scandal.[158] Frightened of not being accorded proper
precedence, Prince Ferdinand of Bulgaria did not attend and spent the day enjoying a
military review and a gala luncheon.[159]

Field Marshal Lord Roberts.[160] And at a special dinner given in his honour by Edward VII at Marlborough House he did his best to cement the two countries by emphasizing how much they had in common and stating his belief that soon England and Germany would get to know one another better and between them keep the peace of the world. He concluded:

> *We ought to form an Anglo-German alliance, you to keep the seas while we would be responsible for the land; with such an alliance, not a mouse could stir in Europe without our permission, and the nations would, in time, come to see the necessity of reducing their armaments.*[161]

It might have been his father speaking. It might even have been the Prince Consort.

CHAPTER ELEVEN

Gallo-Russian Pincers

*'If people in Germany would only sit still, the time would
come when we could all have oysters and champagne for dinner.'*

COUNT PAUL VON HATZFELDT-WILDENBURG
German Ambassador in London, 1885–1901

I

When, by tradition, Edward VII announced his accession to his fellow-
sovereigns in Europe, he chose his friend the Duke of Abercorn to go to
the Courts of Germany and Saxony, Russia, Denmark, Sweden and Norway.
The Kaiser treated the Duke and all his suite with particular kindness.[1] He
also went out of his way to welcome his uncle when he paid a private visit
to the Empress Frederick at Friedrichshof, and bore patiently with King
Edward's unusual lack of tact in including amongst his small suite Sir Francis
Laking, his personal physician. The Empress Frederick's medical attendants
were no more pleased to see an English colleague than their predecessors had
been at William's birth and during the illness of his father. We know now
that Laking had with him large doses of morphia because it was the German
medical practice to be chary in the use of drugs and King Edward could not
tolerate the thought of his sister being in pain.[2] It is also known that the
Empress Frederick made special use of the King's visit. She sent for his
Assistant Private Secretary, Major Ponsonby, who happened to be her godson, and begged him to take her private papers to England. He agreed,
expecting a smallish parcel, but recorded that, to his astonishment, two large
trunks, covered in black oilcloth and corded, were delivered to his room by
stableboys in the early hours of the morning. As a member of the King's
party his luggage was naturally not subject to any sort of scrutiny and the
trunks reached England safely.[3]

By her action the Empress Frederick showed she still had a poor opinion
of William's judgement which was not entirely merited. At his father's death

he had behaved brashly under the influence of Bismarck but not irrationally. It is unlikely that any sovereign when ascending the throne would wish private accounts of controversial family and national affairs to be published for all the world to read. Since then he had mellowed, even if he had not quietened down, and for his part he felt on closer terms with his mother than at any time since they had painted side by side in her studio in the Crown Princess' Palace. But the Empress Frederick was evidently determined that one day her grievances should be aired, her humiliations exposed, and her views made known through publication.

On August 5th, 1901 her tragic life came to an end, and at once the most extraordinary stories began to circulate. It was said that *die Engländerin* had wished to be buried naked wrapped in a Union Jack, and her coffin – an English one – secretly shipped to England for burial at Windsor by an Anglican bishop. A variant rumour said that an Anglican bishop was to be insinuated into the clergy at the funeral.[4] There were rumours in the other direction: that Friedrichshof was surrounded by soldiers as the New Palace had been on the death of her husband and the house ransacked for papers. Some soldiers did arrive, but they were only twelve N.C.Os of the Empress Frederick's own regiment, the Royal Prussian Fusiliers, who were to act as bearers.[5] The facts were much less extraordinary than the rumours. As might have been expected, her affairs were in perfect order. If she was not mourned by many, the depth and intensity of the mourning of the few showed how much she had been loved. On hearing of his sister's death King Edward at once left England with Queen Alexandra. She had with her a wreath of flowers gathered at the Empress Frederick's favourite home, Windsor;[6] he carried a confidential memorandum to be used if, as might happen, the Kaiser brought up the subject of a rapprochement.[7] William went to Frankfurt to meet his royal guests and travelled with them to Homburg. The first part of the funeral took place there, then the mourners accompanied the coffin to Potsdam where the Empress was laid with her husband and her two sons Sigismund and Waldemar in their mausoleum. King Edward was deeply affected, no less emotional than his nephew, and, rather than discuss politics at such a time, he thrust his Foreign Secretary's memorandum into William's hands. The notes were passed on.[8]

The memorandum was of no practical use to Bülow and Holstein, but the English Foreign Secretary was exceedingly angry with his master and King Edward was exceedingly embarrassed. This did not help towards friendlier feelings between the two countries and William's declared intention of fostering some sort of rapprochement was made that much more difficult. It is strange that his policy should have been so unpopular at such a time. Germany appeared to be a progressive country. In manufactures and general economy she was burgeoning. For fifty years she had been the world centre of organized Socialism, and intellectually and culturally she was in the front rank.[9] The capital cradled the formulation of the Quantum Theory and the General Theory of Relativity, and great advances were being made in theoretical physics.[10] Reinhardt was then turning the Berlin theatre upside down,[11] and art nouveau (Jugendstil) was flourishing under Henry van de Velde and Muthesius.[12] A-religious and claiming to be enlightened, the Berliners were also profoundly cynical; for instance, it was said that a famous sculpted lion at the end of the Unter den Linden would roar in the remote possibility of a virgin passing by it.[13] Yet all this inventiveness and revolutionary, social and artistic adjustment and the general ambiency of modern progress seemed to have small effect upon the masses, and only a little upon the intelligentsia. The average German intellectual was chauvinistic and astonishingly complacent. The University of Berlin and other seats of learning were largely staffed by men who felt most comfortable under Junkerbourgeois rule and the umbrella of militarism.[14] It followed that, in wanting to initiate a rapprochement with England and thereby reverse former policies, the Kaiser found himself virtually alone. The executive led by Bülow was against him, as was the vast majority in the Reichstag. Only Eckardstein and Hatsfeldt supported him and they were ignored as having been seduced by their long stay in England.[15] An innate Prussian conversative chauvinism, a national complacency, above all, the great power without responsibility of the German and English press which thundered at each other for years, were utterly opposed to William's plan. Nevertheless he persisted, partly because he had an obstinate streak and partly because he probably enjoyed testing the exact practical measure of his theoretical prerogatives, but chiefly because two months after his mother's death he met at Prince Eulenburg's a man who gave him what was tantamount to a mission.

Houston Stewart Chamberlain shared many of the prejudices of the Kuklux-klan. He could not abide Jews or Roman Catholics, worshipped purity of blood, organization, and what he called 'moral world order'.[16] It is not surprising to learn that he was the son-in-law of the anti-Semite Wagner, nor that his exposition of 'Germandom' *The Foundations of the Nineteenth Century* should have been one of Hitler's favourite books. Born an Englishman, Chamberlain had all the bitterness of a renegade, gloried in everything Teutonic, believed that the future progress of mankind depended on the power of Germany and declared: 'God relies only upon the Germans'.[17]

Prince Eulenburg evidently shared the anti-Semitic prejudice of the Prussian Junkers and no doubt it had been increased by living amongst the even more prejudiced Viennese. He certainly wrote a number of extremely unpleasant anti-Jewish letters to the Kaiser;[18] yet, like him, he had Jewish friends, chief of them Baron Nathaniel Rothschild, head of the Austrian branch of that house, and he made the cynical remark that it was important 'to distinguish between Jews – and Jews'.[19] For all his influence, Eulenburg never succeeded in making the Kaiser anti-Semitic. Nor did Chamberlain. William was adept at picking what he wanted from people's talk and ignoring the rest. Chamberlain's discourse on 'The Mission of Germandom' intrigued him greatly; so did his view that, in a difficult world situation, the House of Hohenzollern was the only trump card held by Germany[20] – a doctrine later suppressed by Hitler. In moments of irritation William execrated the Jews – just as he did the Poles in East Prussia and the French in Alsace and Lorraine, but he never could have been a consistent racialist. And he reckoned religious bigotry was a threat to public order. Nevertheless he happily accepted the sacred trust emphasized by Chamberlain as *le pivot central* of Germany's world policy.

The Kaiser's decision caused consternation at the Foreign Office and the Chancellery, particularly as he continued to conceive it his duty to work for a German-English alliance. Between them Bülow and the Foreign Office killed any possibility of a formal treaty by the simple expedient of asking for far too much. England could not possibly accept the terms and, within twelve months of Chamberlain's opening move, Bülow gave the plan the *coup de grâce*. Some time before Chamberlain had defended the British army against charges of wanton cruelty in the Boer War by saying that the British had never gone so far as soldiers of other nations in Poland, the Caucasus, Algeria, Tonkin, Russia, and in the Franco-Prussian War. Bülow dug up this rotting bone and on January 8th 1902 he gnawed on it in the Reichstag. He accused Chamberlain of having 'a warped mind' and quoted Frederick the Great: 'He is biting on granite'.[22] There was swift repercussion. Chamberlain and King Edward both saw the saddened Eckardstein. They made it clear that an alliance between England and Germany was out of the question. 'It can't be done,' said the King very definitely.[23] At about that time England concluded a treaty with Japan.[24]

William obstinately refused to give up. He did not like his uncle and his uncle did not like him. Nevertheless he still considered it important that at least Germany should have the goodwill of England if it could be obtained. Accordingly, when the Boers surrendered in May, 1902, William's new Ambassador, Count Metternich, was instructed to offer congratulations to the King.[25] A month later the three leading Boer generals arrived in Europe to ask for donations to a relief fund. They saw King Edward, were received well in Holland, less well in France, and ended up in Berlin hoping to be received by the Kaiser. When William learnt that his uncle hoped this would not happen he refused the generals an audience although Richthofen, his new Foreign Secretary, strongly disapproved.[26] After that he warmly welcomed Lord Roberts and the Secretary of State for War to the German manoeuvres, being 'profuse in compliments and hospitality'.[27] Finally he accepted an invitation to go to Sandringham to shoot and celebrate the King's sixty-first birthday on November 9th, 1902, and inspect his own regiment, the Royal Dragoons, on the way.[28]

The Wilhelmstrasse viewed the Kaiser's diplomacy with mixed feelings. There was concern there that Germany's world policy would fail if England, the greatest Power in the world, was made too much of. Richthofen and Bülow were particularly worried because that summer Eulenburg's resignation was at last accepted. William still tried to resist the inevitable but the pleading of Princess Eulenburg and a battery of physicians persuaded him that his old friend had to retire. A fiction was maintained that he was still in the Kaiser's services by keeping the Prince *en disposition* and liable to recall for consultation.[29] But clearly he seldom would be, and he and the Kaiser had fallen out of the habit of writing to one another.[30] William, fortified by his sense of mission, believed that he could manage on his own without the steadying hand of his friend. Officials at the Foreign Office and the Chancellery had their doubts.

The visit to England was not a great success although King Edward went out of his way to make it one. The shooting was excellently managed. Jan Kubelik, the violinist, Albert Chevalier, an illusionist, and Sir Henry Irving were invited to entertain the Kaiser. But William was never happy in his uncle's presence. He was by far the abler of the two yet he had a less integrated personality. King Edward's suavity and air of sophistication unsettled him and made him prickly and seem unappreciative of all that had been specially prepared for him. Moreover his own contribution to the visit, a lecture on the virtues of potato spirit as opposed to petrol as a fuel for motor cars, jarred on his uncle's nerves. When William left to go north to stay with the Lonsdales at Lowther Castle the King was heard to remark 'Thank God he's gone'.[31] No doubt his nephew had an equal feeling of relief. At Lowther there was momentary panic when the special imperial train arrived early. An agitated station master telephoned the Castle to ask for instructions. 'Shunt him!' said Lord Lonsdale immediately.[32] After another brief visit to a former Liberal Prime Minister, the Kaiser embarked on the *Hohenzollern* at Queensferry and went home.

William returned to find Germany deep in a scandal. His friend, the industrialist Alfred von Krupp, immensely rich and generous, whom he had personally visited at Essen and at his villa on Capri, had been pilloried by *Der Vorwärts* the newspaper of the Social Democrats. An article called 'Krupp on Capri' had described an investigation by the Italian police into the 'nest' where Krupp and German friends were alleged to have debauched young boys, as a result of which King Victor Emmanuel's government had decreed he must never return to Italy. On seeing the *Vorwärts* article, Krupp telegraphed Bülow who agreed to confiscate all copies of the paper and institute proceedings against the editor for criminal libel. Copies of the issue which had printed the story became collector's pieces. Through the Imperial Chamberlain Krupp appealed to the Kaiser to ask for an explanation from the Italian government. This was on the 21st November. By six o'clock in the morning of the 22nd, Krupp was dead. It was given out that he had had a stroke but the death certificate was full of contradictions.[33] It is doubtful that the editor of *Der Vorwärts* could have used an Italian police report in a German court even if he had been able to get hold of a copy; doubtful too, if, as a leading Socialist, he would have prised anything from the files of Hans von Tresckow, Commissioner of Police in Berlin. It was widely believed, and is so still, that Krupp had not confined his orgies to foreign soil but had imported a quantity of young Italian waiters to the Hotel Bristol in Berlin, and that, suddenly realizing his case was hopeless, he had committed suicide. Possibly it is significant that his widow had the prosecution for criminal libel withdrawn on the grounds that Krupp was no longer in a position to defend his honour.[34] Nevertheless, the Kaiser, either quite genuinely or because he believed some truths were better suppressed for the good of Germany, refused to credit the story. He personally attended the funeral and emphasized that he had been Krupp's friend. His influence did much to keep the Krupp industrial empire intact. Nothing however could stop rumours swelling – that Krupp had, in fact, slipped quietly away from Germany* – though when a Social Democrat deputy attempted to bring the matter up in the Reichstag two months later he was not permitted a hearing.[35]

Incredibly, as it appeared to William, his uncle had initiated much friendlier relations with England's historic enemy, the Republic of France. And it had been a personal triumph for the King, not a diplomatic move on the part of his ministers. King Edward had arrived on a visit to Paris to be greeted by cries of *'Vivent les Boers'* and, after spreading his suave charm for four days, he left to cries of *'Vive notre Edouard'*, *'Vive le Roi!'*[36] And this was scarcely two months after *l'Assiette au Beurre* had published a vitriolic anti-English cartoon of a woman lifting her shift to reveal a naked and hirsute fundament which closely resembled the features of His Britannic Majesty.[37]

William saw his own chance. Japan was England's ally, France was Russia's – and if England came to an agreement with France she might well

---

* For four years there were newspaper reports of him being seen in the United States, the Far East, South America and Jerusalem.

be putting her head into a noose because Russia and Japan both had large and colliding interests in the Far East and it could only be a question of time before they went to war. If France then joined Russia, Britain would have to side with Japan and thus be cut off from the Dual Entente for ever. The Crown Prince had been sent to Russia that winter to strengthen family ties with the Tsar and Tsaritsa and had been very well received. Now, to underline the cordiality which he believed ought to exist between their countries, he sent his cousin Nicholas II an allegorical painting which he had designed though not executed, and which showed him standing in shining armour and holding a large Crucifix, while the Tsar lay comfortably reclining in a Byzantine robe looking up at him. In a seascape background cruised Russian and German battleships. It was a tribute, said William, from 'the Admiral of the Atlantic to the Admiral of the Pacific', honorary titles he claimed for each without reference to any other nation.[38] Simultaneously he decided to fasten Germany to the United States before England moved in that direction. He had the advantage in that on the whole German expatriates in America cared more for their country of origin than did the English, Irish, Welsh and Scotch. It also happened that the assassination of President McKinley in 1901 by an anarchist in the Temple of Music at Buffalo had brought a president into office who was extraordinarily like the Kaiser. Theodore Roosevelt was three months older than William. Both 'killed mosquitoes as though they were lions'. Both 'wanted to put an end to all evil in the world between sunrise and sunset'. Both were histrionic, conspicuous, conversationally brilliant, and had electric personalities. Both were fidgets and indiscreet and hearty.[39] Weirdly, both shared many opinions. Each was progressive and socially conscious, but an absolute realist. Roosevelt the social reformer said the only way to check the anarchical spirit of the proletariat was to shoot ten or a dozen of their leaders.[40] William II, the social reformer, had no patience with strikers who were inconveniencing a majority of the public. Once troops were called out to deal with a tramway strike and he telegraphed his hopes that five hundred would be 'snuffed out' before the soldiers returned to barracks.[41] William seized the opportunity to become better acquainted with the man who was so like him and entered on a lengthy correspondence.* He also went out of his way to be friendly to Americans who visited his country. Very often he conducted them personally round the New Palace, fixing their attention by mentioning an object's worth in money or its fascinating historical associations. Unlike many of his subjects he found

---

* Baroness Spitzemberg, a highly intelligent, well-informed diarist of the day, who had no liking for the Kaiser, declared that he wrote to Roosevelt in the manner of 'an infatuated fifth-former to a housemaid'. It is legitimate to wonder how she got a sight of the imperial letters.[42]

Americans amusing and appreciative of his courtesies, but their habit of wanting to buy everything was hard to bear. He was made offers for any part of his uniform or a feather from the Kaiserin's hat to take home as souvenirs and one exceedingly rich man asked what price he would take for the Brandenburg Tor, which he proposed to shift piece by piece to the Middle West. He permitted Americans familiarities which he would have allowed no-one else – to clap him on the shoulder for example, as Mr Armour of Chicago did, or to be called 'a good fellow' by a Vanderbilt in open company.[43] One of the Vanderbilts was less well received when he called without an appointment at the New Palace and was marched back to his carriage at rifle point by a zealous sentry who connected the word 'American' with 'republican'.[44] Two months after King Edward's success in Paris, the Kaiser made a very favourable impression on influential Americans at Kiel Week; amongst them the Goelets who arrived on *Nahma* and the Cornelius Vanderbilts on *North Star*.[45] Two years later he was still making himself agreeable – and defying Court protocol in doing so – by gallantly offering his arm at the Opera to a colourful citizen of the United States, Dr Claribel Cone, one of the two Cone sisters of Baltimore, who had collected no less than forty-three Matisses and, though she carried a briefcase even at the opera, was described as 'duchess-like' with an arched, pointed nose, Hindu skewers in her hair arrangement, Renaissance jewelry, and shawls from Africa, India, Italy and Spain around her shoulders.[46] The Americans in return appreciated the Kaiser's friendliness. He was one of the least stuffy of monarchs.

2

William's personal diplomacy as *le pivot central* was not approved of by the trained diplomat who was now his Chancellor, but Bülow, with the highly-skilled assistance of Baron von Holstein, had small difficulty in undoing things done by their master which were not in line with Wilhelmstrasse policy.

Bernard von Bülow deserved his nickname. He was indeed as slippery as an eel. The fourth Imperial Chancellor, he was also the youngest. Certainly he was the most charming, a wit who could and did delight his master with endless anecdotes, introduce him to amusing people in his own home – for the Kaiser, unlike most monarchs, was happy to drop in on those whom he considered his friends and literally take pot-luck.[47] Bülow also gave the illusion of being extraordinarily talented. To his gift for foreign languages was added a knack of finding the right thing to say to the right person. Momentarily he stored useful facts and figures in his mind and used them to such good effect that he gave the impression of being encyclopaedic,[48] but his reputation as an impressive speaker and the originator of such memorable phrases as 'a place in the sun' was actually owing to the deftness and the hard work of his clerks in the Chancellery. They provided him with a portfolio of neat turns of phrase, suitable for a variety of situations which he used to enrich his oratory and earn the title of Bülow the silver-tongued.[49] He could not, of course, deny his Prussian Junker background which automatically put him to the right in politics but he was so very acute at being all things to all men that although by no means were they always prepared to support him, six out of the seven political blocs in the Reichstag* mostly thought of him as 'dear Bernard'. To the Social Democrats he was of course an implacable enemy. He considered himself a second Bismarck,[50] but Bismarck had been a great statesman and Bülow was simply a highly skilled politician with just that touch of the mountebank which a successful politician always has. The most damaging thing about him so far as Kaiser and country were concerned was his purposelessness. World Policy sounded all very well as a slogan but the Chancellor had no positive plan as to how it should be carried out. Holstein, for all his other faults, had an unrivalled knowledge of the workings of diplomacy and could be relied on to manage the Secretary of State and the Ambassadors, yet Germany's aim to continue Bismarck's non-aggressive strategy in a patently deteriorating international situation was myopic to say the least. It really was a non-policy. Bülow considered idea after idea, emphasized some, dropped others, accepted fresh suggestions then abandoned them, and never managed to produce any coherent and continuous policy all the time he was in power.[51] His whole chancellorship rather resembled a duff, liberally sprinkled with currants of good schemes, but uncooked and therefore of no use at all.

'Dear Bernard' went to some trouble to demonstrate that he had the Kaiser's full confidence. At Chancellery receptions guests would see on a little table beside the entrance a large number of picture postcards, or views as they were then called. All were from the Kaiser sending greetings from his gadabouts. It is alleged that two detectives guarded this table of imperial views from the depredations of souvenir-hunters.[52] In fact, of course, for a very long time the Chancellor really did enjoy his master's favour. Being younger than his predecessors and apparently more patient and anxious to carry out orders, Bülow appealed to the Kaiser. William was actually the cleverer of the two; that is, he had outgrown his callow limitations and now could seize on the bones of a subject with amazing rapidity and digest the salient points of a long and complicated report or interview. He was excellent

* These were the Centre Party; the Social Democrats; the Conservatives and Free Conservatives; the National Liberals; the Progressives; the Poles, Danes, Alsace-Lorrainers and Hanoverians; and the Anti-Semites.

at summing up.[53] But this perception was perhaps too quick, so rapid that he naturally preferred superficiality to profundity, and this made it easy for Bülow to take him in.[54] The Chancellor's superficial intellectualism dazzled him. He actually believed Bülow was his intellectual superior and his political mentor, and on him he showered every honour it was within his power to bestow. They walked together each morning when the Kaiser was in Berlin, enjoying frank conversations. This was how William described them in his political memoirs. He recorded advising the Chancellor that *'finesseing'*, at which Bülow was a master, was all very well with Slavs and Latins, but it did not suit the English.[55] He also warned him against Holstein when he suddenly made the painful discovery that if affairs went well Holstein took the credit for the Foreign Office but mistakes and disasters were blamed on 'the young master'.* Holstein further offended by being furtive and secret. William declared that his memoranda, though unquestionably ingenious and attractive, were generally as ambiguous as utterances from the Delphic oracle.[56] Bülow accepted the advice but eventually the Kaiser noticed that he did not work on it. He *'finessed'* with the English and – *'In spite of my warning . . . Bülow worked a great deal, or was obliged to work, with Holstein'.*[57] This was written in the early 'twenties with the advantage of hindsight. By then William must have heard the rumours that Holstein had something about Bülow in the 'Poison Cupboard' either because of homosexual activities or, more likely, because Bülow's wife before their marriage had behaved indiscreetly and compromising letters had found their way into Holstein's hands.[58] If these rumours were unfounded – and there is no mention of them in the Holstein Papers – the most obvious reason for Bülow co-operating with Holstein was simply that he depended upon his skill and knowledge as a diplomat. In the early 1900s, however, the Kaiser would not have been aware that Bülow did not take his advice. Saying yes to his master and doing what he himself wanted was a characteristic of this Chancellor who in duplicity, undependability and faithlessness had scarcely a rival in the Empire. To begin with William was happy to leave him at the helm and accept his flattering attentions. He failed to observe that his own suggestions were charmingly turned down or altered so that they bore little relation to what he had actually said. He then believed things could safely be left to 'Dear Bernard' and he himself was therefore free for more gadabouts; but, in time, his mind changed He became less confiding and more critical. When it was too late he realized what an exceedingly devious Chancellor he had.

At this period however the Kaiser was far more concerned about his eldest

---

* In *My Memories* the ex-Kaiser did not say how he had come by this information, but it would not be too fanciful to suggest that his source was Prince Eulenburg.

son. Dona's anxieties many years before that her eight-year old boy was showing too precocious an interest in the ladies had been quite justified. As a willowy roué with the profile of Frederick the Great he misbehaved himself with monotonous regularity. His first love was for horses, his second for women, and in his lifetime he had a long string of each.[59] His mother shared his passion for horses, but she was far too pious to condone fornication, let alone adultery. His father ought perhaps to have been more tolerant of the situation in which the Crown Prince found himself; young, flattered, rich, with every opportunity to get into mischief while he waited for the throne; but William himself had hardly had to wait at all for his throne and he was angry at his son's lack of moral fibre. He was to live long enough to see the Crown Prince's reputation as a compulsive womanizer play a political rôle in German history, for it weakened the royalist party's cause at a time when there was a real possibility of a return to monarchy.[60] To him the young man was decadent, and for this in large measure he blamed the example of the Crown Prince's godfather Edward VII who, as another waiter in the wings, had filled his time with high living. It was in England that the Crown Prince first kicked over the traces in some style. He went there privately to visit London and Liverpool and a number of country houses. Amongst the last was Blenheim, where he fell in love with an eighteen-year-old American girl called Gladys Deacon. On his way home he wished to visit Paris and asked his father's permission, but William refused. A tour of Holland was proposed instead, presumably in the naif supposition that the young Prince was less likely to misbehave in the flat Netherlands than in the heady atmosphere of France. A few weeks after his return a flood of newspaper criticism throughout Europe exposed the Crown Prince's escapades. *Le Matin* mentioned his penchant for Gladys Deacon. The *Daily Telegraph* said he had given her a valuable ring, a Confirmation present from Queen Victoria.[61] The Kaiser was exceedingly angry; so much so that the Crown Prince was not allowed to represent Germany at King Edward's postponed coronation. William's brother Prince Harry went instead and was pushed into the background because he was not the eldest son of a sovereign, which the German press considered an insult. An unrepentant Crown Prince continued his life of pleasure. He achieved no distinction as a student and seldom acted officially for his father. In 1903 he took up with the American prima donna, Geraldine Farrar, left Bonn, and there was talk of his going round the world with his brother Prince Eitel-Frederick. This was squashed by the Kaiserin, who did not often put her foot down but, in this instance, was quite determined that her sons should not be subjected to mortal sin all round the globe. The tour was restricted to the Near East. They were the honoured guests of Abdul the Damned who, after a violin recital by the Crown Prince, awarded him the

Golden Medal of Turkey for Art and Science; then they were made much of by their aunt Sophie in Athens, met their great-uncle King Edward in Naples, and went on to Rome to be with their parents during a State Visit to Italy and to the Vatican.[63] Their mother was happy to see them safe and well though, as a strict Evangelical, she was not at all happy to visit the Supreme Pontiff Leo XIII. She showed this by refusing to wear the mantilla protocol demanded and wore one of her vast picture hats instead; and she was not exactly cordial to the old gentleman with snuff stains down the front of his white soutane woven from the wool of unborn lambs.[64] Nevertheless William made up for her lack of enthusiasm, and the Pope, conscious of how much the Kaiser had done for his many Roman Catholic subjects, hailed him as 'the spiritual heir of Charlemagne'.[65]

Having behaved themselves with decorum in the Eternal City, the two young princes returned to Germany, both to lead idle lives in the Officer Corps. Neither had the vitality of their father. Their brother, Prince Ethelbert had chosen the Navy, but they were followed into the Army by Princes August-William, Oscar and Joachim. It was the Prussian way of life.

3

Kaiser William was now in the prime of life and it is interesting to study his portrait as it was painted by his contemporaries, preferably those who were most objective.

Princess Alice, Countess of Athlone, was often at the German Court while her brother the Duke of Albany and Coburg was learning to be a German officer at the Lichterfelde Military Cadet School. In her memoirs she has painted in some parts of the picture. Frankly she thought her first cousin William temperamentally unstable, 'a strange man who always blew hot and cold', though if he had been rash he at once regretted it and would try to make up for any harm he had done.[66] She also thought him – in the words of that era – 'shy-making' and considered that he enjoyed being formidable; though she saw through his sabre-rattling.[67] She agrees with the majority of historians of the period that in 1914 the Kaiser was used by those who were bent on war and that he was not a man of violence. She wrote: 'William was the last person to want war'.[68] Finally she called him naturally kind and generous and a prince of considerable moral courage.

Equally discerning brush strokes were painted in by someone who had an observing eye and a long acquaintanceship with the Kaiser. In August 1902 an English lady, Miss Anne Topham, arrived at Wilhelmshöhe to take up her post as English preceptress to the Kaiser's only daughter, Princess Victoria Louise.[69] In her book *Memoirs of the Kaiser's Court* Miss Topham described the Imperial Family and their favourite homes in a series of charming vignettes, and from it she herself emerges as an eminently sensible, fair-minded and fun-loving Englishwoman who enjoyed her work. She had no cause or wish to toady to her imperial employers in her book, nor did she include Court gossip which, if she had been disposed, no doubt she could have done. The result is that her pictures have a flavour of authenticity lacking in many of the other memoirs of the period, and it is of particular interest to note her candid views of the Kaiser as she came to know him better. Her book was written during the long hot summer directly before the First World War and published three weeks after it had broken out and she refrained from commenting on the situation which had developed. She mentioned that one of the first discoveries she had made on arriving in Germany was that no nation was more patriotic and that this emotion centred almost entirely on the Kaiser.[70] She noted that like his daughter he had his share of what Carlyle called 'Hohenzollern choler', and that occasionally he would fall into Napoleonic attitudes.[71] When he became fond of lawn-tennis (played in Germany on composition courts) and sent down to the neighbouring barracks for players or asked his sons for a game, no-one really enjoyed it. The young officers and the princes were extremely conscious that the figure on the other side of the net wearing a loose flapping shirt, a tie and a panama, was the Kaiser, and he could never be certain if they were really giving him a game or allowing him to win or making sure that he lost. Yet still he persevered. Evidently Miss Topham found him not in the least like the figure of fun or dangerous lunatic excoriated by certain sections of the press in her native land. He could astonish, but then royalty suffers from few inhibitions and can be splendidly eccentric. For example, the English royal family, with few exceptions taken as a model of domestic normality, has managed to astound. Even William's grandfather the Prince Consort wandered round Windsor during a typhoid epidemic in 1858 urging everyone to keep calm by employing the unusual English idiom: 'Keep your pecker up! Keep your pecker up!'[72] His grandmother, Queen Victoria, dumbfounded the Eton boys who had come to serenade her on Mafeking night when, towards the end of the concert, an Indian servant appeared at her elbow and handed her a large whisky.[73] William's uncle Edward VII weighed and measured all his visitors to Sandringham and kept records, and he was the terror of the Brighton road, imploring his chauffeur to drive faster as they roared south, shaking his fist at other motorists.[74] And the Kaiser's cousin King George V died, not with that well-phrased last sentence 'And how are things in the Empire?' on his lips, but, disgusted by a suggestion from one of his attendants that he would soon be well enough to recuperate again at Bognor Regis, with a quiet grumble: 'Bugger Bognor!'[75] William, with typical Prussian thoroughness, was the biggest astounder of them all. On a visit to Italy he surrounded himself with tall aides which rather emphasized the minuteness of the new King of Italy.*[76] He was equally tactless at a colonial expedition on being shown a reconstructed chief's hut decorated with shrunken heads and declared he would like to do the same to all members of the Reichstag.[78] He donned a surplice, whitened his face and preached hour-long sermons to a captive congregation aboard the *Hohenzollern*;[79] and had his guests on the deck at an early hour for a round of physical jerks.[80] On a number of occasions he replaced the bandmaster of the band of the Potsdam Guards and conducted himself. Contrary to those of his Ministers who nervously wondered what and when a fresh imperial jack would pop out of the box, Miss Topham much approved of this independent line.

> *One of the great charms of His Majesty that he has no stereotyped line of conduct – if he doesn't feel like walking around and making himself agreeable he doesn't do it.*[81]

She admired his enormously wide range of interests for he followed his mother and his grandfather the Prince Consort in having an insatiable appetite for information[82] and was on terms of friendly intimacy with painters, architects, sculptors and writers, scientists, theologians, philosophers, archaeologists and classical scholars. She also approved of his liking for fresh air. Every afternoon, when the Kaiser was at home, he walked with the Kaiserin,[83] and he still shot, rode, drove, hunted, boated, skated and tobogganed with extraordinary energy. The main meal of the day at Court was luncheon and therefore attended by much ceremonial and had to be indoors. But, if the weather permitted, the Kaiser breakfasted, had tea and supper *al fresco*. Picnics were a family passion and they varied from the simplest, when the children and their parents took a turn at cooking, to sumptuous banquets when cooks and footmen were sent ahead in waggons to a favoured picnic place and the imperial party followed at leisure in carriages.[84] Supper parties would go from Potsdam by river steamer to one or other of the islands where plagues of mosquitoes and midges were partially kept off by burning braziers of charcoal scattered with juniper berries.[85] If the weather was bad, and the Kaiser, like many sensitive men, detested cold, damp and rain, he would work off his bad humour with a fast game of tennis in a covered court or ride with his suite round and round the covered royal riding-school to military music or selections from the latest operettas.[86] Miss Topham soon discovered what a difference it made if the Kaiser was at home. If he was at

---

* In this he was like the father of Frederick the Great who bought, kidnapped and bribed giants of close to seven feet high into his famous Potsdam Grenadiers, and even tried to breed them by obliging giants to marry giantesses.[77]

a meal it passed pleasantly and quickly because he was an excellent raconteur, and he gave vitality to some ceremonies which could have been supremely boring to sophisticated courtiers. The Halloren presentation on New Year's Day when, by ancient right, a guild of Saxon salt-workers presented him with hard-boiled eggs and a special sausage, he infused with an infectious enthusiasm.[87] Likewise the garrison *Schrippenfest* on Whit Monday, and egg-hunts at the Bellevue Palace at Easter, when he personally hid chocolate eggs and large cardboard eggs containing toys, postcards, and fal-lals, and specially invited children searched all over the palace and through the sooty bushes in the grounds to find them.[88] But Miss Topham permitted herself at least a sigh because when the Kaiser was at home the pace of life trebled and everyone had to be ready to go anywhere at any time in the appropriate dress, and this was somewhat enervating. One lady-in-waiting complained: 'We are like Israelites at the Passover, we must always have our loins girt, or shoes on our feet – shoes suitable for any and every occasion, fit for walking palace floors or down muddy roads – our staff in our hand'.[89] And Miss Topham allowed herself some other small grumbles. Presumably herself a feminist, she disapproved of the fact that, like most men and women of his generation, the Kaiser had not the slightest interest in the suffragette movement, and it appalled her that he actually chose the Kaiserin's picture hats.[*90] She also found his dread of infection inconvenient because, at the discovery of measles or mumps in the palace, he would at once move elsewhere and at half an hour's notice everyone had to follow. On one occasion the Court were settling into the Bellevue Palace for the winter instead of the Old Palace in Berlin – a change of plan welcomed by everyone – when Prince Oscar, who had just returned from Italy, went down with chickenpox. All the repacking and moving to another palace proved fruitless because no sooner had they arrived in their new refuge than Prince August William went down with the same disease. Again there was uproar. As if this sudden flight was not bad enough, it was discovered it had been quite unnecessary. Lack of communication had caused the Kaiserin to insist on the moves for the Kaiser's sake, but afterwards to everyone's vexation and surprise he announced that in fact he had had chickenpox years before and had simply done what the doctors had ordered.[91] This sort of inefficiency was trying to an English lady. She also disapproved because the Kaiser indulged his daughter and a spoilt pupil was that much more difficult to handle. He even went so far as to send Princess Victoria Louise a newly scrubbed piglet complete with a blue bow on its tail. Miss Topham foresaw trouble when the normal fate of pigs drew near but she need not have worried. The Princess was quite unsqueamish. When the pig grew up she sold it to a butcher, kept the money for herself,

* It is noteworthy that Browning too invariably chose bonnets for his wife.

and thoroughly enjoyed the sausages made from her pet.[92] Yet the English mistress could forgive the Kaiser almost anything because he had such a strong sense of humour.[93] When he laughed it was impossible not to join in, and he emphasized his pleasure by stamping his foot on the ground. He found a great deal to laugh at. Occasionally he was a chaffer – which can be a cruel form of fun if the butt cannot reply in kind, but it was also a way of pricking the balloon of false conceit. In banter he nicknamed Miss Topham 'the Dreadnought' – not, we must suppose, on account of her figure but because of her nationality and English naval rearmaments – and she did not mind in the least.[94] Like Queen Victoria he was a good mimic, his pièce de résistance, beautifully copied by his daughter, being to imitate the sound of champagne being opened and poured into a glass.[95] Best of all, in the test of a true humorist he passed well: he could laugh at himself. He quite embarrassed Miss Topham by producing copies of *Punch* in which he was caricatured as a sea-serpent, an organ grinder, or as himself with hideously exaggerated moustaches, and asking whether she thought them good likenesses. Whenever she could she tried to hide *Punch* to avoid these difficult moments.[96]

Then there were less desirable traits in the Kaiser's character possibly unknown to his cousin Princess Alice and to Miss Topham. For example, the cruelty inherent in his liking for chaff found physical expression in the way he sometimes deliberately hurt people by turning his finger rings round and shaking their hands with a grip of iron.[97] And his bossiness sometimes reached extraordinary proportions. Another cousin, Princess Marie-Louise of Schleswig-Holstein, recorded that William issued orders that bicycling was not seemly for a Princess of Prussia, and when one disobeyed, he promptly put her and her husband under house arrest for a fortnight.[98] He liked the company of women but there are only vague rumours that he was ever unfaithful to his wife. Mr Michael Balfour in his fine study of the Kaiser gives the plausible view that 'intellectual curiosity had to take the place of mistresses';[99] less reliable sources suggest that he was a hand fetishist.[100] Princess Daisy of Pless in her vapid and often inaccurate *Private Diaries* reveals that her husband was a member of the Kaiser's 'White Stag' dining club.

> *To gain admission everyone had to kneel over a chair and tell a dirty story and be smacked on his behind with the flat of a sword by the Kaiser. Then a chain of stags' teeth was hung round the candidate's neck and he was a member* –[102]

Which probably has no more sexual connotation than the initiations of Freemasons, Water Elks, or any other quasi-secret society of men. The

Kaiser appreciated the Princess of Pless' large and voluptuous hour-glass figure but not her scribblings. When she published a book entitled *What I Did Not Say*, he remarked dryly: 'It's a great pity she did.'*

Finally, in any assessment of his character, William's courage must be noted. In the autumn of 1903 the Kaiser began to lose his voice. At the same time his left ear gave him pain and discharged matter. The ear trouble was quickly cleared, but the hoarseness remained. It was not long before William was reduced to whispering. His doctors urged him to take a sea voyage. Inevitably he must have remembered his father in exactly the same state in the winter of 1887. It was strongly believed that a tendency to cancer could be hereditary, and William's feelings may be imagined especially when the physicians found he had a growth on his larynx. An operation was advised, the very one his father had refused. Lister's work on asepsis had brought surgery into a different sphere, but the old dread of an operation still persisted and especially, we must suppose, in the mind of an emotional and imaginative man like the Kaiser. It was not that he feared the knife. The orthopaedic 'cures' of his boyhood and the horrific experience of learning to keep his balance on a horse had taught him to bear pain, a fact to which his dentist testified. Nevertheless he was of a nervous disposition with the capacity to imagine the worst and, being only too familiar with the horrible details of his father's disease and death, his acceptance of the doctors' advice was especially courageous. The operation took place. A polypus was removed from his throat. It was found to be benign. He had exceptional fortitude, recovered rapidly, and energetically rushed back to work.[103]

In appearance William had not greatly altered since his young manhood. True, there were streaks of grey in his fair hair, and though his eyes were more watchet-coloured than before, they still sparkled. His figure was neat and trim; he had a rowing machine in his dressing room, took hard and regular exercise and – unlike many of his generation – he was extremely sparing in what he ate and drank. Often he sat through course after course not accepting a dish – a fact which worried his aunt Queen Alexandra.[104] His one self-indulgence was a great liking for mince pies with brandy sauce.[105] It speaks much for his fitness that, when he was in his fifties, at a *bal costumé* given by his sailor son Prince Ethelbert at Kiel, he attended dressed as the Great Elector and was actually mistaken for the Crown Prince, a man so lean that he was nicknamed 'the Greyhound'. His partner, believing she was

---

* An example of her inaccuracy is the statement: '*As far as I could discover no-one, except the Kaiserin in the privacy of their bedroom, ever saw the Kaiser in mufti. In my own mind I am quite certain that he must have had a uniform even for the private occasion. I must find out.*' In fact after the death of his grandmother the Kaiser was frequently seen in plain clothes.[101]

The New Palace at Potsdam, the Kaiser's favourite home
Landesbildstelle Berlin

A happy snapshot of the Kaiser with his six sons at a Whitsun *Shrippenfest* in Potsdam
Radio Times Hulton Picture Library

Maximilian Harden, editor of *Die Zukunft*
Radio Times Hulton Picture Library

The Kaiser's friend, Philip zu Eulenburg-
Hertefeld *Radio Times Hulton Picture Library*

Prince von Bülow, nicknamed the Eel
Radio Times Hulton Picture Library

Chancellor Theobald von Bethmann-Hollweg
Landesbildstelle Berlin

The Kaiser in the uniform of the Death's Head Hussars. Unlike the majority of his
official photographs, this portrait was not posed

Radio Times Hulton Picture Library

The Kaiser visiting the Eastern Front near Ternapol in July, 1917
Imperial War Museum

Hindenburg, the Kaiser and Ludendorff on the Western Front in June, 1918
Imperial War Museum

The Kaiser's last public duty at Kiel in October, 1918, where he took an interest in the cutting of armour plates. Within days the fleet had mutinied and a Sailors' Soviet was formed

Imperial War Museum

Charles Liebknecht, a demagogic deputy to the
Reichstag. He, and German Socialism, became
the victim of his volatile, impatient nature

Landesbildstelle Berlin

Rosa Luxemburg, who was as influential as
Lenin in international Socialism in 1914 and
highly critical of his use of terror, tried
unsuccessfully to hold the Spartacists in
check in the German Revolution

Landesbildstelle Berlin

Frederick Ebert, former saddlemaker and
publican, Chairman of the Majority
Socialists in the Reichstag, then ruler *de
facto* of Berlin as Chairman of the Council
of People's Commissars, and finally first
President of the Weimar Republic

Landesbildstelle Berlin

The ex-Kaiser with his second wife, Princess Hermione Reuss, whom he created Princess Liegnitz
Radio Times Hulton Picture Library

Doorn House, William's home in Holland
Radio Times Hulton Picture Library

The elegant exile, William II in his old age   *Radio Times Hulton Picture Library*

speaking to the Crown Prince,* asked how he had padded himself. Was it with a cushion? 'Of course there was no cushion,' said the Kaiser telling the story against himself. 'There was only me.'[106]

4

Exactly four weeks after the removal of his throat polypus the Kaiser was busy writing in English to the Tsar about ships and guns and enclosed a report that the Japanese were secretly being supplied by China. This provocative despatch ended with a flourish: '*Ta, ta, best love to Alix from your devoted friend and cousin* toujours en vedette. *Willy.*'[108] Evidently William was continuing to practice private diplomacy.

His next move was in support of Count Alfred von Schlieffen, Chief of his General Staff, who had devised a plan for the reduction of France should it ever be necessary. This was based on Hannibal's strategy at Cannae, and followed the Clausewitz principle, which in Germany military circles had almost the authority of Holy Writ, that speed and decisiveness mattered more than all else. In the event of a war against the Dual Entente he regarded it as essential to smash France while Russia was lumbering into mobilization, and then, by a perfect system mapped out by the Military Railway Division,† move the victorious armies to the eastern front.[109] A frontal attack on the French fortresses along the frontier would be too slow. Schlieffen decided, and rightly, that he would have to seize on the weakest point and this was the frontier between France and Belgium. That, so far as he was concerned, was that. The political aspect, that Belgium's neutrality had been guaranteed by Prussia, Austria, Russia, France and England as long ago as 1839, had nothing to do with the Army. William decided it was his duty to deal with this in person and in January, 1904, he invited King Leopold to Berlin and put it to him that, in the event of a war with France, Germany would need to pass through neutral Belgium. For permission to do so he would make full compensation for any damage caused by troop movements and undertook to enlarge Belgium by adding French Flanders, Artois and the French Ardennes to her territories. To William it probably seemed a fair offer, too fair indeed to so detestable a monarch as Leopold. What he failed to comprehend was that though Leopold had not a shred of reputation left, all his malpractices against his own wretched family and the natives of the Congo had

---

* She addressed him as 'Your Imperial Highness' a distinction which only he enjoyed. His five brothers and other Prussian princes of the blood were Royal Highnesses.[107]

† It was an army joke that the most intellectual officers served in the Railway Division on their way to retirement in mental asylums.[110]

been just within the law. To his vexation the old villain put on a high-minded air and read him a lecture on constitutional government saying that the Belgian Chambers would never consider such an idea. William made some sour observations about sovereign rulers and parliaments and let the matter drop. The proposal can scarcely have shocked Leopold, yet it is maintained that afterwards he was so stunned by the outrageousness of the suggestion he put his hat on back to front when he left for the station.[111] More likely he was greatly alarmed by the possibility of a war being fought over his country. For thirty years he had been organizing the defences of Belgium, ordering the biggest and best cannon from Krupp. When he arrived home from Berlin he wrote to London, gave an audience to his ministers and ordered the fortification of Antwerp. To allay William's suspicions he bribed sections of the German press to report that the new defence measures were necessary because Belgium dreaded an attack from France.[112] But neither William nor his General Staff were particularly suspicious or even interested. They had the view that Schlieffen's great onslaught would be irresistible – with or without the co-operation of Belgium.

Bülow strongly disapproved of this conference between princes. William was pained. He had expected praise and approval. Bülow was unforgiving. He pointed out that a military plan, to be effective, needed to be kept secret. The King of the Belgians now had a broad idea of Germany's intentions and would have informed the protecting powers.* But though chastened the Kaiser was not going to relinquish what he regarded as his prerogative. When, three weeks afterwards, the long-expected war broke out between Japan and Russia he showed plainly which side he supported. He hoped that France might become embroiled as an ally of Russia and thus diminish the chances of an entente with England which had an alliance with Japan. But, so far as non-European powers were concerned, France's treaty obligations were merely to consult with Russia. This she did, while at the same time she made a formal alliance with England which ironed out many differences between the two countries. Next to the Yellow Peril, William's particular dread was of what he called 'the Gallo-Russian Pincers', a war on two fronts, encirclement. The *Entente Cordiale* between Paris and London announced in April 1904 increased his fears. No doubt he confided in Prince Eulenburg when, soon afterwards, he was at Liebenberg for the wedding of his old friend's eldest son, but by this time Eulenburg was in a distressing state.[114] His health had almost entirely given way. In his place William had two frank advisers.

---

* In fact that year an officer of the German General Staff had already sold the Schlieffen plan in its entirety to the French. He did it melodramatically, handing over parts in Paris, Nice and Brussels, always swathing his head in bandages so that only his eyes and moustache could be seen.[113]

One was Albert Ballin, the German-Jewish industrialist who owned the prosperous Hamburg-American Line; he cruised with the Kaiser and shot at Rominten.[115] The other was a member of William's own family, his young sister-in-law Princess Féodora of Schleswig-Holstein, an unmarried eccentric who lived at the Bornstedt Farm where he had been so happy as a boy. Princess Féodora refused to be given preferential treatment merely because she was the Kaiserin's sister and went shopping in Berlin like any other woman. She was the best water-colourist in the family, wrote rather sombre books on poverty and the life of the peasantry, and, of all pleasures, she most enjoyed games of hide-and-seek in the farm buildings.[116] She and her brother-in-law disagreed on many subjects but William appreciated her humour, and her readiness to take his difficult children on one side and read them an appropriate lecture.[117] He also appreciated her candour. She and Ballin between them were of greater service to him than perhaps he realized. In 1904 General von Mackensen, who deeply cared for William, began the practice of kissing his master's hand at Court.[118] William made no objection. The Pope and the Sultan had their hands kissed and he saw no harm in it. Yet somehow the practice was not in character with the German spirit, and it scarcely went with William's bottom-slapping, cheek-pinching bonhomie. There were grumbles about Byzantinism at the Imperial Court, but Ballin and Princess Féodora helped to keep the centre of it all at a more mundane level. Their frankness served as a counterpoise.

King Edward was invited to Kiel Week in 1904. It pained William that his uncle had paid visits to France, Portugal, Italy and Austria but, so far, he had only been privately to Germany. Nevertheless he was determined to make the visit a success, just as his uncle had done his best at Sandringham. He supervised menus to please the gourmet King. He showed his attentiveness by adding the luxury of a canopy over the promenade deck of the *Hohenzollern* and decorating it with banks of potted plants and artificial pools and waterfalls. He made sure the High Seas Fleet and auxiliaries were in top form and ready for the King's inspection, and large numbers of troops were ordered to Kiel to do him honour.[119] But again there were misunderstandings, muddling and unfortunate accidents. The English party arrived in teeming rain and pitch dark. For an elderly gentleman to have to step at once ashore and inspect troops was asking a great deal. Then the English, who gave few decorations, were not prepared to conform with the continental custom of lavish distribution to royal suites when sovereigns met and they had to be pressed to relax some of their stringent rules.[120] Finally, King Edward, who had come to Kiel with the good intention of placating his nephew and persuading him that the Anglo-French *entente* did not constitute a threat to Germany, interpreted the demonstration of German strength as a deliberate provocation. His suite of Naval officers agreed. Having seen the potential of the German Navy, these gentlemen returned home to press the politicians and the public that a larger British naval programme was essential. William was less than prudent in his speech of welcome, quite openly showing his hand and arousing the hostility of his English guests. He let himself go and described his fleet, though the youngest in point of creation amongst the navies of the world, as 'an expression of the renewal in strength of the sea-power of the German Empire.'[121]

The King's reply was quiet, in excellent German, polite, but utterly deflating. He said that he had been glad to come to Kiel as he had always been interested – and here he paused fractionally – in yachting. He was glad he added to see how successful the Kaiser had been in interesting so many of his subjects in the sport. And at that he sat down.[122] It was a public humiliation which William could not forgive. Suspicious that his brother was becoming too anglophile, he insisted on attending a dinner which Princess Henry was giving for the King at their Kiel home, Hemmelmark, and made a long speech which bored everyone. King Edward made this offensively obvious.[123] The last straw came when William suggested that Russia's cause in the war against Japan was really that of Europe because the Yellow Peril was a very dreadful menace and his uncle, far from troubling to support his ally Japan, merely laughed out loud.[124] Here was another public setdown William could not forgive.

In the succeeding months uncle and nephew pecked at each other like angry bantams.

The King called the Kaiser 'the most brilliant failure in history'[125] and when, to his parents' relief, the Crown Prince fell in love with an eligible *parti*, Princess Cecile of Mecklenburg-Schwerin, he scraped up an inadequate excuse for not permitting the Prince of Wales to be present at the wedding.[126] Angrily William called his uncle 'the old peacock',[127] made censorious comments about his liaison with Mrs George Keppel,[128] and, aware that the King sometimes enjoyed the hospitality of Sir Thomas Lipton at Cowes, he maddened him by describing it as 'boating with his grocer'.[129] It seemed that for about eighteen months they agreed on only two matters:[130] that the suffragette movement was unbecoming;[131] and, as the King put it succinctly to the German Naval Attaché in London: 'The press is mad in all countries'.[132]

The German and British press certainly exacerbated the bad feeling between the two monarchs and their peoples. Trying to discover where the blame first lay is a chicken-and-egg speculation; nevertheless it is noteworthy that no single German newspaper ranked in influence or authority with *The Times* or *The New York Times* or *Figaro* or even *La Prensa* of Buenos Aires, and that in England and America a new type of industrialist was emerging, the newspaper magnate, who had no responsibility to anyone and exercised powerful anti-German influence. They whipped up the less powerful German press into a retaliatory furore.[133]

Acutely aware that his personal influence had waned in England, the Kaiser leant even more towards his cousin the Tsar. Politically it was expedient, and, when the news reached Europe that the Japanese had destroyed the Russian Pacific Fleet and afterwards her Vladivostock squadron, William was profuse in his condolences. He was also surprised and disturbed. That Russia with all her resources should be humbled by an emerging oriental power alarmed him. The Russian Baltic Fleet, on its way round the world to blow the Japanese out of the water caused an international incident when, mistaking them for the enemy, they fired on British fishing vessels in the North Sea. The Russians' chief fault was that, on realizing their mistake, they did not stop to pick up survivors and two men were drowned and others wounded. The English, and notably their King, were in a turbulent state of indignation. The Tsar telegraphed his regrets to London but this was not enough. Provocatively ships of the Royal Navy shadowed the Russian fleet until the Tsar angrily demanded that they be called off. They were.[134] No doubt England had hopes of a future rapprochement with Russia as France's ally. William seized on the opportunity and offered to coal the Baltic Fleet since it could hardly reach the Far East without such assistance. The Tsar accepted. Britain protested. William repeated his offer. The Tsar, angry at England's behaviour, said it was high time to put a stop to it.

> *The only way as you say* [he wrote] *would be that Germany, Russia and France should at once unite . . . would you like to lay down and frame the outline of such a Treaty? . . . France is bound to join her ally.*[115]

It was the sort of invitation that the Kaiser had been waiting for, but he insisted that a treaty be made without first consulting France. Rightly he suspected that the French ministers would not agree to smashing the *entente* with England so soon. He cloaked his doubts characteristically:

> *They* [the French] *not being Princes or Emperors I am unable to place them . . . on the same footing as you, my equal, my cousin and friend.*[136]

But private negotiations between them had to cease for a while as the Tsar was flooded in a tide of disasters. In January 1905 the Russians at Port Arthur surrendered to the Japanese. It was so unexpected and undignified a reversal that a wave of discontent ran through the Empire. It sparked off an anti-Jewish pogrom in Bessarabia, for the Jews were invariably blamed for any national disaster and anti-Semitism has always been endemic both in Tsarist and Soviet Russia. The pogrom was stopped after the third day, but universal criticism of the mismanagement of the war was seized on by revolutionaries as a means to cause trouble. Many workers went on strike. In St Petersburg a demonstration led by Fr Gapon, a priest who was a strange cross of visionary and police agent, approached the Winter Palace to beg the Tsar to deliver them from the economic tyranny of industrialists. It was a badly bungled affair. The Tsar was actually some miles away at Tsarskoe Selo and therefore geographically unable to receive the deputation; and, though the demonstrators carried Icons and sang 'God Save the Tsar', the troops at the Winter Palace fired on them. 'Bloody Sunday', as the day was called, began a period of riots, mutinies, strikes in schools and factories, the assassination of government officials and the murder of policemen. Gapon escaped, denounced the Tsar as a tyrant, but was then hanged by his own supporters as an agent of the police.[137] Three weeks afterwards Duke Serge, the Tsar's uncle, was assassinated in Moscow. His widow was Ella, the Hesse cousin to whom William had once lost his heart. It was typical of her that when she ran from the palace to find her husband had quite literally been blown to pieces, she busied herself with comforting the dying coachman; that she visited the assassin in prison and offered to plead for his life, which he would not allow; and that she afterwards founded a convent for nursing sisters, the Order of Martha and Mary, where she retired with one faithful maid to live the rest of her life caring for the destitute and poor of Moscow.[138] No record survives of William's feelings when he heard this tragic story but they may be imagined. It was but one of many in that bloody year which drew Tsar and Kaiser closer together. It was an agonizing time for Russia and her friends.

The Tsar's preoccupation with fighting the Japanese and quelling outbursts of revolution made Russia politically a negligible quantity, and Bülow and Schlieffen, pressed to it by Holstein, seized on the opportunity to make a trial of strength with France and England. The *Entente Cordiale* stipulated that England's principal Mediterranean interest should be in Egypt and that of France in Morocco. Holstein pointed out that German rights in Morocco had been recognized by the Great Powers fifteen years before and a door ought to be kept open there for the advantage of German commercial interests, or their rights bartered for solid colonial possessions. Bülow saw this as the perfect outward expression of his world policy and brought pressure upon the Kaiser to go there in person and stake Germany's claim. He happened to be taking a spring cruise in the Mediterranean in a chartered liner and could well land at Tangier. William demurred. He approved of standing firmly, but he scented real danger in Bülow's diplomatic lark. German rights in Morocco were not worth a war. He made this limpidly clear in a speech delivered at Bremen in March, 1905 before he left for his cruise:

My study of history has given me no encouragement to seek an empty world rule. . . . The world empire I have dreamed of consists above all in the enjoyment by the newly-erected German Empire of complete trust, as a quiet, honourable and peaceful neighbour.[139]

The Kaiser's quieter, thoughtful speeches were never given the press accorded his more exotic fanfaronades and exploits. Most European newspapers missed or excluded the Bremen speech, but scarcely one failed to report the news when, eight days later, William actually set foot on the disputed soil of Morocco.

The business of setting foot ashore was by no means easy. When he saw what it involved William must have regretted even more permitting himself to be persuaded by Bülow. A high sea was running and his chartered liner was too large to dock in Tangier. Therefore he had to make the journey in small boat and that, judging by the state in which his Consul-General arrived to greet him, was not going to be pleasant. The Consul-General, hampered by the full-dress uniform of a Bavarian Uhlan regiment, clawed his way up the rope-ladder and then, in his own words, approached his Sovereign 'on hands and knees and laying all at his Majesty's feet'.[140] Somehow, despite his atrophied arm, the Kaiser got down into the bobbing boat and in a very short time he felt as ill as his Consul-General. Ashore he was greeted by the Sultan's uncle and expected to mount a high-spirited Arab stallion which again was a test of the strength of his one good arm and his own agility. Once mounted, he found the stallion difficult to manage. The beast hated the crowds – 'Italian and South-French anarchists, swindlers and adventurers' – who showed their enthusiasm for the Kaiser by yelling and firing off rifles. Somehow William got to the German Legation. There he dismounted from his whirling steed, and shouting above the cheers and fusilade of rifle shots and a band which had been added to the hubbub, he assured the Sultan's uncle and the French Minister that the Germans demanded free trade; he would treat with the Sultan as the sovereign of an independent country; and European customs and practices should not be introduced without good reason. Afterwards the excitable stallion took him back to the heaving motor-launch.[141] The liner then took him to Gibraltar – one of the escort vessels accidentally ramming a British cruiser on arrival[142] – where he saw Prince Louis of Battenberg, confirmed that Germany had no designs on the Mediterranean but did not conceal his dislike of France. 'We know the road to Paris,' he said 'and we will get there again if need be.'[143]

It had been a somewhat shattering experience for a one-armed man of forty-six. He said so in no uncertain way to his Chancellor, who replied:

*I shook with fear. When the news reached me that Your Majesty had
come away alive out of Tangier, I broke down and sat weeping at my
desk while I uttered a thanksgiving to Heaven.*[144]

Having been bombarded on the way to Tangier by no fewer than five telegrams from Bülow to keep him resolute, William considered this a piece of
hypocrisy. No doubt he was thinking of Bülow and Holstein when, a few days
later, he was in one of Frederick II's castles and considering how much that
Stupor Mundi had achieved, and he told his suite: 'If I were able to have people
beheaded as easily as he could, I would do more.'[145] One consolation of the
cruise was a visit to Corfu, where he saw the late Empress Elizabeth's villa
standing untenanted and he conceived the idea of approaching Emperor
Francis Joseph with a view to buying it. The Achilleion, named after his
favourite Greek hero, was a pink pastiche with Pompeian interiors and
extensive grounds. William saw it as an excellent cruising base in the springtime.[146]

Germany's move to claim rights in Morocco turned into a mild diplomatic triumph. The Sultan invited the Powers to confer and decide on the
future of his country. Germany at once agreed. England, Italy and Spain
temporized, saying they would follow the lead of France; but, when the
anglophile French Foreign Secretary, M. Delcassé, refused to attend any
conference, Berlin brought pressure to bear on France. Though Delcassé
had been an architect of the *Entente Cordiale*, he was forced out of office.[147]
On the day of his resignation, June 6th, William characteristically forgot
his resentment at having been made to land at Tangier, and he made
Bülow, once more 'dear Bernard', a prince.[148] He also refused an invitation from President Loubet to visit France, and peppered up the formal and
courteous diplomatic reply in an imperial speech at Cassel which left
no-one in any doubt about his feelings: 'The Order of the Day is, keep your
powder dry – keep your sword sharp – and keep your fist on the hilt!'[149]
France with her bourgeois government and her bourgeois vanity was antipathetic to him.

The same June Norway split from Sweden, voted in favour of the monarchical system, and the Kaiser was delighted. He had more of a social conscience than most of his contemporary heads of state and he was undoubtedy
more enlightened than the majority of capitalists who did very little to
improve the lot of their workers, but he had no time for egalitarianism.
Quietly, in case he was unsuccessful, he pushed the candidature of one of his
own sons for the throne of Norway, but King Edward pushed harder and his
nephew and son-in-law, Prince Charles of Denmark, was elected by the
Norwegians as King Haakon.[150] The Kaiser was disappointed but not dis-

pleased. That Norway was now an hereditary monarchy, however limited in power, was the important thing. He would have no truck with the least suspicion of jacobinism.

Tsar Nicholas' dreadful experiences that year were something the Kaiser never forgot. The second Russian fleet from the Baltic met the fate of the first. It was destroyed in the Straits of Tsushima by Admiral Togo in the largest naval action fought since Trafalgar.[151] President Roosevelt offered to mediate and the Tsar was forced to comply. He sent his Minister of Finance, Sergius Witte, to America to negotiate on behalf of Russia.[152] Meanwhile revolutionary pustules continued to break out all over Russia and could only just be contained. Leon Trotsky emerged to lead the Menshevik party. The exiled Lenin was waiting impatiently for an opportunity to slip back and lead the Bolsheviks. In July William judged the time was ripe to further his proposal for a German-Russian agreement. He privately telegraphed the Tsar inviting him to meet in one of the Finnish fjords. The Tsar thought it important to go. The Russian Imperial yacht *Standart* met the *Hohenzollern* by appointment off the island of Björkö. The two sovereigns were not accompanied by their Foreign Ministers, though Tschirschky, a representative of the German Foreign Ministry, was with the Kaiser and acquainted with the terms of the treaty his master was to propose. The two cousins dined together on the first day of their meeting and the next morning William produced a draft of his proposals. They contracted Russia and Germany to mutual military and naval aid in case of attack by another European power and not to make a separate peace. Two other articles were added: that the treaty should not come into effect until peace between Russia and Japan had been concluded and would operate until the conclusion of one year's notice given by either contracting party; and that Russia would confidentially inform France of the agreement and invite her to join it. It was strikingly simple and appealed to the Tsar. He agreed to sign it. His signature was witnessed by Admiral Birilev, his Minister of Marine; the Kaiser's was witnessed by Tschirschky of the Foreign Ministry.[153]

Both monarchs were delighted with the success of their meeting and returned home. They were not warmly welcomed by their ministers. The Tsar was respectfully told that he could not pledge his support to France against Germany in one treaty and by another pledge his support to Germany against France. Less respectfully – though in fact the treaty was far more to Germany's advantage than to that of Russia – Bülow complained because the treaty only applied to Europe and Germany's best defence against England was for Russia to attack India. He promptly resigned.

William was deeply shocked. He had steamed from Finland in the firm conviction that, as he put it:

By God's grace the morning of 24th July, 1905 at Björkö has witnessed the turning point in the history of Europe; a great load has been lifted from my dear Fatherland which has finally escaped from the terrible Gallo-Russian pincers.[*][154]

There is a theory that Baron von Richthofen his Foreign Minister had insisted on the Kaiser being taught a sharp lesson that he must not interfere. If so, it was extremely effective. Very often with William, as is frequently the case with imaginative people, the blackest depression followed euphoria; but this time William was so alarmed at the thought of being deprived of Bülow's solid, comforting presence that his nerve gave way. He wrote an hysterical, pathetic letter begging his Chancellor to take back his resignation and actually threatened suicide.[155] It was a Micawberish letter. No sooner had it been dispatched and he had been reassured by telegram that Bülow would stay on, than he bounced up again; not immediately into an euphoric state, but undoubtedly with all thoughts of suicide banished from his mind.

Far from joining the two cousins in closer intimacy, their attempt to exercise true autocratic government proved to be divisive. Count Witte concluded peace with Japan on exceptionally favourable terms for Russia, and was bidden to call on the Kaiser at Rominten as he travelled home. Witte had already refused official invitations from William as Kaiser, Bülow as Chancellor, and from the King of England on the grounds that he must hurry home to report to his master. This therefore was a compliment from his cousin which William appreciated.[157] He thought highly of Witte, who was a mathematician and an expert on infintesimal quantities as well as statecraft, and he was not surprised when Witte recommended to the Tsar that the only way to contain the pockets of revolution was to turn Russia from an autocracy into a semi-constitutional monarchy. This was done at the end of October and Witte was put in charge of the government. Assailed from left and right he lasted only a short time,[158] and his successor who had a bored air and Piccadilly whiskers and spent most of his time reading French novels,[159] lasted even less. It was left to a bearded country squire, Peter Stolypin, to keep the revolution at bay by creating a new class of millions of peasant landowners and executing so many terrorists that the hangman's noose was renamed 'Stolypin's Necktie'.[160] With genuine concern William watched the Tsar struggle with his difficulties, but his cousin's abandonment of the Björkö treaty – he refused to admit he was bound by its terms – drew a shrewd remark from the Kaiser. 'The Tsar is not treacherous [he minuted]

* One of the more remarkable imponderabilia of history is the idea that, had the Treaty of Björkö been upheld, the Houses of Hohenzollern and Romanov might have survived, and the First World War and the economic collapse which followed might have been avoided.[156]

but he is weak. Weakness is not treachery, but it fulfils all its functions.'[161] This view was amply demonstrated by Nicholas' conduct while his country went through disaster after disaster. And he allowed himself to be battered by a private tragedy, that his year-old heir Alexis was haemophilic. The disease had been transmitted by Queen Victoria through her daughters to many of the reigning houses of Europe,* and the knowledge that his son had the disease had a profound effect upon the Tsar. He became a fatalist and retreated more and more within himself.[162] While Witte and his successors did all they could to maintain the established order in Russia, the head of that order led a secluded life in a small palace at Peterhof and at Tsarskoe Selo living as a private person.[163]

Even had he dared to brave Bülow, the Kaiser would have found little satisfaction in continuing to negotiate personally with so weak a sovereign, and their correspondence dwindled in scope, size and importance.[164]

5

The result of a British General Election held in January 1906 showed the world the way the wind was blowing. It was shown not so much by the fact that power shifted from the Conservatives to the Liberals but in the actual constitution of the new House of Commons. As King Edward's Private Secretary put it: 'The old idea that the House of Commons was an assemblage of "gentlemen" has quite passed away'.[165] Many members were of humble origin. Labour was well represented. It was significant that 180 members were non-conformists and therefore anti-establishment; in fact more dissenters were returned than at any election since the days of Cromwell.[166] A. J. Balfour, who had taken over the leadership of the Conservatives from his uncle Lord Salisbury, minded less the defeat of his party than this emergence of a meritocracy. He confided to the King through his Private Secretary that England now faced 'socialist difficulties' and concluded: 'Unless I am greatly mistaken the election of 1906 inaugurates a new era.'[167]

The Germans, so much more at the mercy of that self-inflicted scourge bureaucracy, were partly blind to the emerging power of the proletariat. William Voigt's extraordinary escapade at this time demonstrates how far bemused the Germans were by bureaucracy – even when authority was aped. Voigt, who had served several prison sentences, pulled the nose of officialdom and set all Europe laughing. He hired a captain's uniform, went to the nearest barracks and ordered a detachment of ten men to go with him by train to the Berlin suburb of Köpenick. There he and his men occupied the

---

* Two of the three sons of the Kaiser's brother Prince Harry had haemophilia, as had two of the sons of the Queen of Spain.

town hall, arrested the mayor and his clerk, claimed that certain irregularities needed to be cleared up and pocketed 4,000 marks from the municipal treasury. He then marched back his men and disappeared. Later he was caught and explained that what he had really been after was a passport. The extraordinary thing is that no-one at the barracks, at the station guichet, or at the town hall ever thought of questioning his power or disobeying his orders. He was a captain and that was sufficient.[168] To the despair of the few activists the Social Democrat workers were far less belligerent than their brethren in other countries. The few who were vocal had little power and when the Kaiser blandly suggested that any really discontented 'Sozis' (from *Sozial-demokraten*) should emigrate, his solution was applauded.[169] It is significant that like England Germany also had a general election that year, but the result was very different. A leading Social Democrat once scornfully described the Reichstag as 'the figleaf of absolutism',[170] and the Kaiser himself was equally scornful, calling it the 'Gossip Shop';[171] but it did, in fact, have some power. Bülow, who generally managed the Reichstag so tactfully, found himself opposed when he asked for monies to put down the Herrero Rebellion in German South-West Africa. His only recourse was to dissolve the Reichstag and there followed what were called the 'Hottentot Elections'.[172] The results were as remarkable as those of the British election but for a very different reason. In the 1890 election the Sozis had taken sixth place out of the seven groups of power, but then had moved gradually upwards, being fifth in 1893, third in 1898, and second in 1903. Now they thudded back to fifth place again.[173] It was not until five years later that they reigned first place.

At the beginning of the year Schlieffen retired as Chief of the General Staff and a second Helmuth von Moltke, nephew to the first, took his place. He was larger and less languid than his elegant uncle. He was also inclined to melancholy. When the Kaiser appointed him he said mournfully that he had no idea how he would manage a campaign and that he was extremely self-critical. 'I lack the capacity for staking all on a single throw'.[174] William cheered him up, affectionately nicknamed him Julius, and put up with his un-Prussian eccentricities of 'cello playing, painting in oils, reading German and French verse and following the teachings of Mary Baker Eddy. That Moltke was able to reconcile the irreconcilable, the profession of arms and Christian Science, and that he was a Colonel General who frequently fell off his charger, in no way lessened his efficiency as a soldier or his loyalty to the Kaiser.[175] In his new Chief of General Staff William found another invaluable adviser who was not afraid to say what he thought. One of Moltke's first gloomy prophecies was an echo of his uncle's warning that any future war would probably be a lengthy affair. The military oracle Clausewitz dreaded a war of attrition and Schlieffen's plan was based on the bold stroke, but both Moltkes had a premonition that a large-scale war in the post-industrial revolution age would drain all national resources and any victory be pyrrhic.[176] Though it was to the Kaiser's own personal advantage to have a candid Chief of General Staff it was questionable whether such a melancholy visionary was the right man for the post.

A far less controversial appointment, in fact one of the Kaiser's best in 1906, was his friend William Bode to superintend all the galleries and museums in the capital. Bode's ability to nose out art treasures was unsurpassed even by the American Berenson and the Englishman Duveen who bought principally for exporting to the United States. The Kaiser with his own capital encouraged Bode, and used his influence to persuade high-ranking Germans to make suitable gifts to the national museums. He would grant a title if necessary to secure the reversion of a private collection to the state; and he was not beyond asking for an outright gift. With his master's help Bode made the galleries and museums of Berlin the envy of many European countries.*[177]

A third appointment was less successful. Richthofen had died in office and William rewarded Tschirschky, who had witnessed the Björkö Treaty, by making him Foreign Minister.[178] It was unlucky for Tschirschky that the Algeçiras Conference almost coincided with his appointment. It is alleged that the Conference was convened by President Roosevelt, for which and because he had mediated between Russia and Japan, he was awarded the Nobel Peace Prize;[179] but the real pressure from the Conference came from Germany, who hoped to prise France from England. In this she was defeated by the inadequacy and arrogance of her own envoys and the shrewdness of the British delegate, who quickly managed to isolate Germany. Only the Austrians and Moors stood by her.[180] Holstein still wanted to press Germany's rights. The Kaiser, now joined by his Chancellor, sought to be more conciliatory. By the Act of Algeçiras, France and Spain were authorized to police Morocco for the Sultan under a Swiss Inspector General,[182] and Germany had the small satisfaction of winning concessions and establishing the principle that nominally the country was under international, not solely French, control.[183] How much the Americans understood of the real situation was demonstrated by the President sending William his 'heartiest congratulations on this epoch-making political success at Algeçiras'.[184] Having strengthened not weakened the *Entente Cordiale* and shown Russia that there might be advantages in having an understanding with Britain, William hardly

* Neither, of course, had faultless taste. One of the Kaiser's blind spots was impressionist painting. Another was his taste for monumental sculpture 'in the classical model'. Defending his Avenue of Victory led him to make one of his more startling utterances: 'An art which transcends the laws and barriers outlined by me, ceases to be an art.'[181]

considered it an epoch-making success.[185] He blamed Bülow who in turn blamed Holstein. Angrily Holstein handed in his resignation.

One story has it that the Senior Councillor had fallen into the habit of resigning to make his point. Tschirschky, for example, had annoyed him by locking his office door so that he could not wander in unannounced as he had done in the old days, and Holstein had sent in his resignation over that.[186] Whichever particular resignation this may have been, and for whatever cause, one was accepted by the Kaiser on the recommendation of the Chancellor on April 6th. The day before Bülow had collapsed in the Reichstag while trying to soothe deputies who were angry about the Algeçiras Conference. Therefore conveniently he was in bed and out of everyone's reach while the unhappy debate dragged on and Holstein found himself virtually dismissed from office.[187]

Holstein was sixty-nine and had had two operations for cataract but to lose, at a stroke, his work and the power he had wielded for years was a blow from which he never recovered. Long after Holstein's end Prince Eulenburg wrote to a friend about his 'thirst for slaughter', his 'impulsive sort of smothered inward fury',[188] that he was 'often seen at night, all alone, in the Wilhelmstrasse, gazing up at the windows of the Foreign Office',[189] and that he had gone 'disappointed, embittered and exhausted to his lonely death'.[190] Eulenburg was to learn precisely how bitter and vengeful the dismissed Senior Counsellor could be. So was Bülow. And so was the Kaiser.

CHAPTER TWELVE

Débâcles

'I am a dog on Fate's vivisection table'

PRINCE PHILIP ZU EULENBURG

I

On the day after Holstein left the Foreign Ministry the Kaiser bestowed on Prince Philip zu Eulenburg the highest of all Prussia's honours, the Order of the Black Eagle.[1] Less than a month afterwards the Prince received from the dismissed Senior Counsellor Baron von Holstein a registered letter in which he was accused of scheming: 'After many years you have attained your end – my removal from office.' Together with this flight of fancy was the accusation that 'for certain reasons' his company was objectionable.[2] Holstein was unlocking the Poison Cupboard once more.

The Prince decided on a bold stroke. He went at once to Berlin and appointed a second who took a challenge to Holstein: 'Exchange of pistol shots until disablement or death'. Being still *en disposition* and attached to the Foreign Office he also formally informed Tschirschky that he had called out Holstein in an affair of honour.

Holstein's reaction was peculiar. Though short-sighted he was an expert with the pistols and regularly practised at a shooting range. To answer the challenge he spitefully chose an old friend of Eulenburg's to act as his second, an obligation which the poor man could not refuse. Then he turned volte face and sent a satisfactory apology.

> *Prince Eulenburg having assured me, on his word of honour, that he had neither hand, act, nor part in my dismissal ... I hereby withdraw the offensive remarks made upon him in my letter.*
>
> *HOLSTEIN.*[3]

That same day, with a sombre clarity of vision, the Prince noted that this was not the end of the affair. He was right. Holstein, copying the example of

Bismarck, began contributing articles in a South German newspaper which attacked the Foreign Office and the Emperor and occasionally Bülow. They were not simply an extended apologia but groundwork for a most thorough campaign of vengeance for his dismissal. On August 16th he boldly mentioned that he had been challenged to a duel, but neatly twisted the facts so that they were to his advantage.

> *I took very sharp measures against a man considerably younger than myself – calling him amongst other things a despicable person. His response was to send me a friend who merely said to my representative that [he] was ready to declare on his word of honour that he had never done anything . . . against me . . . I required that this declaration should be given me in his own handwriting – and I got it. Voilà!*[4]

The somersault baffled and frightened Eulenburg, but not half so much as the discovery he made two days later that Holstein had allied himself to the editor of *Die Zukunft*, who up to that time had been one of Holstein's declared enemies. He wrote in his diary: 'What can such a pair be brewing now?'[5]

The editor of *Die Zukunft* was one of the most enigmatic journalists of his day. Born Arnold Witkowski in 1861 as the sixth son of a Jewish merchant, he broke from his family in adolescence, was baptized a Christian and changed his name to Maximilian Harden. The stage was his first vocation, a choice which one historian argues might account for his 'deep-seated tendency towards exhibitionism'.[6] Significantly in the year of Bismarck's dismissal he changed his profession to journalism. Eulenburg believed that he had once offered his pen to the Kaiser and met with a painful rebuff: 'H.M. has no intercourse with anyone belonging to the Press, nor does he wish to have any.'[7] Bismarck was less particular. He was delighted to pass on to Harden all his views on Caprivi's 'New Course' and his bitter feelings for the Kaiser and the Court. From that year, 1892, Harden wrote in opposition to the German establishment. He was also anti-bourgeoisie and anti-Sozi, though he had tender feelings for non-political workers. The weekly newspaper which he controlled and mostly wrote, *Die Zukunft*, was widely read. He gathered distinguished contributors not only from Germany but from Russia, France and England, and his sources of information were unusually good – other leading journalists, theatre associates, painters, politicians, bankers and industrialists. For thirty years he never ceased his carefully arranged pattern of denigration, though what his personal motives were for being so consistently anti-establishment have never been satisfactorily explained. It seems unlikely that he was gorged with moral disgust at the failings of humanity, unlikely that he was simply a hypocritical sensationalist. Possibly he relished power and opposition for the sake of opposition.[8] An alliance with his old enemy

Baron von Holstein was mutually agreeable to both. It gave Holstein the sour pleasure of revenge and enabled Harden to blow a favourite warning bugle blast against rule by coterie.

This shrewd, and totally unsqueamish editor began his campaign in November 1906, in an article ominously called 'Praeludium'. Harden attacked what he called the 'Liebenberg Round Table' and 'the effeminate camarilla'.[9] Eulenburg was charged with pushing through policies detrimental to the Empire, plotting the replacement of Bülow with a Chancellor more amenable to his views, and encouraging the Kaiser's absolutism.[10] The word 'effeminate' was stressed. Eulenburg himself escaped any direct accusation of being homosexual, though there were innuendoes; but another member of the supposed 'camarilla', his friend Count Kuno von Moltke, Military Commandant of Berlin and first cousin of the Chief of General Staff, was less fortunate. He was openly accused of being homosexual, Harden claiming that Moltke's ex-wife, an hysterical woman who had remarried, was his source of information.[11]

Just before this printed attack William had been at Liebenberg. Amongst his fellow guests were Kuno von Moltke and the French Counsellor of Legation, Raymond Lecomte, who was a notorious homosexual. Harden's article was clearly aimed at the Kaiser through his friends.[12]

To Eulenburg's amazement Bülow made a statement in the Reichstag only four days after the Kaiser had left Liebenberg, not to refute Harden's statement or deny the accuracy of his open charge that an undesirable clique had influence over the Kaiser but simply to declare that a 'camarilla' was a poisonous foreign weed which had never been planted in German soil 'without great injury to Prince and people.'[13] This was gammon, a characteristic example of Bülow's dissembling, though it appears it was the first indication to Eulenburg of his supposed friend's unreliability.* A real friend, Baron Berger, tried to persuade Harden to stop his campaign but he failed. Bülow merely advised Eulenburg to remove himself temporarily from the country.[15] In fact it was good advice, but it was not disinterested. The Prince left with his family to winter in Switzerland and Harden, having won the first round, was content to wait in his corner of the ring for the next.[16]

How much or how little the Kaiser knew of what was going on is uncertain. It is unlikely that such news would have been allowed to percolate

---

* Bülow had secretly supplied Harden with the evidence he needed to initiate the campaign, that Eulenburg and Moltke habitually referred to the Kaiser as *das Liebchen*, the pet or the little dear. Moreover, to cement Holstein's determination Bülow led the vengeful old man to believe that Eulenburg really had been responsible for his downfall.[14]

through to him and in any case, William had had a more strenuous round than usual in 1906 and at the beginning of 1907.

He was much preoccupied by the anarchist's attempt on his cousin Princess Ena after her marriage to the King of Spain, the birth of his first grandson, another Prince William of Prussia, a mad two-day scare at Kiel when it was believed the English were about to descend in force and destroy the German Navy,[17] the bad behaviour of the Crown Prince and Princess at St Moritz where they neglected their own countrymen for English guests,[18] and a decided worsening in his relationship with King Edward. He blamed his uncle for a great deal, not least for trying to undermine his authority with the Crown Prince,[19] and his resentment at last boiled over in a very public place, at a banquet of the Knights of the Order of St John. He was suffering from nervous indigestion and the rich food gave him searing heartburn. For most of the evening he endured the discomfort and pain in virtual silence but then he became agitated. He began to talk excitedly about England's policies and the intrigues of his uncle. To their amazement, a number of his fellow Knights heard him declare: 'He is a Satan; you can hardly believe what a Satan he is.'[20] Such gaffes in public were in character but not likely to ease the existing tension between Germany and England. Less and less was the Kaiser able to stand a long haul. The nervous excitement of the winter and then his duties during the Season, which he found increasingly tedious, had made him exceedingly fraught, and he was barely able to cope when, halfway through April, Prince Eulenburg left Switzerland and went home to Lieben-berg and a second Camarilla scandal rocked Berlin.

True to his promise, as soon as the Prince returned to German soil Harden immediately bounded from his corner with renewed energy and the gloves on, and he proceeded to pound his opponents in *Die Zukunft*. In the issue of April 27th he listed notable members of the aristocracy alleged to have committed homosexual acts, thereby offending against Article 175 of the Criminal Code, for which the punishment was a severe prison sentence. The name of the Military Commandant of Berlin, Count Kuno von Moltke, again appeared, as did that of Prince Philip zu Eulenburg – this time directly and without any innuendo.[21] To these were added two Counts Hohenau, A.D.Cs to the Kaiser and related to him by blood as they were the sons of his great-uncle Prince Albert by a morganatic marriage. A third A.D.C. appeared on the list, Major Count Lynar, as well as the Court Master of Ceremonies, Count Wedel; and an intimate of Eulenburg's who was a veteran of the 1870 war, General Paul von Leszczynski.[22]

From a newspaperman's point of view it was a scoop, for an exposé of moral decadence in high society was an impressive piece of muck-raking. That the alleged homosexuals were the Kaiser's relatives, friends and closest servants, and that eighteen years before two of them, Count William Hohenau and Count Lynar, had been chosen to represent Queen Victoria's regiment of 1st of Garde Dragoner and had actually been presented to her at Osborne by the Kaiser, added considerable spice to the scandal.[23] Compared to it the Krupp affair had been a crocus to a tulip. Inevitably fingers pointed to the Kaiser himself.

One of the less admirable characteristics of Anglo-Saxons and Teutons is the deep delight they take in an occasional public purge. Then there is a sense of mass outrage; with or without reason everyone is righteously indignant, and, for a time, very cruel and unforgiving. Nevertheless it is questionable whether this scandal gratified the German public at large. It was a *cause célèbre* motivated by a journalist on information received from Holstein's 'Poison Cupboard' as well as other sources – for the foibles of public men are seldom inviolate – and it discredited the personal régime of the Kaiser because it assaulted many who were very close to him. Harden also asserted that Eulenburg had pressed the Kaiser to be conciliatory at the Algeçiras conference (a policy which matched Bülow's but was opposed by Holstein and Harden), noting that the homosexual French Counsellor of Legation, M. Raymond Lecomte, had been a crony of Eulenburg's since the eighties and that he had been acquainted with the Kaiser since 1895. The inference, that French influence had subverted German interests in Morocco, was plain to see.[24]

If the general public was lethargic, the Court was shattered by the scandal. Those who did not like Harden's victims pressed that the Kaiser must be told, yet everyone was reluctant to inform him. The Chief of the Military Cabinet, Count Hülsen-Haeseler, was no friend of Eulenburg's, but he refused to act because Eulenburg was the chief amongst the accused and he was not an army man. Even the Kaiser's General Adjutant, General von Plessen, who was noted for his loathing of the press ('Set the guns on them; then they'll shut up!'),[25] and noted, too, for his affection for his master, could not find the courage to inform him of this latest press exposé. Finally on May 3rd the Crown Prince showed his father Harden's two accusing articles. The Kaiser read both, thanked his son, and after that was silent. The Crown Prince later came out with the idea that his father's moral purity was so great 'that he could hardly imagine the possibility of such abnormalities',[26] but this is scarcely credible. Emil Ludwig, William's first biographer, stated emphatically: 'The Kaiser was not ignorant of any phase in the interrelated phases of perverted practices and unnatural tendencies.'[27] Ludwig claimed too that some time before the Criminal Inspector at Court had handed the Kaiser a sealed envelope containing the names of over a hundred homosexuals in the highest circles, together with proof, and the Kaiser had refused to open it, abruptly ordering that it be handed to the police as it was their business not his.[28] This story, though it is not mentioned elsewhere, is consistent with William's dislike of facing up to unpleasant facts. Now he was forced to it. He had to make a decision.

William was too perceptive and intelligent not to realize what many people must be whispering behind his back. His subsequent actions have caused many, Ludwig amongst them, to accuse him of faithlessness to his oldest friend.[29] Whether it was to demonstrate that he himself had had no part in the alleged perverted practices, or to protect the throne from any further mud-slinging, William determined that strong action must be taken. He made it clear at Court that he did not believe the allegations against Eulenburg,[30] yet he asked for his resignation and for that of Moltke. He then insisted they should fight back and sue Harden for criminal libel. Failing that they were to leave the country. The remaining accused were dealt with by a military enquiry.

The effect upon the Kaiser was all that Harden could have wished. It was a shattering blow both to his self-esteem and to his self-confidence. He was quieter, less restless. His old tutor died and, because it was expected of him, he attended Hinzpeter's funeral.[31] He met his uncle King Edward at Cassel and half-heartedly accepted a very half-hearted invitation to visit England in the autumn. Closer to the time he felt he could not stand the strain and, pleading illness, he asked to be excused. King Edward understood the real reason but he insisted that, as all the arrangements had been made, bad feeling between their two countries would result if there was a sudden cancellation.[32] Reluctantly William and Dona made their state visit and the change turned out to be good for him. The King and Queen of Spain were also in England and there were shoots and dinners and entertainments.[33] When Dona returned to Germany William went on to Bournemouth to stay in a house he rented from Colonel E. J. Montagu-Stuart-Wortley. He liked the Colonel and so asked him back to his own house as a guest. But on going home to Germany his nervousness returned. This was much increased when he heard that King Carlos of Portugal and his heir had been shot to death in an ambush before the eyes of the Queen and her younger son.[34] Each time an anarchist struck, surviving sovereigns were filled with apprehension and depression. A small sop to console William was his acquisition of the Achilleion on Corfu which the Emperor Francis Joseph agreed to sell him. He planned to use it as a regular retreat each springtime.[35] Yet nothing, really, could raise his spirits as the protracted and degrading legal processes unfolded the great scandal in Berlin.

Moltke's first suit failed but he sued again and this time Harden was sentenced to four months' imprisonment. Harden at once appealed. His information was accurate and his sentence quashed.[36] Moltke, covered in obloquy, retired into private life.

A sudden and startling turn was the action of a homosexual journalist named Brand who claimed in a pamphlet that the Imperial Chancellor had also offended against Article 175 of the Criminal Code. Bülow moved like lightning. He caused the Crown Prosecutor to bring an action and Brand was sentenced. Eulenburg was cited as a witness and, in the course of his testimony, he denied on oath all that had been attributed to him in Harden's case against Moltke.[37]

Seriously ill, Prince Eulenburg was fated to suffer a longer and more squalid battle with the journalist than any of the other victims of *Die Zukunft*. A Munich newspaper printed a story that Harden had received hush money from the Prince. Harden promptly sued the paper and, in the course of the hearing, he cleverly managed to trap the Prince. Two witnesses, neither of much probity – for one had thirty-two convictions against him and the other was a nervous, stupid man who repeatedly changed his mind – swore in the Munich court that fifteen years before the Prince had been guilty of indecent, though not legally punishable relations with them. If this evidence was true then Eulenburg had committed perjury in Bülow's action against Brand.[38] The Prussian Crown Prosecutor took note of what had happened in the Bavarian court and proceeded against Eulenburg for perjury.[39] The Prince, ill in bed at Liebenberg, was examined by a commissioner and a police-surgeon on three occasions. On the third he was confronted by the two men who had borne testimony against him. They held to their depositions. The police surgeon had noticed a great deterioration in the Prince's health. In addition to his usual ailments he had a violent attack of angina pectoris. In a feeble state he scribbled the facts in his diary. Already he and his family had been irredeemably ruined by the constant press attacks and neither suicide nor flight abroad nor even committal to a lunatic asylum would alter this. To his further wretchedness Bülow as Chancellor and Prussian Minister President signed an order that he be arrested and, ill as he was, he was confined in the Charité in Berlin.[40]

Those who were close to the Kaiser noted that during this period he had never shown such anxiety and irritability. He followed the hearings in the newspapers and special court reports, and could take little pleasure in anything.[41] It is to his discredit that he never once saw Eulenburg or Moltke to give them an opportunity to deny the charges or offer some sort of explanation.[42] It is also to his discredit that when Eulenburg was imprisoned in the Charité William was not disposed to permit Princess Eulenburg to be with her husband. For this he received an angry letter from the Princess which charged him with forsaking an old friend and informed him that, as the one person who had remained faithful to him, she claimed the right to be near her husband and share his fate. William changed his mind. Princess Eulenburg was allowed to remain with her husband.[43] But Eulenburg's physical and mental state deteriorated still further. He was required to return the Order of the Black Eagle so that it should be kept 'in safety' until the case had been concluded. With some spirit he gave orders that the Order should be sent to the Black Eagle Chancery from Liebenberg, together with four other Orders and decorations. In a letter to the Order's Chancellor he gave his reason:

> *I have set an entirely personal value on the conferring of these several Orders and decorations. Hence these objects became wholly valueless to me in the moment when His Majesty, urged thereto by public and private opinion, suddenly deprived me of his countenance and support.*[44]

The Kaiser maintained his grim silence while the preliminary evidence against Eulenburg was sifted. No fewer than 145 witnesses against him were collected. The evidence of 133 broke down. Still there was sufficient for the Prussian Public Prosecutor to indict the Prince for perjury.[45]

Thereafter William endeavoured to lead his normal life. With all the Federal Princes he went to Vienna to congratulate the Emperor Francis Joseph on his Diamond Jubilee. King Edward proposed to visit the Tsar off Reval, and his nephew concluded – wrongly as it happened – that he was going to make a secret treaty and determined to show him an impressive display of German might. When the English royal yacht drew close to the approaches of the Kiel Canal the King was surprised to be greeted by his nephew Prince Harry and almost the entire Grand Fleet; and, as they steamed along the canal, the English royal party was continuously cheered by squadron after squadron of German cavalry which lined both banks its entire length of sixty-one miles.

William was at the Kiel regatta when the case against Eulenburg finally opened.[46] The proceedings continued, while 'grounds for suspicion' were solemnly registered until the only remaining witness for the prosecution was one of Eulenburg's old servants, a man who had acted as his boatman, rowing him about the Starnberg Lake where King Louis of Bavaria had drowned himself at the time Eulenburg was chargé d'affaires at Munich. People came forward to give character witness – the Master of the Royal Household, Baron Albert Rothschild from the Vienna branch of the family, old friends from Munich, officials who had worked with him, and the Prince's own servants.[47] But by now his health had entirely given way. For more than a fortnight he had been carried from his cell in the Charité to the court room. Then he suffered a relapse.[48] The court was moved to the prison and the proceedings continued until the doctors declared that pain and fever and fainting fits made the defendant incapable of understanding what was going on. The court considered, and, finally, the presiding judge declared the proceedings were adjourned. Regular reports from the police surgeons and one futile attempt to continue the cause resulted in a permanent adjournment.[49]

Not able to appear in court, and a physical wreck, Prince Eulenburg was released from the Charité after almost five months' imprisonment.[50] Thereafter he lived a secluded life at Liebenberg and the adjourned case was never reconstituted. His health improved sufficiently for him to become an acute observer and analyser of many of Germany's problems until his death in 1921. Not unexpectedly in his memoranda, letters and other papers, his views of the Kaiser and Maximilian Harden with all his race were very harsh.[51]

At no small cost to himself Harden had won a victory, though it is questionable if he had actually done any good. It was the summit of his journalistic career. Through *Die Zukunft* he continued to snap and carp at authority – at the Court and the Kaiser and High Command for as long as they lasted, and at the Weimar Republic thereafter – but he never had another scoop of such magnitude. In 1922 S.A. thugs beat him up in the street because he was a Jew, and he retired to Switzerland where he died in 1927.

The Kaiser continued to maintain his chilly exterior. Evidently he felt it was his duty to bear with the unspoken criticism that he had behaved badly to his former friends, but the affair had affected him profoundly. Never again did he trust anyone as he had trusted Eulenburg. Significantly it was to Houston Stewart Chamberlain that he revealed most of what he had suffered in the loss of a valued circle of friends through the machinations of a Jewish journalist, and how terrible and humiliating it had been to stand there helpless while their good names had been dragged through the mud.[52] Significantly, too, when he was an old man and the fires of controversy had been damped down he acknowledged his debt to Eulenburg:

> *Whenever he came to our Potsdam home, it was like a flood of sunshine shed on the routine of life. Such a friend as he then was to me he remained through decades of unchanging loyalty. As to the many and various accusations levelled against him, history will one day deliver her verdict. For my part I shall always hold him in grateful remembrance.*[53]

2

Just after Prince Eulenburg had been released from the Charité, the Kaiser's host-guest from Bournemouth, Colonel Montagu-Stuart-Wortley, paid a visit to Germany. He had with him some notes of their conversations of the year before and told the Kaiser that he found his views so interesting they deserved wider appreciation and ought to be published. William was flattered and gave his consent. An article in the form of a mock interview with Montagu-Stuart-Wortley was worked out and a copy formally submitted to Bülow for his approval.

Bülow received the article while he was on holiday. It is questionable if even in those days of more leisurely diplomacy an Imperial Chancellor ever could really take a holiday, and just at that moment it must have been even more unlikely. There had recently been a revolution in Turkey which required his attention. The Sultan, unable to beat his enemies, had sensibly joined them although it had necessitated a considerable reduction in his staff of spies, guards, musicians and A.D.Cs.[54] Then Austria had annexed the two Turkish provinces of Bosnia and Herzegovina, which precipitated an European crisis.[55] This, however, had not prevented the Chancellor from going to the north German coast to enjoy the benefit of sea air, and there he received a transcript of the Kaiser's interview with his English friend. He was required to read and comment on it, but he did neither and sent it to the Foreign Office where a few minor alterations were made to the text before it was returned to him. Once again Bülow failed to read the article, and, in the full belief that it had ministerial approval, the Kaiser permitted it to be published in *The Daily Telegraph* on October 28th, 1908.[56]

Basically the interview covered little fresh ground. William's indignation that England obstinately refused to see him as her best and most consistent friend on the Continent was well known. His claim to have sacrificed his own country's interests by supporting the English in the Boer War was equally well known – though not generally admitted in England and quite certainly disliked in Germany. He also claimed to be cruelly misunderstood by his mother's nation, who did not appreciate that he alone was capable of restraining the anti-English feeling amongst his subjects. Though the general public was unaware of it, King Edward, his ministers and well-informed people undoubtedly knew that the Kaiser and his General Staff had worked out strategic plans for the English in the Boer War and these had been sent to Queen Victoria and Lord Roberts. The fact that they had not been well received was as yet *sub rosa*. Finally the Kaiser reasserted that the German Fleet was intended for potential use in the Far East – which did not deceive the smallest ship's boy in either Navy.[57]

William's aim having been to draw the two countries together, he was at first affronted and then alarmed by the hullabaloo which blew up. What Colonel Montagu-Stuart-Wortley's motives were in encouraging the expression of such views cannot be guessed at, though he might have known that his fellow countrymen would object to being described as 'mad as

March hares' by a foreign sovereign because they did not recognize him as their best friend.[58] There was an even greater outcry in Germany. The chauvinistic right wing said the Kaiser had betrayed them. The left, who wanted his powers checked, said he had considered the interests of a foreign power before that of his own.[59]

If ever there was a time for the constitution to be altered and the Kaiser's powers limited, this was it. That, despite a great deal of noise, it did not take place may be explained in a variety of ways. Probably the most convincing is that many of the intelligentsia believed that the Kaiser as policy-maker was already a spent force. William's old enemy Maximilian Harden underlined this in *Die Zukunft*: 'The empire is sovereign not the Kaiser . . . the constitution does not need to be changed. . . . It offers the people enough.'[60] There was also the Army to be considered. The Officer Corps owed no obedience to any authority other than the Kaiser. All soldiers were outside the jurisdiction of civil law.[61] In theory the Kaiser could have torn up the constitution and ruled absolutely through the Army. Another consideration, generally overlooked, is that the majority of Germans of all classes, except possibly the Bavarians, liked their Kaiser. Few sovereigns have rushed about doing the tedious chores of monarchs as well as William did. Few sovereigns have so frequently carried out one of the most essential obligations of a monarch, to be visible to his people; and to a nation who named their ruler the All Highest and Supreme War Lord it was something to have a Kaiser who could so convincingly look the part. At this stage in his life William was regarded as an exotic cocktail of Don Quixote and Parsifal, and, while on some occasions his speeches and pronouncements were taken seriously and appreciated, on others they were not. The *Daily Telegraph* interview was a singularly unfortunate example of the latter.

William's bewilderment quickly turned to rage. He was furious when he discovered that his Chancellor had not even read the article twice submitted to him for approval. He was even more furious when he discovered slippery Bülow had him in a trap. Correctly the Chancellor proffered his resignation which, because of the present state of public opinion and the continuing Bosnian crisis,[62] he knew the Kaiser could not accept. The only comfort he offered was the promise that he would explain the full facts to the Reichstag and thus silence the critics; and he suggested the best thing his master could do was to maintain a calm exterior and carry on with his prearranged plans.[63] William agreed. No doubt he wished to get away from his weeping wife, reproachful friends, and violent criticism. He left Potsdam for Austria. There he shot with Archduke Francis Ferdinand at Eckardsau, killing 65 driven stags in a battue; stayed with Emperor Francis Joseph at Schönbrunn; and hunted foxes and shot at Donaueschingen in Baden as the guest of Prince Max zu Fürstenberg.[64] His hosts and his suite did everything they could to lift him out of his depression, but a report from Berlin deepened it. His Chancellor had failed him. The promised explanation of the full facts to satisfy the Reichstag turned out to be a pro-Bülow, schoolmasterly report on the Kaiser's waywardness. The Chancellor declared that in future, even in private conversations, the Kaiser would be more reserved because it was essential to the interests of a common policy between him and his ministers. He concluded: 'If this were not so, neither I nor my successors could accept the responsibility.'[65] William perhaps did not know Tirpitz's opinion that 'an oiled eel is a leech compared to Bülow'.[66] At any rate his Chancellor's betrayal and scornful impudence was too much for him. He broke down and cried on Prince Fürstenberg's shoulder.[67] It was symptomatic. His nerves were going to pieces. The Prince and Princess tried by every means to calm him but a grotesque accident after dinner on the last night of the Kaiser's stay at Donaueschingen put him into an even worse state of excitement. The chief of his Military Cabinet, Count Hülsen-Haeseler, did his special turn to delight the company, dancing gracefully a *pas seul* or two dressed in a ballerina's tulle tutu, and then dropped dead. Two doctors tried to revive him but had to give up and, as he had died of a form of apoplexy and by this time rigor mortis was setting in, the General's A.D.Cs and servants had the greatest difficulty in getting him out of the tutu into uniform. He lay in state in the large saloon of the castle and was buried the next morning. The Kaiser was distraught. Not only had he lost a valued friend and counsellor, but he also recognized that the circumstances of Hülsen-Haeseler's death could and probably would be misconstrued. He was in a deplorable situation and he left Baden a changed man.[68]

Dazed by the turn of events, or in a desperate attempt to improve his position, it is alleged he gave an even more disastrous interview to an American journalist in which to prove, as it were, his devotion to his own people, he verbally lambasted the English.[69] The journalist got his copy through to the *New York World* and a synopsis was printed which stated that the Kaiser considered his uncle King Edward corrupt, his Court rotten, his country heading for disaster, and that an Anglo-German war was inevitable.[70] This explosive matter was denounced by the German Foreign Ministry as 'a baseless invention's and, after an investigation in New York, the newspaper proprietors sent a cable to the Imperial Chancellor to say no convincing basis had been found for its published synopsis.[71]

The Kaiser's comments on this journalistic hoax are not known, but his spirits could hardly have been lower than they were. On his return to the New Palace Bülow asked for an audience. The Chancellor's position had become difficult because he had roused the wrath of the left for not seizing the opportunity to change the constitution and he had roused the wrath of the right for making a fool of the Kaiser. It is scarcely credible but he arrived at the New Palace to lecture William and demand his signature to a most humiliating document. In it the Kaiser ensured the continuity of present policy, approved of the Chancellor's Reichstag speech, and assured him of his continued confidence.[72] Still in the same trap of 'sign or I resign' William did as he was bidden and a highly satisfied Bülow, now to all intents and purposes dictator of the Reich, published the declaration. The Kaiser made one act of defiance. A short time afterwards he was due to make a speech at the Berlin City Hall and insisted that the Chancellery compose it. He then took the draft from Bülow's hands in full public eye, read it out in a monotone, and returned it.[73] But it was simply a gesture. Bülow was still virtually his master, and the realization sent William into a state of nervous collapse.

The débâcle on top of the homosexual scandals drained him of all energy. He suffered from giddiness and long bouts of shivering.[74] He took to his bed tortured by facial neuralgia. Then, abruptly, he decided he could endure it no longer. He sent for his eldest son and told the Court Chamberlain to announce to Bülow that he was abdicating. In great alarm the Kaiserin sent to beg Bülow to see her first. She asked him directly if he really wanted the Kaiser to abdicate. Bülow tried to calm her. The Crown Prince then arrived and went directly to his father. He sat with him for over an hour listening to a stream of self pity and acrimony. Afterwards the Crown Prince visited the Chancellor who recorded that he believed the young prince wished for the throne. But someone, possibly Dona, steeled William. He changed his mind and made no further mention of abdication. Listless, quiet and suddenly aged, he could not throw off a deep depression which followed the *crise de nerfs*. He functioned like an automaton, behaved as if he were in deep mourning, and everyone near him spoke in whispers not liking to break the silence which surrounded him. The Kaiserin sent for her two younger sons Oscar and Joachim from Plön, thinking that their high spirits might cheer their father. She also sent for her eldest unmarried son from Kiel, but neither the younger boys nor Prince Ethelbert, though he talked cheerfully of naval affairs, made any impression. Christmas passed. No-one could recall such a joyless feast. Inevitably such a drastic change in the Kaiser and the subsequent dislocation of his programme and the proper functioning of his Court caused some people to believe he was quite out of his wits. Rumours spread and persisted for years.* But, in fact, his breakdown was almost over.[75]

---

* 'We all have our breakdowns' said the late Noël Coward, and not in fun but because he himself suffered from two. He made the point that anyone driven too hard and living under tension can succumb but the breakdowns need cause no permanent

On New Year's day the Season began and by custom the Court moved from Potsdam to Berlin for the Kaiser to receive New Year wishes from the Diplomatic Corps and other officials. It was obvious that he was dreading it, especially the drive through the city. Yet it turned out to be his cure. To his surprise he was received with an ovation. Brooding on the stings of criticism from largely left-wing intellectuals who regarded his office as an anachronism and his behaviour as irresponsible, William had overlooked the fact that they represented a very small proportion of the community. Now the larger part showed their loyal enthusiasm and as the Season proceeded he was left in no doubt that the majority of his subjects really cared for him.[76] Except that he looked much older, the Kaiser was himself again by the time his uncle King Edward made his first and only State Visit to Germany.

3

The middle of February in 1909 was a singularly ill-chosen time for a bronchitic old gentleman to visit frozen Berlin but the King's ministers regarded the visit as essential. It was also unfortunate that the King had chosen to regard the *New York World* hoax as authentic and that he was deeply hurt and resentful.[79] He was also asthmatic and short-tempered and, though his nephew tried to make the visit a success,[80] a chapter of incidents upset the King. The first was on their arrival at the frontier of Brandenburg where a Guard of Honour awaited the King and he had not been woken by his valet. It took him ten minutes to struggle into his tight-fitting Prussian uniform during which a military band played 'God Save the King' again and again.[81] This bad beginning, which made the King furious, was followed by a misunderstanding at the Lehrter station in Berlin where the King descended from the Queen's coach and the Kaiser and Kaiserin with all their family were expecting them both to alight from his own and were some distance down the platform.[82] Then there was difficulty with the horses drawing the carriage of the Kaiserin and Queen Alexandra. They jibbed and refused to move and Dona and her guest had to transfer to another carriage which caused a reshuffle through the whole procession. This pleased neither the Kaiser, who was mortified, nor the King, who was impatient to get on.[83] The programme was extensive. The King's greatest success and most notable contribution to better relations between the two countries was a visit he paid to the Berlin

---

damage. Two illustrious examples may be cited: Queen Victoria's 'madness' after the death of her mother in 1861,[77] and President Wilson's dramatic collapse at a vital point of the Paris Peace negotiations in 1919.[78] The spryness and acuteness of the Kaiser in exile and the even tenor of his life thereafter show how stable he really was.

City Hall. There, though breathless with climbing many stairs, he received the gift of a golden goblet of wine from the mayor at the hands of his small daughter, drank to the Berliners in the galleries, and made a memorable speech in mellifluous German.[84] But the weather was vile, and, though the arrangements were well managed, they exhausted the King. To everyone's astonishment he fell asleep at table during a family dinner, and again at a gala ballet performance of *Sardanapalus*, when he was woken by the realistic fires on the stage and was much alarmed. After a luncheon at the British Embassy he collapsed in a choking fit and fainted.[85] It was not however serious and he was able to attend a State ball that evening in the White Hall of the Old Palace, where he watched the state lancers, quadrilles and minuets faultlessly performed by long rows of dancers.[86] After the free-and-easy ways of his own Court he found the Prussian protocol very stiff. He wished to smoke, but could not. He wished for a whisky and soda but was told none was available. When he asked to retire and play a game of cards he was informed it was not the custom at the Prussian Court.[87] On the next day, before the royal train left, the Kaiser spoke to his uncle about Bülow's treacherous behaviour and said that when an opportunity occurred he would dismiss him, but this was the only political discussion they had.[88] King Edward's Assistant Private Secretary noted how uneasy the Kaiser was in the presence of his uncle: 'There were always forced jokes, and the whole atmosphere when the two were together seemed charged with dangerous electricity.'[89] It was their last meeting.

King Edward returned home to a world of trouble: budget problems, social problems, and great naval problems. In order to surpass German naval armament programmes no less than eight dreadnoughts were ordered to be laid down at a staggering cost to the British public purse. This, plus Bülow's persistence in supporting Austria's annexation of Bosnia and Herzegovina, which drew Russia closer to England, augured badly for the future peace of Europe. Europe had finally settled into two great blocks. Compared with the other Powers, Italy was of small account, and the old Triple Alliance in effect had become a dual alliance of Germany and Austria, while France and England had scooped in Russia to make a Triple Entente. Bismarck's lynch-pins of foreign policy: refusing to be involved in the Balkans, leaning in friendship towards Russia, and being one of three in a world of five Powers had been totally abandoned by his former pupil Bülow.[90]

Not until March would the Kaiser have anything to do with his Chancellor beyond what was absolutely necessary for the running of affairs. Bülow felt this deeply. Eventually, after repeated requests for a private audience, William agreed to see him in the Picture Gallery of the Old Palace in Berlin. There the Chancellor attempted to defend his conduct in the previous

November, and the Kaiser bluntly told him that he had expected better support. But a kind of reconciliation took place.[91] The Kaiser telegraphed his brother Prince Harry, presumably in cypher:

HAVE JUST FORGIVEN BÜLOW WHO BEGGED MY PARDON IN FLOODS OF TEARS

And he consented to dine that night with the Kaiserin at the Chancellery as a public sign that his differences with Bülow had been made up. For a time it must have seemed that the Kaiser had again been taken in by 'the Eel', but when a pamphlet was published which 'unmasked Prince Bülow's baseness' William described it as 'very good' and pointedly recommended it to his friends.[92]

In May 1909 Baron Frederick von Holstein died. As the vengeful destroyer of Prince Eulenburg, Count Kuno von Moltke, and many others in the Kaiser's closest confidence, and as an assiduous collector of material for his 'Poison Cupboard' over so many years, he could not have been much mourned. Possibly Bülow had reasons to be grateful to him for not revealing publicly what he would have preferred kept silent; and no doubt the owner and waiters of Borchardt's missed the old gentleman. A cartoon in the satirical Bavarian newspaper *Simplicissimus* was the Spider's most famous obituary notice. The Bavarians had liked Eulenburg. Bavarians did not like Jews. A combination of the two resulted in a drawing of a gigantic Maximilian Harden standing beside a laboratory bench holding up a phial. Attached to a draining apparatus lay a shrivelled and defunct Holstein, recognizable by his pebble glasses and bowler hat. The caption read: 'After Harden had Extracted his Poison Holstein Died.'[93]

Only a month later Bülow's policy to introduce death duties was defeated by the Reichstag. With the support of the Kaiser behind him he could have continued in power and returned to the attack another day, but patently he did not have the Kaiser behind him. He went to the *Hohenzollern* lying at Kiel, where William was enjoying the regatta, and handed in his resignation. Politely the Kaiser thanked him, pocketed the note, and to avoid the possibility of any further talk took Bülow with him to luncheon aboard the Prince of Monaco's yacht. Not knowing how he stood, Bülow afterwards returned to Berlin. For three miserable weeks he waited. He had enjoyed being Chancellor. Knowing how changeable the Kaiser could be, it was conceivable that he might not accept the resignation after all. Then Bülow saw his resignation announced in the press. He was to be awarded the Order of the Black Eagle in brilliants for his services to the Empire. William added a touch of irony to the retirement. After their official farewell in the Old

Palace gardens, he proposed himself and Dona to dine with the Bülows on the following night.[94]

Some time afterwards William was with the King of Württemberg in the Old Palace gardens and showed him exactly where the official farewell had taken place. His words showed how deeply he had felt the treachery of 'dear Bernard'. 'It was here, on this spot,' he said, 'that I threw the rotter out.'[95]

CHAPTER THIRTEEN

The Iron Dice Roll

'There seems to be sulphur in the air'

CHARLES FÜRSTENBERG, Head of the
Berliner Handelsgesellschaft

I

The replacement of Prince Bülow was not an easy task. The Kaiser considered and rejected a number of possible candidates and eventually his choice rested on a man Bülow recommended, whom he had known personally since his boyhood and who for the past two years had been Secretary of State for the Interior.

Theobald von Bethmann Hollweg was a large man, six feet three inches in height, big boned and well-fleshed. His hair was cropped in the Prussian peg-top fashion, and he cut a great dash in uniform. Towering over most of his ministers and five inches taller than the Kaiser, he looked like a second Bismarck, massive and formidable. In fact he was almost the exact opposite of Bismarck, mild-mannered, courteous, consistently hard-working, and, having spent most of his life in the Prussian civil service, he was an administrator rather than a leader.[1] Moreover he lacked any constructive policy of his own, and shouldered as best he could the world policy of his predecessors.[2]

Because he knew little about Foreign Affairs and felt he could not rely upon Bülow's last Foreign Secretary, Baron von Schön, he asked the Kaiser for Kiderlen-Wächter, who had been 'Dumpling' in the *Kladderadatsch* attack on the Foreign Office and had wounded that journal's editor in a duel. At one time Kiderlen had enjoyed William's favour. On Norwegian cruises he had earned his keep by coarse jokes and slapstick amateur theatricals, generally clowning with enormous strings of sausages;[3] but when it came to William's knowledge that Kiderlen was also fond of laughing at him behind his back and talking disrespectfully of the Kaiserin, he was sent off into virtual exile as Ambassador to Bucharest.[4] After thirteen years he was brought back to the

Wilhelmstrasse as an adviser during the Bosnian crisis, and showed that, far from atrophying his talents, his Roumanian exile had actually sharpened them. He was grosser, more vulgar than ever, and drank too much, but he was Germany's most informed expert on foreign affairs. William warned Bethman that he would soon find his ear had a flea in it, and gave his grudging consent.[5]

Kiderlen immediately turned his attention to the most leprous spot in foreign affairs, German relations with England, and chose as intermediaries Ballin the Jewish shipowner who was the Kaiser's friend and Sir Ernest Cassel who was King Edward's Jewish banker.[6] Admiral von Tirpitz had at last shown himself willing to negotiate some sort of reasonable agreement about naval rearmament. Both he and the Kaiser wished England to abandon her 'Two-Power Standard' whereby she determined that her Navy should be stronger than the next two navies put together, and which in effect was already out of date.[7] Ballin and Cassel worked hard. Tirpitz wished for a 3:4 ratio in shipbuilding. It would reduce England's fantastic shipbuilding expenses, still leave her with the largest Navy in the world, and, in Tirpitz's words, Germany would have 'reasonable prospects in a defensive war against England'.[8] But Kiderlen tied to this proposal a request that there also be a political agreement and this did not suit the Liberal Party in power in England. A general election was due and they foresaw that any sort of political commitments to Germany would not increase their popularity.[9] So the matter was allowed to drop and it was not brought up again until 1912. Meanwhile Kiderlen looked towards Russia, aiming for an agreement to maintain the *status quo* in the Balkans.[10]

The new Chancellor himself set about the virtually impossible task of managing the Reichstag, the Junkers and industrialists, and the General Staff. He also took the trouble to anticipate his master's penchant for dropping bricks, and tried to reduce the areas of aggravation. In environments or circumstances which might encourage the Kaiser's impetuosity he either gave him a friendly warning beforehand or had the programme arranged so that speech-making was cut to the bone and opportunities for discussion almost eliminated. Failing all else, he attempted to prevent any indiscretions from being reported in the press.[11] In exercising this kind of gentle censorship he served William well. It was a new departure. Previous Chancellors had either scolded the Kaiser, or given him his head, or made him look a fool in public.

At first William feared that Bethmann would be bossy, but he soon took comfort in his common-sense and stolid Prussianness. Being cultured and sympathetic and honest, Bethmann could be relied upon, though unfortunately he lacked a sense of humour. His work was endless because neither he nor any

single man could manage the explosion of the imperial economy and population. Germany's national wealth was larger than any other country in the
world, her population about sixty-five million, her armaments vast; and it
is a tenable hypothesis that given time and patience both France and Russia
would have become politically and economically dependent on her friendship.[12] Unfortunately the Pan-Germans were aggressive and had no patience at
all. The Chancellor's efforts to restrain them were constant but largely fruitless. In private the Kaiser scorned their vulgarity and strongly disapproved of
the way sections of the German press supported their extreme nationalism.
In public he tried to maintain his distance from them, and, picking up his
energy, he resumed his apparently tireless round with breaks here and there
to relieve the monotony.

Always interested in progress, he applauded the General Staff's decision to
have a number of officers instructed in aviation; in fact, he was so carried
away by enthusiasm at an airship trial that, overlooking the fact there were
still more than nine decades to run, he declared Count Ferdinand von
Zeppelin was the greatest German of the twentieth century.[13] He was equally
delighted by a flying display given by the American pilot Orville Wright in
September 1909 over the huge parade ground at Potsdam. For half an hour
against a brilliant sunset he watched Wright's biplane circling and diving
overhead and warmly congratulated him on his descent.[14] He was not,
however, so pleased to hear that his eldest son had persuaded Wright to take
him on a seven-minute flight and, as a result, was thinking of buying himself
an aeroplane. The Crown Princess was also highly alarmed. Flying was still
very much in the experimental stage. Only four months previously the
French aviator Blériot had achieved a triumph by flying over the Channel in
a monoplane, but he had actually lost his way and, instead of being greeted
by an excited and expectant crowd, he was met by a single English constable
on patrol duty.[15] The idea of a future Kaiser needlessly risking his life was
quickly scotched.[16]

Royal mortality was very much before William at this time. The mis-
anthrope Leopold II of the Belgians died in his Brussels hothouse, the Pavillon
des Palmiers, accompanied only by a French street-walker he had picked up
seven years before and who, even before he was cold, was hurled screeching
from the room.[17] Then on a Friday afternoon in May King Edward collapsed
while playing with two pet canaries in a cage by an open window, and that
night, surrounded by his family and Household and the highest officers of
state, he died.[18] His death made more of a mark on the history of Europe than
that of Queen Victoria. Related to or personally acquainted with most of the
sovereigns and leading statesmen of his day, he had earned the title 'Edward
the Peacemaker'. William did not think he deserved it. He was convinced

that his old uncle had sown the seeds of war in Europe,[19] a view which was reciprocated. On his way home from Biarritz only a few days before his death the King had seen an old friend the Comtesse de Greffuhle in Paris and said: 'I have not long to live. And then my nephew will make war.'[20] Neither had had much patience or understanding of the other. William attended the funeral as a chief mourner, one of nine reigning sovereigns, five heirs apparent, and scores of princes and princesses who followed the gun carriage. His feelings were very mixed. He was proud to be in his 'second home', proud that the crowds cheered him, angry with King Ferdinand of Bulgaria and Archduke Francis Ferdinand of Austria who bickered about precedence,[21] doubtful that although he got on so well with his cousin, now George V, there would be any change in English policy, and at the same time he was deeply moved by his uncle's funeral. Lord Esher, who had been one of King Edward's closest friends and advisers and the man who knew his deepest thoughts, recorded: 'My firm belief is, that of all the royal visitors the only *mourner* was this extraordinary Kaiser'.[22]

During his father's absence the Crown Prince deputized for him, reviewing the great spring parade when a Russian anarchist, later found to be insane, threw a tin can at him.[23] But he was less dutiful a son than William could have wished. There were special centenary celebrations that June to mark the death of Queen Louise in 1810. She was a dearly-loved figure in Prussian history but her great-great grandson took no part in the celebrations and was put under temporary house arrest by his irritated father.[24] Far more serious, the Crown Prince was allowing himself to be used by the Pan-Germans, and Crown Princess Cecile, though certain aspects of her married life were not what the Kaiser and Kaiserin would have wished, entirely supported her husband in his association with an emerging war party.[25] Twice William had refused his son permission to go to England and only the year before had vetoed, on political grounds, a private visit to the United States although President Taft had already given his enthusiastic approval.*[26] But now he decided they were both better out of the country, and he planned to send them on an extended tour. His first intention was that they should visit India on the way to the Far East but he modified the programme so that they should travel incognito to Ceylon and from Colombo the Crown Prince would make a State Visit to India and the Crown Princess go to Egypt for a

* The Kaiser's friend Theodore Roosevelt retired from office in 1909 to hunt big game in East Africa and write (he had already published fourteen books). He visited Berlin in April 1910, and it was only with difficulty that his Court officers dissuaded the Kaiser from rushing to the station to meet him personally, an unprecedented honour for a commoner and one no longer in office. However a great dinner was given for Roosevelt at the New Palace and the two met again the next month in London for King Edward's funeral.[28]

private holiday. It has been suggested that this was because the Crown Princess one day turned on her father-in-law and said it was strange that he expected absolute obedience from his sons when he himself had been so undutiful to his own parents.[27] But it is unlikely that the Crown Princess would have dared touch so sensitive a nerve and invite the Kaiser's wrath for the sake of a husband who regularly humiliated her by his unfaithfulness. More likely the Kaiser, realizing they were getting on badly, thought that a short separation with his full approval would quieten gossip and perhaps draw the two closer again. He wrote to ask George V if his son might visit India and arrangements were made for his reception by the India Office.[29]

Before leaving the Crown Prince seized a chance to win applause from the Pan-Germans when he was invested as Rector Magnificentissimus of the Albertina University in Königsberg. In his inaugural speech he pleaded that youth should be given patriotic feelings and concluded:

> We long for a stressing of our German national characteristics in contrast to the striving for internationalization which threatens to blot out our healthy national individuality.[30]

No doubt it was with some relief that the Kaiser and Kaiserin saw off their bellicose son and his wife on November 2nd, but even at a distance of over three thousand miles the Crown Prince still caused them concern. At a ball in January he was vastly attracted by a Burmese princess, so much so that with almost unbelievable irresponsibility considering he was on a State Visit, he slipped from his escort a few days later and returned to the scene of the ball. There he found his princess but surrounded by her entire family. A specially arranged gala dinner had to take place without him, and both German and English officials were greatly perturbed.[31] So was his father when he heard the news. What the young man might have succeeded in doing had his world trip continued can only be a matter of conjecture for, owing to plague in the Far East, the tour had to be cut short. A last report from the German General-Consul before the Crown Prince's official visit ended in Calcutta said that His Imperial Highness had been surprised to find quite a number of presentable young ladies in the German colony. Against this the Kaiser scribbled one of his shorter marginal comments: 'Aha!'[32] When the Crown Prince and Princess arrived home in Germany there was no evident sign that the breach between them had been healed. To his great disappointment the Crown Prince was given none of the military appointments he had asked for, which would have kept him in Berlin. Instead he was to be sent into virtual exile away in East Prussia as commander of a regiment in Danzig.[33] However he was not due to take up his appointment for several months and during this period he could perhaps have won a reversal of the decision by proving more responsible and dependable. He went with the Crown Princess to Russia for Tsar Nicholas' birthday celebrations, canoed daily with the Tsar, and felt thoroughly oppressed by the security arrangements made for his safety. No doubt they interfered with his pleasures. The German Ambassador's report on the visit was scarcely encouraging to a worried father: 'The princely couple met a friendly, almost warm atmosphere, which was not marred by any unpleasantness.'[34]

Their reception was better in England, where they went to represent the Kaiser at the coronation of George V, but there the freedom of movement gave the Crown Prince a false impression that he could do what he wanted. Out of great kindness and at some trouble King George had arranged for his young relative to be entertained by the Duke of Buccleuch and other special friends, but the Crown Prince refused to go, saying that he preferred to play polo at Ranelagh. He would not listen to the Crown Princess' pleadings, and caused the German Embassy staff a great deal of embarrassment and trouble. Eventually the Naval Attaché told him to his face he had to go to the Buccleuchs as a matter of duty to the King. Though still grumbling, he at last consented.[35]

The Crown Prince's behaviour in London did not reassure his father. There was no chance now that his tour of duty in Danzig would be altered to something more agreeable to him. He had a certain position in society as Crown Prince, but he was sadly deficient in the qualities expected in the Prussian Officer Corps – self-discipline, a sense of duty and dedication, and loyalty, and the Kaiser was anxious to remove him from the centre of affairs as much as possible. Above all he wanted to prise him from the Pan-German League and their unwholesome nationalism.

Under pressure from the League and from industrialist entrepreneurs a second Morocco Crisis occurred just after the Coronation in England. Through the Kaiser and George V – the latter presumably speaking under ministerial advice – the Chancellor had checked that the English regarded the Algeçiras Agreement as no longer valid because to all intents and purposes the French were still colonizing Morocco just as the English were establishing their rights in Egypt.[36] This did not suit Germany. The entrepreneurs wanted to make money in Morocco. The Pan-Germans wanted to wag the flag there. Bethmann had no intention of losing influence in Northern Africa, but he could not fathom what motivated his Foreign Secretary. In the end he had to make him drunk to get at the truth that Kiderlen was really after colonies in Central Africa in exchange for Germany waiving her rights in Morocco. The Kaiser, who had by no means forgotten the humiliation of the empire at the time of the first Morocco Crisis, was fearful of a second.[37] He said so to Bethmann in May. However, Kiderlen caught him when he was in an ebullient mood at the end of Kiel week and explained that he and M. Cambon, the French Ambassador to Berlin, were almost in agreement but that a little physical pressure would make all the difference. Eager to get rid of Kiderlen and be off on his Norwegian cruise William forgot his misgivings and consented to the German gunboat *Panther* being sent to the port of Agadir on the Atlantic littoral of Africa.[38] The English instantly conceived the idea that the wily Germans intended setting up a naval base which would threaten Gibraltar and they asked for an explanation.[39] Kiderlen refused to answer. Instead he continued negotiating with M. Cambon, explaining that Germany now wished for the whole of the French Congo, not merely part of it. M. Cambon was speechless.[40] When the Kaiser received a report of the negotiations he was exceedingly angry. He ordered the *Hohenzollern* to be turned about, and telegraphed Bethmann to say that France was not to be threatened in his absence. He feared war. As did France. 'London will turn nasty,' William minuted.[41] She did in the person of Mr Lloyd George, who, in his capacity as Chancellor of the Exchequer, spoke at the Bankers' Dinner in the City of London. He stressed the need for settling disputes otherwise than by the sword, yet added:

> If a situation were to be forced upon us in which peace could only be preserved by the surrender of the great and beneficent position Britain has won by centuries of heroism . . . then I say emphatically that peace at that price would be intolerable.

The bankers had no idea what he was talking about, but the German Ambassador did when he read a report of the speech in the press.[42] Bethmann Hollweg sent a formal remonstrance to London. It was couched in such terms that the Admiralty ordered a concentration of the Fleet.* In fact for quite a long period, while the French and the Germans thrashed out their problems, England remained constantly prepared for war. All tunnels and bridges on the vital South Eastern Railway were patrolled day and night.[43] Finally there was a Franco-German agreement. In return for German recognition of French rights in Morocco, France ceded part of the French Congo which gave the Germans river outlets for exports from the Cameroons. But no-one in Germany was really satisfied, certainly not the Kaiser, who was as good as called a coward by Maximilian Harden in *Die Zukunft*, and certainly not those thoughtful Germans who had hoped Bethmann would not follow Bülow's jingoistic policies. Kiderlen had not separated France from the Triple Entente. They were closer than ever. The great industrialists who bought

* This was more of a gesture than an effective remedy as the ships were widely scattered, reserve crews were being paid off and colliers were laid up because of a coal strike.[45]

French iron ore and holdings in French companies now found their task far more difficult. The entrepreneurs who had stakes in Morocco were wildly dissatisfied. But the most vocal of all criticism came, as might have been expected, from the Pan-German League. Bethmann was attacked in the Reichstag, accused of timidity, not being up to his job, and generally humiliated,[44] and to the Kaiser's dismay, one of the Chancellor's detractors was his eldest son.

Hardly had he settled into his quarters in Danzig under the command of his father's faithful friend and A.D.C., General von Mackensen, than the Crown Prince took unofficial leave and appeared in the capital. He went to the Reichstag, and after a fiery anti-Chancellor speech by a Prussian conservative, he drew everyone's attention by applauding loudly, smiting the pommel of his sword and nodding his approval. As soon as the Kaiser heard of this extraordinary behaviour he sent for his son to the Old Palace and gave him a piece of his mind. He also sent for the Chancellor and directed him to correct the Crown Prince's misapprehensions as to what had gone on in Morocco and explain the exact situation.[46] Neither rebuke nor explanation affected the Crown Prince. On the day following he delighted the Pan-Germans by appearing in a zeppelin over Berlin and that night he occupied the Imperial Box at the Circus to be greeted by a great ovation.[47] Overnight he had become the hero of young officers, students and nationalists for his dare-devil, aggressive policy.[48] He was ordered back to Danzig but the Kaiser and the Chancellor knew he would be used by those who were obsessed with the aggrandizement of the Second Reich. The German Ambassador to St James's reported that the Crown Prince would no longer be welcomed in England. A humiliating note came from King George that he could not understand that an heir to the throne could interfere in the policies of his father to such an extent.[49] William did not care to explain that his son was out of control. The Crown Prince did as he pleased: used the long-reins, long-legged riding posture which was considered 'smart' but was entirely contrary to Army Regulations,[50] travelled about, flirting with English girls, hunted, played tennis, enjoyed water sports; and the anti-Prussian Bavarian paper *Simplicissimus* printed a cartoon which showed him dressed in tennis clothes with the caption 'Danzig? Danzig? I've heard that name somewhere before!'[51] He also continued to interfere in state affairs, telegraphing the Foreign Office both to ask for information and give his forthright views on the inadequacy of their news service. Kiderlin begged him not to send critical telegrams *en clair* but it made little difference.[52] The Crown Prince refused to accept the responsibilities of his position. His amorous adventures were a scandal to his mother. His political views repugnant to his father. It seemed that all he had done for Germany was to provide male heirs.* William had often been a thoughtless and unfeeling son, but he had never been disobedent to authority nor to what he believed was his duty. His own son was a rogue elephant amongst German princes, not simply different but an actual danger to the fatherland.

2

At what point the Kaiser became aware that war was inevitable is a controversial point.

There were elections in January 1912 and the Social Democrats, after their rejection in the Hottentot elections, returned 110 deputies. It was a sweeping victory, though a combination of the other parties prevented any drastic Socialist legislation being put forward. Amongst the deputies was the son of William Liebknecht, a founder member of the party who had been a personal friend of Marx and editor of *Vorwärts*. But Charles Liebknecht went a step further than anyone. He was a full-blooded revolutionary, dedicated to the overthrow of the state, and violently anti-militarist. He had an ingenious Jesuitical scheme for unfastening the Army's grasp on Germany by indoctrinating boys before they were called up so that, as informed conscripts, they could reject the military system from within. In 1907 he had published this idea in a pamphlet and been imprisoned for lèse-majesté, and like many another revolutionary leader had been elected to the Prussian parliament while still in gaol. Now he was a deputy of the Reichstag, not liked or trusted by his own party, but the fact that he had been elected at all was a sign of the times.[53] Many people were no longer satisfied with Bismarck's peculiar constitution of the Empire. They wanted change. For example, the *Frankfurter Zeitung*, a highly regarded liberal newspaper, had a large circulation and consistently and vigorously criticized the failure of the central government, and it is doubtful if individual readers would ever have considered sacrificing their liberalism for nationalism.[54] Yet the opposition not only lacked the organization but it also lacked the drive to force power from the few who had it, and the intellectuals who might have fired the opposition were like their Kaiser in that they lacked a sustained sense of proportion.[55] Germany was a political cloud-cuckoo-land.

Because a new Navy Bill was coming up for ratification, Ballin and Cassel arranged for fresh conversations to take place between Germany and Britain. Haldane was sent by the British on an informal mission to Berlin in February. He had been chosen because he had such an excellent command of German, but though he talked with the Kaiser and Tirpitz and the Chancellor, each

* William was born in 1906, Louis Ferdinand in 1907, Hubert in 1909, and Frederick George in 1911. Two daughters were born later.

side was convinced that the other was not being frank. The conversations broke down, and Haldane was accused of being pro-German while Bethmann was accused of being pro-British.[56]

In October that year the Balkans, as not infrequently happened, were ablaze. Bulgaria, Serbia and Montenegro joined by Greece attacked Turkey and within a month they had won several campaigns. Prince Charles von Lichnowsky, the Kaiser's new Ambassador to the Court of St James's, later noted: 'The disposal of the Turkish heritage raised the spectre of a European war.'[57] Indeed it did. In November both Russia and Austria mobilized.[58] England did nothing spectacular. Nor, surprisingly, did Germany though on December 8th, a Sunday, the Kaiser convened a War Council to which members of his Army and Navy staffs were admitted but the civilian members of his government were not. William was concerned about a report from Lichnowsky in London. The Ambassador had been talking with Haldane, who had uttered a solemn warning that 'England could not tolerate Germany becoming dominant on the continent and uniting it under her leadership'. He had added that as a result England would naturally side with France in the event of a European war.[59] How much or little reliance could be placed upon Lord Haldane's remark in that December of 1912 was a matter for conjecture, but, bearing it in mind, it was important for the Germans to make a plan.

Professor Fritz Fischer, Professor Adolf Gasser and other German historians who broke the patriotic self-censorship policy in 1961 because it no longer had a raison d'être, state categorically that this War Council there and then made a decision to fight a major war, not two years later in 1914.[60] A short time before the Council met, General Frederick von Bernhardt had startled Europe by the publication of his book *Germany and the next War*, in which he stated:

> In one way or another we must square our account with France if we wish for a free hand in our international policy. . . . France must be so completely crushed that she can never again come across our path.[61]

Though the General had been dismissed by Schlieffen,[62] there was more to his book than the other war-scarers such as Childers's *The Riddle of the Sands*, August Niemann's *The Coming Conquest of England*, and Le Queux' serial in the *Daily Mail* about a German invasion of England.[63] In fact Professor Fischer believes it represented the main thinking of the General Staff from which the author had been dismissed.[64] Whether or not this was a dress rehearsal for what ultimately happened in 1914 must remain a matter for the historians but non-specialists will appreciate that as three of the Powers were mobilizing on account of the crisis in the Balkans, and England had declared her support for France, some sort of German War Council was clearly necessary.

Certain premises were accepted by the General Staff. Since the débâcle with Japan Russia had been reorganizing her forces; that is, so far as the Minister of War, General Vladimir Sukhomlinov, permitted. This was virtually nil. His Court nickname 'General Fly-off' was a misnomer.[65] As bald and oval as an egg, no-one less liked work or more liked play. Most of his attention was given to his fourth wife, who was thirty-two years younger than he; and some of it to amassing a fortune through corruption.[66] He had a sentimental regard for the charge – by sabre or bayonet – and wasted no money on modern weapons. The idea that war might be a duel of firepower he held in contempt, and he made no effort to build up armaments factories or supplies. Though Russia's manpower was vast, she had few railways and her lumbering attempts at mobilization in 1912 showed she was far behind other European armies. Fully aware of all this, German intelligence had calculated that Russia could not be ready for a full-scale European war until 1916.[67] German intelligence also had a fairly low opinion of the French, who had had no fewer than forty-two war ministers in forty-three years and whose Army was chiefly officered by the bourgeoisie, even by promoted rankers. The German Military Attaché in Paris reported that the Director of the École Supérieure de la Guerre, Ferdinand Foch, was an abstruse thinker on military scientific principles and only rarely concerned himself with the humdrum matters of drill, discipline, cover and guard, fire-power, and tactics on the ground; and in December 1912, even during the European crisis, the French were chiefly concerned about a proposed change in uniform from the cherry-red trousers worn since 1830. In parliament a deputy cried passionately: 'Le pantalon rouge c'est la France!'[68] The German Army itself was in excellent trim; in fact at this stage the Prussian Minister of War was actually complaining that barracks and training grounds could not digest any more recruits. This view was unacceptable to the Head of Mobilization Section of the General Staff, General Eric Ludendorff, who was an organizer without peer and was stuffing more and more recruits into the Army at that very moment.[69]

On the strength of all this, and despite his melancholy prognostication that any future war would be a long, wearisome business, Colonel General von Moltke had come to the conclusion that the sooner it was started the better. He told the War Council that a better opportunity had not occurred since the formation of the Triple Alliance. It would at least give his armies time to settle the French and the English with the Schlieffen plan before dealing with Russia.[70] In other words it would be a preventive war. His view as Chief of General Staff weighed heavily. His motto was well known: 'First ponder, *then dare!'*[71] The Kaiser recognized the menace of Russia, however badly prepared, yet there was a hope that the four victors over Turkey would join Austria-Hungary, which would leave Germany free to attack France in full force. To meet Lord Haldane's challenge the German Navy would have to torpedo English troopships in the Scheldt or by Dunkirk and mine the approaches to the Thames. It was Admiral von Tirpitz who reminded the War Council that even if war was unavoidable it would be wiser postponed until the Kiel Canal had been widened to take unladen dreadnoughts and the base being built on Heligoland was completed.[72]

That concluded the War Council; and Lichnowsky's spectre of a European war on account of the situation in the Balkans was dismissed by an agreement of the Powers in London in 1913. By this the Turks surrendered most of their European territory on the understanding that a new and independent state of Albania was created. This failed to please the victors, and the peace treaty did not and could not insure against a repetition. The Balkan states smouldered and erupted with the regularity of a live volcano.[73]

Kiderlen had died in office between the two wars and on his deathbed he begged Bethmann to make it clear to the Emperor Francis Joseph that only if Russia were involved would Germany feel obliged to render military assistance; if it were merely to douse down a flare-up in the Balkans she would not.[74] For all his expert knowledge gained from long exile in Bucharest Kiderlen obviously failed to realize three new developments: that separatism in the Dual Monarchy had become such a threat to peace that the Emperor Francis Joseph regarded his Slav subjects as potential troublemakers and, if the need arose, he was determined to teach them a lesson; that Russia with her Pan Slav feelings was by now inextricably bound up with the fate of all Slavs in the Balkans; and that Bethmann and the Kaiser, unable to control the Pan-German League and a Prussian war party, recognized that war was now inevitable; it was simply a question of waiting to see how it would be touched off and when. William was sometimes quite overwhelmed at the thought of a European war and frequently he was depressed and edgy. The Chancellor was by no means heartless but, being an expert civil servant and quite certain of the outcome, he later tabulated his plans for a Greater German Empire.[75]

3

Sir Winston Churchill in *The World Crisis* described western civilization as it was then in his stately prose somewhat reminiscent of parts of *Genesis*:

> *Nations and Empires, crowned with princes and potentates, rose majestically on every side, lapped in the accumulated treasures of the long peace. All*

*were fitted and fastened, it seemed securely, into an immense cantilever.
The two mighty European systems faced each other glittering and clanking
in their panoply, but with a tranquil gaze. . . . The old world, in its
sunset, was fair to see.*[76]

Berlin was the scene of the last grand royal occasion before this old world
disintegrated. The year before the Duke of Cumberland and Teviotdale,
Brunswick-Lüneburg,[77] asked his eldest son to go to Denmark to represent
the family at the funeral of King Frederick VIII. On the way to his uncle's
funeral, the thirty-one year old Prince, driving far too fast, met with an
accident in Germany and was killed outright.[78] As soon as he heard of this
the Kaiser sent his sons the Crown Prince and Prince Eitel-Frederick to give
all the help they could, watch by the body, and escort it on its way to burial.[79]
It was an act of courtesy which the Duke was obliged to acknowledge. It is
unlikely that he did so willingly for he was heir to the blind King George V
of Hanover who in 1866 had lost his kingdom to Prussia and his immense
private fortune* to Bismarck's private fund for bribing the German press.
For forty-six years the Duke had ostentatiously lived out of Germany, at
Gmunden on the Traun See in Austria and had refused to end the family
feud with any of his fellow Knights of the Garter, William I, Frederick III or
William II. The last had tried very hard to bring about some sort of reconciliation but whenever he arranged a meeting the Duke either failed to appear
at all or disappeared again before William arrived, thereby earning himself
the name the Vanishing Duke.[80] However it was incumbent upon him to
thank the Kaiser for his kind attention on the death of his heir, and he sent his
third son Prince Ernest Augustus to Berlin to convey his gratitude in person.
There the Prince met the Kaiser's only daughter Princess Victoria Louise and,
though they only spent an hour or two in each other's company and their
families had been implacable enemies, they found themselves in love and
announced that they wished to marry.[81]

The Kaiser could deny his daughter nothing, but how the Vanishing Duke
was prevailed upon to give his permission to such an arrangement has not
been disclosed. Doubtless his Duchess, who was a sister of Queen Alexandra
and of the Dowager Tsaritsa of Russia, brought great pressure to bear upon
him and possibly he thought that after so very long it was time for Guelphs
and Hohenzollerns to be at peace with one another. At all events he gave his
consent, which delighted his many relations and the Court at Berlin. William
was thrown into a high state of excitement, so much so that, the King of

---

* It was the patrimony of the old Royal Family of England because although the
throne of England passed from William IV to Victoria in 1837, her uncle Ernest who
became King of Hanover took with him the family fortune and remained Head of the
Guelph family.

Bulgaria* happening to be in Berlin to place a large order with Krupps of Essen, the Kaiser could not resist exuberantly slapping his fellow monarch on the bottom. King Ferdinand was infuriated and promptly took his large order to the French armaments firm of Schneider.†[82] This unfortunate contretemps occurred just at the time when Professor J. A. Cramb, an authority on Germany, was giving a series of lectures in London in which he foresaw the imminent approach of war.‡[83] But planning his daughter's wedding had temporarily liberated the Kaiser from his gloomy forebodings and he refused to be upset by the King or by the Professor. He was determined the wedding should be as splendid as Prussian efficiency and his large fortune permitted.§

The chief guests were the Kaiser's cousin George V and Queen Mary. King George had been warned by his Foreign Secretary that in view of the unsettled state of Europe their visit would have to be a private one. No doubt his father would have seized on this as a reason for excusing himself with suitable regrets from accepting the invitation, and both his ministers and the British press would have been content. But King George and Queen Mary had a genuine affection for the Kaiser and were determined to be in Berlin for the wedding. Moreover William interpreted the word private in his own way. He and the Kaiserin and all the Princes and Princesses of Prussia were at the station to meet the King and Queen of England in state.[87]

From Russia came the Tsar and Tsaritsa, both sadly changed; he with lines of suffering on his face, for it was now impossible to keep faith with his coronation oath; Peter Stolypin his Minister had been murdered before his eyes; a religious fanatic named Rasputin – whom the secret police had shown to be most unwholesome – had his grasp upon the imperial family, and his beloved wife's name had been defamed in the press and her honour degraded.[88] She was no longer the vivacious Princess so well remembered in Germany but a neurotic and difficult woman, bent with sciatica and totally absorbed in grief that her only son had haemophilia.[89] William appreciated the honour they did his daughter and judged correctly that being away from Russia for a little time would be good for them.

Other guests included the Kaiser's sister and brother-in-law, Prince and Princess Frederick of Hesse, his widowed aunt the Grand Duchess of Baden

---

* The Sovereign Principality had been raised to a Kingdom in 1908.

† He was not alone in suffering this particular indignity. The reigning Grand-Duke of Mecklenburg-Strelitz once received an imperial slap on the bottom in the mess of the Guard Uhlans, and took strong exception to the Kaiser's joie de vivre.[84]

‡ He drew to the attention of his audience the fact that whereas rather less than 20 books on military science were published annually in England, nearly 700 books a year were published in Germany. 'If', his argument concluded, 'Germany has not declined from her ancient valour the issue is certain and speedy. It is war.'[85]

§ The Almanack of German Millionaires, published early in 1914, assessed William's private fortune at £19,700,000.[86]

and her nephew Prince Max, and many other relatives of the Hohenzollerns, Cumberlands, Holsteins, Hesses and Coburgs. As they had grown up each of the Kaiser's sons had been given quarters in Berlin and a palace at Potsdam, and besides the Crown Prince, Eitel-Frederick and August William were married. Each kept open house for their relations and wedding guests. Before the wedding there was much exchanging of visits. The guests took tea and drives together and went riding, re-met old acquaintances and made new ones. It was a gossipy, happy time, the last of its kind, and a strain upon valets and maids, who prepared several different changes of clothing a day for the official festivities. There were balls, banquets, gala operas, a Defilir Cour which taxed everyone's strength and a grand military parade at Potsdam.[90] The Cumberlands, or Brunswicks as they were sometimes known, behaved impeccably. The Vanishing Duke, though almost in his seventieth year, remained constantly visible. Very correctly he had sent a message to the people of Hanover that they must join with him in rejoicing over the union of the two royal Houses, and though his immensely long neck and narrow shoulders made him look a fright in any sort of uniform,[91] he was amiability itself and very popular with everyone in the wedding party. The torch dance after the wedding was spectacularly beautiful, and had an historic moment when the young bride took her father and father-in-law by their hands to lead them round the White Hall. It seemed that then, even more than at the wedding itself, there was a physical healing of the feud between the two royal Houses.[92]

William suffered a reaction after the wedding guests had gone. Not only had his only and deeply-loved daughter left him but he was heavily conscious that many who had enjoyed his hospitality and shown their friendship and affection would soon be ranged against his Empire. An old friend of Queen Victoria's, Bishop Boyd-Carpenter, called on him not long afterwards. He found the Kaiser swinging from one mood to another: from confidence to deep despair and back again. He concluded that 'he was under the influence of a great fear'.[93] The fifteenth of that month was the twenty-fifth anniversary of William's accession. The jubilee was marked in an appropriate way, but the Kaiser himself took little pleasure in the celebrations. He was in the grip of a melancholy which made life itself insipid, and his despondency was deepened when his daughter-in-law, the wife of Prince Eitel-Frederick, ran off with another man.[94] It was deepened still further by the idiocy of his eldest son. The Crown Prince took it into his head that his inheritance was being threatened and without thought of the pain he might cause to his family he telegraphed *en clair* to the Chancellor demanding that his brother-in-law should not use the title of Duke of Brunswick until he had formally renounced the Crown of Hanover for himself and all his descendants. William briefly instructed Bethmann to cool the hothead by saying that the oath of loyalty Brunswick had sworn on entering the German Army was perfectly adequate.[95] The Crown Prince did not agree. At Leipzig on October 19th all the Federal Princes met to commemorate the Battle of Nations against Napoleon in which the Kaiser's grandfather had fought as a sixteen-year-old youth. To show his independence the Crown Prince drove off to Bavaria for a holiday. Angrily his father telegraphed him to return and in such terms that he obeyed. On returning to Leipzig he was severely reprimanded.[96] That same month a retired Bavarian general sent the Crown Prince the draft of a revised constitution which contained strong anti-Semitic clauses and expressed the hope: 'May the man come soon who will lead us along this path';[97] flattered, and in full agreement with the proposals, the Crown Prince forwarded the document to the Chancellor, who would have nothing to do with it and begged the Kaiser to discipline his son. Wearily William tried to do so. He agreed that a Jewish-influenced press could be harmful, but to impose censorship would be even more harmful because free expression was a safety-valve, and he treated the notion of expelling the Jews from the empire with scorn. '[It] would strike a blow against our national welfare and economy which would put us back 100 years.'[98] But the Crown Prince was not susceptible to reason. He continued to flout royal conventions and did his best to undermine the authority of Bethmann Hollweg. A meeting of Pan Germans was addressed by a bitter opponent of the Imperial Chancellor and the Crown Prince telegraphed his best wishes and congratulations. And only a few days afterwards, when there was an exchange of insults between German soldiers and civilians in the Alsatian town of Zabern, far from understanding that because of the ignorance and stupidity of a certain German lieutenant the whole nation was held up to obloquy and there was a real danger of war, the Crown Prince sent congratulatory telegrams to the lieutenant's commanding officers.[99] The Kaiser was highly incensed though he kept his feelings from the public, an action which many people found hard to understand.* He realized it had been a mistake to leave his son theoretically at Danzig where he was far from strict supervision. In the Crown Prince's *Memoirs* he noted:

> *His Majesty took my dear regiment away from me and ordered me to Berlin, in order to clip my independence which had become all too great.*[100]

His recall from Danzig was the subject of some public comment. At a Berlin theatre the audience laughed nightly at the words 'When father whistles then

* It is surprising that they should. Naturally there was gossip in the press and a general awareness that the Kaiser and the Crown Prince were not on good terms, just as in England there was an awareness that King George did not approve of the behaviour or views of his son the Prince of Wales; but a decent reticence was expected and maintained.

I dance'.*[101] But though technically he was busy with the General Staff in Berlin and under closer supervision, nothing could stop the Crown Prince from associating with ardent Pan Germans and sending off telegrams. The son's impudence appeared to increase in direct proportion to the aggravation it caused his father. Both were at the same shoot in March 1914 when the new Foreign Secretary Theophilus von Jagow begged Prince Ratibor in mock seriousness not to kill the Kaiser – 'for the young one is much, much worse'.[103]

4

The Dual Monarchy of Austria-Hungary, Germany's sole ally of any consequence, was in a parlous state, seething with political and social unrest which was only just being contained by the energies of the secret police, and the Imperial and Royal Army was itself discredited by the revelation of a scandal which blew up in 1913. A package directed to a box in the Vienna General Post Office was unclaimed and returned to Berlin where it had been franked and there opened. It contained a very large sum of money and a list of names and addresses. Berlin at once formed the Vienna Evidence Bureau and secret police returned the package to the box and waited for it to be claimed. Weeks passed and the police vigilance slackened. When the package was collected they were informed by telephone but arrived too late at the Post Office to seize the man. Then by an incredible series of coincidences they discovered who he was: Colonel Alfred Redl, the late head of counter-espionage and military secret police who had been highly decorated for his work in detecting and arresting spies and who was now in command of the Eighth Army in Prague and on the General Staff. If he had not panicked and tried to bolt the secret police would have found the notion preposterous that he was a spy himself.[104] The fact that he was a practising homosexual was no secret and accepted by the Army authorities who were tolerant when officers were as discreet as Redl. He had passed off a good-looking lieutenant as his 'nephew', and avoided the rowdier elements of the male demi-monde of Austria and Bohemia. But then it was recalled that he had had a brief affair with a Russian nobleman who was Military Attache at Vienna, that at one time he had often been in debt because he had expensive tastes and not quite the income to indulge them, but that he now appeared to be comfortably off. These facts and his attempted flight forced the secret police and the Officer Corps to conclude he was a traitor. How much damage he had done was not then known. In fact he had betrayed to the Russians spies who

* In the German there is a pun, a form of joke much loved by Berliners: 'Wenn Vater pfeift, dann danz-ick'.[102]

had sold information to Austria and he himself had sold details of highly important secret plans. Moreover, to bolster Redl's reputation as a spy-catcher the Russians with oriental ruthlessness had systematically supplied him with victims who went to their death in total ignorance that they had been sacrificed by their masters. The disgrace was keenly felt by Redl's brother officers who went through the performance of waiting on him at night-time and leaving him with a loaded revolver. He did what was expected of him, to the gratification of the Chief of General Staff but to the fury of Archduke Francis Ferdinand who as a devout Catholic was appalled by 'official' suicide. He also had the sense to see that Redl had been allowed to die before saying exactly how much he knew about Russian espionage.[105] This army scandal, together with the increasing political unrest in the months which followed, much alarmed Austria–Hungary's allies.

In June, 1914 the Kaiser went to stay with the Archduke Francis Ferdinand at Konopischt. Ostensibly it was a private visit to enjoy the famous Konopischt roses and arranged battues – for the heir to the Dual Monarchy was so devoted to the sport that even in the heat of June he had shoots and, unable to contain his enthusiasm, would fire at crows from the carriage on his way to the first stand.[106] It was also a friendly gesture on William's part because he was one of the few reigning sovereigns who afforded the Archduke's morganatic wife the same courtesies as an Archduchess of the Blood,* and he liked their three children. But it was not simply a country house party. Although the absolute ruler of Austria-Hungary was the old Emperor and his heir complained that he knew less of affairs than 'the meanest boot-boy in Schönbrunn',[108] and though the absolute rulers of the German Empire were by now the Junker-Military-Industrialist combination intent on war and not the Kaiser, the two talked of the Triple Alliance and treaty obligations. The Archduke loathed Hungary and planned that, on succeeding to the throne, he would make the Dual Monarchy into a trialism, adding a Southern-Slav block with its own parliament to complement the parliaments of Magyar Hungary and German Austria.[109] He was also planning to reform the Austro-Hungarian Army and reorganize it on German lines with a General Staff like that of Prussia.[110] It is alleged he made his views very clear, and put William, as a guest, in an uncomfortable position by asking direct what Germany would do in the event of the Austrians being forced to discipline the Serbs and crush Slav terrorists. William is said to have evaded the question.[111] Nevertheless the Archduke persisted. From descriptions of his manner and behaviour he appears to have suffered from blood pressure and extreme irritability and was

* The Kaiserin, though, was less magnanimous and her reception of the Archduke's wife on a visit to Berlin was noticeably cool.[107]

just the sort of man who would persist. He asked again what Germany would do if Austria became involved in a Balkan dispute. Allegedly William then made a specific declaration that Germany neither could nor should engage in a life and death war on two fronts.[112]

On June 16th, the Kaiser left Austria. On June 24th, when everyone gathered at Kiel for the regatta, including a British naval squadron, he opened the newly widened canal.[113] His brother Harry was in England that summer and so was his sister Sophie, now Queen of Greece. They had informal talks with the King and Queen, were regarded as 'diplomatic channels', and sent sanguine reports to William.[114] But he sensed they were wrong. He did not trust Sir Edward Grey, the English Foreign Secretary, and considered his habit of going off fishing during international crises as play-acting not a sign of British phlegm.[115] He was sure that a war was coming. So was the shrewd American Colonel House who two years before had steered Woodrow Wilson from a professorship in jurisprudence to the White House and since had been his most intimate, in fact his only close adviser.[116] He was in Berlin on a peace mission, acting for Wilson, and was a strangely un-Texan Texan, stumpy, enigmatic, mouse-quiet, unobtrusive, with the features of an eastern khan.[117] He reported: 'The whole of Germany is charged with electricity. Everybody's nerves are tense. It only needs a spark to set the thing off.'[118]

On Sunday, June 28th William was racing in his splendid yacht *Meteor*. An Admiralty launch put out from Kiel and overtook the yacht sailing on a northerly course. There was news from Austria. On the fourteenth anniversary of their marriage, the Archduke Francis Ferdinand and his wife had been shot and killed by Slav terrorists in the capital city of Bosnia-Herzegovina, Sarajevo.[119] William was greatly distressed, the more so as he had been with them and their three children at Konopischt only a fortnight before.*

He immediately ordered the Imperial Standard to be lowered to half mast, cancelled the remainder of the Regatta, and hurried to Potsdam.[120] He condoled with the Emperor Francis Joseph by telegraph and indicated his intention of going to Vienna for the funeral. To his surprise he was asked not to do so. The Austrian Ambassador revealed that the Crown Prince and Princess of Roumania had also been put off. In this way it was hoped to keep

---

* By grim irony the Archduke's vanity in being sewn into his uniforms for great occasions and thus show a perfectly uncreased appearance was ultimately responsible for his death. He might have been saved had the bleeding been stopped but his jacket could not be unbuttoned and by the time the reason was discovered and scissors found it was too late.[121] By grimmer irony still the man who was prepared to give the Slavs their own parliament within the Empire was slain by orders of the Chief of Intelligence of the Serbian General Staff. This was not known at the time. The outrage was put down to Serbian student terrorists belonging to the Black Hand.[122]

away King Peter of Serbia should he wish to attend. There was also the Emperor's delicate state of health to be considered.*[123] William was obliged to stay away, but he was amazed and distressed by Francis Joseph's reaction to the murder of his heir. King George V had noted on the day of the Sarajevo murders: 'Terrible shock for the dear old Emperor'.[124] But, as a matter of fact, the Emperor expressed no sort of sorrow and accepted the outrage as providential, as Divine judgement upon his nephew for marrying morganatically against the imperial will. Aware that, in the event of her death before the Emperor, his wife would never be allowed to rest in the tomb of the Hapsburgs, the Archduke had directed in his testament that they were to be buried together at Arnstetten, one of his country castles; but at their brief lying-in state the Archduke's coffin was deliberately placed at a higher level than that of his wife. The Emperor attended the Requiem but no other part of the ceremonies. The Grand Master of the Imperial Royal Court directed that though the dead Archduke had been Inspector General of the Army he was not to be permitted military honours, nor the tolling of bells, nor acolytes and cantors beside the funeral cortège. A few members of the aristocracy bravely defied the order and walked on foot in a disorganized procession behind the hearse to the railway station. The new heir, Archduke Charles, and his wife, Archduchess Zita, were ordered to be present at the final interment but they travelled in a separate carriage from the three orphaned children.[126] A ferry took the bodies over the Danube at dawn and during the crossing there was a violent electric storm and the coffins were almost lost in the river. Because Francis Ferdinand had kept his wife and family apart he was not popular with the family. Amongst the pathetically few wreaths there was a large one of roses sent by special order of the Kaiser.[127]

5

On July 4th, Count von Szögyény-Marich, the Austrian Ambassador, asked for an audience and was invited to luncheon at the New Palace and afterwards delivered two letters to the Kaiser. One concerned the Triple Alliance's general policy with regard to the Balkans. The other was a personal letter from the Emperor in which he blamed the Serbs directly and the Russian Pan-Slavism indirectly for the assassinations at Sarajevo and spoke of punishing 'this gang of criminal agitators in Belgrade'.[128]

Less than three weeks had passed since William had made his non-committal declaration to the Archduke at Konopischt that his country neither

* The German Consul at Sarajevo reported there was a Serbian plot to assassinate the Kaiser if he went to the funeral, but it is more than likely this was an Austrian hoax to keep him away from Vienna and from witnessing the Emperor's spiteful behaviour.[125]

could nor should engage in a life and death struggle in a war on two fronts. Now he told Szögyény that uninvited he would not presume to comment on what he regarded as a domestic affair of the Dual Monarchy but, as he had been asked, he offered the opinion that Russia was in no position to interfere with any punitive action the Emperor might carry out. In general terms, as always, Germany would honour her treaty obligations. Very correctly William had sent for his Chancellor on receiving the two letters and when Bethmann arrived he agreed with his master's statement, emphasizing that Germany considered an Austrian-Serbian conflict as a domestic matter and entirely the affair of the Emperor. Only in the unlikely case of Russian intervention would Germany also intervene.[129] Count von Szögyény left the New Palace very satisfied, and understandably so. It was possibly a mistake on the Germans' part not to require further consultations.[130]

In view of the situation William proposed postponing his Norwegian cruise but Bethmann begged him not to do so. The annual July cruise was so fixed in the German Kaiser's routine that any break in the pattern would probably cause alarm and undoubtedly arouse suspicion. The Secretary of State for the Navy, Admiral Tirpitz, was holidaying in the Engadine and Moltke the Chief of General Staff was taking a cure at Carlsbad. Neither the Chancellor nor the Kaiser considered recalling them, but their representatives, the Acting Secretary for the Navy and the senior officer of the General Staff then in Berlin were summoned to Potsdam to hear a summary of what had taken place. Afterwards the Kaiser climbed into his car and left for his summer cruise. Later the Entente were to describe this as a Crown Council held at Potsdam on July 5th for the purpose of inciting Austria-Hungary and making war plans.[131] It was a grandiose conception of two consecutive meetings at which besides the summoned officers there were present the Kaiser, the Kaiserin and a footman.[132]

It was a very hot July, which a few thought foreboding. That shrewd monarch Ferdinand of Bulgaria scented what was about to happen. Charles Fürstenberg, the Berlin banker, remarked that there was a smell of sulphur in the air. Even as far away as Tokyo the German Naval Attaché said there was a feeling as though an inescapable death sentence had not yet been announced.[133] But the majority in all lands were less percipient. In England the government was struggling to avoid a Civil War in Ireland, but most of society was enjoying the season, county and state dinners, the Horse Shows at Richmond and Olympia, sipping that fashionable wicked drink pink champagne, called *oeil de perdrix*, and looking forward to Goodwood Races and afterwards Cowes. In France President Poincaré and the Prime Minister were preparing for a state visit to Russia at the end of the month; there was a financial crisis, and the farmers were up in arms despite the excellent weather; but almost everyone's interest was concentrated on the trial of the wife of a former Finance Minister who, to protect her husband's honour with regard to some compromising letters to a young lady, had called on the editor of *Figaro* and shot him dead.[134]

In the Dual Monarchy there was a dispute between the Hungarian Prime Minister who pleaded for a moderate policy and the Austrian Prime Minister who wanted to send the Serbs an ultimatum which must lead to a quick, punitive and local war. Efforts were being made not to provoke either Russia or France, and because of the French State Visit to the Tsar from July 20th it was decided to hold up the ultimatum until the visit was over and the leaders were separated again. On July 10th the Austrian Minister to Belgrade was sent for to receive his instructions. To his surprise he received an unexpected evening call from the Russian Ambassador in Vienna who was understood to know a good deal about the Serbian Black Hand organization and who wielded great power over the Serbian Government. Whether or not he was planning to cool down Slavic nationalist ardour in the cause of European peace – as a number of historians have surmised – can never be known because, no sooner had he gone through the polite formalities of offering condolences to the Austrian minister for the murders at Sarajevo than he dropped dead from natural causes.*[135]

Most of this, though by no means all, was faithfully reported to the Kaiser by Bethmann. The Chancellor also complained that the Crown Prince had publicly applauded a printed lecture in which he, Bethmann, had been denigrated. He asked the Kaiser to discipline his son.[137] William did as he was asked, begging his son to be more circumspect, especially at such a nerve-racking time. It seemed to him that the tongue of the scales weighing peace against war was jerking backwards and forwards out of all control. On the despatches and signals which he received on board he scribbled hectic marginalia. He was irritated by Austria's ponderousness, by the Hungarian Prime Minister's timidity, and by a British offer to mediate. The waiting and the tension excited him. His thinking was very much under the influence of his military entourage aboard the *Hohenzollern*. It was really their voice which spoke through his marginalia.†[138]

On July 22nd Sir Edward Grey, the English Foreign Secretary, received word from his Ambassador in Vienna that any ultimatum to Serbia would be couched in such terms as to make it unacceptable. Grey sent for Prince

---

* His daughter doubted this. She aired her suspicions so loudly that rumours spread he had been poisoned by the Austrian war party.[136]

† This is made abundantly clear by letters written in 1919 by Prince Philip zu Eulenburg discovered in a washing-basket in the attic of Hertefeld in 1970 by Dr. John Röhl of the University of Sussex.[140]

Lichnowsky, the German Ambassador to the Court of St James's, and informed him the English expected that Germany would not identify herself with impossible demands. The Kaiser received the forwarded despatch with dismay. Evidently Grey did not see the Austro-Serbian crisis as a domestic affair and was setting Serbia on an equal footing with the Great Powers.

> *British insolence!* [he scribbled] *I am not called upon to prescribe à la Grey to His Majesty how to preserve his honour!*[139]

He wished to return home but Bethmann continued to advise against it, re-emphasizing that it was important to avoid causing alarm and suspicion, but no doubt in reality because an excitable and unpredictable Kaiser in Berlin would not make his own task any easier. Certainly the war party wanted William well out of the way just then.

On the evening of the 23rd, at the conclusion of his visit to Russia, M. Poincaré gave a banquet aboard his battleship *France* to the Tsar and Tsaritsa and their suites. Four raised 304cm guns towered over the guests. The Tsar gave it as his considered opinion to the President, and afterwards repeated to the French Ambassador, that the Kaiser was too cautious to launch his country into a wild adventure and that Emperor Francis Joseph's only wish was to die in peace.[141] But already an ultimatum was on its way to Belgrade and, at the direct order of Emperor Francis Joseph, who wanted to teach the Slavs a lesson, the note was so phrased that its acceptance was practically an impossibility. The British Foreign Secretary described it as the most formidable document ever addressed by one state to another.[142]

Significantly the Kaiser was not even sent a copy of the text and happened to read it in a Norwegian newspaper. By then half the time limit of 48 hours had already gone. Angrily he gave orders for the *Hohenzollern* to be turned about and make for Kiel.[143] He was aware that the British First and Second Fleets had been joined by the Reserve Third Fleet, some 20 000 officers and ratings, and that there had been a concentration of forces at Spithead for a Grand Review and summer exercises,[144] and he ordered his own dispersed High Seas Fleet to make for home ports at Wilhelmshaven and Kiel, and there coal up.[145] Bethmann objected to the Fleet Order as a provocative act and still expressed the opinion that the Kaiser should continue his cruise. William paid no attention. 'Things get madder every minute!' he exploded. 'Now the man writes that I am not to show myself to my own subjects.'[146] As he was steaming home the Social Democrats published a pacifist manifesto. It concluded: 'Down with war. Long live the solidarity of the people.'[147] And, believing their party would be proscribed, they made hurried arrangements to transfer their treasury to Switzerland.

On Saturday, July 25th, the first German ship of war passed through the newly-widened Kiel Canal.[148] This and the order for the concentration of the German High Seas Fleet put the First Sea Lord of the Royal Navy, Prince Louis of Battenberg, in an unenviable position. His fleets were at Spithead but, unless ordered to the contrary, they would separate on the Monday and the officers and ratings of the Reserve Fleet would return home. His political chief, Winston Churchill, had judiciously gone for a weekend holiday, leaving the decision to him. Courageously he sent a signal to the Third Reserve Fleet not to demobilize, cancelled all leave and kept the First and Second Fleets concentrated. He also sent despatches to the King and English Foreign Office to say what he had done.[*][149] That afternoon his wife's brother-in-law, Prince Harry of Prussia, called at Buckingham Palace and was advised by the King to get back to Germany as the news was bad. King George added that the English had no quarrel with anyone and hoped to remain neutral but treaty obligations might drag them into a European War. Prince Harry was sufficiently confident to go down to Eastbourne and call on his sister Queen Sophie of Greece rather than hurry home. When he did reach Kiel he sent word to his brother William that King George had said: 'We shall try all we can to keep out of this and remain neutral.' William misinterpreted it to mean that England would stay neutral,[†][150] but by the time he received this dilatory message much else had happened.

He had reached Potsdam, as had Moltke and Tirpitz, to find the Chancellor disturbed by their arrival at the centre of affairs, a view which irritated William profoundly; and a telegram came from London proposing that Grey confer with the Ambassadors of Germany, Italy and France. Lichnowsky urged that the suggestion be adopted. Realistically he no longer believed any war would be 'local'. Realistically he believed that the concept of 'Loyalty to the Alliance' need not determine Germany's political orientation. In his own words, looking back on these fraught days six months after the beginning of the war: 'In politics, "partly-partly" is more applicable than "either-or"; we, however have held to the latter.'[‡][151] At the time he earnestly begged:

[*] Naval historians have agreed this was a master stroke, but the man who made it was shabbily rewarded. He had worked his way up from cadet to First Sea Lord not through nepotism but by sheer hard work; had been a full British citizen for forty-six out of his sixty years; and for thirty years had been married to a first cousin of George V; yet, a little more than two months after the outbreak of war he was relieved of his post, simply because he had been born a German, and later on was obliged to renounce his title of prince and change his surname to Mountbatten.

[†] Presumably he continued to do so until 1938 when the full text of what King George had said to Prince Harry was published.

[‡] Lichnowsky's memorandum written in January, 1915, did not contain this and other deletions. They only came to light as a result of Dr John Röhl's treasure hunt for documents in 1970. He was extraordinarily lucky. Having discovered the important Eulenburg documents in a washing basket in an attic at Hertefeld near Holland, he

that our policy be guided solely and alone by the need of sparing the German nation a struggle which it has nothing to gain from and everything to lose.

Allegedly Bethmann cut this last sentence from the despatch which he forwarded to the Kaiser, and his master approved of the reply which had already been sent stressing the domestic nature of the Austro-Serbia crisis and urging Lichnowsky to advocate in London the need to 'localize' any danger.[152]

The Chancellor's handling of the crisis seems somewhat peculiar. Perhaps this was because he was an administrator rather than a leader. Lord Haldane, a trained philosopher and advocate and an unusually good judge of character, considered him 'an honest man struggling with adversity'.[153] Without a doubt he had the General Staff sitting on his shoulders and they were unlikely to allow him much independence of action, but the private diaries of his confidential associate Kurt Riezler, first published in 1972, disclose that Bethmann did once have the idea of trying for a diplomatic grand slam – nothing less than wrecking the Triple Entente and forming an alliance with Russia by threatening a major war.[155] When he saw what cards he actually held in his hand he took the fatalist view that Germany might as well go to war. At least it would hold the Russian hordes at bay and shake up the status quo in Europe, which he appeared to consider moribund and in need of a stir.[156] It is difficult to reconcile such heartless cynicism with what is known of Bethmann's character, but at least he was honest in facing the situation thrust upon him by the war party and in acting as he thought in the best interests of Germany. No doubt he would have preferred to resign, but, as a trained Prussian civil servant and a member of the Reserve Officer Corps, he would have been strongly conscious of where his duty lay at a time of crisis. Evidently he did not wish the Kaiser to take a too large hand in the conduct of affairs; his motives most probably being mixed, at the lowest level because his master would hinder more than help, and at the highest because by taking an active part the Kaiser might damage his reputation. Consistently Bethmann played down the seriousness of the situation, kept his master in ignorance of facts and held up important information. For instance William did not see a copy of the Serbian reply to Austria's ultimatum until twenty-four hours after it had reached the German Chancellery. When he did see it, he was much relieved. It struck him as conciliatory and a great moral success for Vienna which removed any cause for war. Indeed the

---

then found the Lichnowsky memorandum in a chest in the cellar of a Württemberg castle at Hemmingen.[154]

Serbs had bent to the will of Austria in an unprecedented way. He gave written instructions to Bethmann to ask the Austrians to wait and he offered to mediate. But by the time his despatch reached Vienna it was too late. Austria had declared war on Serbia.[157]

Though only half informed of what had been going on, William knew enough to realize that by her refusal of Serbia's handsome note Austria had lost the sympathy of the Powers and there was no longer any possibility of localizing the quarrel. To his dismay he then found that none of the Triple Entente believed that the disintegrating Dual-Monarchy had either the will or the power to force a war, and they blamed Berlin for her bellicose encouragement rather than Vienna for her intransigence.[158] To exculpate herself Germany would have to claim that the new circumstances entitled her to withdraw from her treaty obligations to the Triple Alliance. But Bethmann did not suggest it. Nor did the German Foreign Secretary. At this point William decided to intervene. He still had faith in the supreme powers of sovereigns and, believing he had been assured by King George that England would try to stay neutral, he sent a long peace-searching telegram to the Tsar on July 28th. On the next day he sent a second.[159]

It is said that on that same day the Crown Prince telephoned the editor of a newspaper and informed him that the Russians had already mobilized. Whether or not it was the Crown Prince in person who did this was beside the point. His name was sufficient. He was recognized as a leader of the Prussian war party, and well known for his indiscretion.[160] The choice of the newspaper was also telling. The *Berliner Lokalanzeiger* was a daily with a large circulation which had no political affinities but wooed subscribers by stunts, sensational reporting, and sentimental stories in instalments.[161] The editor was impressed and rushed out a special edition of his paper. After thousands of copies had been sold the mistake was rectified but the damage had been done.[162] Meanwhile Austria was already bombarding Belgrade over the Danube, and the Tsar, only a little time after copies of the *Berliner Lokalanzeiger* had been called in, did in fact order partial mobilization in the four military districts on the Austrian frontier.[163]

The news appalled William. Worse was a despatch from Count Pourtalès, his Ambassador in St Petersburg, to say the Russian Foreign Minister had declared his country's military decisions could not be altered and Serbia could not be left to her fate.[164] William knew the Tsar's weakness. He knew of the corruption and inefficiency of the Russian War Minister. He knew how inadequately the Army was provisioned and equipped for a modern war. But he was also aware that the Russian General Staff was determined to fight and wipe out the disgrace of their campaign against Japan, and that, however well- or ill-equipped, the Russian army was vast. On a regular basis it had 1,400,000 men. The mobilization of trained reservists would bring it up to four and a half million. [165]

That night, on July 30th, confronted with the absolute certainty of war, William was overwhelmed. His nerve gave way and in a long passionate memorandum he poured out his bitterness and his misery, his conviction that Germany was the victim of a plot, his disappointment that his own efforts were continuously disregarded by the Triple Entente, and, in a burst of anger, he swore vengeance against the villains at the back of it all – not Serbia or Russia but England and her empire.[166] It was a pitiful document, hurriedly scribbled by an overwrought and fearful man close to the end of his tether. It could not have been written by the stock figure of the Kaiser, who has been vilified for propaganda purposes as the man who willed war on Europe and gloried in it.

Somehow William pulled himself together and found reserves of strength to face the following day. It was eventful. The Emperor Francis Joseph ordered general mobilization. There was news from East Prussia of Russian troop movements near the frontier. William made yet another effort. Choosing his words with great care, he telegraphed the Tsar a third time, begging him to reconsider. The reply was evasive, and there were further reports of troop activities in the east. William telegraphed Count Pourtalès in St Petersburg instructing him to warn the Russian Foreign Minister that 'a state of threatening danger of war' had been declared in Berlin. It was an expression not found in diplomatic protocol and an invention of his own to create a delay. If within twelve hours the Russians had not ceased all warlike measures William said he would order mobilization.[167] After that, in a highly tense state, he attended his son Oscar's wedding. The twenty-six year old Prince had fallen in love with one of the Kaiserin's ladies-in-waiting and William had refused to agree to such an ineligible *parti* until, practising her customary power, his daughter the Duchess of Brunswick had asked for his consent as a Christening present to her own first child. Though won over he still did not care for the idea of a morganatic marriage which this had to be, and at such a time it can scarcely have been a happy occasion.[168] In the evening the Kaiser learnt the worst, that the Tsar had already ordered general mobilization the day before. There was only one course left. On August 1st he himself ordered mobilization and an hour later declared war on Russia.*
Bethmann Hollweg made a Chancellor's statement which concluded:

If the iron dice roll, God help us.[169]

They were already rolling. France called for mobilization to begin at midnight. Crowds milled in the streets of Berlin, amongst them paid-up members

* He signed the declaration on a writing table made from the timbers of Nelson's flagship, H.M.S. *Victory*.

of the Social Democratic Party. The German party was the largest group in the whole Socialist International and had turned a sudden doctrinal somersault. They were committed to a general strike in the event of war, but this the majority disavowed*.[170] Not quite sure of their allies the English, the French withdrew all troops to ten kilometres from the frontier, inviting Germany to be the aggressor.[171]

William was still terrified of a war on two fronts and for a short time on August 1st a hope was held out to him that there would only be one war on the east. Prince Lichnowsky telegraphed to say he had been asked by Grey if Germany would refrain from attacking France should France agree to remain neutral. The Kaiser seized on this with joy. He ordered champagne for his Chief of General Staff and told him to cancel the movement westwards.[174] Moltke was aghast. For days he had been in a highly agitated state because Russia was stealing time from Schlieffen's plan. To smash the French in the allotted number of days was going to be extremely difficult but, because of superb staff work, mobilization was moving along rapidly; train after train was transporting troops, guns and supplies to the front, and the General Staff was in the extraordinary position of barely having anything to do.[175] Moltke declared it could not be done. Such a gigantic military manoeuvre planned for years and kept up to date annually was irreversible.† The Kaiser did not spare him. 'Your uncle would not have given me such an answer,' he said. The Chief of General Staff was deeply upset, but he would not change his mind. A telegram was drafted to England by Bethmann and Jagow the Foreign Secretary. For good measure William added another addressed to his cousin the King to say that if France offered neutrality supported by the English, he would refrain from going into France. In a short space of time King George replied. Briefly he said that there had been a misunderstanding about Grey's proposal. It had included Russia as well as France. The Kaiser sent for Moltke. 'Now you may do as you like,' he told him.[176]

Ten months before at a dinner in the New Palace with the Kaiser and Kaiserin, the tables covered with imperial violets, the young King Albert of the Belgians had been warned that in the event of a war with France the

---

* Their action has been called a landmark in the Marxist calendar.[172] So extraordinary was it that Lenin in exile refused to believe it had happened and afterwards he never forgave the Social Democrat leaders. It resulted, too, in the fragmentation of the party into Majority Socialists, Independents, and the International Group; and it removed a deep-seated anxiety from the minds of the war party.[173]

† The German railway strategists were so expert that technically, although 11,000 trains were involved, four out of the seven armies then being transported to the west could have been deployed within hours for fighting on the eastern front, but Moltke could not visualize an operation of such magnitude.[177]

Germans would need to pass through his kingdom. Like his uncle before him he had gone home and prepared.[178] King Albert shared with the Kaiser Coburg blood. His mother belonged to the Hohenzollern-Sigmaringen branch of the Kaiser's family. His wife's father was a Bavarian duke. On August 1st he appealed to William both as a Sovereign and as a kinsman to respect Belgium's neutrality. On August 2nd the Grand Duchy of Luxembourg was occupied by German troops and the German Ambassador in Brussels received a telegram from Berlin and opened a sealed envelope sent by despatch carriers on July 29th.* It was an ultimatum which, according to instructions, he delivered at 8 o'clock that evening to the Belgian Foreign Office. The prologue was a flim-flam to throw the blame on the French. The meat was that Belgium should adopt 'a benevolent neutrality' towards the German troops marching through her territory and guarantees were given that damage should be amply compensated and the country's sovereign rights upheld. It ended with the request that Belgium should reply within twelve hours.[179] The King presided at a Council of State. Exactly within the stipulated time the German Ambassador was given the Belgian reply to the ultimatum. It was a refusal.[180] At this point the Kaiser replied to the young King's personal appeal. In effect he replaced the baby in the Belgians' lap by trying to persuade them to allow his army through.[181] King Albert's response was to assume supreme command and order the Meuse bridges and the railway tunnels and bridges on the Luxembourg frontier to be destroyed. William promptly declared war on France. As Germany was the aggressor Italy was freed from her treaty obligation to the Triple Alliance and refused to mobilize. The last piece fell into place on August 4th. The German troops marched into Belgian territory and the British Ambassador was instructed to call on Bethmann Hollweg and demand that they cease to violate neutral territory. Failing to do so would result in war being declared on Germany at midnight.[183]

Thus Germany began a major war as a single Power latched to one ineffectual ally against three Powers – and when Italy cast her lot with the Entente there were four. She had six million fighting men and a Navy against ten million and the largest Navy in the world.[184] It was a fantastic contradiction of Bismarckian policies forced on the nation by men who considered him their hero. William genuinely considered he had been let down by his fellow sovereigns the Tsar and King George. 'If my grandmother had been alive,' he said indignantly, 'she would not have allowed it.'[185] But much more he must have felt the humiliation of having been theoretically in com-

---

* This was the day on which the Kaiser sent his second peace-searching telegram to the Tsar. The telegram had been drafted on the 26th which demonstrates the efficiency of the General Staff and the determination of the German war party.[182]

mand and able to stop the war, and yet prevented from exercising that power by the strength of the war party.

The Berliners excitedly swarmed to the Old Palace and called for the Kaiser. Eventually he appeared on the balcony above the great entrance already dressed in field-grey uniform and looking white and strained. He was cheered and re-cheered. He was the people's symbol of victory and hysterically they saluted him. His response was untypical but appropriate. He raised his hands and in the silence he called: 'I commend you now to God. Go into the churches, kneel down, and pray for help for our soldiers.'[186]

The Reichstag had agreed unanimously to vote war credits, and declared a truce so that the parties would neither criticize one another nor the government. The Kaiser sent for the deputies to the White Hall of the Old Palace and formally announced that Germany was at war. By a happy touch of informality he also announced: 'I no longer know any parties – only Germans.'[187]

M. Paul Cambon, French Ambassador to Germany, remarked with some feeling to his English colleague: 'There are three people in Berlin tonight who regret that war has broken out; you, me and Kaiser William.'[188] It was an acute observation. Equally acute was King George's remark to the Austrian Ambassador when they said goodbye: 'I don't believe William wanted war, but he was afraid of his son's popularity. His son and his party made the war.'*[189]

When Prince Lichnowsky and his staff were leaving England one of them lamented Germany's isolated position. He asked if no-one was well-disposed towards their Fatherland. A cynical colleague replied: 'Siam is friendly, I believe.'†[190]

* King George's statement was not known until 1970.[191]
† As it turned out Siam entered the war on the side of the Entente.[192]

CHAPTER FOURTEEN

The Gory Game of Might and Chance

'It was neck and neck to the very end'

WINSTON CHURCHILL on the First World War

I

Long before the First Great War military science had altered the character of war but had not altered the spirit of soldiers. In the battle of Königgrätz in 1866 both sides had fought gloriously. An Austrian Reserve Corps advanced with colours flying and to the music of fife and drum, and in twenty minutes 276 officers and 10,000 men were lost. One Prussian regiment marched into battle with 30 officers and 9,000 men and emerged with 2 officers and 400 men.[1] In 1870 at the battle of Sedan the King of Prussia watched a great French cavalry charge under Gallifet being shot to pieces and the survivors rally, form squadrons and charge again and again. Such heroism moved him to exclaim: 'Ah! Les brave gens! Les brave gens!'[2] So it was in 1914. The Germans believed, as did their enemies, that it would be a brisk campaign and in the first few months there were acts of extraordinary bravery. German Uhlans, armed with sabres and lances, tried to take Haelen Bridge in Belgium, and charged repeatedly into volleys of rifle fire from eight in the morning until six in the evening, by which time all their finest squadrons had been slaughtered.[3] At Onhaye a French brigade in a daredevil rush with fixed bayonets slew a far larger force of Saxon troops.[4] At Mons, and in holding back the Germans at Ypres, the original British Expeditionary Force lost many of its men, amongst them some of the finest in Britain.[5] On the eastern front in the initial skirmishes the 18th Russian Division lost 330 officers out of its total complement of 370, and the most famous of all Russian regiments, the Preobrajensky Guard, lost 48 of its 70 officers.[6]

Viewed from the fourth quarter of the twentieth century this calamitous loss of life appears to most people a tragic waste and a spectacular example of human folly. It is most necessary to recall that it did not seem so then. In the breast of everyone who practised the profession of arms there was a longing if not for war then at least that when war came he should behave with honour and if possible achieve glory. Because in 1914 Officer Corps and cadres of all nations were composed of professional soldiers and willing volunteers and they were the first to fall, their loss was a tragedy to the whole of Europe but there was no resentment then about dying;[7] none of the disillusion and disgust and hatred of bungling generals, place-seeking politicians and profiteering industrialists which, in all armies, came to the fore when the dedicated soldiers were nine-tenths dead and their replacements, as H. G. Wells put it, felt they were fighting 'a war without a point'.[8]

The Kaiser well understood the nobility of sacrifice and he wished to identify himself with it. He has been charged with deserting his people at a needy time and it is interesting to speculate that the history of the House of Hohenzollern might have been quite different had William remained in his capital as the focal point of authority and met the need for a visible leader both in victory and in defeat.[9] This was precisely what his cousin King George did with conspicuous success; paying occasional visits to the front and to the fleet but generally identifying himself with his people at home, cultivating potatoes at Frogmore, visiting the victims of air raids, touring munitions factories, living strictly on rations like everyone else, and even voluntarily giving up alcohol for the duration as a token of self-sacrifice.[10] The Kaiser's other cousin, Tsar Nicholas, who seemed doomed to make mistakes, spent part of his time getting in the way of his generals and part with his family at Tsarskoe Selo entirely cut off from everyone. He too set an example by giving up vodka and he issued a ukase prohibiting its sale to speed up mobilization. As vodka was a government monopoly he thereby cut off a third of the national income and the ukase had to be rescinded.[11] Certainly at Headquarters thereafter vodka went down throats 'like a torchlight procession'. William was in an entirely different position. His enemy *The Times* sneered that his knowledge of military science 'might be taken as equivalent to those of a Staff Trumpeter',[12] but as Supreme Warlord he had a constitutional function to approve or disapprove all military and naval strategy. Actually he was by no means as ignorant of military affairs as *The Times* suggested, and he was considerably more intelligent than either King George or the Tsar, but wisely – and contrary to many expectations – he left the decisions to others and, save on rare occasions, he signed the Orders placed before him.[13] But, to accomplish this with the least waste of time, he had to be at or close to Supreme Headquarters and believed it was his duty to show himself to the armies and the fleet on tours of inspection and encouragement. Therefore, though politically it was misfortunate, from the time Supreme Headquarters moved to Koblenz on August 16th, 1914 Berlin saw little of him. He was on a sad gadabout, often on his royal train, its splendour dimmed by dull green paint, or in armed motor cars, and travelling with the High Command in turn to Luxembourg, Charleville, Posen, Pless, Bad Kreuznach and finally to Spa.

The Kaiserin was frequently with him and his suite of advisers (called 'the Hydra' by its opponents) was in constant attendance.[14] Count von Plessen had been his A.D.C. since he came to the throne in 1888 and, at seventy-three, was still with him. He was a firebrand reactionary, described in the old days by Prince Eulenburg as 'Nothing but Gunfire'.[15] As a reward for his services William made him Adjutant-General at the beginning of the war. There were three others in the suite: the Military Secretary, Lyncker; the Naval Secretary, Müller; and the Civil Secretary, Valentini.

The Kaiserin and his suite all served him badly in wishing to serve him well. Because she believed he must keep up his strength Dona frustrated his wish to live on rations,[16] not a difficult thing to do as, although he knew the exact constituents of an army ration he was probably unaware of what most of his subjects were eating – or, rather, not eating. Then his suite, with their mistakenly kind intention of not wanting to upset him,[17] often kept him in ignorance of what was going on. This had little effect on the actual procedure of the war save in the case of the Navy. By naval regulations the Fleet was ultimately responsible to the Kaiser through his Naval Secretary. The volatile Admiral von Tirpitz, Secretary of State for the Navy, was thus sidetracked and not able to persuade the Kaiser to make full use of the force they had created together. From a distance the Royal Navy was blockading Germany and carefully rationing supplies to neutrals and, apart from small engagements at Heligoland Bight and Skager Rak (Jutland) of little strategic importance, and a lightning foray to shell towns on the East Anglian coast, the German Grand Fleet was scarcely used. William dared not risk it.[18] Bitterly Tirpitz called the Kaiser's entourage who stood between them 'the Watchmen on the Wall'. It was a fitting description. They had committed themselves to cushion their master from the worst aspects of war.[19]

The amount of information William did receive made him difficult to live with. There was no telling how well or ill he would be from day to day; no way of telling why the barometer of his moods moved up and down so rapidly, nor how long he would be in euphoria or depression. Generally he was tenderhearted, full of knightly feelings towards his enemies but occasionally he was the reverse, bursting with a savage bravura when he talked of taking no prisoners and killing swine. He had moments when he felt he was being really useful if only as a figurehead, someone to cheer when the days were dismal. But there were also times when setbacks at the fronts or an imagined slight from a busy staff officer would make him abject with melancholy. Someone once brought out a picture and enquired if he had painted it. He shook his head and remarked that if he had had that much talent he would have been an artist and not an emperor in such awful circumstances.[20] So sensitive was he that once, when the news from the eastern front was bad, he took the blame upon himself. He was walking with two of his suite in a garden and suggested they sat for a moment on a bench. It was really too small for three and one of them went to get a chair. At once the Kaiser asked: 'Am I already such a figure of contempt that no one wishes to sit next to me?'[21]

As week succeeded week he followed the action on both fronts with great care and with characteristic reactions. More hopeful of the Schlieffen plan in the west, his primary concern was for his armies in the east. There, though the Russian War Minister was venal, the commissariat futile, and the armies ill-equipped with weapons,[22] the enemy appeared to have two great advantages. One was an apparently limitless supply of manpower, the other was a leader in the Commander-in-Chief, Grand Duke Nicholas, who was loved and trusted by all ranks. His armies pounded the Austrians on the Galician front but his main attack was against East Prussia. The northern First Army was under the command of a general with the German-sounding name of Rennenkampf, and the southern Second Army under an asthmatic melancholic, General Samsonov. Rennenkampf charged down along the Baltic coast and because the majority of German troops were being employed in the west, he did reasonably well – penetrating some distance into East Prussia. The Kaiser was in a highly excitable state until Moltke dismissed the German general who had failed and replaced him with two who were to play a notable part in German history: General Paul von Hindenburg und Beneck-endorf, a veteran of the 1866 and 1870 campaigns, who was ordered out of retirement; and General Eric Ludendorff, who had already distinguished himself by capturing the fortified Belgian city of Liège.[23] The latter, though second in command, was really in charge, Hindenburg deferring to him so much that he earned the nickname of 'General what do you say?'[24] Ludendorf gambled. He left Rennenkampf to enjoy the fruits of his small victory and hurled the greater part of his forces on Samsonov. In five days he had pulverized the Russians, driven Samsonov to commit suicide, killed 110,000 soldiers and taken 90,000 prisoners. This was called by the Germans the Battle of Tannenberg in revenge for the ancient defeat suffered there by the Teutonic Knights at the hands of the Slavs. Then Hindenburg and Ludendorff turned on Rennenkampf and in the Battle of the Masurian Lakes drove him out of East Prussia.[25] On the Austrian front the Russians were doing better but on an appeal from France to put pressure on the Germans they chivalrously withdrew in Galicia and transferred two of their four southern armies to batter hopelessly against the better-trained, better-equipped, infinitely better-led German troops. By the end of 1914 over one million Russians had been killed, wounded or taken prisoner.[26]

German intelligence reports confirmed that the French had pleaded for this Russian sacrifice because Paris itself appeared to be in danger. In fact it was not. To the Kaiser's dismay and Moltke's uneasiness, General von Kluck, the field commander in the van, had decided Paris must wait. It was essential to the Schlieffen Plan that the enemy should be rapidly scooped up from the rear and destroyed, and to include Paris within the scoop would extend the German front for more than fifty miles. Kluck knew this was out of the question. The transfer of two Army Corps to the eastern front and the ferocity of the enemy's resistance had thrown everything awry. Moltke admitted to the Chief of Austro-Hungarian General Staff that the advance in Belgium had been brutal, but the use of terror against *franc-tireur* warfare was Clausewitz's method of shortening war and had been proved in the 1870 campaign. Yet now the great military oracle seemed to be failing them. Moreover the General Staff was finding it exceedingly difficult to adapt itself to the totally unexpected delays and Kluck, mesmerized by the Schlieffen Plan, had outstripped his supply trains and his heavy artillery. It was then August 31st and the Schlieffen Plan called for a complete victory on the western front by September 9th. Kluck knew that his hot, hungry and exhausted army could not take in Paris on the way. He ordered the men on to the south-east, force-marching them in the tracks of the French and the British. They were not informed of the change of plan in case they lost heart. They sang in chorus to keep themselves awake as they marched on blistered feet.

On September 1st Kluck's van finally ran into the heels of the retreating British, who turned and fought for two days until they slipped away over the river Marne. Two days cut from Schlieffen's schedule spelt disaster to Kluck. He urged on his wretched men in pursuit of the French though they had not rested for nineteen days. He was only twenty miles from Paris and wheeling right away from the capital. His movements had been observed and reported, but the French suspected a trick. A map found on the body of a dead German cavalry officer showed that his overall plan was to leave Paris untouched, but still the French could not believe it. On September 2nd, the anniversary of their humiliation at Sedan, the French government left by a special train for Bordeaux, and the French Paris garrison hurled itself on to Kluck's flank, six thousand of them being transported by taxicabs. He turned to meet this thrust and a gap opened between the First and Second Armies. On September 9th – when Schlieffen's time limit expired – Kluck was ordered to fall back. The Germans were forced to retreat to a line which left all Belgium within their grasp and all north-east France down to the Aisne.[27] Moltke, who was racked by the pains of an incurable kidney disease and in despair at his failure, was relieved of his command. With barely any consultation William appointed in his place as Chief of General Staff the Prussian Minister of War, General von Falkenhayn,[28] a tough hard-fighting dandy who, with the Kaiser's full support, tried to effect a breakthrough at Ypres. It failed.[29] The Germans dug in. Clauzewitz's bête noire, a war of attrition, began in the trenches.

The Crown Prince had been given command of an Army, the Fifth, and instructed to do exactly what his Chief of Staff advised. It was an order he obeyed so well that the Kaiser gave him the Iron Cross, Second and First Class, when the Fifth Army took Longwy. Relations between father and son had never been better.[30] But there was a rapid deterioration when with the reversal in the Battle of the Marne the Crown Prince had to move his head-quarters back to Stanay and there began to live expensively and elegantly, womanize, and – unfortunately for Germany – to be his old indiscreet self. He actually announced to an American newspaperman: 'We have lost the war. It will go on for a long time but it is lost already'.[31]

2

Quite certain now that Moltke had been right to prophecy the war would be a long and wearisome business, the Kaiser doggedly continued what he considered his duty. Yet like many others he was a baffled man. Bismarck had thrice used war as a hammer to get what he wanted and called it 'the gory game of might and chance', but his wars had been quite unlike this present war against the Entente. To William it seemed to bear small relation to the practice of the profession of arms which he had been taught. Civilians, who in previous wars had played so small a part that it had barely affected the issue, were now equally important as, and in some absurd cases more important than, the fighting soldier and sailor. There were for example two people amongst his enemies who altered the whole concept of chivalry by the power of the press they controlled: Lord Northcliff owner of the *Daily Mail* and *The Times*, and Mr Horatio Bottomley in *John Bull*. They started a campaign against 'Enemy Knights of the Garter' and because of the pressure they were able to bring to bear, King George was forced to strike eight names from the roll of the Order and command the removal of their banners from St George's Chapel at Windsor. They included the Kaiser, the Crown Prince, the Duke of Cumberland, his son the Duke of Brunswick, and the young Duke of Albany and Saxe-Coburg-Gotha.*[32] At a later stage in the war a similar sort

---

* It is interesting that neither the Tsar nor the King of Italy did this, nor was there any reciprocal action taken by the Kaiser or Emperor Francis Joseph to deprive their enemies in the field of Orders of chivalry.

of agitation was whipped up by the English press because their own King and Queen and very many of the royal family were German by blood or marriage or both. At the behest of the proprietors of newspapers the Battenbergs – seven of whom were or had been on active service – lost the title of prince and became Mountbattens. The Queen's family changed from Teck to Cambridge, and the King altered the name of the Royal House to Windsor.[33] To William the whole thing was farcical. He threatened to order a Command Performance of '*The Merry Wives of Saxe-Coburg-Gotha*'.[34] He better understood the courtly world in which inevitably it happened that during wars cousins, even brothers, were on opposing sides. The dilemma they faced was not restricted to the combatants. Wives and sisters were also confronted by special difficulties. For example, William's first love the Grand Duchess Ella and her sisters the Tsaritsa Alexandra and Princess Louis of Battenberg were suddenly alienated from their native land and from their fourth sister Irène who had married his brother Harry; and as a purely practical measure, Princess Louis and Princess Harry had hurriedly exchanged maids at the outbreak of war, the German maid going to Kiel and the English maid to the Isle of Wight. For the princes on active service their duty was clear, but nonetheless presented heart-searching problems. William's own six sons were temporarily obliged to fight many of their cousins. The brothers-in-law of the Emperor Francis Joseph's heir were lieutenants in the Belgian artillery.[35] The Duke of Saxe-Coburg-Gotha was serving on the East Prussian front[36] while his brother-in-law, who was Queen Mary's brother, was on the British Military Mission to Belgium.[37] Whatever his private feelings each did his best for his own country and was magnanimous to enemies. There was also a code of behaviour to follow if a relative or friend was lost in battle no matter in which army or navy he was serving. When the Kaiser's first cousin, Prince Maurice of Battenberg, was killed in action fighting against Germany he immediately sent a telegram of condolence, and when his own nephew, Prince Maximilian of Hesse-Cassel, was killed while serving in the Death's Head Hussars, the locket from his neck was returned to his mother through the British Medical Service and Queen Mary. These things happened in the old-fashioned, courteous world which the Kaiser so thoroughly understood and which evidently was beyond the comprehension of Northcliff and Bottomley. Yet this sort of people now had the power to create new climates of opinion, and, as the war progressed, they were by no means the only offenders. The political press in all countries, including his own, became vulgarized. The apolitical material was thrust aside not only because of paper shortage but because aggressive propaganda began to have an appeal. As a result primitive emotions were roused and decent people began to speak of their enemies in terms which would have been unthinkable before the war.[38] William found this general lowering of standards very painful, above all the tendency for people to carp and whine.

There was, of course, a great deal to complain about behind the front lines. Owing to the failure of the Schlieffen Plan and the subsequent lengthening of the campaign on the western front there was a serious shortage of supplies at home. The average soldier was far better off than the civilian. First there was rationing by price, then by the issue of coupons, the amount of food varying from city to city and from state to state. The word *Ersatz* entered the international vocabulary. People sold and bought synthetic drinks, coffee, tea, preserves, tobacco and 'soup flavourers'. There was also a lack of fuel, clothing and medicines. Black marketeering and profiteering flourished.[39] As the hunger and cold grew worse criticism mounted. It was perhaps inevitable but the Kaiser considered it a disgraceful innovation into the conduct of a nation at war. The Prussian–Spartan ideals had been deeply impressed on him since childhood and while he was seriously concerned for the cold and hungry civilians and considered the British blockade far more barbaric than the use of poison gas or submarine warfare, he did not approve of the breach of the agreement made by all parties at the beginning of the war that there should be no criticism for the sake of the fatherland. They had decided on *Burgfrieden* – 'a truce within the citadel' – and had gone back on their word. Against an article in the *Frankfurter Zeitung* he scribbled a note which summed up his views: 'In war politics keeps her mouth closed until strategy permits her to speak again.'[10] It was a blinkered, old fashioned view, certainly no longer tenable and perhaps naive even in his own day, and it caused William intense irritation. The true irony of the situation was that had he been permanently in the capital in personal contact with his people there might well have been less criticism. Because he was out of sight everyone believed he was living on the fat of the land in comfort and safety, and the Reichstag, as the visible embodiment of authority, came to play a more important role in affairs.

The most damaging critics of all were revolutionaries, once described by Metternich as 'Snakes in the Grass of the State'. Two in particular were hard at work trying to alter the status quo. One worked from within the Reichstag. Charles Liebknecht was a notorious demagogic deputy. He was no longer considered politically respectable by those who had honoured his father. He was the first Socialist to vote against continuing war credits. He went personally to Belgium on a fact-finding tour and came back with embarrassing questions about shot hostages and looting. He was always on his feet. 'Liebknecht's little interpolations', as they were known, became pestiferous to the government. He could not be silenced in the Reichstag but he was partly gagged by being called up in the Army he hated. Even then he was entitled to be in Berlin whenever the Reichstag was sitting and he continued to harass the government from within.[41] From without he had a few ardent supporters. Chief of them was Rosa Luxemburg, a small middle-aged lady with a limp who wore picture hats and carried a parasol. She looked neat and elegant and quite harmless. In fact in 1914 she was as well known in the world of international Socialism as Lenin himself and was far better liked. His intellectual equal, she had a wit and warm charm which he lacked, and she was highly critical of his theory of the use of terror and defamation of character. Moreover she considered no small group of conspirators had the moral right to seize power in the name of the revolution – and believed that the whole proletariat had to be led to see the true benefits of socialism before power could be properly assumed.[42] The highly intelligent daughter of a rich Jewish merchant in Russian Poland, she led an adventurous life before settling in Berlin to work for the Social Democratic Party. There, to avoid the risk of deportation, she contracted a purely formal marriage with the son of a party worker, and settled to a life dedicated to the party. She proved to be its intellectual giant, one of its most powerful orators, and at the beginning of the war its most caustic critic. Arrested for trying to publish an unauthorized newspaper, she was imprisoned without trial in protective custody. Being so forlorn and small and a cripple and so obviously a lady, she roused the chivalrous feelings of the authorities. They called her the Red Rose. She was made as comfortable as possible, allowed writing materials, and given permission to write to her friends. Thus Rosa had the leisure to draft a formidable document, nothing less than the blueprint for the German International Group and she was in constant touch with the firebrand in the Reichstag.[43]

Doubtless the Watchers on the Wall kept the petty annoyances of 'Liebknecht's little interpolations' from the Kaiser. But he could hardly have failed to be aware of the revolutionary group when on his fifty-seventh birthday in 1916, amongst the posters and bills traditionally pasted up on walls to greet him there was a far from complimentary sheet signed 'Spartacus'. The classical allusion would not have been lost on him either. The gladiator who led the slaves' revolt against the Romans had been named Spartacus.[44] Thereafter quite a number of seditious handbills were pasted on walls and Liebknecht invited the publicity of martyrdom by shouting 'Down with the war! Down with the government!' in the Potsdamer Platz and getting himself a four-year prison sentence.*[45]

This brazen smashing of the *Burgfrieden* was highly damaging at a delicate time. The winter had been hard. Reduced to famine foods and subsisting mainly on vegetables, the Germans called it the Turnip winter. The British

* The Red Rose had already been released by the authorities as 'relatively harmless', though later she had another spell in prison.

Blockade had proved the strongest weapon in the war. The Kaiser and the Chancellor had been pressed to authorize unrestricted sinkings by submarines to break the blockade but they had consistently refused. It was not simply that such an action would almost certainly add America to the Entente, which by now also included Japan and Italy, but that, despite disasters like the sinking of the liner *Lusitania* with a large loss of life which horrified the civilized world, Germany still had a fractional margin of moral ascendancy over the Entente because the blockade was causing intense suffering to a huge civilian population, which horrified the civilized world even more.[46] Furthermore, though the people at home were suffering cruelly, the armies were poised on the edge of victory. Reinforced by troops which could be ill-spared from the western front, Hindenburg and Ludendorff had driven the Russians from Poland, Lithuania and Courland – the territory of the old Teutonic Knights. Galicia, too, had been freed of Russians, and Bulgaria had joined the Alliance and secured rail communications with Turkey. In the west the Chief of General Staff, General von Falkenhayn, was pounding the forces of the Entente in a massive offensive against Verdun and was just succeeding in holding his own. As the battle continued it was vital that the morale of his armies should be sound, and when they were at their most tired and jaded Liebknecht made his public anti-war demonstration. Falkenhayn lost the battle. Defeatism being highly contagious, the whole country began to wonder if the war could ever be won in the traditional fashion, by armies in the field. By the end of the battle of Verdun Germany had lost two and a half million men in two years.[47]

Neither the Kaiserin nor his suite could hide from William that public opinion – spurred on by the breakers of the party truce – was pressing for some sort of change of policy. Three events underlined it. Tirpitz angrily offered his resignation because the Kaiser would not allow unrestricted submarine warfare and he was allowed to go.[48] Then in November the aged Emperor Francis Joseph died, to be succeeded by his great-nephew Charles.[49] Finally Roumania entered on the side of the Entente and was quickly despatched by a German–Austrian army. Bethmann proposed that honour would not be lost and good sense shown if they seized the opportunity to make a peace offer. William agreed. In his note to the Entente the German Chancellor underlined the military strength of the Alliance and said they proposed negotiations because a policy of annihilating their enemies was repugnant. He finished by disclaiming responsibility before mankind and history should the offer of peace and conciliation be refused.[50]

Unfortunately for the world, a few days earlier a climax had been reached in the internecine war amongst the English Liberals. Asquith had been ousted and Lloyd George, a man of very different stamp, had become Prime

Minister. Shrewd, a hard fighter and a brilliant organizer, he was to lead his country to victory, but there is no question that he vulgarized political leadership.[51] He remained a Liberal at heart, had an unquestionable love for Wales, but he loved Lloyd George most of all; and at that critical moment of his career he had to establish himself as a forceful leader. In the House of Commons on December 19th he dismissed the German peace offer as a trap[52] and asked:

> What hope is there . . . that the arrogant spirit of the Prussian military caste will not be as dominant as ever if we patch up peace now?[53]

A superb orator, Lloyd George soon had the Commons with him, and thus he consolidated his own position – but at the expense of a chance, however faint, of peace. President Wilson, acting as mediator, urged that there should be an exchange of views between the Entente and the Alliance. Lloyd George said he did not trust the Germans. He denounced the Chancellor's peace offer as a war manoeuvre, and President Wilson was given a list of the Entente's minimum demands which had to be met before any armistice was possible.[54] These were so extensive and humiliating, and took so little regard of Germany's strong military position, that their acceptance was out of the question. The President was shocked, so much so that had the Germans then sent him a note of more reasonable peace terms there is a high probability he would have put pressure upon England to enter on negotiations. He had the power to lay an embargo on exports to England and he had the will to make peace.[55] But, again unhappily for Europe, the Alliance failed to grasp the opportunity; partly because both the Kaiser and the Chancellor considered that Wilson's feeble acceptance of the blockade made him pro-English, but chiefly because a demagogue was taking control in Germany who believed in total victory and substantial annexations. This was General Eric Ludendorff, with Hindenburg one of the two heroes of the eastern front.

Ludendorff's ambition and exceptional brilliance had carried him from the Cadet Corps, which he had joined at the age of ten, to the General Staff. From a middle-class background and with no private income he had doggedly proved his abilities to his superiors and, while he could never be Chief of General Staff, he was determined to be second in command.[56] His chance came when, after his failure at Verdun, Falkenhayn was dispensed with and, at the recommendation of the Chancellor, the Kaiser appointed Hindenburg as Chief of General Staff. With him of course travelled the real commander, Ludendorff, who achieved his life-long ambition and was made Quartermaster-General. William had personally appointed Falkenhayn and he did not relish being told by Bethmann to appoint Hindenburg and Ludendorff because they were popular heroes.[57] Nor did he care for the idea of sitting in the shadow of the great pair. He did not even like them.[58] Hindenburg was dull and stolid and must have vastly irritated a nervous, mercurial man like the Kaiser. Ludendorff was worse. He could not help his physical appearance and he was decidedly unattractive, being short-legged, tubby, with a peg-top hair crop, wispy moustache, thickish pouting lips, hooded eyes and a ripple of shotaway chins; but he could have been better mannered. As it was the Supreme War Lord found himself being condescended to by his own Quartermaster-General, and Ludendorff made no secret of the scorn he felt for the smarter section of the Officer Corps whom he called 'the children of protection'.[59] He was not at all a comfortable officer to mess with and people kept out of his way. When he made reports to the Kaiser in the map-room he did so briskly, thrusting an eyeglass under his hooded right eye, expertly using mathematical instruments, and was never caught out in a single question concerning troop strengths, dispositions, objectives, obstacles or anything at all.[60] He disconcerted William, who was glad to see the back of him and always apprehensive when Ludendorff, with pouting lips, made one of his famous requests. These were almost as gentle and quiet as a sergeant-major's order on parade.

No sooner had Lloyd George made his speech in the House of Commons than Ludendorff demanded that the Kaiser sanction submarine warfare without delay. For eighteen months William and Bethmann had resisted the pressure. Now, at a Crown Council held at Pless on January 9th 1917, William was hammered with facts. Hindenburg stated that a blow at England would sustain the morale of the Army. The English could be starved within a few months. The Americans would declare war but they had no army of any consequence, and training and equipping one would take a long time. Moreover, as they were shipped over to Europe they could be torpedoed by submarines. Against this was the moral question of the obloquy the nation would incur for using submarines on an unrestricted scale. Besides the Kaiser there were six at the Crown Council, his Military, Naval and Civil Secretaries, the Chancellor, the Chief of General Staff and the Quartermaster-General. William, in a high state of nervousness, noted that only two out of the six – Bethmann and Valentini, his Civil Secretary – were against Ludendorff's proposal. He signed the decree, which had already been drawn up.[61]

Ten days afterwards, when the Americans were as yet undecided whether to break their isolationism, a telegram from the German Foreign Office to the Chargé d'Affaires in Mexico was intercepted by the Americans. He was to offer an alliance, financial aid, and the promise of territories lost to the United States in New Mexico, Arizona and Texas.[62] Nothing came of the telegram but its publication drove a large number of isolationists to support

Wilson when he turned a political somersault and declared war on Germany on April 6th.*

William had expected this since the day he signed the decree for unrestricted submarine warfare, but, recalling Hindenburg's reassurances, at first he was not unduly alarmed. His chief concern at that time was for Russia, where revolution had forced the Tsar to abdicate both for himself and his thirteen year old son.[63] His brother, the Grand Duke Michael, Tsar for a few hours, also abdicated.[64] Russia was not yet a Communist state. The government of the Duma of elected representatives announced its determination to continue the war. Rasputin had been murdered, troops had mutinied, and there had been bread riots and wild demonstrations in Petrograd (as St Petersburg was now called), and the most powerful ruler on earth with an army of fifteen million men had been imprisoned in his own palace and was plain Citizen Romanov.[65]

The governments of the United States and France and England showed small sympathy for the Tsar. Nor did they show much understanding of the delicate situation in which the Russian Provisional Government found itself. Soviets of workers, soldiers and sailors had considerable power and were obviously determined to use it if their new rulers deviated a millimetre from the path of the wishes of the proletariat. The United States officially recognized the new government with almost indecent haste because it permitted President Wilson when asking Congress to vote for a declaration of war to say that it was to make the world 'safe for democracy'.[66] The French telegraphed congratulations and fraternal greetings.[67] This might have been expected from republics, but not from a constitutional monarchy. Only fourteen years had passed since King Edward had refused to resume diplomatic relations with Serbia after the assassination of the King and Queen, claiming that he and they happened to belong to the same trade union, he was going to observe union rules, and under no circumstances would he overlook the outrage. And he had maintained this position for three years.[68] But much had altered since 1906. In 1917 England received the news of the Tsar's enforced abdication with joy. Those who knew the Tsar personally, as his cousin George V did, were aware that he was a kindly man, 'a thorough gentleman who loved his country and his people'[69] even if he had been weak and ineffectual; but press propaganda had for years defamed him as a tyrant with a knout in his hand.[70] Lloyd George sent off a telegram of congratulations to the Prime Minister of the Russian Democratic Republic expressing 'sentiments of the most profound satisfaction' that Russia had adopted 'responsible government'. King George reproached him, saying he had pitched it 'rather strong'.[71] H. G. Wells pitched it even stronger by writing a letter to The

* Only two months before he had been re-elected to the Presidency on the slogan 'He Kept You Out Of The War'.

Times that now was the time for the English to rid themselves of 'an alien and uninspiring Court'. This fired the King to retort: 'I may be uninspiring, but I'm damned if I'm alien!'[72] His hands, of course, were tied. When later there was a likelihood of sending a British destroyer to bring off the Tsar and his family to safety, the King strongly approved. But Lloyd George identified himself with the people of Russia and would not have it.[73] The late Duke of Windsor recalled taking tea with his parents when a message arrived from Downing Street. The King read it and passed it to Queen Mary. She read it carefully and then said 'No', with which the King concurred. The message had been a question as to whether there would be any objection from the Palace if a destroyer was not sent to Russia and asylum not offered. To say no was not a callous act. The Queen, conceiving it her prime duty to protect the English throne, was aware that it could not be put at risk even for dear cousins. The Palace could not object.[74] Lloyd George sent instructions to Russia. The British Ambassador 'with tears in his eyes and scarcely able to control his emotions' informed the head of Provisional Government that his country would not give refuge to the former Tsar 'due exclusively to considerations of international British politics'.[75] When later they heard of Tsar Nicholas' fate the British royal family was greatly distressed. The King was also angry. He confided to his son: 'Those politicians. If it had been one of their kind they would have acted fast enough. But merely because the poor man was an emperor —'[76]

The most genuine and persistent offers of help came from the Tsar's enemy in arms, the Kaiser. He telegraphed offering Nicholas and his family a free and protected passage through Germany.[77] Before April 19th, when the English finally refused to offer asylum, he made it clear through the Danish government that German submarines would not attack any warship of the Royal Navy carrying the Russian exiles.[78] When the Entente simply left them to the mercies of the revolution William was both disgusted and enraged. He vowed vengeance on his cousin's rebellious subjects. Being a devout man, and still holding the naive belief that sovereigns ruled by the Grace of God, he was also baffled that a crowned and consecrated Tsar should have been overthrown and treated not merely as a common man but as a criminal. Had he been less confident in the German Army and Navy with absolute trust in the personal oath made to him by each serving man, he might possibly have seen Tsar Nicholas' enforced abdication as a portent. As it was he made his feelings very plain to everyone and, could he have given physical aid to the fallen Tsar and his family, there is no doubt he would have done so. Because their countries were at war and Russia itself was in such a divided state, it was even difficult to obtain news though through neutral sources it became known that the soviets were becoming more aggressive and resentful and the red soldiers delighted in humiliating the imperial family shut away at Tsarskoe Selo.[79] William was especially concerned about Ella. In the popular Russian view she and the Tsaritsa were 'the Hessian witches', though they made a point of speaking English, French or Russian and never German; and only the sick and the wounded for whom Ella cared in her convent knew she only lived for her faith and her work.[80] The Provisional Government begged her to move to the safety of the Kremlin, but she refused and continued working. Several times William tried to save her at first through Sweden and then, after the Russian defeat, through his Ambassador, but all attempts failed. His feelings may be imagined when he read in the newspapers that, without any reference to him, Lenin and eighteen other Bolsheviks had been permitted to travel through Germany so that they could further agitate the Russians with their revolutionary ardour. Churchill, whose opinion of Lenin matched the Kaiser's, described him as 'the most grisly of all weapons' and as 'a plague bacillus'.[81] That the Kaiser had not been informed of the plan either by the Foreign Office or his General Staff showed they were aware he might raise powerful objections. By the time he read it in the newspapers Lenin had begun on his reign of terror and was doing exactly as the German General Staff had hoped; demanding an end of the war and urging all troops at the front to begin fraternizing with the enemy. A prophetic warning came from William's fellow monarch, the Emperor Charles of Austria.

> If the monarchs of the Alliance are not able to conclude peace during the next few months, the people will go over their heads and the wave of the revolutionary flood will sweep away everything for which our brothers and sons are still fighting and dying.[82]

It made sense, but the Emperor Charles' views were not then much valued by his allies. Only a little time before he had made himself unpopular in Germany by announcing that in any peace treaty he would support the French demand for the return of Alsace-Lorraine. Offering to return territory which was not his while simultaneously refusing to entertain any Italian demands for part of his own empire had enraged even the imperturbable Bethmann. William paid no attention to the warning because his High Command assured him that the war would be over by August. In fact, so satisfactory was the German position militarily that he and Bethmann once again put out peace-feelers through the mediation of the Pope, the King of Spain and the Queen of Holland. None was successful. Aristide Briand, the French Prime Minister, sank them by exciting wide suspicion amongst his allies: 'The call for peace is only the voice of weakness'.[83]

The war aims of the chief protagonists varied. The French, still obsessed by *l'affaire d'Alsace* and the huge loss of life in this war were bent on the obliteration of Germany and any possibility of her resurgence. Lloyd George announced in the House of Commons his own conviction 'that this war is at bottom a struggle for popular government as much as for liberty'.[84] The Americans as non-belligerents had been concerned how to ruin German vested interests without at the same time damaging their own. Now technically combatants though not a single American soldier had as yet arrived in Europe, the President refused the Pope's offer of mediation, declaring:

> The object of this war is to deliver the free peoples of the world from the menace and the actual power of a vast military establishment, controlled by an irresponsible Government. . . . This power is not the German people. It is the ruthless master of the German people. . . .[85]

The Kaiser himself equally claimed to be fighting for freedom. On the thirtieth anniversary of his accession he described the war as

> a conflict between two approaches to the world. Either the Prussian–German–Germanic approach – Right, Freedom, Honour, Morality – is to remain respected, or the Anglo-Saxon which would mean enthroning the worship of gold.[86]

But he, whatever President Wilson believed, was not 'the ruthless master of the German people'. General Eric Ludendorff had slowly tightened his demagogic grasp on the nation. Though Hindenburg was permitted to receive the acclaim of the people and became a splendid father-figure,* Ludendorff had the effective power. He had won and kept it through sheer talent and hard work and his amazing powers of concentration and grasp of detail, and by filling all the vital military and civil posts with his own nominees. Most of these were selected because they were yes-men,[87] a few like General William Gröner for their great ability. Gröner as head of the Railway Section of the General Staff, with every railway, road and waterway under his personal control, had the most intellectually distinguished post in the Army. Ludendorff, aware of the bureaucratic muddle which needed to be disentangled, created a new office, literally the amalgamation of dozens of offices all concerned with weapons, ammunitions, rolling stock, food and other vital supplies, and put Gröner at the head of it.[88]† Ludendorff himself was peerless as an organizer. He directed all strategy, drafted all military communiqués and penetrated government departments with acute memoranda on the most

* To keep him perpetually in mind a colossal wooden statue of Hindenburg was carved and erected near the Reichstag. There hand on sword pommel he brooded over the capital. Berliners drove a nail into the carving at a mark a time to raise funds for charity.[91]

† It was a superb appointment but Ludendorff could not bear criticism and when Gröner said in 1917 that Germany 'should be satisfied with a draw' he found himself exiled to the eastern front as Chief of Staff of the army of occupation.[92]

diverse subjects from postwar rural resettlement to the establishment of V.D. hospitals – called by the soldiers Knightly Castles.[89] Inevitably he became concerned with every section of German life, civilian and military. His aim was the 'Hindenburg Peace' which was to win the war by force of arms, and take territories and indemnities to prepare for the next one.[90] The Entente said the Junkers and greater industrialists of Prussia were their principal opponents, yet, while the General Staff and the majority of high-ranking officers were still largely of the Junker class, most of the younger Junker officers had already been slain in the early part of the war. Their replacements were bourgeois officers who copied the Junkers' arrogance but had few of their qualities. Ludendorff's hold on the Army was in no sense a continuation of the rule of the Junkers.[93] He held them in contempt.[94] The Prussian system had been subordinated by the Pan-German ideal of a dominated Europe, and Ludendorff was the demagogue of the masses.[95]

Ludendorff's only obstacles to supreme power were the Kaiser and the Chancellor. The former was unassailable but the latter was not. The High Command came to the conclusion that Bethmann had been over-tolerant of the defeatists and made too many concessions to the parties of the centre and the left, and they were especially critical of his undertaking to increase the franchise in Prussia. Both Hindenburg and Ludendorff lacked the Kaiser's fairly open mind to a rational argument and could not agree that some mild concessions must be made to the majority party in the Reichstag. William's open declaration they found intolerable: 'After the massive contributions of the entire nation in this terrible war, I am sure there is no room left for Prussia's class suffrage.'[96] William called a Council to meet in Berlin to discuss the project on July 9th. Ludendorff wasted no time, nor many words. He went to his master and told him that Bethmann must be dismissed and replaced by Prince Bülow. The proposal to reinstate Bülow was so preposterous to William that he found the nerve to order Ludendorff back to Headquarters and told him to mind his own business.[97] He then held the Council at which it was agreed that in Prussia there should be universal suffrage. On July 11th this was proclaimed. On the 12th, still in Berlin, William received a despatch from Supreme Headquarters. Unless Bethmann was dismissed Hindenburg, Ludendorff and the whole General Staff would resign. In the prime of life William would probably have sent for the two chief rebels and told them bluntly where their duty lay. But after three years of war his nervous vitality was sapped.[98] He managed to say to his Naval Secretary, Admiral von Müller, that nothing so preposterous had been heard of in the whole history of Prussia, but he took no decisive action.[99] Bethmann, as ever loyal to his master, solved his dilemma by resigning.[100] Had William been well-advised he would have seized the initiative politically and confounded Hindenburg and Ludendorff by giving the choice of a chancellor to the Reichstag; and had the Reichstag deputies been more united and more spirited they could, on their own account, have forced the issue. As it was neither happened. William's Watchers on the Wall urged him to protect his prerogatives and no doubt intensified his mistrust of the Socialists. He still indignantly refused to consider the treacherous Bülow, but no-one else seemed to suit the High Command. Eventually the Kaiser lost on swings and roundabouts. He was forced to tell his Civil Secretary Valentini to find a chancellor acceptable to Hindenburg and Ludendorff, and Valentini, being on bad terms with the High Command, deputed the Military Secretary to act for him. Eventually it was the Kaiser's aged A.D.C. Count von Plessen who triumphantly hauled from the obscurity of the Prussian Food Office a civil servant named George Michaelis, such a nonentity that neither the right nor the left wings of the Reichstag nor the High Command found him in the least objectionable. The Kaiser had not even met him before appointing him Chancellor.[101] Then, still anxious about his prerogatives, he told Reichstag deputies that, where his guards were, there was no room for democracy. The truth was there was no room for anything nor anyone save Ludendorff. The press were not disposed to be friendly to Michaelis. He was described as resembling 'the administrator of an orphanage' and 'a schoolteacher shuffling about in carpet slippers'.[102] He lasted for exactly ninety-nine days. His successor Count Hertling was Prime Minister of Bavaria and in age, origin, elegance and experience not unlike Prince Clovis zu Hohenlohe but without his staying power or knowledge.[103]

The Kaiser, it is alleged, then escaped into a world of fantasy.[104] Certainly he began to rush about inspecting troops, distributing Iron Crosses in person, and addressing parades with long speeches. His vigour and stamina were remarkable. He moved so fast that his generals could hardly keep pace with him and one, on a hot day, fainted with fatigue. He went as close to the front as Ludendorff permitted, driving through the shelled and burnt villages in a motor car displaying the yellow imperial standard.[105] He said he was much encouraged by the mutinies in the French Army, encouraged by the final defeat of Russia and the massive territorial gains granted by the treaty of Brest–Litovsk, and encouraged in March 1918 by the successful German offensive in the west in which 90,000 British prisoners of war, 1,300 guns and 2 million bottles of whisky were taken.[106] But, just as at some point before 1914 he began to realize and shy from the fact that war was inevitable, so now he had to face his conviction that the war was lost. He could reveal this to no-one. Dona and he were closer than they had ever been but it is unlikely that he confided his full feelings even to her, and since the Eulenburg scandal he had never given the same trust to any subject. It was noticed that he had aged perceptibly. His hair had greyed and his face had become lined. Attacks of sciatica obliged him to walk with a stick. It is said he had become much more serious and thoughtful and that, knowing everyone was watching him, he strove to infuse confidence.[107] He conceived it his chief duty to keep up people's spirits and give the impression that all was well and, being the man he was, no doubt he overdid it and gave some people the impression that he was in a state of euphoric delusion. Yet, though Dona and his suite still kept much from him, he knew sufficient to realize how bad things really were.

To him even the good news contained touches of rottenness like bad fruit. His eldest son and the Crown Prince of Bavaria had command of the armies on the western front and, taking advice from their staffs, they did well – but his heir's private life was a public scandal. By command of the High Command his mistress was forcibly removed from the area of his army group headquarters and deported to Lille.[108] Ludendorff was said to have the Socialists under control and yet, beneath his very nose, Der Vorwärts published an appeal from the Bolsheviks for peace, and German Communists, calling themselves the Spartacists, caused a general strike.[109] And for William the victory over Russia was clouded by the wrangling between the demi-gods, as Hindenburg and Ludendorff were now called, and the civilian government. The generals wanted more than the statesmen and the Kaiser sided with the latter; so much so that his excellent Foreign Secretary – the Richard von Kühlmann who had been his Chargé d'Affaires at Tangiers on the unhappy occasion of his landing there – declared the Kaiser was the 'only sensible person in the whole of Germany'.[110] Once more the generals had won by threatening their resignation and had demanded as a pourboire the dismissal of the Kaiser's faithful Civil Secretary Valentini who, like Bethmann, chose to resign to ease his master's position. William was so angry that he told Hindenburg he did not wish for any more paternal advice and he called Ludendorff a malefactor, but they had him in thrall.[111] One of the ugliest aspects of the affair was that the despicable Lenin had overthrown the Provisional Government and made Russia into a Bolshevik state, and that it was with his government the Germans had treated and imposed their hard terms. Only a ruthless and dishonourable leader such as Lenin could have accepted them. One Russian general, on hearing the humiliating terms of the treaty of Brest-Litovsk had shot himself as the only way of retaining his honour.[112] Worst of all to William was the knowledge that from the moment of signing the Romanovs were doomed. It mattered nothing to the demi-gods, but it mattered a great deal to the Kaiser. He did what he could to rescue the family but met with no success.* According to tradition they were

* The fate of the Tsar and his family has always excited a grisly interest and in 1976 it was the subject of intensive research by two British television journalists. They

murdered.[114] Certainly the Tsar, the Tsaritsa and their children, with the Grand Duke Michael disappeared from the European scene. Equally positive is that at some time before the end of the war, probably halfway through July, 1918, Ella, with her devoted maid, and five grand dukes – four of them boys – were dropped alive down a disused mineshaft, heavy timbers thrown down afterwards and then two hand grenades.[115] No fruit was as rotten as the ignoble treaty of Brest-Litovsk, bruised as it was by so much brutality.

There was also a bitter irony in the fact William had not wished to order the offensive in the spring of 1918 which brought the great victory. The people called it 'the Kaiser's Battle', contemptuously implying that he had had nothing to do with any of the others.[116] After that campaign there were no more victories. A second offensive beginning on May 7th 1918 took the Germans back to the Marne. They crossed it. Then they fell back. The very, very few of the professional soldiers who were still alive after almost four years of war were exhausted and disillusioned. The fresh troops were green boys or elderly reservists or strikers who had been mobilized to get them away from the centres of agitation. All were debilitated by the strict rationing. So hungry were they that they stole the barley issued as horse fodder. Most were the victims of concentrated Bolshevik propaganda. The conscripted strikers and the indoctrinated troops drafted from the eastern front were a positive liability. Pamphlets signed by 'Spartacus' were reaching the trenches.[117] Rosa Luxemburg still had no opinion of Bolshevik authoritarianism and the use of terror she continued to condemn as inhuman and 'theoretically incorrect';[118] but the titular leader of the German Spartacus group, Charles Liebknecht, 'lived in a gallop, in eternal haste' and was in far too much of a hurry to theorize and be dainty.[119] Just so long as there was a revolution he did not mind if it was Bolshevik or Menshevik. The poison of Leninism which the High Command had so irresponsibly spilt in Russia was seeping back into their own country and it was only by chance that most of the proletariat were not yet disposed to assimilate it.

---

offered the hypothesis that the official stories have all been distortions of the truth. This may or may not be true, but the section on the all-important German part in this piece of history is marked by some notable omissions. For instance, there is no mention of the Kaiser's special concern for his cousin Ella, nor of his greatly diminished power and Ludendorff's ascendancy at this stage of the war, nor that he was against the heavy demands made by Germany at Brest-Litovsk nor even of the true relationship between Lenin and the German Spartacists – Liebknecht is called Lenin's 'old friend' and Rosa Luxemburg is left out altogether. Such important omissions suggest that the work cannot be regarded as a serious contribution to historical studies, and it seems unlikely that leading scholars should have been duped by *suppressio veri* which two investigating journalists magically managed to avoid.[113]

In April 1917 the German trade union leaders had instructed their members to have nothing to do with the Spartacus League because it 'endangered the German labour movement'.[120] But in the cities the people were close to starvation. They were ill-clothed and, in winter, seldom warm. Nevertheless they still had some spirit. As a symbol of their disapproval they made a butt of the sort of man who makes money out of other people's misery, personifying him as Herr Raffke, Mr Profiteer, and there were many clever and crude stories about this unwholesome man and Frau Raffke.[121] They made a huge joke of it when, on January 26th 1918, the American president made a solemn proclamation – for all the world like a Tsar issuing a ukase – establishing 'one meatless, two wheatless, and two porkless days per week'.[122] For blockaded Germans in their great hunger this rationing on so celestial a scale was indeed a joke, and laughter helped. Yet though the perfect revolutionary situation had not arrived, a good many workers and soldiers and sailors showed an interest in the promises held out by the Bolsheviks, and even the most loyal people thought privately that something should be done. Besides his rationing proclamation, President Wilson had addressed Congress listing fourteen points which he would require to be met for peace,[123] and copies had found their way into Germany by balloons, aeroplanes and pamphlet rockets.[124] Finally on June 25th, 1918 the Foreign Secretary spoke openly in the Reichstag what many people had been thinking privately for a long time: that peace would have to be negotiated, not fought for. This made Ludendorff so angry that he demanded Kühlmann's dismissal. Battered by events the Kaiser consented.[125] The theory that for twelve months he had been enjoying a species of comfortable nervous breakdown, is barely tenable.

On July 15th Ludendorff began his third offensive in the west. It was a last throw to win the war. Eight thousand field pieces shelled the enemy in the largest barrage then known to history. But within a week the attacking forces foundered. Marshal Foch, Generalissimo of the French, British, Imperial and American forces, counter-attacked. The line wavered and then, on August 8th, the British broke through using tanks. Not surprisingly the fighting morale of the German soldiers in the face of such a new weapon was at its lowest. Ludendorff in his *Memoirs* terms it 'the Black Day of the German Army'. But the Germans were still on French territory and Hindenburg believed they could force a peace on their own terms.[126] He proposed asking the Queen of the Netherlands if a peace conference could be held in The Hague.[127] William, showing commendable self-control, spent the evening reading an article on the Hittite language. His unusual calmness when Germany faced defeat moved an aide into suggesting there might be more important subjects to study than the Hittites. On the contrary, said the Kaiser, if France and England had kept their minds on the east as he was doing they would have realized the peril of coming to an entente with a half oriental nation like Russia and so avoided the war.[128] Nevertheless appearances were deceptive. He was becoming increasingly nervous. Temporarily he moved from General Headquarters at Spa to be with Dona at Cassel. She was suffering from heart trouble. In September he went to Krupp factories and spoke to the munition workers but, accustomed like a clergyman to captive audiences and not feeling himself, he was thrown by their obvious hostility and failed as a propagandist. Albert Ballin tried where others had failed to make the Kaiser more aware of the real conditions both at the fronts and in the cities, but the new Civil Secretary, a creature of Ludendorff's, was present at the audience and Ballin's warnings were effectively suffocated by a discussion on the Second Punic war.[129] Nonetheless in the last few days of September when the French, Americans and British began different offensives William showed he knew quite well what was happening. The news so distressed him that, significantly, he suffered from an attack of neuralgia and went to bed for twenty-four hours, refusing to see anyone. He was in the grip of the same nervous melancholia as he had been at the time of the Eulenburg trial and when Bülow had betrayed him, but this time his breakdown quickly passed. The short rest soothed him. When he re-emerged he told his Naval Secretary that he felt a new man and, judging from his subsequent behaviour, this was true.[130]

3

Many commentators have concluded that Ludendorff's power-hunger was pathological. Whatever the truth, the fact that he had been driving himself relentlessly for a long period resulted in a violent mental disturbance. In the past months his irritability had grown more noticeable. On the afternoon of September 28th, having received nothing but bad news from the western front, he erupted into a frenzy of rage. His aides were aghast. Quickly they closed the door of the map-room to drown his hysterical raging. He screamed curses at the Kaiser, the Reichstag, the ministers and those who were working against him. At length the torrent of abuse died down. It is legitimate to wonder why he did not go right off his head. Instead he somehow called up reserves of self-control and by that evening the fit had passed.[131] So, temporarily, had his confidence. His policies turned turtle. The next day there was a Council at Spa. The Kaiser, the Chancellor, the Foreign Secretary were told bluntly by Ludendorff that as Bulgaria had just collapsed, Austria-Hungary was about to collapse and the German Army was in a desperate strait – Bavarian and Saxon divisions already surrendering wholesale – the war was lost, an armistice must be negotiated, the present government changed and the constitution liberalized so that effective power passed to the Reichstag. Hindenburg confirmed these views. It is said Ludendorff added as a rider that in the final treaty Germany should be given the French mining districts of Briey and Longwy – which, if true, does cast serious doubts upon his sanity.[132]

The Naval Secretary, Admiral Müller, held the opinion that the Kaiser had been 'humbugged' and had no idea of the extent of the catastrophe,[133] and others have reported he was appalled by this disclosure.[134] Yet it is worth noting that he was not so ignorant of the state of affairs, nor so unprepared for the announcement, that he flew into a state of excitement which frequently happened when he was faced by unpleasantness. He showed little surprise and remained calm, though he did remark he would have preferred to have had full information earlier. He gave orders for an armistice to be sought and announced that in future his subjects should have a larger hand in the conduct of affairs.[135]

A representative of the High Command called together the party leaders of the Reichstag in Berlin and gave them the news. They showed immense surprise and consternation. Careful censorship had hidden the real state of affairs. The Conservative party leader declared: 'We have been deceived and betrayed'; another right-wing deputy asked for nothing but a bullet; and even the leader of the majority Socialists, Frederick Ebert, whose party stood to profit most from the new dispensation, was so shocked that he could not utter a word. Only the leader of the Independent Socialists saw in the nation's defeat a promise of better things to come, a vision which he expressed with the blunt words: 'Now we've got them!'[136] Meanwhile the Kaiser had taken advice on who should be the last chancellor of his own choosing. He was discussing the problems with Chancellor Hertling when Ludendorff abruptly burst in on them to ask if the new Government had yet been appointed – an infraction of military etiquette and good manners which, from so circumspect a man, casts further doubts upon his sanity. William replied with cold dignity that he was not a conjurer.[137]

n October 3rd William's kinsman, Prince Max of Baden, was nominated Chancellor. Things might have been different if he had been summoned to power earlier. He was a likeable man, trusted by the politicians, liberally-minded, heir to the most enlightened Grand Duchy in the empire, and was known to have favoured peace without annexations for some time. After being invalided out of the Army he had been working for the Red Cross and had done a great deal for prisoners of war. Such a man was likely to be acceptable to the Entente negotiators and he had the great advantage of being acceptable both to the High Command and to the Socialist deputies in the Reichstag.

Ludendorff insisted that his first act should be to ask for an armistice on the basis of President Wilson's fourteen points. Prince Max demurred. Conceivably through his Red Cross connections he may have been aware that the enemy was in as bad a state as Germany. By the end of that month all the Entente commanders were recommending the politicians to come to an acceptable agreement with the Germans because they had reached the end of their strength, and the President's close associate Colonel House said later it was a miracle that the German authorities had been in ignorance of the true condition of affairs.[138] But even if the new Chancellor was ignorant of these facts he had enough savoir faire to know that a government asking for an armistice on the first day of its existence had hardly any bargaining advantage at all. He must first appoint his ministers, settle them in and afterwards approach President Wilson. Ludendorff however persisted, and the Kaiser agreed. William wanted to break off the battle without delay.[139] Resisting the temptation to walk out, Prince Max did as he was told. He sent word to the American President asking for an armistice, made up his Government which included the representatives of the four largest political parties and excluded the extreme right and extreme left. On October 5th the new Chancellor announced to the Reichstag that future chancellors would only serve with the approval of that elected body, that Prussian electoral reform would quickly be implemented, that the Army would be a less dominant feature in everyday life, and that he had sent his note to President Wilson.[140] The majority of deputies was satisfied.

The President's reply was not reassuring. He wanted to know with whom he was dealing, if the Germans thoroughly understood the fourteen points, and he expressed mistrust of their appeal for an armistice because a German submarine had sunk a ferry boat between Ireland and England after its despatch.[141] This was but the first of a number of exchanged notes between the Chancellor and the President. Meanwhile neither much trusted the other. Wilson examined every German note for traces of Prussian duplicity. Prince Max came to the conclusion that the President was asking for far more than fourteen points. Meanwhile the war continued. The German economy was collapsing. In Berlin influenza married to a starvation diet caused no less than seventeen hundred deaths in one day.[142] The Chancellor made more constitutional amendments so that the Reichstag now had the sole power to make peace or war, had command of the Army, and he proclaimed a general amnesty in which Liebknecht and Rosa Luxemburg were released from prison.[143]

William was at last where he ought to have been all along, in the capital.

On October 21st he met the members of the Reichstag at the Bellevue Palace and said he felt at one with them in leading the country out of its present deplorable state to peace and better things. He was always at his best on such occasions, unlike many hereditary sovereigns, and made a good impression. He had conceded the constitutional amendments under Prince Max's advice without a grumble, but he complained bitterly when he rightly read into Wilson's wordy notes that the Entente was demanding his abdication. Enraged he cried that the President was aiming directly at the overthrow of the monarchy.[144] Dona was equally angry and railed against 'the audacity of the parvenu across the sea who thus dares to humiliate a princely house which can look back on centuries of service to people and country'.[145] Thrones were toppling. As the leader of the Independent Socialists put it: 'Crowns are rolling about the floor'.[146] But it is unlikely that either William or Dona had contemplated the remotest possibility of being themselves involved.

On October 23rd President Wilson finally consented to submit the German peace proposal to his allies. These now amounted to twenty-seven sovereign states, though what contribution was made to the Entente's cause by remote nations like Liberia, Nicaragua, Panama and Peru the Germans could scarcely have known. They were to be reduced to what was called the Big Four.[147] It was at this point that Ludendorff came to life again. He had not read the fourteen points, but at last he realized their implication. Possibly he had had at the back of his mind the idea of using an armistice and a period of negotiation, as a time for recouping before attacking the enemy in greater strength.[148] Prince Max had feared he might play such a trick. It was the sort of thing Caesar had done, and Napoleon, and Ludendorff might well have developed delusions of grandeur. To the Chancellor's fury the High Command drafted telegrams to Army Commanders at the front denying that they had insisted upon an immediate armistice and ordering 'resistance with every means in our command'. At the last moment Ludendorff hesitated and he cancelled the order, but the Army was not the loyal and disciplined body it once had been. A Bolshevik indoctrinated signaller who saw the draft telegraphed it to the headquarters of the Independent Socialists in Berlin. An Independent deputy read it out in the Reichstag. The Chancellor at once telephoned Supreme Headquarters and was told that Hindenburg and Ludendorff had gone to Berlin. Prince Max then went to the Kaiser and said unless Ludendorff were dismissed he and his ministers would resign. Unaware of what had taken place, the demi-gods arrived at the Bellevue Palace to demand that the war be continued. William let them talk and sent them away telling them to return the next day. When they did so he referred to the High Command's telegram to Army Commanders and insisted that such a grave decision should not have been made without consultation with the civil government. In a suggestive silence both Hindenburg and Ludendorff offered their resignations. The Field Marshal's was refused, the General's accepted. Outside Ludendorff was so angry that Hindenburg was still in power that he refused to share his motor-car. He went off to spend the rest of the war in a Berlin boarding-house until political events forced him to escape from Germany in heavy disguise. 'The operation is done,' said William. 'I have split the Siamese twins.'[149] On the following day, October 27th, the Emperor Charles informed him that Austria was giving up the fight.

William told the Imperial Chancellor: 'I shall remain in my place and co-operate loyally with the government.' Within twenty-four hours, prompted by Dona and his suite, and 'at the urgent request of Field Marshal Hindenburg' he had gone to Spa and settled at the Château de la Fraineuse, a white-colonnaded villa with beautiful pleasure grounds.[150]

Prince Max had influenza. When he heard the Kaiser was leaving he telephoned, begging him to remain. When the Kaiser had gone he telegraphed begging him to return. But by now the Kaiser must have heard rumours that pressure was to be put on him to abdicate. In fact no one dared approach him on the subject and Prince Max insisted that any abdication must be voluntary. William was unwise not to heed his kinsman. Had he been more approachable, and could they have talked the matter over, there is a high probability Prince Max could have kept the monarchy. He could not save the throne for William, nor for his feckless son, but his idea was to set up the Crown Prince's twelve-year old son William with one of the Federal Princes as Regent. This, had the sovereign's powers been limited in the English fashion, would have been acceptable even to the Majority Socialists.[151] But in the first instance, all depended upon the Kaiser's abdication. To its inevitability only a very few were still blind. William's frank Jewish friend Albert Ballin was within a month of dying. He wrote at the time: 'We caused the war and the Kaiser, like a dummy editor who has to accept responsibility for it, will not be able to escape abdication.[152]

On November 1st the Prussian Minister of the Interior, Dr William Drews, took a train to Spa and asked for an audience. Bravely he told the Kaiser that there was a strong feeling in the empire that he should abdicate. William turned on him: 'How comes it that you, a Prussian official, have the insolence and effrontery to appear before me with a request like this?' Dr Drews returned to Berlin.[153]

From the serious state of affairs in Germany William had come to the conclusion that Bolshevism was a greater enemy to the Fatherland than the Entente. He even hoped that possibly England would assist in crushing the forces of disorder. It was this which preoccupied him. He spoke of it frequently, and he was appalled when a mutiny broke out at Kiel on November

4th. The Navy, which he and Tirpitz had built up with such care and at great expense, became an officerless rabble waving red flags and declaring a Sailors' Soviet on the Russian pattern.[154] William felt personally betrayed. The men had sworn to be *kaisertreu* as had his soldiers. There is no evidence that he suspected the Army could ever possibly do the same. On the contrary the General Staff at Supreme Headquarters was continuing to function smoothly and reassuringly.

Ludendorff's successor as Quartermaster General was William Gröner, formerly Head of Railway Section, then special co-ordinator at the War Office until Ludendorff sent him off to the eastern front. Now he was back again in Ludendorff's place. They had two things in common: both were intellectually formidable and neither were 'children of protection'. Gröner, in fact, had non-commissioned officer background, but he was now virtually in command of the Army and was liked by all ranks for his integrity and his good humour.[155] He was a Swabian from the south of Germany where the people were said to be imaginative and brave and have a pleasing touch of naiveté about them, and he was actually in the Württemberg Army. The Kaiser thoroughly approved of his new Quartermaster General, calling him 'a jolly little chap'. Hindenburg was quite prepared to let Gröner manage the intricate situation in which they found themselves and which hourly grew more difficult.

As soon as he heard of the Kiel mutiny Gröner went to Berlin to confer with the Chancellor and his ministers. He was informed that if no armistice could be arranged within four days the German Army would have to surrender and that President Wilson would not move an inch as long as the Kaiser was in power.[156] While he fully understood the serious situation Gröner made it clear that the Officer Corps would not easily accept the impertinent claim of a foreign head of state to decide arbitrarily, like a nurse with an infant, how a former Great Power should be governed. On the next day he met Frederick Ebert, Chairman of the Majority Socialists, with other leading members of his party and some trade unionists. They were in a great state of alarm about the establishment of a Sailors' Soviet and the responsibilities which inevitably would soon devolve upon them. The Russian Ambassador, Adolf Yoffe, who, according to Trotsky, had been completely cured from lunacy by the glorious revolution, was expelled that day by Prince Max's government for persistent agitation; but Ebert and his colleagues knew the strength of the Independent Socialists and the Spartacus League and dreaded a full-scale revolution. Gröner they liked. He was approachable. With his understanding and experience he was prepared to talk and listen to Socialists, and unlike most of his fellow generals he did not regard them as enemies of the state. They begged him to move the Kaiser to abdicate and entrust one of his younger sons with the regency. Gröner maintained his position with great correctness and told them abdication was out of the question. The Army was engaged in combat and fighting a most difficult battle and it could not be deprived of its Supreme Warlord at such a point. He also informed them that none of the Kaiser's sons would act as regent if their father was forced to abdicate.[157] Meanwhile Prince Max had decided that with or without the President's approval he was sending an Armistice Commission to treat with Foch. Ordinarily it would have been the responsibility of the High Command but the Chancellor had taken Gröner's point. He chose a retired General, Hugo von Winterfeldt,* a Foreign Office Counsellor, and as their chairman, Matthias Erzberger, his Minister without Portfolio and leader of the Catholic Centre, the second largest party in the Reichstag. Within hours they were despatched by special train to Spa to receive their credentials. A tardy note arrived from Wilson to say that Marshal Foch had been authorized to receive accredited representatives and inform them the terms of the armistice.

On November 8th Foch handed to the German Armistice Commission conditions which were tantamount to a complete surrender.[159] Simultaneously King Louis III of Bavaria was deposed, his country separated from the empire and taken over by a charming, cultured Prussian Jew named Eisner who was tiny, heavily bearded, wore steel-rimmed pince-nez and an immense Left Bank black hat. His Workers' Republic was more concerned with aesthetic than practical matters for Bavarian politics always had a flavour of opera bouffe.[160] Far more dangerous were the revolutionary régimes which on that same day seized power in Düsseldorf, Frankfurt-am-Main, Stuttgart, capital city of the King of Württemberg, Leipzig, Magdeburg, Osnabrück, Lauenburg, Oldenburg, Brunswick, Cologne and Darmstadt.[161] The German capital was like a besieged fortress. Railway lines between red cities and Berlin were being ripped up. Stations, gas works and electric stations were occupied by troops and armoured cars moved about the centre of the city.†[162]

By now it was clear to everyone, except apparently to the Kaiser, that if he did not abdicate there would be total social revolution. The alternative was that he should go to the front and get himself killed. It is alleged that Gröner proposed this but, in view of the general's character, it seems most improbable.[163] At all events William knew of it and he was deeply upset. The whole structure on which his life had been based was falling to ruins but he had no

---

* The imperial A.D.C. who, thirty years before, had so tactlessly announced Kaiser William's accession and had been given an icy reception by Queen Victoria.[158]

† Nevertheless that night Richard Strauss conducted the Egmont Overture at the Opera House, and the concert was extremely well attended.[164]

intention of committing suicide to solve the problem of his High Command. Realistically he regarded it as an abnegation of duty and a pathetic and sinful means of escape, not as a Roman virtue.

On the night of November 8th after many attempts the Chancellor finally managed to talk to the Kaiser on the telephone. Speaking as a kinsman he advised William that his obstinacy was leading the country to Civil War. Rightly or wrongly people were laying the blame for all their miseries on his shoulders and the troops were no longer reliable. Then, speaking as Chancellor, he asked permission to resign. William angrily refused his resignation and told him that if necessary he himself would subdue the revolutionaries.[165]

It was about this time that General Gröner came to the conclusion Prince Max's government was virtually defunct and power would soon pass either to Frederick Ebert and the Majority Socialists or to the Independent Socialist and their close ally the Spartacus League. Only the Majority Socialists would consider permitting the Officer Corps to exist and even then in a modified form, but Gröner believed that, shorn of its Prussian vices, the Officer Corps with its Prussian virtues should be kept intact for the benefit of the nation; that its continuance was more important to the future of Germany than the continuance of the monarchy, and that the Kaiser's abdication could only be forced by the Army. He knew precisely what he was doing and was aware that for the sake of what he regarded as an ultimate good he would have to make unpleasant personal sacrifices and draw upon himself the odium of his Supreme War Lord, the conservatives and monarchists, even many members of the Officer Corps for which the sacrifices were being made, but once his mind was made up he hesitated no longer. Somehow it would have to be arranged that the Kaiser's mantle as War Lord should fall upon Hindenburg; and, by now certain that the Kaiser's conviction that his Army would follow him and that he must not let them down was the reason – or the excuse – he gave for not doing as the civil government asked, Gröner quietly set about disillusioning him. He ordered to Spa fifty field officers. Only thirty-nine were able to arrive by the morning of the 9th. Colonel William Heye, Chief of Staff of an Army, was deputed to interview these officers.[166] Meanwhile amongst other papers a telegram had arrived at the Château de la Fraineuse from the desperate Prince Max. It stated that, failing abdication, Germany would be without a Chancellor, a government, a clear majority in the Reichstag, and therefore incapable of negotiating with the enemy. William scribbled on the form one of his acute marginalia: 'This is what has happened already'[167] and went for a walk through the mist patches and thin rain with an A.D.C. He was recalled by a runner to say that the Chief of General Staff and the Quartermaster General with five other officers had arrived at Imperial Headquarters to report. He returned and received them in a room overlooking the garden. The log fire smoked and gave out little heat. He stood close to it and waited.

Hindenburg as Chief of General Staff had to speak first. There was much to report: that the Armistice Commission was still with Foch in the Forest of Compiègne; that the supply dumps on the Rhine had been seized by revolutionaries; that, in the rear, the Army was in a poor state and at the front it was tired out and demoralized; that large parts of the Empire had fallen to the Spartacists.[168] But Hindenburg was not normally loquacious, not a happy bearer of sad tidings, and though he quite agreed with the Quartermaster General he was not prepared to make any sacrifice himself. All he did was mutter about the bad state of affairs and suddenly proffer his resignation. Then he lapsed into silence. The Kaiser neither accepted nor rejected it. It was left to the Quartermaster General to be charged with not being *kaisertreu*. Gröner told his master the solemn facts of the case: that the army could no longer be relied upon and that the soldiers were not prepared to go on fighting.[169]

William was in no way helped at this critical and painful moment by the kind intention of his staff and other officers who vigorously opposed Gröner.[170] The decrepit senior A.D.C. Count von Plessen said it would be intolerable for the Kaiser and the Army to give way to the revolutionaries. He spoke of 'a band of vicious sailors'. He was supported in his view despite the fact that Gröner insisted the revolutionaries had control of most of the big cities, the coast, the west, and the south, and most ammunition dumps and railway junctions. There were rations and munitions for a few more days of fighting. If the army was ordered to march against the homeland they would be fighting a civil war as well as continuing the war with the Entente. Moreover the soldiers would not accept the order.

All that morning the Kaiser's advisers argued. He himself vacillated. He did not want civil war. Nor did he want the Army to continue suffering. He was clearly coming to the conclusion that the best thing would be for him to lead his soldiers home after an armistice had been concluded. The Crown Prince arrived and assured his father of the Army's support. With this fresh encouragement the Kaiser asked Gröner for facts and figures and not simply his opinions.[171] Gröner at once summoned Colonel Heye who, pledging the field officers to secrecy, had asked them if the Kaiser at the head of his troops could reconquer Germany by force, and if their soldiers would fight against Bolsheviks on the home front. Many of the replies had been conditional but the consensus of opinion was that the troops wanted only one thing – to go home, enjoy rest and peace – and that an armistice should be concluded at the earliest moment.[172] Though deeply shaken by this representative view, the Kaiser was helped to make up his mind: that he would lead his troops back to the Fatherland. Gröner then showed great courage. He told the Kaiser that the troops would indeed march home behind the officers, but not under his command. They no longer stood behind their Supreme War Lord.[173]

It was perhaps the first time that anyone had dared to tell the Kaiser the exact truth. He was shocked. He was genuinely bewildered that men who had sworn a solemn oath could break it. Then angrily he burst out and demanded how such an unbelievable thing could happen. He insisted on seeing evidence of it with his own eyes. All commanding generals should be required to state their apostasy in writing. The Army had taken an oath. Gröner, once in his opinion 'a jolly little chap' replied clearly and sadly: 'Sir, in times such as these, oaths are but words'.[174] The Kaiser whitened. He was about to make some cutting remark but he controlled himself in time and maintained his dignity. At this point Admiral Paul von Hintze, the Foreign Secretary, reported the latest information from Berlin. A general strike had been called. The Majority Socialists had left the government. Prince Max and he himself advised instant abdication.[175] Count von Plessen suggested a compromise; that his master give up the imperial crown but remain King of Prussia. By a word or gesture to Admiral von Hintze William agreed to this. Hintze and a small committee sat down to draft the announcement while the Kaiser and the Crown Prince led the remainder in to luncheon. Scarcely anyone ate a mouthful. Hintze brought the draft for signature and at once telephoned Berlin on a special line. He began to read the text, was interrupted and told that it was impossible for the Kaiser to remain as King of Prussia. Then to his astonishment he heard the text of another abdication announcement which Prince Max on his own initiative had issued two hours before.[176] At about the same time Frederick Ebert with some other Majority Socialists had arrived at the Chancellery and told Prince Max that for the preservation of order it was essential that the office of Imperial Chancellor be held by one of their party.[177] Prince Max had reviewed the situation and handed his office to Ebert. Philip Scheidemann, one of the two Majority Socialists in Prince Max's ministry, was taking an early luncheon in the Reichstag building where he heard the news and had gone to the large windows of the library and announced to the huge crowds outside that Frederick Ebert was now Chancellor. He ended by crying: 'Long live the Great German Republic!' and returned to his luncheon.[178]

This spectacular news was received at Spa with dismay. The Kaiser was not simply angry that Prince Max had acted in such a way, he was engorged with rage. 'Treason, gentlemen!' he stormed. 'Barefaced, outrageous treason! I am King of Prussia and I will remain King. As such I shall stay with my troops.'[179]

Hindenburg had already returned to his quarters. Three officers were sent to tell him what had happened. The Kaiser rushed to a desk and completed

many telegraph forms of protest. He ordered his servants to prepare the Château for defence. When Hindenburg returned to his master he had General
Gröner with him. In his fury William refused to acknowledge Gröner's presence. Offensively he remarked that he was merely a Württemberg General.
Gröner stepped back.* It was left to Hindenburg, who had conferred with his
officers, to give advice at long last as the Kaiser's Chief of General Staff. He
said that he could not guarantee his master's safety at Spa; that he might
be seized by mutinous troops and handed over to the revolutionary
government; that if he went to Holland a Civil War might yet be averted.[180]
William objected. He could not leave his troops, his country, his family.
The Kaiserin was in Berlin itself with Prince Eitel-Frederick. But Hindenburg
persisted. The Kaiserin and the Duchess of Brunswick were being guarded at
Potsdam and were less likely to come to any harm if the Kaiser was out of the
country. As for the Kaiser himself, the words were not spoken but it was
hinted that in Berlin he would stand no better chance than the Tsar had in
Petrograd. William began on a long agony of indecision. At one moment he
would go, at the next not. At ten that night he was officially informed that the
local troops were no longer reliable. In order to reach Holland some diver-
sionary strategy might be necessary. Possibly this finally decided the Kaiser,
but it is equally possible that he never did actually make up his mind but
simply permitted himself to be taken from his Imperial Headquarters. The
imperial motor-car, stripped of insignia, with nine others, left Spa at five the
next morning. The imperial train which had been ordered for five, actually
left at 4.30. But William was in neither the motor convoy nor the train. He
was travelling with three of his suite in an eleventh car and had circled to meet
the convoy at some distance from Spa.[182] At about seven they reached the
Dutch frontier at Eysden where a Dutch sergeant asked for passports. Each
member of the Kaiser's suite carried identity documents but none had a passport. The sergeant telephoned his officer who arrived in great haste and in
some embarrassment received the German Kaiser's request for asylum and his
sword. On his own authority, and presumably at the request of William's suite
who were concerned that a Soldiers' Soviet patrol might be in the vicinity, he
ordered the Eysden frontier station to be sealed pending instructions from
The Hague. He then begged the Kaiser to accompany him to the nearby railway station where they would be more comfortable out of the fog in a waiting room.[183]

The Government of the Netherlands could not have been taken quite by

* Gröner accomplished what he set out to do, contacting Chancellor Ebert that
evening and concluding an alliance between the Majority Socialist government and
the High Command. Hindenburg was given supreme command and served as a
figurehead. The Officer Corps, much reduced in size but pared of its weaknesses, was
maintained.[181]

surprise. A Dutch General had visited Supreme Headquarters at Spa just at the time when Gröner had decided that the Army itself mattered more to Germany than the Kaiser. It is unlikely to have been a coincidence. Nevertheless the rapidity of events and the Kaiser's abrupt arrival did cause some consternation at The Hague. Queen Wilhelmina took a personal interest in the matter as it concerned a fellow sovereign.* There were cabinet consultations. Telegrams passed to and fro from Berlin clarifying the situation.[184] William was still *de jure* Kaiser if not *de facto*. He had not abdicated nor renounced his rights, nor had he been deposed by act of a legitimate government. Ebert had been given office by his predecessor without the consent of either the Kaiser or the Reichstag, and his position as Imperial Chancellor of an unofficially proclaimed republic was ambiguous to say the least. Furthermore while Ebert held the Chancellery, a red flag hung over the Old Palace, which had been seized by Liebknecht's Spartacists. It was questionable if Germany had a legitimate government at all.[185] Yet, as almost invariably happens even in most massive political upheavals, there was a hard core of civil servants in the capital who continued the accustomed routine as well as they could.[186] From them and from the Netherlands Minister in Berlin Queen Wilhelmina and her cabinet understood that to offer the Kaiser asylum would not be regarded as an unfriendly act. William was then officially informed. For six hours he had had to wait, uncertain of his prospects, partly in the railway station and, after his own train steamed in, in the greater comfort of familiar surroundings. Once he knew that his request had been granted he conveyed his thanks to Queen Wilhelmina and expressed himself ready to comply with any instructions her government might care to give.[187]

Considering that he was accompanied by his suite of fourteen officers and a large number of functionaries and servants it is astonishing how rapidly the Dutch Government found him accommodation. Having spent the night on his train he was told that for the time being he was to be the guest of Count Godard Bentinck who was a fellow Knight of the Order of St John.[188] He was also part English, the Duke of Portland being titular head of his family, and, in the European aristocracy, *Erlaucht*, or belonging to a *maison comtale*. He was a courteous host and his castle at Amerongen was ideal. Like many traditional Dutch country houses it was surrounded by a double moat and could therefore be more easily guarded from curious sightseers. It was also an apposite refuge for a King of Prussia. In the reign of William's ancestor the Great Elector, the Netherlands Ambassador to his Court had been a Count de

* Philip Scheidemann, Prince Max's minister who had proclaimed the German Republic in the middle of his luncheon, asserted that King George V had earlier asked Queen Wilhelmina to grant the Kaiser asylum: a probability but unproveable until the archives of the Royal Netherlands Government are opened.[189]

Bentinck. He had refused to return home to entertain Louis XIV of France who was pillaging the Low Countries and his castle was burnt to the ground. The Great Elector had immediately sent loads of timber from the *Tiergarten* for its rebuilding. William was surrounded on all sides by wood from his own capital.[190] It could not have been easy for Count Godard but William, even at this tense and unhappy time, was true to his training and quickly put the Bentinck family at their ease. He was an easier guest than they might have expected.[191] Arrangements were made for a large part of the imperial entourage to be housed beyond Amerongen Castle and come in daily to do their duties.

We know that William's staff largely kept in the background and left him to nurse his misery alone, but what his feelings and thoughts were during the first few days of his exile can only be imagined.[192] Again and again he must have relived the events of November 9th and questioned if he had made the wrong decision. He had been repeatedly advised it was his duty to the fatherland to leave and that he could best serve Dona's interests by going, but now he must have wondered. Almost certainly his enemies would accuse him of cowardice. Dona and their daughter with two faithful ladies-in-waiting were at the Villa Liegnitz – the place Queen Victoria had castigated as 'unfit for an empress' – and they must still be in great peril. Only by the goodwill of the new people in power could she join him. His fall had the piquancy of true pathos. He had ruled sixty-five million Germans, now he had forty faithful followers. Utterly convinced that the bond between him and his Army had been indestructible, he had seen it destroyed. Born to the purple and trained to believe he owed his place to God alone, he now found himself in a foreign land and with nothing to do. His disillusionment must have been bitter, and as each piece of news came in he could only marvel that such things could be.

The fatherland had become like a lunatic asylum left in charge of the patients. There was no coherence in the pattern of revolution and it seemed that only a miracle could save the country from total dissolution. On the day of his formal entry into Holland the Berlin workers had voted delegates to represent them at a meeting which would choose a new government. A Council of six People's Commissioners had been appointed by the delegates as the supreme authority not only in Berlin but in the whole country. Surprisingly there were no Bolsheviks amongst them and Ebert was still at their head.[193] It held some promise of moderation if he could stay in power. He had already returned two truckloads of wheat sent by Lenin as a gesture of international Socialist solidarity saying that as there was famine in Russia it should be distributed at home.[194] And he had refused to allow into the country a Russian delegation to the German Workers' and Soldiers' Councils.[195] But, far more important, now that Germany once more had a *de facto* government, an armistice could be signed. This was done in Foch's railway carriage on the day the Kaiser moved into Amerongen Castle. Its terms were so hard that it was almost a surrender, but it was not an unconditional surrender and Germany's honour was maintained. At once there began a massive withdrawal of troops from the occupied zones. As the railway system was in chaos, most of Germany on strike, the soldiers were hungry and tired, and they and their supplies and equipment had to be clear of France, Belgium, Luxembourg and Alsace and Lorraine and the German Rhineland within one calendar month, it was amazing that they managed it at all. Even more amazing was the dash with which it was done. Probably the most efficient General Staff the world has ever known went into action at Spa, then moved to Cassel, where Supreme Headquarters was set up in an hotel.* The retreating men, nursed back to discipline by the promise of going home, were obedient and marched in order to the music of military bands. The armies of the Entente were amazed. So rapid was the German retreat that Foch's advance parties, going forward to accept weapons which, by the armistice, had to be handed over, frequently found the men had already gone leaving a tidy pile of arms behind them. It was a perfect retirement *selon les règles*.[196] At Amerongen William could be sadly proud of his soldiers' exemplary behaviour, though it must have aroused further burning questions in his mind.

Only one commander was not retiring at the head of his army. Through an adjutant the Crown Prince had made enquiries if he could lead his troops home and then retire into private life at his Silesian home at Oels. A representative of the Ministry of the Royal House said it was out of the question – 'The farmers would beat him to death'.[197] He then appealed to Ebert for permission to return, undertaking not to take any kind of action against the government. Through his Minister of War Ebert refused, and the new Supreme Military Commander relieved him of his military post. His friends advised him not to follow his father into exile. The Kaiser had had to leave to save the country from Civil War. It was questionable if it would be correct for the Crown Prince to do so. Nevertheless on November 12th he presented himself at the Dutch frontier. He had with him only two adjutants, a secretary and his chauffeur. They were not offered asylum as the Kaiser and his suite had been but were interned and treated correctly if coolly.[198] The difference soon made itself plain. The Netherlands' government made the place of their internment an abandoned parsonage at Wieringen† on an island at the north-east edge of the Zuider Zee and there were guards to prevent their

* Hindenburg would not permit the High Command to use Wilhelmshöhe as it was the Kaiser's personal property.
† It is no longer an island and now has the more melodious name of Hippolytushoef. It stands on the motorway which runs along the Ijsselmeer Dam and joins North Holland and Friesland.

escape. A bleaker, more sorry place of confinement for a man who loved horses and women and fast sports cars could hardly have been chosen. It showed how truly disliked he was for his flashy, feckless undependability that Queen Wilhelmina made no attempt to ameliorate his lot; neither did his father nor the German government make any attempt to appeal on his behalf; nor, though she was at liberty to do so, would the Crown Princess join him, preferring to remain at Potsdam with her four sons and two daughters.[199] Even the Pan German League, to which he had given such enthusiastic support, in a pharisaic – and fruitless – attempt to make itself respectable, disowned Crown Prince William.

The humiliation of knowing his son had voluntarily fled from the fatherland for no good reason and that he was now interned eighty-three miles away from Amerongen was an additional burden to the Kaiser. Technically he himself was free but the arrival of a large number of reporters and photographers imprisoned him in the castle. The Netherlands Government answered an appeal by Count Godard and sent a detachment of soldiers to guard the drawbridges. Thereafter no one could pass either without an authorization signed by Count Godard. Frustrated by Dutch rifles, the journalists sent in background copy. A rumour spread that the Kaiser had been driven mad by grief and was in a padded cell guarded by male nurses.[200]* William was in fact worrying about his wife, who was still at Potsdam with their daughter, worrying about his country, and worrying about his future. In Berlin the Council of People's Commissioners was rapidly making social legislation. An eight-hour day was brought in, labour was given the unrestricted right to form unions, welfare benefits were raised, the wartime censorship of the press was abolished and there was a political amnesty. The last two were dangerous, for it enabled Rosa Luxemburg to issue *Die rote Fahne*, the Red Flag, and appeal for proletarian solidarity, and many wild activitists were freed to agitate and encourage strikes and anarchy; but to the Independent Socialists on the Council they were doctrinally necessary. Fortunately all the Commissioners and the Ministers they appointed were determined to cut the ground from under the Spartacists until there could be a general election and a new assembly created. Equally they were determined not to hand power to the monarchists.[202] One of their principal difficulties was that the Kaiser was still Kaiser. He had not abdicated and it was the opinion of many jurists that until he did, it might be impossible to make a legal peace with the Entente. There was a possibility that he might refuse and main-

---

* The rumour persisted for some time. When the ex-Kaiser's attention was drawn to it he remarked wryly to one of the Bentinck family: 'The world says I am mad, but if it knew what tremendous difficulties I have had to put up with, it would perhaps be surprised that I am at all sane.'[201]

tain the fiction of being a *de jure* Kaiser in exile, but doubtless he would respond to certain pressures which need not even be expressed. Hindenburg had not necessarily set a precedent in maintaining that Wilhelmshöhe was the Kaiser's property. William would be acutely aware that the security of his possessions and his income and those of all his family, and that possibly even their safety depended upon the goodwill of the government. He was not so naive as to think that, had she wished, the Kaiserin could simply have taken a train from Berlin to Spa without careful preparation and arrangement. It was important that the Commissioners send an envoy as soon as possible and important to choose the right man to act for them.

William was far too grand to be a snob but, at this sensitive time, he would better appreciate talking with an aristocrat than with a torch-carrying Socialist and it so happened that during the war Ebert and Scheidemann had become well acquainted with a representative of one of the most illustrious of German families. As Socialists they had gone to Denmark in the hope of wheedling bread supplies from their neutral comrades and Count Ulric von Brockdorff-Rantzau the German Ambassador to Copenhagen had been extremely helpful. Though he looked like a caricature of the Prussian Junker, politically he was to the left of the centre and Ludendorff's dictatorship had sharpened his life-long detestation of militarism.[203] But he had the distinct advantage of being related to Countess Brockdorff, who for thirty-eight years had been Mistress of the Robes to the Kaiserin and her most intimate confidante, and he was the son of the Kaiser's first battalion commander when he began regular service with the Foot Guards in 1877.[204] Ebert prudently decided that Count Ulric himself might be too domineering a negotiator for the Kaiser's taste but he had a twin brother, a less sharp man who would put the Kaiser at his ease. Count Ernest von Rantzau accepted his appointment and went to Amerongen.

Records were not kept by either party of the conversations, nor are we aware if the Kaiser took advice from anyone. The known facts are three. First, for many years Count Ernest von Rantzau was legal administrator of the Kaiser's property.[205] Second, on November 28th the Kaiserin arrived at Amerongen from Potsdam with frightening tales of her experiences. Her guards had worn the red cockade in their hats and been unable to keep out drunken sailors who attacked the Villa Liegnitz. By sheer force of character she had subdued them and afterwards she had been left in peace. But the tense situation, her anxieties for William, and the sudden collapse of the Empire had broken her. Suddenly she had aged. She was a changed woman.[206] The third fact is that on the very same day Count Ernest headed a government delegation to the Kaiser. He carried a document with an agreed text. In this William renounced for all time his right to the Crown of Prussia and the

Imperial Crown and freed all officials, civil military and naval from their oaths of allegiance while bidding them assist the *de facto* power 'to protect the German people from the dangers threatening through anarchy, famine and foreign rule'.* This he read and re-read, then he affixed his seal and signed firmly 'William'.[207] No longer did he add the letters 'I' and 'R' and thenceforth his legal status was Head of the Royal House of Prussia and ex-Kaiser and a guest, under supervision, of the Queen of the Netherlands. He himself expected to continue being addressed as Kaiser on the grounds that though he wielded no power the rank was no more destructible than the baptism of a man who later renounces his faith.†

A compromise evidently had been reached. Chancellor Ebert's government, although still on a tightrope, had become legitimate. After the Crown Prince's formal renunciation of all rights to the Prussian and Imperial crowns signed at Wieringen on December 1st, 1918, the rule of the House of Hohenzollern, which had had supreme power in the Mark of Brandenburg for more than five hundred years, came to an end.

* In point of fact he abdicated far more than this simple document suggests. Great titles, rights and holdings had accrued to the House of Hohenzollern for centuries. Besides being an Emperor and a King William was also twice a Sovereign Grand Duke, twice a Grand Duke, eighteen times a Duke, a Princely Count, fifteen times a Prince, three times a Margrave, eleven times a Count, as well as the holder of an early twelfth-century Barony and a late nineteenth-century Lordship.

† A point made by legal experts at the time of the abdication of Edward VIII. It appears he was one of the very few monarchs who relinquished his title with the throne.[208]

CHAPTER FIFTEEN

The Silent One of Europe

*'I do not mean to say that everything I did was right, but
everything I did during the thirty years of my reign cannot
have been wrong.'*

THE EX-KAISER AT DOORN

I

Conceivably the rest enforced upon the Kaiser by his new life was precisely
the medicine his nervous system required. The war and increasing age had
played their part in quieting his tempestuous nature, but exile and the
restrictions imposed by the Netherlands government that he should not
travel beyond a certain distance 'for his own safety', finally obliged him to
slow down. Quickly he established a regular routine, getting up at seven,
taking a walk in the garden before morning prayers and breakfast, then writing letters and reading the newspapers and studying the Dutch language,
which he soon mastered. After a simple luncheon he exercised, sawing logs
and chopping wood – a practice he had begun in the war – or, on rare occasions, he rode or drove out. One of the Bentinck family noted how he loved
to be driven fast: 'He is gone almost before one realizes he is there!'[1] But, to
begin with, he was virtually imprisoned by newspaper reporters and the
insistence of the Government that he remain fast at Amerongen because of
threats to his person. The soldiers on guard were instructed that the Queen's
illustrious guest must be protected not only from the nuisance of sightseers
and reporters but also from the danger of kidnappers and assassins. Their
rifles were loaded. At 4.30 p.m. tea was taken with the Bentincks, English-
fashion. The household dined at 8 p.m. and afterwards everyone met in
Count Godard's library for coffee and discussion.[2] The Kaiserin kept to her
rooms and was seldom seen. She was too ill and far too anxious. It could not
be hidden from her that her husband stood in considerable danger.

In England there was to be a general election. The existing parliament was
eight years old and the electorate had increased from eight to twenty mil-

lions.* Though he must have known that to continue in coalition with the Conservatives would be the death of the old Liberal party, Lloyd George had no intention of giving up power. To ensure victory he campaigned by slogan. His first aim was worthy: 'To make Britain a fit country for heroes to live'. So was 'No more war!'[3] Subsequent ones were less worthy and it was those which led a new electorate who lacked settled party principles to sweep Lloyd George to the pinnacle of power: 'Make Germany Pay!' 'Search Their Pockets!' 'We will squeeze the German lemon until the pips squeak!' 'Hang the Kaiser!'[4]

William at Amerongen took in with his German and Dutch newspapers *The Times* and read it carefully although by then it was four days old. It appeared that 'Hang the Kaiser!' was not simply a vengeful vote-catching slogan – which would have been quite unthinkable in any previous election – but that the leading legal authorities in Britain considered it was right and proper to proceed with a trial and then hang him.† A cartoon was published which showed a rope stretched from the Eiffel Tower in Paris to Cleopatra's Needle in London and from this, suspended by tied wrists, was a caricature of himself.[6] What effect this had upon the Kaiser and the Kaiserin can be surmised. G. S. Viereck, an American journalist who became acquainted with the Kaiser in 1921 and wrote an ingenious apologia for his actions, maintained Lloyd George's electioneering campaign was a daily torture to the Kaiserin and a chief cause of her ultimate death.[7] His view was largely confirmed by someone who frequently visited Doorn and, under the pseudonym of 'Joachim von Kürenberg', wrote a study of the Kaiser.[8]‡ At the very least there must have been a sense of deep uneasiness at Amerongen. Even in Britain, the Prime Minister's scramble back into office by appealing to national hatreds and base instincts was regarded by many of his contemporaries as indefensible, and is so still.[9] Therefore at Amerongen, where magnaminity to the conquered was still regarded as the norm of civilization, Lloyd George's unprincipled manoeuvre must have seemed a disconcerting innovation in the conduct of international affairs.§

* Though the British had lost almost a million men in the war, the population had still grown and a limited franchise had been given to women.[5]

† Almost immediately after the Armistice the Attorney-General, later Lord Chancellor and the First Earl of Birkenhead, advised the British Cabinet to bring the Kaiser to trial.[10]

‡ Unknown to the Kaiser this gentleman had served a prison sentence as a confidence trickster. Presumably his technique was still up to the mark when he interviewed the maleable ex-sovereign for he managed to get sufficient information to make his book both interesting and colourful.

§ Possibly it needs to be re-emphasized that in the fourth quarter of the twentieth century it is no more easy for many people to sympathize with this old-fashioned view of magnanimity than with the military concepts of honour and glory held at the beginning of the First Great War.

It was a harrowing and lowering period for the Kaiser. Difficult topics were never openly discussed. The Bentinck family realized that only time could heal the shock he had experienced. He was also agitated about his ailing wife, and their family and friends in Germany, and the Crown Prince much embarrassed him by fecklessly lending himself to a rescue plot only four days after his formal renunciation of rights. A group of officers had planned to snatch him from Wieringen and place him at the head of a reactionary movement and had only abandoned the project when the Dutch discovered the plot and intensified their security precautions.[11] William believed that it reflected on his son's honour and certainly it exasperated the Netherlands Government. Then he was deeply troubled by the grave condition of his country and the humiliating terms of the Armistice. The greater part of his High Seas Fleet had been ordered to sail to the British port of Scapa Flow in the Orkneys with empty magazines, no breechblocks in the guns and manned by skeleton crews.[12] His Army had been left with the minimum of arms for the maintenance of order. Such was the confusion in Germany that sources of communication were unreliable. But the civilian population, unless engaged in revolutionary or counter-revolutionary agitation, continued to work. There was nothing like total chaos. The postal and telegraph and telephone services were still manned and newspapers were printed and distributed as regularly as could be devised. Even cut off at Amerongen William must have been aware of the chief items of news. Most of this was bad. The field army had continued its organized withdrawal and marched into the capital where it was obviously the High Command's intention to disarm all civilians and the newly formed People's Naval Division. Yet no sooner had the last division completed its march into the city than ninety-nine per cent of the army disintegrated. Regimental insignia were cut off, arms given away, and the soldiers made for home.[13] By a series of ruses, flukes, tricks and mircales the six People's Commissioners clung on to power. Chairman Ebert, as he was called, consistently opposed Leninism as a perversion of Marxism unsuitable to the Germans, and made no concessions to Liebknecht's Spartacists. The Commissioners summoned a National Congress of Workers' and Soldiers Councils and three hundred out of the 488 returned delegates were Majority Socialists. This majority forced through a resolution calling for a general election to be held on January 19th so that a truly representative national assembly could assume power.[14] But the Congress also passed other, less desirable resolutions. One was that the existing Army and its Officer Corps should be replaced by a People's Army officered by elected rankers. The High Command's reaction was so vigorous that Ebert was forced to agree that the resolution should not be implemented, whereupon the three Independent Socialist Commissioners resigned,[15] the People's Naval Division marched against the government, and one of the few trusted regiments still left, the Imperial Horse Guards, was ordered to take the Sailors' headquarters in the Old Palace.* They succeeded but then were surrounded and dominated by a huge crowd of civilians including women and children cleverly collected by the Spartacists.[16]

Christmas passed and 1918 drew to a close. At Amerongen the ice was regularly broken in the moats to keep out journalists. The Kaiser's suite was much reduced. Many of his gentlemen had found the cost of living in Holland too expensive and had returned to Germany.[17] The Crown Princess was still in Potsdam. The Duchess of Brunswick was back at Gmunden. The Kaiser's brother, Prince Harry, was living quietly at Hemmelmark wondering what lay in store for him and his family. Pilsudski and Ignace Paderewski were forming units of Polish militia, arranging for the elections of a Parliament, and seizing what could be seized in the German provinces of Posen and Silesia and the Austrian provinces of Galicia and Teschen.[18] The Peace Conference had not yet begun in Paris though the American President had already arrived in Europe aboard a confiscated and renamed German liner to be greeted rapturously in the capitals of his allies, and eulogized by Herbert Hoover:†

> *Woodrow Wilson had reached the zenith of intellectual and spiritual leadership of the whole world, never hitherto known in history.*[20]

Clemenceau and the French government were pressing that, although by Article 26 of the Armistice the Entente had accepted responsibility for provisioning Germany, the Germans must not be permitted to pay for food with gold which later would be required for reparations. The Germans had been obliged to hand over her merchant fleet into an international pool but it had not yet been agreed how this was to be administered. Until these difficulties were ironed out the blockade continued. There had been a disastrous harvest and Germany was threatened by starvation. Ebert's government, facing the possibility of coups from right and left, were forced to cut the tiny bread ration by two thirds. Manufactured articles were equally in short supply.[21] Some of the officers of the Entente armies sent angry reports home about 'the stress of hunger and malnutrition' in Germany;[22] but the majority of the French did not greatly care, and the English were inclined to regard the

---

* There was a secret telephone which bypassed the Chancellery switchboard and kept the Chancellor in constant touch with the High Command at Cassel.[19]

† A member of the committee of economic advisers to the American Delegation and himself President of the United States from 1929 to 1933, Hoover believed that 'other nations were morally and economically inferior [to the U.S.] and deserved to be'.[24]

report of 'privations' as yet another example of Prussian duplicity. In January the *Morning Post* printed articles on the German shortages under such headings as

'GERMAN WHINES – LIMIT OF ENDURANCE REACHED'

and

'FEEDING THE BEAST'[23]

Nevertheless Lloyd George's government believed the stories of starvation in Germany. Pressure was brought to bear on France so that as soon as possible food might be paid for with gold. It was almost too late.[25] In Berlin the Army garrison consisted of less than 200 trained soldiers. Germany was close to a state of anarchy.

2

The history of Germany in the months before the Peace Treaty was signed at Versailles was never forgotten by those who cared for their country. Amongst them, and powerless to do anything, was her former Kaiser.

Rosa Luxemburg worked tirelessly to hold back a Spartacist revolution against the government[26] but Liebknecht was carried away by his own fervour and on January 5th a manifesto was issued calling for the arming of the workers and the launching of a general strike.[27] As Rosa Luxemburg had warned, the proletariat was badly organized, ill-prepared, and not ready; and Ebert's government was able to call up a new type of irregular force which had sprung like sown dragon's teeth from the privileged stormtroop battalions of the Imperial Army. They were mercenaries paid by and theoretically under the supervision of the High Command and called Free Corps or the Black Army. Yet though they owed no duty save personal loyalty to the leader of each Corps and a general duty to the government, they were not – as has often been supposed – reactionaries dedicated to the restoration of the monarchy. Their only politics were anti-Bolshevik.[28] The Free Corps smashed the revolution in a week. The Spartacists had small arms but the Free Corps soldiers and sailors had trench mortars, machine-guns, howitzers, grenades and flame throwers. White flags meant nothing to them. Prisoners were not taken. The general strike was called off, but the Free Corps continued a ruthless campaign against anyone suspected of being a Communist. On January 15th Liebknecht and Rosa Luxemburg were betrayed, taken to a sharpshooter division headquarters for questioning, beaten, their heads smashed with a rifle butt, shot, and the Red Rose's body was thrown into a frozen canal.[29] Ebert was genuinely revolted by this White Terror and ordered an investigation but it was frustrated by the Free Corps commanders, and he himself was too preoccupied with the general election in four days' time to force the issue.[30]

The election provided no surprising results. All the main parties save the Majority and Independent Socialists had changed their names but not their politics. The Majority Socialists dominated the new assembly which for safety's sake met provisionally in Goethe's city of enlightenment Weimar, but, in order to govern, it had to ally itself with the centre bourgeois parties. Ebert formally handed over power to the assembly which formed a new constitution incorporating parliamentary sovereignty, the referendum and proportional representation.[31] Ebert was honoured by being voted first President of the German Republic.* He appointed Philip Scheidemann as Chancellor who made up a cabinet from his own party, the old Catholic Centre (now called the Christian People's Party) and the old Progressives (now called German Democrats).[32]

The establishment of order, the reintegration of Bavaria, Brunswick and Saxony into the Republic, and preparing to treat with the Entente were the chief problems which confronted the government. Public order was the most pressing. Free Corps soldiers and sailors suppressed red revolutions in the North Sea ports, and stopped strikes in the Ruhr and Berlin. Brunswick and Saxony were reintegrated but Bavaria was more stubborn. The idealistic and likeable Eisner was assassinated by a young man, Count Arco-Valley, who simply wished to prove himself,† and for six weeks Bavaria was scarcely governed at all.[34] Then the leader of the Independent Socialists, a poet as Eisner had been, declared a Republic of Councils with the idea of joining Communist Hungary and revolutionary Austria. But this idea never got anywhere and his government's programme was so lunatic that it was affectionately known as 'The Rule of the Coffeehouse Anarchists'. The study of history was forbidden, new art forms were encouraged, homes were not permitted to have more than three rooms, the Foreign Minister telegraphed a protest to Lenin that his lavatory had been stolen, and he declared war on Switzerland and Württemberg.[35] The Republic of Councils was swiftly replaced by a Bavarian Commune led by a Russian named Axelrod, and, confusingly, a Russo–German Jew named Levien, and a Russian Jew named Leviné. They created a Red Guard of 30,000 men by paying them more than any other soldiers in history, and declared that their government programme was Red Terror.[36] The Bavarian majority Socialists who had an alternative

* From being a saddlemaker and then a publican he had come far, and without clawing his way to the top. He was first a German and second a Socialist, had lost two sons in the war, and a third was to die in a concentration camp.[33]

† He had applied for membership to the Thule Society of Bavaria – an anti-Semitic organization which used the swastika as their emblem and greeted each other with the cry 'Heil!' – and had been turned down because his mother was of Jewish descent.[37]

government out of Munich, raised an army, marched on the Commune and were routed. They appealed to the Republican Government at Weimar which decided that this opera bouffe situation in Bavaria could no longer be tolerated. Free Corps in large numbers were ordered into the country but by this time the Free Corps had altered. There were still a few patriotic, order-loving old soldiers amongst them, but the majority were young toughs who paid only lip service to President Ebert and gave all their loyalty to their leader, their Führer. They swept through Bavaria and the Red Guard melted away. In Munich a demented communist began to execute hostages which gave the Free Corps a reason, but no excuse, for the bestial and never-to-be forgotten reign of White terror which followed.[38] In May, 1919 Bavaria was bludgeoned back into the Republic.

By this time the Germans had been invited to send a delegation to meet the Supreme War Council in Paris. The Peace Conference had not passed happily. The victors disagreed about almost everything save that the Germans must be made to pay.[39] The chief delegates were antipathetic to one another and the strain of being obliged to give an appearance to the world of unanimity had told on them all.* The chief strain had fallen on President Wilson who, under pressure, had contorted his orignal fourteen points.[40] Because of his unique position as the only rich man at this meeting of virtually bankrupt and certainly war-exhausted victors, he was deferred to like a judge in ancient Israel. Up to twenty delegations a day would call on him to ask for this, that or the other. By March he was exhausted. In April he had a physical and nervous breakdown. He threatened to leave the Supreme Council rather than compromise any further with his principles, and this was reported in the press, but Clemenceau and Lloyd George and Orlando of Italy called his bluff. They knew he would never surrender his chief aim, the institution of a League of Nations. Wilson stayed.[41] The Germans believed the backbiting in Paris must be to their advantage. For over a year, that is through the last month of the war and through revolutions and Red and White purges, the German Foreign Office had been carefully collecting information to be used in the event of defeat or victory, and when the former came, in preparations for the peace conference.[42] At their head, as Chancellor Scheidemann's Foreign Secretary was Count Ulric von Brockdorff-Rantzau. He had accepted office because he believed it was his duty and most carefully prepared himself and his delegation for their work at Paris.

When the Germans arrived in the French capital they were kept confined to

---

* Lord Riddell, owner of the *News of the World* and appointed by his friend Lloyd George as British Press Liaison Officer in Paris, noted in his diary on April 9th, 1919: 'No four kings or emperors could have conducted the Conference on more autocratic lines.'

an hotel for almost a week and then it was made clear there was to be no negotiating of terms in the ordinarily accepted sense. On the anniversary of the sinking of the *Lusitania*, the German delegation was summoned to the Galerie des Glaces where, forty-eight years before, William, King of Prussia, had been hailed as German Kaiser, and there they were bluntly told by Clemenceau that they would be given a list of the conditions on which the Entente was prepared to grant peace. Any German observations on the terms must be made within fifteen days, at which time final unalterable terms would be offered by the Entente. In his brusque way Clemenceau was about to close the meeting when Brockdorff–Rantzau put up a protesting hand. Though he had not had time to read the terms he insisted on making certain points. Unhappily though he was at the height of his powers as a diplomat, and in private conversation was witty and urbane, public-speaking terrified him. He trembled so much when standing that invariably he spoke sitting, and fright made him stammer and gave a raven harshness to his voice. At this meeting he could not delegate the responsibility of speaking. To sit when Clemenceau had stood seemed an impertinence to the Peace Conference, and his harsh voice seemed to represent all the Prussian arrogance they most detested.[43] Nor were the things he said likely to soothe their anger. He touched on a nerve when he claimed Germany's victors had already broken the terms of the Armistice:

> *The hundreds of thousands of noncombatants who have perished since the eleventh of November by reason of the blockade were killed with cold deliberation, after our adversaries had conquered and victory had been assured to them.*[44]

He spoke to mounting excitement in the Galerie des Glaces and when he finished there was a buzz of outrage. Clemenceau rapidly closed the meeting.

The one copy of conditions which had been handed to the Germans was torn apart and given to translators. Then copies were sent to Germany while the delegation went through the peace articles one by one. At first sight they seemed to offer virtual slavery for two generations in the German Republic.[45] She was to lose her colonies, most of her coal fields and iron-ore deposits, a third of her blast furnaces, and all her merchant marine; a large number of Germans were henceforth to be ruled by Poles, Czechs and the French; her army and navy reduced to the size of those of a fifth-rate petty state; the demanded reparations would ruin her economically, she was to admit full responsibility for the war and hand over some 900 of her chief nationals for trial as criminals.[46]

On the Treaty's publication in Germany there was an outcry. To many it seemed as vengeful as the Romans' act of ploughing a furrow through the

ruins of Carthage to demonstrate the complete destruction of their enemy.*
Brockdorff–Rantzau did all he could in the short time allowed to mitigate the
severity of the terms and insist that they had strayed so far from Wilson's
original fourteen points that the Entente had illegally altered the original
terms of the Armistice.[47] It was no use. On June 16th the German delegation
was formally given an amended and final draft treaty for acceptance or rejection in five days.[48] So few were the amendments that a new draft had not
even been printed. An old one had been used, the alterations being written in
red ink. Brockdorff–Rantzau begged for and obtained two extra days. He
then ordered the delegation to return to Germany. On the way to the station
French patriots stoned the delegates' cars. Windows were smashed and
several delegates cut by glass. For the two–day journey east the delegation
worked on their report for the cabinet. When they arrived in Weimar only
five days remained of the time limit. Exhausted and pale the Foreign Secretary with two of his Counsellors went to recommend the Cabinet that the
German government must reject the treaty.[50]

There followed five days of intense activity. The reaction of the Officer
Corps and the Free Corps commanders to the military clauses was violent.
There was wild talk of resisting the Entente forces which were assembling on
both east and west fronts. But Gröner, the realist, had already been looking
into this possibility. For days past his best staff officers had been travelling
through Germany making searching enquiries and all reported that, though
no-one had a good word to say for the treaty, people lacked the heart to
resume war.[51] By accepting the military clauses Germany would have an
Army of 96,000 long service troops and non-commissioned officers and 4,000
officers, a Navy of 15,000 officers and men, and the Free Corps were to be disbanded. Worst of all, her most precious asset, the General Staff was dissolved,
and the Prussian cadet schools and staff colleges were to be closed down. It
was a heavy imposition to force on a nation trained to arms for centuries.
Nevertheless Gröner saw that acceptance would at least guarantee a tiny
nucleus of the Officer Corps and a continuation of its best traditions. For this
he was prepared to make an unpopular decision and advise Hindenburg to tell
the government that though in the east the Army might hold the old frontier,

---

* Its ferocity was justified by the majority of members of the Peace Conference,
who maintained it was not as crushing as the Treaty of Brest-Litovsk imposed on the
Russians early in 1918–49.[49] The difference was that the Entente was dealing with a
reorganized sovereign republic which was putting its affairs in order at the behest of
President Wilson, while Hindenburg and Ludendorff had been treating with Bolsheviks who had overthrown the legal Provisional Government by a revolutionary coup.
Lenin had voluntarily sacrificed honour, his country's policies, and vast tracts of terri-
tory to keep political power for himself. President Ebert had concluded an honourable
Armistice with the Entente so that Germany should not be entirely ruined.

in the west it would be doubtful. The old Field Marshal did this, adding, to exculpate himself:

As a soldier I would rather perish in honour than sign a humiliating peace[52]

The crisis was acute at Weimar. Gröner had made known the results of his investigation and the Field Marshal's warning was clear enough, yet few of the civilians would consider signing the treaty. Eventually, four days before the time limit expired, the Cabinet was exactly divided. Chancellor Scheidemann resigned and was followed by five others. Amongst them was Brockdorff-Rantzau, who on accepting office had reserved the right to resign if a treaty was accepted which would 'deprive the German people of a decent livelihood'.[53] Germany had no government.

The next day as President Ebert tried to form a suitable government came news which must have put muscle into those who were determined Germany should not sign the treaty. The guarding Royal Naval squadron at Scapa Flow steamed out for a day's sea-training and the German admiral ordered a prearranged signal to be run up his flagship's halyards. The officers of all ships ran below, opened the seacocks and smashed them with hammers. By the time the guard squadron returned fifty capital ships lay on the bottom.[54]

Ebert found a colourless Chancellor. A compromise was proposed: that the treaty should be signed if the articles relating to war guilt and war criminals were withdrawn.[55] These were the most shaming of all. But the scuttling of the Imperial Fleet at Scapa Flow had enraged the Supreme Council in Paris. Ebert's proposal was refused. On hearing this the Minister of Defence pressed him that Germany must fight. The Free Corps leaders did the same. Many of the generals agreed. In a last throw the President telephoned the High Command to know if there had been any change in Hindenburg's evaluation. Typically the old man would not himself vouchsafe an opinion. To Gröner he said 'You can give the answer to the President as well as I can'.[56] And so the Quartermaster General once more had to speak for his chief and incur the odium of many of his fellow officers as a result. Gröner stuck to his carefully collected estimate that there could be no *levée en masse*. Ebert accepted this as final, as did the government and National Assembly. Making the strongest protest at 'the unheard-of injustice of the conditions of peace',[57] Germany yielded.

It seemed to many that the nation had lost her honour. When Brockdorff-Rantzau lay dying nine years later he murmured to his brother, who was the Kaiser's administrator: 'Do not grieve. After all I have been really dead since Versailles'.[58] And even amongst Germany's enemies there were feelings that the load laid on her had been too heavy. The English economist Maynard

Keynes described the Entente's policies as 'abhorrent and detestable',[59] and mild Colonel House, estranged by the tensions at the Council from the man he had put into the presidency wrote in his journal:

How splendid it would have been had we blazed a better trail.[60]

The Kaiser, quite correctly, made no public comment on the treaty. Nevertheless he confided to Count Godard his personal antipathy to Wilson. He had expected the French and Italians to be merciless. They were Latins. And from his daily reading of *The Times* he can hardly have expected much from the British. But from America with her ideals and the much-talked of probity of her president he had expected justice as had many other Germans. He considered that Wilson had broken his word, that his inflated sense of importance was absurd, and that his dictatorial methods while talking endlessly of democracy nothing but hypocrisy. 'Wilson,' the Kaiser told his host, 'is a greater autocrat than I or the Tsar of Russia ever were. He has got more power than either of us had. I'll call him Kaiser Wilson!'[61] And he did for quite a long time.

3

At the beginning of 1920 the Kaiser and Kaiserin with their Households were still official guests at Amerongen. It was a situation which could not continue. The Bentincks had been welcoming and patient but William realized other arrangements must be made as soon as possible. There was no question of his being allowed to return to Germany. He had been gratified to hear that a Majority Socialist deputy had said in the National Assembly the Kaiser's intentions had always been good and pure and that there was no point in attacking a man stricken with misfortune.[62] Yet, although after his abdication they had treated him with fairness, the Socialists were not disposed to permit him to return home. But plans he might have made for leaving Amerongen were changed on January 5th.

Late that night when everyone had gone to bed an American colonel with seven of his younger officers arrived in two cars at the castle. They had passports and permits for the motor cars issued in Brussels and so had been allowed to cross into Holland. Claiming to be emissaries with a high mission they penetrated to the library of the castle where first Count Charles Bentinck and afterwards his father Count Godard asked them polite but searching questions. The Mayor of Amerongen was telephoned and asked to bring help. When he and police and military detachments arrived the Colonel confessed they had planned to steal away the Kaiser and take him as 'a surprise present' for President Wilson in Paris. The Mayor indignantly informed the Americans that their horseplay was callow and not that of responsible officers. They were escorted by troops to the border and their misbehaviour reported to General Pershing who commanded the American Forces. He was incensed but, to keep the matter quiet and his Army unembarrassed, he treated the matter as more of a prank than a serious breach of discipline, shipped the eight officers home and there for a short period they were imprisoned. Because of the shrewdness of the Bentincks no real harm had been done, but the escapade made the Dutch authorities double their guard at Amerongen, and they insisted that the Kaiser remain within the castle grounds.[63] This depressing restriction soon included everyone because the Rhine, which flowed less than a mile away, overflowed its banks and the countryside was flooded for days. A local notable was drowned when he toppled off a flooded road in the dark and Amerongen Castle had to be regularly pumped like the bilges of a ship. Faggots were laid on top of the outer moat wall to keep back some of the flood waters and the Kaiser was out of doors each day, giving orders as sharply as Count Godard – though, as one of the family noted, his were not always obeyed.[64] For weeks no-one could go anywhere except in a boat and the Kaiser was in no danger from kidnappers. Nevertheless a worse danger was resurrected that January. The Supreme War Council in Paris required implementation of Articles 227 to 230 of the Versailles Treaty and demanded from the Weimar Republic* the surrender of more than 900 leading Germans.[65] The Crown Prince promptly sent a verbose telegram to Paris protesting that:

THE CONSEQUENCES OF AN EXECUTION OF THEIR DEMAND BY FORCE ARE INCALCULABLE FOR EUROPE. HATE AND REVENGE WOULD BE MADE ETERNAL BY IT.

And he volunteered to stand trial himself if a victim was required. His biographer, Klaus Jonas, suggests that he made this offer in an effort to retrieve his honour which had been stained by his needless flight for safety, or that he was popularity-hunting. Most likely he was simply being himself and unable to resist the temptation to poke his finger into affairs. No-one has given him the benefit of the doubt and suggested that he might have meant the offer. The Kaiser was angry because his son's offer implied the proposed trial had some sort of validity which he himself denied.[67] However there was no chance of the nine hundred being sacrificed. The demand aroused such fury in Germany that the Entente was forced to realize the Weimar Government would be overthrown if it attempted to obey, and the Officer Corps would

* Although named the Weimar Republic the government soon returned to Berlin and no other city was ever considered as a capital for the new state.[66]

resume the war. It was obliged to give way and permit the German government to try the accused in its own courts.*

However one of the 'Big Four' in Paris had been returned to power on a mandate to try and hang the Kaiser and so successfully had Lloyd George worked on the primaeval feelings of vengeance in his country that in the past twelve months more than fifty thousand separate indictments had been lodged with the English Public Prosecutor against the Kaiser by private citizens.[68] In the event of his escaping the hangman's noose, the Peace Conference had already selected the Dutch island of Curaçao as his place of perpetual imprisonment; and his judges were to be chosen from Great Britain, France, Italy, Japan and the United States.[69] The Netherlands Government was invited to hand him over with the Crown Prince. The nations of the Entente were prepared to 'relieve the Netherlands of the irksome care for the internment of both persons'. The Dutch refused. They said that the German Kaiser was enjoying the hospitality of their country. Neither he nor the Crown Prince were prisoners of war. Queen Wilhelmina had graciously returned their surrendered swords. Heavier pressure was brought to bear. If the Dutch should shield such international criminals they would become 'participants in the Kaiser's guilt'. The guilt had yet to be proven, but the Kaiser, anxious not to embarrass the Netherlands government considered surrendering himself to the Entente. Then he remembered Vercingetorix's gesture in surrendering to Caesar and changed his mind. The Dutch newspapers reported each diplomatic note between Paris and The Hague. Some were for handing the Kaiser over. Others, the great majority, declared it would be an abuse of hospitality.[71] Long before the Armistice William had been regarded by foreign newspapers as the personification of 'all real and invented horrors of this war', and ever since the agitation against him had increased. For the rest of his life he was sensitive to the charge that he personally was responsible for causing the deaths of ten millions, the maiming of thirty millions, and the wasting of hundreds of square miles of territory.† He resented the Entente's accusation that he had been a type of Cromwell who in red rage ordered the sack of Drogheda, because his own faults were very different. He had been stupid in allowing himself to be led by the nose and weak in not being able to resist the power of the war party, and culpably provocative in his sabre-rattling speeches and in indulging his longing for a large German Navy; but his family and closest courtiers and advisers were all aware he had

---

* In the end only six obscure officials were tried and given short sentences. The 'unbearable and unfulfillable' terms were already proving unworkable. The brief official American decision underlined it: 'It was useless'.[70]

† Exact figures are deceptive but the following are generally taken as fairly accurate. By the end of the war France had lost one person in every twenty-eight; Germany one in every thirty-two; Great Britain one in every fifty-seven; Russia one in every 107.[72]

not wanted a war, and, knowing the real truth of his supposed power in German policy-making, even under the gentle Bethmann, he rejected the theory of final responsibility and never did he regard his hands as blood-stained. It has been suggested that the exchange of notes between the Supreme War Council in Paris and the Netherlands Government was mere diplomatic moonshine and that all had been quietly arranged beforehand, but William could not have known this. His wife was in a state of deep distress. She would wake at night and call for help.[73]

Momentarily however both William and Dona were encouraged to believe the unbelievable, that the monarchy would be restored in the father-land. On March 15th Count Godard told his guests that five thousand of the best-trained and disciplined Free Corps soldiers, who refused to be disbanded either by Paris or Berlin, had marched on the capital and set up as Chancellor a nonentity named Wolfgang Kapp. They were not resisted by the regular Army. Hindenburg had retired to Hanover and the new Chief of General Staff told the Minister of War: 'Troops do not fire on troops!' but, being at heart a monarchist, he solved his personal dilemma by promptly going on leave.[74] The Kaiser mistakenly thought that this was a monarchical move-ment. In great delight he said: 'Tonight we shall have champagne!'[75] But within a few days his hopes were dashed. The puppet régime fell. The legiti-mate government continued to operate from temporary quarters in Stuttgart and there was no popular enthusiasm for the Free Corps' declared intention 'to create order with force and set up a type of dictatorship'. The workers settled the matter by successfully calling a general strike. Chancellor Kapp fled to Sweden by air, the government returned to Berlin, and the Free Corps soldiers sullenly left the capital, terrorizing Berliners as they went. It was noted that the majority used the swastika as their emblem – like the members of the Munich Thule Society – and that General Ludendorff chanced to be in Berlin at the time of the coup to receive the acclamation of the troops. Prudently he left for the Bavarian capital when the attempt failed.[76]

Though balked the Free Corps soldiers continued their thuggish activities. Political assassinations became increasingly common. Hundreds were murdered. A story was told that the Bavarian Chief of Police, himself a former Free Corps leader, actually complained there were not sufficient political assassination societies. Possibly it was not apocryphal.[77] The illustrious historian Frederick Meinecke heard Free Corps soldiers whistling in contempt the old imperial hymn 'Heil Dir im Siegerkranz'.[78] But the ground was not being prepared for the return of the Hohenzollerns but for what Meinecke himself described as an 'eruption of the Satanic principle in world history' – Adolph Hitler.[79]

Quite unknown to his father, for the past six months the Crown Prince had been in correspondence with Colonel Max Bauer, Ludendorff's chief political officer, who was a principal officer on Kapp's staff, and when the coup failed he received reports from Bauer on what had happened. But wisely he had refused to be associated with it. Nonetheless the Netherlands authorities evidently believed he was involved for there were local rumours that he was to be seized from his place of internment either by submarine or aeroplane. Wieringen was guarded by a torpedo boat and when, shortly after the coup, an aeroplane flew over the area it was shot down. Unfortunately it was Dutch.[80] This did not make the Crown Prince any more popular as an internee. His father must have been deeply mortified.

The Kaiser's own position was at last made clear when, on March 24th, the last note, appropriately signed by David Lloyd George, laid upon the Netherlands all responsibility for him.[81] This was accepted by Queen Wilhelmina who courteously assured the Kaiser and Kaiserin that henceforth they were to regard themselves as her protected guests. Certain restrictions, again for their own safety, had to be imposed, but these were only of a temporary nature, the inference being that should they be recalled to Germany nothing would be put in their way. Captain Sigurd von Ilsemann, the young A.D.C. at Amerongen, had noted his master's disappointment after the failure of the Kapp coup and saw that in his heart the Kaiser now knew there was no chance of a restoration.[82] The Socialists would never permit him to live in Germany. Therefore with great sense William made up his mind not to fret but to lead a new and full life in Holland. For a year and four months he and the Kaiserin and their Household had been billeted on the Bentincks, who had treated them with conspicuous kindness. Now William was free to find a permanent home of his own. Quite quickly he did so, a small, unpretentious estate, once the summer palace of the Bishops of Utrecht, a mediaeval country house largely re-built in the eighteenth century with outbuildings and the traditional double moat. He at once sized up the situation and reckoned that if he had a gatehouse built there would just be enough room for his family and small Household and about six guests. This was at Doorn, a little more than six miles from Amerongen on the road to Utrecht and Amsterdam.[83] It had formerly belonged to the Labouchère family of which the English branch had produced a famous radical* who stung Queen Victoria by proposing that Buckingham Palace be made into a home for fallen women.[84] Gardens and a large park surrounded the main house and there were plenty of trees to cut down – an essential now for William's daily exercise.†

---

* Henry Labouchère, Liberal M.P., proprietor and editor of *Truth*.
† The Kaiser with the aid of his A.D.C. and a gardener had sawed 17,000 pines at Amerongen.[85]

Whatever feelings he had about settling for ever away from the fatherland he suppressed. He also kept to himself any views he might have had on the startling change in his fortunes. Lady Norah Bentinck was amazed by his adaptability.

> The observed of all observers, as he had contrived to be for most of his life, was to become the Recluse, the Silent One of Europe.[86]

Clearly William thought there was no point in fighting the inevitable or dwelling on misfortune. Instead he dwelt enthusiastically on his liking for Holland which in some respects resembled the Mark of Brandenburg, and on the fact that, because on both his father's and mother's sides he was related to the House of Orange, he really felt comfortably at home.[87] Arrangements were made by his legal administrator, Count Ernest von Rantzau, for selected items to be sent from Berlin and Potsdam for the furnishing and decoration of Doorn. Much had been lost in the revolution but as the Hohenzollerns were one of the richest and best endowed of European dynasties there was still a great deal left. William himself supervised alterations to Doorn House while, as one of the Bentincks reported, waggons laden with precious and beautiful possessions streamed from the German frontier to Doorn. There were pictures, statuary, tapestries, gold and silver plate, looking-glasses, porcelain, crystal, books, and a complete marble staircase for reassembling in the house.[88]

By May, which appears an extraordinarily short time, all was ready at Doorn. The Kaiser gave the town of Amerongen a small but fully equipped hospital as a token of his gratitude for their hospitality.*[89] The parting from the Bentincks was not without sorrow on both sides, though they were often to see one another in the future and their friendship had been sealed by the engagement of the Kaiser's A.D.C. Captain von Ilsemann to Count Godard's daughter, Countess Elizabeth Bentinck.

Once settled into their new home, the Kaiser and his Household began a round which varied only slightly from his former life at Amerongen. The diversions he now allowed himself were dining out on rare occasions, more motoring, walks to Doorn town, and entertaining his family and friends, which, out of consideration for the Bentincks, had been impossible at Amerongen. He also busied himself with tree planting as well as felling and sawing and he made an arboretum which still thrives.[90] He grew many rhododendrons and in dry seasons the morning exercise of woodcutting was changed to irrigating his collection. He and two of his suite plus gardeners would give the plants between 700 and 800 pails of water.[91] Meals were simple. The Kaiser had always been abstemious, disliking the rich, heavy food

* The people were so impressed by the gift and in such awe of the donor that it was a long time before any of them dared to use it.

of the Wilhelminisches Zeitalter.* His table was good, the food being plain but plentiful and rich in variety. This was for his Household and guests. Generally he ate alone or with the Kaiserin and believed he had reached the age when he could indulge his preference for frugality. He had a cooked dish at breakfast or cold meats but not beef – 'Black meat! Gives gout and constipation!',[92] a glass of port and a sandwich after physical exercise, one hot dish at luncheon and one at dinner, on great occasions champagne but generally fruit juices or a sparkling burgundy – an inferior wine but 'I drink it because I was never allowed it as a little boy'.[93] Daily he kept abreast of affairs by reading the newspapers in German, Dutch, English and French, and reports and digests made by his Private Secretary Baron von Sell.† Nevertheless he had a sensible rule that nothing which had taken place after November 9th, 1918 should ever be discussed in the public and state rooms.[94] In his study in the tower of Doorn House, where he sat at his writing table on a saddle seat, he would occasionally talk to specially chosen people or members of his family of what had happened since, but he knew that recriminations would simply disturb the peace of the house. Though sometimes troubled by sciatica he held himself as erect as ever and his imperial dignity was enhanced because the famous upstanding moustache ends had lost themselves in a close-clipped, full beard and this, like his fine head of hair, was silver.

In many ways his was an ideal existence. It was noted by those who knew him well that while the Kaiser had played the histrionic, imperial part of his life almost to perfection, he had always wanted to be an English country gentleman. With his Household of six, and still served by the two valets Schulz and Vieke he had inherited from his father, he was comfortable and healthy and seemed to have found himself.[96] He was, though, very concerned about Dona. Once he had been the more egoistical, excitable and nervous of the two; she calm – if not tormented by imagined jealousies – and always dependable. Now their rôles were reversed. Like Macbeth and his wife, he had become the stronger partner in the marriage, she the weaker. She lacked his adaptability and he realized that, having originally come from humbler surroundings than Potsdam she could not reconcile herself to living modestly again in Holland. Her pride, nourished by her position as one of the great ladies of Europe, prevented her from accepting with resignation the topsy-turvydom of the new society. Moreover she was ill. Her nerves constantly went astray under the weight of adversity and anxiety, and her heart trouble forced her to keep to her rooms for days on end. Because she grieved

---

* The period which corresponds to the late Victorian and Edwardian eras in England.
† After the Kaiser's death the Baron returned to Germany and, being involved in the abortive attempt against Hitler's life in July, 1944, he was executed.[95]

for her rose gardens at New Palace William made rose beds at Doorn and many were planted with the rose named for her in 1890, Kaiserin Auguste Viktoria, a delicately scented rose with white petals edged with green.[97] These were also grown under glass and in heat so that as often as possible a fresh bunch of the roses could be placed on her writing table. There was little else to be done for her. She worried incessantly about the eldest and the youngest of her children who were especially dear to her, though both the Crown Prince and Prince Joachim had consistently infringed her strict Evangelical rules of good conduct. Both were estranged from their wives and were notorious womanizers; both had left Germany, the Crown Prince to be interned, Prince Joachim to buy a villa in Switzerland where he spent much of his time gambling across the Italian frontier; and she felt the disgrace keenly. But she was still their mother and when, a month after settling in at Doorn House the Crown Prince was permitted to leave Wieringen and visit his parents, and at the same time Prince Joachim came to Doorn, the Kaiser must have hoped it would raise her spirits. Momentarily it did, but the close confinement and boredom of his internment seemed to have had a coarsening effect upon her eldest son, and her younger, who had been wounded in action in the war, had been thoroughly demoralized by the failure of the Kapp coup. He could not be persuaded to return to Germany and look after the farm and estate at Bornstedt which had been made over to him on the death of his aunt Princess Feodora, nor persuaded to take any interest in life at all. He was distant, listless, unutterably depressed. Even so it came as a great shock to his parents when on July 18th, only three weeks after leaving Doorn, he took his own life. They could not be at his funeral. Prince Joachim was buried in the presence of four of his brothers and Hindenburg and Ludendorff.[98] From that date there was a noticeable deterioration in the Kaiserin's health. The news that the Crown Princess Cecile and her four sons had visited Wieringen failed to cheer her. She could not even share in the joyful event when Countess Elizabeth Bentinck, to whom she had grown greatly attached at Amerongen, married Captain von Ilsemann on October 7th. The Kaiser was present, doing his best to behave like an ordinary wedding guest and put people at their ease but not entirely succeeding on this occasion because he was held in considerable awe. Thereafter Countess Elizabeth lived at Doorn,* and, with Countess Brockdorff and Countess Keller, she did

* She continued to do so until some time after the Second War, her husband being in charge of the house which was impounded by the Netherlands Government in 1945 as enemy property (viz. that of the Crown Prince). In 1949 the confiscation was confirmed and an order made to turn Doorn House into a museum. As the Crown Prince had begun to sell off family treasures at absurd prices it remains the last existing Hohenzollern museum. On the death of her husband Captain von Ilsemann, Countess Elizabeth returned to her family home at Amerongen.[99]

her best for the ailing and grief-stricken Kaiserin. Theirs was not a long vigil.

On the 27th February in 1921 William and Dona celebrated the fortieth anniversary of their wedding. Many congratulations arrived at Doorn. The Crown Prince was permitted to be present for the occasion and other members of the family were there. The Kaiserin scarcely had the strength to put in a formal appearance. She found it unbearable that so much had altered since the master butchers of Berlin had greeted her bridal carriage and led her into Berlin and, in the flicker and smoke of resin torches, she had paced out the stately wedding dance in the White Hall of the Old Palace. Six weeks later, on April 11th 1921, she died.

William's grief was controlled but touchingly sincere. After the old fashion he ordered that her room be preserved exactly as if she still had need of it and immortelles to be placed on her bed. For Dona's sake he managed to say he was glad she had been released from her sad memories. But her death added to his own. He keenly felt the new loneliness especially as she had directed in her will that she wished to be buried at Potsdam and he was thereby deprived of the small comfort of being able to visit her grave. Neither he nor the Crown Prince could even go to her funeral. They were present at the short house service taken by the Court Chaplain, and at the more elaborate service at which were representatives of the Dutch royal family, but they could go no further and had to wait, an ill-matched pair, until the family and Household mourners returned from Potsdam to tell them that large crowds had lined the way of the cortège to the Antique Temple where the Kaiserin was laid to rest.[100]

The Crown Prince went back to his island prison. Lacking the character to lead a full and ordered life as his father did at Doorn, he took to drink. His loneliness, frustrations and self-pity were temporarily rendered painless by large quantities of strong Dutch beer.[101] His father tried to deaden his sorrow in hard physical work and intellectual exercise but he keenly felt the loneliness of being a widower. His daughter and daughter-in-law dutifully visited him but they could never stay for long.[102] It was a sad year for him made sadder by the death of Count August Eulenburg, still at the head of the Ministry of the Royal House in his eighty-third year,[103] and then the loss of someone who once had meant so much to him, of Philip Eulenburg who died on September 17th, 1921.[104] He took small pleasure in the rare visits of his increasingly tipsy son from Wieringen, and was critical of his Joseph Surface methods of trying to obtain permission to return to Germany. Between drinking bouts the Crown Prince was writing open letters to the newspapers expressing strong left-wing sentiments which he did not feel, entertaining Gustav Stresemann who was leader of the German People's Party, sending an appeal to his kinsman King George of England itemizing twelve points in his own favour, and hiring an Austrian journalist to ghost his memoirs in order to quell the propaganda stories that as 'Little Willy' in Belgium he had murdered children and drunk their blood.[105]

In May, 1922 the Crown Prince paid one of his unwelcomed visits to Doorn and was somewhat startled to be told by his father that he was planning to re-marry.[106] Dutiful children try to prevent elderly parents from being caught by scheming females, but though this lady had brought herself to the Kaiser's attention through a letter of loyalty written by her thirteen-year-old son – a piece of deviousness which opens her to some suspicion – she was, in fact, eminently suitable as a replacement for the late Kaiserin. On her deathbed Dona had urged both Countess Brockdorff and Countess Keller that the Kaiser should not remain alone but ought to marry.[107] Now only thirteen months afterwards William informed his son that in the autumn he would marry the Princess Hermione, born in the ruling house of Reuss and widow of Prince Schönaich-Carolath-Beuthen. Princess Hermione had neither the stateliness nor the air of ripe magnificence of her predecessor, but she had many of her qualities; the same comfortable embonpoint and strong maternal feelings – she had five young children of her own – and the same capacity for supervising the affairs of a large household and a desire to make life comfortable for William. Another advantage was that the Princess had her own fortune and considerable estates and was quite prepared to make a formal renunciation both for herself and for her children of any claim upon the Hohenzollern fortune. There was a discrepancy in their age for she had been widowed at thirty-three and was twenty-eight years younger than he, but to William and all at Doorn it seemed an eminently suitable match. The Crown Prince however did not really care for the idea. His wife disliked it so much that she said she would not attend the wedding.[108] The monarchist party in the fatherland sent a deputation to Doorn begging the Kaiser to change his mind as a re-marriage so soon after the late Kaiserin's death would be a further blow to the dynasty. William did not ask them what the party had been doing on November 9th, 1918 to allow the dynasty to get into such a position. Nevertheless he told them their interference was unwarranted and impertinent.[109] As he was now theoretically a private person he intended to enjoy the liberties of one.

On November 5th he gave Princess Hermione the same style and title which his great-grandfather Frederick William III had given his second wife. She was to be Her Royal Prussian Highness the Princess Liegnitz,[110] though at the wedding breakfast his brother Prince Harry proposed a toast 'To Her Majesty the Kaiserin and Queen'. The Hohenzollerns and the small Court at Doorn officially recognized William's second wife as Kaiserin Hermione and that was how he expected her to be addressed.[111]

On November 10th, five days after his second marriage, the Kaiser received formal notification from the Crown Prince that he had left Wieringen at four o'clock that morning to return to the fatherland. Simultaneously the Netherlands government was officially informed though they had known beforehand and winked at his departure. Gustav Stresemann, leader of the German People's Party – the old National Liberal Party of the Second Reich – had been made Chancellor in August and it was he who had made the return possible. William was angry, claiming that as the Head of the Royal House he should have been consulted by the German government and that he had a clearer right to repatriation than his eldest son. But he maintained his dignity by making no formal complaint.[112]

4

Obeying the imperial command that current events must not be discussed in public must have imposed a severe strain upon the little Court at Doorn because so many day-to-day events in the Weimar Republic were highly controversial. Culturally it was a rich period for Germany. Klee, Gropius, Rohe, Mendelssohn and Brecht were all at work. For the rich it was also a rich period as few taxes were levied and scarcely any were paid. The notion was current that taxes would leave Germany as reparation payments and tax avoidance came to be regarded as morally justifiable and even patriotic. Successive governments paid their way by issuing more and more paper money. By the time Stresemann came to power an article which before the war had cost one mark now cost exactly one million million marks, and people went to the baker's with a suitcase full of Weimar banknotes. In this ludicrous inflation the savings of the bourgeoisie had been swallowed up and the untaxed industrial magnates became the masters of German economic growth.[113] Stresemann was determined to make expenditure balance revenue and he stabilized the currency so successfully that the economy suddenly flourished like Jack's beanstalk. By 1929 Germany had a higher standard of living than ever before but her prosperity depended chiefly on heavy industry which collapsed in the world depression of the 'thirties.[114] The social effect of ruin followed by affluence followed by ruin was disastrous. The old-fashioned bourgeois standards were disregarded. Acts of primitive violence went unpunished. Corruption was widespread. A wave of sexual permissiveness washed over Germany and made Berlin 'the vice centre of Europe'.[115] The political effects were equally drastic. The abandonment of principle was widespread and two 'national' parties waited very noisily and impatiently to seize power by brute force.

One was the new German Communist party, a respectable marriage of many Independent Socialists and the rump of the Spartacists. But it lost its respectability by then prostituting itself to 'Asiatic Leninism'.* By the direct order of Stalin German Communists purged themselves of the Luxemburgists, that is those who followed the Red Rose's non-terrorist and humanely rational exposition of the doctrines of Marx and Engels. At a stroke the party was deprived of its most enlightened members. The rest were craven enough to obey a Kremlin command to drive a wedge between Russia and the Western Powers by attacking democracy, the 'slave treaty' of Versailles, and instituting Red Terror. This they did so thoroughly that they destroyed any chance of peaceful democracy in Germany.[116] At the extreme right of politics were the National Socialists led by Adolf Hitler, a demagogue with a genius for creating and managing mass emotion. His lieutenants were an odd lot; amongst them the crazy Ludendorff; Hermann Göring, commander of the famous Richtofen air squadron who had won the Pour le Mérite and been friendly with the Crown Prince during the war; two members of the Munich Thule Society, Hess and Rosenberg; Strasser, a chemist; Paul Joseph Goebbels, a talented and charming secretary to a Reichstag deputy; and Ernest Röhm, prototype of all Free Corps leaders whom Göring described as 'fighters who could not become debrutalized'.[117] Observed objectively the aims of the Communists and the National Socialists were very similar: both were totalitarian, sworn to avenge the humiliation of the Versailles Treaty, and both used systematic terror. But the National Socialists had a supreme advantage in being backed by many rich industrialists. Both, however, had to wait for the final attempt to seize power until the Republic itself began to disintegrate.

Honest President Ebert died of peritonitis in 1925 at the early age of fifty-five, a disappointed, weary man.† To take his place Field Marshal von Hindenburg was once more tempted from retirement. Hindenburg had tried to make his peace with the Kaiser by sending loyal congratulations every time William celebrated his birthday and by admitting in writing that he accepted full responsibility for advising him to go into exile; but William had never liked him nor trusted him and saw no reason to change his mind. In the following year the Prussian Parliament made provision for the Hohenzollerns from their confiscated estates, returning fourteen royal establishments, amongst them the Kaiser's farm at Cadinen and his hunting lodge at Rominten. It was not an ungenerous settlement but William felt no cause to be

---

* Ebert's phrase.

† He had been spat on in Munich for permitting the Versailles Treaty and imprudently brought an action. This prompted dozens of others to play the game of insulting the President and at one point he was bringing 150 slander actions simultaneously.[118]

grateful. The restoration merely served to remind him of places he loved but could never visit.[119]

The financial crisis in 1930 clearly demonstrated that while Germany had a sovereign Reichstag, a Chancellor and a President, no-one was really in authority. The country was being administered not governed and the difference was noticeable when a national policy was called for to deal with unemployment. The Army was the only power in the Republic. It chose Henry Brüning, a sympathetic ex-member of the Officer Corps, now a leader of the Centre party, to rule as Chancellor by emergency decree. Each Sunday there were bloody clashes between the Communists who sang the Red Flag and Röhm's National Socialist brownshirts who sang *Horst Wessel Lied*. The republican 'Blue Police' tried to keep order, but Hitler was gaining more and more support.[120] At Doorn William found himself listening with some doubt to his second wife's expressed admiration for the Nazis. Some of his gentlemen were equally enthusiastic about the National Socialists. Their programme under the slogan 'Germany awake!' promised order, revenge for Versailles, and the uniting of all Germans of pure Aryan stock under one leader, their Führer. Göring paid a special visit to Doorn to tell the sceptical Kaiser that it was Hitler's aim to restore the monarchy.*[121] As an old friend of the Crown Prince, Göring was treated politely but no definite assurances were given either way. However, simply because Hitler was anti-Bolshevik, the Kaiser did allow two of his sons, Prince August and Prince Oscar to join the party, and the Crown Prince with equal lack of prudence allowed himself to be photographed wearing the uniform of Röhm's brownshirts.[124]

When the 1932 Elections came along only Hindenburg stood between Hitler and the Presidency. A notion that the Crown Prince should stand as a candidate was quickly scotched. Although the Field Marshal was by then in his eighty-fifth year Chancellor Brüning persuaded him to stand for re-election. The Crown Prince declared that because a national front was vital he himself would vote for Hitler.[125] In the event Hindenburg won but he tipped Brüning out of office and replaced him with the reactionary Franz von Papen who made up a 'Cabinet of Barons'.[126] His government declaration was described by a contemporary, Count Harry Kessler:

* According to the Kaiser's nephew, H.R.H. Prince Philip of Hesse, the majority of the family were inclined to approve of Hitler because he wished to restore order and rejuvenate the country. The Führer even managed to persuade them that his anti-Semitism was simply an attempt to reduce the preponderance of Jews in medicine and teaching, the law, the arts and the press etc.[122] Each was disillusioned in turn, Prince Philip most painfully of all. His wife, although she was a daughter of the King of Italy, died in Buchenwald Concentration camp.[123] It is difficult to believe that the Kaiser's well-known distaste for the Nazis' forbears, the Pan-Germans, permitted him to regard Hitler as anything other than a political guttersnipe.

*A hardly credible document. . . . of darkest reaction, compared with which the declarations of the Kaiser's government seem like the brightest Enlightenment.**

He lasted long enough to destroy the Communist Headquarters in Karl Liebknecht House with armoured cars and machine guns, and rule through two general elections within five months in which it was made clear that to avoid civil war Hitler would have to be made Chancellor.

On March 21st, 1933 – the anniversary of the opening of the first Reichstag of the Second Reich – the first Reichstag of the Third Reich was opened in the Garrison Church at Potsdam. One of the galleries was entirely filled by field marshals, generals and admirals all wearing their pre-war imperial uniforms. The Crown Prince in full dress uniform sat behind a vacant throne. The National Socialist and Centre deputies were flanked by armed brownshirts. Hindenburg and Hitler marched together into the church and, as they passed the empty throne, the old Marshal turned and saluted it with his baton. In a skilful, short and modest speech Chancellor Adolf Hitler then tied a knot between 'symbols of the old greatness and the new strength' and he and Hindenburg prayed together beside the tomb of Frederick the Great.[128] William appreciated the compliment to the throne but he was contemptuous of the National Socialists' claim to be in direct political descent from Frederick the Great and Bismarck.† He waited upon events.

In June Hitler consolidated his position in a bloodbath of friends and enemies alike. Strasser was shot in Berlin. Röhm was shot in a Munich cell,‡ and many of his officers met with the same fate. It did not escape the Hohenzollerns' notice that Prince August was put under house arrest by Göring's order. Hitler announced in the Reichstag that 77 people had been executed. Probably it was far more. Hindenburg thanked him for his 'determined and gallant personal intervention',[129] and in August the old Field Marshal died. Hitler took his place as President-Chancellor, and ordered that all officers and men in the Army should take a personal oath to him as Commander-in-Chief.[130]

---

* In Roman history it was commonplace that the supposed saviours of nations turned out to be far more draconian than the despots they replaced. Instances may also be found in modern history. Cromwell became more tyrannical than Charles I, Washington than George III, Lenin than Nicholas II, and Hitler than William II.

† This was accepted by many in the west and underlined by William Shirer's 'unbelievably crude'[131] book *Rise and Fall of the The Third Reich: A History of Nazi Germany*; though it has been refuted by leading historians of the quality of Gerard Ritter and Klaus Epstein – the former stating categorically that Hitler had nothing to do with 'the monarchic power of princes' and was more in line with such demagogues as 'Danton, Lenin and Mussolini'.[132]

‡ A notable cell. It had once confined Kurt Eisner, then Eisner's assassin, Count Arco-Valley, and for a short time, Hitler himself.[133]

That summer the Indemnification of Princes Law was cancelled. No Hohen-zollerns could draw income from their estates, which were again sequestered. Instead handsome provision was made for any member of the family who would guarantee not to criticize the régime.[134] William made one final at-tempt to come to terms with Hitler, requesting that he be permitted to return to his homeland. It was refused.[135] On his birthday in 1935 there were loyal celebrations in public which were brutally suppressed at Göring's orders.[136] Three days later Hitler announced in the Reichstag that Germany would be happier without hereditary princes, and four days after that all monarchical societies were dissolved, the privileges of the royal house were shorn, and Göring took over the royal hunting lodge at Hubertusstock and built a country house there, annoying the Kaiser most of all by renaming this ancient part of the appanage of the Hohenzollerns after his own wife Karin Hall.[137]

The Kaiser found it not only more tolerable but actually necessary to dwell more on the Second Reich than the Third. He was never left in peace all the years of his exile by detractors and admirers. The former far outnumbered the latter, but from the many letters which descended upon him it was clear that .friends and enemies alike showed little appreciation of what had actually occurred in Germany before his abdication. The letters were appropriately dealt with by Baron von Sell and William himself.

More important, because they had a wide circle of readers, were articles in journals in newspapers which anatomized the Kaiser in every particular. Gradually, as the years passed and he became of less interest to the public, the spate died down but, while it lasted, it was so painful that William felt obliged to appoint a number of people to give his point of view. In effect they were his public relations officers.

Still more important, as they were less ephemeral, were the books which poured from the presses both in Germany and abroad. The third 'suppressed' volume of Prince Bismarck's *Gedanken und Erinnerungen*, Count Herbert's much prejudiced account of his father's fall, was issued by the publisher Cotta despite protests from the Bismarck family,[138] and the public was diverted by this bitter attack upon the Kaiser. William was not. With the aid of a journalist named Rosen who ghosted his books William wrote his own memoirs in 1922 and in 1926 published *My Early Life*. With admirable detachment he told his side of the story and in the opinion of some historians he did it effectively.[139] Other critics rose from the tomb and retirement to denigrate their former master and, in some cases, attempt to plaster him with war guilt. Anything really damaging to the fatherland was diluted because of the policy of self-censorship imposed by both politicians and historians,[140] but peripheral matter which threw mud at the exiled Kaiser scarcely fell into this category. The memoirs of Tirpitz, Bethmann Hollweg and Jagow, Moltke, the former Court Marshal Count Robert von Zedlitz-Trützschler, Philip Eulenburg and Waldersee were followed by Haller's work *Philip Eulenburg: the Kaiser's Friend*. William read them one by one and showed surprising restraint, though even the volume written in his favour by Emil Ludwig contained passages which must have made him wince. Not until his mother's memoirs *The Letters of the Empress Frederick* appeared in 1927 did he decide something must be done. These letters were a selection of the documents smuggled from Germany by her godson, Sir Frederick Ponsonby, and issued by him with a commentary on his own responsibility.*[141] There was no doubt that Ludwig had been sharp in his criticism of the Empress. Equally there was no doubt that her letters went too far in making public many private family affairs and, rather than balance the facts for historians as Ponsonby intended, they distorted them. At Doorn William considered his position. Under the Act of Settlement he was a British citizen and could have brought an action in the English Courts,[143] but in England the damage was already done. The newspaper hounds were quickly on to this fresh anti-Kaiser scent and ran joyfully in full cry after their quarry with edition after edition of commissioned and unsolicited articles, editorial comment and full correspondence columns. They were however prevented from making a killing in Germany by a clever ruse of the Kaiser's. He himself bought the German rights of Ponsonby's book and wrote a short preface. In this he emphasized how sensitive and easily moulded his mother had been, how quick to take offence and imagine hostility where none existed and that:

'her temperament made her use bitter words about everybody'

Having drawn its sting he then published the book in translation exactly as it stood without altering a word.[144] In 1929 the treacherous Bülow died. William was aware that his memoirs were ready for the presses. He sent a wreath to the funeral with the laconic inscription: 'To my Unforgettable Chancellor'.[145] Very soon afterwards the memoirs were issued in four blue volumes. Had they not been studded with inconsistencies and contradictions, and so scratchy and screechy they might have been a devastating attack upon the Kaiser. As it was the attempt rebounded and discredited the author. When he had finished the last blue volume William was moved to remark it was the first case he knew of a man committing suicide after he was dead.[146]

All this critical work was, so to speak, from his own, the German side. From other countries came even more books, some in his favour, the great

---

* At first George V and his aunt, Princess Beatrice, were opposed to the idea of publication, though another aunt, Princess Louise, and his uncle, the Duke of Connaught, approved. Then the King said he would not stand in Ponsonby's way, but neither would he say yes or no. When the book came out he showed some interest, and afterwards 'joined in the general abuse of it'.[142]

majority not. He bore the abuse with dignity even when he was called 'the mad dog of Europe', 'this fabulous monster', 'an imperial clown', and, rather curiously, 'a Valkyrie with a fierce moustache'.

Less bearable were the antics of his family. His Nazi sons were rescued from their folly by Hitler's own disagreeableness, but the Empress Hermione remained a devoted supporter of National Socialism, as did some of his nephews and nieces. His third son, Prince Ethelbert, who had served in the Imperial Navy, abruptly decided to have nothing more to do with the fatherland and, calling himself Count Lingen, went to live privately in Switzerland.[147] William's widowed sister Moretta brought shame on the Hohenzollerns by marrying a Russian wastrel who in age could have been her grandson; and two years later in 1929 she died deserted, penniless and utterly wretched in Bonn.[148] That same year the Crown Prince's second son Prince Louis Ferdinand fell in love with an American film star. He was due to go to the Argentine to study and his grandfather gave him two thousand marks and advice on how to behave as a Hohenzollern abroad. Then he discovered the young man had slipped off to Hollywood on his way to South America and was in the eye of the newspapers.[149] However he redeemed himself by being thoroughly anti-Nazi and writing to ask his grandfather's advice on current political affairs,[150] and he became the family ambassador to the English Court where his good qualities and charm made him a welcome guest.[151] Soon he had to replace his elder brother as heir presumptive to the headship of the family. The Kaiser dearly loved his eldest grandson, a quiet, understanding and sober young man who had been formally presented at Doorn on his coming of age and who was the hope of the monarchical party in Germany. Therefore he was all the more distressed when he heard that the young Prince had lost his heart to an ineligible *parti* and was determined upon marriage. The lady of his choice, Dorothea von Salviati, belonged to the lower nobility and it is controversial whether a marriage between them was morganatic or not. Significantly Prince William was required to make a formal renunciation of his rights of primogeniture before the wedding and Klaus Jonas, the biographer of the Crown Prince, claims that everyone was deeply upset by this enforcement 'according to the laws of the House'.[152] Jonas also states that by protocol, Princess William, as she had become, was set apart with another morganatic wife at the wedding of her brother-in-law four years later.[153] But it is also significant that Dorothea von Salviati was permitted to use her husband's rank and that she and her daughters have always been addressed as Royal Highness and accounted Princesses of Prussia, for this is not usual in the case of morganatic marriages. Morganatic or not, William was not at all pleased by his grandson's marriage. Prince Louis Ferdinand, now heir presumptive, did better by forgetting his American actress and marrying the Russian Grand Duchess Kira in 1938 – the civil ceremony taking place at Potsdam, and the Church service at Doorn in the presence of the Dutch and German royal families.

To compensate for family troubles and the perpetual vilification of his own character, the Kaiser received many visitors who generally were received with great cordiality.* They varied in type from the Benedictine Abbot of the huge German monastery of Maria-Laach,[154] who doubtless tactfully failed to mention that the High Altar given by William in 1901 was considered so hideous by the community that it had been hidden away in a vault, to young Randolph Churchill who, besides being a politician was also a journalist and arrived with the express purpose of getting copy on the Kaiser's views on Hitler, but who found himself adroitly side-stepped and led into a discussion on that recurring imperial theme the Yellow Peril. Neither this, however, nor protocol prevented Churchill from giving his own views on the Nazis to the distress of Kaiserin Hermione.[155] There were also many souvenir hunters who went away satisfied with a small log cut by the Kaiser and a large 'W' scribbled on the end in indelible pencil.[156] But the visits William enjoyed most were from his daughter and daughter-in-law and his grandchildren. He was and is spoken of with great affection as a grandfather.[158] Then there were the unofficial visits on his birthdays which were always made great occasions. His most constant visitor was August von Mackensen, who had initiated the custom of kissing his hand and who had been promoted Field Marshal by William for his conspicuous service during the war. On the Kaiser's seventieth birthday the Field Marshal led a deputation of thirty members of the old Prussian Officer Corps who went to Doorn to congratulate their master. They still considered him their Supreme Commander.[159] On his eightieth birthday the Führer showed hostility and forebad all active and reserve officers to congratulate their former Commander-in-Chief. But nothing would have kept Mackensen away nor, for this special birthday, another of William's former Marshals, the Crown Prince Rupert of Bavaria.[160] It was a gala occasion. The Imperial Standard and the flag of Prussia flew from the tower of Doorn House. The gentlemen were all in dress uniform, the ladies in *grande toilette*. Many members of the Kaiser's family were with him as well as representatives of the Imperial Officer Corps, and the presence of the elderly Crown Prince Rupert of Bavaria, the Grand Duke of Mecklenburg, the Grand Duke Vladimir of Russia and Prince Frederick Christian of Saxony, a representative from Queen Wilhelmina, and congratulatory telegrams from the King and Queen of England and the Queen Mother showed that he was still accepted by the people who mattered

* No British subjects were admitted to Doorn until after the British Army of Occupation had left the Rhineland in 1929.[157]

to him. There was a thanksgiving service at which the Court Chaplain preached, a dinner, the showing of a film *The Life of Frederick the Great,* a small Defilir Cour, and a ball.[161] Yet even by then the campaign against the Kaiser had not died away. On the day before his birthday a photograph of the Kaiser was printed in the *Eclaireur de Nice* with the caption:

> *This is the eighty-year-old Herr Wilhelm Hohenzollern, guilty of the premature deaths of many millions of people.*[162]

It is doubtful if the Kaiser suffered the sting of the attack. A long time before he had taken a great deal of trouble working out a Comparative Historical Table to show what each Power was doing and aiming for politically in each year up to the war. But it had persuaded no one. He had grown wiser with age and no longer wasted his time in fruitless polemics. Though eighty he was as alert as ever and his enquiring mind was never quite satisfied, though his studies over the years had been deep and extensive. He had written and published his memoirs of Corfu,* dedicating the volume to the memory of Dona, and portraits of his forbears from the first Zollerns to his father Emperor Frederick, dedicating this to Hermione. Just as he had calmed himself on 'the Black Day of the German Army' by reading an article on the Hittite language at Supreme Headquarters, so he soothed the worst smarts and frustrations of his exile by researches into the past. He corresponded with archaeologists, founded the Doorn Study Group, and interested himself in a wide variety of subjects: a gorgon's head once found near the Achilleion, Babylon in Biblical times, monarchy in ancient Mesopotamia and the laws of Hammurabi, human culture in ancient western Asia, and the possible origin and meaning of the two symbols, the Chinese Monad and the swastika. Largely he had controlled the grasshopper leaps in his thinking but he by no means confined himself to the past and to modern affairs. He read and re-read his favourite books. He had a special affection for the works of P. G. Wodehouse and if his Household displeased him he had a puckish way of punishing them by reading Wodehouse aloud and watching their reactions. It was largely his English inheritance which made the adventures of Jeeves, Mr Mulliner, Uncle Fred and Gally Threepwood so enjoyable to him – and totally incomprehensible to the more Prussian members of his suite. Possibly, in living out his dreams of being a country squire he saw a parallel between his simple life of study, exercise and feeding the ducks on the moats and that of one of the most remarkable of all Wodehouse's creations, Clarence, Earl of Emsworth, whose chief joy was the fattening of his prize sow, pottering in the rose gardens, and reading up his valued text book, *Whiffle On the Pig.* The great difference between them was that Emsworth lived in a perpetual Shrop-

* His estate on the island had been sequestrated by the Greek government.

shire summer, while the calm of the Kaiser's retirement was subject to many outward interruptions.

As it became clearer and clearer that Hitler was taking the Third Reich into war, William joined in the general sense of relief when the Munich crisis passed. For the first time since the war he wrote a letter in indelible pencil to Queen Mary for forwarding to King George VI saying how relieved he was that Chamberlain had succeeded.[163] But he knew perfectly well the peace could not last. Despite his wife's approval of Hitler he said the Nazis' brutal treatment of Jews was an outrage and declared: 'For the first time I am ashamed to be a German.'*[164] But a German he was and could not escape it.

The Second World War began. Of all the Hohenzollerns fifteen Princes were in army service at the front. Within two days of the declaration of hostilities by England and France the Kaiser's grandson Prince Oscar was killed in Poland.[165] When the invasion of the west began Hitler proposed that the Kaiser should return to Germany as an honoured guest of the Third Reich.[167] Alarmed for his safety King George VI offered him refuge in England. An aeroplane would be sent to Holland if he accepted. Meanwhile, Queen Wilhelmina, still conscious of her duties as the Kaiser's host although she herself and her government were obliged to fly to London, offered him sanctuary in a Dutch colony overseas. William refused all these offers on the principle that the Dutch had been good to him during his long exile and he would not desert them now, and he had no intention of being accused of running away a second time.[168]

The Germans swept through Holland and on May 14th, 1940 a special detachment was assigned to guard the Kaiser and prevent him from leaving the Doorn estate. They were given strict orders not to fraternize but William's quiet courtesy and his dignified demeanour charmed them. The army detachment was quickly replaced by a Gestapo guard but even these crack troops failed to be as strict as Hitler required. Their colonel was soon snapping to attention, saluting and addressing the Kaiser as 'Your Majesty'.[169]

On May 23rd 1940 William heard that his eldest grandson William had been severely wounded in the fighting near Valenciennes and three days afterwards he died in a military hospital. At the funeral in Potsdam, where Prince William was laid to rest in the Antique Temple, a huge crowd of 50,000 sympathizers followed the cortège. The ubiquitous Marshal von Mackensen was there, despite his ninety-two years, and was admitted with a few others

* We may be certain that, had he heard of it, William would have much approved of the anti-Nazi attitude of his first Chancellor's grand-daughter, Countess Hannah von Bismarck, by then Frau von Bredow. Invited by Hitler to launch the huge battleship named for her grandfather she coldly replied that she had already done the same thing for His Imperial Majesty the Kaiser, and saw no good reason for repeating herself.[166]

to the Antique Temple for the last rites. Afterwards he saw a general he recognized and in his loud voice sympathized with him for being on the sick list and unable to get up to the front. The general confided that the real reason was because the party did not favour him, at which the ancient Marshal warmly shook his hand and cried: 'In that case I can only congratulate you with all my heart.'[170]

Hitler was exceedingly angry at this massive demonstration in favour of the monarchy. He ordered all Hohenzollern princes to send in their papers and accept civilian employment.[171] It has been said that he also threatened reprisals upon them and their families and that, in order to placate him, the Kaiser was persuaded to join the Crown Prince in sending congratulatory telegrams when the Germans took Paris.[172] Characteristically the Kaiser's telegram was brief, his son's verbose.[173] It has also been claimed that it was under pressure from Kaiserin Hermione that William made this inept gesture.[174] Most probably the latter is the truer explanation – but, for a man who had been so regularly exposed to the opportunities of being indiscreet that Chancellor Bethmann Hollweg actually took precautionary measures against the danger, the fact that William held his tongue for twenty-one years of exile was an astonishing feat. He ought, perhaps, to be permitted one final gaffe.

In the following months he was largely silent. He was comparing the two great wars and seeing a pattern emerge which foretold the ruin of Germany a second time. Hitler was underestimating the effective force of blockade. During the spring of 1941 he began to feel unwell. He suffered from pains and tiredness. It was scarcely surprising. William had already outlived most of his contemporary heads of state and the great majority of the people who had contrived to deprive him of his crown and box him up in Holland for the last quarter of his life. King George of England had died as had Albert of the Belgians and the Emperor Charles of Austria–Hungary. The detestable Lenin was gone, his embalmed and painted cadaver on perpetual show in the Kremlin. President Wilson, unable to persuade his own people to endorse the Versailles Treaty, had been struck down by illness and, for the last year of his term of office, the United States was ruled by his wife and his physician.[175] All William's chancellors had died, including Prince Max, as had Scheidemann, Hindenburg, Ludendorff, Gröner, Clemenceau, and Foch. Out of William's seven brothers and sisters only his youngest sister was still living. Like Queen Victoria it must have seemed that all had fallen around him – though in fact he was to be survived by the foxy King Ferdinand of Bulgaria whose bottom he had slapped thereby almost causing an international situation, and by the slippery Welshman who had threatened to hang him, David Lloyd George.

As a Kaiser in power William had frequently cast a long shadow and, even in exile, his vigour and alertness were conspicuous. But now he had begun to fail. He no longer studied archaeology, nor even Baron von Sell's digests and reports. A cold turned to pneumonia, though not for some time was a bulletin issued that he was seriously ill. Then it was understood he would not recover. He lay in his bed, barely conscious but restful.

What filled his mind during the long hours may be imagined from the common experience of elderly people. He was eighty-two and he had had an eventful life but even the most dramatic moments had probably given place to the memories of his childhood – the ones made sharp by the senses; the irons and belts, for instance, being fixed to his neck and his leg, and being forced to ride by the willpower of his tutor, made to get up again and again and again; and he and Harry munching rain-soaked bread in a Cassel inn yard, and boating with their bearded father on the Havel, and firing the brass cannons at Osborne when Waldemar laid a pet crocodile at the feet of Queen Victoria; and painting with his Mama in her studio, their two easels side by side, and the family holiday at Norderney when there was much swimming and shell collecting and a voyage in a rattling paddlesteamer; and dining with his grandfather the old Emperor at a little table, watching him mark the wine bottle; and listening to the mournful croaking of the bright green Unken frogs at Cadinen.

It would have been very different had he lain dying as a reigning Kaiser, the room filled for hours upon end by his entire family and Household, officials of the Court and Army and the State, chaplains, physicians and servants, all there to witness the exact moment when the sceptre power passed to another hand. William was saved that imperial indignity, the invasion of privacy when privacy mattered so much.

On May 31st he began to lose strength. On June 3rd he lost consciousness. On the morning of June 4th, and quite simply in the presence of his wife, his daughter and three of his grandsons, he died.

Reference Notes

Chapter One (pp. 1–9)
HOHENZOLLERN AND SAXE–COBURG–
GOTHA

1 Longford, Elizabeth, Countess of:
   Victoria R.I. (1964), p. 223.
2 Masur, Gerhard: *Imperial Berlin*
   (1970), paperback British ed.; p. 45.
3 Balfour, Michael: *The Kaiser and His
   Times* (1964), p. 58.
4 Longford, *op. cit.*, p. 194.
5 Goltz, Friedrich Baron von der, and
   Stiefenhofer, Theodor: *Unsterbliches
   Deutschland* (1936), pp. 45 *et seq.*, q.v.
   an historiographical collection Röhl,
   J. C. G.: *From Bismarck to Hitler*
   (1970), cited as Röhl I.
6 Heer, Friedrich: *The Mediaeval
   World*, tr. J. Sondheimer (1962).
7 Longford, *op. cit.*, p. 223.
8 Pound, Reginald: *Albert* (1973),
   p. 231.
9 Longford, *op. cit.*, p. 223; Pound,
   op. cit., p. 230.
10 Queen Victoria: *Letters*, I, i, p. 53.
11 Longford, *op. cit.*, p. 225.
12 Fulford, Roger: *The Prince Consort*
   (1949), cited as Fulford I, p. 233;
   Pound, *op. cit.*, p. 434; Longford,
   op. cit., p. 225.
13 Longford, *op. cit.*, p. 172.
14 Bennett, Daphne: *Vicky, Princess
   Royal of England and German Empress*
   (1971), p. 38.
15 Longford, *op. cit.*, p. 205.
16 Pound, *op. cit.*, p. 279.
17 Masur, *op. cit.*, p. 44.
18 Rochau, Ludwig von: *Grundzüge
   der Realpolitik* (1853).
19 Knight, Alfred E.: *Victoria, Her Life
   and Reign* (1901), p. 183.
20 *ibid.*, p. 217.
21 Aronson, Theo: *The Kaisers* (1971),
   cited as Aronson I, Corgi ed., p.
   39.
22 Queen Victoria: *Journal*, 14th September, 1855.
23 Longford, *op. cit.*, pp. 259–60.
24 Pound, *op. cit.*, p. 286.
25 Aronson I, *op. cit.*, p. 41.
26 Macalpine, Ida and Hunter, Richard:
   George III and the Mad-Business
   (1969), pp. 247–54.
27 Queen Victoria: *Letters*, I. iii, p.
   321.
28 Bennett, *op. cit.*, p. 54.
29 Cowles, Virginia: *The Kaiser* (1963),
   p. 15.
30 *ibid.*, p. 16.
31 Strachey, Lytton: *Queen Victoria*
   (1921), Phoenix Library ed., p. 92.

Chapter Two (pp. 10–25)
CRADLE AND NURSERY

1 Kürenberg, Joachim von: *The Kaiser*
   trs. H. T. Russell and Herta Hagen
   (1954), pp. 1–2.
2 Bennett, *op. cit.*, pp. 84–5.
3 Nowak, Karl Friedrich: *Kaiser and
   Chancellor* trs. E. W. Dickes (1929),
   p. 9; Bennett, *op. cit.*, p. 85.
4 Bennett, *op. cit.*, p. 61.
5 Pound, *op. cit.*, p. 309.
6 *ibid.*, p. 313.
7 Duff, David: *Hessian Tapestry* (1967),
   cited as Duff I, pp. 29–30.
8 Nowak, *op. cit.*, p. 10.
9 Bennett, *op. cit.*, p. 87.
10 *ibid.*
11 Queen Victoria: *Letters*, III, i, p. 440.
12 Rich, N, and Fischer, M. H. (eds.):
   The Holstein Papers, in 4 vols.,
   (1957–1963), cited as Holstein Papers,
   II, p. 254.
13 Pound, *op. cit.*, p. 291.
14 Strachey, *op. cit.*, p. 164.
15 Balfour, *op. cit.*, p. 144.
16 Kaiser William II: *My Early Life*
   (1924), trs. of 1926 cited as Kaiser I,
   pp. 85–6.
17 Bennett, *op. cit.*, p. 73; Aronson I,
   op. cit., pp. 34–5.
18 Hough, Richard: *Louis and Victoria,
   The First Mountbattens* (1974), p. 41.
19 Aronson I, *op. cit.*, pp. 33 and 101.
20 Kaiser I, *op. cit.*, p. 86.
21 Balfour, *op. cit.*, p. 57.
22 Aronson I, *op. cit.*, p. 148.
23 Bülow, Bernhard, Prince von:
   Memoirs, English Ed. in 3 vols.
   (1929), II, p. 529; Kurenberg, *op. cit.*,
   p. 5; Aronson I, *op. cit.*, p. 98;
   Balfour, *op. cit.*, p. 58.
24 Fischer, Henry W. (ed.): *The Private
   Lives of William II and his Consort*, one
   volume abridged ed. (1904), cited as
   Fischer I, p. 29; Kennedy, A. L. (ed):
   *My Dear Duchess, Social and Political
   Letters to the Duchess of Manchester,
   1858–1869* (1956), p. 169.
25 Aronson I, *op. cit.*, p. 99.
26 Mitford, Nancy: *Frederick the Great*
   (1970), pp. 254 and 259; Topham,
   Anne: *Memories of the Kaiser's Court*
   (1914), pp. 36–9 and 76; Fischer I,
   op. cit., p. 62.
27 Aronson I, *op. cit.*, p. 123.
28 Kürenberg, *op. cit.*, p. 11.
29 Pound, *op. cit.*, p. 235.
30 Bolitho, Hector and Baillie, A. V.
   (ed.): *The Letters of Lady Augusta
   Stanley* (1927).

31 Longford, *op. cit.*, p. 314.
32 Fulford, Roger (ed.): *Dearest M
   Letters between Queen Victoria an
   Crown Princess of Prussia, 1861–
   (1968), cited as Fulford II, p. 67.
33 Bennett, *op. cit.*, p. 95.
34 Fulford II, *op. cit.*, p. 161; Po
   op. cit., p. 328.
35 Bennett, *op. cit.*, p. 113.
36 *ibid.*
37 Aronson I, *op. cit.*, p. 3.
38 Wilson, Lawrence: *The Incre
   Kaiser, A Portrait of William II (19
   p. 14.
39 Masur, *op. cit.*, p. 52.
40 Duff I, *op. cit.*, p. 97.
41 Taylor, A. J. P.: *Bismarck, The I
   and the Statesman* (1955), cited
   Taylor I, New English Libr
   Mentor ed., p. 41.
42 Longford, *op. cit.*, p. 316.
43 *ibid.*
44 Gernsheim, Helmut and Alis
   Edward VII and Queen Alexar
   (1962), p. 23.
45 Fulford II, *op. cit.*, p. 181.
46 Bennett, *op. cit.*, p. 125.
47 Fulford II, *op. cit.*, p. 214.
48 *ibid.*, pp. 224–9; Balfour, *op. cit.*,
   67–8.
49 Bennett, *op. cit.*, pp. 127–8; Fulf
   II, *op. cit.*, p. 215.
50 Zedlitz-Trützschler, Robert, Co
   von: *Twelve Years at the Kais
   Court* (1923), p. 199.
51 Fulford II, *op. cit.*, p. 36.
52 *ibid.*, p. 203.
53 *ibid.*, p. 216.
54 Kaiser I, *op. cit.*, p. 3.
55 *ibid.*, p. 6; Pope-Hennessy, James (e
   Queen Victoria at Windsor and Balmo
   (1959), cited as Pope-Hennessy
   p. 57.
56 Aronson I, *op. cit.*, p. 123.
57 Kürenberg, *op. cit.*, p. 27; Benne
   op. cit., p. 138.
58 Epton, Nina: *Victoria and I
   Daughters* (1971), p. 122.
59 Kaiser I, *op. cit.*, pp. 16–17.

Chapter Three (pp. 27–43)
BOYHOOD

1 Taylor I, *op. cit.*, p. 67: Masur, *o
   cit.*, p. 78.
2 Ponsonby, Sir Frederick (First Lo
   Sysonby) (ed.): *Letters of the Empre
   Frederick* (1928), cited as Ponsonby
   p. 64.
3 *ibid.*, p. 60.
4 Taylor I, *op. cit.*, p. 87.

Middlemas, Keith: *The Life and Times of Edward VII* (1972), pp. 20–1.

Fulford II, *op. cit.*, p. 239.

Cassels, Lavender: *Clash of Generations* (1972), p. 92.

Kaiser I, *op. cit.*, p. 17.

ibid., p. 19.

Aronson I, *op. cit.*, p. 71.

Kaiser I, *op. cit.*, p. 23.

ibid., p. 24.

ibid., p. 19.

ibid., p. 18.

ibid., p. 34.

ibid., p. 35.

Masur, *op. cit.*, p. 88.

Taylor I, *op cit.*, p. 66.

Kürenberg, *op. cit.*, p. 9.

Hough, *op. cit.*, p. 32.

Kaiser I, *op. cit.*, pp. 35–7.

ibid., p. 38.

ibid., p. 54.

ibid., p. 39.

ibid., p. 41.

Fisher, Admiral of the Fleet, Lord: *Memories* (1919), p. 230.

Aronson, Theo: *The Fall of the Third Napoleon* (1970), cited as Aronson II, p. 107.

ibid., p. 149.

ibid., p. 128

Martin, Ralph G.: *Lady Randolph Churchill*, in 2 vols. (1969), I, p. 28.

Aronson I, *op. cit.*, p. 98.

ibid., p. 86.

ibid., pp. 88–9.

Böhme, Helmut (ed.): *Die Reichsgründung* (1967), pp. 25–6, q.v. Röhl I.

Masur, *op. cit.*, p. 60.

Balfour, *op. cit.*, p. 69.

Epton, *op. cit.*, p. 127.

Kaiser I, *op. cit.*, p. 44.

ibid., p. 45.

Ponsonby I, *op. cit.*, p. 118.

ibid., pp. 119–20.

Kaiser I, *op. cit.*, pp. 54–5.

Queen Victoria: *Letters*, II, i, p. 297.

Queen Victoria: *Letters*, II, ii, p. 99.

Hansard's Parliamentary Debates, Third Series, Vol. CCIV, February–March, 1871, p. 82, q.v. Röhl I.

Masur, *op. cit.*, p. 63.

Aronson I, *op. cit.*, pp. 97–8; Bennett, *op. cit.*, p. 192.

Kaiser I, *op. cit.*, p. 49.

ibid., pp. 60–61.

Epton, *op. cit.*, p. 141.

Kaiser I, *op. cit.*, p. 51.

ibid., p. 65.

53 *ibid.*, p. 52.

54 Masur, *op. cit.*, p. 74.

55 Palmer, A. W.: *A Dictionary of Modern History, 1789–1945* (1962), Penguin ed., p. 269.

56 Kaiser I, *op. cit.*, pp. 71–3.

57 Bennett, *op. cit.*, p. 193.

58 Longford, *op. cit.*, p. 393.

59 Bennett, *op. cit.*, p. 194.

60 Kaiser I, *op. cit.*, p. 70.

61 *ibid.*, pp. 76–80.

62 Masur, *op. cit.*, p. 77.

63 Kaiser I, *op. cit.*, p. 77.

64 *ibid.*, p. 79.

65 Magnus, Sir Philip: *King Edward the Seventh* (1964), cited as Magnus I, p. 128; Ponsonby I, *op. cit.*, pp. 134–35.

Chapter Four (pp. 44–49)

SCHOOLDAYS

1 Kaiser I, *op. cit.*, p. 100.

2 *ibid.*, p. 99.

3 Wheeler-Bennett, Sir John: *Knaves, Fools and Heroes* (1974), cited as Wheeler-Bennett I, p. 185.

4 Cowles, *op. cit.*, p. 44.

5 Bülow, *op. cit.*, II, p. 450.

6 Kaiser I, *op. cit.*, p. 102.

7 Cottrell, Leonard: *The Bull of Minos* (1953), pp. 37 ff. and 72.

8 Kaiser I, *op. cit.*, pp. 109, 111–13.

9 Aronson I, *op. cit.*, p. 107.

10 Martin, *op. cit.*, I, p. 102.

11 Kaiser I, *op. cit.*, p. 114.

12 Jowett, Benjamin: *Letters* (1899), p. 198.

13 Ponsonby I, *op. cit.*, pp. 174–5.

14 Kürenberg, *op. cit.*, p. 36.

15 Kaiser I, *op. cit.*, p. 154.

16 *ibid.*, p. 115.

Chapter Five (pp. 50–72)

THE YOUNG PRINCE

1 Clark, Sir Kenneth (Lord Clark): *The Nude* (1956), Pelican ed., p. 366; Groenewegen-Frankfort, H. A. and Ashmole, Bernard: *The Ancient World* (1967), Mentor ed., pp. 222–3

2 Masur, *op. cit.*, p. 102.

3 Ludwig, Emil: *Kaiser Wilhelm II*, trs. E. C. Mayne (1926), p. 9.

4 Kaiser I, *op. cit.*, p. 126; Queen Victoria: *Letters*, II, ii, p. 543.

5 Queen Marie of Roumania: *The Story of my Life*, in 2 vols. (1934), I, pp. 222–5.

6 Queen Victoria: *Letters*, II, ii, pp. 592–3.

7 Bennett, *op. cit.*, p. 211.

8 Kaiser I, *op. cit.*, pp. 119–22.

9 Taylor I, *op. cit.*, p. 9.

10 *ibid.*, pp. 11–12.

11 Fraser, Lady Antonia: *Cromwell, Our Chief of Men* (1973), p. 404.

12 Balfour, *op. cit.*, pp. 105–6.

13 Taylor I, *op. cit.*, pp. 39–41.

14 Kaiser I, *op. cit.*, pp. 188–9.

15 *ibid.*, pp. 127–38.

16 Duff I, *op. cit.*, pp. 187 and 192–3; Hough, *op. cit.*, p. 53.

17 Tuchman, Barbara W.: *The Guns of August* (1962), Dell ed., p. 91.

18 Queen Victoria: *Letters*, II, ii, p. 626.

19 Aronson I, *op. cit.*, p. 115.

20 Kaiser I, *op. cit.*, pp. 140–41.

21 Aronson I, *op. cit.*, pp. 118–19.

22 Maurois, André: *Disraeli*, trs. Hamish Miles (1927), ed. of 1962, p. 290.

23 Cassels, *op. cit.*, p. 26.

24 Maurois, *op. cit.*, p. 291.

25 Churchill, Winston, *The World Crisis*, revised and abridged ed. in 2 vols (1939), I, p. 107.

26 Taylor I, *op. cit.*, p. 138.

27 Aronson I, *op. cit.*, p. 119.

28 Kaiser I, *op. cit.*, pp. 141–4.

29 Pound, *op. cit.*, p. 113.

30 Kaiser I, *op. cit.*, p. 144.

31 *ibid.*, p. 146.

32 Duff I, *op. cit.*, p. 178.

33 Queen Victoria: *Letters*, II, ii, p. 647.

34 Duff I, *op. cit.*, p. 181.

35 Leslie, Anita: *Edwardians in Love* (1972), pp. 203–4; Longford, *op. cit.*, pp. 425–6.

36 Ponsonby I, *op. cit.*, p. 173.

37 *ibid.*, p. 215.

38 Kaiser I, *op. cit.*, p. 147.

39 Aronson I, *op. cit.*, p. 122.

40 Kaiser I, *op. cit.*, p. 183.

41 Duff I, *op. cit.*, p. 193.

42 *ibid.*, p. 197.

43 Bennett, *op. cit.*, p. 133.

44 *ibid.*, p. 212.

45 Kaiser I, *op. cit.*, p. 263.

46 Balfour, *op. cit.*, p. 64.

47 Masur, *op. cit.*, p. 72.

48 Pulzer, P. G.: *The Rise of Political Anti-Semitism in Germany and Austria* (1964), pp. 50–2.

49 Kaiser I, *op. cit.*, pp. 149–50; Ponsonby I, *op. cit.*, p. 215.

50 Passant, E. J.: *A Short History of Germany, 1815–1945* (1971). p. 97; Palmer, *op. cit.*, p. 111.

51 Taylor, A. J. P.: *The Course of German History* (1945), cited as Taylor II, University Paperback ed., pp. 141–2.

52 Masur, *op. cit.*, p. 107.
53 Taylor I, *op. cit.*, p. 151.
54 Magnus, Sir Philip: *Gladstone* (1954), cited as Magnus II, 1974 ed., p. 264.
55 Fulford II, *op. cit.*, p. 65.
56 Thaddeus, H. Jones: *Recollections of a Court Painter* (1912), pp. 113–17
57 Longford, *op. cit.*, p. 116.
58 Gernsheim, *op. cit.*, p. 64.
59 Topham, *op. cit.*, pp. 147–9.
60 Keller, Mathilde, Countess von: *40 Jahre in Dienst der Kaiserin* (1935), p. 22.
61 Kaiser I, *op. cit.*, p. 184.
62 Aronson I, *op. cit.*, p. 103.

Chapter Six (pp. 73–93)
MARRIAGE

1 Private Information.
2 Aronson I, *op. cit.*, p. 141.
3 Ponsonby I, *op. cit.*, pp. 206–7.
4 Kaiser I, *op. cit.*, p. 200.
5 *ibid.*, pp. 198–9.
6 *ibid.*, p. 200; Holstein Papers, op. cit., II, p. 317;Wheeler-Bennett, Sir John: *Three Episodes in the Life of William II* (1956), cited as Wheeler-Bennett II, p. 12.
7 Kaiser I, *op. cit.*, p. 221.
8 Baily, Leslie: *The Gilbert and Sullivan Book* (1952), p. 196.
9 Fischer, Henry W. (ed.): *Private Lives of William II and His Consort and Secret History of the Court of Berlin, June 1888–Spring 1898, papers and diaries of Ursula, Countess von Eppinghoven,* 1 unabridged vol. and in 2 vols. (1904), cited as Fischer II and Fischer III, III, p. 327.
10 *ibid.*, pp. 334–5.
11 *ibid.*, p. 327.
12 *ibid.*, p. 322.
13 Balfour, *op. cit.*, p. 89.
14 Mitford, *op. cit.*, pp. 16–18 and 26.
15 Fischer I, *op. cit.*, p. 25.
16 *ibid.*, p. 48.
17 *ibid.*, p. 47.
18 Fischer III, *op. cit.*, p. 198.
19 Topham, *op. cit.*, p. 59.
20 Wilson, *op. cit.*, p. 183.
21 Fischer I, *op. cit.*, p. 68.
22 Kaiser I, *op. cit.*, pp. 232–3.
23 Cotterell, *op. cit.*, p. 93.
24 Magnus I, *op. cit.*, p. 177; Gernsheim, *op. cit.*, p. 64.
25 Bennett, *op. cit.*, p. 214.
26 *ibid.*, p. 216.
27 Lee, Sir Sidney: *King Edward VII* in 2 vols (1925), I, p. 478.

28 Poschinger, Heinrich von: *Conversations with Bismarck* (1900), p. 164, q.v. Röhl I.
29 Apsler, Alfred: *Iron Chancellor, Otto von Bismarck* (1968), Folkestone ed. of 1972, p. 145.
30 Taylor I, *op. cit.*, p. 153.
31 Masur, *op. cit.*, pp. 187–9.
32 Taylor I, *op. cit.*, p. 153.
33 Kaiser I, *op. cit.*, pp. 237–8.
34 *ibid.*, pp. 222–4.
35 *ibid.*, p. 236.
36 Bennett, *op. cit.*, pp. 216–17.
37 Duff, David: *The Shy Princess* (1958), cited as Duff II, p. 110.
38 *ibid.*, p. 111; Ponsonby, Arthur (Lord Ponsonby of Shulbrede): *Henry Ponsonby. His Life from His Letters* (1942), cited as H. Ponsonby, pp. 300–303.
39 Epton, *op. cit.*, p. 171.
40 Kürenberg, *op. cit.*, pp. 42–3.
41 Balfour, *op. cit.*, p. 100.
42 Kürenberg, *op. cit.*, p. 43.
43 Hough, *op. cit.*, p. 128.
44 Corti, Egon Caesar, Count: *The English Empress* (1957), cited as Corti I, pp. 225–7.
45 Pope-Hennessy I, *op. cit.*, p. 18.
46 Kaiser I, *op. cit.*, p. 263.
47 Ludwig, *op. cit.*, p. 16.
48 Aronson I, *op. cit.*, p. 130.
49 *ibid.*, p. 131.
50 Cecil, Lady Gwendolen: *Life of Robert, Marquis of Salisbury,* (1931–32) IV, p. 124.
51 Taylor I, *op. cit.*, p. 152.
52 Kürenberg, *op. cit.*, p. 89.
53 Ponsonby I, *op. cit.*, p. 383; Balfour, *op. cit.*, p. 191.
54 Pless, Daisy, Princess of: *Daisy Princess of Pless,* coll. D. Chapman-Huston (1928), p. 225.
55 Nowak, *op. cit.*, p. 50.
56 Holstein Papers, *op. cit.*, I, p. 137.
57 Balfour, *op. cit.*, p. 91.
58 Kaiser I, *op. cit.*, p. 190.
59 Kürenberg, *op. cit.*, p. 118.
60 Haller, Johannes: *Philip Eulenburg, The Kaiser's Friend,* English Ed. in 2 vols., trs. E. C. Mayne (1930), I, p. 187.
61 Kürenberg, *op. cit.*, p. 120.
62 Haller, *op. cit.*, I, p. 39.
63 Taylor, Edmond, *The Fossil Monarchies* (1963), cited as Edmond Taylor, Penguin ed. of 1967, p. 202.
64 Kaiser I, *op. cit.*, pp. 244 and 246.
65 Pound, *op. cit.*, p. 36; Private Information.

66 Pound, *op. cit.*, p. 243.
67 Aronson I, *op. cit.*, p. 139.
68 Communication from Cecilia, Gr von Sternberg.
69 Harrison, Michael: *Clarence* (19 pp. 210 and 217.
70 Ludwig, *op. cit.*, p. 32.
71 Kaiser I, *op. cit.*, pp. 261–2.
72 Hough, *op. cit.*, pp. 138–40.
73 Cassels, *op. cit.*, pp. 159–60.
74 *ibid.*, p. 161; Aronson I, *op. cit.*, p.
75 Kaiser I, *op. cit.*, p. 185.
76 Thimme, Friedrich (ed.): *Dir Gr Politik der Europäischen Kabin 1871–1914,* cited, by docum number, as Die Grosse Politik, 982 (1922–27).
77 Kaiser I, *op. cit.*, p. 289.

Chapter Seven (pp. 94–112)
THREE KAISERS

1 Aronson I, *op. cit.*, p. 148.
2 *ibid.*, p. 149.
3 Bennet, *op. cit.*, p. 222.
4 Ponsonby I, *op. cit.*, p. 225.
5 Kaiser I, *op. cit.*, p. 274.
6 Aronson I, *op. cit.*, p. 154.
7 Bennett, *op. cit.*, p. 223.
8 Ponsonby I, *op. cit.*, p. 225.
9 *ibid.*, p. 226.
10 Rodd, Sir Rennell (Lord Rennell Rodd): *Social and Diplomatic Men ories,* in 3 vols (1922), I, p. 112.
11 Ponsonby I, *op. cit.*, p. 229.
12 Kaiser I, *op. cit.*, p. 275.
13 Ponsonby I, *op. cit.*, p. 284.
14 *ibid.*, pp. 228–30.
15 *ibid.*, p. 284.
16 Bennett, *op. cit.*, p. 230.
17 Ponsonby I, *op. cit.*, p. 284.
18 Corti I, *op. cit.*, p. 244.
19 Bennett, *op. cit.*, p. 230.
20 Balfour, *op. cit.*, p. 109; Aronson op. cit., p. 165.
21 Kaiser I, *op. cit.*, pp. 276–7.
22 Bismarck, Otto, Prince von: *Recol lections and Reminiscences* in 2 vols ed. A. M. Gibdon (1940), II, p. 329
23 Kaiser I, *op. cit.*, pp. 225–7.
24 Corti I, *op. cit.*, p. 244.
25 Kürenberg, *op. cit.*, p. 50; Ludwig *op. cit.*, p. 37; Benson, E. F.: *The Kaiser and his English Relations* (1936) p. 51.
26 Kaiser I, *op. cit.*, p. 215.
27 Holstein Papers, *op. cit.*, III, p. 219.
28 Duff II, *op. cit.*, p. 147.
29 Leslie, *op. cit.*, p. 33.
30 Gower, Lord Ronald Sutherland: *Old Diaries, 1881–1901* (1902), p. 57.

1 Kaiser I, *op. cit.*, p. 228.
2 Ponsonby I, *op. cit.*, p. 240.
3 *ibid.*, pp. 243–5; Holstein Papers, *op. cit.*, II, p. 351.
4 Kürenberg, *op. cit.*, p. 55.
5 Kaiser I, *op. cit.*, p. 278.
6 Ponsonby I, *op. cit.*, pp. 250–51.
7 Balfour, *op. cit.*, p. 457.
8 Ponsonby I, *op. cit.*, pp. 251–2.
9 *ibid.*, p. 254; Rodd, *op. cit.*, I, p. 123.
10 Nowak, *op. cit.*, p. 8.
11 Ponsonby I, *op. cit.*, pp. 339–41.
12 *ibid.*, p. 260.
13 Kaiser I, *op. cit.*, p. 279.
14 *ibid.*, pp. 280–81.
15 Ponsonby I, *op. cit.*, pp. 256 and 257.
16 Rodd, *op. cit.*, I, p. 123.
17 Balfour, *op. cit.*, p. 113.
18 *ibid.*, p. 115.
19 Balfour, *op. cit.*, pp. 115–16.
20 Jonas, Klaus W.: *The Life of Crown Prince William*, trs. C. W. Bangert (1961), p. 3.
51 Taylor I, *op. cit.*, p. 179.
52 Kaiser I, *op. cit.*, p. 285.
53 Bennett, *op. cit.*, p. 223.
54 Ponsonby I, *op. cit.*, p. 276.
55 Kaiser I, *op. cit.*, p. 286.
56 Ponsonby I, *op. cit.*, p. 279.
57 Aronson I, *op. cit.*, p. 169.
58 Wilson, *op. cit.*, pp. 24–5.
59 Haller, *op. cit.*, I, p. 55.
60 Kaiser I, *op. cit.*, pp. 288–9.
61 Kürenberg, *op. cit.*, p. 61.
62 Schwering, Axel, Count von: *The Berlin Court Under William II* (1915), pp. 25–6.
63 *ibid.*, p. 21.
64 Kaiser I, *op. cit.*, pp. 289–90.
65 Corti, Egon Caesar, Count: *Alexander von Battenberg*, tr. E. M. Hodgson (1954), cited as Corti II, p. 288.
66 Ponsonby I, *op. cit.*, p. 299.
67 *ibid.*, p. 300.
68 Queen Victoria: *Letters*, III, i, p. 403.
69 Longford, *op. cit.*, p. 506.
70 *ibid.*
71 Balfour, *op. cit.*, p. 118.
72 Busch, M.: *Bismarck, Some Secret Passages of His History*, in 3 vols. (1898), III, p. 187.
73 Ponsonby I, *op. cit.*, p. 311.
74 Aronson I, *op. cit.*, p. 184.
75 Haller, *op. cit.*, I, p. 54.
76 Nowak, *op. cit.*, pp. 21–3.
77 Duff I, *op. cit.*, p. 222.
78 Aronson I, *op. cit.*, p. 186.

79 Kaiser I, *op. cit.*, p. 292.
80 Duff I, *op. cit.*, p. 222; Hough, *op. cit.*, p. 147.
81 Bennett, *op. cit.*, p. 258.
82 Kaiser I, *op. cit.*, p. 327.
83 *ibid.*, p. 295.
84 Aronson I, *op. cit.*, p. 186.
85 Kaiser I, *op. cit.*, pp. 296–7.
86 Aronson I, *op. cit.*, p. 187.
87 Ponsonby I, *op. cit.*, p. 313; Aronson I, *op. cit.*, pp. 188–9.
88 Kaiser I, *op. cit.*, p. 299.
89 Bennett, *op. cit.*, p. 262.
90 Fischer I, *op. cit.*, pp. 348–9.
91 Magnus I, *op. cit.*, pp. 202–3.
92 Balfour, *op. cit.*, pp. 118–19.
93 Aronson I, *op. cit.*, p. 299; Bennett, *op. cit.*, pp. 263–4.
94 Cecil, *op. cit.*, IV, p. 96.

Chapter Eight (pp. 113–140)
THE GREAT STEALER OF OUR PEOPLE'S HEARTS

1 Princess Marie Louise: *My Memories of Six Reigns* (1956), Penguin ed., p. 53.
2 Nowak, *op. cit.*, p. 111.
3 Topham, *op. cit.*, p. 210.
4 Fischer I, *op. cit.*, pp. 25–6.
5 Jonas, *op. cit.*, p. 4.
6 Aronson I, *op. cit.*, p. 215.
7 Princess Alice: *For My Grandchildren* (1966), p. 93.
8 Cowles, *op. cit.*, p. 175.
9 Topham, *op. cit.*, p. 210.
10 Ponsonby I, *op. cit.*, p. 214.
11 Wilson, *op. cit.*, p. 102.
12 Topham, *op. cit.*, p. 45.
13 Kürenberg, *op. cit.*, p. 75.
14 Balfour, *op. cit.*, p. 138.
15 Kürenberg, *op. cit.*, p. 72.
16 Masur, *op. cit.*, p. 92.
17 Cowles, *op. cit.*, p. 175; Gore, John: *King George V, A Personal Memoir* (1941) Albemarle Lib. ed., p. 61.
18 Queen Marie, *op. cit.*, I, p. 285.
19 Ponsonby I, *op. cit.*, pp. 322–3.
20 Balfour, *op. cit.*, p. 335; Spitzemberg, Baronin: *Tagebuch* (1960), p. 398.
21 Aronson I, *op. cit.*, p. 193; Ludwig, *op. cit.*, pp. 54–5; Ponsonby I, *op. cit.*, p. 318.
22 Queen Victoria: *Letters*, III, i, p. 417.
23 Hough, *op. cit.*, p. 144.
24 Ponsonby I, *op. cit.*, p. 318.
25 *ibid.*, p. 319.
26 Ludwig, *op. cit.*, p. 57.
27 *ibid.*, p. 56; Nowak, *op. cit.*, p. 26; Kaiser I, *op. cit.*, pp. 298–9.

28 Queen Victoria: *Letters*, III, i, pp. 418–19.
29 Balfour, *op. cit.*, p. 120.
30 Haller, *op. cit.*, I, p. 57.
31 Ludwig, *op. cit.*, p. 56.
32 Balfour, *op. cit.*, p. 121.
33 H. Ponsonby, *op. cit.*, pp. 110–11.
34 Ponsonby I, *op. cit.*, p. 324.
35 Queen Victoria: *Letters*, III, i, p. 423.
36 *ibid.*, p. 425.
37 *ibid.*, p. 429.
38 Nowak, *op. cit.*, p. 45.
39 *ibid.*
40 *ibid.*, p. 50.
41 *ibid.*, p. 28.
42 *ibid.*, p. 50.
43 *ibid.*, p. 27.
44 Schwering, *op. cit.*, p. 151.
45 Masur, *op. cit.*, p. 88.
46 Nowak, *op. cit.*, p. 29.
47 Pless, Daisy, Princess of: *The Private Diaries of* (1950), Albemarle Lib. ed. combining selections from *Daisy Princess of Pless* (1928) and *From My Private Diary* (1931), cited as Pless II, pp. 64 and 106.
48 Ponsonby I, *op. cit.*, p. 322.
49 Masur, *op. cit.*, pp. 93–4.
50 Kürenberg, *op. cit.*, p. 157.
51 Topham, *op. cit.*, pp. 30 and 107–8.
52 Fischer I, *op. cit.*, p. 88.
53 Ludwig, *op. cit.*, p. 78.
54 Taylor I, *op. cit.*, p. 184.
55 Ponsonby I, *op. cit.*, p. 327.
56 Longford, *op. cit.*, pp. 507–8.
57 Ponsonby I, *op. cit.*, p. 330.
58 Masur, *op. cit.*, p. 177.
59 Taylor I, *op. cit.*, p. 182.
60 Magnus I, *op. cit.*, p. 208.
61 Kürenberg, *op. cit.*, p. 129.
62 Kaiser I, *op. cit.*, pp. 229–30.
63 Magnus I, *op. cit.*, p. 209.
64 Röhl, John C. G., Ed.: *Philipp Eulenburgs Politische Korrespondenz*, in 3 vols., Vol I *Von der Reichsgrüdung bis zum Neuen Kurs 1866–1891*, cited as Röhl II (1976).
65 Fischer I, *op. cit.*, p. 30.
66 Ponsonby I, *op. cit.*, p. 352.
67 Pope-Hennessy, James: *Queen Mary* (1959), cited as Pope-Hennessy II, p. 331; Fodor, Eugene (ed.): *Fodor's Germany* (1971), p. 122.
68 Ponsonby I, *op. cit.*, p. 364.
69 Princess Alice, *op. cit.*, p. 70.
70 Queen Victoria: *Letters*, III, i, p. 451.
71 Zedlitz-Trützschler, *op. cit.*, p. 114.
72 Pless II, *op. cit.*, pp. 294–5.
73 Topham, *op. cit.*, p. 135.

74 Balfour, *op. cit.*, pp. 152–5.
75 Topham, *op. cit.*, p. 182.
76 Cassels, *op. cit.*, pp. 200–3, 205, 207–209.
77 Balfour, *op. cit.*, p. 120.
78 Pope-Hennessy I, *op. cit.*, p. 44.
79 Epton, *op. cit.*, p. 193.
80 Fulford, Roger: *Queen Victoria* (1951), cited as Fulford III, p. 134.
81 Leslie, *op. cit.*, p. 136; Gernsheim, *op. cit.*, p. 67.
82 Queen Victoria: *Letters*, III, i, p. 504.
83 *ibid.*, pp. 520–22.
84 *ibid.*, p. 485.
85 Ponsonby I, *op. cit.*, p. 369.
86 Haller, *op. cit.*, I, pp. 83–4.
87 *ibid.*, p. 47.
88 Taylor I, *op. cit.*, p. 183.
89 Röhl, J. C. G.: Review article on 'Friedrich von Holstein by Norman Rich (1965),', *The Historical Journal*, ix, 3, (1966), cited as Röhl III, p. 380.
90 Taylor I, *op. cit.*, p. 187.
91 Viereck, G. S.: *The Kaiser on Trial* (1938), p. 124.
92 Nowak, *op. cit.*, p. 134; Kürenberg, *op. cit.*, p. 134; Wilson, *op. cit.*, p. 51.
93. Rich, Norman: *Friedrich von Holstein, Politics and Diplomacy in the Era of Bismarck and Wilhelm II*, in 2 vols. (1965).
94 Wilson, *op. cit.*, p. 51.
95 Balfour, *op. cit.*, p. 168.
96 Nowak, *op. cit.*, pp. 131–4.
97 Kürenberg, *op. cit.*, pp. 134–5.
98 Nowak, *op. cit.*, pp. 141–2.
99 *ibid.*, p. 129.
100 Viereck, *op. cit.*, p. 100.
101 *ibid.*, p. 102.
102 Röhl IV, *op. cit.*, pp. 381, 387, 388.
103 Ponsonby, I., *op. cit.*, pp. 400–2.
104 Princess Marie Louise, *op. cit.*, p. 75.
105 Nowak, *op. cit.*, p. 192.
106 Taylor I, *op. cit.*, p. 191.
107 Röhl IV, *op. cit.*, pp. 382, 383.
108 Taylor I, *op. cit.*, pp. 196–7; Kürenberg, *op. cit.*, pp. 80–2; Apsler, *op. cit.*, pp. 171, 172. Balfour, *op. cit.*, p. 132.
109 Kürenberg, *op. cit.*, p. 82.
110 Balfour, *op. cit.*, p. 133.
111 Kürenberg, *op. cit.*, p. 83.
112 *ibid.*, p. 82.
113 Wilson, *op. cit.*, p. 80.

Chapter Nine (pp. 141–164)
FULL STEAM AHEAD
1 Ponsonby I, *op. cit.*, pp. 413–14.
2 Balfour, *op. cit.*, pp. 133–4.

3 Kürenberg, *op. cit.*, p. 83.
4 Kaiser William II: *My Memories 1879–1918* (1922), cited as Kasier II, p. 18.
5 Balfour, *op. cit.*, pp. 136–7.
6 Taylor I, *op. cit.*, p. 152.
7 Balfour, *op. cit.*, p. 177.
8 Kürenberg, *op. cit.*, p. 232.
9 *ibid.*, p. 83.
10 Pope-Hennessy II, *op. cit.*, p. 147.
11 *ibid.*, p. 239.
12 Pope-Hennessy I, *op. cit.*, p. 101.
13 Fischer I, *op. cit.*, p. 31.
14 *ibid.*, pp. 49–51.
15 Jonas, *op. cit.*, p. 6.
16 Fischer I, *op. cit.*, pp. 330–1.
17 Corti I, *op. cit.*, p. 337.
18 Bennett, *op. cit.*, p. 301.
19 Lee, Arthur Gould (ed.): *The Empress Frederick writes to Sophie, Letters 1889–1901* (1955), p. 21; Epton, *op. cit.*, p. 199.
20 Fischer I, *op. cit.*, p. 142.
21 Kaiser II, *op. cit.*, p. 53.
22 Balfour, *op. cit.*, p. 125.
23 Ponsonby I, *op. cit.*, pp. 417–18.
24 Masur, *op. cit.*, p. 231.
25 Ponsonby I, *op. cit.*, pp. 422–4.
26 Haller, *op. cit.*, I, pp. 200–1.
27 *ibid.*
28 Balfour, *op. cit.*, p. 158.
29 Haller, *op. cit.*, I, p. 197.
30 Magnus I, *op. cit.*, p. 228.
31 Balfour, *op. cit.*, pp. 180–1.
32 Whyte, A. F. (trs. and condenser): *A Field Marshal's Memoirs from the Diary, Correspondence and Papers of Alfred, Count v. Waldersee* (1924), pp. 167–8.
33 Goerlitz, Walter: *History of the German General Staff*, trs. B. Battershaw (1955), p. 129.
34 Fischer I, *op. cit.*, pp. 322–3.
35 Ponsonby I, *op. cit.*, p. 429.
36 Haller, *op. cit.*, I, pp. 202–3.
37 Balfour, *op. cit.*, pp. 158 and 463.
38 Queen Victoria: *Letters*, III, iii, p. 621.
39 Kürenberg, *op. cit.*, p. 165.
40 Balfour, *op. cit.*, p. 155; Haller, *op. cit.*, I, p. 205.
41 Haller, *op. cit.*, I, p. 206.
42 *ibid.*
43 *ibid.*, I, pp. 208–9.
44 *ibid.*, I, p. 190.
45 *ibid.*, I, pp. 178–9.
46 Gower, *op. cit.*, p. 174; Balfour, *op. cit.*, p. 181.
47 Hough, *op. cit.*, p. 175.
48 Haller, *op. cit.*, I, p. 144.
49 *ibid.*, I, p. 146.
50 *ibid.*, I, p. 145.

51 Queen Victoria: *Letters*, III, pp. 293–4.
52 Massie, Robert K.: *Nicholas Alexandra* (1968), p. 23.
53 *ibid.*, p. 30.
54 Princess Alice, *op. cit.*, p. 41.
55 Massie, *op. cit.*, pp. 31–2.
56 Paléologue, Maurice: *An Intimate Journal of the Dreyfus Case* (195_), p. 180.
57 Cowles, *op. cit.*, p. 147.
58 Bernstein, H.: *The Willy-Nic_ Correspondence* (1918).
59 Fischer I, *op. cit.*, p. 21.
60 Balfour, *op. cit.*, pp. 163–4.
61 Fischer I, *op. cit.*, pp. 203–4.
62 *ibid.*, pp. 33–5.
63 *ibid.*, p. 199.
64 *ibid.*, pp. 202–3.
65 Topham, *op. cit.*, p. 177.
66 *ibid.*, p. 195.
67 Fischer I, *op. cit.*, pp. 310–11.
68 Kürenberg, *op. cit.*, p. 96.
69 Fischer I, *op. cit.*, p. 211.
70 Bennett, *op. cit.*, p. 306.
71 Fischer I, *op. cit* pp. 288–9.
72 Kürenberg, *op. cit.*, p. 96.
73 Fischer I, *op. cit.*, p. 217.
74 *ibid.*, p. 221; Kürenberg, *op. ci_* p. 97.
75 Ludwig, *op. cit.*, pp. 136–8; Fischer *op. cit.*, p. 221; Eyck, Erich: *D_ Persönliche Regiment Wilhelms _ Politische Geschichte des deutsche_ Kaiserreiches von 1890 bis 1914* (1948_ p. 84.
76 Fischer I, *op. cit.*, p. 224.
77 Fischer III, *op. cit.*, pp. 322–3.
78 Fischer I, *op. cit.*, p. 224.
79 H. Ponsonby, *op. cit.*, p. 391
80 Queen Victoria: *Letters*, III, i_ p. 424.
81 Fischer I, *op. cit.*, pp. 23–4.
82 Passant, *op. cit.*, p. 117.
83 Taylor II, *op. cit.*, p. 157.
84 Balfour, *op. cit.*, pp. 170 and 173.
85 Taylor II, *op. cit.*, p. 160; Passant *op. cit.*, pp. 118–19.
86 Ludwig, *op. cit.*, p. 130.
87 Passant, *op. cit.*, p. 118.
88 *ibid.*, p. 119; Balfour, *op. cit.*, pp 170–1.
89 Balfour, *op. cit.*, p. 174.
90 Haller, *op. cit.*, I, p. 112.
91 Nichols, J. Alden: *Germany after Bismarck* (1958), p. 357.
92 Balfour, *op. cit.*, pp. 177–8.
93 Kürenberg, *op. cit.*, pp. 91–2; Haller, *op. cit.*, I, p. 177.
94 Kürenberg, *op. cit.*, p. 93.

Balfour, *op. cit.*, p. 178.
Spitzemberg, *op. cit.*, p. 386.
Eyck, *op. cit.*, p. 84.
Balfour, *op. cit.*, p. 179.
Haller, *op. cit.*, I, p. 287.
Passant, *op. cit.*, p. 119.
Haller, *op. cit.*, I, p. 114.
ibid., I, p. 252.
Balfour, *op. cit.*, p. 167.
Haller, *op. cit.*, I, pp. 260–265.
Balfour, *op. cit.*, p. 186.

Chapter Ten (pp. 165–193)

THE STUMM ERA

1 Haller, *op. cit.*, I, p. 217.
2 Zedlitz-Trützschler, *op. cit.*, p. 39.
3 Thaddeus, *op. cit.*, pp. 302–3.
4 *ibid.*, p. 131.
5 Balfour, *op. cit.*, p. 187.
6 *ibid.*
7 Haller, *op. cit.*, II, p. 192.
8 Schwering, *op. cit.*, p. 167.
9 *ibid.*
10 Taylor II, *op. cit.*, pp. 164–5.
11 Passant, *op. cit.*, p. 120.
12 Kürenberg, *op. cit.*, p. 94.
13 Balfour, *op. cit.*, p. 169.
14 *ibid.*, p. 170.
15 Passant, *op. cit.*, p. 121.
16 Röhl I, *op. cit.*, p. 33.
17 Schwering, *op. cit.*, pp. 103–4.
18 Boehlich, Walter: *Der Berliner Antisemitismusstreit* (1965), p. 81.
19 Die Grosse Politik, *op. cit.*, XX 6376.
20 Schwering, *op. cit.*, pp. 141 and 145
21 Balfour, *op. cit.*, p. 164.
22 Röhl I, *op. cit.*, p. 33.
23 Masur, *op. cit.*, p. 112.
24 *ibid.*, pp. 159–60, and 169.
25 *ibid.*, pp. 145–6.
26 Balfour, *op. cit.*, p. 159.
27 Die Grosse Politik, *op. cit.*, XIII 3399.
28 Balfour, *op. cit.*, p. 190.
29 *ibid.*, p. 191.
30 *ibid.*, p. 194; Röhl III, *op. cit.*, p. 379.
31 Carrington, Charles: *Rudyard Kipling* (1955), Pelican ed., p. 281.
32 Balfour, *op. cit.*, p. 195.
33 Queen Victoria: *Letters*, III, iii, pp. 8–9.
34 Carrington, *op. cit.*, p. 281.
35 Balfour, *op. cit.*, p. 193.
36 Lee, *op. cit.*, I, p. 727.
37 Carrington, *op. cit.*, p. 451.
38 Balfour, *op. cit.*, p. 196.
39 Queen Victoria: *Letters*, III, iii, p. 198.
40 *ibid.*, p. 173.
41 Gower, *op. cit.*, p. 306.

42 Haller, *op. cit.*, II, p. 10.
43 Cowles, *op. cit.*, p. 156.
44 Balfour, *op. cit.*, pp. 159 and 464.
45 Haller, *op. cit.*, I, pp. 378–9.
46 Balfour, *op. cit.*, p. 198.
47 Haller, *op. cit.*, II, pp. 27–8.
48 Balfour, *op. cit.*, p. 201.
49 *ibid.*, p. 203.
50 Taylor I, *op. cit.*, p. 206.
51 *ibid.*, p. 105.
52 Tirpitz, Alfred, Grand Admiral von: *My Memoirs*, in 2 vols (1919), I, p. 102.
53 Taylor I, *op. cit.*, p. 206.
54 Jonas, *op. cit.*, p. 8.
55 Kürenberg, *op. cit.*, p. 106.
56 Duff I, *op. cit.*, p. 290.
57 Queen Victoria: *Letters*, III, iii, p. 244.
58 Die Grosse Politik, *op. cit.*, XV 4195.
59 Wilson, *op. cit.*, p. 77.
60 Queen Victoria: *Letters*, III, iii, p. 257.
61 *ibid.*, pp. 260–1.
62 *ibid.*, pp. 259–61.
63 Balfour, *op. cit.*, p. 211.
64 Queen Victoria: *Letters*, III, iii, p. 262.
65 Magnus II, *op. cit.*, pp. 437–8.
66 Taylor I, *op. cit.*, p. 207.
67 Kürenberg, *op. cit.*, p. 108.
68 Apsler, *op. cit.*, p. 178.
69 Taylor I, *op. cit.*, p. 43.
70 *ibid.*, p. 207.
71 Cowles, *op. cit.*, p. 161.
72 Balfour, *op. cit.*, p. 147.
73 Marek, George R.: *The Eagles Die* (1974), English ed., pp. 368–70.
74 Princess Alice, *op. cit.*, p. 76.
75 Longford, *op. cit.*, p. 373.
76 Martin, *op. cit.*, p. 114.
77 Benson, E. F.: *As We Were* (1930), cited as Benson II, Penguin ed., p. 144.
78 Martin, *op. cit.*, p. 114; Edmond Taylor, *op. cit.*, p. 122.
79 Cassels, *op. cit.*, p. 44.
80 Duff II, *op. cit.*, pp. 187–8.
81 Edmond Taylor, *op. cit.*, pp. 134–5, 146–50 and 158.
82 Bentinck, Lady Norah: *The Ex-Kaiser in Exile* (1921), p. 38.
83 Balfour, *op. cit.*, p. 216.
84 Wilson, *op. cit.*, p. 80.
85 Cowles, *op. cit.*, p. 164.
86 Kaiser II, *op. cit.*, pp. 210–11.
87 Desmond Stewart, personal communication.
88 Balfour, *op. cit.*, p. 216.
89 Kaiser II, *op. cit.*, p. 211.

90 *Illustrated London News*, October, 1975.
91 Masur, *op. cit.*, p. 111; Blake, Robert: *Disraeli* (1966), p. 10.
92 Esher, Reginald, Viscount: *Journals and Letters*, in 3 vols. (1934), II, p. 255.
93 Desmond Stewart, personal communication.
94 Balfour, *op. cit.*, pp. 297 and 477.
95 *ibid.*, p. 217; Wilson, *op. cit.*, p. 80; Edmond Taylor, *op. cit.*, p. 156.
96 Balfour, *op. cit.*, p. 213.
97 Lee, *op. cit.*, I, p. 740.
98 Queen Victoria: *Letters*, III, iii, p. 336.
99 Gower, *op. cit.*, p. 361.
100 Kürenberg, *op. cit.*, p. 112.
101 Queen Victoria: *Letters*, III, iii, pp. 371–4.
102 *ibid.*, p. 359.
103 Lee, *op. cit.*, I, p. 741.
104 Queen Victoria: *Letters*, III, iii, p. 358.
105 Balfour, *op. cit.*, p. 220.
106 Lee, *op. cit.*, I, p. 743.
107 Queen Victoria: *Letters*, III, iii, pp. 377–8.
108 *ibid.*, p. 381.
109 Die Grosse Politik, *op. cit.*, XV 4195; Cowles, *op. cit.*, p. 167.
110 Haller, *op. cit.*, II, p. 57.
111 *ibid.*, II, pp. 59–63.
112 *ibid.*, II, p. 64.
113 *ibid.*, p. 57.
114 Queen Victoria: *Letters*, III, iii, pp. 387–8.
115 *ibid.*
116 Balfour, *op. cit.*, p. 221.
117 Röhl II, *op. cit.*, pp. 35–47.
118 Haller, *op. cit.*, p. 23.
119 *ibid.*, I, p. 345; Bundesarchiv Koblenz, Bülow Papers, folder 76 (q.v. Röhl III).
120 *ibid.*, II, pp. 192–3; Marek, *op. cit.*, pp. 57 and 340.
121 Haller, *op. cit.*, II, p. 129.
122 *ibid.*, II, pp. 127–8.
123 *ibid.*, II, p. 128.
124 *ibid.*, II, pp. 79 and 81–3.
125 Röhl II, *op. cit.*, pp. 35–47.
126 Haller, *op. cit.*, II, p. 83.
127 *ibid.* II, pp. 88–9.
128 *ibid.*, II, p. 128.
129 *ibid.*, II, pp. 90–1.
130 Kaiser II, *op. cit.*, pp. 181 and 192; Masur, *op. cit.*, pp. 188–9.
131 Taylor II, *op. cit.*, p. 169; Passant, *op. cit.*, p. 121.
132 Pope-Hennessy II, *op. cit.*, p. 288.

133 Queen Victoria: *Letters*, III, iii, p. 489.
134 Magnus I, *op. cit.*, p. 265.
135 Queen Victoria: *Letters*, III, iii, p. 555.
136 *ibid*; Aronson I, *op. cit.*, p. 235; Courles, *op. cit.*, p. 182.
137 Cowles, *op. cit.*, p. 184.
138 Masur, *op. cit.*, pp. 211–12.
139 Kürenberg, *op. cit.*, pp. 221–2.
140 Queen Victoria: *Letters*, III, iii, p. 571.
141 Kürenberg, *op. cit.*, p. 118.
142 *ibid.*, p. 177.
143 Haller, *op. cit.*, II, p. 68.
144 *ibid*
145 *ibid.*, pp. 67–8; Bülow, *op. cit.*, II, p. 357.
146 Wilson, *op. cit.*, p. 90.
147 Balfour, *op. cit.*, pp. 226–7.
148 Queen Victoria: *Letters*, III, iii, pp. 583–4.
149 Balfour, *op. cit.*, p. 227.
150 *ibid.*, p. 228.
151 Haller, II, *op. cit.*, p. 39.
152 Röhl III, *op. cit.*, p. 380.
153 Leslie, *op. cit.*, p. 147.
154 Röhl III, *op. cit.*, p. 380; Balfour, *op. cit.*, p. 232.
155 Balfour, *op. cit.*, p. 231.
156 *ibid.*, p. 64.
157 Lee, *op. cit.*, II, p. 9; Jonas, *op. cit.*, p. 16.
158 Fulford, Roger: *Hanover to Windsor*, cited as Fulford IV (1960), Fontana ed., p. 147.
159 Lee, *op. cit.*, II, pp. 10 and 268.
160 *ibid.*, p. 12.
161 *ibid.*, p. 11.

Chapter Eleven (pp. 194–224)
GALLO-RUSSIAN PINCERS
1 Lee, *op. cit.*, II, p. 15.
2 Ponsonby, Sir Frederick (first Lord Sysonby): *Recollections of Three Reigns* (1951), cited as Ponsonby II, p. 109.
3 *ibid.*, pp. 110–11.
4 Aronson I, *op. cit.*, pp. 237–8.
5 Bennett, *op. cit.*, p. 334.
6 Battiscombe, Georgina: *Queen Alexandra* (1969), p. 239.
7 Magnus I, *op. cit.*, p. 300.
8 *ibid.*
9 Masur, *op. cit.*, p. 102.
10 *ibid.*, pp. 199–200.
11 Reinhardt, Max: *Augewählte Briefe, Reden, und Schriften* (1963), p. 89; Sayler, Oliver: *Max Reinhardt and his Theater* (1924), pp. 346 et seq.

12 Masur, *op. cit.*, pp. 215–17.
13 Spender, Stephen: *World within World* (1948), p. 114.
14 Vassili, Paul, Count: *Hof und Gesellschaft zu Berlin* (1884), p. 130. q.v. Masur.
15 Cowles, *op. cit.*, pp. 189–90, quoting Die Grosse Politik.
16 Chamberlain, Houston Stewart: *Briefe* (1928) II, pp. 137 et seq., q.v. Röhl I.
17 *ibid.*
18 Haller, *op. cit.*, I, p. 51; Eulenburg, Philip Prince zu: *Eulenburg Papers* Vol. 37. pp. 591d – 591e, q.v. Röhl I.
19 Haller, *op. cit.*, I, p. 229.
20 Chamberlain, *op. cit.*, II, pp. 138–9.
21 *ibid.*, II, p. 137.
22 Lee, *op. cit.*, II, p. 137.
23 Eckardstein, Hermann, Baron von: *Ten Years at the Court of St. James's* p. 230.
24 Lee, *op. cit.*, II, p. 143.
25 *ibid.*, II, p. 145.
26 *ibid.*, II, p. 147–9.
27 *ibid.*, II, p. 149.
28 *ibid.*, II, p. 151.
29 Haller, *op. cit.*, II, pp. 134–5.
30 *ibid.*, I, p. 133.
31 Lee, *op. cit.*, II, p. 153.
32 Duff I, *op. cit.*, p. 117.
33 Manchester, William: *The Cannons of Krupp* (1968), Mondadori ed., pp. 274–80.
34 *ibid.*, pp. 282–3.
35 *ibid.*, p. 283.
36 Lee, *op. cit.*, II, pp. 236 et seq.
37 Middlemas, *op. cit.*, p. 159.
38 Cowles, *op. cit.*, pp. 203–4.
39 Montgomery-Massingberd, H. (ed.): Burke's *Presidential Families of the United States*, cited as Burke's Presidential Families (1975), pp. 413–17.
40 Massie, *op. cit.*, p. 95.
41 Balfour, *op. cit.*, p. 158.
42 Spitzemberg, *op. cit.*, p. 464.
43 Kürenberg, *op. cit.*, pp. 199–200.
44 Duff I, *op. cit.*, p. 291.
45 *ibid.*, pp. 291–2.
46 Saarnen, Alice B.: *The Proud Possessors* (1958).
47 Kaiser II, *op. cit.*, pp. 93–4.
48 Viereck, *op. cit.*, pp. 146–7.
49 Taylor I, *op. cit.*, p. 167.
50 Viereck, *op. cit.*, p. 147.
51 Taylor I, *op. cit.*, p. 167.
52 Viereck, *op. cit.*, p. 147.
53 Kühlmann, Richard von: *Lebenserinnerungen* (1952), p. 233.

54 Balfour, *op. cit.*, p. 161.
55 Kaiser II, *op. cit.*, p. 95.
56 *ibid.*, pp. 95–7.
57 *ibid.*, p. 95.
58 Viereck, *op. cit.*, pp. 152–3; Kürenberg, *op. cit.*, p. 175.
59 Jonas, *op. cit.*, p. 6.
60 *ibid.*
61 *ibid.*, pp. 20–1.
62 *ibid.*, p. 26.
63 *ibid.*, pp. 24, 25.
64 Keller, *op. cit.*, p. 151; Thaddeu *op. cit.*, pp. 319–20.
65 Viereck, *op. cit.*, p. 394.
66 Princess Alice, *op. cit.*, pp. 99 an 149.
67 *ibid.*, p. 92.
68 *ibid.*, p. 151; Taylor I, *op. cit.*, p. 191 Wilson, *op. cit.*, p. 104; Balfour *op. cit.*, p. 355; Röhl, John: *1914 Delusion or Design?*, cited as Röhl IV (1971), revised and expanded Englis ed. 1973, pp. 66, 87, 112, 126, 131–2 and pp. 13–14, introd. to Röhl IV b Hugh Trevor-Roper.
69 Topham, *op. cit.*, pp. 1 et seq.
70 *ibid.*, p. 30.
71 *ibid.*, pp. 17 and 226–7.
72 Pound, *op. cit.*, p. 314.
73 Bolitho, H: *The Reign of Quee Victoria* (1949), p. 350.
74 Lee, *op. cit.*, I, p. 179; Magnus I *op. cit.*, p. 423.
75 Private Information.
76 Bülow, *op. cit.*, II, p. 237.
77 Mitford, *op. cit.*, p. 21.
78 Holstein Papers, *op. cit.*, III, p. 658.
79 Wheeler-Bennett I, *op. cit.*, p. 181.
80 Balfour, *op. cit.*, p. 148.
81 Topham, *op. cit.*, p. 82.
82 *ibid.*, p. 211.
83 *ibid.*, p. 91.
84 *ibid.*, pp. 166–7.
85 *ibid.*, pp. 169–71.
86 *ibid.*, p. 224.
87 *ibid.*, p. 89–90.
88 *ibid.*, pp. 99–101.
89 *ibid.*, p. 206.
90 *ibid.*, pp. 229 and 95.
91 *ibid.*, pp. 221–3.
92 *ibid.*, pp. 52–3.
93 *ibid.*, p. 45.
94 *ibid.*, pp. 131–2.
95 *ibid.*, p. 13.
96 *ibid.*, pp. 218–19.
97 Hohenlohe, *op. cit.*, II, 411, q.v. Balfour.
98 Princess Marie Louise, *op. cit.*, p. 69.
99 Balfour, *op. cit.*, p. 148.
100 Duff II, *op. cit.*, p. 193, quoting

Fischer, *op. cit.*, and Legge, E: *The Public and Private Life of Kaiser William* (1915).

Pless II, *op. cit.*, p. 291.

ibid., p. 289.

Kürenberg, *op. cit.*, pp. 161-2.

Balfour, *op. cit.*, p. 139.

Princess Marie Louise, *op. cit.*, p. 73.

Topham, *op. cit.*, p. 160.

ibid., p. 219.

Cowles, *op. cit.*, p. 204.

Tuchman, *op. cit.*, p. 36.

ibid., p. 100.

1 Bulow, *op. cit.*, II, pp. 82-5.

2 Bauer, Ludwig: *Leopold the Unloved*, trs Eden and Cedar Paul (1934), p. 201.

3 Tuchman, *op. cit.*, p. 60.

4 Haller, *op. cit.*, II, pp. 148-9.

5 Masur, *op. cit.*, pp. 115-16.

6 Topham, *op. cit.*, pp. 136-7.

7 *ibid.*, *op. cit.*, p. 138: Balfour, *op. cit.*, p. 150.

8 Balfour, *op. cit.*, p. 152.

9 *ibid.*, pp. 247-8.

20 Ponsonby II, *op. cit.*, pp. 178 *et seq.*

21 Sitwell, Sir Osbert: *The Scarlet Tree, Left Hand, Right Hand!* Vol. II (1946) p. 271.

22 *ibid.*

23 Duff II, *op. cit.*, p. 292.

24 Magnus I, *op. cit.*, p. 338.

25 Edmond Taylor, *op. cit.*, p. 208; Magnus I, *op. cit.*, p. 204.

26 Lee, *op. cit.*, II, pp. 335-6.

27 Fulford III, *op. cit.*, p. 115.

28 Gernsheim, *op. cit.*, p. 142.

29 Zedlitz-Trützschler, *op. cit.*, p. 80.

30 Magnus I, *op. cit.*, p. 338.

31 Leslie, *op. cit.*, p. 335; Topham, *op. cit.*, p. 229.

32 Lee, *op. cit.*, II, p. 335.

33 Masur, *op. cit.*, pp. 73 and 186.

34 Magnus I, *op. cit.*, pp. 341-2; Hough, *op. cit.*, p. 190.

35 Grant, N. F. (ed.): *The Kaiser's Letters to the Tsar* (*The Willy-Nicky Correspondence*) *Copied from government archives in Petrograd* (1920), p. 138.

36 *ibid.*

37 Massie, *op. cit.*, 94-8; Radziwill, Princess Catherin : *Nicholas II, The Last of the Tsars* (1931), pp. 158-9.

38 Massie, *op. cit.*, p. 99.

39 Balfour, *op. cit.*, pp. 253-4.

40 Wheeler-Bennett I, *op. cit.*, p. 94.

41 Schoen, William, Baron von: *Memoirs of an Ambassador* (1922) quoted

in Cowles, p. 210; Edmond Taylor, *op. cit.*, pp. 204-5.

142 Valentini, Rudolph von: *Kaiser u. Kabinettschef*, ed. Schwertfeger (1931), p. 81.

143 Hough, *op. cit.*, p. 188.

144 Edmond Taylor, *op. cit.*, p. 205.

145 Balfour, *op. cit.*, p. 256.

146 *ibid*; Kürenberg, *op. cit.*, pp. 160-61.

147 Lee, *op. cit.*, II, p. 343.

148 *ibid.*

149 Kürenberg, *op. cit.*, p. 125.

150 Magnus I, *op. cit.*, p. 346.

151 Lee, *op. cit.*, II, p. 306-7.

152 *ibid.*, II, p. 307.

153 Massie, *op. cit.*, pp. 92-3; Viereck, *op. cit.*, pp. 198-201.

154 Balfour, *op. cit.*, p. 258, quoting Die Grosse Politik XIX 6193.

155 Bülow, Bernard Prince von: *Letters*, trs. and ed. by F. Whyte (1930), cited as Bülow Letters, p. 173; Die Grosse Politik XIX 6237.

156 Viereck, *op. cit.*, pp. 193-4.

157 Lee, *op. cit.*, II, pp. 307-8.

158 Massie, *op. cit.*, p. 105.

159 *ibid.*, p. 205.

160 *ibid.*, pp. 204-6.

161 Magnus I, *op. cit.*, p. 344, quoting Die Grosse Politik 23A, 161.

162 Massie, *op. cit.*, p. 107.

163 Lee, *op. cit.*, II, p. 311.

164 Massie, *op. cit.*, p. 93.

165 Magnus I, *op. cit.*, p. 348.

166 *ibid.*, p. 353.

167 Lee, *op. cit.*, II, p. 449.

168 Heidelmeyer, Wolfgang (ed.): *Der Fall Köpenick* (1968), q.v. Masur, *op. cit.*, pp. 96-7.

169 Kürenberg, *ép. cit.*, p. 165.

170 Balfour, *op. cit.*, p. 23.

171 Kürenberg, *op. cit.*, p. 163.

172 *ibid.*

173 Balfour, *op. cit.*, p. 447.

174 *ibid.*, p. 263.

175 Tuchman, *op. cit.*, pp. 98-9.

176 *ibid.*, p. 38.

177 Masur, *op. cit.*, pp. 207-11.

178 Balfour, *op. cit.*, p. 263.

179 Burke's Presidential Families, *op. cit.*, p. 418.

180 Nicolson, Sir Harold: *Lord Carnock* (1930), pp. 189-94.

181 Masur, *op. cit.*, p. 211, quoting Johann, Ernest (ed.): *Reden des Kaisers* (1966), p. 102.

182 Palmer, *op. cit.*, p. 23.

183 Cowles, *op. cit.*, p. 222.

184 *ibid.*, quoting Die Grosse Politik.

185 Palmer, *op. cit.*, pp. 23-4.

186 Haller, *op. cit.*, II, p. 299; Cowles, *op. cit.*, p. 223.

187 Rogge, Helmuth: *Holstein und Harden* (1959), p. 70.

188 Haller, *op. cit.*, II, p. 292.

189 *ibid.*, II, p. 313.

190 *ibid.*, II, p. 312.

Chapter Twelve (pp. 225-241)

DÉBÂCLES

1 Haller, *op. cit.*, II, p. 154.

2 *ibid.*, II, p. 174.

3 *ibid.*, II, p. 175.

4 *ibid.*, II, p. 177.

5 *ibid.*, II, p. 179.

6 Masur, *op. cit.*, p. 179.

7 Haller, *op. cit.*, II, p. 179.

8 Masur, *op. cit.*, pp. 179-82.

9 Haller, *op. cit.*, II, p. 195.

10 Cowles, *op. cit.*, p. 227.

11 Haller, *op. cit.*, II, p. 196.

12 *ibid.*, II, pp. 149-50.

13 *ibid.*, II, p. 183.

14 *ibid.*, II, p. 197.

15 *ibid.*, II, p. 198; Ludwig, *op. cit.*, p. 328.

16 Röhl III, *op. cit.*, pp. 380-1.

17 Magnus I, *op. cit.*, p. 358.

18 Jonas, *op. cit.*, p. 38.

19 *ibid.*, pp. 32-3, 36.

20 Zedlitz-Trützschler, *op. cit.*, pp. 177-8.

21 Jonas, *op. cit.*, p. 43.

22 Ludwig, *op. cit.*, p. 331; Cowles, *op. cit.*, p. 228; Röhl II, *op. cit.*, p. 58.

23 Queen Victoria: *Letters*, II, ii, p. 521.

24 Masur, *op. cit.*, p. 184; Haller, *op. cit.*, II, p. 150.

25 Haller, *op. cit.*, II, p. 49.

26 Jones, *op. cit.*, p. 43.

27 Ludwig, *op. cit.*, p. 330.

28 *ibid.*, p. 329.

29 *ibid.*, pp. 332-3.

30 Haller, *op. cit.*, II, p. 203; Ludwig, *op. cit.*, pp. 332-3.

31 Balfour, *op. cit.*, p. 78.

32 Magnus I, *op. cit.*, p. 398.

33 Duff II, *op. cit.*, p. 234.

34 Lee, *op. cit.*, II, pp. 574-5; Magnus I, *op. cit.*, p. 399.

35 Balfour, *op. cit.*, p. 284.

36 Harden, Maximilian: *Köpfe*, in 4 vols (1911-1924), III pp. 441 *et seq*; Tresckow, H. von: *Von Fürsten und anderen Sterblichen, Erinnerungen eines Kriminalkommissars* (1922), pp. 115 and 164; Ludwig, *op. cit.*, pp. 329 and 331; Lange, Annemarie: *Das wilhelminische Deutschland* (1967), p. 347.

37 Haller, *op. cit.*, II, p. 213.
38 *ibid.*, II, pp. 219–21.
39 *ibid.*, II, p. 227.
40 *ibid.*, II, pp. 228–32.
41 Schwering, *op. cit.*, p. 246; Ludwig, *op. cit.*, p. 333.
42 Ludwig, *op. cit.*, p. 332.
43 Schwering, *op. cit.*, pp. 246–7.
44 Haller, *op. cit.*, II, pp. 346–7.
45 *ibid.*, II, p. 234.
46 *ibid.*, II, p. 234.
47 *ibid.*, II, p. 239.
48 *ibid.*, II, p. 247.
49 *ibid.*, II, pp. 248, 254–5.
50 *ibid.*, II, p. 233.
51 Röhl IV, *op. cit.*, pp. 57 and 58.
52 Chamberlain, *op. cit.*, II, pp. 226–7.
53 Kaiser I, *op. cit.*, p. 187.
54 Edmond Taylor, *op. cit.*, pp. 162–3.
55 Palmer, *op. cit.*, pp. 53–4; Lee, *op. cit.*, II, pp. 637 and 638, quoting Die Grosse Politik.
56 Balfour, *op. cit.*, p. 289.
57 *ibid.*
58 Lee, *op. cit.*, II, p. 620.
59 *ibid.*, p. 621; Kürenberg, *op. cit.*, p. 196.
60 Masur, *op. cit.*, 185 quoting issues of Die Zukunft of November 1908 and Haacke, Wilmont: *Die Politische Zeitchrift*(1968), pp. 236–47.
61 Watt, Richard M.: *The Kings Depart* (1968), Pelican corrected ed. 1973, p. 276.
62 Balfour, *op. cit.*, p. 290; Lee, *op. cit.*, II, p. 644.
63 Cowles, *op. cit.*, p. 264.
64 Kürenberg, *op. cit.*, p. 196.
65 Balfour, *op. cit.*, p. 290.
66 Cowles, *op. cit.*, p. 262.
67 *ibid.*, p. 266.
68 *ibid.*, p. 267; Balfour, *op. cit.*, pp. 290–1; Kürenberg, *op. cit.*, p. 197.
69 Lee, *op. cit.*, II, p. 622.
70 Magnus I, *op. cit.*, p. 400.
71 Lee, *op. cit.*, II, p. 623.
72 Balfour, *op. cit.*, p. 291.
73 *ibid.*, Kürenberg, *op. cit.*, p. 198.
74 Balfour, *op. cit.*, p. 149.
75 Cowles, *op. cit.*, pp. 270–2; Jonas, *op. cit.*, p. 47.
76 Cowles, *op. cit.*, p. 272.
77 Longford, *op. cit.*, p. 290.
78 Watt, *op. cit.*, p. 106.
79 Lee, *op. cit.*, II, p. 622; Magnus I, *op. cit.*, pp. 400–1.
80 Ponsonby II, *op. cit.*, p. 258.
81 *ibid.*, p. 255.
82 *ibid.*, p. 256.
83 *ibid.*

84 Lee, *op. cit.*, II, pp. 674–5, quoting Grenfell, Field-Marshal Lord: *Memoirs*(1925), p. 185.
85 *ibid.*, pp. 675–6.
86 Princess Alice, *op. cit.*, p. 97.
87 Balfour, *op. cit.*, p. 296.
88 Magnus I, *op. cit.*, p. 418.
89 Ponsonby II, *op. cit.*, p. 258.
90 Lee, *op. cit.*, II, p. 644; Taylor II, *op. cit.*, p 180
91 Kürenberg, *op cit.*, p. 198.
92 Cowles, *op. cit.*, p. 276.
93 Viereck, *op. cit.*, p. 139.
94 Cowles, *op. cit.*, p. 277.
95 Kürenberg, *op. cit.*, p. 204.

Chapter Thirteen
THE IRON DICE ROLL (pp. 242–271)
1 Balfour, *op. cit.*, pp. 303–4.
2 Taylor II, *op. cit.*, p. 181.
3 Ludwig, *op. cit.*, p. 144.
4 Kürenberg, *op. cit.*, p. 137.
5 Balfour, *op. cit.*, p. 305.
6 *ibid.*, p. 306.
7 *ibid.*, p. 205.
8 *ibid.*, p. 301.
9 *ibid.*, pp. 306–7.
10 *ibid.*, p. 309. .
11 *ibid.*, pp. 304–5.
12 Taylor II, *op. cit.*, pp. 182–3.
13 Balfour, *op. cit.*, p. 290.
14 Topham, *op. cit.*, pp. 139–40.
15 Laver, James: *Edwardian Promenade* (1958), p. 138, quoting Berriman, E. B. *Aviation* (1913).
16 Jonas, *op. cit.*, p. 51.
17 Bauer, *op. cit.*, pp. 322 and 335.
18 Leslie, *op. cit.*, p. 337–8.
19 Middlemas, *op. cit.*, p. 174; *Die Deutsche Dokumente zum Kriegsausbruch* (1914) cited as Deutsche Dokumente, II, p. 132; Lee, *op. cit.*, II, pp. 732–3.
20 Leslie, *op. cit.*, p. 337.
21 Gernsheim, *op. cit.*, pp. 151–2.
22 Esher, *op. cit.*, III, p. 4.
23 Jonas, *op. cit.*, p. 51.
24 *ibid.*
25 Schwering, *op. cit.*, p. 73.
26 Jonas, *op. cit.*, pp. 49–50.
27 Schwering, *op. cit.*, p. 74.
28 Burke's Presidential Families, *op. cit.*, pp. 418–19; Cowles, *op. cit.*, pp. 281–2.
29 Jonas, *op. cit.*, p. 52.
30 *ibid.*, pp. 52–3.
31 *ibid.*, p. 61.
32 *ibid.*, p. 63.
33 *ibid.*, p. 53.
34 *ibid.*, p. 66.

35 *ibid.*, p. 67.
36 Kaiser II, *op. cit.*, pp. 140–1.
37 *ibid.*, p. 142; Röhl, J. C. G 'Admiral von Müller and the Approach of the War, 1911–1914'; T Historical Journal, XII, 4 (1969 p. 653.
38 Cowles, *op. cit.*, p. 289–90.
39 Palmer, *op. cit.*, p. 18.
40 Cowles, *op. cit.*, p. 291.
41 *ibid.*, quoting Die Grosse Politik.
42 Owen, Frank: *Tempestuous Journey Lloyd George His Life and Time* (1954), p. 211.
43 Cowles, *op. cit.*, pp. 293 and 363.
44 Taylor II, *op. cit.*, pp. 185–6 Bethmann Hollweg, Theobald von *Reflections on the World War*, trs. G Young (1920), I, p. 37.
45 Hankey, (Maurice Pashal Aleis Lord: *The Supreme Command 1914 18*, 2 vols, (1961), I, p. 78; Marder A. J.: *From the Dreadnought to Scap Flow, the Royal Navy in the Fishe Era 1904–19* in 5 vols (1966–70); I p. 244.
46 Jonas, *op. cit.*, pp. 70–1.
47 *ibid.*, p. 72.
48 Salis, Jean Rodolphede; *Weltgeschicht der neusten Zeit* (1955), pp. 459–60.
49 Jonas, *op. cit.*, pp. 72–3 and 74.
50 *ibid.*, p. 70.
51 *ibid.*, p. 76.
52 *ibid.*, pp. 78–9.
53 Watt, *op. cit.*, pp. 139–40.
54 Epstein, Klaus: 'Shirer's History of Nazi Germany' in *The Review of Politics*, 23, No. 2 (April 1961), pp. 230 et seq, q.v. Röhl I.
55 Balfour, *op. cit.*, pp. 334–5.
56 Haldane, Richard Burdon, Viscount: *An Autobiography* (1929), Popular ed., pp. 239–45; Balfour, *op. cit.*, p. 322.
57 Röhl IV, *op. cit.*, p. 96.
58 Balfour, *op. cit.*, p. 337.
59 Röhl IV, *op. cit.*, p. 29, quoting Fischer, Fritz: *Germany's Aims in the First World War* (London, 1967).
60 Röhl IV, *op. cit.*, p. 28.
61 Bernhardi, Friedrich von, *Germany and the Next War* (1914), p. 106. q.v. Röhl I.
62 Balfour, *op. cit.*, p. 338.
63 *ibid.*, p. 266.
64 Röhl I, *op. cit.*, p. 65.
65 Massie, *op. cit.*, p. 272.
66 Tuchman, *op. cit.*, p. 81.
67 *ibid.*, *op. cit.*, pp. 43, 77 and 83, *op. cit.*, p. 272; Röhl II, *op. cit.*, p. 28.

Tuchman, *op. cit.*, pp. 48–9 and 55.
Röhl IV, *op. cit.*, p. 30; Ritter, Gerhard: *Staatskunst und Kriegshandwerk, Das Problem des Militarismus in Deutschland*, in 4 vols (1954–1968), II, pp. 270–00.
Röhl IV, *op. cit.*, p. 29.
Kürenberg; *op. cit.*, p. 235.
Röhl IV, *op. cit.*, pp. 29–30.
Palmer, *op. cit.*, p. 42.
Balfour, *op. cit.*, p. 335.
Fritz Fischer, *op. cit.*, p. 103–6.
5 Churchill, *op. cit.*, I, p. 107.
7 Pope-Hennessy II, *op. cit.*, p. 109.
8 *ibid.*, p. 326.
9 Topham, *op. cit.*, p. 237.
9 *ibid.*, p. 234.
ibid., p. 237.
2 Wheeler-Bennett I, *op. cit.*, p. 179.
3 Cramb, J. A.: *Germany and England* (1914), pp. 64–6, 131–2, q.v. Röhl I.
4 Kürenberg, *op. cit.*, p. 114.
5 Cramb, *op. cit.*, p. 132.
6 Bentinck, *op. cit.*, p. 94.
7 Pope-Hennessy II, *op. cit.*, pp. 479–80.
8 Massie, *op. cit.*, pp. 212, 214–15 and 218.
9 Hough, *op. cit.*, p. 262.
0 Pope-Hennessy II, *op. cit.*, p. 480.
1 *ibid.*, p. 153.
2 Topham, *op. cit.*, p. 238.
3 Cowles, *op. cit.*, p. 305.
4 Radziwill, Princess Marie: *This Was Germany* trs C. S. Fox (1937), p. 279.
5 Jonas, *op. cit.*, p. 85.
6 *ibid.*, p. 86.
7 Gebsattel, Konstantin, Baron von: 'Gedanken über einen notwendigen Fortschritt in der inneren Entwicklung Deutschlands', *Deutsches Zentralarchiv*, Potsdam, Alldeutscher Verband, 204 (q.v. Röhl I).
98 Strandmann, Hartmut Pogge-von: 'Staatsstreichpläne, Alldeutsche und Bethmann Hollweg', *Die Erforderlichkeit des Unmöglichen* (1965), p. 38 q.v. Röhl I.
99 Jonas, *op. cit.*, p. 87.
00 *ibid.*, p. 88.
01 *ibid.*, p. 89.
02 *ibid.*
03 Redlich, Joseph: *Schicksalsjahre Österreichs 1908–1919* (1953), II, p. 15.
04 Marek, *op. cit.*, pp. 416–18.
05 Hirschfeld, Magnus: *The Sexual History of the Great War* (1946), pp. 110–11; Edmund Taylor, *op. cit.*, pp. 233 *et seq.*

106 Kürenberg, *op. cit.*, p. 225.
107 *ibid.*, p. 223.
108 *ibid.*, p. 226.
109 *ibid.*, p. 224.
110 *ibid.*, p. 227.
111 *ibid.*, p. 225.
112 *ibid.*, p. 227.
113 Röhl II, *op. cit.*, p. 32; Cowles, *op. cit.*, p. 310.
114 Duff I, *op. cit.*, p. 295.
115 Cowles, *op. cit.*, p. 304 quoting *British Documents on the Origin of the War 1898–1914*.
116 Watt, *op. cit.*, pp. 24–6.
117 *ibid.*, p. 23.
118 Gooch, George Peabody, *Before the War. Studies in Diplomacy* 2 vols (1935–38), p. 56.
119 Balfour, *op. cit.*, p. 342.
120 Kürenberg, *op. cit.*, p. 236.
121 *ibid.*, p. 226.
122 Balfour, *op. cit.*, p. 344 quoting Ritter *op. cit.*, and Albertini Luigi: *The Origins of the War of 1914*, in 3 vols (1952–1957).
123 Kürenberg, *op. cit.*, p. 237.
124 Massie, *op. cit.*, p. 244.
125 Balfour, *op. cit.*, p. 343.
126 Marek, *op. cit.*, pp. 436 and 437.
127 Kürenberg, *op. cit.*, p. 229.
128 Deutsche Documente, *op. cit.*, I, p. 13.
129 Balfour, *op. cit.*, pp. 344 and 345.
130 *ibid.*, p. 346.
131 *ibid.*, pp. 345–6.
132 Kürenberg, *op. cit.*, p. 238.
133 *ibid.*, pp. 240–1.
134 Edmond Taylor; *op. cit.*, p. 281.
135 *ibid.*, p. 283–4.
136 *ibid.*
137 Kruck, Alfred: *Geschichte des Alldeutschen Verbandes, 1890–1939* (1954), p. 48.
138 Röhl IV, *op. cit.*, p. 66.
139 Cowles, *op. cit.*, p. 319 quoting Kautsky, Karl: *Outbreak of the World War: German Documents Collected by Karl Kautsky* (1924) ed. M. Monteglas and W. Schucking, cited as Kautsky.
140 Röhl IV, *op. cit.*, p. 17.
141 Massie, *op. cit.*, p. 248.
142 Edmond Taylor, *op. cit.*, p. 284.
143 Kaiser II, *op. cit.*, p. 242.
144 Hough, *op. cit.*, pp. 278–9.
145 Kürenberg, *op. cit.*, p. 239; Cowles, *op. cit.*, p. 322.
146 Müller, George Alexander von (ed. Goerlitz): *The Kaiser and His Court, the Diaries, Notebooks and Letters of*

Admiral G.v.M., Chief of the Naval Secretariat 1914–1918 trs M. Savill (1961), cited as Müller I, quoted by page number or date of diary entry, p. 8.
147 Müller, Richard: *Vom Kaiserreich zur Republik*, in 2 vols (1924), cited as R. Müller, I, p. 27.
148 Röhl IV, *op. cit.*, p. 32.
149 Hough, *op. cit.*, p. 281.
150 Nicolson, Sir Harold: *King George V* (1952), pp. 245–6.
151 Röhl IV, *op. cit.*, p. 91.
152 Cowles, *op. cit.*, pp. 325–6.
153 Balfour, *op. cit.*, p. 303.
154 Röhl IV, *op. cit.*, p. 17.
155 Reizler, Kurt: *Tagebücher, Aufsätze, Documente* (1972), p. 189, q.v. Röhl IV.
156 *ibid.*, pp. 182 *et seq.* and 186 *et seq.*
157 Balfour, *op. cit.*, p. 348.
158 Cowles, *op. cit.*, p. 327, quoting Kautsky.
159 Kürenberg, *op. cit.*, p. 244.
160 *ibid.*, p. 245.
161 Masur, *op. cit.*, pp. 70–1.
162 Kürenberg, *op. cit.*, p. 245.
163 Balfour, *op. cit.*, p. 349.
164 Cowles, *op. cit.*, p. 346.
165 Massie, *op. cit.*, p. 270.
166 Deutsche Dokumente, *op. cit.*, II, p. 132.
167 Kürenberg, *op. cit.*, pp. 246–7.
168 Schwering, *op. cit.*, p. 92.
169 Kautsky, *op. cit.*, p. 553.
170 Masur, *op. cit.*, pp. 265–6.
171 Balfour, *op. cit.*, p. 353.
172 Nettl, J. P.: *Rosa Luxemburg*, in 2 vols. (1966), II, p. 601.
173 Warr, *op. cit.*, pp. 133–4.
174 Balfour, *op. cit.*, pp. 353–4.
175 Tuchman, *op. cit.*, pp. 94 and 95.
176 Moltke, Helmuth, General, Count von: *Erinnerungen-Briefe-Doukumente 1877–1916* (1922), pp. 19, 23; Kautsky, *op. cit.*, pp. 575, 578, 579 and 612.
177 Staab, General Hermann von: *Aufmarsch nach zwei Fronten* (1925).
178 Beyens, Baron: *Deux Années à Berlin, 1912–1914* in 2 vols (1931), II, pp. 38–43; Galet, General Emile Joseph: *Albert, King of the Belgians, in the Great War* (1931), p. 23.
179 Belgian Grey Book, No. 20.
180 Kürenberg, *op. cit.*, p. 251; Belgian Grey Book, No. 22.
181 Galet, *op. cit.*, pp. 58–9.
182 Kautsky, *op. cit.*, p. 376.
183 Kürenberg, *op. cit.*, p. 251.

184 Balfour, *op. cit.*, p. 359.
185 Blücher, Evelyn, Princess: *An English Wife in Berlin* (1920), p. 14.
186 Kürenberg, *op. cit.*, p. 251.
187 Balfour, *op. cit.*, p. 355.
188 *ibid.*
189 Röhl IV, *op. cit.*, p. 87.
190 Blücher, *op. cit.*, p. 6.
191 Röhl IV, *op. cit.*, p. 79.
192 Viereck, *op. cit.*, p. 2.

Chapter Fourteen (pp. 272–309)
THE GORY GAME OF MIGHT AND CHANCE .
1 Crankshaw, Edward: *The Habsburgs* (1971), Corgi ed. p. 155.
2 Gorce, Pierre de la: *Histoire du Second Empire* in 7 vols. (1894–1905), VII, p. 343.
3 Tuchman, *op. cit.*, p. 218.
4 *ibid.*, p. 285.
5 *ibid.*, p. 487; Laver, *op. cit.*, p. 212.
6 Massie, *op. cit.*, p. 294.
7 Laver, *op. cit.*, p. 212.
8 *ibid.*, p. 222.
9 Müller, George Alexander von: *Regierte der Kaiser?* (1959), p. 177; Balfour, *op. cit.*, p. 356.
10 Gore, *op. cit.*, pp. 169–72; Pope-Hennessy II, *op. cit.*, p. 508.
11 Florinsky, Michael T.: *The End of the Russian Empire* (1931), p. 38; Massie, *op. cit.*, p. 281.
12 Kürenberg, *op. cit.*, p. 254.
13 *ibid.*
14 Balfour, *op. cit.*, p. 357.
15 Haller, *op. cit.*, I, p. 183.
16 Balfour, *op. cit.*, p. 358.
17 Müller, I, *op. cit.*, August 6th, 1914.
18 Balfour, *op. cit.*, p. 360.
19 Kürenberg, *op. cit.*, p. 255.
20 Müller, I *op. cit.*, August 24th, 1918.
21 Cowles, *op. cit.*, p. 355.
22 Massie, *op. cit.*, p. 272.
23 *ibid.*, p. 276.
24 *The New York Times*, May 19th, 1918.
25 Massie, *op. cit.*, p. 277.
26 *ibid.*, pp. 293 and 294.
27 Tuchman, *op. cit.*, pp. 443–6, 452, 455, 461 and 487; Ritter, Gerhard: *The Schlieffen Plan, Critique of a Myth* (1958), pp. 66 *et seq.*; Klück, General Alexander von: *The March on Paris and the Battle of the Marne, 1914* (1920), pp. 77, 82–4, 90, 91, 100, 107.
28 Moltke, *op. cit.*, p. 413.
29 Palmer, *op. cit.*, p. 359.
30 Jonas, *op. cit.*, pp. 92–4.

31 *ibid.*, p. 96.
32 Nicolson, *op. cit.*, pp. 332 and 333.
33 Duff I, *op. cit.*, p. 309.
34 Duff II, *op. cit.*, p. 241.
35 Princess Alice, *op. cit.*, p. 160.
36 *ibid.*, p. 105.
37 *ibid.*, p. 158.
38 Harrod, Sir Roy: *The Life of John Maynard Keynes* (1951), Pelican ed., p. 311.
39 Masur, *op. cit.*, pp. 272–4.
40 Hammann, Otto: *Bilder aus der letzten Kaiserzeit* p. 128.
41 Watt, *op. cit.*, p. 141.
42 *Die Rote Fahne*, December 14th, 1918.
43 Watt, *op. cit.*, pp. 141–4.
44 *ibid.*, pp. 144–5.
45 *ibid.*, p. 146.
46 Cowles, *op. cit.*, p. 365.
47 *ibid.*, pp. 368–9.
48 Kürenberg, *op. cit.*, p. 276.
49 *ibid.*, p. 267.
50 Cowles, *op. cit.*, pp. 374–5.
51 Harrod, *op. cit.*, p. 311.
52 Owen, *op. cit.*, pp. 355–6.
53 Cowles, *op. cit.*, p. 375.
54 Owen, *op. cit.*, p. 356.
55 Cowles, *op. cit.*, p. 376, quoting Grey of Falloden, Viscount: *Twenty-five Years* (1925).
56 Kürenberg, *op. cit.*, p. 264.
57 Cowles, *op. cit.*, p. 374.
58 Balfour, *op. cit.*, p. 368.
59 Cowles, *op. cit.*, p. 381; Kürenberg, *op. cit.*, p. 264.
60 Kürenberg, *op. cit.*, pp. 265–6.
61 Balfour, *op. cit.*, pp. 371–2; Cowles, *op. cit.*, p. 378.
62 Kürenberg, *op. cit.*, p. 275.
63 Massie, *op. cit.*, pp. 395–6.
64 *ibid.*, p. 401.
65 *ibid.*, p. 427.
66 *ibid.*, p. 398.
67 *ibid.*, p. 397.
68 Magnus I, *op. cit.*, p. 341.
69 Gore, *op. cit.*, p. 173.
70 Massie, *op. cit.*, p. 397.
71 Nicolson, *op. cit.*, pp. 392–3.
72 *ibid.*, p. 403.
73 Owen, *op. cit.*, pp. 437 and 439.
74 Private Information.
75 Massie, *op. cit.*, p. 440.
76 *ibid.*, p. 441.
77 Hough, *op. cit.*, p. 328.
78 Massie, *op. cit.*, pp. 439–40.
79 *ibid.*, pp. 421–2 and 432.
80 Duff I, *op. cit.*, p. 322.
81 Massie, *op. cit.*, p. 442.
82 Balfour, *op. cit.*, p. 375.

83 Kürenberg, *op. cit.*, p. 271.
84 Owen, *op. cit.*, p. 376.
85 Balfour, *op. cit.*, p. 389.
86 *ibid.*, p. 390.
87 *ibid.*, p. 369.
88 Feldmann, Gerald: *Army Industry and Labor in Germany 1914–1918* (1966) p. 306; Lutz, Ralph H: *The Fall of the German Empire*, in 2 vols. (1932), I pp. 99–103.
89 Hirschfeld, *op. cit.*, p. 92.
90 Watt, *op. cit.*, p. 152.
91 Masur, *op. cit.*, p. 280.
92 Kabisch, Ernst: *Gröner* (1932), p. 53.
93 Taylor II, *op. cit.*, pp. 196–7.
94 Kürenberg, *op. cit.*, p. 265.
95 Taylor II, *op. cit.*, p. 199.
96 Balfour, *op. cit.*, p. 273.
97 *ibid.*, pp. 378–9.
98 Watt, *op. cit.*, p. 155.
99 Cowles, *op. cit.*, p. 385.
100 Watt, *op. cit.*, p. 155.
101 Balfour, *op. cit.*, p. 380.
102 Kürenberg, *op. cit.*, pp. 277 and 278.
103 *ibid.*, p. 278.
104 Cowles, *op. cit.*, p. 386; Wilson, *op. cit.*, pp. 156 *et seq.*
105 Kürenberg, *op. cit.*, pp. 282–3.
106 Taylor II, *op. cit.*, pp. 104–5; Cowles, *op. cit.*, p. 389.
107 Kürenberg, *op. cit.*, p. 283.
108 Jonas, *op. cit.*, p. 104.
109 R. Müller, *op. cit.*, I, pp. 102, 194, 202.
110 Balfour, *op. cit.*, p. 384.
111 *ibid.*, p. 386.
112 Massie, *op. cit.*, p. 469.
113 Summers, A. and Mangold, T.: *The File on the Tsar* (1976), pp. 273–90.
114 Massie, *op. cit.*, pp. 491–2 and 497.
115 *ibid.*, p. 497; Duff I, *op. cit.*, p. 324; Hough, *op. cit.*, p. 327.
116 Taylor II, *op. cit.*, p. 204.
117 Watt, *op. cit.*, p. 161.
118 *ibid.*, pp. 142 and 265.
119 Meyer, Karl W.: *Karl Liebknecht, Man Without a Country* (1957) p. 167.
120 Röhl I, *op. cit.*, p. 81.
121 Masur, *op. cit.*, p. 274.
122 Burke's Presidential Families, *op. cit.*, p. 447.
123 *ibid.*
124 Watt, *op. cit.*, p. 34.
125 Cowles, *op. cit.*, pp. 390–1.
126 Balfour, *op. cit.*, pp. 391–2.
127 Cowles, *op. cit.*, p. 394.
128 Müller I, *op. cit.*, August 20th, 1918.
129 Cowles, *op. cit.*, p. 394.
130 Müller I, *op. cit.*, September 6th, 1918.

Watt, *op. cit.*, p. 162.
ibid., p. 163.
Cowles, *op. cit.*, p. 394.
Watt, *op. cit.*, p. 163.
Balfour, *op. cit.*, pp. 393 and 394.
Maximilian, Prince of Baden: *The Memoirs of Prince Max of Baden* in 2 vols. (1928), cited as Prince Max II, pp. 11–12.
Hertling, Carl, Count von: *Ein Jahr in der Reichskanzlei* (1919), p. 183.
Kürenberg, *op. cit.*, p. 289.
Balfour, *op. cit.*, p. 396.
Lutz, *op. cit.*, II, p. 382.
Balfour, *op. cit.*, pp. 396–7.
Watt, *op. cit.*, p. 169.
ibid., pp. 171–2.
Niemann, Alfred: *Kaiser und Revolution. Die entscheidenden Ereignisse in Grossen Haupt-Quartier* (1922), p. 100.
Baumont, M.: *The Fall of the Kaiser*, trs. E. I. James (1931), pp. 3 and 4.
Prince Max, *op. cit.*, II, p. 181.
Viereck, *op. cit.*, p. 2.
Taylor II, *op. cit.*, pp. 205–6.
Balfour, *op. cit.*, pp. 399–400.
Kürenberg, *op. cit.*, pp. 293.
Ritter, Gerhard A and Miller, Susanne: *Die deutsche Revolution 1918–1919* (1968) cited as Ritter and Miller, pp. 50 et seq., q.v. Röhl I.
2 Stubmann, P.: *Albert Ballin* (1960), pp. 259 et seq., q.v. Röhl II.
3 Balfour, *op. cit.*, p. 402.
4 Watt, *op. cit.*, p. 186.
5 Wheeler-Bennett I, *op. cit.*, p. 36.
6 Prince Max, *op. cit.*, II, p. 300.
7 Ritter and Miller, *op. cit.*, pp. 50 et seq., q.v. Röhl I.
8 Ponsonby I, *op. cit.*, p. 324.
9 Watt, *op. cit.*, p. 123, 208.
10 Gentizon, Paul: *La Révolution allemande* (1919), pp. 57 and 63.
11 Prince Max, *op. cit.*, p. 340.
12 Kürenberg, *op. cit.*, p. 298; Watt, *op. cit.*, pp. 208–9; R. Muller, *op. cit.*, II, p. 16.
13 Balfour, *op. cit.*, p. 405.
14 Masur, *op. cit.*, p. 236.
15 Prince Max, *op. cit.*, pp. 341–2.
16 Baumont, *op. cit.*, p. 111.
17 *ibid.*, p. 22.
18 Watt, *op. cit.*, p. 212.
19 Balfour *op. cit.*, p.406
70 Westarp, Kuno, Count von: *Das Ende der Monarchie am 9 November 1918* (1952), pp. 42–8, q.v. Röhl I.
71 Baumont, *op. cit.*, p. 99.
72 *ibid.*, p. 111.
73 Westarp, *op. cit.*, p. 48.

174 Baumont, *op. cit.*, p. 112; Wheeler-Bennett I, *op. cit.*, p. 36; Kürenberg, *op. cit.*, p. 301, Jonas *op. cit.*, p. 119; Balfour, *op. cit.*, p. 407.
175 Scheidemann, Philipp: *The Making of a New Germany*, in 2 vols (1929), II, p. 250.
176 Balfour, *op. cit.*, pp. 408–9; Lutz, *op. cit.*, II, p. 537.
177 Prince Max, II, *op. cit.*, p. 354.
178 Scheidemann, *op. cit.*, II, pp. 261–2.
179 Prince Max, II, *op. cit.*, p. 127.
180 Balfour *op. cit.*, p. 409–10; Prince Max, II, *op. cit.*, p. 133.
181 Gröner, Wilhelm: *Lebenserinnerung, Jugend, Generalstab, Weltkrieg* (1957), pp. 467 ei seq, q.v. Röhl I.
182 Balfour, *op. cit.*, pp. 410–11.
183 Kürenberg, *op. cit.*, pp. 308–9.
184 Vierick, *op. cit.*, p. 338.
185 Scheidemann, *op. cit.*, p. 264.
186 Ritter and Miller, *op. cit.*, pp. 320 et seq., q.v. Röhl I.
187 Viereck, *op. cit.*, p. 338.
188 Balfour, *op. cit.*, p. 413.
189 Wheeler-Bennett II, *op. cit.*, p. 17.
190 Viereck, *op. cit.*, p. 344.
191 Balfour, *op. cit.*, p. 413.
192 *ibid.*, p. 411.
193 Taylor II, *op. cit.*, pp. 207–8.
194 Bouton, S. Miles: *And the Kaiser Abdicates* (1920), p. 172.
195 Carr, E. H.: *The Bolshevik Revolution* in 3 vols. (1951–1953), III, p. 101.
196 Volkmann, Erich Otto: *Revolution über Deutschland* (1930), p. 76.
197 Prittwitz und Gaffron, Friedrich Wilhelm von: *Zwischen Petersburg und Washington* (1954), p. 105.
198 Jonas, *op. cit.*, p. 127.
199 *ibid.*, p. 128.
200 Cowles, *op. cit.*, p. 410.
201 Bentinck, *op. cit.*, p. 81.
202 Watt, *op. cit.*, p. 245.
203 *ibid.*, pp. 438–9.
204 Balfour, *op. cit.*, p. 415; Kaiser I, *op. cit.*, p. 117.
205 Watt, *op. cit.*, p. 439.
206 Kürenberg, *op. cit.*, p. 311.
207 *ibid.*
208 Viereck, *op. cit.*, p. 384.

Chapter Fifteen (pp. 310–341)
THE SILENT ONE OF EUROPE
1 Bentinck, *op. cit.*, p. 49.
2 Kürenberg, *op. cit.*, pp. 310–11.
3 Owen, *op. cit.*, pp. 498–9.
4 *ibid.*, p. 501.
5 *ibid.*, p. 498.
6 Viereck, *op. cit.*, p. 3.

7 *ibid.*, p. 346.
8 Kürenberg: *op. cit.*, p. 316.
9 Harrod, *op. cit.*, pp. 309–10.
10 Owen, *op. cit.*, p. 501.
11 Jonas, *op. cit.*, pp. 130–31.
12 Watt, *op. cit.*, p. 541.
13 *ibid.*, pp. 236–7.
14 Ryder, A. J.: *The German Revolution of 1918* (1967), pp. 173–7.
15 *ibid.*, pp. 186, 187; Gröner, *op. cit.*, p. 475.
16 Watt, *op. cit.*, pp. 262–3.
17 Kürenberg, *op. cit.*, p. 312.
18 Watt, *op. cit.*, pp. 399–402.
19 Röhl I, *op. cit.*, p. 87; Watt, *op. cit.*, p. 259.
20 Hoover, H. *The Ordeal of Woodrow Wilson* (1958).
21 Watt, *op. cit.*, pp. 268–9.
22 Owen, *op. cit.*, pp. 535–6.
23 *The Morning Post*, January 20th and 23rd, 1919.
24 Burke's Presidential Families, *op. cit.*, p. 478.
25 Harrod, *op. cit.*, pp. 272–3.
26 Taylor II, *op. cit.*, p. 210; Nettl, *op. cit.*, II, p. 750.
27 Watt, *op. cit.*, pp. 286–7.
28 *ibid.*, pp. 278–83; Masur, pp. 291 and 292; Taylor II, *op. cit.*, p. 210.
29 Masur, *op. cit.*, p. 290; Watt, *op. cit.*, pp. 302–3.
30 Watt, *op. cit.*, p. 304.
31 Taylor II, *op. cit.*, p. 212.
32 Watt, *op. cit.*, pp. 309–10.
33 Taylor II, *op. cit.*, p. 215.
34 R. Müller, *op. cit.*, II, pp. 240–44.
35 Watt, *op. cit.*, p. 364.
36 *ibid.*, pp. 365–8.
37 *ibid.*, p. 326.
38 *ibid.*, pp. 375–9.
39 Owen, *op. cit.*, pp. 534–5.
40 Keynes, Maynard (Lord Keynes of Tilton): *The Economic Consequences of the Peace* (1919), pp. 44–5.
41 Watt, *op. cit.*, pp. 105–7; Keynes, *op. cit.*, pp. 49–50.
42 Watt, *op. cit.*, p. 440.
43 *ibid.*, pp. 453–6; Owen, *op. cit.*, p. 553.
44 *The Times*, May 8th, 1919.
45 Keynes, *op. cit.*, pp. 209–10.
46 Watt, *op. cit.*, pp. 458 and 462.
47 Luckau, Alma: *The German Delegation at the Paris Peace Conference* (1941), p. 308.
48 *ibid.*, p. 419.
49 Sinclair, W. A.: *Changing the Tune*, No VIII in a series of B.B.C. talks broadcast on May 14th, 1940 and

issued as *The Voice of the Nazi* (1940), p. 61.
50 Watts, *op. cit.*, pp. 503–6.
51 Gröner, *op. cit.*, p. 496.
52 Dorpalen, Andreas: *Hindenburg and the Weimar Republic* (1964), p. 39.
53 Luckau, *op. cit.*, p. 55.
54 Watt, *op. cit.*, pp. 541–4; Owen, *op. cit.*, p. 525.
55 Hankey, *op. cit.*, p. 177.
56 Wheeler-Bennett, Sir John: *Hindenburg, the Wooden Titan* (1936), p. 220.
57 Hankey, *op. cit.*, p. 181.
58 Watt, *op. cit.*, p. 580.
59 Keynes, *op. cit.*, pp. 209–10.
60 Watt, *op. cit.*, p. 13.
61 Bentinck, *op. cit.*, p. 79.
62 Kürenberg, *op. cit.*, p. 354.
63 *ibid.*, pp. 316–19.
64 Bentinck, *op. cit.*, pp. 152–3.
65 Kürenberg, *op. cit.*, p. 313.
66 Masur, *op. cit.*, p. 293.
67 Jonas, *op. cit.*, pp. 132–3.
68 Kürenberg, *op. cit.*, p. 313.
69 Viereck, *op. cit.*, p. 3.
70 Owen, *op. cit.*, p. 554; Watt, *op. cit.*, p. 556.
71 Kürenberg, *op. cit.*, pp. 315–16.
72 Tuchman, *op. cit.*, p. 488.
73 Kürenberg, *op. cit.*, p. 316.
74 Wheeler-Bennett I, p. 24; Watt, *op. cit.*, pp. 560–1.
75 Ilsemann, Sigurd von: *Der Kaiser in Holland* in 2 vols (1967), I, p. 149, q.v. Röhl I.
76 Watt, *op. cit.*, pp. 561 *et seq.*
77 *ibid.*, p. 563.
78 Meinecke, Friedrich: *Erlebtes* (1941), p. 345.
79 Meinecke, Friedrich: *The German Catastrophe: reflections and recollections*, trs. Sidney B. Fay (1963) cited as Meinecke II, pp. 9 *et seq.*, q.v. Röhl I.
80 Jonas, *op. cit.*, p. 135.
81 Kürenberg, *op. cit.*, p. 319.
82 Ilsemann, *op. cit.*, I, 149, q.v. Röhl I.
83 Wheeler-Bennett I, *op. cit.*, p. 180; Balfour, *op. cit.*, p. 414; Kürenberg, *op. cit.*, p. 320.
84 Longford, *op. cit.*, p. 567.
85 Viereck, *op. cit.*, p. 486.
86 Bentinck, *op. cit.*, p. 159.
87 Kürenberg, *op. cit.*, p. 320.
88 Bentinck, *op. cit.*, pp. 94–5.
89 Kürenberg, *op. cit.*, pp. 319–20.
90 Balfour, *op. cit.*, p. 417.
91 Viereck, *op. cit.*, p. 486.

92 *ibid.*, p. 485.
93 Wheeler-Bennett I, *op. cit.*, p. 186.
94 Kürenberg, *op. cit.*, p. 321.
95 Wheeler-Bennett I, *op. cit.*, p. 182.
96 *ibid.*, p. 181; Kürenberg, *op. cit.*, p. 320.
97 Kürenberg, *op. cit.*, p. 323–4.
98 Jonas, *op. cit.*, p. 136.
99 *ibid.*, pp. 227–8; Wheeler-Bennett I, *op. cit.*, p. 190.
100 Jonas, *op. cit.*, pp. 137–8.
101 *ibid.*
102 Kürenberg, *op. cit.*, p. 336.
103 Kaiser II, *op. cit.*, p. 23.
104 Haller, *op. cit.*, II, p. 284.
105 Jonas, *op. cit.*, pp. 140–3.
106 *ibid.*, p. 145.
107 Balfour, *op. cit.*, p. 415; Kürenberg, *op. cit.*, p. 324.
108 Jonas, *op. cit.*, p. 145.
109 Kürenberg, *op. cit.*, pp. 336–7.
110 *ibid.*
111 Viereck: *op. cit.*, pp. 383–4.
112 Jonas, *op. cit.*, pp. 147–50.
113 Taylor II, *op. cit.*, p. 227.
114 *ibid.*, pp. 229 and 231.
115 Masur, *op. cit.*, p. 294; Wheeler-Bennett I, *op. cit.*, p. 33.
116 Nettl, *op. cit.*, II, p. 819; Taylor II, *op. cit.*, p. 224.
117 Bullock, Sir Alan: *Hitler, A Study in Tyranny* (1952), Pelican ed., pp. 78–9 and 138; Waite, R. G. L.: *Vanguard of Nazism: The Free Corps Movement in Post-War Germany, 1918–1923* (1952), pp. 25–6.
118 Watt, *op. cit.*, pp. 575–6.
119 Jonas, *op. cit.*, pp. 158–9.
120 Wheeler-Bennett I, *op. cit.*, pp. 41–3.
121 Jonas, *op. cit.*, p. 223.
122 Private Information.
123 Jonas, *op. cit.*, p. 211.
124 *ibid.*, p. 150; Balfour, *op. cit.*, p. 418; Kürenberg, *op. cit.*, p. 345.
125 *ibid.*, p. 170 and 177.
126 Wheeler-Bennett, I, *op. cit.*, p. 57.
127 Kessler, Count Harry: *Tagebücher 1918–37* (1961), p. 670, q.v. Röhl I.
128 Meinecke II, pp. 9 *et seq.*, q.v. Röhl I; Bullock, *op. cit.*, pp. 267–8.
129 Bullock, *op. cit.*, pp. 301 *et seq.*
130 *ibid.*, p. 309.
131 Epstein, Klaus: 'Shirer's History of Nazi Germany', *The Review of Politics*, 23, No. 2, April, pp. 23 *et seq.*, q.v. Röhl I.

132 Ritter, Gerhard: *The Third Re*... Essays pb. International Council f... Philosophy and Humanistic Studi... and UNESCO (1955), pp. 381 *et se*... q.v. Röhl I.
133 Watt, *op. cit.*, p. 317.
134 Jonas, *op. cit.*, p. 189.
135 *ibid.*, pp. 189–90.
136 *ibid.*, p. 186.
137 *ibid.*, p. 187.
138 Taylor I, *op. cit.*, p. 207.
139 *ibid.*
140 Trevor-Roper, *op. cit.*, p. 12, q.... Röhl IV.
141 Ponsonby II, *op. cit.*, pp. 111–12.
142 *ibid.*
143 Balfour, *op. cit.*, p. 416.
144 *ibid.*, Ponsonby II, *op. cit.*, pp. 114... 15
145 Viereck, *op. cit.*, p. 157.
146 *ibid.*, p. 144.
147 Jonas, *op. cit.*, p. 202.
148 Pope-Hennessy I, *op. cit.*, p. 16... Aronson I, *op. cit.*, pp. 211–12... Hough, *op. cit.*, p. 142.
149 Jonas, *op. cit.*, p. 164.
150 *ibid.*, pp. 171–2.
151 *ibid.*, p. 184.
152 *ibid.*, p. 185.
153 *ibid.*, pp. 194–5.
154 Bentinck, *op. cit.*, pp. 147–8.
155 Cowles, *op. cit.*, pp. 424–5.
156 Bentinck, *op. cit.*, p. 34.
157 Balfour, *op. cit.*, p. 417.
158 Confirmed by H. I. H. Prince Louis Ferdinand.
159 Jonas, *op. cit.*, p. 165.
160 *ibid.*, p. 197.
161 Kürenberg, *op. cit.*, p. 347.
162 *ibid.*, p. 348.
163 Pope-Hennessy II, *op. cit.*, p. 592.
164 Balfour, *op. cit.*, p. 419.
165 Jonas, *op. cit.*, p. 198.
166 Personal communication from Cecilia, Gräfin von Sternberg.
167 Wheeler-Bennett I, *op. cit.*, p. 188.
168 *ibid.*, pp. 188–9; Aronson I, *op. cit.*, p. 251; Cowles, *op. cit.*, p. 429.
169 Wheeler-Bennett I, *op. cit.*, p. 189; Cowles, *op. cit.*, p. 429.
170 Jonas, *op. cit.*, pp. 199–200.
171 Wheeler-Bennett I, *op. cit.*, p. 30.
172 Cowles, *op. cit.*, p. 430.
173 Jonas, *op. cit.*, pp. 200–1.
174 *ibid.*, p. 199.
175 Burke's Presidential Families, *op. cit.*, p. 444.

Index (compiled by R. and R. Haig-Brown)

All royal persons are indexed according to their Christian names rather than their titles: thus,
'Arthur, Duke of Connaught' comes under 'A' and not 'C'.
The use of 'W' and 'W's' refers throughout to Kaiser William II.
The letter-by-letter system has been adopted.
'n' refers to footnotes for the page reference given.
All headings are in alphabetical order except those which have been run on and are in chronological
order to assist the reader.

21   32   38   51   65   255